Dynamic Statutory Interpretation

Dynamic Statutory Interpretation

William N. Eskridge, Jr.

Harvard University Press

Cambridge, Massachusetts
London, England
1994

To the memory of the Honorable Edward Weinfeld,
1901–1988

Library of Congress Cataloging-in-Publication Data
Eskridge, William N.
    Dynamic statutory interpretation / William N. Eskridge, Jr.
      p. cm.
    Includes bibliographical references and index.
    ISBN 0-674-21878-7 (acid-free paper)
    1. Law—United States—Interpretation and construction. 2. Law—Interpretation and construction. I. Title.
KF425.E83 1994
348.73'22—dc20   94-14151
[347.30822]   CIP

Contents

Acknowledgments

This book grew out of my collaboration with Philip Frickey on our case-book, *Statutes and the Creation of Public Policy*. One of my contributions in the book was to sketch a theory of "dynamic statutory interpretation," a term I hit on after my friends Owen Fiss and Laurens Walker vetoed "nonoriginalist statutory interpretation" as cumbersome. After publication of this book, my work on statutory interpretation theory continued at the Georgetown University Law Center, where a number of gracious scholars—Wendy Webster Williams, Steven Goldberg, Peter Byrne, G. Edward White, Gary Peller, Richard Posner, Vicki Jackson, William Nelson, Robert Katzmann, Anita Allen, and Jerry Mashaw—helped me find a productive academic home.

There, Deans Robert Pitofsky and Judith Areen and Deputy Deans Goldberg, Williams, and Mark Tushnet made sure that I had more than enough resources and student assistants to produce a stream of statutory interpretation articles. They also provided research assistants specifically for this book. I am indebted to Jill Aranson (Georgetown, class of 1995), Jeffrey Adler (class of 1994), Jarrett Barrios (class of 1995), David Burton (class of 1996), Steven Dubuc (class of 1994), Andrew Goldfarb (class of 1995), Julie Harris (class of 1995), Judith Holiber (class of 1995), Stephen Saxe (class of 1995), Sarah Sheive (class of 1995), Ian Teran (class of 1995), and Elizabeth Wyatt (class of 1996) for their research assistance.

Many people provided useful comments on the articles, a great number disagreed with them, and not a few wondered whether all the articles were consistent with one another (they aren't). This sort of feedback impelled me to write this book. Although I am the nominal author, and take responsibility for glitches, this book is a collective effort. The emotional payoff for the academic life is learning from brilliant people and working with kind ones. When the brilliant people are also kind, and you can learn from collaboration, this life is hard to beat.

Chapters 1, 2, and 9 were developed in part from articles I coauthored with Philip Frickey. Chapter 9 was also in part developed from an article I coauthored with John Ferejohn. Chapter 6 was developed from an article co-authored with Gary Peller. Each has declined coauthorship of his respective chapter(s) but deserves equal credit for whatever insights are there. Indeed, a good case could be made for adding any or all three as coauthors of this book.

All of the chapters involve collaboration with other scholars as well. Warren Schwartz introduced me to the positive political theory used in Chapters 1 and 2, and Roger Noll clarified my thinking on the specific application of such theory to legal issues raised in those chapters. Dennis Patterson and Anita Allen encouraged my use of hermeneutic philosophy in Chapter 2 and provided many valuable references over the years; Philip Frickey and Daniel Farber taught me all I know about pragmatism. Chapter 3 reflects the influence of Daniel Ernst's work, especially his doctoral dissertation and his own book in progress. Conversations and letters with Daniel Farber, Richard Posner, Alex Johnson, and Lawrence Lessig over the years shaped my approach to Chapter 4. Collaboration with Philip Frickey in publishing our first book, a series of articles, and the Hart and Sacks materials, "The Legal Process," framed my thoughts in Chapter 5. Michael Seidman, Peter Strauss, and Mark Tushnet provided brilliant—and conflicting—advice about how I should approach the legal process school in Chapter 5, and Neil Duxbury shared with me the legal process chapter of his work in progress on American jurisprudence. Steven Middlebrook and Heidi Sorenson helped me explore the factual background of the case discussed in Chapter 6. My discussion of feminist theories as applied to statutory interpretation owes much to conversations with Naomi Cahn, Martha Fineman, and Wendy Webster Williams. I have participated with Stephen Breyer, Frank Easterbrook, Abner Mikva, and Antonin Scalia in various panels and events analyzing the value of legislative history, and what I have learned from each of these former law professors (now judges) is reflected in Chapter 7. Akhil Amar provided important advice as well as encouragement toward systematizing my thoughts about vertical and horizontal coherence in Chapter 8. And my work on the canons in Chapter 9 has benefited over the years from exchanging drafts with Cass Sunstein.

For other useful comments or conversations that have contributed to this book, I thank Shirley Abrahamson, Alexander Aleinikoff, Jack Beerman, Gregg Bloche, Rebecca Brown, James Brudney, Ronald Cass, Barbara Child, Linda Cohen, Christopher Edley, Cynthia Farina, Owen Fiss, Erwin Griswold, Hendrik Hartog, Bruce Hay, Heidi Hurd, Willard Hurst, Vicki Jackson, Alex Johnson, Sanford Kadish, Robert Katzmann, Jack Knight, Keith Krehbiel, Sylvia Law, Bill Luneburg, Matthew McCubbins, Harold McDougall, Earl Maltz, Jerry Mashaw, Mari Matsuda, Daniel Ortiz, Robert Post, Daniel Rodriguez, Stephen Ross, Edward Rubin, Edward Schwartz, David Shapiro, Suzanna Sherry, Lawrence Silberman, Joseph Singer, Pablo Spiller,

Matthew Spitzer, John Stick, Lynn Stout, Laurens Walker, Barry Weingast, G. Edward White, Stephen Williams, Wendy Webster Williams, John Yoo, and Nicholas Zeppos.

Chapters in the book, or articles that became the basis of chapters, were presented as faculty workshops at the law schools of Boston University, University of California at Berkeley, Columbia, Cornell, Florida, Georgetown, Minnesota, Tulane, Vanderbilt, and Wisconsin. I am grateful to the workshop participants for their attention and their reactions. Some of the work reflected in this book was also presented as papers at annual meetings of the Public Choice Conference.

I am greatly indebted to Daniel Farber, John Ferejohn, Philip Frickey, Roger Noll, and Richard Posner for reading the entire manuscript and providing excellent comments, which led me to rewrite the book.

I dedicate this book to the memory of the Honorable Edward Weinfeld, a judge in the Southern District of New York from 1950 to 1988. I first thought pragmatically and critically about statutory interpretation during my clerkship with Judge Weinfeld. I dedicate the book to him in memory of his integrity, for which he is justly remembered.

Introduction: Why Statutory Interpretation Is Worth a Book

Statutory interpretation is the Cinderella of legal scholarship. Once scorned and neglected, confined to the kitchen, it now dances in the ballroom. Although the interpretation of statutes has been an ongoing topic of interest since the colonial period, only since the early 1980s have American legal academics become intensely excited about statutory interpretation as an object of theoretical interest.[1] In that time, theories of statutory interpretation have blossomed like dandelions in spring. They now eclipse theories of common law and compete with constitutional law theories for space in the public law agenda.

This efflorescence is overdue. As long as there has been law, there has been statutory interpretation, and insight into the topic is more practically relevant now than ever before. In addition, the subject has been one of great theoretical interest because of its historical connection with general theories of interpretation and meaning. Although statutory interpretation theory has lain in conceptual desuetude here in America, there are intellectual opportunities for the field which can take it well beyond the work that has been done in constitutional and common law theory.

The Practical Importance of Statutory Interpretation

Throughout Western history, obeying the law has depended on the interpretation of statutes—the Code of Hammurabi in ancient Babylonia, the Ten Commandments and other strictures followed by the Israelites, the decrees of Drago and other tyrants in classical Greece, the Twelve Tables of republican Rome, the Justinian Code during the late Roman Empire, the edicts of national monarchs and the Code Napoléon, statutes enacted by parliaments and other popularly elected legislative bodies. In all cases the generality of

1

statutory directives required "interpretation" when they were applied to concrete circumstances. The Roman emperor Hadrian opined that the future of the state depended on an interpretation and application of its laws that ensured both fair and generous treatment of the citizenry. As an example, Hadrian cited a case in which a slave had attacked him with a knife. Such an atrocity carried the death penalty, "[h]ad the law been applied with savage rigor," but the emperor applied the law leniently, thereby gaining the loyalty of an able servant.[2]

Concerns about appropriate statutory applications are no less important today, though statutes operate differently in the modern regulatory state: their numbers are greater; more of them are detailed in their prescriptions; statutes are frequently written as directives not to the citizenry but to the bureaucracy. Statutes today often delegate to agencies the authority to make specific rules. The content of the statute then consists of creating or identifying the agency, structuring its decision making, and suggesting the overall goals or guidelines for the agency's ongoing implementation of the statutory scheme. The legitimacy and operation of the modern state begins, and sometimes ends, with the official whose job it is to apply and interpret the statute.

Statutory interpretation has long been a primary task of courts as well, even in common law countries such as the United States.[3] Although our Supreme Court's constitutional decisions receive more attention, the Court's statutory decisions have been just as important in the evolution of American public law. The Marshall and Taney Courts' most celebrated constitutional decisions were also decisions interpreting federal statutes, for example.[4] During the freedom-of-contract era, the Court implemented its economic libertarian philosophy as much through interpretation of federal antitrust statutes as through interpretation of the due process clause (see Chapter 3). The civil rights agenda of the Warren and Burger Courts was accomplished as much through statutory as through constitutional decisions (see Chapters 1 and 2 for examples).[5] The Rehnquist Court has contributed to the resurgence of interest in statutory interpretation. While relatively passive in constitutional interpretation, the Rehnquist Court may be the most activist Court in our history on issues of statutory interpretation (a case that is made out in Chapters 7 through 9). There is a lot at stake in how statutes are interpreted.

A Short Jurisprudential History of Statutory Interpretation

In addition to its practical importance, statutory interpretation is a field with a much more distinguished intellectual history than that of either common law or constitutional interpretation. Most of that history, presented here in capsule form, has continuing relevance for debates about statutory interpretation in the modern regulatory state.

Aristotle is the first significant Western theorist of statutory interpretation. His *Rhetoric*, for example, introduced the various types of arguments and counterarguments that can usually be invoked in interpreting the written law.[6] The *Nicomachean Ethics* makes clear that Aristotle considered statutory interpretation more than rhetorical point-counterpoint, however, for he used it as an illustration of practical wisdom. Aristotle's practical philosophy emphasized the situatedness of statutory issues. Although general statutes are necessary, their meaning is manifest only when applied to specific factual circumstances. "[Law] is defective owing to its universality. In fact this is the reason why all things are not determined by law, viz. that about some things it is impossible to lay down a law, so that a decree is needed. For when the thing is indefinite the rule also is indefinite, like the lead rule used in making the Lesbian moulding; the rule adapts itself to the shape of the stone and is not rigid, and so too the decree is adapted to the facts."[7] Aristotle also wrote what is arguably the first work of hermeneutics, or the study of interpretation and understanding.[8]

The greatest statute of the ancient world, the sixth-century Code of Justinian and its accompanying *Digest*, represented a compilation not only of Roman statutes but also of commentaries on their interpretation.[9] Just as Aristotle had arrayed various principles of statutory interpretation in the *Rhetoric*, so the *Digest* collected over two hundred precepts suggested by the commentators as guides to statutory interpretation. These precepts are similar to those followed in ancient Hindu, Judaic, and Christian cultures, all of which are in turn similar to modern "canons of statutory construction."[10] These sources suggest that even though general statutes had to be applied flexibly, as Aristotle had taught, their application could be guided, and rendered predictable, by rules of construction. Medieval jurisprudence until the twelfth century largely took the form of further commentaries on the Justinian texts.

The late Middle Ages yielded two important developments in statutory jurisprudence. Saint Thomas Aquinas' *Summa Theologica* argued for a deep relationship between natural or divine law and human or positive law. Although he did not posit a complete overlap between the two, he did indicate that efforts to legislate rules contrary to natural order are subject to nullification or to interpretation more in conformity with natural law.[11] Aquinas' work is the classic statement of a natural law approach to legislation. Subsequent work by secular scholars owes much to the structure laid out in the *Summa*. More broadly, Aquinas' thought suggests the interconnection between what one thinks the positive law is and which moral values one brings to the interpretive process.

The other late medieval development was the revival of interest in Roman law, and with it the foundation of modern legal hermeneutics. Like Aristotle's *Rhetoric* and the Justinian *Digest*, the work of legal hermeneuticists consisted mainly in the development of principles of interpretation for legal texts; the medieval hermeneuticists ensured that the tradition of interpretive principles would not be lost.[12] Although most of them emphasized close textual analysis and advocated an immanent meaning for texts, they also drew from the Roman tradition the idea that literal interpretation has its limits and that statutes must often be interpreted to carry out their overall purpose. This hermeneutic insight showed up in legal decisions of the early modern period, including English decisions, for example: "And the law may be resembled to a nut, which has a shell and a kernel within, the letter of the law represents the shell, and the sense of it the kernel, and as you will be no better for the nut if you make use only of the shell, so you will receive no benefit by the law, if you rely only upon the letter."[13] The shell-and-kernel metaphor finds a parallel in ongoing debates between literal and purposive theories of statutory interpretation.

During the Enlightenment hermeneutics scholars expanded their field into a general philosophy of understanding all utterances, spoken as well as written, aesthetic as well as legal. The first important theory was Friedrich Daniel Ernst Schleiermacher's romantic hermeneutics, which taught that the goal is "[t]o understand the text at first as well as and then even better than its author," by putting oneself both objectively and subjectively in the position of the text's author, imaginatively reconstructing his circumstances and patterns of thought.[14] Schleiermacher's theory offers both the possibility of an objective reading of a text and a linkage between the interpreter and the author of the text. Romantic hermeneutics had almost immediate relevance for statutory interpretation theory because it provided a link between judicial interpretations of statutes and the democratic process which yielded the statutes themselves. Once democratically elected legislatures or parliaments were accepted as the only legitimate "author" of law (as was the case in many Western countries by 1800), the actual and subjective "intent" of that author became important. The method of romantic hermeneutics could most productively be applied to such an inquiry, and theories of imaginative reconstruction of the legislature's intent have been popular in the West since the early nineteenth century.[15]

The jurisprudence of statutory interpretation has since proceeded in several different directions, all of them going beyond the imaginative reconstruction of romantic hermeneutics. Chronologically, the first important development was utilitarianism, the view that social policy should yield the greatest good for the greatest number. Utilitarian theories of statutory interpretation urge the interpreter to construe the statute to yield the maximum social benefit. François Gény's *Méthode d'interprétation*, for example, advocated a method of "free inquiry" into social needs by the interpreter and construction of statutes to advance social goals, overriding contrary authorial intent if necessary.[16] Agencies are often supposed to follow precisely such a utilitarian approach, and judges do the same in practice (but not openly). For both positive and normative reasons, a utilitarian approach to statutory interpretation has been robust in the academic literature, especially in the United States, starting with the legal realists and continuing with law and economics scholars.

Modern hermeneutic theories posit that interpretation is neither the reconstruction of an author's intent nor the interpreter's act of social engineering, but rather a process by which the interpreter and the text reach what Hans-Georg Gadamer terms a "common understanding."[17] Hermeneutics recognizes the difficulty of imaginative reconstruction but treats the text with respect, inviting its instruction. Hermeneutics is an appealing approach to statutory interpretation, for its idea of conversation between judge and text seems consistent with democratic ideals of deliberation, openness, and respect for majority preferences. The most accomplished legal version of such a theory of statutory interpretation was that of the legal process school (see Chapter 5). Legal process theory posits that law, as the means by which interdependent human beings can cooperate with one another, is necessarily purposive; hence, statutory interpretation is the process by which various legal actors work together to apply legislative directives to carry out their purposes under constantly changing circumstances.

Other important intellectual developments of the last one hundred years have significant implications for statutory interpretation theory which have not yet been thoroughly explored. Pragmatism's skeptical approach to grand theory and its interest in weblike reasoning have a relevance for statutory interpretation. Postmodernism has equally interesting, and heretofore less recognized, implications for statutory interpretation theory. Its refusal to privilege the author, its deconstruction of text and textual authority, and its understanding that legal institutions are socially constructed are relevant to the various debates in the field of statutory interpretation. One goal of this book is to bring to bear pragmatic and postmodern theoretical insights on statutory interpretation theory (see Chapters 1, 2, and 6 in particular).

The Plan and Contribution of This Book

Given the practical importance of statutory interpretation, its impressive intellectual history, and the resurgent academic interest in the topic, it remains surprising how much more work needs to be done before statutory interpretation can enjoy a central status in American jurisprudence, like the status it enjoys virtually everywhere else in the world. The plan of this book is to contribute to that project in several ways.

My initial and primary goal is to advance a thesis: that statutory interpretation is *dynamic*. The interpretation of a statutory provision by an interpreter is not necessarily the one which the original legislature would have endorsed, and as the distance between enactment and interpretation increases, a pure originalist inquiry becomes impossible and/or irrelevant. I originally advanced this thesis in 1987,[18] and subsequent scholarship confirms the thesis as a description of what courts and agencies do and has provided tentative support for the thesis as a proposition for what ought to be done with statutes.[19] This book will explore the thesis more deeply.

Part I develops the thesis as a positive, that is descriptive, theory of how courts and agencies interpret statutes. Chapter 1 argues that none of the originalist theories of statutory interpretation describes the practice of statutory interpretation, and suggests some reasons why originalist theories cannot supply coherent foundations for statutory inquiries. Chapter 2 sets forth a constructive (but still descriptive) theory of dynamic statutory interpretation. It draws on positive theories of what original legislative coalitions want interpreters to do with statutes over time; how courts and agencies go about the process of interpretation; and how courts, agencies, and subsequent legislative coalitions interact over issues of statutory interpretation. Case examples in Chapters 1 and 2 illustrate the analytical points. Chapter 3 shows how my positive theory explains statutory cases in one field (labor disputes) over time (1877–1938).

The positive thesis cannot be seriously disputed, in my opinion. But the normative thesis might be. Is it a good thing that agencies and courts interpret statutes dynamically? Or should we be doing all that we can to prevent this? Part II explores these normative questions about dynamic statutory interpretation. Its desirability is evaluated from the perspective of three different schools of political thought: liberal social contract theory (Chapter 4), legal process theory (Chapter 5), and normativist theory (Chapter 6). My main conclusions are that dynamic statutory interpretation is defensible under any of these theories, but that particular dynamic interpretations are open to critique. A concomitant conclusion is that my positive theory of dynamic interpretation provides a basis for criticizing liberal, legal process, and most normativist political theories. The normative political theory I find most congenial for dynamic interpretation is critical pragmatism, developed at the end of Chapter 6.

Part III evaluates doctrines of statutory interpretation in light of the positive dynamics and normative criteria of Parts I and II. The method of Part III is to develop evaluative criteria through a historical exegesis of doctrinal debates in American statutory interpretation—the usefulness of legislative history (Chapter 7), the legislative inaction doctrines and the super-strong presumption of correctness for statutory precedents (Chapter 8), and the canons of statutory construction (Chapter 9).

Some of the argumentation in this book draws on prior work in common law and, especially, constitutional theory. Because statutory interpretation theory languished for so long, its renaissance has borrowed heavily from existing scholarship in these areas. Nonetheless, a secondary theme of this book is that statutory interpretation theory is distinct from, and intellectually independent of, common law and constitutional theory. For example, statutory interpretation involves much richer authoritative texts than common law or constitutional interpretation. Statutes themselves are often particularly detailed, and even open-textured statutes may have rich legislative history—in contrast to the common law (with no foundational text) and the Constitution (whose most interesting provisions are open-textured and little illuminated by background history). More than common law or constitutional interpretation, statutory interpretation is a holistic enterprise, permitting deep involvement of the interpreter in the structure and history of a statutory text, as well as its formal relation to other statutory provisions. This book explores the interesting variety of textual analyses and modes of critique.[20]

Another distinctive feature of statutory interpretation is the importance of theories of legislatures. In the background of every federal statutory case is Congress. The Constitutional Convention in Philadelphia disbanded centuries ago, and the common law enjoys no majority-based legitimating institution. In contrast, Congress, the author of federal statutes, is an ongoing institution. It can rewrite statutes when it disagrees with the way they are interpreted. Although Congress can also override the common law and (sometimes) constitutional interpretations with statutes, it more regularly does so for statutory interpretations. As a result, statutory policy is often doubly dynamic: agencies and courts attend to current as well as historical congressional preferences when they interpret statutes, and when they fail to attend perceptively enough, Congress often rewrites the text to reflect current values.

The institutional features of the law implementation process offer exciting intellectual possibilities for the study of statutory interpretation because that field—much more than common law or constitutional interpretation—demands a theory of Congress (and the presidency) as well as a theory of language and interpretation. Previous literature has explored the relevance of interest-group theories of politics for statutory interpretation, with rather inconclusive results.[21] More useful insights can be gleaned from the theory of institutions, or positive political theory, as it is called.[22] This book draws on work in positive political theory (especially in Chapters 1, 2, 5, and 9) to develop descriptive and normative insights about statutory interpretation.

Finally, statutory interpretation is the most important form of legal interpretation in the modern regulatory state because it is as much agency-centered as judge-centered. Although not inevitably judge-made, our common law as well as constitutional traditions are juricentric. This renders them less relevant for thinking about the creation of public policy in the modern administrative state.

The two main goals of this book are to develop my thesis and to establish the intellectual autonomy of this field as central rather than peripheral to public law scholarship. A final, and perhaps less significant, goal is to show that statutory interpretation is interesting. With many readers this is an uphill battle. But please read on, for I am confident that you will find the stuff of statutes much more engaging than you would expect. Nothing that is human escapes statutory interest.

Thus if you find the law of employment and labor relations interesting, you ought to pay attention to statutory interpretation, which is the main legal forum for struggles over fair treatment of employees (Chapter 1), workplace diversity (Chapters 1 and 2), and the larger historical battles fought by and against organized labor (Chapter 3). If you find international business transactions profitable, there is no more pertinent legal inquiry than statutory interpretation, which dominates issues of immigration (Chapter 2), international trade (Chapter 4), and the regulation of transnational business enterprises (Chapter 9). Environmental law is inconceivable today without reference to statutes (Chapters 5 and 7). Many of you are most interested in issues of national and international human rights. You might think that constitutional interpretation has an edge on statutory interpretation for these issues. You might be wrong.

Statutory interpretation is the critical battleground for most human rights issues in the United States. In the 1990s statutory and not constitutional protections are perhaps the main redress for racial minorities who have been denied fair employment opportunities (Chapters 1, 2, 8, and 9), equal access to education (Chapter 5), and the same property and contracting rights as everyone else (Chapters 7 and 8); for women seeking the information they need to exercise their choice to abort a pregnancy (Chapter 5) or equal employment opportunities (Chapter 8); for lesbians, gay men, and bisexuals petitioning for equal citizenship and protection against private violence and discrimination (Chapters 2 and 6); for religious groups wishing to practice their faith without local interference (Chapters 5 and 6); and for people with disabilities who want protection against discrimination (Chapter 9). Not only is there now a lot at stake in statutory interpretation, but its underlying subject matter ensures that statutory struggles will stimulate your interest in this book, and in the interpretive debates of our time.

I · *The Practice of Dynamic Statutory Interpretation*

THE "ORIGINAL INTENT" and "plain meaning" rhetoric in American statutory interpretation scholarship and decisions treats statutes as static texts and assumes that the meaning of a statute is fixed from the date of enactment. The implication is that a legislator interpreting the statute at the time of enactment would—or should—render the same interpretation as an agency or judge interpreting the same statute fifty years later. This is a dubious description of practical reality, and a dreary aspiration for our polity. These dubieties suggest that we might also doubt the assumptions embedded within the originalist rhetoric of statutory interpretation. Neither constitutional nor common law interpretation is viewed as just an exercise in discovering original intent. Why should statutory interpretation, our third main source of law, be conceptualized as an originalist enterprise?

There is nothing revolutionary about understanding statutes in something other than static terms. Other industrialized countries conceive of statutory interpretation as dynamic: the meaning of a statute is not fixed until it is applied to concrete circumstances, and it is neither uncommon nor illegitimate for the meaning of a provision to change over time. The standard reasons given for dynamic interpretation by scholars in other countries are equally applicable to statutory interpretation in the United States.

At the time of its enactment, a statute usually resolves the most pressing legal questions that gave rise to it, and resolves them in ways that are just as clear to the addressees as to the authors of the statute. For such issues there is no need for "interpretation"; the statute is clear. Interpretation is required for those issues that were either unanticipated or politically sidestepped. Where such gaps or ambiguities exist, a legislator voting for the statute might have a different interpretation than would contemporary administrators or judges (or, indeed, other legislators). Over time, the gaps and ambiguities

9

proliferate as society changes, adapts to the statute, and generates new variations on the problem initially targeted by the statute. The original meaning of the statute or the original intent of the legislature has less relevance for figuring out how the statute should apply to unforeseen circumstances. As legal systems in other countries recognize, the interpreter in these cases is more likely to be influenced by subsequent legal developments, current legislative preferences, and probable future consequences of different interpretations.

Statutory interpretation around the world is dynamic. Common law and constitutional interpretation in the United States is dynamic. The claim in this part of the book is that statutory interpretation in the United States is also dynamic, as a matter of practice and positive theory. This claim is pursued in several different ways.

Chapter 1 critically examines the traditional theories of statutory interpretation that purport to replicate original legislative expectations. Such theories emphasize intent, purpose, or text. They rest on a concept that the nonelected administrator or judge is simply following the directives given him or her by the legislative coalition which reflects some democratically legitimate response to a social problem. Yet, on examination, none of the traditional theories positively describes what American agencies and courts do in statutory interpretation cases. Nor, surprisingly, can any of the theories coherently correlate its methodology with its democratic premises or even with the goals of legislative coalitions. In short, no originalist theory generates results in statutory cases that can objectively be tied to majority-based preferences, and originalist theories collectively cannot exclude evolutive values from statutory interpretation.

In addition to criticizing originalist theories, Chapter 1 also suggests, affirmatively, that statutory interpreters in the United States routinely consider nonoriginalist factors, including statutory precedents, postenactment legal and social developments, and current values and social needs. Chapter 2 presents a more systematic positive analysis of dynamic statutory interpretation, and explains why such interpretation is even more likely in the United States than in other Western countries. Dynamic statutory interpretation is inevitable because of the structure of policy-making in the United States. Because it is hard to enact statutes, the ones that are enacted have to last a long time. As they encounter unanticipated circumstances, the statutes are bound to change. Indeed, the evolution of a statute might be immediate, for statutory implementation is vested in agencies and judges who are institutionally independent of the legislature and whose frame of reference may from the beginning be quite different from that of the enacting coalition. Statutory interpretation is also sequential and hierarchical in our polity. Early interpreters are usually parties at whom the statute is directed; agencies and courts are later interpreters which do not write on a clean slate and which may in turn be overridden by a subsequent legislature. The sequential and hierarchical structure of statutory interpretation means not only that results might change from interpreter to interpreter, but also that the expectations of the current legislature might be more important than those of the enacting one. Originalist interpretation is turned on its head.

Another way of expressing the thesis of Chapter 2 is to say that statutes will be construed dynamically whenever the perspective of the interpreter departs from the perspective of the statute—a departure that often exerts an influence at the time the statute is passed and is inevitable as the statute ages. Over time, the interpreter's perspective diverges from that of the statute as a result of changed circumstances which give rise to unanticipated problems, developments in law and the statute's evolution, and different political and ideological frameworks. The divergence of the interpreter's perspective from the statute's perspective does not suggest that the former will simply displace the latter. It suggests only that the historical text takes on new meaning in light of subsequent formal, social, and ideological developments.

Chapter 2 develops its positive analysis of dynamic statutory interpretation through an analysis of several statutory issues, including the ones introduced in Chapter 1. Chapter 3 shows how the positive theory of dynamic statutory interpretation can provide a framework for understanding a whole subject area over time. Using federal labor cases from 1877 to 1938, the chapter demonstrates how social, formal, and ideological changes affected the interpretation of the federal antitrust laws and other statutes. Like the other chapters in Part I, the argument in Chapter 3 is not that the evolutive interpretation of federal statutes in this period was normatively desirable. The argument is only that my positive theory of dynamic statutory interpretation provides a richer understanding of American practice than prior theories have done.

1 · The Insufficiency of Statutory Archaeology

Theories of statutory interpretation in the United States have in this century emphasized the original meaning of statutes, and debates have focused on identifying the best evidence of that original meaning. The leading treatise states that "[f]or the interpretation of statutes, 'intent of the legislature' is the criterion that is most often cited,"[1] and the Supreme Court sometimes says that its "sole task" is to discover and apply the original legislative intent for the issue in suit.[2] Other authors and judges have emphasized the original text or purpose of a statute as the best evidence of original intent, but their point has been the same: judges interpreting statutes are "honest agents of the political branches" whose role is to "carry out decisions they do not make" but only discover in the materials originally enacted by the legislature.[3] This "archaeological" (Charles Curtis's term) focus of traditional approaches to statutory interpretation is inspired in large part by anxiety that nonelected officials feel when they make policy decisions in a democracy. Each approach starts with a theory of politically legitimate action and uses that theory as a foundation for its particular brand of originalism. These archaeological approaches seek to reconcile statutory interpretation by nonelected judges with the constitutional assumptions of our representative democracy.

As a positive matter, all originalist theories fail, and they fail in similar ways. To begin with, none of them accurately describes what American agencies and courts do when they interpret statutes. The practice of statutory interpretation does not follow any single inquiry (originalist or otherwise), and many important agency and judicial interpretations are not easily defensible under any of the traditional theories. Of course, these decisions may be wrong, but originalist theory provides an insufficient positive or normative basis for attacking nonoriginalist statutory interpretations.

13

Although originalist theories promise that statutory interpretation in concrete cases can be analytically connected with decisions that have been made by a majority-based coalition in the legislature, none of the theories can deliver consistently on this promise. Traditional legal writers have no theory of legislatures in general or of enacting coalitions in particular. Without such a theory statutory archaeologists lack a methodology for linking up their approaches with democratically legitimate expressions of preferences by the legislature, an unruly and incoherent group. In this chapter I outline positive political theories that each archaeological approach might appropriate in support of its methodology, an effort that has profited from discussions with Roger Noll. But even with the best possible political theory of what the legislative process, or an enacting coalition, wants when it passes a statute, none of the originalist schools (intentionalism, purposivism, textualism) is able to generate a theory of what the process or the coalition "would want" over time, after circumstances have changed. Thus, in the tough cases—those that reflect unanticipated circumstances or new versions of the originally targeted problem—none of the methodologies yields determinate results. Consequently, none fully constrains statutory interpreters or limits them to the preferences of the enacting coalition.

In addition to the foregoing positive critiques of archaeological approaches to statutory interpretation, I note a normative difficulty with such approaches, in that they do not reflect the best aspirations for our political system. I postpone detailed discussion of that difficulty to Part II, but the positive analysis here should suggest some of the normative defects of originalist theories in general.

Intentionalism

The most popular foundation for an archaeological theory of statutory interpretation is probably intentionalism, which directs the interpreter to discover or replicate the legislature's original intent as the answer to an interpretive question. Anglo-American scholars from early modern times[4] to the present[5] have argued that original intent is and should be the cornerstone of statutory interpretation. Intentionalism is in some respects a natural way to view statutory interpretation in a representative democracy. If the legislature is the primary lawmaker and interpreters are its agents, then requiring interpreters to follow the legislature's intentions constrains their choices and advances democracy by carrying out the will of the elected legislators.

Nonetheless, intentionalism does not account for the actual practice of federal agencies and courts. A prominent example is United Steelworkers v. Weber.[6] In 1974 Kaiser Aluminum and the United Steelworkers entered into a collective bargaining agreement creating an affirmative action plan designed to eliminate racial imbalances in Kaiser's almost all-white craft work force. The plan established programs to train unskilled production workers to be craft workers, with about 50 percent of the places in the programs reserved for African Americans. Until 1974 Kaiser had hired as craft workers for its Gramercy, Louisiana, plant only persons with prior craft experience. Because black workers had been excluded from craft unions, few of them qualified for the jobs: as a result, only 1.83 percent of the craft workers at the Gramercy plant were African American, even though they occupied 39 percent of the area's work force. Implementing the national plan, the Gramercy plant established a craft training program, selecting thirteen production workers, seven of whom were black. One of those not chosen for the program was Brian F. Weber, a white production worker with greater seniority than the African Americans chosen.

Weber complained to the Equal Employment Opportunity Commission (EEOC) that Kaiser's choice of black workers with less seniority violated section 703(a)(1) of the Civil Rights Act of 1964, which makes it unlawful "to discriminate against any individual" in the terms and conditions of employment because of his or her "race, color, religion, sex, or national origin."[7] The issue raised by Weber was whether this language—or similar language in section 703(d), which applies to training programs—bars the establishment of voluntary affirmative action plans to increase the number of black workers. The EEOC believed that such plans do not violate the statute, and adopted guidelines to that effect. Because the EEOC offered no relief, Weber brought suit in federal court. The Fifth Circuit Court of Appeals held that such plans constitute unlawful discrimination under Title VII. The Supreme Court agreed with the EEOC's interpretation and reversed the Fifth Circuit.

Justice William Brennan's opinion for the Court slighted the original legislative intent and focused instead on the consistency of voluntary affirmative action with the "spirit" and "purpose" of the statute. Based on an exhaustive review of Title VII's legislative history, Justice William Rehnquist's dissent maintained that a provision embodying the Court's result "could not possibly" have been enacted in 1964.[8] Yet Rehnquist drew only one other vote for his position, whose factual underpinnings were not rebutted in any detail by Brennan. *Weber* is no anomaly. The Supreme Court often interprets statutes in ways that reflect statutory purpose or current values instead of original legislative intent,[9] and agencies (like the EEOC) are even more likely to do so.

In addition to its inability to explain either agency or court interpretations in cases such as *Weber*, intentionalism is an incomplete theory of statutory interpretation, at least as traditionally articulated. A central problem is that it is unclear what is meant by legislative "intent." Whose intent governs? How is it established? Because the Rehnquist dissent in *Weber* is an intentionalist classic, I use it to raise and criticize three theories of legislative intent. None of the theories permits Rehnquist to claim that his interpretation is more faithful to democratic principles than the Court's interpretation. My critical examination also suggests reasons why, in the hard cases, statutory interpreters will be unable to derive determinate answers from an intentionalist inquiry.

I do not maintain that legislative intent is never discoverable or is irrelevant to statutory interpretation. The Rehnquist dissent in *Weber* makes arguments that are both relevant and useful, and I believe they can be improved on through the use of positive political theory. Instead, my thesis is that because intentionalism does not yield clear answers in cases such as *Weber*, the approach is more pliable—and therefore less constraining on agencies and courts—than its legal proponents claim.

Actual Intent: Unknowable

The meaning colloquially suggested by the invocation of legislative intent is the actual intentions of the legislative coalition that enacted the statute. If a majority of our elected representatives had a specific meaning in mind when they passed a statute, understanding that meaning has obvious appeal in a representative democracy. One problem is that actual legislative intent is rarely revealed in the historical record, even when the record is as recent and detailed as that of the Civil Rights Act of 1964.[10]

To begin with, legislators usually do not have a specific intention on more than a few issues (if that) in any bill for which they vote. Legislators routinely vote for legislation simply because their president, their party leaders, or relevant interest groups favor it. Even when legislators do have specific intents, the historical record usually does not record them. Most members of Congress never say anything on the record about pending bills, and given the myriad reasons they might have for voting in favor of a bill, no necessary inference can be drawn about their intentions from the remarks of other members. That most members of Congress voted for a bill tells us little about what most members of Congress actually thought about specific issues raised by the bill. Even when legislators state for the record what they think a bill means for a specific issue, their statements may not be reliable because of strategic behavior. A legislator may specifically intend her bill to be broadly construed, but will say that the bill should be narrowly construed to some audiences, such as skeptical interest groups. Problems with identifying the actual intent of individual legislators become overwhelming when these hard-to-figure individual intentions must be aggregated for each legislative chamber and then matched up with the intent of the president.

These difficulties undermine efforts to establish the actual intent of the

1964 Congress on the affirmative action issue. The report of the House Judiciary Committee on the civil rights bill in 1963 simply restated, in summary form, the terms of what was to become Title VII of the act. The minority report, joined by southern Democrats and a few conservative Republicans, argued that if the civil rights bill were enacted, an employer "may be forced to hire according to race, to 'racially balance' those who work for him in every job classification or be in violation of Federal law."[11] The issue of required racial balancing was not a major focus of the House floor debate, but the chair of the Judiciary Committee claimed that the minority report overstated the effect of the bill. Other supporters echoed the view that "[t]here is nothing here as a matter of legislative history that would require racial balancing."[12] After this debate, and with only one material amendment to the jobs title (adding a prohibition against discrimination based on sex), the House approved the bill by a vote of 290 to 130.

What was the actual intent of a majority of the House of Representatives on the *Weber* issue? Unclear. The southerners suggested that the bill if approved would require racial balance for all employers, a consequence more radical than the voluntary affirmative action permitted in *Weber*; but obviously they were trying to scare away potential supporters of the bill. By denying that the bill required racial balance, its supporters were behaving just as strategically, trying to allay concerns that the bill was too radical. Most members of the House said nothing on the issue. Thus, if *Weber* had been brought to a vote as an amendment to the jobs title, it is impossible—contra Rehnquist—to predict how the vote would have gone. Many southerners might have voted in support of affirmative action, hoping to kill the bill by making it too strong. Some Republicans and Democrats might have joined them out of sincere support for affirmative action. Other supporters of the bill might have voted against affirmative action to attract moderate support for the overall legislation. Some would have ducked the issue by not voting.

Moreover, even if it could be discovered, the intent of the House is not the intent of Congress. The intent of the House must somehow be matched to the intent of the Senate. A similar debate about affirmative preferences occurred in the Senate, with similar posturing by interested senators but with a more complete record of their positions. Rehnquist's dissenting opinion cited evidence from eleven senators who said they believed Title VII would require racial quotas, and from eleven who argued that Title VII would prohibit quotas.[13] Although this is an impressive bit of research, it does not tell us what a majority of the Senate believed about the bill, and it tells us very little about what those twenty-two senators believed about *voluntary* affirmative action, as opposed to *required* quotas.

The most useful evidence of the Senate's actual intent was its amendment of the bill to add section 703(j), providing that nothing in Title VII "shall be interpreted to *require* any employer . . . to grant preferential treatment . . . to any group because of the race . . . of such . . . group on account of" a de facto racial imbalance in the employer's work force.[14] This provision was part of the bill that passed the Senate, was accepted by the House, and was signed by the president. Hence, whatever the actual intent of the House was when it originally passed the bill, one might infer that it, like the Senate, agreed to the resolution of the issue in section 703(j). Unhappily, section 703(j) says only that the government cannot "require" employers to grant preferences; it says nothing about whether the government can "permit" employers to do so. The ambiguity of section 703(j) mirrors the ambiguity of Congress's actual intent on the *Weber* issue.[15]

Problematic Assumptions Underlying Conventional Intent

Given the epistemic, vote-counting, and aggregation problems with any inquiry focusing on the precise intentions of legislators, what intentionalists usually mean by the term is conventional rather than actual legislative intent. Although the rhetorical appeal of Rehnquist's dissenting opinion was to suggest that most members of Congress in 1964 did not think Title VII would allow affirmative action, his precise argumentation rested on presumed conventions about legislative intent. Thus, in establishing his case from the Senate debates, Rehnquist emphasized the remarks of the floor manager for the civil rights bill (Senator Hubert Humphrey) that nothing in the bill would "require hiring, firing, or promotion of employees in order to meet a racial 'quota' or to achieve a certain racial balance," and that the bill "encourage[s] hiring on the basis of ability and qualifications, not race or religion."[16] Rehnquist also emphasized the written commentary of the floor managers for Title VII (Senators Joseph Clark and Clifford Case), which said that "[t]here is no requirement in title VII that an employer maintain a racial balance in his work force. On the contrary, any deliberate attempt to maintain a racial balance . . . would involve a violation of title VII because maintaining such a balance would require an employer to hire or to refuse to hire on the basis of race."[17] This is a good argument, but not as majoritarian nor as determinate as Rehnquist thought.

Statements by authoritative speakers (bill sponsors and the reporting committee) can be an adequate surrogate for actual legislative intent, to the extent that legislators are on notice that such statements will be considered binding on them and are in a position to respond to or correct errant ones. In that event, rational legislators who fail to object can be presumed to acquiesce in those statements, and vote-counting problems are ameliorated. It is not clear, however, that legislators in 1964 were on notice that what the sponsors were saying was legally binding on Congress. Senator Everett Dirksen, for example, demanded explicit statutory language—section 703(j), for example—

and not just sponsor assurances before he agreed to support the civil rights bill.

More important, even if vote-counting problems were resolved, the problem of strategic behavior would remain. On the one hand, because committees and floor managers are not necessarily representative of their chamber[18] and are likely to be more supportive of "their" bills than the chamber as a whole, their statements should be read critically. On the other hand, because of the cooperative nature of the legislative process, committees and floor managers have incentives not to lie, lest the chamber ignore their current or future recommendations.[19] In order to acquire a reputation as a trustworthy agent of the chamber, a committee has good reason not to write tricky committee reports. Similarly, the floor manager has incentives to reflect the views of the majority coalition lest his or her reputation for trustworthiness be undermined for future interactions.

Admitting the possibility of either strategic or sincere behavior on the part of sources of conventional intent, the intentionalist inquiry then is: How do we tell one from the other? McNollgast (a Borglike collective author) cogently argue that we look to incentives and consequences.[20] Opponents of a bill have incentives to exaggerate its controversial features, and so what they say about a bill is usually "cheap talk," which has little value in figuring conventional intent. Hence, Rehnquist's *Weber* dissent was justified in discounting the statements by southern opponents of the civil rights bill. But talk by supporters can also be cheap, unless it would be costly for them to exaggerate or lie. Denials by Senators Humphrey, Clark, and Case that the bill would require racial quotas may have been cheap talk meant to counter the rhetoric of opponents without actually weakening the bill. Rehnquist accepted the managers' statements as serious talk, subject to institutional penalties if untrue. But the sponsors' talk is not necessarily less manipulative than that of opponents. Both groups risk their reputation by engaging in hyperbole, and both have an interest in being considered trustworthy. My belief is that the only serious talk on the quota issue was the managers' agreement with Senator Dirksen to add section 703(j) to the bill. Because most talk in Congress is some hybrid of cheap and serious, McNollgastian theory does not help us decide the hard cases.

Theories of conventional intent generally fall back on the simple idea that what the sponsor or committee says about the bill is binding on the legislature. As I argued earlier, that proposition does not solve problems of vote counting, strategic behavior, or aggregation. An independent objection to the proposition is that any theory of interpretation that formally treats the views of a legislative subgroup (a sponsor or a committee) as presumptive or conclusive evidence of the views of a majority of the legislature is in tension with article I, section 7 of the Constitution. Section 7 provides that legislation is not valid law unless it has been passed by both chambers of Congress and presented to the president. The constitutional goal of these procedural requirements is to protect against hasty, faction-driven changes in the status quo.[21] Presuming that statements made by committee reports and floor managers reflect authoritative legislative intent is constitutionally suspect for some of the same reasons that the legislative veto is unconstitutional: it shortcircuits the requirement that statutes reflect a consensus of both chambers of Congress and (usually) the president, and it offers factions and interest groups opportunities to manipulate public policy without subjecting their ideas to the full deliberative process.

The bicameralism and presentment point is more than just a formal problem with conventional intent theory. The requirement that legislation reflect a consensus among the House, the Senate, and the president reimposes problems of aggregation and strategic behavior. Even if the House Judiciary Committee (or the floor manager) is a faithful agent of the House coalition passing a bill, there may be insufficient reason to believe that it is faithful to the Senate coalition, or to the president whose veto can kill the bill. Indeed, loyalty to the coalition within the chamber might impel these actors to behave strategically. The article I, section 7 structure not only renders committee reports and floor statements in one chamber incomplete aids to statutory interpretation, but also suggests that majoritarianism is not enough to establish the legitimacy of a theory of statutory interpretation. The theory must find common ground among two different majority-elected legislative bodies and a majority-elected president. This common ground is difficult to establish not only as a formal matter but also as a practical matter, once one understands the bargaining context within which conventional sources of intent are created.

To the extent that conventional intent is created by agents trying to push legislation through the chamber, one would expect those sources to be singularly unhelpful for the issues typically at stake in the "hard cases" (Ronald Dworkin's term) of statutory interpretation. Hard cases arise when the issue is either unanticipated or conflictual. If an issue is unanticipated by the majority coalition, its agents are unlikely to say anything about the issue, for obvious reasons. If the issue is controversial, the agents are likely to suppress discussion in order to preserve cohesion within the coalition. In fact, the two phenomena are often interrelated: an issue *becomes* conveniently unanticipated *because* it would be controversial to talk about it openly.

Such was the fate of voluntary preferences in 1964. Congress was aware of the possibility that employers might grant racial preferences to African Americans, but most discussion of the issue came from the opponents of the bill. The supporters of the bill avoided the matter because it threatened to fracture their coalition of civil rights groups (generally favoring preferences) and labor unions (against them). The sponsors of the civil rights bill had a perfect dodge that appealed to both wings of their coalition while presenting a plausible view of the world: once employers and unions stopped all discrimination against African Americans, their numbers in the work force would climb on their own, and preferences would not be necessary. In other words, no one in Congress in 1964 would admit, and many could not imagine, the *Weber* situation, in which a work force would remain segregated ten years after the statute's enactment because of the continuing effects of discriminatory structures (Kaiser's requirement of prior craft experience).

This is why Rehnquist's quotations from supporters of the civil rights bill focused on whether Title VII would *require* employers to institute racial quotas, and not on whether Title VII would *permit* employers to adopt voluntary preferences. Indeed, the point of my analysis is sharpened by the best evidence Rehnquist discovered, from the interpretive memorandum submitted to the Senate by the managers of Title VII, Senators Clark and Case:

> Title VII would have no effect on established seniority rights. Its effect is prospective and not retrospective. Thus, for example, if a business has been discriminating in the past and as a result has an all-white working force, when the title comes into effect the employer's obligation would simply be to fill future vacancies on a nondiscriminatory basis. He would not be obliged—*or indeed permitted*—to fire whites in order to hire Negroes, *or to prefer Negroes for future vacancies, or, once Negroes are hired, to give them special seniority rights at the expense of white workers hired earlier.*[22]

Rehnquist considered this quotation his smoking gun, a statement by the floor managers of Title VII that anticipated *Weber.*

But the hypothetical is not *Weber,* for its explicit assumption was that after 1964 employers would no longer discriminate against African Americans. Kaiser in fact continued—perhaps unintentionally—to discriminate against African Americans from 1964 to 1974: blacks were not hired for craft positions, and did not even have a fair shot at them, given Kaiser's criteria. If the company had been successfully sued for this discrimination, section 706(g) of the Civil Rights Act would have permitted a court to order "such affirmative action as may be appropriate" to remedy the post-1964 discrimination. Because Clark and Case were also supporters of section 706(g), their memorandum can be read to permit voluntary preferences (the functional equivalent of that section's remedy) in situations where an employer wants to avoid the costs of a lawsuit. Under this variation of the Clark-Case hypothetical, Rehnquist's assurance that "with virtual clairvoyance the Senate's leading supporters of Title VII anticipated precisely the circumstances of this case"[23] is unfair.

The Indeterminacy of Imaginative Reconstruction

Because of the theoretical and practical problems associated with relying on the actual or conventional legislative intent, intentionalism is pressed toward a more generalized version of the theory, imaginative reconstruction, whereby the interpreter tries to discover "what the law-maker meant by assuming his position, in the surroundings in which he acted, and endeavoring to gather from the mischiefs he had to meet and the remedy by which he sought to meet them, his intention with respect to the particular point in controversy."[24] Some political theorists define the inquiry as discovering the preferences of the "pivotal" players, those participants in the enactment process whose support was critical in helping a bill pass through the various "veto gates" which can kill legislation.[25]

Imaginative reconstruction provides the best way to read the *Weber* dissent, which in turn provides insight into how to do imaginative reconstruction. The most persuasive feature of Rehnquist's dissent was his argument that the probable deal necessary to enact the Civil Rights Act of 1964 included assurances that affirmative racial preferences would be prohibited. To make that argument, Rehnquist did not need to demonstrate (through either vote counting or relying on trustworthy conventional sources) that most members actually believed this. All he had to show is some probability that the pivotal voter did. The pivotal voter for the civil rights bill in the Senate is usually assumed to have been the conservative Republican Senator Dirksen, whose support was needed to break the Senate filibuster.[26] It was to the Senate minority leader that Humphrey was speaking when he condemned quotas, and it was to him that the Clark-Case memorandum appealed when it assured the Senate that there would be no preferences for black workers under Title VII. Dirksen's level of commitment to workplace equality for African Americans was much lower than that of the liberal Democrats and Republicans who actively supported the civil rights bill, but it was his level of commitment that controlled the bill because it could not have been passed without him. This is where the deal lay, and Rehnquist argued that Dirksen would have vetoed a civil rights bill that contained *Weber*.

This is a terrific argument, but misleading in ways that reveal the difficulty of imaginative reconstruction. To begin with, it is not always easy to tell who is the "pivotal" voter on any given issue, and in that case the reconstructor faces most of the vote-counting problems discussed earlier. On the issue of preferences, it is probable that Dirksen was the pivotal voter in the Senate coalition that broke the southern filibuster. But there were other pivotal voters at other "veto" stages of the enactment process—including Representative William McCulloch, the ranking Republican who ensured recommendation of an optimal bill from the House Judiciary Committee; Representative Clarence Brown, the ranking Republican who insisted that the House Rules Committee not block the bill, as its chair had done to past civil rights bills; Senator Mike Mansfield, the Senate majority leader, who maneuvered the bill to the Senate floor; and President Lyndon Baines Johnson, who signed the bill. It is doubtful that any of these other pivots shared Dirksen's preferences on employment quotas, for they were all more enthusiastic than Dirksen about helping African Americans.[27] Why focus on Dirksen? Not only was he not the sole pivotal voter, he was also not the final one. That was the president, whose views are the clearest of all (he was willing to pressure employers to adopt quotas), and who was the last hurdle the bill had to pass. Indeed, historians believe it likely that President Johnson's preferences were more important than those of Dirksen as the bill's end game was being played out.[28] In short, imaginative reconstruction does not necessarily solve the vote-counting problems of stronger versions of intentionalism.

This extended exercise in political analysis suggests how hard it is for intentionalists to maintain the promised linkage between their methodology and the preferences of the enacting coalition. The rhetorical force of intentionalism rests on its ability to link a current interpretation to past legislative majorities. But in the hard cases an intentionalist cannot prove that her interpretation is the one actually intended by most legislators, either through rigorous vote counting, or through conventional sources, or even through reconstruction of the enacting coalition. All the intentionalist can claim is that if she had asked her chosen pivotal legislator the interpretive question, the legislator probably would have answered in a certain way.

The difficulties thus developed are distressing enough, but a final problem suggests how imaginative reconstruction is more "imaginative" than "reconstructive." The methodology of imaginative reconstruction calls for posing counterfactual questions to a long-departed pivotal legislator, for the interpretive issue will usually not have been precisely addressed by the legislator. The counterfactual nature of the questions tends to render the inquiry indeterminate. Every statute carries with it certain assumptions about the nature of law and society. Often those assumptions turn out to be wrong, or simplistic, or obsolescent in light of social change—change that sometimes occurs in response to the statute itself. As the assumptions prove incorrect, the statute inevitably deviates from its original course through an often imperceptible process of implementation and interpretation. Once such changes have occurred, how should an intentionalist even pose the question?

For example, Rehnquist's dissent in *Weber* made its case by asking Dirksen or other members of the enacting coalition in 1964 this question: "Do you want to allow voluntary quotas in hiring?" Rehnquist answered: "No, I want to eliminate racial categories from employment decisions." Brennan's majority opinion asked a different question: "Would you allow voluntary remedial preferences if it could be shown that after ten years an employer had less than two percent blacks in its craft force, even though over thirty-nine percent of the area's work force is black, and that the disparity is probably the result of the continuing effects of past discrimination?" One can quite plausibly say that Dirksen (or McCulloch) in 1964 would have answered yes to this form of the question, even if he had answered no to Rehnquist's question. Which of these questions is truer to the intentionalist approach? Which is the more accurate reconstruction? I do not know. Neither does Rehnquist.

Even if Dirksen had answered no to both questions, he might have answered yes if asked: "Do you think that businesses ought to have the flexibility to comply with the act in various practical ways, including the hiring of blacks in order to avoid possible liability?" As a pro-business Republican, Dirksen would have wanted businesses to have flexibility in complying with Title VII, and in 1964 he could not have anticipated that such voluntary compliance would lead to widespread adoption of quotas such as those chosen by Kaiser. It is for this reason that Justice Harry Blackmun's concurring opinion in *Weber* argued that Rehnquist's strong historical case was undermined by an unexpected dilemma for employers and unions under Title VII.[29] Ten years after the enactment of the statute, Kaiser and the Steelworkers found portions of their work force still segregated, probably because of Kaiser's reliance on recruiting from segregated craft unions. Two formal developments in the law during that ten-year period transformed this moral dilemma into a legal problem.

One involved the interpretation of Title VII.[30] The EEOC as early as 1965–66 recognized the *Weber* problem that had been submerged during the congressional deliberations over Title VII: because many of the barriers to minority employment were structural, a "disparate impact" approach to enforcing Title VII had advantages over a "disparate treatment" approach. That is, many of the officials at the EEOC believed that persistent underrepresentation of minority workers required justification, even without a showing that the employer or union had actively sought to exclude them. These officials drew legal support for their position from section 703(a)(2), prohibiting employment practices "which would deprive or tend to deprive any individual of employment opportunities or otherwise adversely affect his status as an employee, because of such individual's race, color, religion, sex, or national origin." Although this interpretation of Title VII was in tension with some of the statute's legislative history (such as the Clark-Case memorandum), these officials persuaded the EEOC to endorse their interpretation. The Supreme Court in 1971 ratified the EEOC's interpretation in Griggs v. Duke Power Company.[31] As a result of *Griggs*, Kaiser and the Steelworkers faced possible liability in the early 1970s for their bad craft force numbers; the affirmative action plan adopted in 1974 and challenged in *Weber* was a rational response to this legal development because it improved Kaiser's numbers immediately.

Another legal development provided even more tangible motivation for the Kaiser plan. In 1965, President Johnson issued Executive Order 11,246,[32] which directed the secretary of labor to require government contractors to take "affirmative action" to ensure an adequate representation of "minorities and women, at all levels and in all segments of [the] work force where deficiencies exist." Unlike Title VII, which was primarily enforced by the courts, Executive Order 11,246 was interpreted and enforced administratively by the Office of Federal Contract Compliance (OFCC) within the Department of Labor. The Nixon administration and its OFCC aggressively expanded Johnson's Executive Order 11,246 to establish numerical targets that government contractors pretty much had to meet. With federal contracts constituting an important share of its business, and with pressure from OFCC to improve its numbers, Kaiser in 1974 had another powerful incentive to adopt an affirmative action program.

Blackmun's concurring opinion conceded that *Weber* may have sacrificed some of the concerns held by members of Congress in 1964, but maintained that these concerns had been substantially sacrificed years before—by the Johnson administration's EEOC, by *Griggs* and subsequent Burger Court decisions, and by the Nixon administration's OFCC. Of course, the Supreme Court could have overruled those earlier interpretations, but Blackmun believed that such a shift would have been a public retreat from the nation's commitment to improving minority workplace opportunities.

Purposivism

I have suggested many reasons why intentionalism does not work as a foundational theory of statutory interpretation. *Weber* is an important proving ground for intentionalism's failures. Not only did the Court seem to reject intentionalism as a universal approach, but analysis of the apparently strong intentionalist arguments of the *Weber* dissent reveals their insufficient link to their asserted majoritarian premises, their indeterminacy, and their intellectual poverty in explaining what is relevant in statutory interpretation, especially their denying the dynamic features of interpretation. These are the negative implications of my analysis. Of course, there may be affirmative implications as well. Thus, *Weber* may be the basis for a different foundational theory of interpretation—purposivism. The Court's main reason for rejecting Rehnquist's position was that it would "bring about an end completely at variance with the purpose of the statute."[33]

In making this argument Brennan was invoking a robust legal tradition that crystallized during the New Deal. Rejecting the static approach of intentionalism, scholars and judges between 1938 and 1959 developed a more adaptable theory of statutory interpretation. As classically stated by Henry Hart and Albert Sacks, statutory ambiguities can be resolved, first, by identifying

the purpose or objective of the statute, and then by determining which interpretation is most consistent with that purpose or goal.[34] Purposivism is an
attractive alternative to intentionalism because it allows a statute to evolve to
meet new problems while ensuring legitimacy by tying interpretation to original legislative expectations. The Supreme Court appears to rely on this approach frequently, as it did in *Weber*, to reject interpretations that, while plausibly grounded in statutory text and history, would undermine the statute's
purpose.

Nonetheless, purposivism is subject to the same problems as intentionalism. As a positive matter, purposivism does not account for the way in which
agencies and courts do statutory interpretation, nor does its methodology rest
on a sufficient account of what enacting coalitions want. For these theoretical
reasons purposivism can establish no connection with majority-based preferences in the hard cases, is indeterminate in practice, and sometimes sacrifices
important values.

From Original to Attributed Purpose

The Court in *Weber* answered the dissenting opinion by trumping Rehnquist's invocation of Congress's original intent with its own invocation of
Congress's original purpose. This analytical move reconciles a dynamic reading of statutes with deference to majoritarian preferences. Because an inquiry
into legislative purpose is set at a higher level of generality than an inquiry
into specific intentions, statutory interpretation becomes more flexible and is
better able to update statutes over time. But purposivism's apparent majoritarian justification rests on questionable assumptions about the legislative process. As I did with intentionalism, I want to unpack several different versions
of purposivism.

Hart and Sacks assumed that the legislature is filled with "reasonable persons pursuing reasonable purposes reasonably."[35] Whether they thought this
assumption reflects the realities of the legislative process is unclear (see Chapter 7), but it was a plausible working assumption for the intellectual community in the 1950s.[36] When agencies and judges invoke a purposivist approach
(as in *Weber*), they are typically claiming that this assumption is reliable. The
assumption is either trivial or false under modern thinking about the legislative process, however.

Modern theory posits that "reasonable" legislators have a complex bundle
of goals, most notably achieving reelection and prestige inside the Beltway, as
well as contributing to good public policy.[37] To the extent that reelection is
an important goal of legislators, they tend to deemphasize bold policy entre-
preneurship and, instead, seek out popular activities such as pork barrel proj-

ects and constituent service to please important interest groups while avoiding positions that may antagonize constituents or groups, and work out compromises on big issues that cannot be avoided.[38] Given these political realities, reasonable legislators do not always produce reasonable policies. Some statutes are little else but back-room deals which distribute public benefits to groups that legislators want to help. This suggests that identifying the actual or even conventional purpose of a statute is just as difficult as identifying the actual or conventional intent of the legislature, or perhaps even more so, since legislators may have incentives to obscure the real purposes of the statute. Legislators do not say, "This is a back-room deal, distributing rents to a group." Instead they say, "This statute helps America!"

Even if legislators are working for public-regarding ends, the political process all but ensures a complex array of purposes, none of which will be desired at any price, all of which will be compromised, and some of which may undercut others. The compromises endemic in the political process suggest that legislation is frequently a congeries of different and sometimes conflicting purposes. To be enacted a statute must be acceptable to a range of public officials, political parties, and interest groups. As a result, supporters of legislation usually appeal to more than one public purpose in order to maximize political support. And as they encounter roadblocks in the political process, they trade off some of their purposes to ameliorate opposition or woo undecided legislators. The statutes that result from this process of sequential deals and trade-offs tend to be filled with complex compromises which cannot easily be distilled into one overriding public purpose.

Let us reconsider *Weber* in light of this problem. Title VII seems to be one of the most purposive statutes adopted in the last thirty-odd years, and its antidiscrimination purpose is a great purpose. Yet even that commanding purpose was repeatedly compromised in order to pick up the support necessary to pass the bill. Thus, the final version of Title VII guaranteed labor backing by protecting existing seniority systems from challenge,[39] firmed up the support of mainstream churches by excluding them from coverage,[40] headed off potential chamber of commerce opposition by exempting small businesses[41] and providing all employers a "bona fide occupational qualification" defense,[42] and bought off Dirksen with procedural restrictions on the EEOC[43] and with an assurance that affirmative preferences would not be "required."[44] Antidiscrimination was not a principle that Congress was willing to implement at any price.

Moreover, the antidiscrimination purpose of Title VII does not answer the interpretive question in *Weber,* where the issue is the meaning of "discrimination." The reasoning in Brennan's opinion tried to answer the question by seizing on one specific purpose of Title VII to create this syllogism: (1) Congress's purpose was to move African Americans into mainstream jobs; (2) affirmative action is a useful way to speed up the process of getting more jobs for blacks; (3) therefore, affirmative action is permissible under the statute because it is consistent with the statute's purpose. This line of reasoning is possible only if one romanticizes the legislative process and subordinates other purposes of Title VII.

The Court's evidence that the purpose of Title VII was to obtain jobs for blacks was a series of quotations from the Senate debates and from President John F. Kennedy's speech proposing the legislation.[45] All of the Senate quotations came from liberal Democrats—Senators Humphrey, Clark, and Edward Kennedy—and the Court offered nothing on this issue from the House record. If the Court was trying to show that the entire Senate, let alone the entire Congress, believed that the purpose of the employment discrimination title was to obtain tangible results for African Americans, the evidence is thin. Although Humphrey and Clark were key players in the debate, they were not representative of the pivotal legislators who supported the bill (midwestern Republicans and western Democrats). More representative of the pivotal Republicans was Dirksen, who said the bill's central purpose was equality of opportunity, not equality of results. For Dirksen and others the purpose of the bill was to ensure color-blind decisions in employment. That purpose is not carried out by affirmative action, which is color-conscious. By asserting the "results purpose" and ignoring the "color-blindness purpose," *Weber* subordinated one purpose of Title VII to another without making any effort to acknowledge the subordination, much less justify it.

Brennan's opinion in *Weber* cannot easily be linked to any purpose actually or even conventionally held by most legislators in 1964. What was really going on in *Weber* was an interpretive "attribution" of purpose to the legislature, not a "discovery" of the purpose actually held by most legislators. Note, too, that Rehnquist's opinion concluded with an argument that the original statutory purpose supported his interpretation, citing Dirksen's paean to the bill as one "that advances the enjoyment of living; but, more than that, it advances the equality of opportunity."[46] Although Rehnquist smartly suggested that the purpose he invoked was more widely shared than the purpose Brennan invoked, his invocation of original purpose is subject to the same problems as Brennan's: it assumes that there was a single purpose underlying Title VII, that different legislators with different agendas were in agreement as to this purpose, and that they were not willing to sacrifice this purpose. Like Brennan, Rehnquist could not have demonstrated any of these points in any rigorous way. Also like Brennan, Rehnquist was attributing a purpose to Title VII, not discovering one. The arguments of both Justices rested on judicially attributed, not majority-chosen, purposes of Title VII.

Indeterminacy of Purposivism

Like intentionalism, purposivism does not yield determinate answers in the hard cases. The foregoing analysis suggests that arguments from actual or conventional or attributed purpose are usually indeterminate because there is no neutral way to choose a single statutory purpose. Even if there is agreement as to which purpose should be attributed to a statute, the analysis in the hard cases must still be indeterminate. An attributed policy purpose is too general and malleable to yield interpretive closure in specific cases, for its application depends on context and the interpreter's perspective. This idea can be expressed through several paradoxes.

Paradox Number One   Even if I were to agree with Rehnquist that the purpose of Title VII was to provide equality of opportunity, I still might vote for Brennan's result. Conversely, even if I were to agree with Brennan that the purpose of Title VII was to get jobs for African Americans, I still might vote for Rehnquist's result. The reason for this paradox is that a general purpose is elastic enough to encompass a variety of specific applications.

Consider the first prong of the paradox: Is an interpretation of Title VII prohibiting affirmative action programs one that conduces to "equality of opportunity" in the context of the *Weber* case? Recall that without the new training program in Kaiser's Gramercy plant, African American workers had little chance of obtaining desirable craft positions, and for no reason other than their race. Is that the equality of opportunity that Dirksen described as "the mass conscience of mankind that speaks in every generation"? Many scholars have argued from empirical and historical evidence that structural barriers, such as Kaiser's requirement of prior craft experience, have impeded minority opportunities in the workplace and that affirmative action may be a useful remedy.[47] The idea of preferences as a remedy for disadvantages resulting from structural or historical barriers is no radical concept. Recall the Bush administration's position in trade negotiations with Japan. Because American companies feel that they have faced structural barriers to entering Japanese domestic markets, President Bush and his trade negotiators sought quotas, guaranteed market floors, and other preferences as a necessary precondition for having what they considered an "equal opportunity" to crack those markets.[48]

Consider the second prong of the paradox: Is an interpretation permitting affirmative action programs one that will generate more jobs for African Americans? Probably so in the short run, but not necessarily in the longer term. If race-based prejudice or stereotyping continues, the market may negate some or all of the law's efforts.[49] Thus, under a *Griggs-Weber* legal regime companies such as Kaiser may have an incentive not to locate their plants in areas where African Americans constitute a large percentage of the work force. Also, by reintroducing race-based hiring and promotion, affirmative action threatens to marginalize and even demoralize African Americans in the workplace, stigmatizing them as "special hires," in contrast to others hired "on the merits." Notwithstanding affirmative action, African Americans in the 1990s are statistically not much if any better off than they were in 1964; they continue to have double the unemployment rate of white Americans and to earn only a fraction of the income of whites.[50]

Paradox Number Two   The two statutory purposes emphasized by Brennan and Rehnquist are potentially the same purpose. One way to understand the purposivist debate within *Weber* is to see it as the disaggregation over time of two elements of a single statutory purpose. The legislative goal in Title VII was to produce equality of opportunity, and even color-blind hiring and promotion practices, as Rehnquist maintained. As Brennan claimed, however, the goal was at the same time to improve the actual economic integration of African Americans into the work force. Members of Congress who supported the civil rights bill believed, or said they believed, that these purposes were the same—that color-blind hiring and promotion would naturally generate good numbers. Over time that was not what happened, as Kaiser discovered: African-American representation in the work force did not increase, in part because discrimination against blacks was hard to prove and in part because historical and structural impediments worked against them. Once the interpreters of Title VII understood this, their understanding of Title VII's purpose changed, albeit not in predictable ways.

The EEOC in the 1960s and the Supreme Court in the 1970s responded to the disaggregation of Title VII's purpose by recognizing disparate impact liability and permitting voluntary affirmative action. But they could legally have made the opposite choice and left structure-based reasons for discrimination essentially unremedied. Indeed, that is where the Reagan EEOC and the Rehnquist Court were headed in the 1980s—toward essentially overruling *Griggs* and challenging the continued viability of *Weber* (see Chapter 9). The material difference between the Nixon EEOC and Court and the Reagan EEOC and Court lay not in the overall purpose they attributed to Title VII, but in their different judgments about what to do when the purpose ran up against structural socioeconomic problems.

In the Civil Rights Act of 1991, Congress rejected the Rehnquist Court's approach and gave at least a qualified approval of *Griggs*'s interpretation of Title VII to attack employment policies having a disparate impact.[51] It is unpredictable what the EEOC and Court will do with the new law, for one lesson of this experience is that statutory purpose not only permits dynamic interpretation of old statutes but is itself dynamic. The purpose of a statute changes over time as the targeted problem changes, often negating the assumptions critical to the original formulations of that purpose. Statutory purpose also changes as new interpreters approach the issue, often reacting to problems they perceive in prior interpretations. And Congress itself provides feedback, signals that approve or disapprove of the way the agency or the Court is developing the statutory policy or purpose.

Paradox Number Three   Brennan did not believe that the only purpose of Title VII was to gain jobs for African Americans, any more than Rehnquist believed that the only purpose was to provide African Americans with equal employment opportunities. Purpose is dynamic even in the hands of the same interpreter because the interpreter's understanding of the statutory purpose depends in part on the context in which she or he is applying the statute.

Evidence for this proposition came eight years after the *Weber* decision, when the Court interpreted Title VII to permit affirmative action programs to place female employees in jobs where they had been traditionally underrepresented. Brennan's opinion for the Court in Johnson v. Transportation Agency, Santa Clara County,[52] not only reaffirmed *Weber* but gave it a highly expansive reading to sanction affirmative action for female employees whenever there was an "imbalance" in women's representation. This is an extension of the *Weber* reasoning, which rested on (thin) evidence that Title VII's overriding legislative purpose was to gain jobs for racial minorities, mainly African Americans. There was never a discussion of a similar overriding purpose to gain jobs for female employees, since sex discrimination was added to the jobs title by a last-minute floor amendment in the House, offered by an opponent of the bill in an attempt to make it too strong.[53]

Johnson provides a strikingly different picture of Brennan's views about the purpose of Title VII (opening up employment opportunities for gender as well as racial groups underrepresented in a particular job category), and demonstrates that the purpose Brennan attributed to Title VII was quite dynamic and, by 1987, had little if any connection to the original discussions surrounding the enactment of Title VII. Almost as dramatic as Brennan's volte-face in *Johnson* was Rehnquist's silence. Abandoning the fervent attention to Congress's original intent and purpose laid out in his own *Weber* dissent, Rehnquist silently joined Justice Antonin Scalia's dissenting opinion, which flogged the majority opinion for violating the "plain meaning" of the statutory text.[54]

Purposivism and Other Values

My analysis of the *Weber* issue suggests that purposivism shares the same theoretical vulnerabilities as intentionalism. Like intentionalism, purposivism cannot connect its results with original legislative expectations because it has no robust positive theory of enacting coalitions. The Hart and Sacks theory, which attributes purposes to made-up coalitions, is substantially aspirational and (as we shall see in Chapter 5) nonoriginalist. Like intentionalism, purposivism has no good theory for setting its inquiry; intentionalism founders on its inability to pose neutral counterfactual questions, while purposivism founders on the unwieldy generality of its questions.

Thus, we should not be surprised to discover that purposivism is no more a foundational inquiry in statutory interpretation than is intentionalism. The Supreme Court often follows the plain meaning of the statutory text over objections that the literalist interpretation undermines the original intent or purpose of the Congress that enacted the statute.[55] Consider, for example, Griffin v. Oceanic Contractors, Inc.[56] Danny Griffin, a welder working on Oceanic's vessels in the North Sea, was injured during his employment and subsequently discharged. Oceanic withheld $412.50 in earned wages which Griffin claimed were owing to him, and he brought suit under a federal statute that required certain maritime employers to pay wages within a specified period after terminating a seaman's employment. The statute further provided that "[e]very master or owner who refuses or neglects to make payment in the manner hereinbefore mentioned without sufficient cause shall pay to the seaman a sum equal to two days' pay for each and every day during which payment is delayed beyond the respective periods."[57] The trial court found Oceanic liable for the withheld wages and assessed the penalty for the period between Griffin's discharge (April 1, 1976) and reemployment (May 5, 1976); the penalty amounted to $6,881.60. The Supreme Court directed that the penalty be recalculated to reflect the period between discharge and the actual date of payment (which was not until May 6, 1980, the trial court judgment). The Court relied on the literal terms of the statute, which said that the owner "shall pay" penalty wages "for each and every day during which payment is withheld." No pertinent exceptions appeared on the face of the statute. Hence, the penalty for withholding $412.50 became $302,790.40 by the Court's calculations.

This striking result was disputed in a dissenting opinion by Justice John Paul Stevens, who relied on both legislative intent and purpose to argue that the penalty statute gave trial courts discretion to abbreviate the penalty period for equitable reasons. The original statute, enacted in 1872, used mandatory language ("shall") to ensure that additional wages would be awarded, but double wages could be awarded for up to ten days only, and courts had discretion to award even less than that.[58] Congress amended the statute in 1898 to eliminate the ten-day limit, but retained the mandatory language.[59] Given the routine nature of the 1898 amendment and the absence of legislative comment, Stevens suggested that Congress did not intend to abrogate judicial discretion to award less than the maximum amount. Also, the Court's broad interpretation of the 1898 change went well beyond the statute's purpose, which was to compensate seamen for additional expenses incurred after discharge (often in a foreign land), not to afford them a windfall.[60]

Both arguments are subject to the analytical problems developed earlier in this chapter. The critical 1898 amendment did two important things: it eliminated the ten-day cap on recovery, *and* it rewrote the statute as a whole to delete any explicit grant of judicial discretion. Nothing in the committee reports or legislative debates suggests that judges would retain discretion to shorten the penalty wage period. This omission left Stevens with only an argument from legislative silence, which generally reveals very little about legislative intent.

The committee reports do say that the 1898 amendment sought "the amelioration of the condition of the American seamen" and that the strengthened penalty wage provision was "designed to secure the promptest possible payment of wages."[61] If we assume that these statements of purpose can be attributed to Congress (a strong assumption), they do not clearly support Stevens's interpretation of the double wages statute. One problem is that there may be two cross-cutting statutory purposes. Stevens may be right that Congress sought an easy-to-administer formula for compensating seamen for their expenses resulting from an unfair discharge, and the statutory "amelioration of the condition of American seamen" might support his view. Congress, however, also wanted "to secure the *promptest possible* payment of wages," and this purpose suggests a deterrence rationale that might support the Court's interpretation. Moreover, either version of the statutory purpose could support either interpretation of the statute. Truly, the interpretations reached by both the Court (Griffin gets $302,790.40) and the dissent (Griffin gets $6,881.60) ameliorate "the condition of American seamen" and might be expected to "secure the promptest possible payment of seamen's wages" (the $412.50 owing to Griffin). The Court's interpretation accomplishes a lot more amelioration and promptness than does the dissent's interpretation. What makes it hard to choose between the two is that nothing in the legislative materials tells us how draconian Congress expected the remedy to be, nor do the materials tell us when Congress thought the compensatory and deterrence purposes of the statute might be sacrificed for other values, such as unfair surprise.

Even if the original legislative intent or purpose had supported Stevens's position more clearly, a majority of the Justices might have reached the same result in *Griffin* because they value enforcement of clear texts. Citizens ought to be able to open up the statute books and have a good idea of their rights and obligations. When the statute seems plainly to say one thing, courts should be reluctant to alter that directive. Thus, in *Griffin* the Court sent a message to vessel owners that the provisions of the United States Maritime Code set forth clear obligations, which judges will enforce to the letter. This clarity discourages owners, who have greater resources than seamen, from engaging in strategic withholding of wages or dilatory litigation. Furthermore, it signals to the owners and the seamen that the law will be applied to them in a predictable manner. As Philip Frickey pointed out to me, Congress endorsed and relied on this rule of law value when it rewrote the statute in 1983.[62]

Textualism

Legal process thinkers such as Hart and Sacks rejected intentionalism as a grand strategy for statutory interpretation, and in its place they offered purposivism. A new generation of scholars and jurists, most notably Judge Frank Easterbrook and Justice Antonin Scalia, have criticized both purposivism and intentionalism from an originalist perspective and argue for textualism as the foundational approach to statutory interpretation.[63] For these "new textualists," the beginning, and usually the end, of statutory interpretation should be the apparent meaning of the statutory language. Based in part on the theoretical arguments of the new textualists, the Supreme Court in the 1980s increasingly relied on plain meaning as the primary—and sometimes the only—method for determining statutory meaning.[64]

The arguments for textualism as the foundational method in statutory interpretation are strong ones. As I suggested, textualism appeals to the rule of law value that citizens ought to be able to read the statute books and know their rights and duties. Because the actual words of a statute have been voted on and approved by a majority of legislators in each chamber of the legislature, statutory text has the strongest connection to majority preferences. Indeed, the actual text of the statute may be the most reliable and precise evidence of legislative intent and purpose. Nonetheless, textualism falls athwart the same difficulties that plague the other foundationalist theories. Like intentionalism and purposivism, textualism cannot rigorously be tied to majority preferences, does not yield determinate answers or meaningfully constrain the interpreter in hard cases, and is not an accurate description of what agencies and courts actually do when they interpret statutes.

Statutory Text and Majority Cycles

The pitch for textualism is that it is the most concrete evidence we have of the preferences that are supposed to count for article I, section 7 purposes. Theories of "majority cycling," however, question whether there is any single majority whose preferences can be discovered, whether under the aegis of statutory text or legislative intent or purpose.[65] Although statutes do not necessarily reflect the preferences of popular majorities, most people assume that statutes do reflect the preferences of legislative majorities. Yet that is only part of the story. There might not be a single legislative majority on some issues, for legislators do not usually line up their preferences based on a single criterion; instead they consider different criteria, thereby generating preference rankings that are not coherent with any one continuum (e.g., liberal-conservative). This fluidity gives rise to the documented phenomenon of "majority cycling," in which a series of pairwise votes will yield different policy choices depending on the sequence of the voting.[66] Consider this illustration.

Section 703(j) of the Civil Rights Act of 1964 may have been the product of a majority cycle, in which there were three policy choices on the affirmative action issue:

1. Title VII prohibits all affirmative action, including voluntary plans.
2. Title VII allows any and all affirmative action and is open-ended on whether the government can require employers to adopt such plans.
3. Title VII allows voluntary affirmative action by employers but makes it clear that the government cannot require affirmative action.

Different groups of legislators had different criteria for ranking these policies, taking into consideration not only their preferences for affirmative action per se (which dominated the ordering by the liberal supporters of the bill), but also their preferences for transparency in the bill's provisions (a value held mainly by the bill's opponents) and for giving businesses as many options as possible (a value held mainly by the centrist senators, especially the Republicans).

Following this analysis, my imaginative reconstruction of the groups' different rankings can be mapped:[67]

	Strong supporters (42 Senators)	Strong opponents (27 Senators)	Moderates (31 Senators)
First choice	(2)	(1)	(3)
Second choice	(3)	(2)	(1)
Third choice	(1)	(3)	(2)

Under this configuration of preferences, there is a majority cycle. Any of the three choices can prevail, depending on which two pair up last:

A. Choice (1) defeats choice (2) by 58–42, but then loses to choice (3) by 73–27. *Choice (3) prevails.*
B. But if choice (3) had paired up first against choice (2), choice (2) would have prevailed by 69–31, only to lose in the next round to choice (1) by 58–42. *Choice (1) prevails.*
C. But if choice (1) had paired up first against choice (3), choice (3) would have prevailed by 73–27, only to lose in the next round to choice (2) by a vote of 69–31. *Choice (2) prevails.*

This result, in which any of the three proposals can win, represents the "chaos" feature of cycling theory: everything becomes indeterminate or chaotic. Yet chaos does not rule the legislature. Legislative choices tend to be stable ones, and in practice majorities do not cycle, in part because legislative procedures create conditions of stability and equilibrium.[68] Cycling is avoided, for example, when one of the groups controls the chamber's agenda, and hence can protect its preferred outcome against a rival that would beat it. These agenda setters can orchestrate their desired outcome—let's say choice (2)—in one of two ways. One way that would work in the Senate would be to arrange for choice (2) to be the last to pair up, following scenario (C). Thus, the strategy would be to put choice (2) in the bill. If opponents filed an amendment to the bill to replace choice (2) with choice (1) (an amendment that ought to be successful), the agenda setters could file an amendment to the amendment to replace choice (1) with choice (3). Under Senate procedures, senators would first vote on the amendment to the amendment, which would pass 69–31 and would substitute for choice (3) in the amendment, which would then fail against the original bill by a vote of 73–27. Choice (2) would prevail simply because of who had control over the bill and its procedures.

Another way the agenda setters could influence the outcome would work only in the House, where the Rules Committee (now controlled by the House leadership) determines what amendments are even presented. If the agenda setters desired choice (2), they would place it in the bill during committee deliberations, and then would limit amendments to choice (3) through a "modified closed rule" issued through the Rules Committee. Again, choice (2) would prevail. Even if such strategies fail, the agenda setters often have a final opportunity to add their policy choice—during a conference committee required to iron out bicameral differences in a bill. If conferees from both chambers favor choice (2), and it is arguably within the version adopted by one chamber, the other chamber can recede, leaving choice (2) in the bill, subject to an up-or-down vote by its chamber.

This scenario shows one way that cycling can be avoided, but it is not what happened in 1964, when the bill's supporters controlled the agenda in both

House and Senate but were not able to encode their preferred policy, choice (2), in section 703(j). Instead, section 703(j) represents choice (3), and the story about how that happened reflects another way in which legislatures can avoid majority cycles. Cycles can be avoided when one group "buys off" another group, so that the latter gets its preferred policy in return for its agreement to do something for the first group. This is logrolling, and few laws get through the political process without some logs being rolled. Section 703(j) was the result of a logroll in which Senator Dirksen extracted his group's favorite option, choice (3), for the preferences issue in return for his support in breaking the filibuster. Because the selection of choice (3) was part of a logroll to which two groups agreed, it was a stable selection.

The theory of majority cycling has interesting implications for statutory interpretation. The most striking is that even text-based interpretation is hard to link up with majority preferences because there may be several equally plausible majority-based preferences in the legislature. An enacting coalition may be just one of several different possible coalitions, and any particular provision might be in a law only because of which group controlled the legislative agenda or what logrolls were expedient. This conclusion provides a functional justification for my earlier point about article I, section 7: the legitimacy of the statute is derived less from majoritarianism (this policy is what most legislators want) than from formalism (this text was agreed to by both chambers of Congress and signed by the president). But formalism of this sort opens up statutory interpretation. Articles II (the executive power) and III (the judicial power) authorize the president and the Court to implement and interpret the laws enacted by Congress under article I, but they set forth no formal constraints on such interpretation, leaving those institutions a great deal of freedom.

How do agencies and courts use this freedom? It would be irrational to constrain themselves with an originalist methodology; but even if they tried to be originalist, cycling theory suggests they would fail. That is, if legislatures are subject to majority cycles, then so are agencies and courts.[69] In that event there may be instability as to statutory decisions (mainly for agencies), or the order in which issues are decided might affect what the decisions are (especially for courts because of stare decisis). For example, the EEOC in the 1960s vacillated on issues of disparate impact and affirmative action, and its position on the latter issue grew out of its position on the former. The Supreme Court grappled with the *Griggs* issue of disparate impact discrimination before it tackled voluntary affirmative action; *Weber* was a much easier case after *Griggs*. If voluntary affirmative action had come before the Court in 1971 and not 1979, the Court might well have decided the issue differently. This simple thought experiment vitiates all the originalist theories of statutory interpretation. As a positive matter, one would expect agencies and courts to follow a variety of approaches to statutes over time, including explicitly dynamic approaches; as a descriptive matter, that is precisely what Nicholas Zeppos and others have found.[70]

The Indeterminacy of Textual Plain Meaning

Textualists might accept my assertion that the legitimacy of statutory interpretation does not rest on majoritarianism, but would sharply contest my assertion that the Constitution does not require textualism or any other originalist methodology. The new textualist position is that statutory text is the most determinate basis for statutory interpretation. That proposition, important to their theory, is questionable. As I did for other theories, I shall start with the simplest, cleanest version before moving on to a more sophisticated one.

The simplest version of textualism is enforcement of the "plain meaning" of the statutory provision: that is, given the ordinary meanings of words and accepted precepts of grammar and syntax, what does the provision signify to the reasonable person? An initial problem with simple plain meaning is that, for any statute of consequence, the legislative drafting process ensures textual ambiguities, which only multiply over time. Ambiguities arise because there is no single author, because different authors write and rewrite provisions at different times and with different goals or strategies in mind, and because the goals of at least some of the authors are to create rather than avoid ambiguity. This last phenomenon explains the popularity of referring difficult issues to courts and/or agencies through delegation of authority or through the use of highly generalized terms that have to be fleshed out (or both).

The basis for Brian Weber's claim was section 703(a)(1) and (d) of the Civil Rights Act. Section 703(a)(1) states:

(a) It shall be an unlawful employment practice for an employer—
(1) to fail or refuse to hire or to discharge any individual, or otherwise to discriminate against any individual with respect to his compensation, terms, conditions, or privileges of employment, because of such individual's race, color, religion, sex, or national origin . . .

Section 703(d) made it unlawful "to discriminate against any individual because of his race, color, religion, sex, or national origin in admission to, or employment in, any program established to provide apprenticeship or other training." Rehnquist's dissent in *Weber*, and even more pointedly Scalia's dissent in *Johnson*, chided Brennan's opinions in those cases for ignoring what they considered the plain meaning of section 703(a).[71]

Yet this criticism supposes that "discrimination because of race" means any and every kind of differentiation based on race. That is one definition of discrimination (usually the first dictionary entry for the term) but not the only one. "Discrimination" has acquired nuances in our culture that undermine any attempt to confine the term to that definition. For example, in common usage we do not say we "discriminate because of flavor" when we choose chocolate and not vanilla (although this would be a correct dictionary use of the word). Nor do we usually say we "discriminate because of sex" because we spend more time with Jim, to whom we are attracted, than with Elizabeth, who is a good friend. Instead, we tend to use the term only when some "invidious" differentiation is involved. Admittedly, this point only displaces the linguistic conundrum. It is surely an invidious differentiation to exclude an African American from the Kaiser training program simply because the decision maker dislikes blacks, or to exclude Brian Weber because she dislikes whites.[72] Is it legally the same thing—an "invidious" differentiation—to include African Americans in a training program, and thereby to exclude some whites, because the decision maker feels a moral or legal sympathy toward African American workers as a previously excluded group, or simply because the decision maker wants a greater diversity in her work force? This is a contested point. From Brian Weber's perspective it seems like the same thing—it feels unjust.[73] But from the perspective of someone who has herself felt the sting of bigoted actions or suffers the heritage of historical prejudice (including not just African Americans but also Asian Americans, lesbians, gay men, Latinos and Latinas, and women generally), it might seem like something quite different—and just.[74]

Griggs suggests the less obvious point that it is invidious differentiation for an employer to continue to use a nonessential job criterion—one for which there is no business reason—which has the effect of excluding African Americans from consideration for employment. Once *Griggs* defined discrimination in this way, we came to realize the extent to which concepts of subordination and justification are bound up in what choices we consider invidious and therefore prohibited. It isn't disparate impact "discrimination" if the employment criterion has a business justification or does not contribute to the continued economic subordination of blacks. Why, then, should it be disparate treatment "discrimination" if the training program has a justification rooted in compensatory justice or in workplace diversity?[75]

Even those who agree that discrimination in *Weber* is not textually determinate might argue that the double wages statute in *Griffin* was determinate because it was more detailed and did not use terms that have a rich variety of connotations. But is that so? The statute said the owner "shall pay to the seaman a sum equal to two days' pay for each and every day during which payment is delayed beyond the respective periods." The statute did not explicitly provide that "there shall be no diminishment of such recovery of double wages for any reason whatsoever." Thus, the penalty statute could have been interpreted to permit judicial amelioration of the double wage penalty with no greater violence to the statutory language than is routinely done when judges read equitable exceptions into statutes of limitations. In addition, a statutory prerequisite to recovery of the penalty in *Griffin* was the employer's failure to pay wages "without sufficient cause," a vague term that could have been construed to delegate discretion to the court to stop the running of the penalty for equitable reasons. Although the plain meaning of the statute lent support to the Court's interpretation in *Griffin*, it hardly required it. Note that *Griffin* is probably an easy case for textualists.

An additional problem with a simple textualist theory is that the meaning of text is decisively influenced by context. If I were to write you a note saying, "Go fetch me some soup meat," you could not interpret it without knowing and understanding its context. Have you regularly been fetching soup meat for me? If so, you might reasonably assume that I want the same kind of meat you have been bringing me. What is the purpose of the order? If you know from context that I am hosting a fancy dinner party, you might interpret the order to mean prime steak, unless you know that my friends do not eat red meat, in which case you might bring fine boneless chicken, or even fish, which some people do not consider meat at all.

This same sort of analysis readily applies to legal texts. When Congress told us in 1964 that we should not discriminate on the basis of race in employment decisions, did we not know from ten years' experience with *Brown*, from the pictures of Bull Connor's fire hoses pummeling black youths marching aginst racism, from the march on Washington, and from Dr. Martin Luther King, Jr.'s, speeches and letters that the point of the statute was to seek compensatory justice for a group that had systematically been treated unjustly in our society? The thrust of the Court's opinion in *Weber* was that our country's commitment in Title VII was to results as well as process. In the context of unbroken centuries of structural racial injustice in this country, we blink at moral as well as historical reality when we say that differentiation targeted against African Americans is the same as differentiation seeking to redress patterns of prior prejudice and oppression. Indeed, during deliberations on the *Johnson* case,[76] which reaffirmed *Weber,* Brennan circulated a draft footnote that provided historical evidence for *Weber*'s toleration of affirmative action. The 1963 settlement of King's Birmingham boycott included a commitment by stores to hire blacks and to create an "area-wide program for acceleration of upgrading and the employment of Negroes in job categories previously denied to Negroes." This settlement was hailed by the Kennedy administration and the media as a good development—praise that would not have been possible if the public culture in 1963–64, when the civil rights bill was being deliberated, considered this sort of voluntary affirmative action race discrimination.

Not everyone would agree with these sentiments, but one's attitude toward them is an important factor in how one would vote in *Weber*. Brennan agreed with these statements; Rehnquist found them irrelevant or unpersuasive. This is my third problem with a simple, naive texualism: the interpreter's own context, including her situatedness in a certain generation and a certain status in our society, influences the way she reads simple texts. As I argue in greater detail in the next chapter, interpretation cannot aspire to universal objectivity, since the interpreter's perspective must always interact with the text and historical context. This is an inherently dynamic process, as the subsequent history of *Weber* reveals.

Although the Court reaffirmed *Weber* in *Johnson*, the opinions in the latter decision demonstrated a heterogeneity in their interpretation of Title VII and of *Weber* itself. The recently appointed Justice Scalia wrote a scorching dissent, but one that largely ignored the historical points made by Rehnquist's *Weber* dissent, and instead anchored on the injustice he keenly felt for ethnic working-class white men who are made to suffer the costs of voluntary affirmative action.[77] Justice Sandra Day O'Connor, the other post-*Weber* appointee, approached the statute and the record much more sympathetically than did Scalia, not because she is a liberal but because she is more committed to stare decisis,[78] and (one suspects) because the case involved gender preferences. Most of the Justices who were on the Court for both cases brought new perspectives to the proper interpretation of Title VII. As I have noted, Brennan ignored the reasoning in his own *Weber* opinion and greatly expanded allowable affirmative action—so much so that Justice Byron White, who joined *Weber*, not only dissented from that precedent's expansion but called for its overruling entirely.[79] Stevens, who recused himself in *Weber*, announced in his *Johnson* concurring opinion that he would have dissented in the earlier case, but that stare decisis persuaded him not only that *Weber* should be reaffirmed but that Brennan's opinion was too constraining and that there should be virtually no limits at all on voluntary affirmative action under Title VII.[80] One cannot read the nine opinions in *Weber* and *Johnson* without an appreciation for the critical role played by personal perspective in interpreting both statutory texts and statutory precedents.

Indeterminacy and Inadequacy of Holistic Textualism

A simple plain meaning approach to statutory interpretation seems unlikely to yield the determinacy needed for a foundational theory of statutory interpretation. Because textual meaning is so dependent on context, textualism cannot mount a serious effort to be considered the foundational theory of statutory interpretation without developing a theory of contextual constraints on the textualist interpreter. Scalia has developed such a theory, which I call holistic textualism.[81]

Scalia's goal in statutory interpretation is to produce text-based interpretive closure even when the statutory provision being interpreted is itself ambiguous. He accomplishes this through reference to three different contexts: textual authorities (dictionaries) and established traditions (case law) in place when the statute was written; the text of the statute as a whole, as well as related statutory provisions; and statutory clear statement rules setting forth policy presumptions that will govern absent clear textual contradiction. The leading statement of his approach to statutory interpretation is Scalia's concurring opinion in Green v. Bock Laundry Machine Company:

> The meaning of terms in the statute books ought to be determined, not on the basis of which meaning can be shown to have been understood by a larger handful of the Members of Congress; but rather on the basis of which meaning is (1) most in accord with context and ordinary usage, and thus most likely to have been understood by the *whole* Congress which voted on the words of the statute (not to mention the citizens subject to it), and (2) most compatible with the surrounding body of law into which the provision must be integrated—a compatibility which, by a benign fiction, we assume that Congress always has in mind.[82]

This holistic textualism is the best effort textualism can make to be the foundationalist method for statutory interpretation. This methodology, too, fails because it does no better than plain meaning to yield determinate interpretations, because the interpreter's perspective remains critical, and because even the most ardent new textualist is willing to sacrifice plain meaning for other values.

Holistic textualism suggests a rich array of arguments for the *Weber* issue by asking which interpretation is most consistent with the whole statute and with statutory policy generally. Rehnquist's view that Title VII prohibits any race-based differentiation in the terms or conditions of employment finds support in the overall structure of section 703. Subsections (a)–(d) set forth broadly phrased prohibitions, not only against efforts to "discriminate" because of race (section 703[a] and [d]) but also against any programs "to limit, segregate, or classify employees" because of race (section 703[a][2]). The prohibitions seem deliberately broad, to set up the baseline rule that employment decisions cannot take account of race and other prohibited criteria. Then, subsections (e)–(i) set forth permissible departures from the presumptive baseline. For example, section 703(h) allows seniority systems to continue, so long as their race-based effects "are not the result of an intention to discriminate because of race."[83] This exemption suggests that Title VII considers "intention to discriminate" different from merely "discriminate," consistent with Rehnquist's position that Congress meant to prohibit all race-based differentiations. His position is also supported by section 703(e), which creates an employer defense "where religion, sex, or national origin is a bona fide occupational qualification reasonably necessary to the normal operation of that business or enterprise."[84] It is notable that section 703(e) assumes that race and color (the two omitted categories) are never the basis for a "bona fide occupational qualification."

Similarly, the structure of section 703 works against Brennan's view that an employer does not "discriminate" when it sets up voluntary racial preferences: by establishing specific policy-based exceptions to the broad antidiscrimination rule, Congress was implicitly discouraging the creation of additional exceptions such as the one created by *Weber.* This reading of section 703 is suggested by the canon of construction, "expressio unius est exclusio alterius" (expressing one thing implies that all other things are excluded). Yet this same canon suggests that Brennan's interpretation finds support in section 703(j), which provides that nothing in Title VII "shall be interpreted to require any employer . . . to grant preferential treatment to any individual or to any group because of the race, color, religion, sex, or national origin of such individual or group on account of an imbalance" in their representation in the work force. Section 703(j) is the only provision in section 703 that speaks directly to preferences, and it prohibits only an interpretation of Title VII that "requires" preferences; it does not prohibit any interpretation that "permits" voluntary preferences. Thus, Brennan argued from the *expressio unius* canon that Congress implicitly permitted voluntary preferences in section 703(j).

A lesson I draw from *Weber* is that even a holistic understanding of textualism does not yield determinate results in the hard cases. This is confirmed by Scalia's *Johnson* dissent, which paid insufficient attention to Scalia's own textualist theory and practice. Citing only section 703(a), Scalia found the statute "unambiguous" against voluntary race-based preferences, and lambasted the majority opinion for rewriting the statute. It is remarkable that, in making accusations about the Court's good faith, Scalia not only failed to consider the structural arguments supporting his position (detailed earlier) but also ignored Brennan's section 703(j) argument, which had been fully developed in *Weber.* Although I do not consider the section 703(j) argument dispositive, it is the sort of parsimonious textual argument—give priority to the provision specifically focusing on the issue (section 703[j]) over the general provision (section 703[a]) and presume that any gaps are left unregulated *(expressio unius)*—that Scalia has elsewhere found dispositive to reject broad interpretations of statutes protecting racial minorities and consumers.[85]

Although Scalia refused to analyze section 703(j) in his dissent, he did rely on its policy. He argued that *Griggs* in combination with *Weber* had turned section 703(j) on its head: the former decision put pressure on employers (such as the Santa Clara Transportation Agency) to diversify their work forces, which the latter decision allowed employers to accomplish through quota programs.[86] This is a neat point, but again not the sort of rigorous textual argument that Scalia has demanded from those seeking expansive interpretations that help, rather than hurt, minority interests. *Griggs* does not "require" quotas in any formal sense. If an employer feels it might lose a disparate impact lawsuit, the employer knows that section 706(g) would permit a court to order broad "affirmative action" to correct the violations. While that knowledge gives an employer incentives to adopt voluntary preferences, it is just as much section 706(g) as *Griggs* that practically "requires" such a move; and there is every reason to believe that Congress in the 1970s and 1980s considered section 703(j) consistent with *Griggs*.[87] Given the tools of strict textual analysis Scalia has deployed in other cases, it is hard to see why he was so vexed in *Johnson*—until the end of his dissenting opinion, which is a heartfelt appeal against shifting the costs of historic patterns of discrimination onto people such as Brian Weber and Paul Johnson, blue-collar (often ethnic) white men who get bumped by management's plans to improve their Title VII numbers.[88]

Scalia's performance in *Johnson* is Exhibit A for my suggestion that holistic textual analysis is no more determinate, objective, or constraining than other archaeological approaches to statutory interpretation. Relatedly, my analysis suggests that current values, including those widely shared as well as those more particular to the interpreter, will influence any interpreter's approach to statutory text. Current values cannot easily be excluded from statutory interpretation, a proposition supported by the ode to blue-collar white men that climaxed Scalia's impassioned dissent in *Johnson* (my Exhibit A). Exhibit B is Scalia's performance in *Bock Laundry*, his main statement of the new textualist position.

In that case the laundry operation being sued for failure to warn an employee against putting his hand in a dangerous dryer sought to impeach the credibility of the plaintiff employee by bringing up his prior criminal felony convictions. Federal Rule of Evidence 403 permits a federal court to exclude relevant evidence "if its probative value is substantially outweighed by the danger of unfair prejudice." Rule 403 would probably have excluded the impeaching evidence, but the lower courts and the Supreme Court held that a more specific provision, Rule 609(a), trumped the general precepts of Rule 403.[89] Rule 609(a) provided:

> For the purpose of attacking the credibility of a witness, evidence that a witness has been convicted of a crime shall be admitted if elicited from the witness or established by public record during cross-examination but only if the crime (1) was punishable by death or imprisonment in excess of one year under the law under which the witness was convicted, and the court determines that the probative value of admitting this evidence outweighs its prejudicial effect to the defendant, or (2) involved dishonesty or false statement, regardless of the punishment.

Section 609(a)(1) had a plain meaning in the case: Bock Laundry's evidence impeaching Paul Green "shall be admitted," because the crime was punishable by more than a year in prison and because admitting the evidence would have had no prejudicial effect on the defendant (Bock Laundry!).

Although the statute's meaning was plain, it was also peculiar—and arguably unconstitutional in civil cases because it set up a discrimination between civil plaintiffs such as Paul Green (who could always be impeached for their convictions for serious crimes) and civil defendants such as Bock Laundry (who could often escape impeachment by showing that introducing their prior convictions would have a countervailing prejudicial effect on their cases). If Rule 609(a)(1) were unconstitutional, it should not have been applied in the case, and Rule 403 would have applied to exclude the impeaching convictions. But no Justice read the statute *that* literally. Stevens, writing for five Justices, rewrote the statute to reflect what he thought was the probable intent of Congress in 1974: to exclude convictions for serious crimes only when unduly prejudicial to a *criminal* defendant. Blackmun, writing for three Justices, rewrote Rule 609(a) to reflect what he thought was the overall purpose of the rules of evidence: to exclude convictions for serious crimes when unduly prejudicial to any party. My focus, however, is on the separate opinion by the ninth Justice.

Concurring only in the Court's judgment, the arch-textualist Scalia *also* rewrote the statute because he agreed with the Court that Rule 609(a)(1) was absurd as written, that the absurdity was unintended, and that the Court was right to depart from the statute's plain meaning.[90] This is itself significant. By creating an exception to textualism when a statute requires unintended "absurd" consequences, Scalia conceded that following statutory text is not all that is going on in statutory interpretation, and that current interpretive values also have a role to play. Though Scalia believes that plain meaning can be sacrificed only in the rare case of absurd results, there is no logical reason not to sacrifice plain meaning when it directs an "unreasonable" result that was probably unintended by Congress. Indeed, this is one way to interpret Brennan's *Weber* opinion, which Scalia deplores. But, I submit, he is outraged mainly because he disagrees with Brennan about what is a "reasonable" result in a case such as *Weber*, not because he can claim that he or anyone else always applies statutory plain meaning.

Although Scalia agreed to rewrite the statute in *Bock Laundry*, his opinion dismissed the dissenting opinion's rewrite in favor of the majority's rewrite because the latter "does least violence to the text." Scalia framed the issue this way:

> The available alternatives [for rewriting the statute] are to interpret "defendant" to mean (a) "civil plaintiff, civil defendant, prosecutor and criminal defendant," (b) "civil plaintiff and defendant and criminal defendant," or (c) "criminal defendant." Quite obviously, the last does least violence to the text.[91]

Not obviously—not at all. Fairly read, Blackmun's dissent rewrote Rule 609(a)(1) to permit impeaching convictions only when "the court determines that the probative value of admitting this evidence outweighs its prejudicial effect to a *party*" (new language emphasized).[92] This rewrite did no more "violence" to the text than Scalia's, which permitted impeaching convictions only when "the court determines that the probative value of admitting this evidence outweighs its prejudicial effect to the *criminal* defendant" (new language emphasized).

Indeed, from a textualist perspective, Blackmun's rewrite was a better version than Scalia's, for Scalia left the statute more chaotic than it was originally. Rewritten Rule 609(a)(1) would still have applied in a civil case such as *Bock Laundry*, and Scalia's version would have told the judge to follow a very strange rule: allow plaintiff Green to be impeached by his prior felony convictions, but only if the probative value outweighs prejudice to the "*criminal* defendant."[93] Which criminal defendant? Should the judge pretend that the civil defendant is a criminal one? Or should she import one from another case? Although the original Rule 609(a)(1) favored civil defendants over civil plaintiffs without apparent justification, it at least set forth a rule that could be applied by the district judge. Under the pretense of doing "least violence" to the text, Scalia's rewrite deprived the judge of an intelligible rule. After consultation with Philip Frickey, I would opine that the shortest way for Scalia to rewrite Rule 609(a)(1) without making it more textually nonsensical would have been something like this: allow impeachment by prior felony convictions "only if the crime (1) was punishable by death or imprisonment in excess of one year under the law under which the witness was convicted, and, *in a criminal case*, the court determines that the probative value of admitting this evidence outweighs its prejudicial effect to the defendant" (new language emphasized). This of course flunks Scalia's announced test of doing "least violence" to the text. In *Bock Laundry*—the leading statement of his new textualism—Scalia's actual performance demonstrates the plasticity of textualism.

For practical as well as theoretical reasons, textualism fails as a foundational, constraining methodology for interpreting statutes. As do intentionalism and purposivism. What are courts and agencies doing in statutory interpretation? Not just archaeology. The cases analyzed in this chapter suggest that interpreters are interested in statutory text and the expectations of the enacting coalition, but that interpreters are interested in other things as well—the facts and equities of the case, precedents interpreting the statute and legislative feedback, and the consequences of accepting one interpretation over another. The analysis also suggests that originalist theories are not capable of explaining or predicting statutory interpretations, even when interpreters are rhetorically invoking one or more originalist theories to justify their interpretations. In the remainder of this part of the book, I suggest positive reasons and theories for how statutes will be interpreted dynamically.

2 · The Dynamics of Statutory Interpretation

Chapter 1 demonstrated, critically, that archaeological theories do not and cannot satisfactorily describe what courts and agencies do in statutory interpretation. Its analysis also suggests positive features of statutory interpretation in practice. Problems identified with originalist theory can help us understand the dynamism of statutory interpretation. Chapter 1 argued that originalist theories cannot limit statutory interpretation to a single factor or exclude postenactment considerations, do not yield objective and determinate answers in the hard cases, and cannot convincingly tie results in statutory cases to the expectations of original legislative majorities. Here I argue that statutory interpretation is multifaceted and evolutive rather than single-faceted and static, involves policy choices and discretion by the interpreter over time as she applies the statute to specific problems, and is responsive to the current as well as the historical political culture.

There is nothing revolutionary about understanding statutes in dynamic rather than static terms. American scholars have long recognized that the Constitution and the common law are interpreted dynamically, and early in this century applied this insight to statutory interpretation as well.[1] Scholars in other industrial countries have long recognized that statutory interpretation is evolutive.[2] The standard reasons given for evolutive interpretation by scholars in other countries are equally applicable to statutory interpretation in the United States.

Because they are aimed at big problems and must last a long time, statutory enactments are often general, abstract, and theoretical. Interpretation of a statute usually occurs in connection with a fact-specific problem (a case or an administrative record) which renders it relatively particular, concrete, and practical. As an exercise in practical rather than theoretical reasoning, statutory interpretation will be dynamic. It is a truism that interpretation depends heavily on context, but the elasticity of context is less well recognized. The expanded context of cases and problems engenders dynamic interpretations. Because statutes have an indefinite life, they apply to fact situations well into the future. When successive applications of the statute occur in contexts not anticipated by its authors, the statute's meaning evolves *beyond* original expectations. Indeed, sometimes subsequent applications reveal that factual or legal assumptions of the original statute have become (or were originally) erroneous; then the statute's meaning often evolves *against* its original expectations.[3]

Under a system of separated powers, the statutory interpreter (an administrator or judge) is a different person from the people enacting the statute (legislators). The interpreter's perspective makes a difference in statutory interpretation: two different people acting in good faith often interpret the same text in different ways. Because of differences in perspective, dynamic interpretation can occur early in the statute's evolution, especially if the statute submerges or fails to resolve controversial issues. As time passes, the interpreter's perspective is likely to diverge in an increasing number of ways from the perspective of the statute's authors, and changing societal and legal contexts afford her more discretion to interpret the statute in ways not anticipated by its authors. To the extent that people rely on official interpretations to structure their conduct and expectations, their reliance may be a practical or equitable barrier to efforts by subsequent interpreters to reestablish the statute's original meaning.

Statutory interpretation is hierarchical and sequential. Interpretations by private parties can be corrected by administrators, who can be reversed by judges, who can be overridden by the legislature. Even if agencies and courts seriously sought to enforce original intent, text, or purpose, they would not do so because of a hydraulic process of feedback and anticipation which occurs as the system works out statutory meaning for issues that arise. Thus it is that agencies and courts are constantly pressed from below—by private communities of interpretation, by interest groups, by ground-level implementers of the statute—to interpret the statute in ways that are responsive to new facts, new needs, new ideas. They are also pressed from above—by congressional committees, by the threat of legislative override, by the president—to interpret the statute in ways that are responsive to current rather than historical political preferences.

As Francis Bennion of the United Kingdom put it in 1984, a statutory act "takes on a life of its own . . . [T]he ongoing Act resembles a vessel launched on some one-way voyage from the old world to the new. The vessel is not going to return; nor are its passengers. Having only what they set out with, they cope as best they can. On arrival in the present, they deploy their native endowments under conditions originally unguessed at."[4] Based on the reasons set forth in this chapter, I think Bennion's description holds for statutory interpretation in the United States as well.

Pragmatic Dynamism: Applying Statutes under Changed Circumstances

Article I, section 7 of the Constitution requires bicameral legislative approval and presentment to the president before a bill can become law. Because this structure makes it hard to enact or amend statutes, they must usually last for a long time. As a consequence, statutes are often general and abstract. But the circumstances to which they are applied are specific and concrete. Aristotle urged that application of general statutes to unanticipated cases requires the interpreter "to correct the omission—to say what the legislator would have said had he been present, and would have put into law if he had known."[5]

An Aristotelian approach to statutory interpretation is suggested by the American pragmatic tradition.[6] Pragmatism argues that there is no "foundationalist" (single overriding) approach to legal issues. Instead, the problem solver should consider the matter from different angles, applying practical experience and factual context before arriving at a solution. Practical experience in both Europe and the United States (see Chapter 1) suggests that when statutory interpreters apply a statute to specific situations, the interpreter asks "not only what the statute means abstractly, or even on the basis of legislative history, but also what it ought to mean in terms of the needs and goals of our present day society."[7]

In this part of the book I construct a pragmatist-inspired argument for why this is so. The argument is based on an Aristotelian theory of application and changed circumstances: a statute is relatively abstract until it is applied to a specific situation. Especially over time, the circumstances will not be ones that the statute or its drafters contemplated, and any application of the statute will be dynamic in a weak sense, going *beyond* the drafters' expectations. Sometimes the circumstances will be materially different from those contemplated by the statutory drafters, and in that event any application of the statute will be dynamic in a strong sense, going *against* the drafters' expectations, which have been negated because important assumptions have been undone.

Application and the Unfolding of Statutory Meaning

Pragmatism emphasizes the concrete over the abstract and is problem-solving in its orientation. For the pragmatist, a statute is a political response to a problem or cluster of problems, and the statutory drafters expect their product to be applied in a manner that advances the overall political enterprise as well as its specific goal. Indeed, they realize that, in an important sense, statutory meaning is not fixed until it is applied to concrete problems. Pragmatic thought understands application as a process of practical reasoning.[8] Every time a statute is applied to a problem, statutory meaning is created.

Application is easy for most immediate applications of statutes, for there is a close connection between the text of the statute, the expectations and assumptions of the statutory drafters, and the problems faced by interpreters. The problem(s) targeted by the statute, and its directed response(s), will usually be clear to all concerned. Yet even the immediate application of a statute can materially change the statute in at least three circumstances. To begin with, there may be unresolved issues in the statute, namely, those recognized by the legislative process as important but about which the legislative process was unable to reach clear resolution in the statute's text or its authoritative legislative history. The enacting coalition may also be in general agreement as to the way a social problem should be regulated but may disagree as to collateral issues. To enact the statute the factions often will submerge their disagreements and leave ambiguities to be resolved by other decision makers. This is in part what happened with the Civil Rights Act of 1964: the supporters of the bill had different views about voluntary affirmative action and so fudged the issue, essentially leaving it to future resolution (Chapter 1's analysis of United Steelworkers v. Weber).

In addition to suppressed or unresolved issues, many other issues may simply be overlooked or unanticipated by the enacting coalition. This is another way of looking at *Weber:* the legislative and public debates focused on government-required quotas and overlooked the possibility of voluntary quotas. This is probably what happened in the drafting of Rule 609(a), the statute interpreted in Green v. Bock Laundry Machine Co. (also discussed in Chapter 1): the legislative debates focused on possible prejudice to criminal defendants in allowing their impeachment by reason of prior convictions, so the issue of impeaching civil litigants and their witnesses was simply forgotten by the time the conference committee crafted the final compromise.[9] A third reason why a statute may be applied dynamically from the beginning is that the statute's integration into the social and political culture may be met with resistance.

A new example illustrates how statutes may evolve immediately after enactment. The Immigration and Nationality Act of 1952 provided in section 212(a)(4) that "[a]liens afflicted with psychopathic personality, epilepsy, or a mental defect" shall be excluded from the United States.[10] Section 212(a)(4) was one of seven medical-based immigration exclusions, administered by the Public Health Service (PHS) in coordination with the Immigration and Naturalization Service (INS). Congress had written the exclusion in this way at the suggestion of the PHS that this provision was "sufficiently broad to provide for the exclusion of homosexuals and sex perverts."[11] The PHS's suggestion represented its view, widely held in the medical and psychiatric profession during the 1950s, that homosexuality is a mental "disease," a type of "psychopathic personality."

The 1952 act was subject to evolution because it was abstract, to the point of coyness, about exactly what "psychopathic personality" entailed. For practical reasons, such as the difficulty of identifying "homosexuals and sex perverts" in medical examinations, the PHS applied the statutory exclusion in a small minority of cases where "homosexuals" tried to enter the country. Curtailing the statute further, the Ninth Circuit, in Fleuti v. Rosenberg,[12] held that the term "psychopathic personality" was too vague to be constitutionally applied to "homosexuals" generally. In 1965 Congress amended section 212(a)(4) to override *Fleuti*, rewriting the statute to exclude aliens "afflicted with pschopathic personality, *or sexual deviation*, or a mental defect."[13] The 1965 statute was slightly less open-ended than the 1952 one, and gave the PHS (which again wrote the statute) the same discretion to apply the exclusion to as many "sexual deviants" as it could or would find. Again, the PHS did not find many.

Just before enactment of the 1965 amendment, the PHS and INS interpreted section 212(a)(4) to exclude Clive Michael Boutilier, a Canadian who had been convicted of homosexual sodomy while visiting in this country. But Boutilier's case presented an unanticipated issue, for he was apparently a "bisexual."[14] Was a bisexual a "homosexual" afflicted with "psychopathic personality" for purposes of the 1952 statute? The legislative process had been completely oblivious to this issue, and any resolution would have represented an important evolution in the statute. Agreeing with the PHS, the Supreme Court in Boutilier v. INS[15] interpreted the pre-1965 version of section 212(a)(4) to exclude the Canadian. This was a striking expansion of the 1952 statute, giving it a potential breadth that might reach millions of the world's population and that rendered the 1965 amendment superfluous.

The Evolution of Statutes When Circumstances Change

Because of gaps and ambiguities for issues unresolved or unanticipated by the legislative process, statutes begin to evolve from the moment people start applying them to concrete problems. Over time that statutory evolution becomes ever more striking because the world changes, often as a result of the statute itself. Changed circumstances have important consequences for statutory interpretation. Statutes are enacted by their drafters with certain consequences in mind, but whether those consequences actually occur (or undesirable consequences do not occur) depends on a series of assumptions about people and institutions, about society and its mores, and about law and policy. If those assumptions unravel over time, the statute will not have its intended consequences, and however the statute is applied by decision makers, it will be interpreted dynamically—that is, subsequent interpreters will apply the statute in ways unanticipated by the original drafters.

At the level of society and culture, changed circumstances include new understandings about individual, group, or institutional behavior; revised professional consensus or popular mores; and fresh factual information or intellectual paradigms. When the assumptions of a society or culture underlying a statute are discredited, the interpreter will think about the statute differently than the original drafters, or earlier interpreters, would have. To fulfill the original statutory functions, the interpreter must consider the new circumstances, and that often leads to a dramatically dynamic interpretation of the statute.

Let us say that I direct you: "Fetch me some soup meat from Store X" (recall a similar hypothetical in Chapter 1). The directive is filled with unstated assumptions about the existence and location of the store, reimbursement for your trouble and expense, exactly what "soup meat" is, and so forth. If we are of the same mind about all the assumptions, as is the case when the directive is recent and the parties know each other, there is little room for interpretation of the directive, much less dynamic interpretation. But once an important assumption changes, one's application and interpretation may also change. Thus, if you learn on the way to the market that only Store Y has soup meat today and that you need to hurry because it is running low, you will go to Store Y notwithstanding the directive. In this example the dynamic interpretation is straightforward; in the realm of statutes it is rarely so. Reconsider the *Boutilier* issue.

The function of the medical exclusions in the Immigration and Nationality Act of 1952 was to prevent the entry into the United States of people with severe medical problems. Congress's and the PHS's targeting of "homosexuals" under one of the medical exclusions rested on the belief, widely held in the 1950s, that "homosexuals" are mentally ill.[16] This view became more controversial by the 1960s, as empirical studies found no correlation between pathology and homosexuality, and the Ninth Circuit in *Fleuti* explicitly relied on newer medical studies in its effort to curtail application of the psychopathic personality exclusion.[17] In the *Boutilier* litigation, dissenting opinions by judges on both the Second Circuit and the Supreme Court rejected the PHS's expansive view of the exclusion because they were skeptical of its sweeping factual underpinnings.[18]

Although the view of homosexuality as disease was still widely held in the medical community throughout the 1960s, everything changed—almost immediately—after the Stonewall riots in 1969, which triggered gay activism against traditional penalties based on sexual orientation. After Stonewall, it was much harder to dismiss lesbians, gay men, and bisexuals as psychotics, for they not only were showing their faces and talking back, but were working within the medical profession to discredit the earlier views. Within four years of Stonewall the American Psychiatric Association removed "homosexuality" from its list of mental disorders, after intense debate over the evidence.[19] Other medical associations followed suit immediately, and the prior medical consensus collapsed. Responding to the new views within the medical establishment, the PHS announced in 1979 that it would no longer carry out examinations or issue certificates to exclude gay men, bisexuals, and lesbians pursuant to section 212(a)(4) because there was no reliable basis for considering homosexual orientation a medical disorder.[20]

The PHS's about-face represented a dynamic interpretation of section 212(a)(4) based on changed societal and cultural circumstances. The PHS's decision was itself a new legal circumstance that undermined other assumptions made by the immigration statute. Just as statutes are enacted under certain assumptions about society and culture, so too are they enacted under certain assumptions about law and policy; when those assumptions become obsolescent, the statute's application changes. A critical assumption made in section 212(a)(4) was that the PHS would be an enthusiastic enforcer of the exclusion of gay men, lesbians, and (after *Boutilier*) bisexuals, for the imprimatur of the medical profession lent an aura of scientific respectability to the policy. Therefore, the statutory scheme for enforcing section 212(a)(4) was built around the PHS, which was charged with examining immigrants for physical and mental defects,[21] and a PHS certificate was required for the INS to exclude an immigrant for "medical" reasons.[22] When the PHS refused to participate in the exclusion, the statutory scheme was thrown into turmoil.

In light of *Boutilier* and the legislative history of section 212(a)(4), the Department of Justice advised the president that the PHS was "without authority" to remove bisexuals, gay men, and lesbians from the section 212(a)(4) exclusion, and indicated that the INS must try to enforce the exclusion without the aid of the PHS.[23] In response, the INS announced it would apply the statute in 1980 to exclude gay men and lesbians, but only if the person made an unsolicited declaration of his or her sexuality.[24] Relying on the statutory requirement of a PHS certificate in order to exclude noncitizens under section 212(a)(4), the Ninth Circuit in Hill v. INS[25] interpreted the immigration law as not permitting the INS to exclude gay men and lesbians without the cooperation of the PHS. Relying on *Boutilier*, the Fifth Circuit interpreted the law to permit the INS to enforce the exclusion without the PHS's cooperation, in In re Longstaff.[26]

All these different interpretations of the statute were dynamic in the weak sense that they went *beyond* Congress's original expectations about the statute—expectations that were shattered by the PHS's new interpretation (itself impelled by changed social circumstances) which undermined a key assumption of the statute. All of the interpretations except for the Department of Justice's (discussed in the next paragraph) were also dynamic in a stronger sense, in that they went *against* Congress's original expectations about the statute. Even the conservative interpretation of the INS effectively repealed the exclusion of lesbians, gay men, and bisexuals, who now had to rub the agent's face in their homosexuality before the INS would exclude them.

The experience with section 212(a)(4) in the 1980s suggests one final way in which circumstances can change. In addition to changes in society and culture, law and policy, there may be sea changes in the community's general cultural assumptions and framework of thought. Notwithstanding the Department of Justice's insistence that *Boutilier* was still a valid authority, that interpretation was a dead letter by the 1980s. Virtually no bisexual, gay man, or lesbian was excluded by the INS in the 1980s, and in 1990 Congress overrode *Longstaff* and *Boutilier* by revamping the entire web of exclusions.[27] The end result—no policy to exclude people based solely on their sexual orientation—could have come about in several different ways. What drove the statute's evolution (and ultimately drove the statute into an early retirement) was a sea change in American attitudes about sexual orientation, from hysterical intolerance to partial toleration.

When the world changes, there are several things that can happen to a statute. It can become irrelevant and basically wither away, like the mythological Tithonus, who was given eternal life but not eternal youth by the gods and thereupon shriveled into a grasshopper. This is what happened to section 212(a)(4) even before it was repealed. Or the statute can remain relevant but, like the mythological Proteus, can change its form to deal with the policy chasms introduced by the obsolescence of some of its assumptions. This is what happened to Title VII, which evolved to meet new challenges, through agency implementation and interpretation, judicial construction, and congressional amendment.

Statutory Interpretation as Practical Reasoning

The dynamic approach of the PHS, the Ninth Circuit, and even the INS and the Fifth Circuit can be generalized as a description of what interpreters consider when they interpret statutes. Philip Frickey and I constructed the model in Figure 2.1 from our study of Supreme Court decisions;[28] Nicholas Zeppos has kindly provided empirical support for our model.[29]

Our "funnel" reflects both the multiplicity of considerations and the conventional hierarchy ranking those considerations against one another. An important point is the pragmatic idea that our intellectual framework is not single-minded but consists of a "web of beliefs," interconnected but different understandings and values.[30] It suggests that human decision making tends to be polycentric, spiral, and inductive—not unidimensional, linear, and deductive. We consider several values, and the strength of each in the context of the problem at hand, before reaching a decision. As Charles Peirce taught,

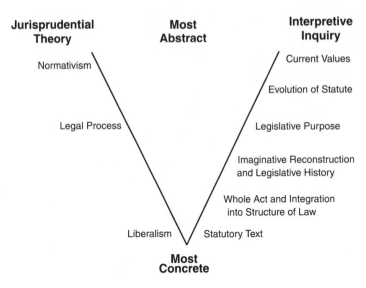

Figure 2.1   The Frickey and Eskridge funnel of abstraction

problem solving ought to "trust rather to the multitude and variety of its arguments than to the conclusiveness of any one. Its reasoning should not form a chain which is no stronger than its weakest link, but a cable whose fibers may be ever so slender, provided they are sufficiently numerous and intimately connected."[31]

Moreover, our model suggests the interactive process by which a practical interpreter thinks about the various sources of statutory meaning. She will slide up and down the funnel, considering the strengths of various considerations, rethinking each in light of the others, and weighing them against one another along conventional criteria. The interpreter does not view the statutory text in isolation, but reads it in connection with the legislative history, statutory practice and precedents, and current norms and values. Thus, a clear text whose plain meaning is unreasonable and apparently unanticipated by the legislature may be interpreted to be consistent with that legislative history (*Bock Laundry*) or that purpose and current values (*Bock Laundry* dissent). By contrast, a clear text that does not yield unreasonable results will not be undone simply because it is contradicted by some legislative history, for the text, as the most concrete factor, has conventionally been more heavily weighted (*Griffin*).

Recall the soup meat hypothetical. Because we share common understandings about all the relevant terms, the text of the directive itself tells you all you need to know in most cases. Even minor surprises (such as a heavy rain) will not change that, especially if you and I have talked about those surprises specifically ("I want you to go to Store X, through hell or high water") or generally ("It is very important for me to have soup meat for tonight's party"). Bigger surprises might derail the textual command entirely (Store X burns down) or substantially (Store X has raised its price for soup meat 100 percent). Substantial changes in circumstances present the most difficult interpretive issues as a matter of theory.

Theory ought not paralyze you as it did Buridan's ass, the animal who starved to death because he could not choose between equally distant haystacks. You are in the middle of your errand and have to make a decision that will satisfy me, or at least seem defensible. You will go through a process of practical reasoning to figure out a satisfactory response to the situation. You might consider my reasons for wanting soup meat today and for sending you to Store X. If you don't know my reasons (and my hypothetical does not allow you to call me up), you might impute to me those reasons that seem probable to you, and consider what people generally do in this situation. You might recall whether this situation has happened before, and how I (or how others) responded then. Even if you thought shopping for soup meat at Store Y would save me a lot of money, you might go to Store X and pay its unexpectedly high price if you recall that I disapproved of your buying soup meat at Store Y in the past. Generally, if you proceed in this way, there is a good chance that your ultimate choice will be acceptable to me, not because you followed my original directive to the letter, but because you made an intelligent response to unexpected circumstances. You adapted to the predicament better than Buridan's ass.

Just as a directive that was relatively clear when issued becomes unclear once a material assumption has changed, so too the directive of section 212(a)(4) to exclude "sick homosexuals" (apparently clear from the legislative history) became unclear once it appeared that gay people are no sicker than any other group. For the legal interpreter, as for my soup meat interpreter, practical reasoning suggests considerations that are relatively reliable in guiding interpretation under conditions of such uncertainty: How would a legislature composed of reasonable people pursuing reasonable purposes respond to the changed circumstances? What has been the past practice or precedent, and have people relied on it to their detriment? What interpretation is most coherent with present social and legal rules and policies? This process of practical reasoning will not necessarily yield one determinate answer, in part because different interpreters will bring different perspectives to the reasoning process, as the PHS, INS, and other interpreters of section 212(a)(4) revealed in the 1980s. Indeed, these different perspectives suggest a second structural reason why statutory interpretation is inevitably dynamic.

Hermeneutic Dynamism: The Critical Role of the Interpreter's Perspective

Our Constitution divorces statutory interpretation (given to the executive and the courts in articles II and III) from statutory enactment (by Congress under article I). This division of responsibility ensures that statutes will evolve because the perspective of the interpreter will be different from that of the legislator. Just as the changing factual contexts for interpretation render it dynamic for reasons best explained by philosophical pragmatism, so the independent and changing identity of the interpreter ensures dynamic interpretation for reasons best explained by philosophical hermeneutics.[32] The interpreter's role involves selection and creativity, which is influenced, often unconsciously, by the interpreter's own frame of reference—assumptions and beliefs about society, values, and the statute itself.

At the time the statute is enacted, the interpreter is a stranger to the statute in a way the legislator is not. Even if she shared the same cultural framework with legislators, the interpreter might approach the statute somewhat differently than the legislator would because of her different institutional role (recall *Fleuti*). The dynamism introduced by the interpreter's perspective tends to be more pronounced over time, as her cultural and political framework diverges from that of the original drafters (recall the PHS's changing viewpoint in the 1970s). If that framework becomes irreconcilable with that of the drafters, statutory interpretation becomes a discontinuous process of rupture and dramatic political shifts (the collapse of section 212[a][4] in the 1980s, when the PHS abandoned its policy and the Ninth Circuit nullified the INS's tepid effort to enforce the statute without the PHS's cooperation).

The Importance of the Interpreter's Perspective

Philosophical hermeneutics is concerned with the ways in which current readers interpret and understand historical texts.[33] The meaning of the text does not take form until an interpreter understands it, and different interpreters will read the same text differently. Each interpreter brings to the text her own point of view, her own framework of thought, her vision. Our attention might be focused on one thing, but we also have a field of vision—our horizon—that conditions what we focus on, what we look for, what we see.[34] Hermeneutics gives rise to the commonplace observation that an author's text usually says much more than the author herself thinks it does, even to a contemporary audience. The interpreter's understanding is also a historically situated event. Because our horizons are conditioned by the world into which we have been thrown, an interpreter of a different time or culture from the author's may have a vastly different interpretation of the same written text.

Consider Charlotte Brontë's *Jane Eyre* as an example of how a text changes over time. Published in 1847, *Jane Eyre* became one of the most widely read and reread novels in Western history. This lifetime tale of an intelligent and independent-spirited woman and her struggle for survival in an unpredictable and often hostile world is one that has gripped the imagination of generations of readers. Although the text of the novel has not changed in numerous reprintings, its interpretation has changed dramatically from generation to generation. Brontë herself was surprised at the charges of early critics, most of them male, that the novel is "vulgar" in its depiction of the sexual feelings Jane has for her employer Edward Rochester, his effort to trick Jane into a bigamous marriage, and their eventual marriage after his mad wife's death.[35] Brontë would have been just as surprised with the interpretations by twentieth-century critics, many of them female, that emphasize the ways in which her intelligent, independent, and plain heroine stands in contrast to— and to some extent triumphs over—society's traditional view of women as submissive and ornamental.[36]

Brontë surely would have been astounded at my own reading of her novel. Some analysts of *Jane Eyre* emphasize the ways in which older women played a nurturing role in helping young Jane to grow into a sustaining, mature woman. Specifically, during her education at the Lowood Institution, a charity school, Jane draws strength from her friendship with Miss Temple, the superintendent, and Helen Burns, an older student. I interpret the love between Jane and Helen as at least partially erotic. Although a modern lesbian relationship is never discussed in the novel, the novel's broader horizon suggests its possibility, as in Jane's declaration to Helen that "to gain some real affection from you, or Miss Temple, or any other whom I truly love, I would willingly submit to have the bone of my arm broken, or to let a bull toss me, or to stand behind a kicking horse."[37] To interpret Jane as a modern lesbian would be anachronistic, but to see the "lesbian in Jane" is, I think, a useful way of thinking about her.

The example can be pursued one step further. The meaning of *Jane Eyre* will not only change from generation to generation and from interpreter to interpreter but will change for the same reader over time. For example, Anita Allen has contrasted her interpretation of *Jane Eyre* as inspirational when she read the novel as a child with her disappointment, when she reread the novel as an adult feminist, in Jane's inability to transcend the gender- and class-subordinating attitudes of her era.[38] Even though Allen read the same text as a child that she reread as an adult, its meaning had changed for her, since she brought to the text different pre-understandings drawn from her life experience as well as her intellectual interests. Like Allen's, my view of *Jane Eyre* has changed. To consider Jane and Helen's relationship in romantic terms, as I do now, would have been inconceivable to me when I was younger, and is inspired by scholarship concerning female friendships in the nineteenth century[39] and my own identity as a gay man. The experience Allen and I have had illustrates the dynamic nature of our horizons. In the words of Hans-Georg Gadamer, "The historical movement of human life consists in the fact that it is never absolutely bound to any one standpoint, and hence can never have a truly closed horizon."[40]

From this analysis of *Jane Eyre* and the dynamic nature of the interpreter's horizon, one might be tempted to conclude that interpretation is wholly subjective and adventitious. At the same time, however, that an interpreter seeking to understand a text projects possible meanings onto it, the interpreter is herself trying to learn from the text. Although her own vision influences what she chooses to emphasize, she will still look to the text to guide her emphasis, and she will be curious about the circumstances of the text. The discriminating interpreter realizes, too, that her first impression of the text may be superficial (just her own projections), and that she should subject that first impression to a critical scrutiny to make more certain that she is learning what the text has to offer her. "A person trying to understand something will not resign himself from the start to relying on his own accidental" pre-understandings, but will instead be "prepared for it to tell him something."[41] That interpreter also profits from listening to the reactions of others to the text, including her contemporaries, as well as understandings of the text reached by prior generations.

Just as the interpreter's horizon changes over time, so too "the horizon of the past, out of which all human life lives and which exists in the form of tradition, is always in motion," as Gadamer puts it. "When our historical consciousness transposes itself into historical horizons, this does not entail passing into alien worlds unconnected in any way with our own."[42] Although Brontë and Allen are separated by a gulf of more than a century, their horizons are not mutually exclusive: *Jane Eyre*'s horizon is expanded by 150 years of interpretation and application to current interests, while Allen's horizon is very much informed by tradition, including Brontë and her commentators.

Hermeneutics suggests the intellectual impoverishment of the view that interpretation simply re-creates departed meaning. On the contrary, interpretation is a way in which texts live and we evolve. The interpreter is not adrift in an alienated present, seeking to re-create a dead past, but is linked to a generative past through interpreting its canonical texts. Interpretation in this way involves a "fusion of horizons," says Gadamer, in which the "old and new are always combining into something of living value. In fact the horizon of the present is continually in the process of being formed because we are continually having to test all our [prejudgments]. An important part of this testing occurs in encountering the past and in understanding the tradition from which we come."[43]

A Hermeneutical Model of Statutory Interpretation

Literary interpretation is not legal interpretation, and so it is not immediately clear that hermeneutics generally, and specifically my use of *Jane Eyre*, provides any insight into statutory interpretation. The traditionally emphasized difference between the two derives from the normative force of statutory interpretation: what we learn from interpreting statutes has a coercive effect on us that is not the same as what we learn from interpreting novels.[44] From this follows the need for authoritative statutory interpretations, since we often disagree with one another about the best interpretation of a statute (just as we disagree about the best interpretation of *Jane Eyre*). Because a statute has coercive force and is usually meant to provide some collective order to our individual activities, the state wants to suppress this multiplicity of interpretations, through reference to an authoritative interpretation by state organs, primarily agencies and courts. The agency or court stands as an arbiter of interpretation—the official whose special role it is to validate one interpretation, choosing it from among several alternatives. Unlike a literary critic, the agency or court is both interpreter and censor: it chooses one interpretation and suppresses others.

Surely there is some truth in this traditional distinction between legal and literary interpretation, but it is usually expressed too strongly. Many literary texts have a substantial normative force, and the most frequently interpreted ones have a normative force often exceeding that of legal texts. This is particularly true of scriptural texts, which present themselves as having a special authority and whose interpretation carries great meaning for the faithful. It is also, though less obviously, true for texts such as *Jane Eyre*, which carry powerful normative messages for many readers. An important reason why interpreters are still drawn to the novel today is its resonance with women's lived experience, and therefore its relevance to women's evaluation of that experience.

Similarly, it is possible for the nonlegal interpreter to wield more power than the legal interpreter. Recall our polity's exclusion and persecution of bisexuals, gay men, and lesbians. *Boutilier* represented the Supreme Court's authoritative interpretation that Congress meant to exclude these outsiders from entering the country as a medical threat. Because of difficulties in medically "diagnosing" homosexuality[45] and the reluctance of some doctors to cooperate in this policy, I doubt that the Court's antihomosexual interpretation affected the lives of bisexuals, gay men, and lesbians as much as the equally antihomosexual interpretations of Freud by private psychiatrists and doctors, who locked up "homosexuals" and subjected them to institutionalized torture (including castration, lobotomy, and electroshock treatments) for most of this century.[46] While I do not maintain that nonlegal or literary interpretation is coercive in the same way as legal interpretation, I do insist that there is not necessarily less at stake in the interpretation of literary or religious texts than there is in the interpretation of legal texts.

Even if there were less at stake, the central insight of hermeneutics would be relevant for legal interpretation: the horizon of the interpreter affects the way she approaches the text—what questions she asks of it, how she responds to words and phrases, and what text and surrounding context she finds important.[47] Hermeneutics suggests that statutory interpretation, whatever its differences from other interpretations, involves an interaction between interpreter and text that creates new and perhaps unexpected meaning over time. Contrary to originalist legal theory, hermeneutics posits that statutory meaning is constructed, not discovered, by the interpreter.

Consider the Second Circuit's internal debate in *Boutilier.*[48] Judge Leonard Moore dissented from the Court's willingness to exclude as "psychopathic" anyone who had engaged in same-sex intimacy. His dissent expressed a reluctance to read the vague language of section 212(a)(4) broadly enough to reach not only the obscure Mr. Boutilier, but also such celebrated figures as Leonardo da Vinci, John Maynard Keynes, and Ludwig Wittgenstein, whom historians say also engaged in same-sex intimacy.[49] Judge Irving Kaufman, author of the majority opinion, dismissed Moore's interpretation as "permitting the emotions to overwhelm reason and enacted law." In contrast, Kaufman thought his exclusionary interpretation was the one "Congress has made [as] its judgment."[50]

Hermeneutics suggests that Kaufman's interpretation was no less constructed, no less dynamic, and if anything more emotional than Moore's interpretation. For instance, Kaufman chose to ignore the ill fit between his interpretation and the statute's text, which hardly seemed to target well-adjusted bisexuals like Boutilier (recall *Fleuti*). Kaufman ignored this anomaly and focused on the legislative history of section 212(a)(4). The critical event was the decision by the Senate Judiciary Committee to reject Senator Patrick McCarran's original provision, which excluded "homosexuals and sex perverts," and to accept the PHS's recommendation to exclude instead persons "afflicted with psychopathic personality," a medical term.[51] Holding that Congress thereby intended to exclude all "homosexuals," Kaufman emphasized the committee report's statement that the "change of nomenclature is not to be construed in any way as modifying the intent to exclude all aliens who are sexual deviates."[52] This is hardly the smoking gun that Kaufman considered it to be. Instead, his treatment of the legislative history represented his choice to assume, first, that vague statutory language should be interpreted broadly so as to apply Congress's original "specific intent" even if that seemed unreasonable in light of the current technical literature *(Fleuti)*; second, that a focused committee report is sure evidence of Congress's specific intent even though a decision was made by the sponsors to abandon the more targeted language; and third, that the quoted passage is the relevant evidence for Congress's specific intent as to *Boutilier*. As a matter of statutory interpretation theory, the first two assumptions made by Kaufman are questionable (see Chapter 7).

Moore focused on the third assumption and revealed it to be the most questionable. His dissent emphasized the PHS report, which both the Senate report and Kaufman relied on as a statement of the policy embodied in section 212(a)(4). The PHS explained what it meant by "psychopathic personality," namely, "developmental defects or pathological trends in personality structure manifest by lifelong patterns of action or behavior," a category *"frequently includ[ing]* those . . . suffering from sexual deviation."[53] This understanding of what was originally meant by "psychopathic personality" supported a more cautious interpretation of section 212(a)(4), one that would exclude only those whose same-sex intimacies represented a dangerous inability to adjust to society. Boutilier's lawyers produced affidavits by qualified medical experts attesting to the utter lack of psychiatric or mental pathology. In excluding Boutilier, the PHS had not even bothered to evaluate his psychiatric health, beyond asserting his "psychopathic personality" based only on his having enjoyed intimacy with another man. To Moore, Congress did not target mentally healthy people like Boutilier, whose bisexuality made his status under the 1952 legislative history even more unclear. To interpret section 212(a)(4) to exclude anyone who has been intimate with someone of the same sex seems well beyond any specific intent harbored by Congress.

Boutilier illustrates how statutory interpretation is dynamic in the ways in which literary texts are dynamic: the horizon of the text changes over time as the text is interpreted, and the horizon of the interpreter changes over time as new interpreters replace old ones and as the world into which all interpreters are thrown also changes. Hermeneutics further suggests that statutory interpretation is dynamic in a third respect: the interaction between text and interpreter changes as the statute is applied to new factual contexts. For Moore the application of section 212(a)(4) to Boutilier was an occasion to cut back on the statute's ambit, to insist that the PHS be more careful about applying the statute. For Kaufman the *Boutilier* facts were an occasion to expand the statute to cover situations not anticipated by Congress. Regardless of which interpretation had prevailed, the statute would never be the same after the court's decision.

These lessons of legal hermeneutics—the importance of the interpreter's horizon, the evolving nature of the text's horizon, and the importance of application to new factual circumstances—make possible the construction of a model of statutory interpretation that builds on my earlier discussion of pragmatism (Figure 2.2). The model recasts the traditional textual, historical, and evolutive inquiries as more explicitly interconnected and mutually influencing. The inspiration for this is the concept of the hermeneutical circle, which posits that we can understand the whole text only by understanding its

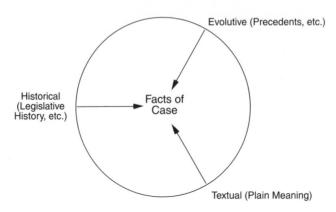

Figure 2.2　The hermeneutics of statutory interpretation

various parts, whose meaning in turn depends on our understanding of the whole.[54] Thus, the statutory interpreter's understanding of the plain meaning of a statutory text depends on her understanding the whole story of the statute, including its historical circumstances and its evolution, which themselves cannot be understood without reference to the statute's plain meaning.

This hermeneutical model deepens our pragmatic understanding of statutory interpretation in two additional ways. By representing the interpreter's horizon of thought as the field on which this back-and-forth process proceeds, the hermeneutical model recognizes the critical role played by the interpreter's framework. Different interpreters will ask different questions of the text and will read the legislative history and statutory precedents differently because they bring different pre-understandings to the text. By representing the facts of the case as the focal point for the back-and-forth process by the interpreter grappling with the text, the hermeneutical model explicitly recognizes the link between understanding a text and applying it to a specific situation. "The work of interpretation is to *concretize* the law in each specific case—i.e., it is the work of *application*."[55]

Continuity and Rupture in Statutory Evolution

Hermeneutics insists on the relativity of statutory interpretation: a statute's meaning depends on the evolutive considerations in the hermeneutical circle, the interpreter's particular horizon, and the facts of the case to which the statute is applied. Contrary to the warnings of some critics,[56] the relativity of interpretation should not be alarming.

To begin, the relativity of interpretation is potentially productive. Temporal distance may produce a better understanding of what is good or useful about the statutory text and what is not.[57] Most of us have had the experience of writing some text we thought was truly insightful and then returning to it some years later, only to find that most of what we originally thought were insights appear trivial or slightly wrong. Yet sometimes after the passage of time, one of the original points will appear even more striking—"truer"— than it did at first. Similar experiences occur with statutes, which are constantly tested by application to unanticipated facts. The process by which interpreters struggle with making the statute work in new factual and even legal settings permits statutes to grow in a constructive way. That the interpreters are different people from those enacting the statute potentially pushes the statute's evolution in more evenhanded and less partial directions.

The productivity of temporal distance and of case-by-case development of statutes through subsequent interpreters does not completely answer the related charge of subjectivism—that meaning will not only vary over time and new circumstances but will be idiosyncratic across different interpreters as well.[58] Yet hermeneutics rejects the idea that individual beliefs necessarily dominate interpretation; the interpreter's horizon is itself dominated by traditions and not by prejudices idiosyncratic to the interpreter. One lesson of hermeneutics is "how little interpreters and their points of view matter, for even where interpreters attempt to break with tradition and approach their subject-matter without preconceptions, the tradition retains its normative force."[59] Thus, the relativity of interpretation does not mean that it is unpredictable. At a specific historical moment in a particular culture, a range of interpreters will read a text in the same way because of their shared understandings.

The limits imposed by tradition are if anything more characteristic of statutory interpretation. The statutory interpreter is constrained—often unconsciously—by the traditions of the surrounding culture and of her professional culture, just as all interpreters are.[60] In addition to, and complementing, these constraints is the one imposed by the *reliance* of others on authoritative legal materials. An important reason why statutory interpreters start with and pay such close attention to the text's plain meaning is their pre-understanding that people rely primarily on the statutory text when they figure out what the law requires and plan their activities accordingly (recall Griffin v. Oceanic Contractors, discussed in Chapter 1). When the statutory text reveals a drafting error (as in *Bock Laundry*), statutory interpreters will follow legislative history if they believe it sufficiently clear, reliable, and available, such that people have probably relied on it. Courts and even agencies follow their prior interpretations in large part because people rely on them, and statutory precedents provoking widespread reliance are less likely to be overruled (recall Johnson v. Transportation Agency, which reaffirmed *Weber* notwithstanding doubts that some of the majority Justices had about the original opinion).

In short, an agency or court interpreting a statute is influenced by a reasonable consensus of private opinion as to what a statute means, especially if people in apparent good faith have relied on this consensus. This explains the result in *Boutilier*. For more than a decade the PHS and the INS had relied on their understanding of Congress's intent. When the Ninth Circuit interfered with that understanding in *Fleuti*, Congress overrode that decision and supported the PHS's and INS's position. Even though the congressional override was not applicable to the facts of *Boutilier*, it must have reinforced the Court's inclination to affirm what it perceived to be the long-standing agency practice and to believe that there was a public consensus that "homosexuals" (broadly defined) were not welcome in this country. Although *Boutilier* was a dynamic interpretation of the immigration statute, it was both continuous with its evolution and fairly predictable.

Of course, the statute's evolution did not stop with *Boutilier*. Within five years of the decision the medical consensus about homosexuality had evanesced, and within twelve years the PHS had ended its cooperation. There was no controversy when Congress overrode *Boutilier* in 1990, for the social and professional consensus that underlay both the decision and the original statute had all but dissipated. The death of *Boutilier* was as predictable in 1990 as its birth was in 1967. Yet in the interim there was a "rupture," a discontinuity, in the statute's interpretation which corresponded to society's and the medical community's changing attitudes toward homosexuality, and the replacement of the closeted homosexual with the openly lesbian or gay person.

The idea of rupture presents more clearly the importance of ideology in statutory interpretation.[61] By ideology I mean the web of cultural as well as political understandings and beliefs held by the interpreter. An interpreter's ideology includes not just her specific beliefs about an issue, but also the broader web of interconnected ideas and biases that condition the way she looks at an issue, the bases for her pre-understandings. The ideology of a government official is rarely idiosyncratic, for her pre-understandings can be constructed only by years of collective discussion and exchange. Though an ideology is necessarily collective, it need not be universal and uncontested. The toughest cases of statutory interpretation tend to be those where the issue is ideologically contested within the larger society. An important reason why statutes evolve, sometimes dramatically, is as a result of shifts in ideology because of new information and/or new interpreters.

Thus, Senator McCarran and the 1952 Congress which enacted section 212(a)(4), the PHS and the INS in the 1950s and 1960s, the 1965 Congress which overrode *Fleuti,* and the authors of the Second Circuit and Supreme Court opinions in *Boutilier,* for all their differences, shared an ideology about homosexuality that was not much contested in American society before 1969. Supported by medical "experts" in the 1950s, this ideology defined homosexuality as a psychologically and medically distorted form of "normal" heterosexuality; "homosexuals" were considered "the Other," people who were sick, perverted, immoral—threatening from the perspectives of medicine, psychiatry, and religion.[62] Under this ideology it was easy enough, almost a reflex, to interpret an exclusion of people afflicted with "psychopathic personality" (and many other malignant signifiers) to mean "homosexuals."

This ideology was publicly contested after the Stonewall riots in 1969, when many gay men and lesbians came out of the closet. They not only proclaimed their homosexuality, but also demanded a reconsideration of prejudiced views, stereotypes, and policies adopted under the old ideology. Once the ideology was questioned, even medical experts began to see "homosexuals" no longer as mysterious aliens but as colleagues, family members, real people. Consequently, they turned a more critical eye on previous "evidence" of homosexuality as mental illness and, suddenly, found it untenable.[63] This ideological rupture came like a tidal wave within the medical community, which abandoned its earlier position. Though many Americans continued to believe that homosexuality is a disease, the medical community's reversal exposed the exclusion of bisexuals, gay men, and lesbians to the charge of simple bigotry and sapped people's enthusiasm for enforcing the exclusion. Conservative Republicans as well as liberal Democrats supported its repeal in 1990.

The role of ideology not only illuminates *Boutilier* and the evolution of section 212(a)(4) but also provides a useful way of looking at the issues discussed in Chapter 1. Interpreting the Civil Rights Act of 1964 to permit voluntary employment preferences, *Weber* was a hard case because its resolution would have to depend on a contested ideology of racial justice (discussed more thoroughly in Part III). Justice Rehnquist's dissent rested on an ideology of color-blindness, in which the main problem to be attacked was personal racial prejudice and the remedy was to screen race out of employment decisions entirely. Justice Brennan's opinion for the Court rested on an ideology of results, in which the main problem to be attacked was socioeconomic structures that perpetuated patterns of racial inequality, and the remedy was to press employers toward more representative percentages in their work force. This ideological clash has only sharpened since *Weber,* and is the backdrop to continuing efforts to overrule *Weber* (recall *Johnson,* and see Chapter 6).

Interpreting an 1898 statute to require a maritime employer to pay a seaman $302,790.40 as a penalty for unlawfully withholding $412.50 in wages, *Griffin* was a superficially easy case, even though it is an even more dynamic interpretation than *Weber* was.[64] But the ideological assumptions needed to decide *Griffin* are much less contested in our legal culture: follow the plain meaning of the statute unless it generates an "absurd" result. A statute which says that the shipowner "shall pay" penalty wages "for each and every day during which payment is withheld," with no listed exceptions, presumptively requires the calculation to continue until the owner actually pays. Although that period was several years in *Griffin*, the large penalty is not an absurd one because it serves well-accepted punitive and deterrent purposes of this sort of statute, and because we have little sympathy for a shipowner that strands a seaman abroad after he was injured on the job. Some of these propositions would have been sharply contested in 1898 (and an 1898 Court would probably have reached a different result), but the Court deciding the case in 1983 was virtually unanimous because the propositions are no longer seriously contested.

Interpreting the Federal Rules of Evidence to permit impeachment of civil plaintiffs' credibility on the basis of their prior criminal convictions, *Bock Laundry* was (unlike *Griffin*) a hard case, for its resolution involved taking ideological positions that were sharply contested. Interestingly not contested were the propositions that, as written, Rule 609 (which on its face allowed the possibility of excluding such impeaching evidence against civil defendants but not civil plaintiffs) was unconstitutional, that this was the result of a drafting error, and that the Court should rewrite the rule. The Court splintered on how to do so, and its ideological division reflected the division within Congress fifteen years previously.[65] Believing that Congress had operated under a moralist ideology whereby the jury "ought to know" about a litigant's or a witness's scrapes with the law as part of its moral evaluation of her or his credibility, the Court majority interpreted the rule to allow such impeachment routinely in civil cases. Believing that Congress was too sharply divided to make such a choice, the dissenters operated under a scientific ideology, which posits from psychological studies that prior convictions (unless for perjury or some other *crimen falsi*) tell juries little about a witness's credibility and that juries tend to punish civil plaintiffs unduly once they know about their criminal convictions. Hence, the dissenters urged that the rule be interpreted to allow impeachment only if the relevance of the conviction outweighs probable prejudice. *Bock Laundry* is particularly interesting because within a year of the decision the Court rewrote the rule under its Rules Enabling Act powers and adopted the ideological framework of the dissenters.[66] Thus, unlike the ideological divisions in *Weber*, those in *Bock Laundry* have been resolved within the Court.

Institutional Dynamism: Statutory Interpretation as a Sequential Process

Thus far I have told two stories of evolution and constraint in statutory interpretation. One is largely from a practical perspective, in which changes in society and law drive statutory interpretation in dynamic directions, though the interpreter is constrained by clear texts, authoritative legal materials, and reliance interests. The other story is largely from a cultural perspective, in which the changing culture or ideology of interpreters drives statutory interpretation in dynamic directions, though the interpreter is in turn constrained by cultural or ideological consensus. Consider now a third story, from a political perspective, in which changing political pressures drive statutory interpretation in dynamic directions, though the interpreter remains constrained both by the way the issue is framed for her from below and by the prospect that her interpretation will be overridden from above.

My case for this third story rests on a simple claim: that we should stop looking at statutory interpretation just from the perspective of the Supreme Court and instead consider statutes from the "bottom up,"[67] from the perspective of private parties, agencies, and lower courts, whose work most shapes statutes and influences what the Court hears and how it will resolve cases. Conversely, to the extent that we view statutory interpretation from the "top down," we need to remember that the top is not the Supreme Court but the current Congress and president, whose ability to override Supreme Court decisions is another political influence or constraint on how the Court interprets statutes.

This claim suggests how statutory interpretation is dynamic, but in a more complex way than has been suggested thus far. The mediation between original expectations and dynamic application occurs at the retail level first, and the statute's application to unforeseen circumstances works its way through the system before the wholesalers (agency heads and the Supreme Court) even get a crack at it; by then the statute's evolution is often strongly directed, and the Court's role is just to ratify or modify the dynamic consensus that exists from below. Also, the interpreters whose horizons matter so much in statutory interpretation are not just judges but also include citizens, interest groups, and administrators. This variety of interpreters not only ensures that the statute will grow and develop over time, but reduces the likelihood that any one individual's idiosyncratic interpretation will prevail. Finally, and perhaps most paradoxically, statutory interpretation ends up as a sequential political game, pushing judicial as well as agency interpretations in dynamic directions, typically more responsive to the current preferences of Congress and the president than to the historical preferences of the original enacting coalition.

Statutory Interpretation from the Bottom Up

Statutory interpretation has almost universally been viewed by legal scholars *(moi inclus)* from the top down. That is, we have approached the subject from the Olympian perspective of the Supreme Court. Under the top down approach the Court sets policy to reflect its own interpretation of the law and then monitors everyone else (agencies, private parties, lower courts) to enforce its choices; the Court's interpretations are then considered the final word, with little interest given to how the rest of the political system reacts to the Court's ruling. The Court's interpretive practice is presented in a stylized way. What has happened lower down in the hierarchy matters far less than the Court's own prior interpretations and its general practice.

Viewed from the top down, statutory interpretation is presented as little if anything more than the common law with an unusual first precedent.[68] While this is not an irrational way to approach statutory interpretation, it is not the most useful way. Statutory interpretation can be more usefully viewed from the bottom up. That is, scholars ought to consider statutory interpretation as occurring everywhere all the time, with no one interpreter having the final word on what a statute means. The bottom up perspective emphasizes interpretations by the person or institution that must initially apply the statute at the ground level—private persons and firms, bureaucrats and law enforcement officers, and dispute resolution centers (such as arbitrators and administrative law judges). Because different interpreters at the ground level will often reach different interpretations of statutes, the bottom up perspective must take into account the resolution of interpretive conflicts, but will not unduly privilege the Supreme Court as the last word. For practical purposes, agencies and lower courts will have the final word on most interpretive matters. Even when the Supreme Court does rule, the issue will be framed by the preexisting discussion.

The bottom up approach is a particularly useful perspective because it highlights important intellectual issues obscured by the top down approach. Its primary contributions are its focus on interpretation by private parties and agencies and its revelation of the contingency of the Supreme Court's own interpretations, which can be overridden by Congress. The next two sections demonstrate how these insights of the bottom up perspective press even the Supreme Court's statutory interpretation in dynamic directions. On the one hand, the Court is often decisively influenced by how the people and institutions below it in law's hierarchy want the statute to be interpreted. On the other hand, the Court is also often decisively influenced by how it thinks the institution above it (Congress and the president) would want the statute interpreted. Both ways reveal how normal politics (not just ideology but good old interest group partisan politics) exerts continuous pressure on statutory interpretation. For institutional reasons, statutory interpretation over time will reflect shifting political preferences.

Retail Politics: Political Struggle among Communities of Interpretation

Viewing statutory issues from the perspective of actors lower in the legal hierarchy enables us to see more clearly how statutory interpretation reflects the dynamics of political conflict and balance. For example, the bottom up perspective reminds us that courts are not the primary officials interpreting most statutes. Edward Rubin criticizes the juricentric bias of statutory interpretation scholarship and reminds us that most statutes in the modern regulatory state are not directives to the citizenry but "intransitive" directives addressed to agencies.[69] Even transitive statutes, addressed directly to the citizenry, are often implemented by agencies, the first-order interpreters of statutes such as Title VII and the immigration statute. Because agencies approach statutory interpretation from a pragmatic and (shifting) political point of view and because courts defer to agency interpretations, the primacy of agencies as statutory interpreters makes the pragmatic, political, and dynamic nature of statutory interpretation more transparent.

Section 212(a) of the 1952 immigration law was an intransitive statute, consisting of directives to the INS and PHS. As a consequence, the critical interpretive battles over excluding bisexuals, gay men, and lesbians pursuant to section 212(a)(4) occurred within agencies, not courts. So long as the PHS believed that bisexuals, gay men, and lesbians are mentally ill, the statute was interpreted that way (as in *Boutilier*); once the PHS changed its mind, it was only a matter of time before the earlier interpretation was abandoned (as in the 1990 override of *Boutilier*, which had been a dead letter throughout the 1980s). The PHS's 1979 change of mind was openly evolutive and policy driven, decisively influenced by the shift in medical opinion. The Justice Department and the INS did not see the matter that way and sought to adapt what they saw as their duty to exclude with the PHS's opting out, but the INS resolution was an obvious practical compromise (exclude only those who volunteer their sexual orientation). The courts were left with a choice between two dynamic agency interpretations, not so much interpretations of what the statute meant as interpretations of what their respective duties were under the statute. The forty-year interpretive life of section 212(a)(4) was dominated by politics and not neutral principles, agencies and not courts.

Looking at statutory interpretation from the bottom up would press Rubin's insight further than he does. Not only are agencies the key interpreters, but the critical developments for the agency's interpretation often occur at the ground level, not at the top of the agency hierarchy. Most interpretation is done in the lawyer's office, on the police officer's beat, and at the bureaucrat's desk. What is done with the statute by private persons and institutions, lower-level administrators, and on-the-spot commentators strongly frames the issues presented to the higher-ups (agencies and courts). It is exceptional for a judicial or agency decision to cut against a strong consensus of those interpreting the statute at the bottom. The critical event in the evolution of section 212(a)(4), the PHS's reversal in 1979, was the result of extended debate within the medical and psychiatric community over homosexuality, and the Surgeon General (who heads the PHS) was probably responding to pressures from within his own agency when he adopted the new policy.[70]

The most important consequence of the bottom up approach is to show how the evolution of a statute is driven by socioeconomic and cultural developments more than by formal legal developments. Rather than being imposed from the top, power and legal change come from below.[71] Thus, the PHS's reinterpretation of section 212(a)(4) was not the turning point. It was possible only because of other events: the Stonewall riots in 1969 and the gay rights movement, which propelled many gay and lesbian doctors and psychiatrists out of the closet; Dr. Franklin Kameny's seizing the microphone at the American Psychiatric Association's (APA) meeting in 1971 and refusing to give it up until the APA agreed to review its persecution of gay men, lesbians, and bisexuals; and the APA's striking of homosexuality from the list of mental defects in 1973 and the accompanying ferocious debate within the medical community.[72] These events, and the underlying cultural and social developments, made the PHS's 1979 reversal possible (and some kind of change inevitable), and fueled the policy debate of the 1980s which overrode *Boutilier*.

Looking at law from the bottom up reveals the cultural and political struggle for meaning that generates and underlies the most interesting stories of dynamic statutory interpretation. The struggle for meaning occurs when different communities of interpretation form around a statutory issue. The communities of interpretation contest with one another about what the statute should mean, each one jockeying for position within and without the formal channels of government and developing arguments for their different interpretations. Sometimes a consensus develops among those most interested in the statutory issue, and it is never resolved through formal administrative or judicial interpretation (as in the *Griffin* issue before the Supreme Court unsettled the consensus). Sometimes a consensus interpretation exists early on but dissolves when a new community of interpretation becomes prominent (the gay community's dissent from *Boutilier*) or an existing community changes its mind (the medical community). Other times one community of interpretation will temporarily capture the agency and/or the courts (as the civil rights community did in *Weber*), but other communities or new communities continue to contest the official interpretation (as in *Johnson*).

The struggle for statutory meaning at the retail level can easily be understood as political and dynamic. What is not so easily understood is how the retail politics drives statutory interpretation in agencies and courts—by determining which issues are contested and how sharply they will be contested, by framing the issues, and by supplying information and political signals to the decision makers. Consider the interpretation of Title VII to prohibit employment practices that have a "discriminatory effect" on racial minorities.[73] The statute that was enacted in 1964 focused on intentional discrimination[74] and set up a cumbersome administrative apparatus designed to minimize the role of the Equal Employment Opportunity Commission (EEOC) in the statute's development,[75] both trade-offs that had to be made to break the southern filibuster in the Senate. Nevertheless, the dynamic interpretation of Title VII started shortly after the statute went into force, and it began at the declawed EEOC, as the activists who had worked to enact the statute—civil rights leaders and litigators, bureaucrats, law professors—turned to the task of making the statute work to implement President Johnson's goal of "not just equality as a right and a theory but equality as a fact and equality as a result."[76]

From its first year in operation, key players at all levels of the EEOC came to believe that racial inequality in employment was the result of structural factors, not just intentional discrimination, and that affirmative results were more important than formal requirements.[77] Based on her labor law experience, EEOC staff member Sonia Pressman argued that it would be impractical to expect evidence of discriminatory intent in most cases. Just as litigants challenging racial discrimination in jury selection could rely on statistical underrepresentation of minorities, Pressman urged that plaintiffs could make out a prima facie claim of employment discrimination based on statistical underrepresentation of minorities.[78] Although the EEOC legal staff was candid about the tension between their views and the compromises adopted in the 1964 statute, they urged their approach as the most practical way to enforce the law. By the end of the Johnson administration, the EEOC commissioners publicly interpreted the statute to bar employer practices "which prove to have a demonstrable racial effect."[79]

The EEOC's rationale for an effect-based approach was that such an interpretation better served the statutory purpose. This position was shared by the NAACP Legal Education and Defense Fund, Inc. (Inc. Fund). Directly encouraged by the EEOC, which filed helpful amicus briefs, civil rights litigation groups challenged employer testing and union seniority arrangements which had disproportionate and negative effects on African Americans. These groups sometimes found a receptive audience in Eisenhower- and Johnson-appointed federal judges who were struggling with similar issues of racially discriminatory effects of arguably "neutral" state policies in the areas of education, voting, and jury selection.[80]

What turned out to be the critical litigation was Griggs v. Duke Power Company,[81] a class action challenging employee tests used by Duke Power for hiring and promotion, on the ground that they had a discriminatory effect against African Americans. The Inc. Fund lost in the district court and in the Fourth Circuit Court of Appeals, but over a powerful dissent by Judge Simon Soboloff, President Dwight Eisenhower's Solicitor General, who had argued *Brown*. In *Griggs* he endorsed a disparate impact approach as the only way to fulfill the goals of Title VII.[82] On appeal to the Supreme Court, the Inc. Fund worked from Soboloff's dissenting opinion, other lower court cases adopting a disparate impact approach, the EEOC's 1966 guidelines on employment tests, and a supportive amicus brief filed by Solicitor General Erwin Griswold for the Nixon administration. Although the legal world was stunned by the Supreme Court's unanimous adoption of a disparate impact approach in *Griggs*, careful observers should not have been too surprised by the Court's opinion, which closely followed the analysis suggested by the nation's most eminent Republican lawyers (Soboloff and Griswold), the leading civil rights group, and the agency charged with implementing the statute.

Griggs assuredly represented a dynamic interpretation of Title VII, but its interpretation did not leap out of the blue. It filtered up from the brains of EEOC and Inc. Fund attorneys, round after round of discussions and conferences within and outside the EEOC, debate among lower court judges and within the Nixon Justice Department. Like the PHS's dynamic interpretation of the 1952 Immigration and Nationality Act, the Supreme Court's dynamic interpretation of Title VII in *Griggs* (and, in a similar process, later in *Weber*) was the result of a battle for meaning—which ideology would dominate Title VII enforcement?—that was fought step by step through the federal government (where a substantial consensus developed in the 1970s) and within the private sector (where there was less consensus).

Wholesale Politics: Statutory Interpretation as an Anticipated Response Game

A further implication of viewing statutory interpretation as a sequential process is the importance of "anticipated response." That is, a legal actor's interpretation of a statute will be guided not only by her own preferred interpretation, but also (in varying degrees, depending on the context) by what the actor anticipates will be the interpretation of some individual or institution higher up in the hierarchy of lawmaking authority. For example, a lawyer giving tax planning advice to a client will interpret the Internal Revenue Code with an eye to her client's interests, but she will also be attentive to what she anticipates the agency's interpretation will be. The agency's interpretation, in turn, will often be attentive to its judgment about what a reviewing court (such as the Tax Court) and Congress would consider an acceptable interpretation of the statute. In turn, the Tax Court will be attentive to its judgment about the likely interpretation the Supreme Court would give the statute. Last, and perhaps most surprisingly, the Supreme Court's interpretation will often be attentive to the possibility of a congressional override, which the Court will tend to avoid. Just as private parties, agencies, and lower courts anticipate preferences of institutions higher up, the Supreme Court may anticipate congressional preferences when it interprets the statute.[83]

To develop this hypothesis, I draw on positive political theory models that view statutory interpretation as a sequential political game.[84] The game is played across a linear space (the possible statutory policies) in which a position to the right represents relatively conservative policy preferences and a position to the left relatively liberal policy preferences. The agency makes the first move in the game by choosing a point on the policy line which represents its preferences as to the statute's interpretation for some issue (A). Once the agency has made its move, the losers have recourse to the courts, and ultimately to the Supreme Court, which has a raw preference of its own about the best interpretation of the statute ($\mathcal{J}$). Although the Court can substitute its interpretation for that of the agency, the House and Senate (H and S) can, in turn, override the Court's interpretation, subject to veto by the president (P), which Congress can override by a two-thirds vote in each chamber (h and s). In equilibrium, each player in the game will try to impose its policy preferences on the statute, to the extent that its result is not overridden by a subsequent player.

The operation of this game, and an important elaboration, can be illustrated by *Boutilier*. The application of the statutory exclusion to a bisexual with no "psychopathic personality" was a dynamic interpretation by the PHS. In making this move the PHS was reading into the statute its belief that a "bisexual" is not materially different from a "homosexual" for medical purposes. According to the model I have just outlined, the PHS would also have considered the political viability of its position. In the mid-1960s it would have anticipated that Congress and the Court would go along with its enforcement of section 212(a)(4) against virtually any kind of sexual orientation minority,[85] and it would have been correct: the Court agreed with the PHS in *Boutilier*, and there was no congressional effort to override the Court or the agency.

In the 1970s the PHS felt professional pressure to ameliorate its policy, which contributed to its 1979 reversal. Although the Department of Justice disagreed with the new policy, it did not have the authority to override the PHS, and the latter again correctly anticipated that its new policy would find support in the courts and in Congress. Figure 2.3 reveals the new configuration of preferences during the 1980s, with A and $\mathcal{J}$ representing the original

	x*		x
	A*		A
	J*	J*	J
	(H*, S*)		(H, S)

Figure 2.3   The *Boutilier* issue, 1967–1990: Statutory policy shifts from $x = A$ to
$x^* = A^*$

agency and judicial preferences on the gaylesbian exclusion; A^* the PHS's new position; J^*, J^* the split in the courts on the PHS position; and H^*, S^* the ultimate congressional consensus in favor of the PHS. Under the conditions of the game in 1979, the equilibrium position shifted from x (in the 1960s) to x^* (in the 1980s).

It is important to note that the history of the *Boutilier* issue suggests that the preferences of the various players are not necessarily independent of their participation in the game.[86] Especially where the players are all working toward the same policy objectives but have some uncertainty about how best to achieve those objectives, they seek out useful information and are open to arguments from other players before they determine their preferences.[87] On medical issues, Congress, the INS, and the Court were all willing to defer to the PHS, which was the main source of medical information for official organs of government. The agency's position of perceived expertise gave it great power to avoid overrides and move policy toward its own preferences, which changed in response to pressures from the PHS's own professional community.

For institutional reasons, statutory interpretation has especially dynamic qualities when primary interpretive responsibility is given to an agency that is responsive to new circumstances and norms, and to which the other branches defer (Figure 2.3). But statutory meaning can be just as mobile when there is no player to which the others defer and when preferences are less malleable. Institutional dynamics alone will generate dynamic statutory interpretations.

One reason for this phenomenon is that the judges and administrators interpreting the statute may from the beginning bring a perspective different from that of the enacting Congress. Recall the immediate efforts within the EEOC to interpret Title VII to prohibit at least some employer policies having a "demonstrable racial effect." The statutory bargain struck to enact Title VII represented a compromise between the House's preferences and the Senate's more conservative preferences on issues such as how intrusive the government should be in an employer's hiring and promotion decisions. Indeed, the compromise (x) was skewed to the right of even the preference of the median senator because the need to obtain a two-thirds majority in the Senate rendered conservative Senator Dirksen the pivotal voter (recall Chapter 1). But once Title VII was enacted into law, the agency (dominated by Johnson administration liberals) could move statutory policy to the left of Dirksen's preferences, for Dirksen did not have enough votes to override the agency. Dynamic statutory interpretation can occur immediately after a law's enactment (and did occur in the Johnson and Nixon EEOC) because the ideology of the implementing agency may be different from that of the enacting coalition.[88]

The EEOC moved cautiously, however, both because it was internally uncertain as to the best way to enforce the statute and because it was concerned that either the Court or Congress would override a dramatic policy shift. The EEOC took a risk by supporting the Inc. Fund's *Griggs* litigation, but the risk paid off when the Supreme Court confirmed a new Title VII policy that represented a dramatic shift to the left of the policy voted in 1964. Figure 2.4 diagrams the preference configurations and the new equilibrium.

Three different political dynamics enabled Title VII's policy to shift to the left between 1964 and 1971. One was the internal politics of the EEOC (*A**) and the Supreme Court (*J**), both of which were pressed from below by an academic consensus in favor of vigorous enforcement of Title VII. A second dynamic was a slight shift to the left in congressional preferences between 1964 (*H* and *S*) and 1971 (*H** and *S**), owing in part to the increased electoral power of African Americans following enactment of the Voting Rights Act of 1965. When the preferences of Congress shift in the direction of the interpreter's, the latter has more freedom to apply the statute dynamically, for the only Congress to which it is accountable is the current one. But any change in legislative preferences between 1964 and 1971 was modest[89] and does not explain how the EEOC and the Court could shift Title VII's policy so much further to the left.

My judgment is that *Griggs* represented a policy more vigorous than that which Congress—*H** and *S**—would have wanted in 1971 (see Figure 2.4). Yet Congress did not override *Griggs*, even though it amended Title VII immediately after *Griggs*, and even though the employer community wanted *Griggs* curtailed or overridden. The key to this nonevent was the endorsement of *Griggs* in committee reports drafted in 1971 by the House and Senate labor committees (*C**).[90] Those reports may not have been representative of

$$
\begin{array}{l}
\text{x*} \qquad\qquad\qquad\qquad\qquad\qquad\quad \text{x} \\
\overline{} \\
\text{A*}\quad \text{C*}\quad \text{H*}\ \text{H}\quad \text{S*}\ \text{S} \\
\text{J*} \\
\text{C* (H*)}
\end{array}
$$

Figure 2.4   The *Griggs* decision, 1971: Statutory policy shifts from *x* > *S* to
$x^* = A^* = J^*$

the views of the median member of Congress, however, because the House and Senate labor committees have since the 1970s been dominated by representatives with preferences to the left of their chambers on civil rights.[91] Because those committees exercise "gatekeeping" power over issues on the legislative agenda, they have substantial ability to head off overrides, especially if they are supported by the majority party leadership (which was similarly liberal on civil rights).

Under the foregoing analysis, the EEOC and the Supreme Court can set policy at the point reflecting the preferences of the median member of the House Committee on Education and Labor ($x^* = C^*$) rather than the median member of the House ($x^* = H^*$). This institutional dynamic alone gives the agency and the courts substantial discretion to move statutory policy away from the original equilibrium ($S < x$). The EEOC and the Court may have moved Title VII's policy to the left of the labor committees' preferences in 1971. The committees went along either because they were persuaded by the EEOC-Court (C^* shifts to the left) or because the new policy was no more distant from the median committee preference than was the policy preferred by the median House member. Figure 2.4 suggests the latter explanation, but either is plausible. Although the preferences of the current Congress limit interpretive options, the existence of supportive congressional gatekeepers affords a greater leeway for dynamic interpretation, as occurred in *Griggs*.

Of course, *Griggs* was itself subject to interpretation. After Justices Lewis Powell and William Rehnquist started voting in 1972, the Burger Court became more ambivalent about broadly defined antidiscrimination duties. In constitutional cases, where the Court is better protected against political overrides, the Burger Court rejected the *Griggs* approach and held that race-based or gender-based effects do not amount to unlawful discrimination.[92] While the Burger Court cut back on *Griggs* by tightening up the burden of proof on plaintiffs, it did not directly attack the decision. The survival of *Griggs* through the 1970s is remarkable because the decision was poorly reasoned and vulnerable to the charge that it represented a significant leap away from the expectations of the enacting Congress (x^* is a long way from x), and because a majority on the Court in the 1970s was unenthusiastic about outlawing discriminatory effects. I hypothesize that *Griggs* remained safe from an overruling in a period when the Court was moving to the right because Congress had moved to the left on civil rights issues in the 1970s.[93] Thus, the new policy ($x^* = A^*$) was one that was acceptable to the median House member by the late 1970s. Any open retreat from *Griggs* would have generated controversy, since the civil rights community, the EEOC, and the gatekeeping (labor) committees would have mobilized for an override. In fact, when the Court retreated from *Griggs* by refusing to treat pregnancy discrimination as sex discrimination under Title VII, the Court suffered a firestorm of protest and was promptly overridden.[94]

This institutional logic also accounts for the conservative Court's liberal response to voluntary affirmative action. The Burger Court was ambivalent about affirmative action, as we see from its constitutional decisions.[95] In *Weber*, and even more obviously in *Johnson*, the Court broadly sanctioned voluntary affirmative action, accommodating its interpretation of Title VII to the preferences of the current rather than the enacting Congress.[96] The liberal interpretation of Title VII by a conservative Court between 1972 and 1986 suggests that the Court is sometimes more responsive to the preferences of the current Congress than to those of the enacting Congress.[97]

The political changes in the 1970s—the Court moved to the right on civil rights issues while Congress moved to the left—tended to cancel each other out on Title VII issues, but *Griggs* was left vulnerable in the 1980s because of the election of conservative presidents. Figure 2.5 maps the new configuration of preferences. The insight illustrated in Figure 2.5 is that not only may the current preferences of Congress (H^* and S^*) make a difference in statutory interpretation, but so may the current preferences of the president (P^*) when those preferences line up with the Court's preferences in periods of divided government.

After the election of Ronald Reagan as president in 1980, the Court had more discretion to cut back on liberal civil rights precedents because its decisions would be overridden only if they were more conservative than the veto medians in both chambers of Congress (h^* and s^*). It should therefore not be surprising that immediately after 1980, the Court's statutory civil rights decisions became more conservative.[98] By the late 1980s the Court's preferences had moved to the right with the appointment of Justices Scalia and Kennedy. These two developments reinforced each other and in 1989 produced a significant change in the Court's interpretation of job discrimination statutes. The main decision was Wards Cove Packing Company v. Atonio,[99] which narrowed *Griggs*, though it did not move statutory policy all the way back to the original balance.[100] *Wards Cove* was a more conservative policy than that desired by Congress, but it had only to satisfy the veto median in either the House (h^*) or the Senate (s^*). I think the Court missed the veto medians in both chambers because it underestimated the academic and public perceptions of how radically it was cutting back on *Griggs*. Although the Senate (barely) voted to uphold President George Bush's veto of the *Wards Cove* override in 1990,[101] a less ambitious override might have passed that year.

x*			x**		x	
H*	S*	h*	s*	J**	P**	

Figure 2.5   Overruling *Griggs*, 1989: Statutory policy shifts from $x^* < H^*$ to $x^{**} = s^*$ when president and judiciary shift rightward and Congress remains stable

Wards Cove was substantially overridden by the Civil Rights Act of 1991.[102] Title VII policy did not shift back to the original *Griggs* decision, which the Burger Court itself had narrowed, but did shift to the left.

Questions of the original intent of the Congress that enacted the Civil Rights Act of 1964 remained relevant to the debates over *Griggs* and *Weber*, but they were talking points rather than serious analyses. At the Supreme Court, as at the EEOC, the interpretation of the statute and of its statutory precedents in the 1980s was clearly evolutive. Changes in the law as well as changes in society required, as a practical matter, that the interpreters approach Title VII issues (many of them new and unanticipated) differently than Congress would have in 1964. Changes in Court personnel and EEOC chiefs dramatically affected interpretations of Title VII, for the new interpreters brought strikingly different perspectives to the statute. Additionally, the new institutional context for Title VII litigation, especially the election of conservative presidents in the 1980s, influenced the statute's evolution.

Different intellectual traditions—pragmatism, hermeneutics, and positive political theory—interact to explain the dynamics of statutory interpretation. In this chapter I have applied these theories to discrete issues of civil rights and immigration law. The next chapter takes up the ways in which statutory interpretation can be even more dramatically dynamic when the law's treatment of an important issue, labor strikes and boycotts, is examined over three generations.

3 · A Case Study: Labor Injunction Decisions, 1877–1938

Statutory interpretation is a cultural as well as a legal process. Cultural shifts generate movement of statutory meaning. Changes in society, its values, and its competing ideologies shape and reshape statutory meaning as they reveal new practical problems unresolved by the statute, interpretive horizons distant from those of the drafters, and novel political environments attentive to interpretive developments. This evolutive process is illustrated by the issues examined in Chapters 1 and 2. Analyzing the federal labor injunction cases from 1877 to 1938,[1] this chapter will provide further evidence—during a different time period and for different issues from those examined earlier—for my descriptive thesis and its pragmatic, hermeneutical, and positive political themes.

No federal statute specifically authorized the federal labor injunction. Instead, it was carved out of bankruptcy law, the Interstate Commerce Act, the Sherman Act, and even civil rights statutes by lawyers, scholars, and lower court judges responding to the new problems that bedeviled industrializing America. Few if any of the leading labor injunction decisions can be cleanly defended under originalist theory. The aforementioned statutes were not passed to deal with labor strikes and boycotts, but interpreters adapted these statutes to new problems and political alignments. The meaning these statutes took on was not the result of any sustained application of original legislative expectations, but was the consequence of a dialogue among regulators, legislators, and judges, as well as private interests, about how best to balance workers' need to organize against employers' need for smooth business operations.

Just as the labor injunction cases provide a useful example of dynamic statutory interpretation, an interpretive analysis of these cases may also contribute (modestly) to American labor law history, which is coming to appreciate the complex way in which interpretations of the Sherman Act, in particular, were part of the sociocultural struggle between labor and management during this period. This chapter shows how evolving discourse in labor-management relations, shifting political attitudes toward unions, and politically responsive changes in the personnel of the federal judiciary contribute to a more complete story about labor injunctions. I proceed in three stages: through an initial formative period (1877–1895) in which judges created the federal labor injunction and read it into the Sherman Act, to a period of experimentation (1896–1921) during which judges and legislators sought consensus limitations on an instrument that had become politically controversial, and a final harsh period (1921–1938) which was reversed by the political revolution preceding and carrying over into the New Deal.

The Creation of the Federal Labor Injunction, 1877–1895

The period after the Civil War witnessed an industrial revolution in the United States. The establishment of a national railway network, large-scale industries, and new forms of corporate organization contributed to a threefold increase in production between 1865 and 1890. The growth of corporate power was accompanied by unprecedented labor organization, first in the railroads and then in other industries. Labor-management strife escalated as a result of workers' better organization, competitive pressures by employers to reduce labor costs, and the tensions engendered by business cycles. On July 16, 1877, at the tail end of America's first major industrial recession, a wildcat shutdown of the Baltimore and Ohio Railroad by trainmen in Baltimore, Maryland, and Martinsburg, West Virginia, triggered the nation's first national railroad strike.[2] The strike shut down much of the nation's rail service and saw pitched battles among strikers, local authorities, and railroad security officers. It was quelled when President Rutherford B. Hayes called out the army at the request of three state governors. The 1877 strike also gave birth to the federal labor injunction.

The roots of the labor injunction lay in the particular economic ideology held by legal elites in the mid-nineteenth century. They assumed that existing holders of private property and capital had rights that were legally "vested," as did every person for his or her own labor. A person's "right to liberty [includes] the right to exercise his faculties and to follow a lawful avocation for the support of life; the right to property [includes] the right to acquire possession and enjoy it in any way consistent with the equal rights of others."[3] These libertarian principles suggested a further baseline: the relations between freely contracting workers and freely hiring (and firing) employers must be insulated from "interference" and "coercion," especially by collectives.[4] State courts in the late 1860s and early 1870s worked from these premises to permit criminal conspiracy or civil damage actions against efforts by labor organizations to interfere with employment relationships.[5] In 1877, Justice Thomas Cooley of the Michigan Supreme Court specifically urged an aggressive use of the courts' equity powers to prevent intrusions into an employer's business by both state regulators and union activists. After 1877 railroad attorneys successfully used this precise argument to persuade state officials to break strikes, much as President Hayes had done in 1877.[6]

During the 1877 strike itself, attorneys for bankrupt railroads made similar arguments to federal courts which were managing their roads while in receivership. Reflecting the view that employer-employee relations should not be disrupted, Judges Thomas Drummund, Walter Gresham, and Samuel Treat entered injunctions ordering marshals to maintain the operation of railroads under their federal receivership and notifying workers that any interference would be treated as a contempt of court. When striking employees continued to prevent operation of the different railroads, all three judges held the workers in contempt. The judges justified their orders in the same terms used by Cooley. By obstructing railroad operations, the striking employees not only invaded their employers' private property but deprived fellow employees of their economic liberty. The strikers' actions also interfered with interstate commerce and therefore implicated the national interest, reasoned these judges.[7]

Although the first federal labor injunctions were grounded on the courts' receivership powers under federal bankruptcy law, these judges were reacting to the same fears of mob violence and outside interference with vested property rights which had impelled state judges to expand the common law of conspiracy to include union activities. Some interested observers opined that federal labor injunctions might be issued to protect railroads not in receivership,[8] and legislative proposals to that effect were offered when Congress was debating the interstate commerce bill in 1887.[9]

Such legislative proposals were not adopted by Congress, but railway strikes between 1885 and 1888 saw federal judges issue labor injunctions to nonreceivered railroads based on dynamic readings of other federal statutes. Gresham, for example, in 1886 enjoined a strike against a nonreceivered railroad, based on the Civil Rights Act of 1871, which prohibited "conspiracies" to prevent citizens from exercising their federal statutory or constitutional rights.[10] This was a dynamic reading of the 1871 statute, which had been passed to protect against Ku Klux Klan violence aimed at African Americans. Several federal judges enjoined worker boycotts as violations of the Interstate Commerce Act's prohibition of discrimination in interstate traffic.[11] This was a dynamic reading of the 1887 law. Although section 3 of the act prohibited discrimination in the interchange of interstate traffic among railroads, that provision by its terms was enforceable only by the Interstate Commerce Commission (ICC) against railroads themselves, not against workers and unions. Moreover, section 16 (the injunction provision) provided merely for federal court injunctions against violations of orders by the ICC (which did not intervene in labor disputes), and Congress had considered but specifically rejected proposals to add remedies against railway workers whose strikes disrupted interstate commerce.

Responding to railroad attorneys pleading public emergency as well as invasion of economic liberty, federal judges were creating public policy out of thin statutory material. Different judges came up with different policies, based on different visions of the interests at stake. Many judges conceded the right of workers to organize and strike to advance their economic goals—but not to disrupt interstate commerce through boycotts. This was the approach of Judge John Love during the 1888 Burlington strike, later adopted by Judge William Howard Taft of the Sixth Circuit.[12] Other judges accepted the railroads' view that "all associations designed to interfere with the perfect freedom of employers in the proper management and control of their lawful businesses . . . by interference with their property or traffic . . . are pro tanto illegal combinations or associations."[13]

Judge David Brewer of the Eighth Circuit issued labor injunctions reflecting this libertarian philosophy. He allowed for "a right to quit work," but not for "interfering with other persons' working, and preventing the owners of railroad trains from managing those trains as they see fit—there is where the wrong comes in."[14] Brewer's philosophy had an audience beyond the railroad attorneys and their alumni on the bench. His writings reveal a nostalgic Jeffersonian vision of America as an arcadian land of rugged individuals. This vision was under siege after the Civil War, when industrializing America threatened to overwhelm the striving individual with the power of collectives. "[T]he drift today is toward the subjection of the individual to the domination of the organization," lamented Brewer. "The business men are becoming slaves of the combine, the laborers of the trades union and organization. Through the land the idea is growing that the individual is nothing, and that the organization, and then the State, is everything."[15]

Given these concerns, conservatives such as Brewer were ambivalent about the role of the state. Although the economic libertarian philosophy was skeptical of state regulation because the state represented collective action, the state was itself a necessary bulwark against private combinations. Responding to labor unrest in the 1880s, Cooley had found that "the best government is that which governs most, which is most certainly present at all times with its protecting arm, and for that reason gives a perpetual sense of security."[16] Such a vigorous view of the government's role gave rise to the Sherman Act of 1890, section 2 of which prohibited combinations or conspiracies "in restraint of trade." While corporate and railroad attorneys were predictably cool toward the statute, proactive libertarians were receptive. "I am by no means satisfied that the old maxim, that the country which is governed least is governed best, may not, in these days of monopolies and combinations, be subject to revision," wrote Justice Henry Billings Brown after the statute's enactment.[17]

Because many economic libertarians in the 1890s feared what they viewed as the coercive potential of labor collectives, there was a receptive audience for the argument that the broadly phrased Sherman Act applied to labor activities. Yet the argument was substantially inconsistent with public expectations accompanying the statute's enactment. Senator John Sherman had assured the Senate that the act would have no effect on workers or farmers.[18] Modern scholars believe that Congress had no intent to render illegal labor combinations or strikes that had as their goal the union shop or the improvement of wages and working conditions,[19] and Congress in 1890 probably expected labor troubles to be handled through arbitral rather than judicial means.[20] The earliest court decisions held the Sherman Act inapplicable to labor combinations and conspiracies. As late as 1893 Attorney General Richard Olney specifically instructed a United States attorney not to use the Sherman Act as the basis for intervening in a local labor dispute, "in as much as it is a matter of public notoriety that the provisions of the statute in question were aimed at public mischief of a wholly different character."[21]

Yet within a year the railroads' position had become the conventional wisdom and black-letter law. What revolutionized legal construction of the Sherman Act was the unprecedented outbreak of labor strikes, boycotts, and violence accompanying the depression of 1893–94. This social unrest triggered near-hysteria within the legal community.[22] The hysteria was immediately translated into legal interpretation, as the Sherman Act was applied to labor controversies after three years of resistance.[23] The debate shifted away from whether the act applied to labor controversies and toward what sort of judicial regulation could be accomplished under the act.

The Northern Pacific Railway litigation illustrates this process. Judge James Jenkins issued a Sherman Act injunction against "combining or conspiring together or with others, either jointly or severally, or as committees, or as officers of any so-called 'labor organization,' with the design or purpose of causing a strike upon the [Northern Pacific] . . . and from ordering, recommending, advising, or approving by communication or instruction otherwise, the employes of said receivers . . . to join in a strike." The court said that there is no such thing as a "legal strike, because compulsion is the leading idea of it."[24] The court reasoned that when a lot of employees quit together, that was just as "malicious" and actionable as employee violence because it amounted to mob activity seeking to coerce the employer. These ideas were similar to those articulated by Brewer (in receivership cases) and some state judges (under the common law and state conspiracy statutes) in the 1880s.

Jenkins's order was reversed, in part, by an opinion written by Justice John Harlan, sitting on circuit duty. Although Harlan was more sensitive to labor's perspective than Jenkins had been, his opinion accepted without discussion the lower court's assertion of Sherman Act jurisdiction and reversed only because the order went too far, effectively imposing an involuntary servitude on workers.[25] Other federal judges echoed Harlan's more balanced vision, and Judge Henry Caldwell of the Eighth Circuit went one step further. When Union Pacific receivers unilaterally lowered wages and then sought federal injunctions against striking workers in 1894, Caldwell rebuffed them in terms similar to Harlan's, but also reinstated the previous wage rate until the receivers were able to work out a deal with the strikers or otherwise demonstrate a need to change.[26] Yet, like Harlan, Caldwell did not question the assertion of Sherman Act jurisdiction over labor conspiracies.

This debate reached a bloody climax in the Pullman strike of 1894.[27] The Pullman Company, which ran sleeper cars, was engaged in a dispute with its employees, who called a strike. The American Railway Union (ARU), headed by Eugene V. Debs, voted in June to support the Pullman workers by striking against all trains using Pullman cars. Pullman was, in turn, supported by the General Managers Association of Chicago. The result was a railway strike that tied up service all over the country and generated escalating violence, especially in Chicago. The political response to the strike was illuminating. At the local level many people sympathized with the strikers, given Pullman's reputation for meanness. Governor John Peter Altgeld openly criticized Pullman and supported the workers' requests. Others—especially at the national level—were alarmed, however. Attorney General Olney, a former corporate lawyer unsympathetic to worker protests, sought to destroy the ARU's strike, and the ARU itself. Olney ordered U.S. attorneys all over the country to obtain injunctions against sympathy strikes, based mainly on the federal power to move the mails (Olney was reluctant to interpret the Sherman Act broadly). Judges issued the injunctions, usually under authority of the Sherman Act,[28] and were willing to enforce them pitilessly through the federal marshals Olney made available to them. Taft—a judicial moderate—wrote his wife: "They [the marshals] have killed only six of the mob as yet. This is hardly enough to make an impression."[29]

Working directly with the railroad attorneys, the U.S. attorney's office in Chicago drafted a petition for an omnibus injunction against the core strikes, based on the Sherman Act. Pressured by his subordinates, his friends in the business community, and his own sense that this was a public emergency, Olney on July 1 authorized the U.S. attorney to file the petition under the Sherman Act.[30] The injunction was issued verbatim by federal Judges William Woods and Peter Grosscup on July 3, 1894. It ordered Debs and other ARU members to "desist and refrain from in any way or manner interfering with, hindering, obstructing or stopping any of the business" of the Chicago roads; the order detailed a wide range of actions that were forbidden, including the "compelling or inducing or attempting to compel or induce, by threats, intimidation, persuasion, force, or violence, any of the employés of any of the said railroads . . . in connection with the interstate business or commerce of said railroads or the carriage of the United States mail by such railroads."[31] Over the objections of Governor Altgeld, the army entered Chicago to enforce the injunction the next day, Independence Day, and the strike was crushed within ten days. Like others, Debs was jailed on July 17. In a decision issued December 4, 1894, Judge Woods justified his power to issue the injunction under the Sherman Act, as well as the Interstate Commerce Act and the Constitution itself, and then upheld Debs's contempt.[32]

On May 27, 1895, the Supreme Court unanimously affirmed Woods's injunction and contempt order. Following the lead of Olney, who argued the case, Justice Brewer's opinion in In re Debs found the "national emergency" and the general federal interest in moving the mail and protecting interstate commerce reason enough to establish federal jurisdiction and justify the broad remedy.[33] Notwithstanding Brewer's willingness to ignore the Sherman Act, the lower courts and the Supreme Court itself read *Debs* as ratifying the lower courts' view that the Sherman Act applied to labor combinations and that strikes interfering with interstate commerce were illegal.[34]

The Refinement of the Antiboycott Injunction, 1896–1914

Debs was the apotheosis of the labor injunction, with the courts accepting an interpretation of the Sherman Act that left a broad range of union activities—from boycotts and picketing to the union shop and sympathy strikes—open to regulation by federal judges. While it is not clear that Congress had completely ruled out application of the Sherman Act to labor activities, as Samuel Gompers of the American Federation of Labor (AFL) argued,[35] the federal executive and judiciary in 1893–1895 cooperated in a dynamic reading of the Sherman Act, a reading in which Congress acquiesced. Of course, any reading of the Sherman Act to permit injunctions against striking workers was itself subject to reinterpretation, and political feedback suggested that *Debs*—which outlawed various "persuasive" as well as "coercive" activities—was too radical an interpretation. As memories of the turbulent nineties receded and labor's voice became more reassuring and politically prominent, the federal executive, legislative, and judicial branches rejected *Debs*'s radicalism.

In the Wake of Debs: Thermidor 1896–1904

Just as suddenly as the omnibus federal antistrike injunction was created to quell the Pullman strike, it became problematic. The labor injunction both transformed and was transformed by organized labor. Between 1897 and 1904 the number of union members increased from about 400,000 to almost 2 million, and the AFL came to speak for a pragmatic business unionism, which sought mainly "short-term material gains—advances purely and simply in the interests of union members—achieved through collective bargaining and political action."[36] Partly out of fear of the labor injunction and partly out of an awareness of the underlying social fear that gave rise to the labor injunction, unions at both the national and local levels abandoned radical talk, were careful to disassociate themselves from violence, and showed themselves sensitive to local political structures. Led by the AFL, unions also focused their efforts on creating a more tolerant political climate, and the first order of business was to neutralize the omnibus labor injunction.

Thus, the AFL vigorously questioned the impartiality of a judiciary that used the federal "antitrust" statute to crush labor strikes (Debs) while refusing in the same term to apply the same law against the sugar trust (United States v. E. C. Knight Co.[37]). "There is," wrote Gompers, "perhaps, no law which can now be enacted which will seek to reach the trusts, but which the courts will construe, however unjustly, to include and affect labor unions."[38] In 1898 the AFL passed a resolution calling for "an impartial judiciary that will not govern us by arbitrary injunctions of the courts, nor act as pliant tools of corporate wealth."[39] At the AFL's urging at least four bills were introduced in Congress to limit federal court jurisdiction to issue injunctions in labor disputes, and the Senate passed a bill that would have limited federal courts' contempt power and would have required jury trials in at least some labor cases.[40]

The labor injunction also became an important issue in presidential politics after Debs. The Democratic party in 1896 renounced the economic conservatism of Olney and the Grover Cleveland administration and nominated the populist William Jennings Bryan. At their July convention the Democrats adopted a platform condemning "Federal Interference in Local Affairs" and "especially object[ing] to government by injunction as a new and highly dangerous form of oppression by which Federal judges, in contempt of the law of the States and rights of citizens, become at once legislators, judges and executioners."[41] The Populist party also nominated Bryan and denounced specific Supreme Court decisions (including Debs and the Income Tax Case[42]) in their platform.[43] Although Bryan made the free coinage of silver the chief issue of his campaign, the Supreme Court became almost as important an issue as the campaign progressed. The Republicans used the Court issue to appeal to conservative Democrats, and to tar Bryan with the charge of anarchism and disorder.[44] The Democrats used the Court issue to appeal to workers and farmers as victims of a system manipulated by economic and professional elites. Although the Republicans won the election, their popular vote margin was slender (50.2 percent to 47.5 percent), and it was apparent that much of the country was unhappy with the Court.

Judges themselves publicly attacked the omnibus injunction. Judge Caldwell wrote in 1897: "What is 'competition' when done by capital is 'conspiracy' when done by laborers. No amount of verbal dexterity can conceal or justify this glaring discrimination ... Whether organized labor has just grounds to declare a strike or boycott, is not a judicial question. These are labor's only weapons, and they are lawful and legitimate weapons."[45] Judges like Caldwell believed that labor unions were a necessary concomitant of industrial America. A government perceived to be partial to management was a government inviting labor turmoil.

Justice Oliver Wendell Holmes, Jr., of the Massachusetts Supreme Judicial Court provided an intellectual basis for the law to be responsive to this political reality. He conceptualized the doctrines of malicious restraint and conspiracy as torts which served the social goal of discouraging unproductive activity. Because these tort rules were policy driven, they should be subject to policy-based exceptions. Holmes offered a line of argument that would leave these doctrines inapplicable to most union activities. First, injuries to economic interests cannot always give rise to liability, elsewise the free market could not operate. Second, actions causing injury to economic interests should be legally cognizable only when they impair public policy; conversely, they should be privileged when justified by public policy. Third, "the policy of allowing free competition justifies the intentional inflicting of temporal damage, including the damage of interference with a man's business, by some means, when the damage is done not for its own sake, but as an instrumentality in reaching the end of victory in the battle of trade."[46] A related argument, privileging collective action pursuing rational goals of organized labor and only incidentally affecting the rights of management, was developed in the British courts at about the same time.[47]

Although many state courts remained hostile to worker efforts to obtain collective benefits such as the union shop, a new political climate, tying into the intellectual structure developed by Holmes, had an immediate impact on common law decisions—most prominently in New York, where the decision upholding union shops in National Protective Association (NPA) v. Cumming[48] became the leading case for the view that labor's needs for collective power should be accommodated by the legal system. In New York and other states the inquiry in strike cases shifted from one generally presuming that concerted labor activity violated economic liberty to one accepting collective action as a valid means of pursuing workers' self-interest and requiring specific allegations of unlawful purpose or coercive means to justify judicial intervention.[49] Within a decade of *Debs*, the AFL found "in our courts a remarkable tendency toward the application of modern enlightened principles to controversies between capital and labor."[50]

The incidental effects approach followed Holmes onto the Supreme Court in 1903. Writing for the Court in Aikens v. Wisconsin,[51] Holmes upheld a state malicious conspiracy law against due process attack, but only after drawing from the incidental effect cases an interpretation that saved its constitutionality: "We interpret 'maliciously injuring' to import doing a harm malevolently for the sake of the harm as an end in itself, and not merely as a means to some further end legitimately desired,"[52] hence suggesting that malice would not be inferred from collective conduct only incidentally harming economic interests. Lower courts (most prominently Judge Taft for the Sixth Circuit) and some Supreme Court Justices were at the same time reading a similar concept of "ancillarity" into the Sherman Act as it applied to businesses.[53] Federal courts of appeals interpreted the Sherman Act in labor cases to permit at least some strikes, peaceful picketing, and demands for union shops in the first decade of the century.[54]

In general, between 1896 and 1906 federal courts' interpretation of the Sherman Act shifted from an aggressive application against organized labor activities to one that was more reluctant to penalize collective action that served labor's self-interested purposes. More important, after the hysteria of 1894–95 and the popular objections to *Debs* in the 1896 election, the Department of Justice was less vigorous in pressing Sherman Act prosecutions against labor activities, largely for practical reasons.[55] The labor injunction was not even an issue in the 1904 campaign, which pitted two pro-labor candidates—Chief Judge Alton Parker of New York (the author of *NPA*) and President Theodore Roosevelt (who had appointed Holmes to the Court in part because of his pro-labor views).

Secondary Boycotts and the Sherman Act, 1904–1912

Just as the federal Department of Justice and courts of appeals were retreating from the implications of *Debs* for strike activities, private employers were seizing on its philosophy as a way to fight labor boycotts. The common law disapproved of boycotts on the ground that "the means used are threatening in their nature, and intended and naturally intended to overcome, by fear of loss of property, the will of others, and compel them to do things which they would not otherwise do."[56] For precisely the same reasons, and usually citing the common law, federal courts applied the Sherman Act against labor boycotts in the same period,[57] and of course *Debs* itself was mainly aimed at enjoining workers who boycotted trains carrying Pullman cars.

The political Thermidor after *Debs* led to a rethinking of the law's regulation of boycotts as well as other union activity. The incidental effect argument provided a possible justification for what were later to be called "primary" boycotts, in which workers urge people not to patronize their employer, because publicity about their grievances could be considered a fair weapon in the economic warfare between employer and employee.[58] One could easily make the same argument for "secondary" boycotts, in which unions engage in sympathy strikes or otherwise refuse to cooperate with other workers' "unfair" employers, simply by characterizing workers' economic self-interest in terms of collective solidarity with others in their national as well as local union and in allied unions. Nonetheless, the conventional wisdom was that such boycotts extended employer-employee economic warfare too far, representing judgments that workers had no direct self-interest in the conditions of other workers or that such boycotts too greatly unsettled the trade of the larger community. Analogously, common law judges considered business boycotts to be unjustifiable restraints of trade,[59] and the English courts which had articulated the incidental effects argument in the 1890s refused to apply that concept to sanction any kind of boycott (labor or business) as a matter of policy.[60]

Notwithstanding these legal dubieties, unions in the 1890s and early 1900s engaged in regional and national boycott campaigns against unfair employers, with some success. The AFL, for example, had a "We Don't Patronize" list. One AFL boycott was against the hatmaking firm owned by Dietrich Loewe in Danbury, Connecticut.[61] The United Hatters of North America had Loewe's firm placed on the AFL's "We Don't Patronize" list and organized a national boycott, in which the union distributed letters urging patrons not to purchase Danbury hats and notified hat dealers that the union would boycott their firms if they carried Danbury hats. Loewe and another Danbury hatter, Charles Merritt, responded by forming the American Anti-Boycott Association (AABA) in 1902, which for the next generation served as a focal point for employer politicking on issues relating to federal labor law. The Danbury hatters also brought several lawsuits against organized labor, winning a Sherman Act injunction against the boycott in 1905.[62]

Loewe also brought a Sherman Act treble damages lawsuit in Connecticut against the United Hatters. Reflecting the new thinking on labor issues, the district court dismissed the complaint, but the Supreme Court overruled that decision in *Loewe v. Lawlor*.[63] Chief Justice Melville Fuller's opinion for a unanimous Court made a number of interpretive moves that reflected the economic libertarian philosophy of the 1890s. Citing only *Debs*, which had skirted the issue, the opinion treated as a settled principle of law that the Sherman Act applied in full force against labor unions. That this holding provoked no dissent was testament to how thoroughly that dynamic reading of the Sherman Act had permeated the legal culture; even Holmes silently joined the Court's opinion.[64] Then the Court held that labor boycotts restraining trade among the several states violated the Sherman Act, curiously ignoring the more nuanced policy focus on secondary boycotts by both state and federal lower court opinions and in its own Sherman Act precedents.[65] Finally, the Court swept aside the objection that much of the complained-of conduct was intrastate rather than interstate, even though the Court had earlier held in Adair v. United States[66] that the federal government could not constitutionally prohibit antiunion clauses in railroad employment contracts because the statute reached intrastate as well as interstate matters.

Gompers and the AFL reacted with alarm to *Loewe*, in part because it came on the heels of an injunction against Gompers himself and the AFL for a boycott in Buck's Stove & Range Co. v. AFL,[67] and in part because *Loewe's* libertarian philosophy left open the possibility that the Court would invalidate other union activities, such as industrywide collective bargaining agreements. Not insignificantly, *Loewe* also assured businesses of a new remedy—monetary damages—against labor boycotts, at the very time when labor injunctions were no longer helpful because the Department of Justice was not willing to enforce them. As a result of *Loewe*, the AFL agreed to support the Hepburn bill, which was developed by big business to amend the Sherman Act and which included a provision stating that nothing in the antitrust laws restricted labor's rights to organize and to bargain collectively with employers.[68] Testifying in the House hearings on the bill, Gompers argued that the Sherman Act was never intended to cover labor's collective actions and that *Loewe's* interpretation confused anticompetitive business restraints with collective practices of labor that were necessary for workers to assume their rightful share.[69] Other witnesses argued that unionization and collective bargaining were not implicated in *Loewe*, and Congress in 1908 was in any event disinclined to move on Sherman Act reform. Gompers then took his case to presidential politics.

As a result of its 1908 decisions in *Adair* and *Loewe*, the Fuller Court was a secondary focus of the 1908 election. Both the Socialist and Populist parties specifically condemned "government by injunction," as part of a "far reaching and unscrupulous conspiracy by the ruling class against the organization of labor."[70] Interestingly, the Republican party refused to defend the Supreme Court in absolute terms, and its platform mildly criticized due process problems with injunctions in labor cases.[71] Its nominee, former Judge Taft, was a moderate on labor injunction issues. He had declared in January 1908 that "organization of capital into corporations with the position of advantage which this gives it in a dispute with single laborers over wages, makes it absolutely necessary for labor to unify to maintain itself."[72] Nominating Bryan (for a third time) in July, the Democrats ran on the theme "Shall the People Rule?" and specifically questioned the impartiality of the federal courts in labor cases.[73] In the same month the AABA lawyers asked Justice Daniel Wright in the *Buck's Stove* litigation to hold Gompers and other union leaders in contempt of court for violating the antiboycott injunction in that case. Gompers campaigned for the Democrats, who once again lost.

Almost immediately after the election, on December 23, Justice Wright held Gompers and the other defendants in civil contempt, haranguing them for over two hours. A divided District of Columbia Court of Appeals affirmed both the antiboycott injunction and the contempt in 1909.[74] Although Buck's Stove and the AFL agreed to settle the case in 1910, Gompers appealed to the Supreme Court, hoping for a clarification of *Loewe* favorable to organized labor. This was not a fanciful hope. Between October 1909 and July 1910 the Court's three most doctrinaire conservatives (Brewer, Peckham, and Fuller) died, and President Taft replaced each of them with someone more to the left on labor matters.[75] Justice Joseph Lamar, one of the Taft appointees, wrote for a unanimous Court in overturning Gompers's contempt citation in Gompers v. Buck's Stove & Range Company,[76] but on a procedural technicality (the trial court had erred in imposing a criminal sentence in the context of a civil case). The decision skirted the substantive issues but suggested that all labor boycotts were actionable in civil lawsuits.[77] Also, the Supreme Court's opinion left open the possibility of criminal contempt proceedings against Gompers, which Justice Wright promptly initiated. Criminal contempt sentences loomed over Gompers in 1912 until the Supreme Court again reversed in 1914, also on a technicality.[78]

At the same time that the AFL and the AABA were doing dirty battle in the courts, labor issues were once again polarizing national politics.[79] Taft's Republicans lost the off-year elections of 1910, both to the Democrats and to insurgent Republicans, who criticized the partiality of the federal courts and some of whom advocated the possibility of recalling judges or their decisions.[80] Although federal circuit courts were adopting Sherman Act interpretations permitting a wide range of boycotts by labor, the federal courts were still considered hostile. The harassment of Gompers by Justice Wright in the *Buck's Stove* litigation contributed to this impression. Also significant was the injunction issued by federal Judge Alston Dayton in West Virginia against the United Mine Workers for unionizing miners in violation of "yellow dog" contracts. Dayton found the union a "conspiracy in restraint of trade" in violation of both the common law and the Sherman Act in Hitchman Coal & Coke Company v. Mitchell.[81] The *Hitchman* decision seemed to confirm Gompers's predictions that *Loewe* left the Sherman Act dangerously open-ended, to be turned against labor's right to organize and bargain collectively. As the election of 1912 approached, the interpretive struggle over the meaning of the Sherman Act had reached a second crisis point.

The election of 1912 was a watershed. It pitted President Taft, the Republican nominee and a fervent law-and-order candidate, against former President Roosevelt, the Progressive party nominee and a critic of the judiciary; the Democratic nominee, Governor Woodrow Wilson of New Jersey, who urged moderation in labor disputes; and Debs, now the Socialist party's nominee and the candidate most critical of the judiciary.[82] Taft and Roosevelt waged a bitter campaign against each other, especially over the courts issue, all but ensuring the election of Wilson. The election of 1912 was important in several respects: all of the candidates were on record in favor of labor's right to organize and bargain collectively; the top two finishers (Wilson and Roosevelt, with three fourths of the vote) were pro-labor; and the candidate supported by the AFL, Wilson, was elected, along with a Democratic majority in Congress.

Judicial Moderation and the Clayton Act, 1912–1914

The election of 1912 reflected a political shift in attitudes toward labor unions. This affected federal statute-based labor injunctions in several ways, some of them unpredictable. Significantly, the legal culture was coming to accept Holmes's framework for analyzing labor cases: unions should not be penalized simply because the incidental effects of their collective activities might affect employers' freedom or restrain commerce; whether their activities should be privileged under the antitrust law depended on a policy determination. In the 1910s this framework pretty much replaced the economic libertarian one explicit in *Debs* and implicit in *Loewe* and *Buck's Stove*. The focal point of the policy debate was secondary boycotts, as to which legal opinion was divided.

NPA, Parker's decision expanding the arena of organized labor's privileged activity, was adopted in other states in this period, including several conservative states.[83] "In the last half century," wrote an Illinois Supreme Court Justice, "the changes in machinery and in social conditions generally have not only greatly affected economic theories, but have required many changes in the law so as to conform to altered social needs. New statutes have been enacted, but, independent of any statute, the courts have gradually adapted the fundamental principles of the law to changing conditions."[84] Under this policy approach primary boycotts were widely approved by state courts, often including in their definition of primary activity the cooperative arrangements by unions to pool their clout. Thus, the New York Court of Appeals in Bossert v. Dhuy[85] held that the United Brotherhood of Carpenters and Joiners could lawfully enforce a rule forbidding its members from working for any employer who hired nonunion carpenters or materials purchased from nonunion stores.

Populated by Roosevelt, Taft, and Wilson appointees, federal courts curtailed the application of the Sherman Act to peaceful labor activities.[86] For the best example, the Fourth Circuit reversed Judge Dayton's Sherman Act injunction in *Hitchman Coal*.[87] Judge Jeter Pritchard's opinion situated the lower court's reasoning within the economic libertarian arguments of the 1890s and noted that "industrial development of the world within the last half century has been such as to render it necessary for the courts to take a broader and more comprehensive view than formerly of questions pertaining to the relation that capital sustains to labor . . . [T]he laboring man is entitled to the fullest protection in the assertion of his right to demand adequate pay for any labor that he may perform." To Dayton's finding that the union's goal of "interfering" with the employer's business was an unlawful restraint, Pritchard responded: "[W]e have not reached the point when capital with its strong arm may adopt a plan . . . for protecting its interests, while on the other hand the laboring classes are to be denied the protection of the law when they are attempting to assert rights that are just as important to their well-being as are the rights of those who have been more fortunate in accumulating wealth."[88]

Also significant were boycott cases decided by the influential Second Circuit. Relying on the incidental effects argument and *NPA*, Judge Charles Hough of the Southern District of New York found no federal policy against either secondary or primary boycotts. He dispatched the old "malice" and "coercion" arguments with the observation that "the priest of the Juggernaut may be glad that the car rolls over a personal enemy, but the car rolls primarily to glorify the god within."[89] Hough's views about boycotts were controversial within the Second Circuit, but the Holmesian framework was adopted by the circuit in National Fireproofing Company v. Mason Builders' Association,[90] which suggested that issues arising out of labor warfare were essentially beyond the realm of judicial competence. More important, *National Fireproofing* indicated that the Sherman Act did not authorize injunctive relief for private parties. In the context of the carpenters' boycott also litigated in *Bossert*, the Second Circuit in Paine Lumber Co. v. Neal[91] squarely held that the Sherman Act did not authorize injunctions at the behest of private litigants; the only remedies under the statute were damage suits and criminal prosecutions.

At about the same time *Hitchman Coal* and *Paine Lumber* were decided, Congress enacted the Clayton Act of 1914.[92] President Wilson made antitrust reform his main legislative initiative in January 1914, and part of his proposal was an antilabor injunction provision. Section 18 of the Clayton bill (ultimately section 20 of the act) prohibited federal courts from issuing injunctions in cases "involving or growing out of, a dispute concerning terms or conditions of employment, unless necessary to prevent irreparable injury to property, or to a property right." The second paragraph of the section directed:

> And no such restraining order or injunction shall prohibit any person or persons, whether singly or in concert, from terminating any relation of employment, or from ceasing to perform any work or labor, or from recommending, advising, or persuading others by peaceful means so to do; or from attending at any place where any such person or persons may lawfully be, for the purpose of peacefully obtaining or communicating information, or from peacefully persuading any person to work or to

abstain from working; *or from ceasing to patronize or to employ any party to such dispute, or from recommending, advising, or persuading others by peaceful and lawful means so to do;* . . . or from peaceably assembling in a lawful manner, and for lawful purposes; or from doing any act or thing which might lawfully be done in the absence of such dispute by any party. (Emphasis added.)

Section 20 reflected the philosophy of Holmes and Parker (an AFL adviser on the Clayton bill). Its approach would have voided most of the *Debs* injunction, as well as labor injunctions against picketing, demanding a union shop, and primary boycotts. At the urging of the AFL, the House Judiciary Committee added at the end (separated by a semicolon) an amendment proposed by Representative Edwin Webb, chair of the Judiciary Committee: "nor shall any of the acts specified in this paragraph be considered or held unlawful." The Webb amendment made section 20's procedural restriction a substantive one as well.

The AFL favored a second labor section that would have stated: "[P]rovisions of the antitrust laws shall not apply to . . . labor . . . associations." The president opposed such an exemption,[93] but acquiesced in a compromise provision which Webb's Judiciary Committee added to the bill (ultimately section 6 of the act):

That nothing contained in the antitrust laws shall be construed to forbid the existence and operation of fraternal, labor, consumers, agricultural, or horticultural organizations, orders, or associations operated under the lodge system instituted for purposes of mutual help, and not having capital stock or conducted for profit, or to forbid or restrain individual members of such organizations, orders, or associations from carrying out the legitimate objects thereof; nor shall such organizations, orders, or associations, or members thereof, be held or construed to be illegal combinations or conspiracies in restraint of trade, under the antitrust laws.

Section 6 overrode at least part of the injunction against the United Mine Workers in *Hitchman Coal.*

The Clayton bill went to the Senate in June 1914, where the Judiciary Committee made several changes in the labor provisions, in response to AABA lobbying.[94] The committee rejected the AABA's demand that the Webb amendment be deleted but changed it to read "nor shall any of the acts specified in this paragraph be considered or held to be *violations of the antitrust laws*" (emphasized material added by the committee), so that section 20 would not override state contract law.[95] Section 6 was amended to add that the antitrust laws did not prohibit unions from "lawfully carrying out the legitimate objects thereof," apparently to emphasize that the Clayton Act did not immunize unions from conduct unlawful under other legal regimes (perhaps to preserve part of the *Hitchman Coal* injunction). Section 6 was further amended on the floor of the Senate to provide that "[t]he labor of a human being is not a commodity or article of commerce."[96]

When President Wilson signed the Clayton Act on October 15, 1914, its effect on existing federal law was unclear. Although section 6 substantially overrode Dayton's injunction in *Hitchman Coal*, that order had already been reversed by the Fourth Circuit. Section 20's override of *Debs* and the earlier cases merely confirmed federal circuit court developments after 1900, and the lower court consensus for allowing collective action when effects on trade were merely incidental (the Holmes framework). One issue that remained controversial was the effect of the Clayton Act on labor boycotts in general, and the secondary boycott such as that in *Loewe* in particular. Former President Taft believed that the Clayton Act changed nothing in the common law, while his former attorney general George Wickersham believed that section 20 legalized the secondary boycott and was unconstitutional as a result,[97] while the AFL and labor leaders claimed that sections 6 and 20 exempted peaceful labor activities from antitrust attack. Gompers hailed the Clayton Act as "the Magna Carta upon which the working people will rear their structure of industrial freedom."[98]

The Curtailment, Revival, and Collapse of the Federal Labor Injunction, 1914–1938

The dynamics of statutory interpretation are not entirely predictable. The year 1914 looks like a turning point. Enactment of the Clayton Act, federal court of appeals decisions in *Hitchman Coal* and *Paine Lumber*, and the refusal of Wilson's Department of Justice to cooperate in the enforcement of labor injunctions signified a changing of ideas about how to regulate the collective action of workers. By 1914 the legal culture (Congress, the president, the courts, commentators) seemed to have accepted the principles that workers ought to be able to organize and exert collective power, that antitrust laws should not apply to organized labor in the same way they apply against corporations, and that collective activity by organized labor should be regulated only when third-party effects are very significant (as when a lot of people not party to the primary dispute are injured by its spillover). Daniel Ernst cogently argues that these were ideas whose time had come in the 1910s.[99] Ironically, it took another generation for those timely ideas to become public policy in the United States. This final section of the chapter begins with the Court's dynamic interpretation of the Clayton Act, which transformed what Gompers had hailed as labor's Magna Carta into labor's Runnymede. The political culture of the 1920s was acquiescent in the Court's interpretation, and it took the Great Depression finally to override the labor injunction.

Dynamic Interpretation of the Clayton Act, 1914–1921

The Supreme Court's first decisions after enactment of the Clayton Act immediately revealed ironic twists in the law. The Court in Paine Lumber v. Neal[100] affirmed the Second Circuit's opinion dismissing a Sherman Act claim to enjoin a labor boycott. Writing for five Justices, Holmes agreed with the Second Circuit that the Sherman Act did not provide an injunctive remedy at the behest of private parties; the only remedies provided by the Sherman Act were injunctions at the behest of the government and treble damages for private parties. Holmes also opined that the Clayton Act represented a labor policy contrary to the prayer for relief but conceded that, as to this issue, "I am in a minority."[101] That meant that the four dissenters—Justices George McKenna, Mahlon Pitney, Willis Van Devanter, and James McReynolds— were joined by at least one Justice from the majority in believing that sections 6 and 20 of the Clayton Act did not override *Loewe* and that the earlier precedent covered this type of boycott. Surprisingly, unions might have been better off without their proclaimed Magna Carta: the labor provisions of the Clayton Act, it seemed, did not provide unions with any more immunity than earlier judicial decisions had accomplished, while the Clayton Act injunction provision now ensured a federal remedy for private parties which would have vanished after *Paine Lumber*'s interpretation of the old Sherman Act.

Just after *Paine Lumber*, a divided Court reversed the Fourth Circuit's decision in *Hitchman Coal*. Because of *Paine Lumber*, the Court did not overrule the Fourth Circuit's Sherman Act analysis, but it did hold actionable as a common law conspiracy the UMW's efforts to persuade employees to break their contracts, which included "yellow-dog" provisions prohibiting them from joining unions.[102] Justice Louis Brandeis's dissenting opinion responded that the record revealed only that the union was trying to get the employees to resign, which was not forbidden by the yellow-dog clauses. Such clauses stipulated that if an employee joined a union, he could be discharged. *Hitchman Coal* disclosed that in arenas where the Court still made the law, six Justices clung to an economic libertarian philosophy: the common law would police labor's efforts to invade the private sphere of employee contracts, and constitutional law might police the state's efforts to open up labor contracting.[103] Four of the Justices in 1917 had economic libertarian records, and the surprise was that moderate Chief Justice Edward White and Justice William Day joined the Court's libertarian discussion. Presumably, White and/or Day provided the swing vote or votes in *Paine Lumber* which prevented Holmes from reading his views into the Clayton Act. In this way the Court in the 1910s walked a fine line between continuing what it considered a useful regulatory regime and riling the political system that had enacted the Clayton Act.

Despite these signals from the Court, Judges Hough and Learned Hand of the Second Circuit took a broad view of the Clayton Act in the Duplex Printing litigation. The litigation arose out of a campaign by the International Association of Machinists against Duplex Printing through boycotts and threats of strikes against firms doing business with the company. Hough's opinion held that "the designed, announced, and widely known purpose of section 20 (perhaps in conjunction with section 6) was to legalize the secondary boycott, at least in so far as it rests on, or consists of, refusing to work for any one who deals with the principal offender." He also argued that the broad phrasing of section 20, prohibiting injunctions in "case[s] between an employer and employees . . . involving, or growing out of, a dispute concerning terms or conditions of employment" plainly covered secondary boycotts.[104]

As signaled in *Paine Lumber*, the Supreme Court reversed. Justice Pitney's opinion in Duplex Printing Press Co. v. Deering[105] emphasized the same statutory language Hough's did, but read section 20 to require that the primary "dispute concerning terms or conditions of employment" be the same as the "case between [the] employer and employees" in the lawsuit, before section 20's prohibition applied. Pitney relied on statements by key players in the legislative process, who denied that the Clayton Act would legalize the "secondary boycott." Representative Webb, the House floor manager for the Clayton bill, opposed an amendment that would have rewritten section 20 to be inapplicable to secondary boycotts. His stated reason was that this was already the meaning of section 20.[106] The obvious import of the Pitney decision, and perhaps a critical argument for one or more Justices in his majority, was that his desire to regulate secondary boycotts was consistent with Congress's expectations in the Clayton Act. Pitney's case is a shaky one, though.

Previous legal scholars have doubted that the legislative history of the Clayton Act provides much support for Pitney's interpretation.[107] But Holmes himself believed that "there was a strong case for holding the Clayton Act to be a piece of legislative humbug—intended to sound promising and do nothing."[108] Daniel Ernst has improved on Pitney's argument, pointing out opposition to secondary boycotts by key members of the Clayton Act coalition, especially President Wilson and Senator Albert Cummins.[109] I remain skeptical and believe that Pitney's interpretation of the Clayton Act is just as dynamic as Hough's. To begin with, criticism of secondary boycotts by some key players can be countered by statements by equally key players asserting that the Clayton Act would completely exempt labor unions from antitrust injunctions. For example, when Representative Robert Henry of the House Rules Committee proposed to amend section 6 of the bill to add what was to become its first sentence, he claimed that he had consulted with members of both the Rules and the Judiciary Committees and that all agreed the amendment would ensure that "the anti-trust laws against conspiracies in trade shall not be applied to labor organizations and farmers' unions."[110]

Moreover, the general background of the Clayton Act might undermine the Supreme Court's reconstruction. This was the argument in Brandeis's dissenting opinion that "the statute was the fruit of increasing agitation, which extended over more than twenty years and was designed to equalize before the law the position of workingmen and employer as industrial combatants."[111] The point of the statute, he argued, was to take federal judges out of the business of issuing labor injunctions, and leave labor relations to the market and the political process. Finally, Pitney's own opinion suggested that his interpretation was inspired by more than Congress's original intent, for he explicitly invoked the common law background articulated in *Hitchman Coal.* Hence, he argued against an expansive reading of section 20 because such a reading "imposes an exceptional and extraordinary restriction on the equity powers of the courts of the United States and upon the general operation of the anti-trust laws, a restriction in the nature of a special privilege or immunity to a particular class, with corresponding detriment to the general public."[112] This view was consistent with former President Taft's prediction that the Court would interpret the Clayton Act's labor provisions narrowly in order to avoid the constitutional problems of class legislation and liberty of contract that would attend a broad reading.[113]

In short, I do not think the holding in *Duplex Printing* had much to do with either the statutory text or the legislative history, in part because the enacting coalition in Congress suppressed the issue in order to avoid internal disagreement. Thus Congress sent mixed signals, leaving the courts with discretion to interpret the statute dynamically from the beginning. *Duplex Printing* was an expression of the Court majority's regulatory ideology, a framework of thought still influenced by common law baselines from the 1890s. Although it was an ideology out of touch with the developments of the 1910s, as the Brandeis dissent argued, it was in touch with those in the next decade. For *Duplex Printing* was decided right after the election of 1920, in which conservative business-oriented Republicans swept the election on the platform of a "return to normalcy." In labor cases the return to normalcy was to be a journey back to the 1890s.

Revival of the Federal Labor Injunction, 1921–1932

Although *Duplex Printing* was a disappointment for labor, it was not an unmitigated disaster, as the opinion could be read to prohibit only secondary boycotts. Later in 1921, newly appointed Chief Justice Taft's opinion in American Steel Foundries v. Tri-City Central Trades Council[114] stated that federal courts could not enjoin peaceful picketing. The opinion was the first Supreme Court case to adopt Holmes's incidental effect approach for labor injunctions:

> Union was essential to give laborers opportunity to deal on equality with their employer . . . To render this combination at all effective, employees

must make their combination extend beyond one shop. It is helpful to have as many as may be in the same trade in the same community united, because in the competition between employers they are bound to be affected by the standard of wages of their trade in the neighborhood. Therefore, they may use all lawful propaganda to enlarge their membership and especially among those whose labor at lower wages will injure their whole guild. It is impossible to hold such persuasion and propaganda without more, to be without excuse and malicious.[115]

Taft showed similar balance the next year in his opinion in the First Coronado Coal Company Case,[116] which held that unions might be liable for actions of its agents but not when the agent (in that case a local union engaged in a wildcat strike) was engaged in actions whose harm to the complainant was "secondary or ancillary" to improving workers' conditions.

Notwithstanding Taft's early effort at balance, the 1920s were the heyday of the federal labor injunction, with hundreds issued.[117] Although in each case carefully avoiding extreme statements such as plagued *Debs* and *Loewe*, the Court's decisions in *Duplex*, *Tri-City*, and *Hitchman Coal* were rebukes to federal circuit judges who sought to remove the judiciary from labor disputes. In each case the Supreme Court laid out litigation strategies for employers to follow in complaining about strikes (allege contract violations under *Hitchman Coal*), picketing (allege violence and threats under *Tri-City*), and boycotts (allege secondary activity under *Duplex*). For cultural and political reasons, employers in the 1920s were more aggressive in using these strategies, and ironically the antitrust laws became bigger threats to organized labor than ever before, as a new generation of receptive judges were willing to grant injunctions against union activity under the authority of labor's Magna Carta, the Clayton Act.

Moreover, the Supreme Court's approach to labor injunction cases discernibly changed after 1922–23. The administration of Warren Harding presided over a revival of economic libertarianism—but a libertarianism more beholden to the interests of corporate America than that of the 1890s. Paradoxically, Taft played a critical role in this shift. He was increasingly obsessed with preserving the status quo against all attacks and with suppressing the views of Holmes and Brandeis on the Court. Taft's candidates for the two vacancies created when Pitney and Day retired moved the Court irreversibly to the right in 1922: Senator George Sutherland of Utah (a former railroad attorney) and Chancellor Pierce Butler of the University of Minnesota were implacable foes of collective labor activity, and along with Justices McReynolds and Van Devanter formed a solid block of Justices (from labor's point of view, truly the "Four Horsemen of the Apocalypse") willing to interpret the antitrust laws broadly in labor injunction cases.[118]

The era's new receptivity to federal labor injunctions can be seen in the Second Coronado Coal Case.[119] The trial following the Supreme Court's first opinion in the case had uncovered grounds for Sherman Act jurisdiction not found in the first trial; there was some evidence that the union's strike had been motivated by an intent to destroy the interstate market for non-unionized coal. Taft's opinion held that this sufficed to establish Sherman Act jurisdiction. Although the Court's judgment was fact-bound, it offered significant opportunities for business to bring labor disputes into federal courts, a phenomenon already well under way.[120]

The retrenchment of the 1920s is epitomized by the history of the boycott in Bedford Cut Stone Co. v. Journeymen Stone Cutters' Association of North America.[121] The defendant was an interstate association of stonecutters' unions; its constitution provided that no member local union could work on stone declared "unfair" because of the employer's labor practices. Bedford, an unfair employer thus boycotted, sued for an injunction under the Clayton Act. The district court refused an injunction, and a Seventh Circuit panel similar to the one in *Tri-City* affirmed. The Supreme Court reversed. Sutherland's opinion was a dynamic interpretation not only of the Clayton Act but also of the Court's precedents. Thus, his opinion expanded upon the Second Coronado Coal Case to assert antitrust jurisdiction with scarcely more than a claim that a boycott was involved.[122] This went beyond the First Coronado Coal Case, which held that the labor activity had to be targeted at interstate commerce, not just incidentally affecting it.

After the jurisdictional hurdle Sutherland reanalyzed a generation's worth of antitrust precedents supporting the union's argument that any restraint of trade was only incidental (Holmes) or ancillary (Taft) to lawful goals. "A restraint of interstate commerce cannot be justified by the fact that the ultimate object of the participants was to secure an ulterior benefit which they might have been at liberty to pursue by means not involving such restraint,"[123] the opinion concluded, dismissing the framework that had ostensibly been accepted in *Tri-City*. Finally, Sutherland claimed only to be applying *Duplex* to the facts before him, an argument that was persuasive to two reluctant concurring Justices.[124] This was striking because *Duplex*'s analysis did not necessarily apply to *Bedford Cut Stone*. Unlike *Duplex*, where the activity in suit (a secondary boycott because of labor disputes in another industry) did not "[grow] out of" any "dispute concerning terms or conditions of employment" between the boycotted "employer and [its] employees," the activity in *Bedford* (a primary boycott because of labor disputes in the stonecutting industry) did. There was no specific legislative history condemning the primary boycott, as there was for secondary boycotts. Brandeis's dissent (joined only by Holmes) argued that *Bedford* was a classic case of primary activity by a national union, "the co-operation for self-protection only of men in a single craft," seeking to defend itself against a "combination of employers."[125]

Sutherland's opinion was a throwback to an era when labor combinations were considered questionable per se. That five Justices unqualifiedly joined the majority opinion and only two openly rejected its analysis boded ill for organized labor, which turned again to the political arena for relief. That the next chapter in the federal labor injunction turned out to be its last was as surprising as any development in the history of that remedy.

The Last Chapter: The Norris–La Guardia Act, 1928–1938

The revival of the federal labor injunction in the 1920s stimulated professional concern. Labor-management experts and leaders of the bar as well as labor leaders questioned the federal judiciary's willingness to regulate labor disputes in ways that systematically helped employers.[126] The Supreme Court's decision in *Bedford Cut Stone* revealed how far the Supreme Court was willing to tolerate labor injunctions, and the decision provoked an immediate reaction in Congress. Senator George Norris, chair of the Judiciary Committee, held hearings the year after *Bedford Cut Stone* to consider legislation restricting the scope of labor injunctions.[127]

But *Bedford* was in no danger of being overridden, in part because the initial override bill focused on the tired AFL claim that the courts' equity jurisdiction should be limited to claims against property and that the labor injunction violated the Thirteenth Amendment by essentially treating people's labor just like property rights. The bill's preclusion of equity jurisdiction in cases where there was no "tangible and transferable" property would have had broad and constitutionally questionable ramifications beyond the field of labor-management relations. Norris abandoned that approach and, with the aid of Felix Frankfurter and others, devised a substitute bill that more directly cordoned off labor disputes from federal judicial regulation.[128] Even as revised the override bill went nowhere in 1928 because the same return-to-normalcy politics that had yielded an antilabor Court ensured that Congress would be reluctant to override the Court. Thus, the majority Republicans on the Judiciary Committee refused to support their chair in reporting an override bill in 1928, and the same corporate-minded Republicans won a landslide victory in 1928, electing Secretary of Commerce Herbert Hoover as president and increasing Republican majorities in Congress.

The Great Depression, which started in 1929, revolutionized American labor law. It sapped the political credibility and energy of the Hoover administration. Hoover suffered a major rebuke, and organized labor won a victory, when the Senate in 1930 narrowly rejected Hoover's nomination of the economic libertarian Judge John Parker of the Fourth Circuit for the Supreme Court, partly because of his supposed antilabor views.[129] In the 1930 off-year elections the Republicans lost fifty-three House seats and control of that chamber, as well as eight senators and working control of that chamber. The new political climate, and the new members of Congress, were more receptive to Norris's anti-injunction bill, which was reported out of the Judiciary Committees of both House and Senate in 1931, with committee report language criticizing "abuses of judicial power in granting injunctions in labor disputes" and specifically repudiating the Supreme Court's decisions in *Duplex*, *Tri-City*, and *Bedford Cut Stone*.[130] The Norris–La Guardia bill passed both chambers of Congress by overwhelming margins early in 1932 and was signed by a reluctant President Hoover. The new law provided: "No court of the United States . . . shall have jurisdiction to issue any restraining order or temporary or permanent injunction in a case involving or growing out of a labor dispute, except in a strict conformity with the provisions of this Act," which were very confining.[131] Organized labor finally got, in 1932, what it claimed to have gotten in 1914—an end to federal judicial interference in most labor-management disputes.

Or did it? Attorney General William Mitchell advised Hoover that tough issues of statutory and constitutional interpretation were raised by the act and that, given the shifting political climate, there was no way to predict how any of them would be resolved in the courts.[132] So long as the Supreme Court was dominated by the Four Horsemen, interpretation and indeed the constitutionality of the statute were up for grabs. In a final irony, the New Deal intervened. The Supreme Court did not address the act's constitutionality until 1938, just after the Court had lurched to the left and two of the Four Horsemen had dismounted.[133] Fortified by a slender but determined New Deal majority, the Court upheld the statute.[134] A third Horseman had hung up his spurs by the time the Supreme Court first interpreted the Norris–La Guardia Act in Milk Wagon Drivers' Union, Local No. 753 v. Lake Valley Farm Products, Inc.[135] Reversing a circuit court opinion that held the statute inapplicable to conduct illegal at common law, New Deal Justice Hugo Black's opinion read the act's exemption of "labor disputes" from federal injunctive relief broadly and overruled *Duplex Printing*, *Tri-City*, and *Bedford Cut Stone*. In 1940–41 the New Deal Court held that no federal injunctions could be granted against disruptive picketing, large-scale secondary boycotts, and worker occupation of a factory.[136] These decisions were substantially broader exemptions for labor than most of the statute's supporters could have imagined in 1931–32, as a few Justices from the Hoover era argued in dissents. In contrast to the dynamic antilabor interpretation the Normalcy Court gave the Clayton Act, the New Deal Court gave a dynamic prolabor reading to the Norris–La Guardia Act.

The victory of the New Dealers did not mean that labor disputes were no longer regulated. For a generation it meant that federal regulation shifted from labor injunctions administered in the courts to the managed conflict model administered by the National Labor Relations Board. The effect of the

New Deal Court was to shift the dynamics of statutory interpretation in labor disputes from the Sherman and Clayton Acts to the National Labor Relations Act for a generation.[137]

This mini-history of the federal statutory labor injunction illustrates the deeply dynamic nature of statutory interpretation. Former President and future Chief Justice Taft recognized this in his book on the antitrust laws. He explained in 1914 how statutes as well as the Constitution evolve for practical reasons, in response to "the changes of business and social conditions"[138] which create contexts and problems not anticipated or not clearly addressed by statutory drafters. The history of the labor injunction shows how changed circumstances influenced both executive and judicial interpretations of the antitrust laws, Taft argued. The history also helps us to understand exactly what constitutes "changed circumstances," for it reveals a deeply ideological component: if lawyers and other elites had not been alarmed to their toes by the labor unrest of the 1893–94 depression, the attorney general and the courts would not likely have seized on the Sherman Act as the vehicle for expanding the labor injunction.

Strikingly, Taft understood how statutory interpretation is also responsive to the hermeneutical and institutional dynamics developed in Chapter 2: "It is not that the court varies or amends the Constitution or a statute, but that, there being possible several interpretations of its language, the court adopts that which conforms to prevailing morality and predominant public opinion."[139] The story of the labor injunction shows how different interpreters—a Holmes versus a Brewer—will approach the same statute from different perspectives, and how much perspective matters in statutory interpretation. Yet interpreters are sensitive to their institutional roles as well. Attorney General Olney sought a Sherman Act injunction against the ARU and Debs in part because of changed circumstances and his own sense of public emergency, but also in part because he thought it would be granted by an equally alarmed judiciary. Judges Woods and Grosscup granted the injunction in part because they believed the Supreme Court would approve, and the Court was unanimous in part because it was certain that Congress would not object to drastic interpretations in (what both Court and Congress considered) drastic circumstances.

Like Part I of this book generally, my story of the federal labor injunction from 1877 to 1938 has been largely descriptive and illustrative, but it raises normative questions because the labor injunction is generally not considered a successful experiment in public policy. It is not enough to say that courts and agencies interpret statutes dynamically. The story of the federal labor injunction recalls Justice William Rehnquist's qualms about the Court's dynamic reading of the Civil Rights Act in *Weber*: Is dynamic interpretation consistent with the rule of law? With democratic theory? With justice?

II · *Jurisprudential Theories for Reading Statutes Dynamically*

Loewe v. Lawlor, Boutilier v. INS, and United Steelworkers v. Weber illustrate the dynamics of statutory interpretation. But they also raise normative qualms about interpreting statutes dynamically. These decisions seem less defensible in retrospect than they appeared to their contemporaries. Using the Sherman Act to regulate labor-management disputes, excluding bisexuals on grounds of "psychopathic personality," and allowing employers to adopt racial quotas are controversial policies. In each case, it can be argued, the agency that devised the policy, and the Court that acquiesced in it, made a bad choice.

In addition to these substantive difficulties there are two procedural concerns. One arises from democratic values: Shouldn't elected legislators, rather than nonelected judges and bureaucrats, be making these important and politically controversial decisions? The other concern arises from the rule of law: If a statute means something different today from when it was enacted, is there not a risk that people will lose confidence in the predictability, reliability, and objectivity of the law? These concerns compel us to confront the normative issue: Is dynamic statutory interpretation justifiable and, if so, under what circumstances?

This normative issue remains important even if, as I suggested in Part I, dynamic statutory interpretation is inevitable. The main reason why statutes change is that some issues are unresolved in the political process and others are not anticipated. When these issues are squarely presented later, interpreters have to go "beyond" the original expectations. This dynamism is unavoidable, but a further dynamism also illustrated in Part I may be less so. In some cases (most strongly in *Loewe* and *Weber*) it can be argued that a subsequent interpreter goes "against" the original legislative expectations on an issue that was anticipated and apparently resolved by the political process. There are

107

often good reasons for doing so—adherence to stare decisis, constitutional difficulties with the apparent resolution, subsequent legal developments—but these reasons may be overridden (at least sometimes) if our political system concludes that dynamic statutory interpretation against original expectations is illegitimate. The normative inquiry is also important because even if dynamic statutory interpretation is sometimes illegitimate, it may not always be so. Hence, there should be some effort to channel law's dynamism in directions that are responsive to democratic theory and rule of law values.

Does democratic theory or the rule of law suggest guidelines for reading statutes dynamically? I have no answer, in part because there is no consensus in our polity as to the precise value and implications of democratic theory and the rule of law. The more modest aim of this part of the book, therefore, is to address these issues of legitimacy from the perspectives of different jurisprudential traditions, which help us evaluate how theories of dynamic statutory interpretation may be carried out. In turn, dynamic statutory interpretation theory helps us evaluate theories of jurisprudence, for this discussion impels us to ask what the rule of law ought to mean, and how law ought to work in a democracy.

Traditional liberal theory (the form of positivism dominant in Anglo-American law) maintains that the polity is a social contract among people seeking to overcome collective action problems; individual autonomy is the baseline, and government regulation requires justification. Dynamic statutory interpretation may be alarming if it amounts to lawmaking outside the legislative process. Some liberals find such a practice inconsistent with the formal processes of lawmaking established in our Constitution, as well as with democratic responsibility for major policy decisions and with a vision of the rule of law as a law of rules. In Chapter 4 I argue that liberal premises support dynamic statutory interpretation as a means of adapting statutes to new circumstances and responding to new political preferences—sometimes even when the interpretation goes against as well as beyond original legislative expectations. As a limiting principle, liberal theory urges greater caution when statutes are being expanded rather than circumscribed or when a new interpretation undermines "justifiable" private or public reliance interests.

Modern deliberative theories, loosely characterized in Chapter 5 as legal process theories, accommodate political thinking to the modern regulatory state. Legal process theories emphasize the community as well as the individual, view politics as essential given human interdependence, and support state activity for the public good. These theories embrace dynamic statutory interpretation and recognize that political choices are made by the dynamic interpreter, but their concern is whether such choices are made by the institution that is the most competent and/or legitimate one to do so. Legal process thinkers tend to be more sympathetic to dynamic interpretation by agencies because agencies are usually more institutionally capable of making such choices and are more politically responsive than courts. Chapter 5 argues that legal process thought justifies dynamic interpretations where the political process has been dysfunctional, and tentatively identifies possible dysfunctions. For example, the interpreter might legitimately protect the interests of groups systematically excluded from the political process.

Antiliberal, or "normativist," theories posit that state legitimacy cannot be ensured by formal or procedural criteria alone; it must be grounded in substance. Accordingly, the rule of law is neither a law of rules nor a law of procedural integrity but a law of justice or right. Under such assumptions, the lodestar for statutory interpretation is good results, which often go against original legislative expectations. Chapter 6 describes and criticizes a variety of normativist theories of dynamic statutory interpretation. The most desirable approach is a critically pragmatic one in which the rule of law is grounded in and follows everyday practice, but which reevaluates practice in light of rank discriminations.

Each chapter in this part starts with a different political theory assumption and yields different arguments for dynamic statutory interpretation, as well as different criteria by which a dynamic interpretation can be evaluated. Hence, each chapter is potentially addressed to a different audience. But each chapter also poses criticisms of these various jurisprudential traditions, suggesting that none fully captures the aspirations of our political system. All three have long coexisted in the United States. Most of us find something attractive in each one, and the three theories together more accurately capture our political society than any one separately. We value individual autonomy (liberalism), but we also understand our interdependence (legal process) and crave a society that stands for values we can be proud of (normativism). As a result, we usually favor limited government, but endorse state regulation to address social and economic problems and to foster national values. State legitimacy is sometimes backward-looking, sometimes present-centered, and sometimes future-oriented. The rule of law sometimes means rules, sometimes means process, and sometimes means values.

This dialectic among the various jurisprudential traditions enables us to view the cases in Part I in different lights and thereby provides a useful way of evaluating those dynamic interpretations. *Loewe* and *Boutilier* fare badly under the jurisprudential approaches examined in this part. Ironically, *Weber*—the most controversial statutory decision of the last thirty years—fares better. Notwithstanding the widely held view that the EEOC's and the Court's acceptance of voluntary affirmative action went against—and not just beyond—original legislative expectations, *Weber* receives different kinds of normative support from liberal theory, legal process, and critical pragmatism. The critical pragmatist is most open to a reexamination of *Weber*.

4 · Liberal Theories

Liberalism views government as a social contract among autonomous individuals who in the distant hypothetical past gave up some of their freedom to escape the difficulties inherent in the state of nature. For liberals the baseline is private activity (property, contract, the market), and government regulation is the exception requiring justification. The justification for government regulation is consent. In the United States consent is embodied in the Constitution, which sets forth the procedures for enacting and implementing laws. Hence, laws enacted by prescribed constitutional procedures are legitimated by the consent expressed in this original social contract.

The Constitution is clear about how statutes are to be enacted but noncommittal about interpreting them. Nonetheless, some liberals (the "formalists") view the interpreter's role as relatively mechanical, reasoning from authoritative sources to reach determinate answers. This determinacy, or at least the pretense, is essential to the rule of law, which enables citizens to know what statutes govern their conduct and how the statutes will be applied to their activities. Such liberals are uncomfortable when they perceive nonelected officials making political choices, as when they interpret statutes. Exemplars of liberal rhetoric in statutory cases are Justice William Rehnquist's dissent in United Steelworkers v. Weber (discussed in Chapter 1), Justice Antonin Scalia's separate opinions in Johnson v. Transportation Agency of Santa Clara County and Green v. Bock Laundry Machine Company (also discussed in Chapter 1), and Judge Irving Kaufman's opinion for the Second Circuit in Boutilier v. INS (discussed in Chapter 2). Steeped as they are in originalist vocabulary, these judicial opinions suggest that liberalism is hostile to the concept that statutory meaning changes over time, and this perception has been the conventional wisdom.[1]

The conventional wisdom is wrong. Liberal premises require that statutes be interpreted dynamically once changed circumstances have undone the legislature's earlier assumptions. Surveying leading liberal-based theories of statutory interpretation, this chapter reveals that most are explicitly dynamic; static theories, in contrast, are the least consistent with liberal premises. Moreover, liberalism provides tentative precepts for evaluating dynamic interpretations. Under liberal premises, dynamic interpretation is most appropriate when (1) there has been explicit or implicit statutory delegation of lawmaking authority to agencies and/or courts, (2) societal and legal circumstances have changed so as to unravel material assumptions made in the statute, and (3) the interpreter is applying the statute consistently with understandings on which private and/or public institutions have relied. But I doubt that these liberal precepts—especially the important third one—constrain interpreters, either theoretically or practically.

Formalist Theories Based on Articles I–III of the Constitution

In a polity with a written Constitution, the exercise of government power must be authorized by the formal terms of that social contract. For this reason many liberal theories of statutory interpretation are formalist in nature. That is, they require that statutory interpretation be justified by reference to the formal limits of government power under the Constitution. This was the point of Rehnquist's critique of *Weber:* the Court was acting ultra vires in adopting an interpretation inconsistent with the expectations of the enacting Congress. In this section of the chapter I analyze several theories of statutory interpretation that are justified solely from the structure, terms, and background of the Constitution's separation of powers among the three branches. Such structural theories must accept dynamic statutory interpretation in many circumstances, and the main theory denying the validity of dynamic interpretation is not supported by liberal arguments.

Separation of Powers and Legislative Delegation of Authority to Update Statutes

Thomas Merrill argues from the Constitution's separation of powers that Congress alone has lawmaking authority and that original intent is the only method of statutory interpretation consistent with this division of functions.[2] Merrill's is a formalist theory that denies the legitimacy of dynamic statutory interpretation, but it is ultimately unpersuasive because it is not rigorously supported by the text and structure of the United States Constitution.[3]

Nowhere does the Constitution say that Congress shall have all lawmaking power. It says only, in article I, that "[a]ll legislative Powers" shall be vested in Congress, leaving the "executive Power" to the president (article II) and the "judicial Power" to the Supreme Court and inferior federal courts (article III). The commonly accepted meaning of "legislative Powers," in 1789 as well as today, is the power to enact statutes, not the power to control their implementation and interpretation.[4]

The Constitution's structure suggests that the executive and the judiciary are coordinate branches of government with lawmaking powers. The president has an explicit lawmaking role in signing statutes passed by Congress[5] and in initiating treaties,[6] and an implicit lawmaking role in his article II capacity as chief executive officer and commander-in-chief of the armed forces.[7] The Constitution also contemplates lawmaking powers for federal courts. Article III, section 2 lists nine areas of federal jurisdiction, only one of which, "Cases, in Law and Equity, arising under the Laws of the United States," requires that federal statutes define the substantive rights of the parties. The Supreme Court was vested with original jurisdiction over two categories, "Cases affecting Ambassadors, other public Ministers and Consuls, and those in which a State shall be a Party," with the implicit power to make law to resolve these disputes.[8] Several areas of federal jurisdiction over which the Supreme Court has appellate jurisdiction similarly contemplate the creation of federal common law.[9]

Even in the lawmaking arena where Congress has primacy under article I, over statutes, the structure of the Constitution contemplates ongoing policy creation as interactive and dynamic rather than unitary and static. The framers established separate branches within the federal government, in part to ensure that no one branch would create law and control policy by itself. James Madison argued in *The Federalist* that tyranny is more likely when state power is concentrated in one department.[10] He also maintained that segregating different lawmaking functions (enactment, enforcement, interpretation) protects liberty because ambition is made to counter ambition.[11] For this reason, branches that are separate can still have some "partial agency in" or "control over" one another, and Madison saw the nature of those powers as mutually encroaching, setting up a competition among ambitious officials seeking to protect the public good as the best way to preserve their own authority.[12] If one body (Congress) enacts the laws, another institution (the presidency) implements them, and yet another (the Court) interprets them, it is less likely that tyrannical or unfair policies will result.[13]

Merrill's formalist theory is particularly unpersuasive in the context of the modern administrative state. Even if Congress held all lawmaking power as well as complete primacy over the executive and the courts in matters of statutory implementation (propositions inconsistent with the Constitution), Congress would still have the authority under article I to enact statutes setting forth general policies and delegating rulemaking authority to agencies or courts to fill in the details.[14] Such statutes are characteristically open-textured, and most of the specific rules are ones generated by agencies or courts, typically with no clear idea whether such rules are those that Congress itself would have adopted. The agency- or court-generated rules change to reflect new circumstances, evolving well beyond those that the enacting Congress could have contemplated.

Agency and judicial lawmaking pursuant to congressional delegation is the way most statutory interpretation and implementation is accomplished in the United States today, with Congress playing only an occasional role. Consider one example. In A. Bourjois & Co. v. Katzel,[15] a French producer of Java face powder sold its U.S. trademark rights to an American producer, Bourjois, which thereafter developed the American market for the world-famous cosmetic. A competing company bought quantities of the face powder in France and marketed it in the United States; Bourjois sought to bar this parallel importation as a violation of its federal trademark rights. The Court of Appeals for the Second Circuit declined to bar importation, holding that trademarks do not confer property rights on the holder but merely operate to prevent deception of consumers; so long as the competing face powder sold as Java was in fact Java powder, there was no violation of law. Congress in the Tariff Act of 1922 overrode the Second Circuit's opinion in *Katzel*. The 1922 act prohibited the importation into the United States of "any merchandise of foreign manufacture if such merchandise . . . bears a trademark owned by a citizen of . . . the United States, and [is] registered in the Patent and Trademark Office by a person domiciled in the United States." Congress recodified this provision as section 526 of the Tariff Act of 1930[16] and vested enforcement in the Customs Service of the Treasury Department.

The agency's regulations simply tracked the statutory language until 1936, when the Customs Service adopted a "same company exception" to the statutory prohibition: foreign-manufactured goods bearing U.S. trademarks could be imported if the foreign and domestic trademarks were "owned by the same person, partnership, association, or corporation."[17] The exception was adopted in part because it was not considered unfair to allow "gray market" trade (when foreign-made trademarked goods come into the United States to compete against U.S.-made trademarked goods) in circumstances where the foreign trademark holder had both the ability and the incentive (as the same company) to prevent intrabrand competition in the U.S. market.

In the post–World War II period many American companies established foreign subsidiaries or divisions which manufactured and sold their trademarked products abroad, sometimes at substantially lower prices than in the United States. Responding to this new development, the Customs Service in 1953 tentatively (and after 1972 permanently) expanded the same company exception to include situations where the foreign manufacturer is a parent or subsidiary of the U.S. trademark holder, or the two companies are subject to common control.[18]

As a result of these business and legal developments, a thriving gray market developed in which brand-name products (such as cameras) purchased abroad were imported and sold at bargain prices in the United States, in competition with domestic-manufactured products of the U.S. parent corporation. At the same time the gray market was expanding, the trend of multinational ownership was shifting. Increasingly, foreign companies were establishing subsidiaries in the United States and charging higher prices here for goods sold more cheaply abroad. Concerned with the intrabrand competition generated by the gray market, a coalition of these foreign subsidiaries sued to overturn the Customs Service regulations. In Coalition to Preserve the Integrity of American Trademarks [COPIAT] v. United States,[19] the Court of Appeals for the District of Columbia Circuit invalidated the agency's "common control" exception as inconsistent with Congress's specific intent in 1922 to bar importation of "merchandise of foreign manufacture" bearing a trademark owned by a U.S. company.

As *COPIAT* suggested, it is hard to tie the agency interpretation of the tariff statute to Congress's specific intent in 1922, but the theory of separation of powers suggests an initial argument in favor of the agency ruling. The intent of Congress in the tariff statutes was both to override *Katzel*, which operated unfairly on American companies purchasing trademark rights from independent foreign firms, and to delegate rulemaking and enforcement authority to the Customs Service. The latter intent suggests that the agency was to have flexibility in its application of the statute, and its creation of a common control exception to the blanket exclusion seems justifiable. New circumstances, in which the American trademark holder was faced with imports bought from its own foreign subsidiary, were materially different from those originally justifying the statutory override of *Katzel*. Allowing the gray market import of merchandise sold by a related company does not involve fraud against the American company by the foreign company (since they are under common ownership), but it does offer advantages to consumers, who can overcome price discrimination by the American company. Although the delegation concept does not resolve the difficult interpretive issues involved in *COPIAT*, it does suggest that the agency's exception was not illegitimate *simply* because it went beyond the statute's original expectations. While an agency application of a statute to changed circumstances may be overturned if it is inconsistent with Congress's expectations, such inconsistency might be hard to establish when Congress has delegated lawmaking responsibility in an open-textured statute. The burden should be on those questioning the agency to establish the invalidity of its interpretation. The Supreme Court in K Mart Corporation v. Cartier, Inc.,[20] reversed *COPIAT* and ratified the Customs Service common control exception for essentially this reason.

The "Judicial Power" and Adapting Statutes to Changed Circumstances

Some liberals believe that when a court interprets a statute, its "judicial Power" under article III constrains it, as Chief Justice John Marshall put it, to do nothing more than "giv[e] effect to the will of the Legislature."[21] Although article III does not define what it means by the "judicial Power," the eighteenth-century background and the debates surrounding the adoption of the Constitution suggest that the framers' views were informed by the same practical, hermeneutical, and institutional considerations that render statutory interpretation dynamic, as I argued in Chapter 2.

Eighteenth-century Anglo-American judicial interpretation of statutes was not dogmatically originalist. Sir William Blackstone's *Commentaries*, a conservative statement of eighteenth-century legal practice, explicitly contemplated that statutes would evolve.[22] Blackstone recognized that gaps and ambiguities are inevitable in statutes. In resolving ambiguities, he urged that "the most universal and effectual way of discovering the true meaning of a law, when the words are dubious, is by considering the reason and spirit of it . . . [f]or when this reason ceases, the law itself ought likewise to cease with it."[23] Blackstone also recognized that as time passed, the statute would be applied to new circumstances not contemplated by the legislature. "For since in laws all cases cannot be foreseen or expressed, it is necessary, that when the general decrees of the law come to be applied to particular cases, there should be somewhere a power vested of defining those circumstances, which (had they been foreseen) the legislator himself would have excepted."[24] In such cases he urged judges "to expound the statute by equity" and to reject unreasonable consequences "where some collateral matter arises out of the general words" of the statute.[25]

Principles like these were recognized in the American colonies and early state courts, some of which went further to tolerate implementations apparently contrary to original legislative expectations. In a striking example, Bracken v. The Visitors of William and Mary College,[26] the Virginia Court of Appeals allowed the governing board of William and Mary to eliminate the chair of grammar, which had been specifically mentioned in the decrees creating the college. The court in one paragraph simply acceded to the position urged by John Marshall, who argued that the primary intent of the authorizing statutes was to delegate policy-making discretion to the Visitors, and that changed circumstances justified the Visitors' adoption of a plan contrary to some of the details of the original grant. "It was proper, that this discretion should be given to the Visitors, because a particular branch of science, which at one period of time would be deemed all important, might at another, be thought not worth acquiring," argued future Chief Justice Marshall. "In institutions, therefore, which are to be durable, only great and leading principles ought to be immutable."[27]

These eighteenth-century precepts of statutory interpretation seem tailor-made for the issues in *K Mart*. Like the judges in *Bracken*, Justice Anthony Kennedy's opinion for the Court in *K Mart* accepted the Customs Service's common control exception out of deference to the agency's delegated rule-making authority to adapt the statute to new circumstances, and Justice Brennan's concurring opinion reads like pages from Blackstone. Brennan argued that Congress in 1922 was focused on overriding *Katzel* and would not have foreseen the application of its statute to situations where the same company controlled both the U.S. and the foreign trademark. Since Congress's core purpose in 1922 was to prevent importers from cheating the American holder out of its bargained-for rights, the legislators would probably have excepted common control situations had they presented themselves.[28]

The framers of the Constitution were at least as pragmatic as Blackstone in their approach to statutes. It appears that one specific reason for separating the enactment of statutes from their interpretation was the framers' belief in the productivity of evolving interpretation to meet new circumstances. This was the point of Marshall's argument in *Bracken*, that the governing board should have the freedom to create new rules "according to their various occasion and circumstances, as to them should seem most fit and expedient," limited only by "the great outlines marked in the charter."[29] Similarly, in *The Federalist*, no. 78, Alexander Hamilton went beyond Blackstone in arguing that courts should not only interpret statutes equitably, but might also respond to "unjust and partial laws" by "mitigating the severity and confining the operation of such law[s]."[30] Whereas Blackstone was willing to interpret statutes *beyond* original legislative expectations, Hamilton was willing to interpret them *against* those expectations. His reasoning was that interpretive curtailment of unjust laws would force the legislature to "qualify" the severity of statutes it enacted, knowing them to be subject to further review. "[N]o man can be sure that he may not be tomorrow the victim of a spirit of injustice, by which he may be a gainer today," and "every man must now feel that the inevitable tendency of such a spirit is to sap the foundations of public and private confidence."[31]

The Federalist, no. 78, also warned against "the substitution of their [judges'] pleasure to that of the legislative body," but that warning was sounded in connection with Hamilton's discussion of judicial review, not of statutory interpretation.[32] Hamilton did believe that courts were constrained in their interpretation of statutes. But his argument was that statutory interpreters are constrained not by the "will of the Legislature" (which Hamilton never mentions) but instead by "strict rules and precedents"; by the purpose of an independent judiciary "to secure a steady, upright, and impartial administration of the laws"; and by the institutional weakness of the judiciary, whose judgments can be overridden by the two more powerful branches.[33] Hamilton's criteria for constraining judges are more pragmatic than the nebulous "will of the Legislature" sometimes bruited about by static-minded liberals today.

Brennan's dynamic concurring opinion in *K Mart* seems consistent with Hamilton's suggested limitations. It goes beyond the original legislative expectations because the statute was being applied to circumstances that were not the focus of the 1922 deliberations; upholds a long-standing agency practice on which numerous businesses had relied; and respects an equilibrium reached within the political process. As to the last point, Brennan noted that Congress was aware of the agency's exception and had rebuffed COPIAT's repeated efforts to have the regulation revised or repealed.[34]

Bicameralism and Presentment and the Evolution of Statutory Texts

My general argument that the structure of the Constitution is inconsistent with static approaches to statutory interpretation finds surprising support in the text-based liberal philosophy of Justice Antonin Scalia.[35] He argues that three features of the Constitution's structure, including the two already surveyed, require judges and other statutory interpreters to follow the plain meaning of statutory text rather than their own often unreliable reconstruction of the enacting legislature's intent.

Scalia reasons from the Constitution's separation of powers that all Congress is charged with doing is enacting statutory texts, and that the text alone—not any concomitant expectations—is binding on the coordinate branches. Moreover, any inquiry based on legislative intent is inconsistent with the bicameralism and presentment requirements of article I, section 7, which posits that the only legitimate statute is one approved in the same textual form by both chambers and presented to the president. The only evidence of the collective agreement of the House, the Senate, and the president is the actual text of the statute they all accepted. Finally, Scalia believes that judges' discretion needs to be tightly constrained, and that focusing on statutory text is more constraining than other methods.

Although textualism is generally an originalist methodology, Scalia's "new textualism" is a consciously dynamic approach to statutory interpretation.

Thus, where Congress has chosen broad, open-textured statutory terminology—such as "restraint of trade" or "fraud"—Scalia believes that Congress is presumptively aware of the terms' "dynamic potential," and courts are free to develop the statute in the same evolutive way that they develop the common law.[36] Moreover, Scalia's textualism is structural, requiring statutory texts to be interpreted in a manner "compatible with the surrounding body of law,"[37] which of course changes constantly. Such a holistic approach thereby opens the door for statutes to evolve "in the light of surrounding texts that happen to have been subsequently enacted. This classic judicial task of reconciling many laws enacted over time, and getting them to 'make sense' in combination, necessarily assumes that the implications of a statute may be altered by the implications of a later statute."[38]

Scalia's is an excessively narrow dynamic theory, however. It pays insufficient attention to the continuous evolution of statutory policy (and attendant reliance interests) and fails to achieve its main stated goal of less judicial discretion in statutory interpretation. These difficulties are revealed in the Court's internal debate over the validity of the common control exception in *K Mart*. The statute prohibits importation of "any merchandise of foreign manufacture if such merchandise . . . bears a trademark owned by a citizen of . . . the United States." Kennedy's opinion maintained that this language leaves the Customs Service leeway to except gray market imports where the American and foreign holders are subject to common control. The opinion reasoned that "merchandise of foreign manufacture" could be read to mean "goods manufactured in a foreign country by a foreign company," which would exempt goods manufactured abroad by a division or subsidiary of an American company.[39] Finding statutory ambiguity, Kennedy deferred to the agency's dynamic interpretation based on the delegation principle suggested by separation of powers.

Kennedy's belief that the statute is ambiguous is subject to several difficulties. First, his reading does not sustain the agency exception for foreign *subsidiaries* (as opposed to *divisions*) of American companies, because subsidiaries are by definition "foreign[-incorporated] companies," and therefore any of their trademarked goods shipped to the United States are "goods manufactured in a foreign country by a foreign company." Second, Kennedy's reading may be strained. In everyday parlance "merchandise" is "of foreign manufacture" if it was made outside this country, whatever the nationality of the manufacturer. Third, the Customs Service itself did not rely on Kennedy's ambiguity; in fact, there is no evidence that the agency ever even conceived of it. Nor is his reading consistent with the agency's unwillingness to apply the common control exception where a trademark owner licenses an American firm in the United States and another American firm in Europe, and the latter tries to crash the U.S. market.[40]

Scalia's dissent relied on the last two points to insist that the common control exception must be overridden as inconsistent with the plain meaning of section 526. Although I agree with Scalia (mainly for the first reason, and less so for the ones he invokes) about the likely meaning conveyed by the statutory language, I am not as confident as he that Congress in 1922 would have read the language that way, for reasons explored in the Brennan concurrence.[41] Moreover, Kennedy's lenient textualism strikes me as more judicially restrained than Scalia's dogmatic textualism. The facts remain that Congress passed a broad statute delegating enforcement and interpretive authority to the Customs Service; the Service created an exception that preserved the core statutory policy; the exception was openly in place for several decades; there is every reason to believe that Congress was satisfied with the agency's exception; businesses had been established in reliance on the agency rule; and those businesses offered attractive deals to American consumers and discouraged transnational price discrimination. Should this long-standing pro-consumer policy have been unsettled because it stretched the plain meaning of the Tariff Act? While a liberal might believe, as Scalia does, that the rule of law is a law of rules,[42] only a scholastic liberal believes in a law of text tyranny.

Moreover, a holistic textualism might support the Customs Service regulation, based on evolving antitrust policy. A broad reading of the Tariff Act prohibition, such as Scalia's, is in tension with modern antitrust law. Antitrust law now applies to international arrangements having effects in the U.S. market (this was unclear in 1922) and is hostile to price discrimination, especially when the discrimination results in higher prices for American consumers.[43] A lenient reading of the Tariff Act, such as Kennedy's, might be supported as a measure to accommodate its trademark-protective policy to the pro-consumer policy of the antitrust statutes. That this reading is a dynamic interpretation of the Tariff Act of 1922, even one running against Congress's expectations, should not be a decisive objection, even to a formalist.

Functional Theories and the Principle of Legislative Supremacy

Theory need not be formalist to be liberal, and most liberal theories of statutory interpretation appeal to functional concerns. The main functional concern is that dynamic interpretation might be inconsistent with the policy-making supremacy of the legislature.[44] In this section I address that objection in some detail by drawing on a whole range of dynamic theories in the literature, including those based on the interpretation of consensual agreements, the ongoing interpretive dynamics of the principal-agent relationship, and the idea of translation. These metaphors and analogies support dynamic readings of statutes—including readings that contradict as well as transcend the legislature's original expectations—by reference to the nature of statutory directives, the role of the directive's recipient, and the process of interpretation itself.

The Dynamics of Consent

One way to think about statutory interpretation from a liberal perspective is to focus on the nature of the directive. A statutory directive is not just a command; according to liberal theory it also entails consent. "We the People" have consented in the Constitution to have Congress enact statutes, and the enactment process involves majority-based consent in both chambers of Congress and usually the consent of the president as well. For formal (the Constitution) as well as functional (democratic theory) reasons, the legislative supremacy precept demands that subsequent statutory interpretation be linked to what Congress (the surrogate for We the People) consented to when it passed the statute. Our system's emphasis on consent as a basis for political legitimacy is why the statutory interpretation literature talks so much of "legislative intent," a term that resonates with consent-based theory.

Although theories focusing on legislative intent are often hostile to dynamic interpretation, this hostility dissipates once one thinks about legislative intent in a complex way.[45] The legislature typically does not have a "specific intent" as to most issues of statutory application, or at least no specific intent beyond delegation of statutory detail and gap filling to other decision makers. Even when one can figure out the legislature's specific intent as to an issue when it enacted the statute, there may be considerable doubt that the legislature "would have" specifically intended that the issue be resolved in that way if it could have predicted future circumstances. When Congress told the Customs Service to stop parallel importation of goods bearing a U.S. trademark, it specifically intended to prevent U.S. trademark assignees from losing the benefit of their bargained-for assignments. Whether Congress had any specific intent is far less clear when foreign multinationals establish U.S. subsidiaries to register their trademarks, resulting in higher prices for American consumers.

The legislature may also have a "general intent" about the goals the statute subserves. Especially when the legislature delegates lawmaking to agencies or courts, its main operative intent is the general policy goal set forth in or implicit in the statute. To implement the legislature's general intent requires dynamic interpretation as circumstances change, because the statute has to adapt to the changed circumstances if it is to achieve its goal, even if that means bending the literal terms or original meaning of the directive. For example, if the goal of the Tariff Act of 1922 was to protect American-owned companies from losing the benefit of their trademark-assignment contracts, the statute ought to be interpreted more restrictively once it becomes clear that most gray market transactions do not harm American-owned companies and actually help American consumers.

Finally, there is a "meta-intent" imputed to the legislature according to fundamental rules of the liberal polity. For example, we presume that when the legislature enacts statutes it intends that the statutes follow accepted conventions of language and grammar, are not mutually contradictory, and are consistent with the rule of law and constitutional limits (a theme I develop in Chapter 9). When the statute is enacted, the legislature's *presumed* meta-intent is the same as the *actual* intent its members. Over time, however, the meta-intent is subject to shifts as linguistic practice changes, new statutory policies are adopted, and constitutional rules evolve. Congress in 1922 was not worried about the antitrust implications of the Tariff Act. One might argue that, as national antitrust policy came to focus on international transactions and price discrimination, Congress's meta-intent about the relationship of the tariff law and the antitrust laws changed as well.

Thus, even liberal theorists who insist on consent- or intent-based theories of statutory interpretation should view the process as a dynamic one. For similar reasons, theorists who analogize interpreting statutes with interpreting contracts,[46] where the parties' intent has been the traditional inquiry, ought to accept the normative desirability of dynamic interpretation. If statutes were contracts, they would be long-term ones, for they usually have indefinite or lengthy lives. Traditional contract law involves all sorts of consent-based default rules that permit or require long-term contracts to be interpreted dynamically as circumstances change, and some of these "suppletive rules" (Hart and Sacks's term) support interpretation not only beyond the drafters' original expectations (as when they leave gaps and ambiguities) but sometimes against those expectations as well.[47]

For example, a contract can be updated by reference to current "usages of trade" generally, or "courses of dealing" specifically adopted by the parties.[48] For long-term contracts, usages of trade often change over time, as may the parties' course of dealing. In addition, contractual performance may be excused or the contract reformulated if performance becomes impracticable and/or the purpose of the contract is frustrated by changed circumstances. Although traditional contract law has been reluctant to invoke these doctrines with great frequency, they are particularly appropriate for updating long-term contracts.[49] General obligations of contractual "good faith" and "unconscionability" protect against stale contract terms no longer considered reasonable,[50] a greater problem for long-term contracts than for short-term ones. More generally, terms can be added to or subtracted from the original contract according to new legal policies.[51]

If interpreters treat the Tariff Act of 1922 as they would a long-term contract, there are good consent-based arguments for interpreting it to allow gray market importation, even if that would not have been the interpretation in 1922. First, there has been a long-standing course of dealing, repeatedly ratified in the courts and known to Congress, which excepts many gray market imports from the strict terms of the statute. Second, it would not serve the original purposes of the statute to extend its protections beyond the *Katzel* facts, and would frustrate at least some of the original purposes (such as helping American industry). Third, evolving antitrust policies that protect consumers against price discrimination support a narrowing interpretation to allow pro-consumer gray market imports.

Dynamic interpretation against as well as beyond original expectations is consistent with other rules for interpreting private agreements. Alex Johnson and David Farber have argued that a theory of statutory changed circumstances is similar to property law doctrines permitting the updating of charitable trusts.[52] "Cy pres" doctrine permits courts to rewrite substantive provisions of charitable trusts, against the donor's original expectations, when changed circumstances frustrate the attainment of the trust's goals. Johnson also points to the more liberal doctrine of "deviation," which allows modification of a trust's administrative provisions when "it appears to the court that compliance is impossible or illegal, or that owing to circumstances not known to the settlor and not anticipated by him compliance would defeat or substantially impair the accomplishment of the purposes of the trust."[53] Even though cy pres and deviation permit interpreters to rewrite the private document against the expectations of the donor or author, they are defensible as default rules that we presume a rational donor "would have chosen" to incorporate in her or his trust if she or he had considered the matter in light of new circumstances.

Scalia recognized the possibility of statutory cy pres in his *K Mart* opinion, but insisted that any such doctrine be limited to cases in which "(1) it is *clear* that the alleged changed circumstances were unknown to, and unenvisioned by, the enacting legislature, and (2) it is *clear* that [the changed circumstances] cause the challenged application of the statute to exceed its original purpose."[54] Yet Scalia presented no reasons why statutory cy pres should be limited to such "clear cases." Especially when the statutory updating is being done by the agency delegated to implement the statute, enacting legislators would rationally want the interpreter to adapt the statute to new circumstances.

Statutory Interpretation as Relational

Another way to think about statutory interpretation from a liberal perspective is to focus on the role of the interpreter carrying out the legislature's directives. Liberal theorists believe that the precept of legislative supremacy requires interpreters "to be honest agents of the political branches. They carry out decisions they do not make."[55] But talk of honest agents is not helpful when there are many uncertainties about the principal's commands. Such uncertainties are inevitable in a long-term agency relationship where the agent must cope with a rapidly changing environment and a slow-reacting principal.

Richard Posner, the honest agent theory's leading early exponent, has responded to this phenomenon with a more sophisticated version of the theory, one that endorses dynamic interpretation. A judge interpreting a statute, says Posner, is like a platoon commander following orders in battle.[56] Not infrequently the commander finds his forces in an unexpected situation not contemplated by existing orders. Given battlefield conditions, he may be unable to communicate with the high command, but he has to do something. In this situation he must go beyond—and sometimes even against—existing orders to ensure the success of the overall battle plan. "The responsible platoon commander will ask himself what his captain would have wanted him to do if communications should fail, and similarly judges should ask themselves, when the message imparted by a statute is unclear, what the legislature would have wanted them to do in such a case of failed communication."[57]

The platoon commander metaphor suggests that even in a strongly hierarchical system subordinate officers must sometimes expand upon their orders, through interpretation, to deal with current problems. Neither the formal nor the functional supremacy of the high command is sacrificed by such a dynamic reading of one's orders. The platoon leader's creativity is born of necessity, and his decision is constrained by efforts to figure out what his superiors would have him do, based on their past orders and their overall plan. Indeed, the platoon commander's *refusal* to interpret his orders dynamically might violate the supremacy of his superiors, who would not want outdated orders implemented in a wooden and counterproductive way that could result in heavy casualties or even defeat. The commander who sent waves of soldiers to certain death in the battle of Gallipoli because his orders were to continue the attack may have been a rigorous textualist, but he was a rotten interpreter. Scalia's textualist opinion in *K Mart* falls into the Gallipoli trap; Kennedy and Brennan were better officers in that case.

Yet the platoon commander metaphor understates the dynamic nature of statutory interpretation, for it assumes a temporal situation not typical of that facing a judge interpreting a statute. The platoon commander has been in recent, perhaps continuous contact with the high command, and the breakdown in communication is usually brief. Hence, he has many clues as to what his superiors would want him to do in the new situation. In contrast, the judge interpreting a statute not only is unable to talk directly with the enacting legislators (indeed she is not supposed to talk with them), but often must deal with orders issued long ago—as in *K Mart*, where the Court was interpreting a statute enacted sixty-five years earlier. It is much harder for her to imagine what the legislature would have wanted her to do, and she may never receive feedback from the legislature about her interpretation of the statute.

The element of time requires the liberal to go beyond Posner's analogy. If a judge is a subordinate officer or agent, how should she deal with directives issued by her superior over time? As time passes, the gaps and ambiguities created by unanticipated circumstances will increase both quantitatively, because there will be more of them, and qualitatively, as unexpected tensions within directives and goals arise. For this reason a metaphor that better reflects the role of the statutory interpreter is that of a "relational agent." A relational contract is one that establishes an ongoing relationship between the parties over time; in many respects the contract is incomplete because of uncertainty about what problems will occur, but the parties understand that all will make their best efforts to accomplish the common objectives.[58] In a principal-agent contract of this type, the agent is supposed to follow the general directives embodied in the contract and the specific orders given her by the principal, but her primary obligation is to use her best efforts to carry out the general goals and specific orders over time.

Like the relational agent, the judge is the subordinate in an ongoing enterprise and follows directives issued by the legislature. Like the relational contract, statutes are often phrased in general terms, written long before an interpretive issue arises; yet they are the most authoritative documents to which the judge may refer when answering an interpretive question. Like the relational principal, the legislature will often speak on a specific question just once, leaving it to the judge (agent) to fill in details and implement the statute in unforeseen situations over a long period of time. Hence, like the relational agent, the judge must often exercise creativity in applying prior legislative directives to specific situations.

As an illustration, consider this variation on the soup meat hypothetical, introduced in Chapter 2. Williams, the head of the household, retains Diamond as a relational agent to run the household while Williams is away on business. The contract is detailed, setting forth Diamond's duties to care for Williams's two children, maintain the house, prepare the meals, and do the shopping on a weekly basis. One specific directive is that Diamond fetch five pounds of soup meat every Monday (the regular shopping day) so that he can prepare enough soup for the entire week. Diamond knows from talking to Williams that by "soup meat" she means a certain type of nutritious beef that is sold at several local stores. When Williams leaves, Diamond has no doubt as to what he is supposed to do. But over time his interpretation of the directive will change if the social, legal, and constitutional context changes so as to affect important assumptions made in Williams's original directive.

Changes in Social Context   There are a number of changes in the world that would justify Diamond's deviation from the directive that he fetch five pounds of soup meat each Monday. For example, suppose Diamond goes to town one Monday and discovers that none of the stores has the precise kind of soup meat he knows Williams had in mind when she gave the order. Should he drive miles to other towns in search of the proper soup meat? Not necessarily. It might be reasonable for him to purchase a suitable alternative in town, especially if it appears in his judgment to be just as good for the children. One can imagine many practical reasons why, in a given week, Diamond should not follow the apparent command. The reasons for deviating are akin to the interpretive creation of "exceptions" to a statute's broad mandate based on the interpreter's judgment about the statute's goals and the extent to which other goals should be sacrificed—just as the Customs Service did in *K Mart*.

As the reasons multiply over time, one can imagine changed circumstances that would effectively nullify Williams's directive altogether, therefore going beyond *K Mart*. Suppose Diamond discovers that one of the children has an allergy to soup meat. That child can continue to eat soup, but not with meat in it. Because Diamond realizes that one of the reasons Williams directed him to fetch soup meat every Monday was to ensure the good health and nourishment of the children, and because he believes that Williams would not want him to waste money on uneaten soup meat, he henceforth purchases only three pounds of soup meat per week. If both children are allergic to the soup meat, and Diamond does not care for it himself, he might be justified in entirely forgoing his directive to fetch it. Although he would be violating the original specific intent as well as the plain meaning of Williams's orders, Diamond could argue that his actions are consistent with her general intent that he act to protect the children's health and with her meta-intent that Diamond adapt specific directives to that end.

New Legal Rules and Policies   The relational agent might receive inconsistent directives over time. Suppose that two months after Williams embarks on her trip, she reads in a "Wellness Letter" that if children do not eat healthy foods, they will have cholesterol problems later in life. She sends Diamond a letter instructing him to place the children on a low-cholesterol diet, which should include Wendy's Bran Muffins and fresh apples. As a faithful relational agent, Diamond complies. He also reads up on the cholesterol literature, including the "Wellness Letter," and discovers that soup meat is high in cholesterol. He discontinues the weekly fetching of soup meat and fetches chicken instead because it is lower in cholesterol. Diamond's action is akin to a court's reconciliation of conflicting statutory mandates, in which one of the statutes is often given a narrow interpretation to accommodate the policies of a later statute. Recall that one justification for the Customs Service interpretation in *K Mart* was to render its policy consistent with developments in federal trademark and antitrust law.

Changed circumstances might further alter Diamond's interpretation of Williams's inconsistent directives. Weeks after he has substituted chicken for soup meat, Diamond learns from the "Wellness Letter" that Wendy's Bran Muffins actually do not help lower cholesterol, and that they have been found to cause cancer in rats. Furthermore, Diamond discovers that 50 percent of the apples sold in his region have a dangerous chemical on them. Diamond thereupon switches from Wendy's Bran Muffins to Richard's Bran Muffins, recommended by the "Wellness Letter," and from fresh apples to fresh oranges. Thus, not only has Diamond overthrown Williams's earlier directive on soup meat because of the new policy in her later directive, but he has also altered her specific choice of low-cholesterol foods in that directive!

New Meta-Policies   The relational agent's interpretation of his orders may well be influenced over time by changing meta-policies. The new meta-policies may be endogenous or exogenous. Endogenous meta-policies are those generated by the principal herself and are just a more dramatic form of inconsistent directives. Suppose that, after several months, Williams writes to Diamond that financial reversals impel her to cut back on household expenses. Food costs must thereafter be limited to $100 per week. Although he has long been directed to fetch soup meat every Monday, and there are other ways to economize, Diamond cuts back on soup meat, in part because it is the most expensive item on the shopping list. This is akin to a court's modifying an original statutory policy to take account of supervening statutory policies.

Exogenous meta-policies are those generated by an authority greater than the principal. Suppose that Diamond has an unlimited food budget and no health concerns about soup meat, yet he stops fetching it on a weekly basis because the town is in a crisis period and meat of all sorts is being rationed; hence, Diamond could not lawfully fetch five pounds of soup meat per week. This is akin to a court construing a statute narrowly to avoid constitutional problems based on the legislature's meta-intent not to pass statutes of questionable constitutionality.

In all of these hypotheticals Diamond, our relational agent, has interpreted Williams's soup meat directive dynamically. Quite dynamically, in fact, because in most of the variations Diamond created substantial exceptions to or even negated the original specific meaning of the directive. Notwithstanding his dynamic interpretation of the directive, I believe that Diamond has been nothing but an honest agent.

The foregoing thought experiment makes clear that a statutory interpreter is a relational agent, either from the beginning of the statute's life or at some point in its evolution, and that a relational interpreter should have freedom to adapt the statute's directive to changed circumstances. In so doing, the interpreter must first understand the assumptions underlying the original directive, including its purpose. Then she must figure out how the statute can best meet its goal(s) in a world that is not the world of its framers. This process, which closely parallels the hermeneutical one explained in Chapter 2, is explored in more detail in the next section.

Translation

A final way to think about statutory interpretation from a liberal perspective is to focus on the process itself. Mark Tushnet has argued that from a liberal perspective constitutional interpretation can be considered a process by which the current interpreter seeks modern "functional equivalents" to the norms and rules of a long-departed world.[59] Other theorists, from Paul Brest to James Boyd White, have argued that constitutional interpretation is a process of "translation" of the framers' goals and principles into our time and application of them to situations the framers did not anticipate.[60] Similarly, statutory interpretation scholars have long argued that legislators can "be presumed to realize that the principle [of their statute] can often be maintained only by adapting the interpretation of details to the changes of external circumstances."[61]

Lawrence Lessig suggests that interpretation which preserves constitutional or statutory meaning over time *must* be dynamic and, conversely, that static interpretation is not faithful to the Constitution or statutes enacted thereunder.[62] The meaning of a text when written is a function of its context. For example, "Meet me in Cambridge" means something different in England than in Massachusetts. Also, the meaning of a text when read is a function of context and may differ from the meaning when written. If I write "Meet me in Cambridge" while I am in England and you read the message while you are in Massachusetts, the received message may well be different from the conveyed message. The task of the reader who wants to implement the writer's directive faithfully is to figure out from the writer's context what she meant.

When the directive speaks well into the future, the task of translation requires more imagination. If I write "Fetch me some soup meat every Monday," what should the reader do when a shortage of soup meat has sent the price sky-high? The challenge is to figure out what meaning in our current context (high prices) is the functional equivalent of the author's meaning in the original context. Some traditional liberal theory argues for what Lessig calls a "one-step" approach to the question: Given the original context, in which soup meat is available at a reasonable price, what did the writer expect the reader to do? Fetch the soup meat. But, Lessig argues, that is misleadingly simple, for fidelity to the original directive requires a "two-step" approach.[63] Step one: Given the original context, what did the writer expect the reader to do? Step two: Given the changed context (a very high price), what application would be the functional equivalent of the original application in the original context?

Tushnet and Lessig argue that the faithful liberal interpreter is the two-stepper and that the one-stepper is unfaithful and stubborn. Like my relational agent analogy and Johnson's and Farber's theories of statutory cy pres, two-step interpretation can be a sharp instrument for criticizing static statutory interpretations within the premises of liberal theory. Let us return to *K Mart*. A secondary issue in the case was whether the Customs Service could also except from the statutory prohibition "articles of foreign manufacture [which] bear a recorded trademark or trade name applied under authorization of the U.S. owner."[64] A five-person majority of the Supreme Court invalidated this "authorized use" exception because they believed that it unambiguously contravened the statutory prohibition.[65] Unlike the common control exception, for which he believed there was statutory ambiguity, Kennedy (the swing vote) found that the statute clearly prohibited importation of trademarked goods made by a foreign company authorized to manufacture the goods abroad. This is a bizarre bit of line drawing on Kennedy's part,[66] but the more interesting criticism is the one made by Brennan, who argued in dissent (on this point) that Kennedy broke faith with the statute's original meaning when he applied it in a current context that had materially changed. Brennan's two-step analysis is an example of Lessig's fidelity in translation.

Brennan argued that, when Congress enacted the prohibition in 1922, the only purpose of trademark law was to identify for consumers exactly who had made the product. Hence, the law had been unwilling to allow a trademark holder to authorize third-party use of the mark because that might constitute misinformation to the consumer. It was not until the 1930s that trademark licensing became widely acceptable, and not until the Lanham Act of 1946 that it became firmly established in statutory law. Indeed, it was the enactment of the Lanham Act that stimulated the Customs Service to adopt its authorized use exception in 1951.[67] This change has serious consequences for the liberal statutory interpreter.

A legislator who voted in 1922 to prohibit importation of foreign merchandise bearing a trademark "owned by a citizen of . . . the United States" might have thought that the prohibition applied to a trademark assigned to a foreign company, in part because the legislator might have assumed that an American company could not have sold the rights to use the trademark abroad without divesting itself of ownership generally. Hence, Kennedy's interpretation replicated the answer that Congress might well have reached in 1922. But once it became possible for an American company to authorize use of its trademark abroad without relinquishing ownership or other rights to the mark, the correct answer in the original context became an incorrect answer in the current context, as Brennan argued. The new circumstance makes the authorized use case much like the common control case: in both instances the American trademark holder is allowing a foreign company (in one case a subsidiary, in the other an unrelated company) to use the mark, and in both cases the holder profits from it and can exercise whatever quality and other control it wants (through either corporate control or contract requirements). One arrangement may well be more efficient for the American holder, but there is little reason for that to make a difference in its ability to prevent gray market importations. By translating what Congress apparently wanted in 1922 into the legal circumstances of 1988, Brennan's two-step analysis seems more faithful to the premises of liberalism than Kennedy's one-step approach.

Liberal Default Rules

The foregoing analogies (private contracts, relational agency, translation) suggest that dynamic statutory interpretation is required by liberal theory when material assumptions of the statute are altered or negated by changed social, legal, and constitutional circumstances. The debate on the Court in *K Mart*, carried out within liberal premises, is among the most illuminating on this question. The case also reveals the way in which a theory of dynamic statutory interpretation can be a normative tool for criticizing or defending different interpretations. Examined from the vantage point of liberal premises, Kennedy's position collapses, and the thoughtful interpreter is left with a choice between the Brennan position, which would permit agency deviation from the statutory language to except both common control and authorized use situations, and the Scalia position, which would hold the agency strictly to the current plain meaning of the statute. I have provisionally suggested that Brennan makes out a better case, but I have not considered Scalia's best arguments against the Brennan position.

The Leave-It-to-Congress Objection

Scalia first objects that an interpretive approach by which a court would trim back the ambit of a statute because of changed circumstances is inconsistent with the limited term of each Congress. Judicial updating invades "the prerogative of each currently elected Congress to allow those laws which change has rendered nugatory to die an unobserved death if it no longer thinks their purposes worthwhile; and to allow those laws whose effects have been expanded to remain alive if it favors the new effects."[68]

One problem with this argument is that it draws the wrong conclusions from the structural limitations on Congress. The reason for liberal government is to avoid collective action difficulties associated with the state of nature. To solve those problems, both liberal theory and the Constitution contemplate that Congress will enact statutes; the assumption in both 1789 and today is that statutes will have an indefinite life—well beyond that of the enacting Congress. An important reason for having an independent judiciary is to reassure Congress that the statutes it enacts will remain efficacious over time and not run wild or expire because of the inattention of subsequent Congresses. Contrary to Scalia, the constitutional design does contemplate that interpreters will "rewrite the United States Code to accord with the unenacted purposes of Congresses long called home."[69]

The Scalia theory is also inconsistent with liberalism, which presumes against government regulation.[70] Brennan's position seems more consistent with this presumption, for it insists that Congress's regulatory decision in 1922 be confined to the core problem (overriding *Katzel*), leaving expansion of the regulation to Congress. Scalia's position expands government regulation of market conduct simply because new economic practices have brought a great deal of conduct within the terms of the broadly written statute. This position is not liberalism but reveals itself as a kind of "text positivism" which can easily justify judicial activism that expands statutes arbitrarily (recall the earlier discussion of the Kennedy-Scalia debate over the meaning of "merchandise of foreign manufacture").

Scalia's text positivism is not redeemed by his assertion that if new Congresses don't like ever-expanding statutory schemes, they can just change them, for the same argument is available to Brennan: if Congress really wants the statute to have Scalia's breadth of coverage, it can amend the statute. Moreover, it may be unrealistic to expect Congress to monitor every nook and cranny of statutory policy from year to year, for that is the reason why Congress delegates policy-making authority to agencies and courts. Indeed, Scalia has it backwards: the traditional rule has been that patterns of statutory interpretations by agencies and courts adapting a statute to changed circumstances are presumptively valid so long as they have been brought to Congress's attention and Congress has not changed them.[71]

Congress had plenty of chances to abolish or narrow the Customs Service exceptions. Exactly what Congress "knew" is uncertain,[72] but it was undisputed in the *K Mart* briefs that (1) there were formal communications to Congress from 1951 onward[73] making it clear to relevant members that the Customs Service was not interpreting the Tariff Act broadly or literally; (2) there were several proposals in Congress to codify or expand the agency exceptions (none was enacted) but not a single proposal to narrow or override them; and (3) on at least two occasions committee reports for enacted laws noted the 1972 regulations with approval.[74] This history reinforces the presumption that the political system was comfortable with the regulations. If there is any burden on Congress in such circumstances, liberal theory would suggest that it should be to correct the long-standing agency interpretation, not to head off the expansion the statute would have followed if the agency had not narrowed it.

Ironically, the leave-it-to-Congress argument is itself a form of judicial activism inconsistent with the Constitution's separation of powers. One reason for separating the power to legislate from the executive and judicial powers is to leave the legislative agenda uncluttered by issues of fine-tuning and application, and relatively free to focus on the major policy issues. This allocation is more necessary than ever today, as an increasing number of socioeconomic problems compete for space on the limited congressional agenda.[75] A theory of interpretation like Scalia's, which requires each Congress to revisit or even just fine-tune the political decisions reached in prior Congresses, is an interference with Congress's power to set its own agenda. In this way Scalia's text positivism is in some tension with the precept of legislative supremacy, and is thus an unsatisfactory liberal theory.

The Indeterminacy Problem

Scalia also attacked Brennan's defense of the authorized use exception by questioning Brennan's factual assumptions. Specifically, Scalia argued that it is unclear that Congress in 1922 would have assumed that trademark owners could not have authorized others to use their trademarks. The Supreme Court before 1920 had determined that unrelated businesses could own a trademark so long as the uses were confined to different regions. Unfortunately, the cases Scalia cited refer only to permanent "assignment" of the property right and not to the temporary "authorization" of a use.[76] The latter was not a common practice until the Lanham Act, as Brennan argued. Hence Scalia was also wrong when he said that the case providing the impetus for the 1922 statute, *Katzel*, involved precisely the sort of interregional trademark authorization that Brennan said was questionable in 1922. Notwithstanding Scalia's erroneous formal point, his analysis does suggest a troubling functional question: *Katzel* is almost the mirror image of the typical authorized use case. The former involves foreign assignment of a trademark to an American company, while the latter involves licensing an American trademark to a foreign company. Brennan conceded that the 1922 statute was aimed at the former case, but contended that the agency can except the latter. Why? In both instances the American company is subject to losing part of its bargained-for deal if it has exclusive rights to the trademark in the United States but then is subjected to gray market importation of cheaper goods from the foreign country. In both instances the only protection the American company has is contractual protection, which may in either instance be unavailing, since most gray market importation is carried out by third parties who buy up the merchandise in the foreign country. The main advantage that the American licensor (the authorized use exception) has over the American assignee (the core coverage of the 1922 statute) is that it can undercut the gray market by refusing to license its trademark abroad, or by licensing it with price assurances.

The last point must be the basis for Brennan's defense of the authorized use exception, and whether it is sufficient depends on exactly how one defines the statute's purpose. If the statute's purpose was mainly to protect American companies that had purchased foreign trademark rights, Brennan's interpretation may be the better one—but not if the statute's purpose was also to protect American sellers of trademark rights abroad, for then Congress would be expected to have sympathy for the reverse-*Katzel* situation as well as for the *Katzel* situation itself. And if the statute's purpose was to protect owners of trademarks generally, then both the common control and the authorized use exceptions are invalid. Although the various judges claimed to be quite certain of their different readings of the statutory purpose, I think that none of them knew for sure, nor do I. There is plenty of evidence for various articulations of the statutory purpose.[77]

This analysis parallels the problems identified in Chapters 1 and 2 with originalist theories: their methodology cannot yield analytically determinate answers in the hard cases. Such indeterminacy creates a dilemma for liberal theories of statutory interpretation.[78] If important policy issues cannot be resolved by an interpretive methodology that is determinate and predictable, then unelected judges and agencies will make political decisions that liberalism leaves to the legislature or some other majoritarian institution. Brennan's purpose-based interpretation in *K Mart* is vulnerable to this objection, as is the original intent approach of the Court of Appeals in *COPIAT.*

Notably, Scalia's textualist approach is no less malleable than the approaches he attacks. Just before Scalia's *K Mart* opinion criticized Brennan for not adhering to statutory plain meaning (on the authorized use exception), it criticized Kennedy for not being dogmatic enough about what is a plain meaning (on the common control exception). As to the latter, Scalia contended that "merchandise of foreign manufacture" cannot plausibly be read to mean "goods manufactured in a foreign country by a foreign company." Yet he offered no evidence for his dogmatic view. "The phrase 'of foreign manufacture' is a common usage, well understood to mean 'manufactured abroad,'" he said, without citing any authority as to "common usage"; even after he admitted that "looking up the separate word 'foreign' in a dictionary might produce the reading the majority suggests," Scalia denied any plausibility to the majority's reading.[79] Though I agree with Scalia as to the probable meaning, I do not find Kennedy's reading completely implausible. If I told you that my tennis racket was "of foreign manufacture," you would likely believe that it was manufactured outside the United States. You might also assume that it was made by a foreign company, unless I qualified the statement, as in "foreign made but American owned." Compare the current

"Made in the U.S.A." slogan, which some would consider misleading if the manufacturer were foreign.

I find the Kennedy-Scalia debate over the common control exception perversely illuminating because it reduces statutory interpretation to a linguistic shell game played by amateurs.[80] This is further illustrated by the Scalia-Brennan debate over the authorized use exception. Arguing that a text's plain meaning can vary with context, Brennan posed a hypothetical statute requiring state inspection of "all ovens" for their propensity to spew flames and asked whether it required the state to inspect all electric ovens.[81] Scalia responded that the statute unambiguously applied to all types of ovens, including electric ones.[82] This retort strikes me as simply stubborn. Although the word "oven" includes electric ovens in *most* contexts ("I am going to bake a cake in the oven"), that is not true for *all* contexts. Thus, if I told you to "check all the ovens for their propensity to spew flames" (parallel to the Brennan hypothetical), you would be justified in checking only the old-fashioned wood-burning ovens.[83]

Oddly, Scalia chose to reach the same answer to the spewing ovens hypothetical as Brennan did, but through a more indirect process of reasoning: because electric ovens do not give off sparks, it would be "absurd to inspect electric ovens for that propensity," and "it is a venerable principle that a law will not be interpreted to produce absurd results."[84] This reasoning seems little more than a different verbal formulation of the Brennan approach: because electric ovens do not give off sparks, their inspection would not serve the statutory purpose. In other words, by allowing an "absurd result" exception to his dogmatic textualism, Scalia allowed for just as much indeterminacy, and just as much room for judicial play, as he accused Brennan of creating with his context-dependent approach to statutory meaning.

Interpretive Precepts Drawn from Liberal Theory

The indeterminacy problem does not mean that liberal theory has nothing to say about how to interpret statutes. Quite the opposite. Because the Constitution does give Congress the authority to adopt statutes entitled to supremacy unless unconstitutional, liberalism requires a connection between the text and/or the legislative history of the statute and the interpretation reached in a particular case. The liberal interpreter starts with the statutory text and its background history, which in most instances (the easy cases) answer the interpretive question in a predictable way. Even when the circumstances of the statute's enactment change, liberalism requires that the interpreter deal with the originalist sources in good faith. The cy pres judge starts with and defers to the original trust instrument, the relational agent is attentive to what she thinks the principal would have her do in the unanticipated situation, and the translator tries to adapt the text by finding functional equivalents consistent with the author's expectations.

For example, Rehnquist's opinion in Griffin v. Oceanic Contractors, discussed in Chapter 1, is an extraordinarily dynamic reading of the nineteenth-century penalty wages statute but may be defensible under liberal theory because it is genuinely responsive to the statute's text. Brennan's opinion in *Weber*, also a dynamic reading, is less defensible under this liberal premise, for the opinion seems cavalier in its treatment of the originalist sources. But Blackmun's opinion in *Weber* provided a liberal justification that the majority did not: while the originalist evidence should not be overridden without justification, the practical problems facing employers seeking to avoid disparate impact liability provided such justification for the affirmative action plan in suit.[85]

Moreover, liberalism's vision of the rule of law requires a statutory interpretation to be one that would be persuasive to other interpreters within the prevailing legal culture. *Griffin* has this virtue as well, for a range of different Justices—including both Brennan and Rehnquist—agreed with the interpretation. Even when circumstances change, the results reached by liberal interpreters are still usually predictable at a given point in time because of cultural or professional agreement about the meaning of the statutory language and the amount of play allowed by the context. In the debate about spewing ovens, both Brennan and Scalia excused regulators from looking at electric ovens. Recall that, in the soup meat hypothetical earlier in this chapter, most relational agents would interpret Williams's directive in roughly the same ways that Diamond did when confronted with all sorts of variations, on account of a shared situation sense.[86]

In the hard cases, such as *K Mart* and *Weber*, it is difficult to extrapolate from the originalist sources to unanticipated circumstances, nor is there a cultural or professional consensus as to the significance of the statute's language or message or the circumstances of its application. In that event the liberal theorist has several choices. One, ably defended by H. L. A. Hart, is to admit that the interpreter is engaged in interstitial lawmaking, and defend its legitimacy based on a concept of rulemaking discretion vested in the officials who have been delegated interpretive duties by the legislature.[87] This choice is consistent with positivism but makes many liberals nervous, for it is an admission that law is often made by unelected officials, is not entirely predictable, and can yield results inconsistent with liberal presumptions against state regulation of the private sphere.

An alternative strategy is to recognize default rules which allocate the burden of interpretive uncertainty in accord with liberal precepts. Default rules are used to fill in contractual gaps to create greater predictability, and such rules may yield greater determinacy in public law as well (see Chapter 9 for elaboration). Consider some provisional default rules suggested by liberal theory (and which in turn reflect some of liberalism's philosophical contradictions).

Presumption against Overenforcement of Statutes   Earl Maltz distinguishes between two different kinds of dynamic interpretations: underenforcement, or the refusal of an interpreter to apply statutes to situations the legislature probably intended to cover, and overenforcement, or the extension of statutes beyond the original legislative understanding.[88] The problems Maltz raises about overenforcement are particularly interesting. Overenforcement of federal statutes is more problematic under liberal premises than underenforcement for reasons of constitutional federalism. Because the Constitution limits federal power to that which is delegated to the national government in articles I–III, the constitutional presumption is that regulation of local affairs should be left to state and local governments.[89] Hence, federal agencies and courts may be more hesitant to overenforce statutory norms (for reasons of federalism as well as legislative supremacy) than to underenforce them (which implicates only legislative supremacy).[90] Because *K Mart* involved international trade issues, this federalism concern was not as significant as it would have been in other cases.

A related concern with overenforcement is implicated in *K Mart*. Liberalism presumes against state interference in private relationships, especially when the interference is for parentalist reasons.[91] Under liberal premises, the risk of underenforcement of legislative interference is therefore less problematic than the risk of overenforcement. This point is the focus of *The Federalist*, no. 78, which counsels that courts should interpret "unjust" and "partial" laws *restrictively*. Placing the burden on a subsequent legislature to reiterate or clarify majority-based expectations is less objectionable when the burden protects private liberty of action until the system has addressed it with more certainty and deliberation. This reasoning reverses the normative comparison made earlier between *Weber* and *Griffin*: because it risked only underenforcement of its statute by declining to apply Title VII's antidiscrimination norm to private affirmative action plans, *Weber* is in this respect more defensible for a liberal than *Griffin*, which risked a great deal of overenforcement by expanding the statutory penalty for withholding a seaman's wages.

Under this precept the agency's rules litigated in *K Mart* might be defensible as interpretive underenforcement. But were the agency rules *under*enforcement? I have assumed that they were because the agency declined to extend the tariff statute to interfere with the operation of the private gray market. But the agency rules might be *over*enforcement (and in tension with liberal premises) if, in combination with other laws comprehensively regulating trademarked goods, they structured a market that, from the point of view of the trademark holder, prevented it from obtaining what it considered the full economic value of its mark. As Wesley Hohfeld argued earlier in this century, any legal rule—including the refusal to issue or change a legal rule—can be viewed as establishing a right for one group that is accompanied by a corresponding obligation for another group.[92]

Hohfeldian thought renders a concept such as overenforcement useless, unless one specifies the baseline for enforcement. As Maltz uses the term, overenforcement probably assumes traditional state common law as the regulatory baseline; hence, a statutory interpretation that disturbs the Hohfeldian rights and obligations created by the common law risks overenforcement. This is a framework that does little to advance liberal policies, for what Maltz calls overenforcement is merely his preference for one regulatory regime (state common law) over another (federal regulation), without any showing that one regime protects individual liberty more than the other. In today's world, moreover, the regulatory choice is often not between the common law and a new federal rule but instead between an old federal rule and a new one. In that context overenforcement becomes even harder to determine. Thus, the issue in *K Mart* was not between the federal tariff law and the common law but between federal tariff law and federal trademark or antitrust law.

Presumption in Favor of Continuity over Change in Legal Obligations David Shapiro has suggested a precept similar to Maltz's, but one that is not subject to the Hohfeldian criticism. Shapiro argues that "in a society in which revolution is not the order of the day, and in which all legislation occurs against a background of customs and understandings of the way things are done," the statutory interpreter should presume against change in preexisting practices and obligations.[93] Such a presumption has several virtues under liberal premises. It reflects the framers' vision that the status quo should be disturbed as rarely as possible and only after new rules have passed through all sorts of filters (not just the legislature but also the executive and the judiciary). It is a good surrogate for what the legislature probably intended in the hard cases. "Thus," writes Shapiro, "in a world in which change is news but continuity is not, a speaker who is issuing an order or prohibition is likely to focus on what is being changed and to expect the listener to understand that, so far as this communication is concerned, all else remains the same."[94] Shapiro's precept contributes to law's predictability and provides fair notice to the citizenry when the law is changed.

A presumption of continuity gives support to Justice Stevens's dissenting opinion in *Griffin*. Conceding that the broad statutory language favored the majority's interpretation, Stevens nonetheless argued that the legislative background of the 1898 double wages statute nowhere indicated the sort of sweeping change in shipowner obligations that the majority had created, and that the draconian liability imposed by the Court went well beyond established custom.[95] Stevens's opinion for the Court in Green v. Bock Laundry Machine Company (also discussed in Chapter 1) is a classic application of a continuity presumption. The opinion canvassed the legislative history for evidence that Congress expected to change the common law rule allowing impeachment of witnesses in civil cases based on their felony convictions and, finding no evidence one way or the other, applied the rule of continuity as a tiebreaker. Stevens joined the Brennan opinion in K Mart probably because that opinion preserved continuity with the pre-1922 federal and common law practice of allowing free importation of marked items, so long as there was no fraud on the consumer or violation of contractual rights.

The main difficulty with a presumption of continuity is that it may ill serve statutory policy in a swiftly changing world.[96] In the soup meat hypothetical the relational agent should not be held to an obligation of continuity once circumstances have materially changed. Fidelity to continuous legal obligations sometimes means updating them to take account of changed circumstances; fidelity can mean discontinuity in legal obligations. A related difficulty is that it is often hard to determine the contours of legal "continuity" itself when both legal rules and the extralegal world are in flux. In 1922 an aggressive importer could sell European-made face powder in the United States even though an American company had the exclusive right to manufacture that powder in this country. After the Tariff Act of 1922, the importer would not have been able to do so—until 1936, when the Customs Service adopted its same company exception, perhaps in response to the importer's desire to engage in this business. The Service expanded this exception to include related companies in 1953. In 1951 the Service adopted the initial version of the authorized use exception. What interpretation did the presumption of continuity support in 1988, when the Supreme Court decided K Mart? Perhaps the Brennan position, which reflected the pre-1922 practice and the practice after 1936. But the Scalia position apparently reflected the practice between 1922 and 1936 (when the same company exception was adopted) or 1951 (the authorized use exception) or 1953 (the common control exception). Continuity is a hard value to implement in a world of discontinuities.

Presumption to Protect Reliance Interests The aversion to overenforcement and the presumption of continuity are most defensible when they protect reliance interests. Private parties often rely on public rules in structuring their behavior, organization, and future plans. Just as such reliance interests are protected in contract and property law,[97] so may they be protected in public law through a presumption in favor of agency or judicial statutory interpretations that have triggered private reliance. Judicial precedents interpreting statutes receive a super-strong presumption of correctness when there is some indication that private interests have relied on those interpretations, even if they are erroneous (see Chapter 8), and agency precedents may enjoy a similar, albeit weaker, presumption.[98]

Government in the liberal state often builds on old rules when it establishes new ones, and there is a general disinclination to overturn rules on which public decision makers have relied in creating other new rules. This reasoning parallels the liberal justification for stare decisis: courts should be particularly reluctant to overrule their own decisions when other decisions and doctrinal developments would be affected. The same reasoning should make interpreters prone to accept agency and court interpretations that have been relied on by the legislature as it goes about its lawmaking tasks. Congress can rely on an agency rule by enacting laws that incorporate it or make no sense if the rule is not valid.[99] Or Congress can enact statutes that assume the validity of the rule even without codifying it.[100]

Reliance interests provide a further liberal justification for Brennan's interpretation in *K Mart*. The Customs Service had by regulation excepted some common control cases from the statute at least since 1936, and had excepted related company and authorized use cases since the 1950s; the current form of its exceptions had been in effect since 1972, after full notice-and-comment rulemaking. International price discrimination and fluctuating exchange rates offered enormous gray market opportunities; by 1988 gray market importation was a multibillion-dollar annual business[101] and was an important contributor to the growth of retail discounting by chains such as K Mart and 47th Street Photo.[102] Based on the Customs Service practice, which was upheld by lower federal courts (until *COPIAT*), firms were established to conduct gray market trade, chains of distribution were developed, and discount retailers came to depend on the availability of such goods. When there has been so much private reliance on a rule, the rule itself is presumed lawful.

The public reliance argument in *K Mart* may be of some weight. When in 1978 Congress created an exception for trademarked goods brought back into the United States for people's "personal use,"[103] the House report indicated that this would not be the first exception to the statute's broad reach, citing the Customs Service authorized use regulation.[104] And when Congress established criminal sanctions against counterfeit trademarked goods four years later, the Senate report emphasized that the legislation did not cover gray market imports, and then cited the Customs Service common control exception for the proposition that "[t]he importation of such goods is legal under certain circumstances."[105]

Liberal theory provides normative support for agencies and courts to interpret statutes dynamically. Liberalism also offers provisional criteria for evaluating different dynamic interpretations. For example, liberal theory on the whole justifies the Customs Service's willingness to create exceptions to the Tariff Act's broad ban on importing trademarked goods and provides a solid basis for criticizing the Supreme Court's invalidation of the authorized use exception. Liberalism does not object to trimming back a broadly written statute through policy exceptions, especially (1) when the exceptional cases were not the focus of the legislative deliberation and reflect equities and circumstances that would not have been accessible to the legislature; (2) when the interpretation runs the lesser risk of underenforcing the statutory policy, for then it is more justifiable to place the burden of changing the statute on the legislature; and (3) when the interpretation has been relied on by private and public decision makers.

Liberal theory also provides criteria for evaluating the interpretations discussed in Part 1. Notwithstanding the EEOC's and the Court's unsympathetic attitude toward Title VII's legislative history, *Weber* emerges as more defensible under liberal premises. The decision resolved an issue (voluntary affirmative action) that the legislative process ducked, and did so by an underenforcing interpretation that preserved employer and union common law rights. Conversely, *Griffin* seems less defensible under liberal premises because the Court's interpretation expanded the statute far beyond prevailing practice and posed substantial risks of overenforcement, without any solid evidence that Congress had mandated draconian remedies. *Bock Laundry* seems more defensible under liberal premises, for the Court's opinion was sensitive to the legislative deliberations and held to the traditional common law rule once it found no real evidence that Congress wanted to displace it. *Boutilier* (expanding the immigration statute to bar bisexuals from entering the United States) and *Loewe* (expanding the antitrust statute to penalize union boycotts) are most inconsistent with liberal baselines, since those decisions overenforced federal statutes far beyond the expectations of statutory framers and inserted the federal government into arenas where the state performed wretchedly.

5 ▪ Legal Process Theories

Like three streams flowing together into a mighty river, three twentieth-century intellectual developments came together to produce the legal process school. One was an organic rationalism, which viewed legal decision making as neither rule-bound and deductive (as the formalists did) nor intuitional and inductive (as some of the realists did), but instead as a search for the expression of coherent reason in the fabric of law.[1] Rationalism yielded a theory of adjudication in which the role of judges is to seek principled bases for legal decisions which can then be integrated into a coherent whole (the law). A second development was the New Deal's administrative state. This spawned a theory of regulation in which complicated social problems could be referred to agencies for solution through the application of expertise over time. The third development was our country's reaction to totalitarianism (the Nazis and the communists).[2] This reaction generated a political theory that viewed the United States as demonstrably superior to other governments because of its open, participatory democracy. Not only is democracy more legitimate than other forms of government, but also its openness ensures better-informed decision making, greater adaptability in responding to problems, and superior flexibility.

Legal process is the synthesis of these theories of judging, regulation, and legitimacy into a school of thought about law and its role in society. This synthesis came together in scholarship written between 1938 and 1959 and was classically expressed in Henry Hart and Albert Sacks's materials, "The Legal Process."[3] Legal process thought rests on a theory of political life that is distinct from nineteenth-century liberalism. Whereas liberal theory posits mutually suspicious humans who form a social contract to escape the state of nature, legal process theory posits humans who recognize their interdependence and cooperate for the advancement of common interests. The state exists to further the interests that the members of a community have in common.[4] Legal process views law as a "purposive activity, a continuous striving to solve the basic problems of social living."[5]

As a purposive system, law includes a number of substantive understandings or arrangements. Certain guiding "principles" have been developed through the legal system, and other "policies" have been adopted to solve specific problems. More fundamental are the "constitutive or procedural understandings or arrangements" by which the substantive arrangements are applied, for process is "at once the source of the substantive arrangements and the indispensable means of making them work effectively."[6] Process, in turn, is conceived of in pluralist-democratic terms, emphasizing the dispersion of problem solving. Although private ordering remains the primary process of social adjustment, most social problems are tackled through the interaction of different state institutions, according to their relative "competence." Procedure is central to legal process theory, both as an effective way to ensure better decision making and as the means by which the interconnected institutional system works in harmony.[7] Procedure is above all critical to law's legitimacy. One may debate the correctness of a legal decision or the degree of popular support for it, but legal process maintains that if a decision is the "duly arrived at result of a duly established procedure," that alone lends it legitimacy.[8]

Legal process theory invites dynamic statutory interpretation. Viewing statutes in rationalist terms, most legal process thinkers accept dynamic interpretation as normatively essential to the implementation of statutory policy. In the first part of this chapter I critically examine leading legal process theories of dynamic interpretation, which adapt a statute's purpose to new circumstances, integrate the statute with the ever-changing principles and policies of the society, and apply the statute in light of evolving background understandings. The main difficulty with the rationalist tradition as applied by legal process writers is summed up by the question: Whose reason? Rather than identifying right answers in the hard cases, the application of law's reason depends on the interpreter's own policy choices, which are themselves guided by the framework she brings to the issue. Reasoned elaboration fares no better than plain meaning or intent (liberalism's lodestars) as a basis for determinately resolving the hard cases, especially those that are hard because of ideological polarization.

The second and third parts of the chapter take up the main legal process objections to dynamic interpretation by judges—the countermajoritarian difficulty and the relatively greater competence of agencies. In analyzing these objections I also tease out further legal process–inspired considerations for dynamic interpretation. The most notable one is that, in close cases, the interpreter should protect interests that have not been or will not be heard in the legislative process. Like the general theories canvassed in the first part of this chapter, though, this one depends on notions of political fairness which the interpreter brings to the case.

The genius of legal process theory is its ability to mediate substantive divisions through procedure and to press the polity toward new consensuses over time. Its danger is that procedural regularity may become a cover for the triumph of a partial substantive position and consensus a shield for an unjust or inefficient status quo. The challenge for a legal process theory of statutory interpretation is to find a balance—one that must be constantly recalibrated—between procedural mediation and substantive responsibility.

Dynamic Process Theories: Statutory Purpose and Legal Coherence

Hart and Sacks's materials known as "The Legal Process" contain the first systematically developed American theory of dynamic statutory interpretation, representing the culmination of twenty years of discussion among law professors and judges. These materials remain the most sophisticated legal process theory of statutory interpretation[9] because they are the most critical and the least dogmatic, and because they synthesize themes that have been the main basis for theories of dynamic interpretation for a generation.

Hart and Sacks are best known for their theory that statutes should be interpreted to carry out their purposes over time, an openly dynamic theory. Yet their materials also contain a coherence theory, according to which statutes should be interpreted consistently with the surrounding legal terrain or legal principles. Because the legal terrain and prevailing principles themselves evolve, statutory interpretation will evolve with them. Better worked-out coherence theories have been developed by the successors of Hart and Sacks in American rationalist jurisprudence. Although subsequent judges and scholars have apprehended Hart and Sacks's conviction that statutory interpretation is evolutive, they have neglected the equally important legal process insight that it is hard to determine the right answer once statutes are interpreted dynamically.

Attribution of Purpose

According to Hart and Sacks, statutes must be understood not solely as directives addressed to the citizenry (the traditional liberal position), but also as directives addressed to government officials who are charged with developing statutory schemes over time. Courts and agencies do this through a process of reasoned elaboration from the statutory purposes. Because "every statute and every doctrine of unwritten law developed by the decisional process has some kind of purpose or objective," the statute or doctrine can be applied to specific problems or controversies by a rational process in which the decision maker first "attributes" a purpose to the statute and the "principle or policy" that it embodies, and then reasons toward the result most consistent with that policy or principle.[10]

In attributing purpose, Hart and Sacks warned against taking a cynical view of the legislative process. Interpreters should assume, "unless the contrary unmistakably appears, that the legislature was made up of reasonable persons pursuing reasonable purposes reasonably."[11] Hart and Sacks conceded that deciding on a statute's purpose is no easy task. Where no clear answer appears, they recommended identifying instances where the statute unquestionably applies and using those easy cases to reason by analogy to the harder ones, in all events avoiding an "irrational pattern" of statutory applications.[12]

Like their contemporaries, Hart and Sacks viewed the enactment of a statute as merely the beginning, not the end, of lawmaking.[13] They honed their purpose-based approach by criticizing examples of static interpretation. For example, in Doherty v. Ayer,[14] a nineteenth-century statute required that cities and towns keep the highways "reasonably safe and convenient for travellers, with their horses, teams and carriages at all seasons." In 1908 the Massachusetts Supreme Court held that the statute did not require cities and towns to maintain roads for use by automobiles, which had been recently developed. Hart and Sacks faulted the Court for focusing mainly on the statute's plain meaning.[15] Since the statutory purpose was to ensure safety and convenience of travel, why shouldn't the statute be extended to the automobile, even though it was an innovation outside the legislators' original expectations?[16]

This was hardly the end of their inquiry, for Hart and Sacks appreciated the possibility that the statutory purpose itself was qualified by the costs local governments could bear.[17] But, they added, "Was this qualification of purpose proper?" Wouldn't it justify abrogation of the maintenance requirement for horse-drawn carriages as well, should the costs of that maintenance skyrocket? Hart and Sacks concluded with no sure answer to this statutory riddle, for it was unclear how carefully the statutory purpose ought to be calibrated. But they did suggest that the Massachusetts Supreme Court—like Hart and Sacks—was necessarily engaged in dynamic policy analysis because "the pros and cons of the problems could not have been considered by the legislature because not then apparent, and therefore the court should consider them and decide what is best."[18]

Hart and Sacks's analysis of the Case of the Carriages is a legal process exemplar of dynamic interpretation,[19] not only for its recognition that judges cannot help but construe statutes dynamically, but also for its insistence that interpreters recognize uncertainties in their attribution of purpose and take responsibility for the policy decisions they make when they determine which interpretation will best carry out the statutory purpose. Unhappily, judges tend to use the Hart and Sacks approach as a method of simplifying their task rather than making it more complicated. This was my complaint in Chapter 1 with regard to Justice William Brennan's use of purposivist interpretation in *Weber*.

Consider also the case of Bob Jones University v. United States.[20] The issue was whether a nonprofit private school following a racially discriminatory admissions policy could qualify as an institution "organized and operated exclusively for religious, charitable . . . or educational purposes" and thereby be entitled to exemption from federal income taxation under section 501(c)(3) of the Internal Revenue Code. Pressed by constitutional challenges, the Internal Revenue Service (IRS) had since 1970 interpreted section 501 to be inapplicable to educational institutions that engaged in racial discrimination.[21] In 1976 the IRS revoked Bob Jones University's tax exempt status because of its discriminations against African Americans involved in interracial relationships.[22] Bob Jones claimed that its activities were "exclusively for . . . educational purposes," thereby entitling it to exemption under the statute's plain meaning; the university also maintained that its antimiscegenation policies should not affect its tax exempt status. Because the charitable organization exemption originated in the 1894 version of the tax code, during an era of racial segregation by law, Bob Jones could also argue that original legislative intent supported its interpretation. The Reagan White House and its Department of Justice agreed with this argument[23] and in 1982 directed the IRS to adopt Bob Jones's interpretation of the statute. This reversal sparked a firestorm of protest in Congress and the media, and even within the administration.[24]

A virtually unanimous Supreme Court rejected these plain meaning and original intent arguments, looking instead to the statute's purpose.[25] Chief Justice Warren Burger's opinion for the Court found the purpose of section 501 to be the provision of tax benefits to organizations serving "charitable purposes" because such organizations afford a substantial benefit to society.[26] This purpose would be thwarted if the exemption were read to exclude any organization whose activity is "contrary to fundamental public policy," such as the *Brown* policy against racial discrimination in education. Therefore, it was not enough for Bob Jones's activities to be "educational" in nature (the explicit statutory requirement) if they were not also "charitable" overall (the additional requirement suggested by the statutory purpose). Bob Jones did not meet this additional requirement, and so it was not entitled to the section 501 exemption.[27]

Although the Court was clearly invoking the sort of dynamic statutory analysis developed in the legal process materials, Hart and Sacks would have been critical of the Court's simplification of complicated policy choices. Was the statutory purpose to encourage organizations that the IRS and the Court thought were contributing to good public policy? The Court's evidence for this purpose was thin, and surely the Court did not mean to turn the exemption into a referendum on the goodness of an organization's purpose. Should I interpret section 501(c) to deny the educational arm of the National Rifle Association tax exempt status simply because I do not consider its functions "charitable"?

Hart and Sacks would also wonder whether there might not be more narrow ways of framing the statute's purpose. Why wasn't the statutory purpose simply to contribute "to the diversity of association, viewpoint, and enterprise essential to a vigorous, pluralistic society," as some Justices have suggested?[28] Or if the statute's purpose was to provide a public benefit, why isn't the list of organizations in section 501—those engaged in religious, educational, scientific, or other enumerated activities—per se evidence of the sort of organization Congress thought met its purpose? And why wasn't the purpose of the statute to encourage education generally, and to promote scholarly dialogue on important issues such as racial discrimination? Under this view of the statutory goal, the Court's decision undermined the statutory purpose by muting the discordant voice of Bob Jones. Though Hart and Sacks might have agreed with the IRS's dynamic interpretation of section 501, they would have conceded "play" in the statute's purpose. By making the interpretive issue more complicated, Hart and Sacks would have undercut the simple majoritarian argument Burger thought necessary to get around an apparently clear statutory text.

Coherence

Hart and Sacks posited that law "rests upon a body of hard-won and deeply-embedded principles and policies" that transcend any one statute.[29] If the underlying statutory purpose were ambiguous, as section 501 might be, the official should interpret it "so as to harmonize [the statute] with more general principles and policies."[30] Hart and Sacks explicitly contemplated that evolving principles and policies would form the basis for dynamic interpretation of statutes and precedents.[31]

This type of analysis has inspired a number of theories arguing that statutory meaning should evolve as legal principles and policies change.[32] Ronald Dworkin has developed this theme in his concept of "law as integrity."[33] Focusing on the necessity and desirability of human interdependence, Dworkin states that "integrity in legislation," by which lawmakers try to make our total set of laws coherent, is central to the legitimacy of government. Dworkin points to our disdain for "checkerboard statutes," which treat different groups of people in different ways, without clear justification in principle or policy.[34]

A corollary to integrity in legislation is "integrity in adjudication," which requires interpreters to "treat our present system of public standards as expressing and respecting a coherent set of principles, and, to that end, to interpret these standards to find implicit standards between and beneath the explicit ones."[35]

Under this conception propositions of law are true if they are consistent with the principles of justice, fairness, and due process that provide the best interpretation of the community's legal practice. Because its principles and policies change as the community changes, Dworkin's theory requires dynamic interpretation. The judge or administrator "interprets not just the statute's text but its life, the process that begins before it becomes law and extends far beyond that moment. He aims to make the best he can of this continuing story, and his interpretation therefore changes as the story develops."[36]

Dworkin's theory provides a legal process defense of *Bob Jones*. The interpreter should be reluctant to attribute to section 501 a purpose that is at odds with fundamental principles and policies of the nation. Although racial desegregation was not a national policy when earlier versions of section 501 were added to the Internal Revenue Code, since *Brown* the right of a student not to be segregated on racial grounds has been recognized as "fundamental and pervasive,"[37] not only in judicial interpretations of the Constitution but also in judicial interpretations of Reconstruction-era statutes, in executive orders and administrative regulations, and in statutes such as the Civil Rights Act of 1964. It would be incompatible with the idea of integrity in legislation for an interpreter to impute to the tax code benefits for an institution whose actions violate constitutional, statutory, and administrative policies against racial discrimination. Under Dworkin's theory the principles that undergird law's integrity required the Court to reach the result it did in *Bob Jones*.

Understanding law as integrity seems to resolve the *Bob Jones* case—until one considers the difficulty of figuring out what principles and policies our political community accepts. Notwithstanding its adoption of a broad antidiscrimination principle in 1970, the IRS's enforcement of section 501 was halfhearted; usually if an educational institution was willing to sign a statement that it did not discriminate, it was permitted to keep its tax exemption, without any further inquiry from the agency. Moreover, the same Court that had trumpeted the nation's commitment to eliminating racial discrimination in *Bob Jones* made it hard for African Americans to sue the IRS to enforce its regulations in Allen v. Wright,[38] a standing case decided the next term. One might expect Dworkin to be critical of the IRS's and *Allen*'s approach to section 501.

But it is not clear that the IRS's ambivalent approach was incoherent with the nation's principles and policies. It was arguably consistent with congressional appropriations pressure in the 1970s, which impelled the IRS to curtail any serious plans for enforcement;[39] with the Supreme Court's own refusal to enforce the antidiscrimination principle at all costs in school desegregation cases[40] or to enforce it at all in cases where racial discrimination is not intentional;[41] and with the Reagan administration's effort to reverse the IRS's interpretation, one of several signals from the administration that it did not consider racial discrimination an urgent national problem.

This analysis suggests general problems with Dworkin's theory of law as integrity: there are few if any principles or policies that we accept at any and all cost, some principles and policies may be in tension with one another, and given this complexity it is hard for an interpreter to weigh these competing concerns determinately. Without an external standard for judgment, which Dworkin does not provide, it is difficult to discern the "best" reading of our nation's antidiscrimination law. The romantic reading, such as that in *Bob Jones*, rings false to the people who are supposed to benefit from the antidiscrimination principle, while the cynical reading does not seem to make the statute the "best" it can be.

Public Values

Also inspired by Hart and Sacks, who revived interest in the canons of statutory construction as a way of contributing to law's rationality, both Cass Sunstein and I have thought about the coherence issue from a different angle.[42] Interpreters always read statutes in context. Part of the context for interpretation is background understandings about overall goals and policies held by our polity, or what Owen Fiss has called "public values."[43] When an official reads and interprets a statute, she thinks about it in light of these background understandings, which predispose her toward one interpretation rather than another.

All interpretation involves background understandings. For example, it is easy to apply the Constitution's requirement that the president be at least thirty-five years old, because we share understandings about (1) the desirability of applying the conventional meaning of a text unless there is justification for doing otherwise, (2) the conventional meaning of "thirty-five years old," and (3) the lack of persuasive justification for departing from this plain meaning.[44] Linguistic, syntactic, and other conventions are background understandings that are widely shared and that generate predictability in our legal culture. Other background understandings order substantive and procedural decision making in the regulatory state. These are the basis for the canons of statutory construction, which variously operate as tiebreakers in close cases; as presumptions of statutory meaning that can be rebutted only if inconsistent with other signals; or as clear statement rules that can be negated only by statutory text to the contrary (see Chapter 9).

Although Sunstein and I have categorized these interpretive canons differently, we both emphasize the ways in which the canons reflect underlying constitutional, statutory, and common law principles; the need for accommodation of statutory policies with one another and for general statutory consistency; and the functional requirements for efficacious government in the modern regulatory state and for counteracting patterns of statutory failure.[45] What sets our project apart from Dworkin's is that we urge statutory interpreters to think about the canons in light of a political theory of the modern regulatory state. Essentially, our systemic aspirations are that statutes respect and protect individual rights, especially those of disadvantaged groups; that broad public interest statutes not be eroded by rent-seeking exceptions; that special interest statutes be narrowly construed; and that statutory schemes be allowed to change over time to adapt their goals to new circumstances and political values.

Background understandings reflected in several established canons help justify *Bob Jones*. Though ignored by the Court, a relevant canon is that exemptions to tax statutes should be narrowly construed in order to protect the public fisc and avoid rent seeking by special interests.[46] *Bob Jones*'s canon that statutes be construed to meet their goals is also relevant. It suggests that the IRS might scrutinize more attentively the link between a "charitable" organization's activities and the public interest (the goal of the statute, according to the Court). Most critical is the canon that interpreters should construe statutes to be consistent with, and not detract from, other statutory schemes.[47] It is illegal for a private school to discriminate against applicants on the basis of their race.[48] The state should not be subsidizing illegal activity through a tax exemption!

Another relevant canon is that statutes should be construed to avoid the constitutional difficulties attendant on state support for race discrimination. Indeed, the IRS changed its interpretation of section 501 in response to constitutional litigation that resulted in a lower court decision disapproving tax exemptions for racially discriminatory private schools.[49] The agency was trying to avoid constitutional problems, as was Congress when, during a decade of hearings, it refused to overturn the new IRS policy. The latter point is also significant because of the canon that congressional failure to change an interpretation after extensive deliberation offers some (weak) evidence in favor of preserving that interpretation (see Chapter 8).

It is striking that the *Bob Jones* interpretation is supported by such a wide variety of background understandings enshrined in canons of construction. This type of argumentation yields a richer understanding of the issues. More important, it provides a normative focus from which to criticize particular interpretations. While the analysis might support the IRS interpretation in *Bob Jones*, it does not support the IRS's foot-dragging in enforcing that interpretation and suggests that the IRS ought to be generally more stingy in according section 501 status to other "charitable organizations."

A public values understanding of statutory interpretation does not necessarily produce determinate answers in the hard cases, however.[50] Cases such as *Bob Jones* are hard because background understandings cut in different directions. At least one canon worked strongly against the result: the plain meaning rule that interpreters should apply statutes as they are written.[51] The Court's interpretation is not the one suggested by the statute's text, as Rehnquist emphasized in his dissent. Other canons support either the Court or the dissent. For instance, the canon urging deference to agency interpretations could support either view: on the one hand, the IRS after 1970 denied the tax exemption to discriminatory schools; on the other, the agency before 1970 allowed an exemption to such schools, and the Reagan administration renounced the post-1970 IRS policy.

The canon to avoid constitutional difficulties was the most ambiguous, for the Court's decision to avoid equal protection problems raised in their place problems of the free exercise of religion and academic freedom. Bob Jones was a fundamentalist Protestant college which as a matter of religious belief did not condone interracial relationships. Although denying it a tax exemption for these beliefs may not be a direct infringement on academic freedom or the free exercise of religion, as the Rehnquist dissent conceded, the actual operation of the state's penalty was troubling. As administered by the IRS (after pressure from Congress), the loss of tax exempt status affected only those schools that admitted to some form of discrimination on a bureaucratic form. Because the IRS did not second-guess this self-reporting, it tended to catch only the schools for which such discrimination was based in principle. Contrast the dozens of tony colleges in the South (including Davidson College, from which I graduated) whose admissions policies in the 1970s yielded virtually all-white classes, while retaining their tax exemptions because they discriminated out of indirection or indifference, not out of principle. Is this a public value?

The foregoing discussion suggests a general difficulty with legal process theories of dynamic interpretation. The legal process school has sought to enable nonelected legal decision makers (agencies and especially courts) to update statutes, but without seeming to make controversial value choices. Such a dynamic but neutral approach to statutory interpretation was to be accomplished by reading statutes in light of reasoning external to the individual interpreter (statutory purposes, legal principles, public values). The problem is that in the hard cases—from the Case of the Carriages to *Bob Jones*—

the interpreter is not constrained by one purpose, one principle, or one public value; hence, she has policy-making discretion. Hart and Sacks insisted that interpreters take responsibility for and justify their policy choices. In practice, however, their rationalist methodology is often used to submerge such choices and deny such responsibility.

The Countermajoritarian Difficulty and Interpretive Principles to Counteract Political Dysfunction

Once courts and agencies are found to have lawmaking discretion, legal process theorists wonder whether these officials are competent for such a task and whether lawmaking by nonelected officials is consistent with the constitutional procedures for statutory policy-making. I defer discussion of the former concern and focus now on arguments based on the "countermajoritarian difficulty" that democratic theory suggests when unelected officials make new law.[52] The countermajoritarian difficulty is not so troubling in statutory as in constitutional cases, and statutory interpretation should often be counter- or nonmajoritarian under the premises of legal process theory. I also suggest some legal process precepts for resolving ambiguities in hard cases. These precepts are based on the idea that statutory interpretation can ameliorate some dysfunctions in the political process.

Allocating the Burden of Legislative Inertia

Legal process theory does not hold that all lawmaking must occur in the legislature but maintains that statutory interpretation should be a cooperative endeavor, in which different institutions work together to create public policy. This suggests one answer to the countermajoritarian difficulty: dynamic statutory interpretation, even against legislative expectations, is subject to override by the legislature and in fact may even be a stimulus to legislative deliberation. Citing the many procedural obstacles to legislation and the ability of groups to block initiatives, legal process scholars have assumed that Congress rarely responds to statutory interpretations.[53] Recent scholarship, however, demonstrates that the override possibility is a tangible one. Congress monitors most controversial Supreme Court statutory decisions and overrides about six of them each year; it influences agency decisions and sometimes Court decisions through oversight; but it is only selectively aware of lower court statutory decisions and does not override them often.[54]

Ongoing congressional monitoring of statutory issues suggests another way in which dynamic interpreters might respond to the countermajoritarian difficulty. Once circumstances have changed beyond those reasonably contemplated by the enacting legislature, it is typically hard to tell how the original legislative majority would have wanted the statute to apply in those new circumstances (see Chapter 1). But if there is congressional monitoring of the issue, it might be easier to guess how the current legislature wants the statute to apply. To the extent that the dynamic interpretation is consistent with current legislative desires, the countermajoritarian difficulty is ameliorated. Of course, it might be hard to figure out what current legislative preferences are. Under traditional legal theory, subsequent legislative developments are most helpful when the legislature deliberates over the interpretive issue and either enacts a statute relying on or consistent with the prior interpretation or authoritatively rejects proposals to override that interpretation (see Chapter 8). Positive political theory suggests, further, that less formal postenactment legislative signals, such as statements in committee reports, can provide useful information to the Court about the nature and intensity of current congressional preferences.[55]

Bob Jones illustrates the relevance of postenactment legislative signals for the statutory interpreter who wishes not to upset political equilibria. In the 1970s the IRS was unconcerned with the original intent of the enacting Congresses in this matter but was keenly interested in the attention given to the issue by current Congresses. In 1970 the IRS was persuaded not only that its old policy of giving tax exemptions to racially discriminatory schools was vulnerable to override in the courts, but also that a new policy of no tax exemptions would not be overridden by Congress. Congress held its first hearings a month after the IRS adopted the new policy in 1970; those and subsequent hearings revealed sufficient congressional support for the new policy.[56] The Supreme Court's decision affirming IRS policy explicitly relied on postenactment legislative signals as evidence of congressional approval. Burger's opinion pointed to Congress's failure to enact any of thirteen bills introduced to override the IRS's interpretation of section 501(c), to Congress's enactment of a provision (section [501(i)]) expanding the IRS position to deny exemptions to racially discriminatory social clubs,[57] and to the explicit endorsement of the IRS interpretation of section 501(c) in committee reports accompanying section 501(i).[58] Although Congress's actions in the 1970s stopped well short of formal ratification, its signaled preferences were more important to the Court than the preferences of the enacting Congress. Such dynamic interpretation is arguably promajoritarian.

Although legislative overrides are more common than legal scholars once thought, most interpretations (especially those below Supreme Court level) are not overridden. One reason is that the losing interests usually do not have sufficient political clout or incentive to place the issue on the legislative agenda, often because the group is poorly organized or politically marginalized. In my study of congressional overrides of Supreme Court and lower court statutory decisions from 1967 to 1990,[59] I found that groups differed sharply in their ability to get their losses in the judicial arena reversed in the legislative arena. These findings are reflected in Figure 5.1.

In close cases the legal process interpreter ought to consider, as a tie-breaker, which party or group representing its interests will have effective access to the legislative process if it loses its case, and to decide the case *against* the party (if any) with significantly more effective access. Thus, if the interpreter believes that the issue is indeterminate yet so important that the legislature ought to resolve it (a standard legal process concern), the interpreter ought to be attentive to the likelihood of various interpretations' actually reaching the legislative agenda. If one interpretation is significantly more likely to stimulate legislative attention because it *hurts* a group with political clout, that provides one, sometimes decisive, reason for adopting that interpretation.

This precept is inapplicable to *Bob Jones*, where the Reagan administration and religious fundamentalists (the losing groups) had about as much access to the legislative process as did the civil rights groups that won the case, and where there had recently been considerable congressional attention to the issue. But consider its application to United States v. Albertini.[60] This was a criminal prosecution based on a federal statute making it unlawful to reenter a military base after having been "ordered not to reenter by any officer or person in command or charge thereof."[61] James Vincent Albertini had been issued a "bar letter" for destroying government property during an antiwar protest. Nine years later he and some friends reentered the base during its annual open house on Armed Forces Day. The friends engaged in a peaceful

Figure 5.1   Group access to Congress to override Supreme Court decisions

demonstration against the nuclear arms buildup, and Albertini took pictures. For this activity he was convicted of violating the criminal reentry statute. A divided Supreme Court upheld his conviction.

The legal process philosophy provides a basis for criticizing the result in *Albertini*. The statute is written broadly enough to include his conduct but does not target people like him. It would be irrational for courts to apply the statute as broadly as it is written, to convict somebody who wandered onto the base completely by accident, for example.[62] The Court, for due process reasons, "has on a number of occasions read a state-of-mind component into an offense even when the statutory definition did not in terms so provide."[63] Such a narrowing of the criminal reentry statute seems appropriate in *Albertini*, where the arrest came in connection with the exercise of First Amendment rights (and with a military invitation for the public to enter the base).

Justice Sandra Day O'Connor's opinion for the Court recognized these difficulties with the prosecution of Albertini, and considered interpreting the statute to avoid the First Amendment problems. Her decision is a careful analysis of First Amendment rights on military bases, forums where the state has greater discretion to limit speech under the Court's precedents. Indeed, O'Connor implicitly invoked public values analysis, her public value being judicial deference to military judgments about security lest our national defense be compromised. Like the dissenters, I am unpersuaded that national security was implicated in Albertini's activity, but the Court's deliberations went the other way.

The Court's decision stimulated no legislative interest because the Albertinis of this country have no access to Congress, and their occasional surrogate (the ACLU) did not put the issue on its agenda—knowing that an override would have been blocked by the opposition of both the Justice and Defense Departments. Given the closeness of this case on the merits, the Court could have stimulated legislative attention to the broadly written statute by construing it narrowly. If the statute really needs to be so broad to serve its security purposes, the Justice Department could have obtained congressional hearings, and its record in winning overrides is the best in the land.[64]

Avoiding Unreasonable Results

A further legal process response, propounded by Guido Calabresi as the best solution to the countermajoritarian difficulty, draws from the rationalist tradition. To the extent that courts follow principles in construing statutes, they may, consistent with majoritarian democratic theory, be given lawmaking tasks based on "the belief that the legal fabric, and the principles that form it, are a good approximation of one aspect of the popular will, of what a majority in some sense desires."[65] Under this theory *Bob Jones* would be defensible as dynamic interpretation if the drumbeat of legal sanctions against school segregation since *Brown* is seen to reflect a consensus that de jure segregation is not right.

I do not have the impression, however, that there was a popular consensus in favor of the particular result and expansive rhetoric of *Bob Jones*, where the college's discrimination in the late 1970s was limited to interracial dating and marriage, controversial activities even today. Nor did other dynamic interpretations, such as agency and judicial approval of voluntary affirmative action (discussed in Chapter 1), reflect any popular consensus.[66] In most cases it is hard to tell what the "popular will" is, and it is even more doubtful that legal elites are able to discern it reliably. While I believe *Albertini* was wrongly decided, I have little confidence that my reasoned view is "a good approximation of one aspect of the popular will."

This analysis raises another difficulty with legal process theory. The early process theorists were writing in a period when American political and legal theory assumed a consensus in American society about underlying values and was optimistic that good procedures would generate agreement about issues that temporarily divided the polity.[67] Although later process theorists continue to make these assumptions, the rage of the 1960s, the shocks of the 1970s, and the multiculturalism of the 1980s and 1990s have undermined our confidence that fundamental social agreement exists on important questions, including what resources government should invest in fighting segregation *(Bob Jones)*, how citizens can protest state actions *(Albertini)*, and so forth. Can reason resolve debates that seem so ideologically polarized? Indeed, might not the reasoned enterprise in cases like *Bob Jones* and *Albertini* obstruct social progress by pretending that there is consensus when in reality we are riven with dissent?

I am not optimistic that courts and agencies can consistently subject hard legal issues to balanced or neutral inquiry, even issues that are not emotionally charged. Consider United States v. Locke,[68] where the Court held that a family that had run a gravel business on federal lands they had legally occupied since 1952 lost their property because they filed a renewal of their claims on the last day of the year (December 31) rather than "prior to December 31," as the statute required. The Court stuck to the plain language of the statute, notwithstanding Justice John Paul Stevens's dissenting argument that "prior to December 31" was probably a drafting error (for "on or prior to December 31") and that it served no rational purpose to enforce it strictly against the Locke family. Moreover, the Lockes had not been neglectful. They had sent their daughter to the Ely, New Mexico, office of the Bureau of Land Management (BLM), whose officials had told her that the filing had to be made "on or before December 31, 1980."[69] Indeed, the BLM in an official document had read the statute precisely that way,[70] and courts and agencies had interpreted similar language in other contexts to mean "the end of the year."[71] Justice Thurgood Marshall's opinion for the Court lamely responded that fixed deadlines are always somewhat arbitrary. The decision is bereft of reason or mercy.[72]

Ameliorating Statutory Failures and Political Dysfunctions

A final response to the countermajoritarian difficulty is to recognize that our polity is not majoritarian. Thus, our system tolerates electoral schemes that permit candidates and parties receiving a minority of votes to win elections.[73] Once representatives are in office, there are perverse incentives that lead them away from majoritarian preferences, and the rules created by a legislature often fail to reflect majority preferences even within the body because of procedural manipulations (see Chapter 1). In short, our political system does not necessarily reflect majority preferences, nor did the framers of the Constitution expect it to.[74]

Had the framers wanted a strict majoritarianism, a system of direct democracy in which people vote on statutory proposals might have been most appropriate. Yet they considered and rejected direct democracy in favor of representative democracy because of their fear that temporary majorities might enact laws that are unjust to the minority and are not in the public interest. In terms of structure, a representative government better protects against this danger because, as Madison wrote, it is able "to refine and enlarge the public views by passing them through the medium of a chosen body of citizens, whose wisdom may best discern the true interest of their country, and whose patriotism and love of justice will be least likely to sacrifice it to temporary or partial considerations." Madison claimed that "it may well happen that the public voice, pronounced by representatives of the people, will be more consonant to the public good than if pronounced by the people themselves."[75]

Madison's argument provides context for Hamilton's argument, expressed in *The Federalist*, no. 78, that one role of statutory interpreters is to act as an additional filter:

> [T]he independence of the judges may be an essential safeguard against the effects of occasional ill humors in the society. These sometimes extend no farther than to the injury of the private rights of particular classes of citizens, by unjust and partial laws. Here also the firmness of the judicial magistracy is of vast importance in mitigating the severity and confining the operation of such laws. It not only serves to moderate

the immediate mischiefs of those which may have been passed but it operates as a check upon the legislative body in passing them; who, perceiving that obstacles to the success of an iniquitous intention are to be expected from the scruples of the courts, are in a manner compelled, by the very motives of the injustice they mediate, to qualify their attempts.[76]

The deliberative democracy envisioned by the framers, therefore, is one in which "the public voice" speaks beyond the private preferences of temporary majorities, and in which nonelected representatives are expected to contribute.[77]

Countermajoritarian statutory interpretation may be normatively desirable if it contributes to the overall legitimacy of the political system. Dynamic interpretation, even against legislative expectations, is justified to ameliorate "unjust and partial laws." But what laws are partial or unjust? Justice Harlan Fiske Stone, an influential rationalist parent of legal process theory, argued for a procedural theory of partiality and injustice. The Court in constitutional cases should entertain less deference to legislative judgments when certain interests are systematically excluded.[78] The idea that courts can serve a "representation-reinforcing" role in constitutional cases[79] provides an even more attractive goal for the dynamic statutory interpreter: to resolve or even create ambiguities so as to counteract distortions in the political process. The problem with Stone's concept is that there is no dominant normative theory of the political process. Positive political theory (introduced in Chapters 1 and 2) is mainly a descriptive theory, but it does have some normative bite. Where its normative implications are confirmed by different theories of politics, we might tentatively identify a dysfunction in our political process.

Minimizing Asymmetrical Distribution of Statutory Benefits and Costs A variety of political theorists argue that legislation is most often socially productive when its costs as well as its benefits are symmetrically distributed.[80] Examples of laws that symmetrically distribute costs and benefits are article 2 of the Uniform Commercial Code (UCC) regulating sales transactions, the generally applicable criminal laws, the antitrust statutes, and legislation to build roads out of public revenues. These laws tend to be efficient and fair because interests and deliberation tend to be evenly balanced when cost payers are the mirror image of benefit receivers.

Our polity therefore needs symmetrical laws but is confronted with countervailing pressures. Public choice theory posits that laws generally distributing benefits and costs will not often be enacted and, once enacted, will not be updated because they do not necessarily stimulate the formation of supportive interest groups and because they offer insufficient opportunities for legislators to advance their chances of reelection.[81] Just as the legislature produces too few statutes that distribute benefits and costs symmetrically, so too does it produce too many statutes that concentrate benefits or costs. Such statutes tend to be rent-seeking, distributing benefits from society as a whole to a well-organized group without a larger social justification.

In a similar vein, institutional theorists argue that legislative policy does not address public problems in an integrated and timely manner. The increasingly decentralized structure of Congress has resulted in problems of coordination and leadership that threaten the ability of the legislature to be responsive to changing policy concerns. The many procedural obstacles to the creation of statutes make legislative policy an adventitious occurrence.[82] Conversely, everyday policy-making tends to be submerged from public view inside "subgovernments" of congressional subcommittees populated by legislators hungry for PAC money, revolving-door or turf-protecting bureaucrats, and lobbyists.[83]

To counteract these biases in the political system, interpreters should update laws that generally distribute benefits and costs, but should approach concentrated benefit statutes more stingily.[84] This idea is a normative justification for courts (especially) to treat the UCC, section 1983, general antitrust law, and antifraud rules as common law statutes, whose rules are developed over time in a case-by-case method by interpreters working from general legislative directives.[85] Because there is a tendency in our system for interest groups to chip away at general rules and create special exceptions, interpreters should approach such exceptions cautiously.

A problem here is that many statutes cannot easily be characterized. The charitable contributions exemption to the Internal Revenue Code, for example, may seem at first glance to be asymmetrical, distributing costs widely (to all taxpayers) and concentrating benefits. This is the way I view section 501, and I would interpret it scroogily. Other observers view section 501 as more symmetrical because they think public subsidies to charity benefit us all; therefore, section 501 might be considered a distributed benefits statute. In response I would say that any public benefits from the subsidized charities are modest in comparison to the subsidies.

Alternatively, these public choice problems could be a justification for the Hart and Sacks approach of attributing reasonable, public-regarding purposes to statutes, even those that were in fact little more than rent-seeking transfers to private groups. Jonathan Macey argues that by applying all statutes "as though" they were public-regarding, the interpreter faithfully carries out the legislative design of statutes that are more or less public-regarding and minimizes the damage done by statutes that are not.[86] Macey's argument may justify Burger's reasoning in *Bob Jones*. The broad exemption in section 501 may well have represented the raw power of educational and religious groups to exclude themselves from taxation. To the extent that their exemption was shrouded in language ("charitable") indicating that these groups were somehow contributing to the public interest, it was perhaps appropriate for Burger to urge a process of weeding out organizations that are not very "charitable."

Interpretation to Open Up the Implementation Process   A related dysfunction is Congress's tendency to delegate policy decisions to agencies, which might then be "captured" over time by regulated groups or other interests.[87] Agency capture happens when the regulated group is significantly better organized than beneficiaries who are widely distributed throughout the polity and whose diffusion and numbers make them less likely to organize politically. The better-organized group is then able to "work" the agency over the years, maybe even turning the regulatory scheme to support its own private goals.[88] Statutory interpretation can operate (at least at the margins) to keep the implementation process open to critical perspectives and even to represent the voice of forgotten beneficiaries.

The Agricultural Marketing Agreement Act of 1937 permits milk producers to agree on minimum prices, subject to orders by the secretary of agriculture setting floor prices that handlers (who process the dairy products) must pay to the producers. In Block v. Community Nutrition Institute[89] the Supreme Court held that consumers cannot seek judicial review of the orders because the statute explicitly allows handlers to seek judicial review but is silent as to consumers. The Court reasoned that Congress's inclusion of review at the behest of handlers implicitly denied it to consumers, whose interests would be effectively represented by the handlers. Functionally, the Court's preclusion of consumer standing undermined the act's purpose of protecting the interest of consumers because the regulated group (milk producers) had built alliances with the regulators in the Agriculture Department and had bought off the handlers. For consumers, a diffuse and badly organized group, the result was higher prices and fewer choices.[90] Allowing judicial review at the behest of consumers might help retrieve the statutory purpose by opening up the calcified administrative process to consumer pressure. *Community Nutrition* is a bad decision because it negates a possible check on the administrative operation of a statute that authorizes price-fixing.

Interpretation to Protect the Interests of Marginalized Minorities   The most obvious application of representation reinforcement theory to statutory interpretation is, unexpectedly, the most difficult. Just as statutes penalizing "discrete and insular" minorities receive heightened constitutional scrutiny under this theory, so may the statutory interpreter presume against a construction that

hurts groups marginalized by the political process. Recall my earlier suggestion that in close cases the Court interpret statutes in favor of the interest
with less clout in Congress. At first glance neither precept helps us decide *Bob
Jones*, for the paradoxical reason that both groups (African Americans and
religious fundamentalists) have been marginalized in American politics in
much of this century, yet both had a robust political presence in the 1980s
and therefore had access to seek a legislative override.[91]

A historical understanding of how a group can come to be marginalized
helps us make more of this point. Although civil rights groups have apparent
political clout, the interests of African Americans are still undercounted in
our system because of the pervasiveness of unconscious racism.[92] Derrick Bell
has argued that from *Brown* onward our national policy has been to celebrate
the antidiscrimination principle in order to placate blacks and the international community, but not to expend real resources to implement the principle.[93] Bell's analysis provides a way of reconciling *Bob Jones* and *Allen v.
Wright:* the former decision (like *Brown*) reflected the distaste that upper-class
whites have for America's being perceived as a land of apartheid, and the desire of these elites to distance themselves from open racism and its ugly connotations, at little cost to themselves (they want to send their children to Davidson, not to Bob Jones). The latter decision (like *Brown II*) reflected the
willingness of the same elites to tolerate substantial nonenforcement of the
antidiscrimination principle in tax exemptions (if a school says it does not
discriminate, give it the exemption even though virtually no minorities are
actually enrolled), since more stringent enforcement of the policy might affect schools like Davidson and not just Bob Jones. This often reflects a country club attitude that is passively rather than actively oppressive. "It just never
occurred to me!" is a cheap excuse for tolerating racist structures.

Bell's historical and cultural analysis reveals deeper problems with legal
process approaches to statutory interpretation. "It just never occurred to me!"
pervaded the culture of the 1950s. Hart and Sacks and their heirs assumed
away problems with the electoral and legislative process, treating legislators
as presumptively reasonable, for example. To the extent that legal process
thinkers took a position, they endorsed open democratic pluralism yet never
thought to ask whether our system really is an open democracy and whether
legislators really are reasonable. The failure of legal process advocates even
to pose this question—in a decade of much-discussed racial apartheid (and
right after the wartime internment of Japanese Americans), McCarthy black-
lists for left-wingers, electroshock as the therapy of choice for "homosexuals,"
and legalized rape within *Ozzie and Harriet* marriages for women—might be
a result of unconscious attitudes held by the narrow constituency of legal
process.[94]

Alternatively, legal process theory's reluctance might be a result of the destabilizing nature of this type of inquiry. For example, the Congress that enacted the original charitable institutions tax exemption in 1894 represented at best a fragment of the American people, given the disenfranchisement of women, African Americans, and poor people. A liberal formalist is unperturbed by these defects, but a legal process functionalist might be expected to ask why she should obey statutes enacted by such an undemocratic process. Legal process theorists from the 1950s through the 1980s have not raised such questions.[95] The failure of legal process to develop a robust normative theory of democratic legitimacy is a striking deficiency in its usefulness in thinking about law, a deficiency that becomes glaring in light of the willingness of legal process theory to turn over so many policy decisions to unelected judges.

The Institutional Competence of Courts and Agencies to Make Statutory Policy

The final important legal process issue is institutional competence. If statutes are to be interpreted dynamically, who should be charged with the primary responsibility? The Supreme Court's decision in Chevron U.S.A., Inc, v. Natural Resources Defense Council[96] suggests outlines for a legal process theory under which it is agencies that do the dynamic interpreting. *Chevron* teaches that courts are second-order decision makers, deferring to agency decisions except when clearly inconsistent with the statutory mandate. Many scholars have embraced *Chevron*'s general point that agencies are usually more competent than courts to interpret statutes dynamically, while others have urged courts to exercise independent judgment.[97] Legal process thinking is sympathetic to *Chevron*'s concept that agencies ought to have wide leeway to interpret statutes dynamically, indeed wider leeway than courts, which are not as close to the political process and hence less acountable to it. Nonetheless, rigid adherence to *Chevron* threatens to unbalance government, a legal process horror. Courts should not defer to new agency interpretations when constitutional or other statutory rights are implicated, when the agency is shifting policy dramatically away from congressional preferences and toward presidential ones, or when the agency itself is acting nondeliberatively (i.e., the agency does not seriously consider the variety of interests at stake in the policy it adopts).

Chevron *and Judicial Deference to Agency Interpretation*

The Clean Air Act, as rewritten in 1977, required states that had not met federal ambient air quality requirements to establish a permit program to regulate "new or modified major stationary sources" of air pollution.[98] Between

1977 and 1981 the Environmental Protection Agency (EPA) experimented with various rules to implement the legislative directive. Industry groups argued for a "bubble concept" defining "stationary source" as a whole plant, thereby allowing firms to avoid applying for permits when they increased emissions in one part of the plant, so long as the plant's overall emissions level did not increase. The EPA rejected the bubble concept, however, and required plants in targeted states to obtain permits for any emissions increase anywhere within the plant.[99] In 1981 the EPA changed its position and adopted industry's bubble concept. The District of Columbia Circuit, in an opinion by Judge Ruth Bader Ginsburg, overturned the agency's dynamic interpretation as inconsistent with the statutory language and purpose.[100] The Supreme Court in *Chevron* reversed, holding that where Congress has not explicitly addressed the interpretive issue, courts should defer to the agency's decision so long as it is "reasonable."

Justice Stevens made three important points in his *Chevron* opinion. First, he found that the traditional indicia of legislative intent—statutory text and history—failed to provide a clear answer to the question whether the bubble concept is a permissible definition of "major stationary source." This finding is an important concession that traditional sources often support a variety of statutory interpretations (even for a recent statute such as the 1977 amendments), leaving substantial policy-making discretion to the interpreter. Second, Stevens found that in such cases, agencies, not courts, are the legitimate decision makers:

> When a challenge to an agency construction of a statutory provision, fairly conceptualized, really centers on the wisdom of the agency's policy, rather than whether it is a reasonable choice within a gap left open by Congress, the challenge must fail. In such a case, federal judges—who have no constituency—have a duty to respect the legitimate policy choices made by those who do. The responsibilities for assessing the wisdom of such policy choices and resolving the struggle between competing views of the public interest are not judicial ones: "Our Constitution vests such responsibilities in the political branches."[101]

Third, the opinion rejected the argument that the agency's change of position dilutes the deference owed to it. "An initial agency interpretation is not instantly carved in stone. On the contrary, the agency, to engage in informal rulemaking, must consider varying interpretations and the wisdom of its policy on a continuing basis."[102]

Stevens's opinion in *Chevron* is a legal process exemplar. It is an important recognition that statutory interpretation often involves policy-making choices, that the best interpretation can change over time, and that agencies are usually in a better position to make those choices than courts. *Chevron* delivers the punch line for Hart and Sacks's purpose-oriented approach to statutory interpretation: especially in complicated technical regulatory statutes, Congress cannot anticipate most problems of application. It can articulate a goal that it is pursuing; that goal is then carried out by statutory interpreters—mainly agencies, which have both the expertise and the political accountability to make the hard political choices Congress has not made. *Chevron* itself involved the sort of issue the political branches are more institutionally competent to handle; the acceptability of the bubble concept rests on judgments about how much extra pollution will be generated, how badly that will compromise the ability of nonattainment states to reach federal air quality standards, what the cost to industry and the country might be if the concept were not adopted, and how administrable are the bubble concept (will it be used as a cover for wider cheating?) and its alternatives (would it be easier just to police the plant as a whole?).

That *Chevron* is a defensible decision from the perspective of legal process theory does not mean that its progeny have been equally defensible. In 1970 Congress added Title X to the Public Health Service Act.[103] Title X provides federal funding for family planning services. Its purpose is to assist in making available "comprehensive voluntary family planning services." Title X authorizes the provision of federal funds to support the establishment and operation of voluntary family planning projects and empowers the Health and Human Services (HHS) secretary to promulgate regulations imposing conditions on grant recipients. Section 1008 stipulates: "None of the funds appropriated under this Act shall be used in programs where abortion is a method of family planning."[104] The 1971 HHS regulations provided that "the project will not provide abortions as a method of family planning" but did not regulate the form of counseling or the distribution of information at federally funded projects.

In 1988 HHS promulgated new regulations preventing personnel in Title X projects from providing any counseling or information about abortion.[105] In Rust v. Sullivan[106] the Supreme Court affirmed the agency's new regulations under *Chevron*, finding that the statute and its legislative history did not clearly answer the question, that the agency's interpretation was a reasonable reading of the statute, and that the agency's change in policy was one that the dynamic administrative interpreter was entitled to make. Stevens, the author of *Chevron*, dissented in *Rust* on the ground that the agency's position went well beyond, and arguably against, Congress's announced purpose of providing counseling and materials to help people plan their families.[107] He argued that the statute's exclusion of plans involving abortion as a "method" of family planning referred only to programs that actually perform abortions, not to those that provide professional information about the possibility. O'Connor dissented on the ground that issues of censorship and women's opportunities to obtain useful information raised constitutional questions that Congress needed to address.[108] Blackmun dissented, saying that the agency regulations were an unconstitutional infringement on doctors' First Amendment rights to provide information and counseling and on women's due process rights to abortion.[109]

However one resolves the constitutional issues, they were serious ones. Legal process theory should not be sympathetic to *Chevron* deference when the agency's interpretation gets the statutory purpose wrong or raises serious constitutional issues. Figuring out statutory purpose and harmonizing applications of statutes with legal and constitutional principles are the traditional strengths of judges, who are statutory generalists; *Chevron*-mandated deference to administrators (statutory specialists) in such instances is not appropriate. The heavy-handedness of the agency's censorship in *Rust* was a particular reason to exercise caution, and O'Connor's suggestion that decisions about censorship ought to be made in Congress if they are to be made at all is a splendid legal process point. (Ironically, it is a position she declined to take in her *Albertini* opinion.)

Constitutional Checks and Balances

Rust raises a second concern, that judicial deference to agency interpretation gives the president too much power to shift statutory policy. Cynthia Farina makes an excellent historical case that deference undermines the balanced lawmaking instinct in the constitutional structure.[110] I want to complement her argument with a game-theoretical analysis similar to the one in Chapter 2. If we look at the article I, section 7 procedures for lawmaking (bicameral legislative approval and presentment to the chief executive) as a sequential game,[111] we can see the implications of a broad reading of *Chevron* for the dynamics of the modern administrative state.

Under the article I, section 7 structure, the starting point for the game is the status quo (SQ), which prevails in the absence of legislation. If the median legislators in both chambers of the legislature (H and S) agree on a similar policy to replace the status quo, the legislature will want to pass a statute implementing the legislative preference. In a parliamentary system this would be the end of the game. In our presidential system the chief executive (P) may not prefer the legislative policy and hence may veto the legislation. The final move would then be that of Congress to override the veto, provided two thirds of the legislators in each chamber (h and s) preferred the median chamber preference to that of the president.

Figure 5.2 maps the apparent political preferences involved in enacting Title X in 1970. The preferences of the president (a budget-conscious moderate

```
                        x
    ─────────────────────────────────────────────
            H         S   P          SQ
```

Figure 5.2   Statutory policy $H < x < P$ when $H, S < P < SQ$

Republican) were more conservative than those of Congress but still sympathetic to a leftward change from the status quo ($H, S < P < SQ$). In that event, the policy equilibrium ($H < x < P$) would not be as sharp a departure from the status quo as in a parliamentary system because the president could credibly threaten to veto legislation that did not accommodate his preferences.

In the New Deal state most lawmaking is accomplished by agencies under the authority of statutory delegations. This shift to agency lawmaking is far beyond, and arguably against, the liberal assumptions of the framers, but is generally acceptable to legal process theory, which was formulated in the shadow of the New Deal. From a legal process perspective agency lawmaking offers potential benefits of expertise and rapid adjustment of rules to meet unforeseen circumstances. But it bears a risk of unbalancing government, of shifting too much policy-making power from Congress to the president.[112] Because the president has a great deal of control over the policy preferences of agencies (especially executive agencies), a regime of agency lawmaking may allow substantial displacement of congressional preferences for presidential ones in the implementation of statutory policy.

In Title X, Congress delegated rulemaking authority to HHS, effectively giving the agency some discretion in setting policy, limited by Congress's ability to override the agency's choice. Thus the agency with policy preferences near those of the president can propose any policy, x', at or to the right of the veto median (h or s) of the more pro-presidential chamber, and Congress cannot successfully challenge this interpretation (as there are not enough votes to override a veto). Instead of x, the original president-Congress compromise, the administrative state may produce x', as in Figure 5.3. This represents a shift in policy toward the preferences of the president and away from those of most members of Congress. We would not expect such a shift to occur immediately. Knowing that the president has this power, Congress would not delegate such power without assurances that its intended

```
                        x         x'
    ─────────────────────────────────────────────
            H         S         P   SQ
                                A
```

Figure 5.3   Statutory policy shifts from $H < x < P$ to $x' = P$ if Congress delegates lawmaking authority to executive-controlled agency

```
              x        x'         x*
    ─────────────────────────────────────
      H    S    P    h      s    P*
                A             A*
```

Figure 5.4 Statutory policy shifts from $x' = P, A$ to $x^* = s$ when president shifts rightward and Congress remains stable

policy (x) would be implemented, at least in the short term. Policy drift toward x' might occur in the longer term, however.

Thus far the discussion has assumed that congressional and presidential preferences do not change over time. But those preferences do change, and elections in 1952 (Eisenhower), 1960 (Kennedy), 1968 (Nixon), 1976 (Carter), 1980 (Reagan), and 1992 (Clinton) produced dramatic shifts in presidential preferences. Figure 5.4 diagrams the big switch in statutory policy statutes when there is a rightward shift in presidential preferences, as there was after the 1980 election. Note that even more dramatic shifts can occur, as illustrated in *Chevron*, where presidential preferences in the Carter administration (and its EPA) were to the left of Congress's (no bubble concept at all), while those in the Reagan administration were well to the right (the bubble concept was embraced).

Consider Figures 5.2, 5.3, and 5.4 as a sequential pattern. Under the procedures of article I, section 7, statutory decisions should cluster around the policy balance set by Congress (x). The administrative state not only skews this in practice toward the president's preferences (x'), but then subjects statutory policy to dramatic shifts when new presidents are elected (from x' to x^*). The sequence from Figures 5.2 to 5.4 roughly describes the shift in statutory policy by HHS that was litigated in *Rust*: the 1980 election left congressional preferences on the abortion issue pretty much where they were—the state should not encourage or assist abortions but should also not stand in the way of private actions—but shifted presidential and agency preferences strongly to the right. HHS moved policy to the right by adopting the "gag rule" (x^*). Although the new policy was contrary to congressional preferences, it was protected against override by the president's veto.[113]

The framers' modest restraints on congressional power to enact statutes reflecting legislative preferences have given way in the modern state to a substantial transfer of lawmaking power from Congress to the president, as illustrated in *Chevron* and *Rust*. This shift concerns legal process theorists because it is in tension with the constitutional lawmaking process and is less balanced and less majoritarian than the process envisioned by the framers. Congress has tried to counteract this reallocation of power in three ways. One mechanism, the legislative veto, has been negated by the Supreme Court.[114] A second response—legislative oversight and appropriations pressure—does affect policy, sometimes profoundly, but may not be as effective against executive agencies (whose heads can be fired by the president) and may doubly unbalance implementation by rendering executive officials more responsive to the preferences of a rent-seeking committee than to Congress generally. Let's focus on the third congressional response, judicial review.

Under traditional liberal theory aggressive judicial review is useful because it enforces the original article I, section 7 deal (x) against executive usurpation. Working from a legal process point of view, *Chevron* (I think correctly) rejects this defense of aggressive judicial review: there is often no clear "deal" to enforce, and for the hard issues of statutory interpretation there is no easily determined x. This was the case in *Rust*, for example.[115]

If statutory interpretation involves lawmaking choices over time, as *Chevron* suggests, the legal process inquiry then becomes one of how best to balance legislative expectations and other inputs into the lawmaking process. A regime of deference to agencies is on the whole less majoritarian than a regime of agency lawmaking checked by nondeferential judicial review. Even when there is no determinate original deal to enforce, judicial preferences concerning the best statutory policy are heavily conditioned by examination of the legislative deliberations leading up to the statute's enactment, and sometimes beyond that point (see Chapter 7). For cases where Congress's preferences have not changed much but those of the president have *(Rust)*, nondeferential judicial review draws policy back toward the original balance (even when the precise location of that balance is unclear). For cases where the preferences of both Congress and the president have shifted in the same direction, nondeferential judicial review tends to accommodate the new consensus, especially when the Court can rely on subsequent shifts in the legal terrain and on subsequent legislative discussions as evidence of a new majoritarian consensus *(Bob Jones)*. This is a simple positive political case for nondeferential judicial review.

More complexly, even if judicial preferences about statutory policy were completely unrelated to legislative preferences (well beyond the assumptions of *Chevron*), aggressive judicial review would not necessarily be countermajoritarian because it would create a new default position relatively less influenced by presidential preferences. Sticking with *Rust*, consider how different judicial preferences would affect the outcome of this new playing of the game.[116] For notational simplicity, assume that x is the original statutory equilibrium; A, P, H, S, and J represent current preferences (we shall omit the asterisks); and x' represents the new equilibrium.

Variation 1: Outlying Judicial Preferences ($J < H, S$)   Figure 5.5 maps the configuration of preferences where those of the current Court (J) are "outlying"—that is, they are not aligned with those of any of the other major players in the game. Judicial review introduces the judge as a decision maker who can create a new default position, much as the agency has done in our earlier

	x'		x			(x')		
J	H		S	h	s	A	P	

Figure 5.5 Statutory policy set at *x'* = *H*, rather than (*x'*) = *s* where *J* < *H*, *S*

examples. Under a regime of aggressive judicial review, the agency loses its policy-making advantage and will set policy at the House median, *H*. If the agency sets statutory policy anywhere to the right of the House median (*H*), the Court will want to overide the agency interpretation with its own preferred policy. Anticipating future moves of the other players, the Court will not set policy to the left of *H* because the House and Senate would override it. Anticipating the Court's moves, the agency will reluctantly set policy at the median.

The situation diagramed in Figure 5.5 is the *Lochner* scenario: activist judicial review implements the preferences of nonelected judges, which seems undemocratic. Figure 5.5 suggests that may be misleading. Even though statutory policy is pressed in the direction of judicial preferences, *J*, the ultimate position might better reflect congressional preferences, *x'* = *H*, than does the alternative without aggressive judicial review, (*x'*) = *s*. More important, in a situation like *Rust* the possibility of aggressive judicial review prevents the president from even trying to shift statutory policy from *x* to (*x'*) without going through the article I, section 7 process.

For many scenarios the existence of aggressive judicial review is relatively *less* countermajoritarian than deference to agencies controlled by the president. Conversely, under various scenarios aggressive judicial review would be relatively *more* countermajoritarian. If under the conditions of Figure 5.5 the House's preferences were significantly to the left of those of the Senate and the president, judicial review setting policy at *x'* = *H* would be more countermajoritarian than deferential review leaving policy at *x'* = *s*. I do not consider this a likely scenario, however.

Variation 2: Judicial Preferences within the Range of Current Congressional Preferences (H < J < s)   If the Court's policy preferences fall between *H* and *s* (a likely scenario), aggressive judicial review ameliorates the constitutional dilemma considerably more than it did in variation 1. Figure 5.6 maps the preferences. Under this configuration the Court has maximum freedom, for wherever it sets policy (such that *H* < *x'* < *s*), its policy will be protected

	x	x'		(x')			
H	S	J	h	s	A	P	

Figure 5.6 Statutory policy set at *x'* = *J*, rather than *x'* = *s* where *H* < *J* < *s*

from override.[117] Given the relative homogeneity of our mainstream political culture, the requirement of Senate confirmation for agency heads, and the attention courts have traditionally given to current congressional preferences, variation 2 is the most likely scenario. If that is so, aggressive judicial review would be promajoritarian—rather than countermajoritarian, as *Chevron* assumes—most of the time.

Variation 3: Judicial Preferences Aligned with Those of the President and Agency ($J > s$) The final variation assumes that judicial preferences are aligned with those of the agency, as mapped in Figure 5.7. Under this configuration the agency is free to set statutory policy at $x' = s$, which the Court will affirm on judicial review; both Court and agency realize that any policy to the right of the veto median, s, can be overridden by Congress with veto-proof margins. In this variation judicial review does not counteract antimajoritarian activism, but it does not contribute to it either.

Figure 5.7 provides a non-*Chevron* model for explaining *Rust* and solves a puzzle associated with the case. Presidential preferences on the abortion issue changed in 1981, but HHS did not adopt the gag rule until 1988. Some theorists would assume that HHS moved slowly because it was responsive to congressional pressures,[118] but in fact Congress moved in precisely the opposite direction (to the left, not the right) between 1981 and 1988, as the Republicans lost control of the Senate and lost seats in the House. My game-theoretical explanation is a better one: HHS would have been deterred by hostile judicial review in the early 1980s, for the Supreme Court's preferences in 1981 were pretty much lined up with the status quo (no abortions in Title X clinics, but no restrictions on giving medical advice).[119] Three years later *Chevron* was a political signal by the Court that it would tolerate a fair amount of policy shifting by Reagan administration agencies, to the detriment of liberal majorities in Congress, a thesis empirically supported by Linda Cohen and Matthew Spitzer.[120] Three new appointments to the Court between 1981 and 1988 (O'Connor, Scalia, and Kennedy) shifted the Court's substantive preferences to the right on both abortion and First Amendment issues (see *Albertini*). Once HHS perceived that the constitutional problems with a gag rule were less threatening, right after Kennedy began voting, the agency acted, with success. The Court in *Rust* upheld the agency by a five-to-four vote, with newly appointed Justice David Souter as the critical fifth vote. Congress was unable to override President Bush's veto protecting the agency

	x		x'				
H	S	h	s	J	A	P	

Figure 5.7   Statutory policy set at $x' = s$ when $s < J$

rule. The rule fell only after the 1992 election produced another shift in presidential preferences.[121]

I would not argue that nondeferential judicial review is invariably promajoritarian or never countermajoritarian. I do insist, however, that *Chevron* overstates the countermajoritarian potential for aggressive judicial review and neglects the ways in which unconstrained agency lawmaking can itself be countermajoritarian, as in *Rust*.

Relative Competence of Courts and Agencies to Make Policy Decisions

A lesson of the New Deal is that agencies are usually better situated to make policy judgments because they have more resources and expertise, are more flexible in responding to changed circumstances with new interpretations, and are better able to deal with the complex balancing involved in solving polycentric problems and to integrate an interpretation into a broader field of policy actions.[122] As statutory decision making has become increasingly technical and complex, the practicalities of the situation impelled courts toward greater deference long before *Chevron* stimulated academic and judicial excitement about the issue.[123] Is it true that courts are relatively less competent to make policy decisions?

Relevant to this inquiry is the debate over whether judge-made common law is efficient. A couple of different lines of argument maintain that it is. One rests on the selective nature of the common law adjudication process.[124] Judicial rules that are socially efficient will over time be recognized as such by litigants, who will tend to follow those rules and settle out cases involving them; hence, efficient rules will tend to yield little appellate litigation and, therefore, fewer chances of being changed. Inefficient rules, by contrast, will yield fewer settlements, more litigation, and more appeals; hence, they will offer more opportunities for change and reversal. This line of argument suggests structural advantages to case-by-case judicial policy-making, as opposed to general agency rulemaking. But it is vulnerable to the empirical criticism that the relative efficiency of legal rules does not demonstrably affect settlement rates.[125]

Gillian Hadfield raises another line of criticism.[126] She maintains that the main effect of common law rules is on primary activity, not settlement rates. The only cases that will get litigated are those involving perceived rule violators, and not rule obeyers or those who drop out of the activity once the rule is announced. Whatever the efficiency of the original rule, the "activity selection bias" of subsequent litigation will provide courts with skewed information about the world, which augurs ill for the efficiency of the rule's evolution. Paul Rubin has argued that the common law also reflects an "interest group bias" because organized groups are more likely to litigate issues of concern to them, perversely squeezing rent-seeking exceptions out of generally efficient rules.[127]

The second type of argument for the efficiency of the common law is that unelected judges are motivated to maximize social welfare,[128] unlike legislators and agencies, which often bow to rent-seeking pressures by interest groups who can assist their personal agendas for reelection or advancement. This argument rests on an overstatement on both sides of the equation. Modern learning about the behavior of agencies in particular belies the inevitability of "agency capture" by regulated interests. And no one has empirically demonstrated exactly what motivates judges.[129] The best empirical analogue is the literature on officials of nonprofit institutions, who accept relatively low salaries in return for increased leisure time, but this analogue provides little support for thinking that judges seek out efficient rules.[130] In addition, Hadfield's and Rubin's arguments undermine motivational theories of common law efficiency, for even if judges were interested only in welfare maximization, they could not achieve it if the information available to them were biased because of activity selection (Hadfield) or interest group strategizing (Rubin).

The economic literature gives us scant reason to believe that policy made by judges is any better or more efficient than policy made by legislatures or agencies. A point of agreement in the debate suggests at least one constructive role for courts in the creation of statutory policy. No one disputes the economic (and legal process) axiom that better information yields better decisions. By "better information" I mean inputs that more accurately reflect the entire range of factual circumstances and group perspectives as they relate to a legal problem. Agencies may well be able to generate better information than courts in most cases, and hence be in a superior position to make policy choices, but courts may be in a superior position to evaluate the extent to which an agency has made a real effort to inform itself and to base its decision on accurate information rather than just political whim. This suggests a legal process evaluation of *Chevron* itself: if one agrees that the EPA's decision to implement the bubble concept was based in good faith on a substantially complete array of information and perspectives, then the Court should defer to the agency's interpretation.

Deference is not appropriate under the legal process philosophy when the agency interpretation is not based on an evaluation of an adequate factual record in which a variety of interests are seriously considered.[131] This may have been the basis for the Court's refusal to defer in Motor Vehicle Manufacturers Association of the United States, Inc., v. State Farm Mutual Automobile Insurance Company.[132] In 1977 the National Highway Traffic Safety Administration (NHTSA) adopted a rule requiring that either air bags or passive seat belts be installed in all passenger vehicles by model year 1984. The Reagan administration's NHTSA issued a new rule revoking the passive seat belt requirement, based on a cost-benefit analysis; because the agency assumed that air bags would be widely used in the 1980s, it made little sense to require seat belts, which do not have to be used and, hence, would not necessarily contribute to traffic safety. Although the agency invoked a classic policy justification, the Court (on the eve of *Chevron*) rejected it because NHTSA did not explain why stricter alternatives—such as requiring air bags or nondetachable seat belts in all cars—were not justified. Legal process theory might support the Court's result and would consider it consistent with *Chevron* because the agency's dynamic interpretation did not seriously consider the traffic safety perspective.

That was the stated justification for overturning the agency's decision, but one suspects that the Court's underlying concern was that the agency had basically changed the policy as a response to the Reagan administration's philosophy of deregulation. If so, the case begins to look more like *Chevron*, and the legal process justification for not deferring becomes more ambiguous. *State Farm*'s refusal to defer is attractive to me because I believe the government should aggressively assert and enforce traffic safety measures; that result is less attractive to others who believe that state traffic safety rules impose unnecessary costs. The same point could be made about the other cases discussed in this and prior chapters: one's willingness to defer to the agency is influenced by one's substantive reaction to the agency's decision.

The foregoing analysis presents a final quandary for legal process theories of statutory interpretation. Such theories are substantive, insisting that statutory interpreters make and defend choices as to statutory purposes, overall principles and policies, and public values. Yet this move toward substance is usually undermined or submerged by legal process's anxiety about letting nonelected decision makers make value choices, which are bound to be controversial. Hence, from the beginning legal process has also craved neutrality in decision making.[133] Because substantive neutrality depends on a confidence in our polity's consensus about underlying norms of discourse which has evanesced since the 1950s, legal process thinkers searching for neutral criteria have been faced with a choice: either take the heat for openly purposivist or rationalist decisions which are going to be controversial where there is no community consensus, or base decisions on procedural grounds such as doctrines implementing the passive virtues (standing, political question, mootness, ripeness); the absence of a cause of action; deference to other decision makers, especially agencies and arbitrators; and requirements that correct procedures be followed, such as rules that habeas corpus petitioners exhaust their state remedies before coming into federal court.

My generation of lawyers is often not willing to take the heat required by the first strategy, but it finds the second one frustrating if not empty. Law and economics has taught us that erecting procedural barriers (such as standing, as in *Allen* and *Community Nutrition*) is the functional equivalent of curtailing the substantive right.[134] Critical theory has taught us that supposedly neutral rules of procedure are not designed nor do they operate randomly; they may be ways for elite culture to pretend to be open and inclusive while in fact remaining closed and exclusive.[135] Critical race theory, for example, is suspicious of neutral principles which eschew any commitment to results, for in a society assertedly stacked against racial minorities the procedural rule or neutral principle will be one that preserves an objectionable status quo.[136]

The *Chevron* literature is beginning to explore these critical insights. Although commentators hailed, or assailed, *Chevron* as a Magna Carta of agency independence and reduced levels of judicial scrutiny, the Supreme Court has applied *Chevron* selectively. In fact, the Court has been more willing to disregard agency interpretations after *Chevron* than before it.[137] The Court's selective invocation of deference is not unconnected with the Court's substantive views. For example, the politically conservative Rehnquist Court has been deferential to Reagan-era agency interpretations that dismantle regulatory and social welfare programs (as in *Chevron, Community Nutrition, Allen,* and *Rust*), while undeferential to agency interpretations that protect the civil rights of racial minorities (see Chapters 8 and 9).

Like the statutory interpretations explored in Chapters 1 through 4, *Bob Jones, Chevron,* and *Rust* are strikingly dynamic, arguably going against as well as beyond original legislative expectations. Legal process provides potential theoretical support for such interpretations, based on the New Deal concept that agencies (the IRS, EPA, and HHS) ought to have discretion to adapt statutory schemes to new circumstances, political regimes, and public values. The rationalist and democratic theory features of legal process thought offer grounds for criticizing those decisions as well. Do they reasonably serve statutory purposes? Are they consistent with other constitutional principles and legislative policies? Do they render statutes less partial? More just?

But these critical inquiries suggested by legal process thought depend on normative frames through which the interpreter approaches the statutory scheme. Because I believe in women's right to control their bodies and am enough of a rationalist to think that women can make better-informed choices if they have access to medical advice, I am unsympathetic to the gag rule in *Rust.* I am undecided as to *Chevron,* because I admire the nondegradation principle but am concerned about industry costs and have little intuition whether the bubble concept is cost-efficient. Inspired by the civil rights movement and *Brown,* I accept *Weber* and *Bob Jones* but remain skeptical that either decision represents anything more than ambiguous progress. Just as liberalism could not escape the normativity of dynamic statutory interpretation, neither can legal process theory.

6 · Normativist Theories

Both liberal and legal process approaches to statutory interpretation are founded on procedure-based theories of the state. Under liberal theory law derives from the consent of the governed, and legitimate rules are those whose authority can be traced back to a majority-based decision, usually made by an elected legislature (the surrogate for We the People). Under legal process theory law depends on its generation by the duly authorized institutions of the state. In Chapters 4 and 5, I suggested not only that liberal and legal process theories require dynamic statutory interpretation, but also that neither theory can prevent unelected interpreters from making value choices when they interpret statutes in the hard cases.

Consent and process are not the only ways to look at law's legitimacy. Their limitations were classically expressed more than a generation ago by Joseph Schumpeter:

> Let us transport ourselves into a hypothetical country that, in a democratic way, practices the persecution of Christians, the burning of witches, and the slaughtering of Jews. We should certainly not approve of these practices on the ground that they have been decided on according to the rules of democratic procedure. But the crucial question is: would we approve of the democratic constitution itself that produced such results in preference to a non-democratic one that would avoid them?[1]

While consent- and process-based theories are not without analytical tools to criticize such a polity (see Chapter 5), Schumpeter's inquiry challenges the state to justify obedience to its laws substantively rather than procedurally. Not only might citizens not consider a law ordering the slaughtering of Jews to be a "law" for which obedience is morally compelled, but the existence of such a law might call into question the polity's overall legitimacy.[2]

An insistence that law's legitimacy must rest on substance and not just procedure has inspired various "normativist"[3] theories of statutory interpretation that are manifestly dynamic. One inspiration for normativist theorizing has been natural law. Natural law theories assert either that a statute is not law unless it is consistent with larger moral precepts, or (more weakly) that statutes are and should be implemented with moral precepts in mind. Accordingly, interpreters will improve the legislative product, and hence will interpret statutes dynamically. A central problem with natural law theories is that we harbor doubts about the existence of natural law or our ability to recognize it even if it did exist.

Feminist and republican theorists assert that law's legitimacy rests on norms that are derived from dialogue among diverse groups in a society. Their "dialogic" theories, like legal process theories, look to procedural features of lawmaking and interpreting to judge legitimacy, but they go beyond legal process by taking a more critical stance toward law's norms. Declining to privilege the legislature as much as legal process theory does, dialogic theories subject the legislative product to ongoing scrutiny. Because dialogue over time brings in new and ever-changing interlocutors, and because its societal focus evolves, dialogic interpretation is dynamic. Dialogic theory makes no strong claims for ultimate or even immediate truth and hence does not suffer from the indeterminacy problem of natural law theory. Instead it suffers from the opposite problems: it may be insufficiently decisive or critical.

Another way of viewing state legitimacy is through the lens of postmodernism, the acid bath of modern political theories. It considers consent, duly established procedures, and moral order to be constructed language games and provides analytical tools that contribute to a lawyer's skepticism about modern theories of democracy, the rule of law, and statutory interpretation. Postmodernism suggests that statutory interpretation cannot help but be a dynamic practice. Though it offers no normative criteria for evaluating dynamic interpretations, postmodern thinking challenges the interpreter to be eclectic, tolerant, and nondogmatic in understanding law's practice. The postmodern skepticism about an objective rule of law and majority-based statutory applications finds support in the analysis in Part I of this book.

I cannot offer a normative theory of dynamic statutory interpretation that satisfies traditional rule of law or democratic criteria, for the criteria are themselves elusive in a postmodern world. I can only offer a theory derived from what I see as a normatively desirable conception of our polity. The theory, critical pragmatism, is one that I think will be attractive to others. Although the rule of law is not a law of preexisting and objectively determinable rules, it can be understood as a professional or social practice that respects commonly held conventions, traditions, and priorities. Statutory interpretation should be pragmatic, in that the interpreter has a responsibility to take practice seriously and to consider the consequences of different interpretive choices. Such interpretation should also be critical, using the interpretive moment as an opportunity to evaluate the practice in which the issue is situated, in light of criteria drawn from different political traditions surveyed in Part II of this book. Will an interpretation unsettle existing practice on which people have relied and institutions have been constructed (liberalism)? Does this interpretation take account of, and reasonably accommodate, a diversity of interests (legal process)? Is this interpretation responsive to social needs and public values (normativism)?

Natural Law

Liberal political theory is positivist, and legal process theory substantially so. Both accept a separation between the "is" and the "ought" in law: we can and should criticize laws as wrongheaded or even immoral, but such ethical criticisms do not undermine law's legitimacy, its claim to obedience.[4] In contrast, natural law theory asserts that positive law is and must be interconnected with overriding ethical principles such as justice, liberty, and equality.[5] Some advocates of natural law (such as Cicero and Aquinas) posit that not all the statutes enacted by the democratically accountable legislature will be "law." This widely rejected proposition does not concern me in this chapter.

I am here interested in the more broadly acceptable proposition that ethical principles do and should affect one's interpretation of statutes.[6] This proposition renders statutory interpretation dynamic, as the statute enacted by the legislature may not perfectly reflect natural law. Because our knowledge of natural law might itself be revealed over time, statutes would evolve even if the legislature's product perfectly reflected our understanding of natural law at the time of its enactment.

A more subtle natural law theory of dynamic interpretation is found in the work of Lon Luvois Fuller.[7] His 1940 Rosenthal Lectures at Northwestern University Law School, published as *The Law in Quest of Itself*, are a classic natural law exposition of statutory interpretation. The point of the first lecture was to contest the positivist claim—in science, law, and ethics—that we can separate description and evaluation or, for short, fact and value. Consider his argument:

> If I attempt to retell a funny story which I have heard, the story as I tell it will be the product of two forces: (1) the story as I heard it, the story *as it is* at the time of its first telling; (2) my conception of the point of the story, in other words, my notion of the story *as it ought to be* . . . If the story as I heard it was, in my opinion, badly told, I am guided largely by my conception of the story as it ought to be . . . On the other hand, if I had the story from a master raconteur, I may exert myself to reproduce his exact words . . . These two forces, then, supplement one another in

shaping the story as I tell it. It is the product of the *is* and the *ought* working together . . . The two are inextricably interwoven, to the point where we can say that "the story" as an entity really embraces both of them. Indeed, if we look at the story across time, its reality becomes even more complex. The "point" of the story, which furnishes its essential unity, may in the course of retelling be changed. As it is brought out more clearly through the skill of successive tellers it becomes a new point; at some indefinable juncture the story has been so improved that it has become a new story. In a sense, then, the thing we call "the story" is not something that is, but something that becomes; it is not a hard chunk of reality, but a fluid process, which is as much directed by men's creative impulses, by their conception of the story as it ought to be, as it is by the original even which unlocked those impulses. The *ought* here is just as real, as a part of human experience, as the *is*, and the line between the two melts away in the common stream of telling and retelling into which they both flow.[8]

"Exactly the same thing may be said of a statute or a decision," Fuller continued. "The statute or decision is not a segment of being, but, like the anecdote, a process of becoming."[9]

Fuller's analysis of the anecdote is a classic exposition of the inevitability of dynamic interpretation.[10] His second point, suggested more than developed in the Rosenthal Lectures, was that the interconnection between law and morality is a good thing. The main argument was one of coherence. Because the "bulk of human relations find their regulation outside the field of positive law," a continuous interpenetration of law and social morality creates a more seamless web of interconnected rights and duties.[11] Fuller emphasized that such interconnection was necessary to the efficacy of law; without a link with changing social mores, law would not be able to achieve its goals or, worse, would lose the respect of the citizenry.[12]

Before we turn to the final issue developed by Fuller (in his later work), let us consider his argument as applied to Gay Rights Coalition of Georgetown University Law Center v. Georgetown University.[13] Georgetown is a Roman Catholic university in Washington, D.C., and the Gay Rights Coalition of the Law Center was one of two groups of gay and lesbian students that sought university recognition in and after 1978. Reasoning that university recognition would imply approval of gay and lesbian activities, contrary to Catholic religious doctrine,[14] Georgetown denied the Coalition's application. The Coalition then sued Georgetown, arguing that its action violated the District of Columbia's Human Rights Act, which makes it "an unlawful discriminatory practice . . . for an educational institution . . . to deny, restrict or to abridge or condition the use of, or access to, any of its facilities and services to any person otherwise qualified, wholly or partially, for a discriminatory reason, based upon ... sexual orientation."[15] Georgetown argued that the statute could not require it to recognize, fund, and provide support to a gay and lesbian group without violating its First Amendment right to the free exercise of its faith.

The seven judges on the District's Court of Appeals who voted on the appeal wrote seven different opinions. All but one of the opinions explicitly recognized the importance of normative considerations in interpreting the Human Rights Act. The judgment of the court was delivered by Judge Julia Cooper Mack, who interpreted the act to require Georgetown to provide the gay and lesbian student groups with access and tangible benefits on the same terms afforded other student groups but not to require it to grant official "recognition."[16] The broad language of the Human Rights Act does not require this interpretation. But Mack was reluctant to turn the statute's broad command into a story in which the state "compel[s] a regulated party to express religious approval or neutrality towards any group or individual," for that would be jarringly inconsistent with our society's commitment to freedom of religion and our discomfort with state-compelled speech.[17] In the context of Georgetown's religious as well as secular educational mission and its plausible belief that recognition carried with it the implication of endorsement, Mack read the statute to allow the Catholic institution some discretion.

But not much. Mack required Georgetown to provide equal access and benefits to the gay and lesbian student groups, which Georgetown had strenuously resisted on the same free exercise grounds on which it had resisted formal recognition. Mack responded that once Georgetown was relieved of the obligation to recognize the gay and lesbian student groups, its free exercise interest became less compelling. Balanced against that interest was the compelling societal interest in protecting lesbian and gay students from tangible discrimination. In a remarkable survey of the medical and sociological literature, Mack debunked antihomosexual prejudices as unfounded and built a powerful normative case for protecting the rights of gays and lesbians.[18]

The dissenting opinions were just as normativist as Mack's opinion for the court. Judges John Ferren and John Terry criticized the court's acceptance of a regime that treated gay and lesbian student organizations differently from other student organizations.[19] To the extent that the court's statutory analysis was inspired by its constitutional concerns, they maintained that university recognition would not have been tantamount to endorsement and that Georgetown's free exercise rights were not abridged. Conversely, Judges James Belson and Frank Nebeker took the court to task for forcing Georgetown "to subsidize activities by those groups that offend the religious beliefs to which the university adheres."[20] They found the state's intrusion into Georgetown's religious freedom unjustified by the nondiscrimination policy, in part because they believed that such discrimination was not as much of a social problem as racial discrimination, for example.[21] Nebeker, in a separate dissent, went further, arguing that there was "no factor favoring a state inter-est under the Act which can be balanced against Georgetown's rights" because the "conduct inherent in homosexual 'life-style' is felonious" under the District's sodomy statute.[22] To make his normative point, Nebeker attached three pictorial examples of "propaganda used to announce dances and gatherings" among gay and lesbian students at George Washington University.[23]

The opinions in *Gay Rights Coalition* illustrate Fuller's point that the "is" and the "ought" are not easily separated in statutory interpretation. Because the various judges had such different normative responses to homosexuality and Catholicism, their accounts of the case are correspondingly heteroge-neous. Yet the opinions' normativity is also a strength because it renders the judges' decisions more transparent and instructive to the parties and to the general public.[24] Unhappily, the different decisions instruct us in different directions. Which is right? Fuller's Rosenthal Lectures offer us no criterion for deciding, and his subsequent work emphasizes a "procedural natural law" or an "internal morality of law" that characterizes a legitimate legal system.[25] Although Fuller's process-based natural law was an important foundation for the legal process school discussed in Chapter 5, a robust natural law theory of statutory interpretation—one that can evaluate rather than just appreciate the normative clash in *Gay Rights Coalition*—seeks something more than pro-cess alone.

A generation after Fuller's work, Heidi Hurd and Michael Moore have taken up this challenge.[26] Their theories of interpretation move toward the view that statutes should be interpreted to reflect underlying moral reality. Moore derives his theory of statutory interpretation from the rule of law val-ues identified by Fuller and from explicit consideration of the social conse-quences of different theories.[27] From these premises he defends a theory of interpretation that presumptively starts with the ordinary meanings of words and phrases in legal texts, and applies those words in light of statutory prece-dents, overall purpose, and values.

Natural law or moral values play a dual role in Moore's theory: not only does the interpreter check her result against moral values, but such values play an important role in helping her determine the meaning of words and phrases, the holdings of precedents, and statutory purpose. The values Moore invokes are not conventional values (widely held beliefs) but "real" values (be-liefs based on underlying moral reality). Moore concedes that we may not fully apprehend moral reality but insists that there is one and that we can know more about it over time.[28] Our improving, or at least changing, under-standing of moral reality alone ensures that statutory interpretation ought to be dynamic. Moore rejects any interpretation that is "glued to the past," for "[t]he meaning of words, the direction of precedent, and the nature of [values] are all items about which we can have developing theories."[29]

Hurd's natural law theory of interpretation rests on a rejection of theories of legal authority that are "content-independent" (Joseph Raz's term), in which law is a command or request to be followed for reasons apart from or in addition to its moral merits.[30] She argues that traditional legal theories of authority are incoherent, "[f]or it appears that to act *because one has been told to*, and not because the balance of reasons favors such action, is definitional of irrationality. How could it ever be rational to act contrary to the balance of reasons as one sees it solely because one has been told to do so?"[31] Hurd's solution to this paradox is that we should treat statutes as advice, as evidence of moral reality, but with no independent normative force.[32]

Hurd concludes that statutes not reflecting moral reality are not authoritative, and therefore are not law. Like Moore, she also argues that a natural law theory of legislation rejects static statutory interpretation in favor of a dynamic approach. Natural law theory "would call upon courts to interpret a statute by seeking to discover and to achieve the optimal state of affairs of which the statute is a natural sign." This "optimal state of affairs" is reached by interpreting statutes "in light of the purposes that they may best be made to serve" rather than "the intentions which legislators had in drafting them."[33]

The theories of Hurd and Moore provide a normative justification for dynamic interpretation of the Human Rights Act in *Gay Rights Coalition*. Because originalist theories of statutory interpretation rest on a command theory of legal obligation, the Hurd-Moore challenge to that theory necessarily rejects originalism. Hurd and Moore insist that statutory obligations are driven by present needs and values, not those of the past. Consistent with their teachings, Judge Mack read the Human Rights Act in light of larger principles—equal treatment of gay men and lesbians and the university's right to the free exercise of religion. Without the second principle it is hard to see how the act could be interpreted to allow Georgetown to refuse university recognition to the plaintiffs. Without the first principle it is hard to see how the free exercise clause of the First Amendment could be interpreted to require Georgetown to make its facilities and services available to the gay and lesbian student groups.

Yet Mack's opinion in *Gay Rights Coalition* reveals difficulties with the Moore-Hurd approach. Two moral values are in conflict, and two communities have radically different ideas about the moral reality underlying the conflict. I am a citizen of both communities, for I am a professor at Georgetown's Law Center and am openly gay. Although Georgetown University was internally divided by the lawsuit,[34] its position in denying recognition was unequivocal: it believed that granting university funds to gay and lesbian student groups, subsidizing them by providing office space, supplies, equipment, and telephone service, or authorizing their use of the university's name would constitute an endorsement of homosexuality inconsistent with Catholic religious tradition.[35] From the university's perspective the court's willingness to require it to subsidize speech with which it disagrees is morally question-able.[36] Georgetown had no necessary quarrel with Mack's analysis of the med-ical and historical literature about the etiology of homsexuality but main-tained that its objections to homosexuality rest on beliefs that same-sex intimacy is contrary to the Bible, is unnatural, and is morally indefensible—beliefs supported by centuries of Roman Catholic natural law literature. In-deed, it would be deeply ironic to force a Catholic institution to subsidize gay rights groups on the basis of "natural law"!

The gay, lesbian, and bisexual students viewed Georgetown's stance as wrong under a reason-based rather than Scripture- or tradition-based natural law. One gaylegal view of Mack's opinion is that it accurately represents mod-ern scholarship rebutting modern stereotypes and establishes a basis for a strong state antidiscrimination policy—which Mack then withheld from gay and lesbian students by interpreting the statute to permit continuing stigmati-zation. Would Mack have been willing to let Bob Jones University (see Chap-ter 5) refuse to recognize an African-American student group because it advo-cated interracial dating, to which Bob Jones objects on moral grounds? By treating gay and lesbian student groups so differently from racial or other groups, Mack's opinion echoed the invidious differentiation and exclusion of gays and lesbians practiced by the Catholic church. It invited the charge that it was just a kinder, gentler homophobia.

What is the morally right answer to *Gay Rights Coalition?* I do not know. Confronting each other in the case were two immiscible moral realities. This dissonance suggests that in some cases there is no underlying moral reality or that moral values will usually be unknowable to us or heavily dependent on context. Moore and Hurd surely have pitches they can make about the moral reality of *Gay Rights Coalition,* but they would be hard-pressed to do a better job than the seven judges of the District's Court of Appeals—seven judges whose different perspectives leave me with a sense that there is no single right answer to this case.

Assume that Moore and Hurd could demonstrate a morally right answer in *Gay Rights Coalition.* They would still confront the problem of the sore loser, a problem inherent in statutory interpretation litigation under a natural law theory. Say their moral resolution were to give the gay and lesbian students recognition and/or access (Mack's position or Ferren's). Under their theory, why should Georgetown obey the judgment, which it would consider con-trary to natural law? Hurd seems to think that the priests might change their minds about moral reality after reading the seven opinions (or even reading the statute), but that was a dim possibility in *Gay Rights Coalition,* and is rarely the losing party's reaction. Nonetheless, the loser obeys the judgment, and for reasons that go beyond the penalties resulting from disobedience. In other words, moral obligation to obey the law typically stems from content-independent reasons, contrary to Hurd's central thesis.

Like Hurd and Moore, Joseph Raz argues that authoritative directives should be based on reasons that would make sense independently of the directives. Unlike Hurd and Moore, Raz argues that citizens (such as Georgetown) have a moral duty to obey directives with which they disagree (such as the Human Rights Act, as interpreted). He posits that "there is no point in having authorities unless their determinations are binding even if mistaken (though some mistakes may disqualify them)."[37] Unless we are absolutely certain of a law's moral error, which is rare given my earlier discussion, deference to other people's judgment itself becomes a content-independent reason to follow the law. Even if we are convinced that the law is morally mistaken, we still might rationally follow it because we consider it in our interest to privilege the rule of law over our own moral evaluations in most cases. This moral concern is particularly important in a pluralist society, where there are always several competing conceptions of "the good" or "the right."

The cogency of Raz's argument is illustrated by the fallout from the court's judgment in *Gay Rights Coalition*. Some within the university community were morally aghast at the judgment and determined to resist it; some supported the judgment; and a critical middle group disagreed with the judgment but believed that Georgetown's interests were best served by making peace with the students. The latter two groups prevailed, and a settlement was reached assuring the gay and lesbian student groups of equal access to university services, facilities, and benefits (but not official recognition). When Congress overrode the *Gay Rights Coalition* judgment with the Armstrong amendment, specifically permitting religious educational institutions to discriminate on the basis of sexual orientation,[38] Georgetown made no effort either to support the amendment or to break its agreement with the students, even though there is no indication that its officials were any more persuaded of the moral correctness of the court's judgment. Georgetown's response was nonetheless a rational one because it believed that its religious as well as its secular educational mission would be compromised by any perception that it was breaking its promises contained in a good faith settlement of the case or, worse yet, "going after" the gay and lesbian students.[39]

A problem that besets the leading natural law theories of statutory intepretation is the problem of normative pluralism. Natural law theories are most appealing in a homogeneous culture, for it is easier to conceive of right answers and universal moral reality in such a culture. The United States in the 1940s and 1950s (when Fuller was writing) may have thought itself such a culture, for legal discourse was defined as well as limited by the world of Anglo-Saxon elites and their assimilated ethnic allies.[40] The United States of the 1990s is not such a culture, for groups excluded or submerged in the 1950s—African Americans, women, religious fundamentalists, consumers, Latinos, lesbians and gay men, bisexuals, Native Americans, Asians—have become insistent, even if often still at the margins. However one characterizes them, whether as different voices or competing interest groups, they have proliferated. On legal issue after legal issue these fresh voices or new groups have unhinged natural law understandings.

Feminist Republicanism

The evanescence of the cultural conditions for natural law reasoning only heightens the importance of devising a useful normative discourse for dynamic statutory interpretation. Legal scholars have drawn on a wide range of sources—especially feminism, pragmatism, and republicanism—to reconcile their desire for a normativist grounding for statutory interpretation, with a recognition of the nation's underlying and indeed deepening normative pluralism. These diverse intellectual backgrounds have fed an overriding impulse toward regarding statutory interpretation as a dialogue among different perspectives.[41]

Dialogic statutory interpretation accepts Fuller's insight that one's normative framework will and should influence one's interpretation but is concerned that the interpreter's framework will be too narrow. Like Fuller and subsequent legal process thinkers, feminist and republican theorists believe that statutes evolve over time, but they conceptualize the process as a more collective project. Like Moore and Hurd, they believe that achieving right answers is more important than deferring to an alienated original meaning, but they are less confident about the possibility of right answers and believe that the accommodation of colliding norms, reflecting the collision of communities of interpretation, should be the central inquiry. The feminist and republican projects recognize incongruent normative communities in statutory interpretation and seek reconciliation and ongoing citizenship. In this section I develop a feminist republican theory of dialogic interpretation from various legal materials, apply the theory to the *Gay Rights Coalition* case, and use that case to suggest the theory's limitations.

Republican Justifications for Government

Under liberal and legal process theory the legitimacy of the state depends on formal or functional theories of consent to certain procedures and institutional arrangements for lawmaking. Under natural law theories legitimacy depends on substance alone, namely, the congruence of the state's laws with moral reality or principle. Under modern versions of civic republicanism legitimacy depends on both substance and procedure because the state exists as a public organism to deliberate (procedure) for the common good (substance).[42] Inspired by classical Athens and Renaissance Florence, the civic republican ideal is a politically hyperkinetic city-state in which citizens share a commitment to debate toward consensus and responsibility for making politics work. In such a republic law is neither social control nor authoritative commands; rather, the political and social cultures continuously interact in what Robert Cover called "jurisgenerative" (norm- or law-creating) moments.[43] Republicanism integrates not only the "is" and the "ought" but also the "what might be," for it contemplates that people's preferences may be transformed through the political experience. Republicanism is a grand aspiration for law but falls athwart the same difficulty as natural law theory: our society does not enjoy the homogeneity and political intimacy of historical city-states. To use Cover's terminology, we are a plurality of normative worlds (*nomoi*) rather than a single one *(nomos)*.

Gay Rights Coalition illustrates our normative heterogeneity. The Roman Catholic community in which the court found Georgetown to exist is a *nomos*, for it draws on a common history and tradition in which its members are educated and which provide the community "a sense of direction or growth that is constituted as the individual and his community work out the implications of their law." Like other *nomoi*, Georgetown is a "strong community of common obligations," and common "initiatory, celebratory, expressive, and performative" discourse.[44] The Catholic *nomos* teaches that homosexual behavior is a serious sin. Although the church offers "homosexuals" compassion as people, it does not tolerate actions it considers sinful. Georgetown University, as part of the Catholic *nomos*, did not ostracize gay men, lesbians, and bisexuals; it refused to include only those groups it thought would encourage prohibited homosexual activity.

To flourish, a normative community needs protections against too much state intrusion; a certain degree of insularity is required for the community to educate its members, discuss issues of importance to it, and adapt its central values and messages to changing times. The conditions of insular autonomy required by religious *nomoi* are ensured in our republic by the free exercise clause of the First Amendment. The clause invalidates some statutes but more often operates as a cautionary canon of statutory interpretation. Indeed, the starting point for Judge Mack's analysis was the "deeply rooted doctrine that a constitutional issue is to be avoided if possible," and the opinion for the court read the Human Rights Act "so as to avoid difficult and sensitive questions concerning the scope of the First Amendment," specifically the free exercise clause.[45]

Mack's opinion also recognized the emergence of a new *nomos*, the gay and lesbian community.[46] Though different in kind from the Catholic church, the gay community shares most of its "nomic" characteristics, including common experiences that have engendered a shared framework of thinking about a wide range of issues; formal organizations for reporting and comparing those experiences, expressing group identity, and developing group positions; and a collective commitment to implementing shared values in people's lives. Like other nonreligious nomic communities, the gay community's insularity is not protected by the free exercise clause, but it is protected by other First Amendment guarantees of free speech and assembly. The equal protection clause potentially shields gay, lesbian, and bisexual communities from arbitrary state intrusion as "discrete and insular minorities," a point explicitly invoked by Mack.[47]

Gay Rights Coalition would be a simpler case for modern republican theory if the state were invading either *nomos*, through meddling in the affairs of the church or in the personal affairs of lesbians, gay men, and bisexuals.[48] Instead, the case involves two normative universes squarely in conflict—colliding norms, if you will. This collision is hardly unusual for statutory interpretation cases in our culturally and economically heterogeneous nation. Indeed, it is the fecundity of jurisgenesis, its proliferation within different nomic communities, that gives rise to the need for law. The role of the judge or the agency in statutory interpretation then tends to be jurispathic; the state arises out of the need "to suppress law, to choose between two or more laws, to impose upon laws a hierarchy."[49]

If this account of *Gay Rights Coalition* is correct, one wonders what republican theory has to offer to the practice of statutory interpretation. Indeed, legal academics have not applied republicanism in its classic form but have instead examined it through the lenses of modern political theories—including pragmatism, hermeneutics, and feminism.

Practical Reasoning and Feminist Theory

Accommodating conflicting and colliding norms is the most difficult problem in statutory interpretation theory and practice.[50] Although republicanism's interest in the common good may not suggest definitive ways to do so, its parallel interest in practical reasoning offers greater promise.[51] A major challenge faced by republican or pragmatic theorists is to develop practical reasoning as a way of treating colliding norms in statutory interpretation.

In this effort feminist theories provide many leads.[52] Early "liberal" feminist theory gave way in the 1980s to theories that share republicanism's skepticism toward liberal theories of individual autonomy, rights discourse, and neutral principles. Prominently, cultural feminism poses an "ethic of care" as a way of viewing problems different from the traditional "ethic of rights."[53] Liberal or legal process jurisprudence, developed by a male-dominated Western culture, assumes the primacy of the individual, whose autonomy is protected and bounded by rights and duties observable from statutes and constitutions; traditional law tends to set bright line rules or utilitarian balancing tests which represent themselves as neutral, objective, and determinate—and tends to deny or suppress the conflicting interests or colliding norms in dispute. Cultural feminism valorizes an ethic of care which recognizes the primacy of the community and of communities within the larger polity, and situates individuals not as autonomous but as connected with one another, and with a variety of communities. This approach considers statutory interpretation an opportunity to understand and reconcile, rather than to deny or suppress, norms in collision. Decision making is not, therefore, rule-based, rights-oriented, or balancing. Nor is it abstract, neutral, or hierarchical. Under the practical reasoning of cultural feminism, decision making is concrete and situated, engaged, and weblike.

Although cultural feminism does not maintain that all women are attracted to an ethic of care, its ideas have been drawn from women's experiences in our society. It may be instructive to compare Judge Mack's opinion with those of her six male colleagues. The four dissenting judges invoked the argot of rights and balancing and adopted rigid denunciatory stances in their opinions. Mack, in contrast, focused on community needs and group interests. Rather than speaking of the "violation" of Georgetown's free exercise "rights," as her dissenting brethren did,[54] Mack discussed the "burden . . . on Georgetown's religious exercise," and the "interest" of the larger community in eliminating discrimination based on sexual orientation.[55] In her treatment of the colliding norms—free exercise of religion and ending discrimination—Mack's opinion was even more distinctive, for she was open to long-submerged voices but also sought reasonable accommodation of their needs. Analyzing the District's interest in antidiscrimination, amply revealed in the legislative history, Mack subjected the legislature's findings to independent but sympathetic examination in light of the history of society's understanding of homosexuality. She expanded the record to consider information about the nonvolitional nature of homosexuality (a subject still being studied), the persecution of gay men and lesbians, and the ways in which such persecution demeans the community.

Significantly, Mack's analysis drew sharp disagreement from concurring Judge Theodore Newman, who argued for simple deference to the District's legislative judgment. He invoked the traditional criticism of courts sitting as "super-legislatures to divine the importance of governmental interests" and urged courts to hew to "what are surely the main qualities of law, its generality and its neutrality."[56] In his emphasis on deference to hierarchy, generality, and neutrality, Newman detached himself from the normative debate in the case. Judges Belson and, particularly, Nebeker shared Mack's inclination to subject the legislative policy to independent normative scrutiny—but their dissenting opinions evidenced a traditional hostility to bisexuals, gay men, and lesbians.[57]

Feminist theory is familiar with the ways in which traditional jurisprudence marginalizes the interests of groups outside the traditional elites, for that is how family law, the crime of rape, and employment law have been constituted to the disadvantage of women. In part because women have directly experienced social domination, feminist thought has been critical of traditional legal theory for its complacency and its failure to understand or recognize "the perspective of the oppressed."[58] As a corollary of their focus on women's marginalization, feminist practice has explored modes of social marginalization generally. Feminists tend to be particularly critical of accepted dividing practices.[59] Their perspective is, again, reflected in Mack's opinion. In contrast to Nebeker, who wrote from the baseline of traditional prejudice, and Newman, who wrote from the baseline of the status quo and its slow-moving legal process, Mack made out a concrete case for treating gay men and lesbians with equal respect.

An important theme of cultural feminism is that one does not have to approach colliding norms from a win-lose perspective (the ethic of rights); one can instead try to reformulate the apparent conflict, approaching it from a different angle which seeks to reconcile various normative commitments (the ethic of care). This theme, too, is prominent in Mack's opinion. The parties posed the issues in the lawsuit in starkly dichotomous win-lose terms: either Georgetown was required to recognize the gay and lesbian student groups, with all the attendant benefits, or it was not. This way of posing the issue sharpened the normative conflict in the case. Over the strong objection of most of her male colleagues, Mack found this an unproductive way of looking at the case, and bifurcated the issue into one of recognition and endorsement, on the one hand, which reflected Georgetown's core objection, and one of access to benefits, on the other, which reflected the students' main demands. In analytical terms this move permitted Mack to save the Human Rights Act from serious constitutional difficulty while preserving its core policy. In practical terms it enabled her to show both sides that she had attended to their key interests and to offer a result that accommodated the most significant needs of each group.

What is most remarkable about Mack's opinion is its effort to minimize the "jurispathic" (literally, law-killing) role to which most statutory and constitutional interpreters are resigned. The parties arrayed themselves in the traditional adversarial postures, in which the lawsuit resembles a jousting match— a battle to the death between two normative visions (free exercise takes on antidiscrimination). The judges themselves seethed with legal bloodlust, most notably in Nebeker's assaultive opinion, but also in the opinions of Ferren and Terry, who insisted on subordinating Georgetown's interests entirely and handing a complete victory to the gay and lesbian students. Most of the judges saw their role as jurispathic—killing the claims of a vibrant (but to each objectionable) nomic community under the aegis of law's empire.

Such authoritarian judging is questionable under republican and feminist theory because it exacerbates the tension identified by Frank Michelman between our ideals of self-government and of a government of laws.[60] The freedom proclaimed in self-government is in tension with the constraint ensured by government of laws. By taking an imperial stance that exercises dominion over one of the two communities at the bar, the authoritarian judge denies one of the two communities the freedom to live by its own norms, thereby abridging that community's citizenship, its part in self-government. Given the assumptions of our nomic pluralism, authoritarian judging and law's empire will undermine self-governance. Set against this is a vision of law's republic, in which the interpreter seeks out a role that is jurisgenerative—offering reconciliation and opportunities for a "dissolution of difference" between clashing communities. Reconciliation can come through dialogue: the interpreter hearing each side sympathetically, experimenting with new ways of posing the problem to protect the interests of each in part, and presenting the communities with opportunities to speak to each other afresh, perhaps with the hope that preferences can change.

Drawing on the feminist republican theories of Martha Minow and Suzanna Sherry in particular, Michelman has suggested some themes characteristic of this "reconciliatory project." He writes:

> The *dialogic themes* express the vision of social normative choice as participatory, exploratory, and persuasive, rather than specialized, deductive, or demonstrative. They emphasize openness to "otherness" as a way toward recognition not only of the other, but also of oneself.
>
> The *historical themes* express the sense that the conversation neither begins nor ends now. We have individual pasts and a collective past, and those pasts raise for us issues of identity and integrity. At the same time we have, we hope, our individual and collective futures, and our conversation now ought not to foreclose future conversations.
>
> The *responsibility themes* express demands for both clear-sightedness and personal engagement. They warn against the comforts of legal abstraction, hiding or overlooking actualities of social disadvantage. They protest against projection of the agency of decision onto a distant force—such as law or state—when the truth is that their distance is what we make it by our deference.
>
> The *identity themes* reflect the tug between the demands for both ethical situation and personal "space" as dual conditions of freedom. They also point most obviously towards the irresolvable tension between generality and particularity that pervades the reconciliatory enterprise as a whole.[61]

Under this vision of statutory interpretation Mack's opinion is an overture to the parties, and its most brilliant move is the creation of a dialogue between the two communities: Georgetown has to let the gay and lesbian students become participants in the intellectual and social community, but on face-saving terms for the university, while the students have to respect Georgetown's perspective even as they seek to persuade other students of its error. As the faculty adviser to the Georgetown University Law Center's student group (Bi-LAGA), I think Mack's opinion has been "jurisgenerative" (law-creating). Openly bisexual, gay, and lesbian students have a forum for mutual support and expression, while Georgetown has become a better educational institution without sacrificing its Roman Catholic identity.

Evaluating Feminist Republican Interpretation

There are three ways to disagree with the foregoing approach to statutory interpretation. One is to challenge its underlying theory of political legitimacy. Contrary to the liberal and legal process theories explored in Chapters 4 and 5, feminist republicanism insists that the legitimacy of state action requires more than following the regularized procedures for the enactment and application of laws. It holds that every time the law is applied, the state must treat all the affected interests with concern and must work to minimize the jurispathic possibilities of law. Liberal or legal process theory would object that feminist republicanism faithfully applied asks too much of government. Newman's posture of deference to legislative judgments may seem less noble than Mack's inquiring stance, but it may also be less taxing and more feasible for overworked state actors.

Natural law theory would object that feminist republicanism asks too little of government. Unlike most natural law theories, feminist republicanism does not insist that state legitimacy be measured against any unitary conception of the common good. The republican revival has all but abandoned classical republicanism's confidence that we can know what the "common good" is. Republicanism substitutes procedural bases to evaluate the legitimacy of state actions for the substantive ones (purpose or moral reality) favored by natural law. Once one embarks on the path of normativity, as Mack does, why not go all the way to the moral judgment of a Ferren or a Nebeker rather than being satisfied with just another procedural way station, albeit a sophisticated one?

Dialogic theorists could invoke feminist analysis in response to either the liberal or the natural law vision of politics, challenging their assumptions that theories of political legitimacy must always choose between procedure and substance, consent and normativity, democracy and coercion. Why can't political theory seek to mediate between values that we cherish and resolve the tensions in different ways, depending on context? This challenge, however, can be turned back upon dialogic theories, because the mediation itself requires justification from context; and when context is expanded, justification sometimes disappears. The republican justification for Mack's opinion in *Gay Rights Coalition* rests on her willingness to listen to both sides and to reconcile colliding norms. But that justification depends heavily on contingent characterizations of the two communities, the norms in collision, and the consequences of the court's judgment.

Based on the testimony of Georgetown president Timothy Healy, general statements in various university booklets, membership in several associations of Roman Catholic educational institutions, and a few policy decisions (e.g., its hospital will not perform abortions), Mack concluded that Georgetown is a Roman Catholic institution,[62] and this characterization permitted her to invoke Catholic religious values throughout her opinion as a justification for a narrowing interpretation of the Human Rights Act. As a professor at Georgetown's Law Center, I find the situation more complicated. The school's Catholic connections have little impact on what I perceive to be the educational experience and academic dialogue at the Law Center. The courses are completely secular; the professors usually take positions on controversial issues such as abortion, gay rights, public aid to parochial schools that are contrary to Catholic doctrine; the traces of religious influence in our scholarship is as likely to be Jewish or Protestant as Catholic; school programs are secular; faculty hiring and student admissions are with few exceptions unaffected by religious considerations; and funded student groups regularly advocate activities that are contrary to Catholic teaching, though such advocacy is sometimes met with administrative resistance. The Law Center faculty voted overwhelmingly to support the gay and lesbian students in *Gay Rights Coalition*. The main campus reveals a greater Roman Catholic presence and social conservatism, but I doubt much more. For example, the undergraduate school's Student Activities Commission and its Student Senate voted in 1979 to recognize the gay and lesbian student groups "for the purpose of providing a forum where all students of Georgetown may come to understand the concerns of Gay Students."[63]

Even at the level of formality and labels Georgetown's Catholic affiliation is ambiguous, for the university participates aggressively in the secular world on secular terms. As of 1979 Georgetown had long tolerated student organizations that openly advocated ideas and actions contrary to Catholic teachings, such as the nondivinity of Jesus Christ. Even the sources cited by Mack emphasize the school's educational mission and state any religious mission in extraordinarily general terms. For example, President Healy's 1979 annual report said: "Any university is a creature of time and is by its nature secular. Our job is to discover what impact the habit of belief in God has on the secular reality of a university, on its teaching, its learning, its research and its service."[64] The clearest specific statement in a university publication of the Catholicism of the institution was, ironically, its commitment to "a basic, widely accepted view of humankind. It sees all men [*sic*] as essentially equal, as endowed with a human dignity always to be respected."[65] If *this* is what Catholicism means to Georgetown, it is hard to see why the school refused to recognize the gay and lesbian student groups.

Indeed, even if Georgetown were considered nothing more than an arm of the Roman Catholic church, the invocation of the church's free exercise of religion as a justification for excluding gay and lesbian student organizations is open to debate and in fact is debated within the church. Although official church doctrine currently maintains that homosexual activity is sinful, this stance is more recent than the Catholic hierarchy admits and is supported by questionable readings of Scripture.[66] Throughout most of the Middle Ages, the church tolerated same-sex intimacy among its clerics and performed same-sex union and possibly same-sex marriage ceremonies between men.[67] The adamancy of the church today against homosexuality strikes me as having less to do with religion than with the defensive reaction of a homosocial institution (the all-male priesthood) to societal homophobia. Such institutional homophobia is cruel because it tangibly contributes to families' hostile attitudes toward their gay and lesbian members. It is also hypocritical, given estimates that between 20 and 50 percent of Roman Catholic priests are gay and that many of them engage in homosexual activity.[68] Bigotry, cruelty, and hypocrisy are inconsistent with the teachings of Jesus Christ—in whose name Christian doctrine is promulgated—as reported in the Gospels.

These characterizations are uncharitable to Georgetown and the Catholic church, but they are as plausible as the characterizations in Mack's perhaps excessively charitable opinion. Her willingness to accept Georgetown's projection of itself as a Catholic institution opposing the students on principle thus infects Mack's normative discussion, turning her admirable concern for the school's religious integrity into a concession to its hypocrisy. And at what price to the gay and lesbian students? Almost all of the judges believed that the students primarily wanted "things"—money for their activities, an office with a phone, places to hang their posters. This, too, seems to have been the judges' projection of their own values, for the record indicated that what the students wanted was intangible. Dissenting Judge Ferren believed that the students' main demand was integration, which the court arguably declined to provide. Ferren charged that the court's interpretation of the statute "permits a 'separate but equal' access to university facilities and services reminiscent of the justification that once permitted blacks on public buses, but only in the back."[69]

This assessment, in turn, may be an unfair charge against Mack's opinion, in part because Ferren too quickly conceptualized the gay and lesbian community as a minority seeking integration into the great melting pot (a characterization also made by Mack). The gay, lesbian, and bisexual community is just as internally diverse as Georgetown itself.[70] One line of division has been between assimilationists, who mainly want acceptance in American society notwithstanding their sexual orientation, and the radicals or separatists, whose sexual orientation provides a stance from which to criticize the institutions of compulsory heterosexuality. Ferren's charge reflects his assumption that the concept of gay rights is essentially assimilationist, but that charge rings false to "queer crits," for whom the university's disapprobation is more like a badge of honor than the back seat of the bus.

The quandary raised by the foregoing analysis is that even the best exemplars of dialogic statutory interpretation—the opinions of Mack and Ferren—suppress complexities within the nomic communities they address. How much more simplifying are the opinions of Newman, Belson, and Nebeker (and how much more typical are their approaches). Law's republic is not with us yet.

Postmodernism and Statutory Interpretation

Liberal, legal process, and most normativist theories of statutory interpretation reflect the "modernist" assumption that an authoritative, legitimate answer to a statutory puzzle can be arrived at through a process of reasoning that itself legitimates the answer. Because the answer is arrived at through a method independent of the specific interpreter, a good interpretation can be replicated by other interpreters and is a legitimate application of the rule of law. Because the answer is linked to work accomplished by a representative legislature, it is authoritative for democratic theory reasons. Part I of this book argues that theories of statutory interpretation resting on originalist methodologies are not able to satisfy these modernist conditions for legitimacy and authoritativeness. Not only is statutory interpretation going to be dynamic, but it is going to be dynamic in ways that are dependent on unpredictable changed circumstances, the perspective of the interpreter, and the current political context.

Part II has continued this modernist story, but in greater depth, arguing that different political theories (liberalism, legal process, natural law) provide normative support for the dynamism of statutory interpretation. The inquiry has taken a turn in Part II, however, as we have discovered little assurance that statutory dynamism will be predictable or that interpretive discretion will be reliably constrained by any of the theories of dynamic statutory interpretation. In short, dynamic theories may not meet the modernist assumptions any better than the originalist theories questioned in Part I. The methods introduced in this book for criticizing modernist-based originalist reasoning can be extended to criticize modernist-based dynamic reasoning.

Conversely, the approaches to statutory interpretation that strike me as most attractive in Part II are those that are the most modest: the invocation of pragmatic, situational metaphors in the theories of Daniel Farber and Alex Johnson (statutory cy pres) and Richard Posner (the platoon leader analogy), the statutory Socratic method of Henry Hart and Albert Sacks's teaching materials on the legal process and Lon Fuller's metaphors and analogies, and feminist-republican dialogue suggested by Suzanna Sherry, Martha Minow, and Frank Michelman. Should statutory interpretation theory abandon or soften its modernist insistence that reason can yield determinate answers, tied to legislative expectations and capable of replication by differently situated interpreters? In this section I explore the implications of postmodernism for statutory interpretation.[71]

The implications are mostly critical. Postmodern theorists believe that traditional legal reasoning is both a malleable language game and a social creation. The analysis in this book lends support to this belief. In the argot of postmodernism, reasoning traditionally conceived depends on hierarchies and concepts which can be "deconstructed," especially those that involve intent, language, and norms central to traditional theories of statutory interpretation and the rule of law. Deconstruction suggests that there are several different "reasoned" solutions to an interpretive problem—or no single one. Social constructionist theory posits that the solution we actually arrive at is constructed by us and by the social practices that we have internalized. It suggests that interpretation is a localizing practice rather than a universalizing method, thereby reinforcing deconstruction's challenge to traditional rule of law theory. In its further emphasis on the way in which law is deployed to create or strengthen subordinating power relations, social constructionism undermines democratic theory as a legitimating device.

The postmodern attitude considers statutory interpretation dynamic because nothing is static. Other than that, and the skepticism it throws on traditional thinking about rule of law and democracy, postmodernism has no direct implications for statutory interpretation theory. Yet it does suggest to us that there has been a theory in this book all along, one that emerges piecemeal from my extended analysis of different cases and problems. We can call my approach a *critical pragmatism*. It is pragmatic because I believe the interpreter's fidelity to the rule of law is nothing more (and nothing less) than a sympathetic effort to understand a statute in the context of the problem at hand and of ongoing practice. It is critical because I believe that our government's legitimacy depends on an ongoing reevaluation of practice, especially dividing practices that marginalize groups of citizens and interest group distributions at the expense of the public interest.

Deconstruction and the Rule of Law

Modernist reasoning rests on various hierarchical relationships and their consequences: one thing precedes another and therefore causes it; one person has authority over another and directs her behavior; an institution is expert in a matter, and other institutions defer to its expertise. The cause, the authority, the expert are all privileged in modernist theory, with the effect, the obedient person, and the deferring institutions being subordinated. Pioneered by Jacques Derrida, deconstruction "flips" hierarchical oppositions, showing that the privileged term depends on the subordinated term, thereby reversing the hierarchy.[72] Deconstruction argues that hierarchical opposites can always be flipped, usually by identifying hidden similarities and mutual dependencies in the terms.

Deconstruction corrodes traditional theories of the rule of law, which posit that the interpreter retrieves direction for real world actions from authoritative materials (text, intent, norms). As such, these theories rely strongly on hierarchies. If the hierarchies can routinely be deconstructed, the rule of law collapses. Consider the familiar concept that "the rule of law is a law of rules," or authoritative texts.[73] Like other articulations of the rule of law, this one rests centrally on a hierarchy: the subject (interpreter) retrieves the right answer to an interpretive problem from the object (the text). That the subject then follows the dictates of the object suggests the subordination of the former to the latter. Judge Mack invoked this hierarchical conception in her opinion, which relied on the text of the Human Rights Act which makes it unlawful for an educational institution "[t]o deny, restrict, or to abridge or condition the use of, or access to, any of its facilities and services to any person otherwise qualified, wholly or partially, for a discriminatory reason, based upon the . . . sexual orientation . . . of any individual."

But as feminist theory emphasizes, texts mean nothing until they are applied in concrete contexts. What does the act mean when it is a Roman Catholic institution that is said to "deny, or to abridge . . . the use of, or access to, any of its facilities and services" to a student group espousing views the institution finds objectionable on religious grounds? Can the group be considered "otherwise qualified" for university recognition and/or facilities when the university has an antihomosexual religious mission? Was the denial "based upon the . . . sexual orientation" of the group (as the students argued), or merely on their advocacy of anti-Catholic views (as the university argued)? The act meant something different to each of the different judges not because the statutory text was different for each judge, but because each read the text in light of his or her own understandings about the free exercise clause,[74] evidence in the trial record relating to Georgetown's objections to the student groups,[75] and the legal and moral status of lesbians and gay men.[76] Because the statute's meaning varied among the different interpreters, we can see how the dominant term (authoritative text) depended on the subordinate term (the interpreter). In this way the hierarchy assumed by traditional rule of law thinking is inverted.

Just as general ideas such as the rule of law can be deconstructed, so can specific constitutional or statutory arguments. For example, Mack's opinion permitted Georgetown to deny recognition to the gay and lesbian student groups but did not permit Georgetown to deny access and services to the groups. Her reasoning was that endorsement more strongly implicated Georgetown's free exercise of religious faith than the access and services because the former would be a signal approving the students' activities.[77] Mack's reasoning rested on a dichotomy between endorsement and access, and for constitutional reasons she privileged the former. Yet the qualities she found in required endorsement can also be discovered in required access. Requiring a Catholic institution to provide money, services, and facilities to a gay and lesbian group would seem to result in a signal of the group's acceptability just as much as requiring the institution to recognize or endorse the group—as Georgetown's officials repeatedly testified in the trial court. Indeed, because it is a forced subsidy and involves scarce resources, required access may be a more intrusive signal than simple endorsement. If the Georgetown University Law Center required me as a condition of my employment to endorse Roman Catholic theology, I would be unhappy because I disagree with much of it—but not nearly so upset as I would feel if I had to open up my house and host meetings in which Catholic priests on the faculty inveighed against gay and lesbian intimacy. The latter would be a greater invasion of my freedom because it would be more concrete and more in my face than an abstract endorsement (as to which I could make a mental reservation).

This deconstruction suggests a deeper hierarchy in Mack's opinion, a dichotomy between speech and conduct, in which the former is constitutionally privileged against state intrusion. The reason given by Mack is that regulating pure speech "invades the sphere of intellect and spirit" more than regulating conduct.[78] Yet speech is itself a form of conduct, by which our mouth, lips, and vocal cords coordinate in issuing utterances. And our conduct may reflect our "sphere of intellect and spirit," just as speech does; nonspeech conduct often has openly expressive elements (flag burning, cross waving, fist shaking) and more often has elements that are expressive if viewed more deeply. The way you treat your children is a reflection of your "sphere of intellect and spirit"—at least as much as any public speeches you may make, yes?

These deconstructions of Mack's appeal to constitutional norms might suggest that the dissenting opinions were right to treat endorsement (speech) and access (conduct) as similar for First Amendment purposes. But one can also deconstruct the dissenters' arguments. For example, in arguing that required access was a "forced subsidy" and therefore unconstitutional, Belson was relying on a dichotomy between voluntary speech or conduct and coerced speech or conduct, in which the first is constitutionally privileged. Does Mack's opinion coerce Georgetown to do anything repugnant to its religious beliefs? Her interpretation of the statute says only that so long as George-town voluntarily decides to fund student groups, it must fund gay and lesbian groups on the same terms as it funds all others. The university can choose to have no student groups (or even to move to Virginia). Within Belson's conception of coercion, therefore, there is a voluntary element. Conversely, within Belson's conception of voluntary behavior there is an element of coercion. Belson necessarily believes that allowing Georgetown to discriminate against gay and lesbian student groups is not state coercion of those groups. Yet the law would protect Georgetown's exclusion of the gay and lesbian students; if the students protested the discrimination, the state could send in the police, for the students would have no right to object. Paradoxically, there-fore, Belson would be willing to allow a great deal of state-supported coercion against gays and lesbians, yet he would be perfectly happy to call it voluntary, because the state intrusion would in his view be justified. Hence, for him there is an element of state coercion in voluntary activity.

Deconstruction corrodes our belief in the rule of law, as traditionally de-fined as a law of rules which are independently binding, universally knowable, and objectively predictable. If the "rules" in the rule of law are subject to the sorts of manipulation or contextualization suggested by deconstruction, then the formalist-sounding rule of law seems implausible. Of course, the rule of law does not have to be formalist (consent-based, positivist, liberal). Margaret Radin, for example, argues that the rule of law can be reconceptualized: "Rule-following can only be understood to occur where there is reiterated human action both in responding to directives and in observing others re-spond. Only the fact of our seemingly 'natural' agreement on the instances of obeying rules permits us to say there are rules. The rules do not cause the agreement; rather, the agreement causes us to say there are rules."[79]

Stanley Fish has developed a similarly conventionalist strategy for under-standing rule following.[80] Even though texts impose no limitations on how they are to be read, Fish maintains that readers are not unconstrained in their readings. What constrains readers, and limits the range of viable interpreta-tions of a text, are conventions about meaning developed by one's "commu-nity of interpretation," or the several of which one is a member. Communica-tion is possible between people "not because [we] share a language ... but because a way of thinking, a form of life, shares us, and implicates us in a world of already-in-place objects, purposes, goals, procedures, values, and so on; and it is in the features of that world that any words we utter will be heard as necessarily referring."[81] Fish's understanding, like Radin's, is similar to that of philosophical hermeneutics, explored in Chapter 2.

Fish not only rethinks the rule of law as practice but gives it more bite than liberal or legal process theory. He posits that administrators and judges are never free to interpret statutes any which way, for they are constrained by the conventions of the legal community and of their particular professional communities. The ability to formulate a decision in terms that would be recognizably legal depends on one's having internalized the conventional norms and professional vocabulary of legal practice. To the extent that the administrator or judge departs from recognizably legal conventions and follows those of another community that she has internalized, her interpretations run the risk of being considered unprofessional, idiosyncratic, or (worst) lawless.

Social Construction and Legitimacy

Radin's and Fish's efforts to rethink the rule of law as practice are distinctly postmodern. Law does not depend on rules that preexist their application. Law following requires one not to "represent" a rule so much as to "*re-present*" it to the relevant community of interpretation in the light of social context. One implication of the view of law as a practice is, of course, that statutory interpretation will be dynamic, for the reasons developed in Chapter 2: as social circumstances change, as new intepreters come to the bench, and as new communities of interpretation form and re-form, the statute's meaning will change. The fluidity of the rule of law was illustrated by the EEOC's and Supreme Court's treatment of voluntary affirmative action in employment (discussed in Chapter 1), the Public Health Service's and the Immigration and Naturalization Service's application of the immigration exclusion of people afflicted with psychopathic personality (discussed in Chapter 2), and the federal courts' and Department of Justice's application of the antitrust laws to labor unions (discussed in Chapter 3). All these examples reveal the plasticity of statutory interpretation, but at any given point in time the choices of interpreters were contextualized by law's practice.

One question presses us: Is law's practice legitimate? A postmodern understanding of the rule of law might undermine the theoretical reasons for obeying the law. Because a text's meaning is plastic and situational, an implication of postmodernism is the death of the author.[82] Yet in statutory interpretation the loss of the author unlinks the interpretation (by judge, agency, or citizen) from what democratic theory has long considered the legitimating source (the legislature, the legal process).[83] Moreover, not only is postmodernism skeptical about traditional concepts of representation, rule making, and rule following, but it views the polity and its traditions not as a social contract but as a social construction.[84] Social constructionist theory posits that the state has neither monopoly nor control over authority. "Power comes from below, and not from the top down," wrote the philosopher Michel Foucault; the "relationships of force" that profoundly affect our lives come not from the state but from the "machinery of production, families, limited groups, and institutions."[85] This postmodern reconfiguration of power only reinforces the insight of Radin and Fish, that rule following is situated in a practice.

But social constructionism poses several difficulties for law as practice.

First, it reveals practice to be not only historically contingent but also unpredictably protean and confusingly pluralistic. Social context (in which practice is situated) is an interconnected web of beliefs, organizations, and institutions. This context is ever changing, for if one strand of the web breaks or shifts direction, the whole web is affected. Moreover, there is not just one web but multiple webs of beliefs, as there are many overlapping interpretive communities in the United States. Finally, law is not a continuous practice but is filled with ruptures as well as uncertainties.

An example of rupture was the social treatment of lesbians, gay men, and bisexuals after 1969. As my discussion of *Boutilier* in Chapter 2 suggests, the legal interpretive community knew what to do with "homosexuals" in the 1950s and 1960s: identify them, exclude them, institutionalize them. This was law's practice until gay men and lesbians fought back, starting with the Stonewall riots in June 1969. Because the new gay liberation movement problematized previous medical and moral stigmas against people who were intimate with others of their gender, it unraveled many strands of the social web and disrupted practice. Georgetown's exclusion of gay and lesbian students was firmly grounded in pre-1969 practice, but by the 1980s that practice was in a state of confusion. What made *Gay Rights Coalition* a hard case was that one social construction ("homosexuals" as sick, immoral, or pathetic people) was giving way to another one (lesbians, gay men, and bisexuals as a minority against whom discrimination is unjustifiable).[86]

The fluidity of practice is the lesser problem. The greater problem is the way in which social constructionism undermines the legitimacy of practice. Social power is exercised through "dividing practices" and "scientific classifications" by which the prevailing culture identifies and stigmatizes groups of people.[87] In contrast to most other cultures in history and to much of Western history, modern industrial cultures have created a category of citizens based mainly on their sexual practices, labeled them "homosexuals" (a nineteenth-century term), justified the label and the creation through scientific theories, all of which wove together in this century to generate feelings of loathing, fear, and exclusion of those found out, thereby forcing most "homosexuals" into "the closet." Is this exercise of social power—one that has also been reflected in numerous legal disabilities—justifiable? The answer in the 1960s was, on the whole, yes. The answer today is shifting toward no. Georgetown University was caught in this cultural shift.

The experience of gays and lesbians can be generalized. I have lived as both a closeted and now an openly gay man. My experience suggests that a lot of categories we take for granted, as part of ordinary social practice, rest on classifications and divisions that are normatively unjustified. A generation ago it was culturally possible to think that women were naturally unequipped to do a wide range of jobs, that interracial marriages were immoral, and that school segregation was acceptable. It was possible, but there were strong objections to those classifications and the abundant "science" that backed them up. Those objections have become widely, even if not universally, accepted. So, too, current classifications and dividing practices are questioned. Although it is no longer culturally respectable to argue for de jure racial segregation, de facto patterns of housing segregation probably rest on "unconscious racism," and a new generation of critical race theorists argue that race remains a dividing practice which yields constant and invidious discriminations in our society.[88] Although it is no longer culturally respectable to argue for the exclusion of women from most occupations, women continue to be severely disadvantaged within the workplace through sexual harassment and hostile work environments, and a new generation of critical feminists argue that gender remains a classification that carries tremendous disadvantages in our society.[89]

If practice is not only contingent but constructed in ways that put down one group of people so that other groups can feel superior, then practice may have little if any legitimacy for the groups put down. Together, deconstruction and social constructionism create a dilemma for the rule of law in a democracy. The former undermines our belief in rules that preexist their application and presses us toward a theory of law as practice. The latter undermines our belief that practice will necessarily yield justifiable "law." What implications does this depressing news hold for statutory interpretation?

Critical Pragmatism as a Postmodern Cultural Form

Perhaps the only implications of postmodernism for statutory interpretation are descriptive ones consistent with the analysis in Part I of this book: statutory interpretation cannot rest on the modernist conception that a subject retrieves a plain meaning or an intent or a purpose from the object (see Chapter 1); interpretation is dynamic, in the sense that the meaning of a statute will change as social context changes, as new interpreters grapple with the statute, and as the political context changes (see Chapter 2); the story of a statute becomes a small part of the larger web of institutions and practices in a society (see Chapter 3).

It is harder to specify the normative implications of postmodernism. Its main implication is negative: modernist theories of democracy or the rule of law do not justify any requirement that we obey the interpretations of a statute rendered by a court or agency. Although we do in fact obey such directives, our obedience is not required by any robust normative theory. Also, because law is socially constructed, it is contingent and subject to rupture at any time; a directive we obey today (lunch counter segregation) we might not obey tomorrow (we shall overcome). I do not contest the conventional wisdom that postmodernism supports no normative "theory" of law or anything else,[90] but I do maintain that a normative theory can emerge from one's practice of statutory interpretation.

Such a normative theory has been emerging from the first two parts of this book. It represents my beliefs about statutory interpretation, as revealed in my practice, which is informed by long-standing study of the cases and extensive reading in the leading jurisprudential theories of our day. My approach can be described as one of critical pragmatism. It reflects a balance among three facets of my life: my thoroughly middle-class background and exposure to legal work through the usual insider institutions (Ivy League law school, clerkship, tony law firm), versus my experience as a gay man (which makes me a pariah looking at legal practice from the outside), versus my fascination with the phenomenon of scarcity and its implications for public life. My experience sweeps widely if not comprehensively across the American political spectrum.

Critical pragmatism is both pragmatic and critical.[91] It is pragmatic in several ways. Following Aristotle, I believe that we can figure out what works best in specific cases even without a general theory of what works. If the rule of law is situated in practice, there is no foundational theory that can capture that protean complexity, but our situation within practice itself may help us figure out which applications work best within the conventions of society and law. And these are themselves plural: no single legal convention governs statutory interpretation, but all are relevant—statutory text, legislative intent or purpose, the best answer. Recall the funnel of abstraction developed in Chapter 2. It takes into account a number of different factors in evaluating interpretations—conventions of language and expression, the statute's background history, its subsequent interpretation, its relationship to other legal norms, and its consequences. The funnel assumes that the strongest interpretation is one that, like a cable, weaves together several mutually supporting threads.

The Supreme Court's interpretation of the seaman's double wages statute in Griffin v. Oceanic Contractors, Inc. (discussed in Chapter 1), might be consistent with practical reasoning as I have outlined it. Justice William Rehnquist's opinion gave a windfall recovery of more than $300,000 to a seaman because the employer unlawfully withheld $412 in wages and did not pay until after the district court's judgment. Rehnquist justified this striking interpretation by a process of practical reasoning, emphasizing the plain text which required that the employer "*shall pay* to the seaman a sum equal to two days' pay for *each and every day* during which payment is delayed beyond" the statutorily specified period, Congress's original purpose to deter employers from leaving seamen high and dry in a foreign land after being discharged, and the reasonableness of penalizing an employer that behaves squalidly. Like a three-legged chair, Rehnquist's opinion rests on no single point but rather on all three working together. Because it appealed to widely held conventions and wove the different inquiries together skillfully, Rehnquist's opinion attracted the votes of all but two Justices on the Court, as well as my vote in an earlier article.[92]

But as a pragmatist I am also interested in an interpretation's consequences for social and political practice. The Roman Emperor Hadrian provided a statement of pragmatism in statutory interpretation when he observed that "[l]aws change more slowly than custom, and though dangerous when they fall behind the times are more dangerous still when they presume to anticipate customs."[93] This feature of pragmatism presses me away from Rehnquist's opinion. I am now inclined to agree with Justice John Paul Stevens, who dissented in *Griffin*, weaving together an equally cogent pragmatic case against the large recovery. The statutory language, he argued, is no plainer than that of statutes of limitations, into which judges have routinely imported equitable tolling exceptions. An equitable exception could have been justified in *Griffin* because the seaman was reemployed about a month after his discharge. The history of the statute suggests that Congress did not expect such draconian recoveries when it made relatively minor amendments to the statute in 1898, and the statute's purpose was just as much to compensate seamen as to deter employers from wrongdoing. Stevens argued that the Court's absurd result was not compelled by any of the legal sources it invoked. A further reason, argued in the briefs but only hinted at in the dissent, is decisive for me: equitable tolling of the double wages period was not only within the expectations of the enacting Congress but was widely accepted within the relevant interpretive communities (shipowners, insurers, labor organizations) during this century. Unsettling this long-standing practice requires justification beyond statutory plain meaning.

A pragmatic interpretation is one that most intelligently and creatively "fits" into the complex web of social and legal practices. My approach is one of "critical" pragmatism, so I am in the exceptional case open to statutory interpretations that press beyond or criticize existing conventions and traditions. For if law's legitimacy is not mechanically established by a rule's pedigree or its process of formulation, the interpreter has a grave responsibility to reestablish the productivity of law every time she construes a statute. What is the productivity of law? A general point is suggested by history: a strength of American law and politics is that it has drawn on several different traditions, including liberalism and its emphasis on individual autonomy, legal process and its interest in considering a plurality of viewpoints, and normativism's insistence on justice and/or efficiency. The critical process is a willingness to reexamine practical and conventional readings of a statute in light of these criteria. Is this interpretation (or this statute) consistent with a plurality of interests, or is it partial? Does it needlessly invade conventionally defined spheres of autonomy? Is it just? Wasteful?

Such an internal critique does not at present impel me to change my conventional interpretation in *Griffin*, but it strongly affects other decisions. Consider three examples from Part I. Affirming a decision by the Second Circuit, the Supreme Court in Boutilier v. INS (discussed in Chapter 2) interpreted the immigration law to exclude a bisexual man because any and every such person was, according to the Court, afflicted with a "psychopathic personality." There is a reasonable pragmatic case to be made for the Court's result: even though the exclusion was not strongly suggested by the statutory text, it fit well into pre-1969 practice, for members of Congress, the Public Health Service and the Immigration and Naturalization Service (the two agencies administering the statute), and most medical and psychiatric experts agreed that same-sex intimacy was evidence of psychopathy. Humane people—including Chief Justice Earl Warren and Solicitor General Thurgood Marshall—went along with this pragmatic approach to the statute, and any other approach probably would have been overridden by Congress, which in 1965 had strengthened the statutory exclusion to include people afflicted with "sexual deviation." Yet Second Circuit Judge Leonard Moore dissented from this application because he was reluctant to read such vague language to reach not only people such as poor Mr. Boutilier, but also such celebrated figures as John Maynard Keynes, Leonardo da Vinci, and Ludwig Wittgenstein, "homosexuals" all.[94] An Eisenhower Republican and former U.S. attorney, Moore was a pragmatist—but in *Boutilier* he was a critical pragmatist, willing to read the statute more cautiously than his colleagues because of normative reservations. Excluding people simply because of their sexual orientation struck Moore as arbitrary; he could not think of a good reason for it. The policy seemed to him unnecessarily hurtful, and indeed wasteful and inefficient in light of the productive people it swept within its exclusionary net. It is his opinion, alone, that inspires admiration today.

Reversing the Second Circuit, the Supreme Court in Duplex Printing Press Co. v. Deering (discussed in Chapter 3) held that the Clayton Act of 1914 did not exempt labor unions from Sherman Act lawsuits against secondary boycotts. Justice Mahlon Pitney's opinion for the Court made out a good conventional case for this result, based on the statutory language, legislative history and purpose, the common law. Unlike in *Boutilier*, however, there were equally strong conventional arguments against the Court's result, including arguments based on statutory text and history. And *Duplex* was handed down just as labor-management practice was evolving toward a socially rather than a legally regulated coordination between unions and employers. Giving employers a treble damages remedy against unions for secondary boycotts was discordant with this developing social practice. Even if the pragmatic case on the merits were not so evenly situated, I could not have joined the Court in *Duplex* because of normative reservations about the efficiency or fairness of federal courts' performance in previous labor injunction cases. Federal judges between 1877 and 1921 had generally shown themselves intemperate and partial, viewing labor-management controversies too much from management's point of view and encouraging private parties to deploy state apparatus in wasteful and socially divisive ways. *Duplex* was, as Justice Oliver Wendell Holmes, Jr., put it, "a public misfortune,"[95] and I would have joined him in dissent.

Consider the continuing viability of United Steelworkers v. Weber (discussed in Chapter 1), which interpreted the jobs title of the Civil Rights Act of 1964 to allow voluntary affirmative action plans. *Weber* has once been reaffirmed by the Supreme Court, in large part for pragmatic reasons.[96] *Weber* faces another round of challenges, however, based on language in the Civil Rights Act of 1991 which added a new section 703(m):

> Except as otherwise provided in this title, an unlawful employment practice is established when the complaining party demonstrates that race, color, religion, sex, or national origin was a motivating factor for any employment practice, even though other factors also motivated the practice.[97]

Because this language outlaws race as a "motivating factor," it has spawned new law review articles and lawsuits arguing that *Weber* has been overridden.[98] A pragmatist would consider these arguments close to frivolous because the legislative context in which the new section was written indicates that it was intended to override part of the Supreme Court's decision in Price Waterhouse v. Hopkins,[99] and not to affect *Weber*. This observation is confirmed by the 1991 act's further provision that "[n]othing in the amendments made by this title shall be construed to affect court-ordered remedies, affirmative action, or conciliation agreements, that are in accordance with the law."[100]

I should therefore be inclined to leave *Weber* alone—and would certainly not overrule it on the evidence just noted—but I am open to critical arguments that *Weber* has contributed to racial polarization and resentment and not to increased economic opportunities for racial minorities.[101] Although the more sophisticated analysts still consider that affirmative action yields beneficial results,[102] I believe the *Weber* debate needs to focus on what the consequences of workplace affirmative action have actually been. Do companies use it as a quick and easy way to avoid disparate impact lawsuits, thereby foisting the costs of past discrimination onto future employees? Does affirmative action primarily affect blue-collar white employees and not the managers making the decisions to engage in diversity hiring? What are the cultural consequences of affirmative action for African Americans, Latinos and Latinas, gay men and lesbians, Asians, blue-collar white men? If dynamic statutory interpretation is to have any positive payoff, interpreters need to test their own preconceptions (mine are supportive of affirmative action) against the operation of their interpretation in the world.

III · *Doctrinal Implications of Dynamic Statutory Jurisprudence*

THE DISCUSSION TO this point has been theoretical, emphasizing hermeneutics, positive political theory, and jurisprudence. But the theoretical analysis has a practical payoff, for statutory practice is chock-full of doctrines that cannot be well understood without an understanding of the ideas developed earlier in this book. This part analyzes these doctrines, such as those concerning the proper use of legislative history and the canons of statutory construction, both historically and critically.

To organize the flow of the doctrinal histories, I follow the jurisprudential sequence suggested in Part II. The key developments were the realist critique of formalism in the 1920s and 1930s, the birth and maturing of legal process from the 1930s to the 1950s, and the development of post–legal process theories during and since the 1970s. Just as they did to common law categories, the realists debunked formal doctrines of statutory interpretation (such as plain meaning, legislative intent, and the canons), showing them to be intellectually incoherent, incapable of constraining judges, and counterproductive to the creation of rational public policy. The realists and allied thinkers created the first sustained theories of dynamic statutory interpretation by judges and agencies, and their ideas were warmly received during the early New Deal.

Chapter 7 uses the legislative history debate to trace the generational movement from the old *Lochner*-era formalists, to their critics such as Holmes and Pound, to the systematically debunking realists, to the succeeding generation of moderates who rejected the old formalist categories while seeking to create conditions that would balance the polity's need for dynamic statutory interpretation with the rule of law tradition. Between 1939 and 1949 this last generation created the jurisprudence that would be classically articulated in the Hart and Sacks materials known as "The Legal Process." Chapter 7 traces

205

the intellectual and historical features of this development, outlines its policy-based theory of legislative history, and describes its impact on the federal courts. Chapter 8 demonstrates how the legal process school moderated the formalist-realist debates over the precedential effect that should be afforded earlier statutory decisions, the significance of legislative inaction, and the conditions under which new legal rules should be retroactive.

Chapters 7 and 8 conclude with the doctrinal debates that have arisen with the collapse of a professional consensus around legal process theory. Chapter 9, analyzing the canons of statutory construction, discusses the various post–legal process schools of thought that now compete for academic attention. The leading theories are more normativist than legal process theory: law and economics seeks rules and doctrines that allow our polity to operate most efficiently; republicanism advocates rules and doctrines that foster public values and a new consensus; and critical theories understand rules and doctrines as expressions of social ideologies that might be undemocratic or unjust.

This Part III suggests one obvious theme: just as statutory interpretation is dynamic, so too are the traditional doctrines of statutory interpretation. Another theme developed here touches on the interesting ways in which dry and dusty doctrines have been intertwined with deeper ideological shifts and debates in American public law. The advent of legislative history as an important guide to statutory interpretation, for example, was associated with efforts by early twentieth-century progressives to limit the discretion of the *Lochner*-era jurocracy, an effort that failed in its goal but nonetheless stimulated a feverish interest in legislative history for the remainder of the century (see Chapter 7). The Rehnquist Court has tried to suppress this cult of legislative materials, and the new textualism ascendant on that Court is tied to other doctrinal developments, such as a retreat from strict stare decisis in statutory cases (see Chapter 8) and a vigorous revival of the canons of statutory construction (see Chapter 9). All of these efforts are related to the Rehnquist Court's political ideology. Part III focuses on civil rights cases, where the Court's distinct ideology is most apparent.

My intention is not just to describe and understand this Court's practice in statutory cases but also to evaluate it as an interpretive regime. The Rehnquist Court is just as dynamic in its approach to civil rights statutes as the Burger and Warren Courts were, but the question I pose is whether its dynamic readings of civil rights statutes are justified under a critically pragmatic philosophy. Do the Court's interpretations accord with professional, social, and political practice? Or do they disrupt the evolution of practice? Is any rupture normatively justified?

7 · Legislative History Values

During the last one hundred years judicial invocation of extrinsic legislative sources to interpret statutes has bloomed like azaleas in April. For most of the nineteenth century, American courts focused on statutory text, policy, and canons of interpretation. But by the turn of the century a number of American judges and commentators had come to believe that the proceedings of the legislature in reference to the passage of an act may be taken into consideration in construing it. Reliance on such materials grew more widespread in the twentieth century and was well entrenched in the federal and some state courts by World War II. By 1983 Judge Patricia Wald could observe that "[n]o occasion for statutory construction now exists when the [Supreme] Court will *not* look at the legislative history."[1]

Yet just as Wald's observation reached the press, the Court was having second thoughts about its use of legislative history.[2] At the same time, a collection of judges, administrators, and scholars (the new textualists) began to mount a systematic attack on the use of legislative history in interpreting statutes, and the ensuing debate has become the hottest one in recent statutory studies.[3] In this chapter I situate the legislative history debate historically and jurisprudentially. This survey suggests several lessons, including this primary one: like previous schools of thought, the new textualism can best be understood as a cultural and political phenomenon, one that is most successful in reviving realist arguments against legislative history's "authority value" but reveals a lack of sophistication in ignoring other legislative history values, such as figuring out statutory policy and exploring the normative issues involved in applying the statute.

The Positivist Era, 1892–1949: Rise and Decline of the Authority Value of Legislative History

Statutory interpretation in American courts during the nineteenth century was billed as a search for legislative intent, but evidence of intent was pretty much limited to the plain meaning of statutory texts, as understood by reference to the canons of statutory construction and the common law. Although publicly available legislative history existed at the federal level throughout the nineteenth century, American courts and commentators followed the "English Rule" that, "for the purpose of ascertaining the intention of the legislature, no extrinsic fact, prior to the passage of the bill, which is not itself a rule of law or an act of legislation, can be inquired into or in any way taken into view."[4] In this part of the book I trace the embrace of extrinsic sources in the generation that came of age during the period of legal formalism, and the lively debate over the appropriate use of legislative history that developed in the succeeding generation, during the period associated with legal realism.

Legislative History as Evidence of Specific Intent, 1892–1921

American public law usually eschewed reference to extrinsic legislative materials in statutory interpretation before 1892.[5] A generation later legislative history was often discussed in federal cases. The turning point can be located in the early 1890s. The first edition of the celebrated statutory construction treatise by Jabez Gridley Sutherland reported in 1891 that the intent of the law is "the vital part, the essence of the law," but followed earlier treatises and contemporary English practice in declaring extrinsic legislative materials inadmissible in establishing legislative intent.[6] That Sutherland went out of his way explicitly to disclaim use of extrinsic sources suggests, weakly, that there was some pressure on the courts by nineteenth-century litigants to consider such materials.

In 1892 the Supreme Court decided Church of the Holy Trinity v. United States.[7] Holy Trinity Church in New York had hired an English clergyman and provided for his transportation to the United States, an action arguably in violation of a federal immigration statute making it "unlawful for any person . . . in any manner whatsoever, to prepay the transportation, or in any way assist or encourage the importation or migration of any alien or aliens, any foreigner or foreigners, into the United States . . . to perform labor or service of any kind in the United States."[8] Although the prohibition against employment contracts facilitating immigration was broad and filled with loophole-plugging language,[9] the Supreme Court refused to interpret the statute to exclude the rector. The Court argued "that a thing may be within the letter of the statute yet not within the statute, because not within its spirit, nor within the intention of its makers." The main evidence of a contrary legislative intent was language in a committee report indicating that the words "labor and service" really should have read "manual labor and service" and assuredly were not meant to cover "brain toilers."[10]

Holy Trinity Church was a sensation. Reflecting this and other decisions, the second edition of the Sutherland treatise, published in 1904, devoted an unprecedented five pages to discussing the proposition that "proceedings of the legislature in reference to passage of an act may be taken into consideration in construing the act," including committee reports, rejected amendments, and legislative journals but not legislative debates.[11] The case and its endorsement induced lawyers and judges in the federal system to offer extrinsic evidence of legislative intent, which in turn provided a receptive Supreme Court with more opportunities to refer to such materials. As a consequence legislative history became common in Supreme Court as well as lower federal court opinions issued in the early twentieth century. The Court relied not only on committee reports but also on preliminary drafts of bills ultimately enacted, changes made in legislation by committees or considered by the legislative chamber, and statements by sponsors or floor managers of enacted bills.[12] Lower courts followed the Supreme Court's lead; commentators overwhelmingly approved. By 1940 there was an academic as well as a federal judicial consensus that "close consideration of extrinsic aids," including committee reports, floor debate, and the evolution of the bill, "is today the dominant feature of the interpretive technique employed by federal judges."[13]

Why the sea change? And why did it begin in the 1890s, when the parol evidence rule held sway over issues of contract interpretation? Any answer must lie in a web of reasons. Part of the story involves the new subject matter of legislation in the United States, which after the Civil War little resembled traditional statutes codifying the common law (recall the regulatory statutes described in Chapter 3). New regulatory statutes even sought to move policy beyond or against common law doctrines. Without the common law to guide interpretation in such statutes, legislative history emerged as another useful context for interpretation.

Some of the new statutes received a surly judicial reception, with courts declaring them unconstitutional or interpreting them narrowly. Turn-of-the-century progressives argued for the superiority of the legislature in responding to new social and economic problems, and asserted that the role of courts was to follow legislative commands faithfully and give up their *Loch-ner*ian obduracy. Roscoe Pound specifically associated what progressives regarded as the outmoded conceptualism of mechanical jurisprudence with "spurious" statutory interpretation, in which courts read outdated judicial values into statutes instead of trying to discern the intent of the legislature.[14] The drumbeat of charges that federal courts, in labor and antitrust cases particularly, were biased and activist is another important background aspect for understanding the appeal of legislative history. Progressive judges used legislative history as a weapon against common law assumptions and spurious interpretations, while conservative judges sensitive to charges of antidemocratic activism felt obliged to defend their common law analyses by reference to legislative sources.

An example of this dynamic was Duplex Printing Press Company v. Deering[15] (analyzed in Chapter 3), which involved a Clayton Act injunction against a secondary boycott by print workers against an "unfair" employer. Relying on a reconstruction of the legislative deliberations surrounding the recently passed Clayton Act, the Second Circuit held that Congress intended to exempt all labor boycotts from antitrust injunctions. The Supreme Court reversed, relying on a narrow reading of the statutory text, on the common law's distaste for secondary boycotts, and on committee report language and floor statements by the bill's sponsor which supported the Court's narrow common law reading of the statute. As was the case in *Holy Trinity Church*, the conservative Court came up with a smoking gun in the legislative history[16] and used it to avoid the charge that the judiciary was thwarting the popular will. The dissenting Justices also relied on legislative history, but for the more general proposition that the Clayton Act was a congressional effort to insulate labor unions from Sherman Act lawsuits, which had proved to be harmful to them.[17] The debate in *Duplex* was carried on with no apparent self-consciousness that all of the Justices were relying on materials that had been considered inadmissible thirty years earlier.

Critiques of Legislative History's Authority Value and the Rise of Imaginative Reconstruction, 1915–1938

Just as federal courts were becoming keen on using legislative history as evidence of specific intention, academics were growing restive. The leading cases invoking legislative history—*Holy Trinity Church* and *Duplex*—used that history to read conservative values into statutes and must have given progressives cause for second thoughts about the utility of legislative history. In fact, from the very beginning of its climb to authority, legislative history was beset by analytical doubts urging a more sophisticated methodology.

The Formalist Critique and the Response (Context and Imaginative Reconstruction)   The obvious problem with considering legislative history authoritative is that only the words of the statute have authority value. Justice Oliver Wendell Holmes, Jr., put it pithily in 1899: "We do not inquire what the legislature meant; we ask only what the statute means."[18] Holmes's point was that there must be an objectivity or an "externality" to law, lest it violate the underlying constitutional norm that our government is a "government of laws, not men." Just as the "prudent man" standard (someone external to the particular actor) should govern private liability, and just as the "normal speaker of English" standard should govern contract interpretation, so, believed Holmes, should statutory interpretation focus on the ordinary meaning of the statute's language.

A related argument was made by Max Radin in 1930. Under the Constitution's allocation of national power, the function of the legislature (according to article I) "is not to impose [its] will . . . on [its] fellow-citizens, but to 'pass statutes,' which is a fairly precise operation," involving the promulgation of words with operative effects. "And once the words are out, recorded, engrossed, registered, proclaimed, inscribed in bronze, they in turn become instrumentalities which administrators and courts use in performing their own specialized functions" under articles II and III.[19] An approach to statutory interpretation that views the legislature as having predetermined the interpretation of its statute in certain cases confuses the functions of the legislature (to enact statutes having general application) with that of courts and agencies (to apply statutes to particular facts).

Frederick de Sloovère responded to Radin with a plea of confession and avoidance: legislative history itself is not law, but law's meaning depends on context, and legislative history is the most authoritative context for determining the probable meaning of the statutory language.[20] Contextualists such as de Sloovère were therefore always willing to look at legislative history, since the interpreter cannot say that there is really a "plain meaning" unless she checks the legislative history. "It is said that when the meaning of language is plain we are not to resort to [extrinsic] evidence in order to raise doubts. This is rather an axiom of experience than a rule of law," conceded Holmes in 1928, "and does not preclude consideration of persuasive evidence if it exists."[21]

If the role of legislative history is contextual, not authoritative, statutory interpretation then becomes an "imaginative reconstruction" of the legislature's original expectations rather than a mechanical search for smoking guns. Under this conception the role of the judge is to discover "what the lawmaker meant by assuming his position, in the surroundings in which he acted, and endeavoring to gather from the mischiefs he had to meet and the remedy by which he sought to meet them, his intention with respect to the particular point in controversy."[22] The classic practitioner of imaginative reconstruction was Learned Hand, one of the judges reversed in *Duplex*.[23]

Imaginative reconstruction was thought to avoid the judicial policy-making inherent in both literalist and equitable statutory interpretation, two forms of activism that progressives thought converged in practice. An example from the period is Caminetti v. United States.[24] The White Slave Traffic Act of 1910 prohibited the interstate transportation of "any woman or girl for the purpose of prostitution or debauchery, or for any other immoral purpose." The Court held that the act criminalized transportation of a woman so that she could be the defendant's "mistress and concubine." This represents little more than a transference of the Court's quaint sensibilities onto the statute. A dissenting opinion relied on the original Department of Justice proposal, the committee reports, and sponsor statements to demonstrate that the act was meant "solely to prevent panderers and procurers from compelling thousands of women and girls against their will and desire to enter and continue in a life of prostitution."[25] *Caminetti* was Exhibit A for the progressives' argument that literalism led to spurious interpretation and judicial activism.

The Reliability Critique and the Response (Conventions and Legislative Notice)
Radin's quarrel with legislative history also argued that there is no "intent" of the legislature, and even if there were, we wouldn't be able to know or discover it.[26] When members of Congress vote on a bill, they usually have no specific intent on any but a few issues, if that. Even when members do have specific intentions about certain issues, those intentions change in the process of compromise needed to enact most legislation. And even if members have unalterable intentions about an issue, those are usually unknowable from the historical record either because there *is* no record or because what was said for the record may have been intended to mislead the interpreter. Finally, even if the intent of some members were known with certainty, it would be impossible not only to aggregate the preferences of large groups of people (the House and Senate), but also to match their preferences up with one another and also with those of the president.

James Landis answered Radin's reliability arguments immediately, denying that defenders of legislative history sought to recover the actual mental intent of the enacting legislature. The best that can be done is to construct a probable intent, based on conventions of the legislative process. Also, at various points in the legislative process—in committee, on the floor, in conference—choices are made, proposals are rejected, and reasons are given for doing so. This, too, is good evidence of "a real and not a fictitious intent," even if it is merely inferred from convention.[27]

Landis maintained that the conventions on which courts base their use of legislative history are sound. Statements in committee reports are particularly probative of legislative intent, for Congress relies on committees to develop legislation and shepherd it through the process, and because House and Senate rules require that members must receive committee reports before they vote. Hence, statements in those reports are assumed to be reliable because they are made by a key group, and because the reports are accessible to everyone involved in the process. Landis's argument seems persuasive even if committee reports and the like cannot be shown to represent the views of chamber majorities. So long as the Supreme Court makes clear to Congress what legislative history it will consider relatively probative of statutory meaning, Congress and its members are thereafter on notice that they must monitor those sources and correct the record if it is misleading. By the 1930s the Court had indeed sent such signals, and Congress was aware that committee reports would be considered in statutory cases.[28]

The Judicial Discretion Critique and the Recognition of the Dynamic Nature of Statutory Interpretation   The published discourse in the first few decades of the twentieth century was dominated initially by debate over whether to consider extrinsic evidence, and if so how much, in discerning legislative intent. The debate was carried on entirely within a positivist framework in which progressive scholars and judges sought to preserve the recent handiwork of progressive legislatures against distortion by reactionary judges who might interpret statutes spuriously. The progressives' goal was to remove as much judicial discretion as possible, a position bedeviled by the difficulty of constraining judges. The legal realists (such as Radin) and allied thinkers (such as Benjamin Cardozo) argued that the nature of the judicial process "in its highest reaches is not discovery but creation."[29] *Duplex* and *Caminetti* supported this insight.

The inevitability of interpretive discretion—the realization that all statutory interpretation may ultimately be spurious—was most apparent for cases not anticipated by the legislature, which was early on recognized as a problem.[30] That problem became more acute as statutes got older and the number of unforeseen circumstances multiplied. If imaginative reconstruction were indeterminate for cases arising under recently enacted statutes (*Duplex* and *Caminetti*), consider how much more difficult it would be to reach interpretive closure in the second generation of statutory cases (the cases interpreting both the statute and the precedents within a wider array of unforeseen circumstances). This realization shot like a riptide through legislative history scholarship in the 1930s, undercutting the antidiscretion arguments of old guard progressives such as Pound, Landis, and Hand. But the younger generation of legislative history defenders—Felix Frankfurter, Frederick de Sloovère, and Harry Willmer Jones—was free to recast the defense in a way that recognized and accommodated interpretive discretion. For they were saved by the New Deal.

Legislative History as Evidence of General Intent, 1939–1949

Although the earlier generation had accepted imaginative reconstruction and its conventions as a sufficient response to Radin, a new generation of scholars did not. Legislative intent was a fiction in the hard cases, and imaginative reconstruction and conventions of interpretation were judicial constructions as much as legislative ones. But that was not troubling to the new generation, who accepted Radin's further point that the role of the legislature was to make general rules, not to dictate specific applications, which was the role of an independent judiciary and of the increasingly powerful administrative agencies.

Radin's arguments were validated retrospectively by the New Deal, which brought progressives of all stripes (from establishment types such as Landis and Frankfurter of Harvard to Young Turk realists such as William O. Douglas and Jerome Frank of Yale) into government and underscored the importance of vigorous and dynamic application of statutes over time by administrators as well as judges. Legislative intent looked musty indeed from the perspective of the New Deal, and interpretive discretion was attractive so long as New Dealers were doing the interpreting. Although they essentially adopted Radin's critical arguments, the new generation avoided the overall cynical stance of Radin's article, the sense that law depends on official fiat or whim. In the shadow of an alarming fascism, realist positivism was morally unattractive. By 1940 intellectuals were insisting that the legitimacy of law depends on its reasonableness and justice.[31]

As a result of academic retreat from both Pound's reconstructionist ideal and Radin's cynical positivism, legal intellectuals turned en masse from an emphasis on legislative history as evidence of *specific* intent to an emphasis on legislative history as evidence of *general* legislative intent or purpose. This turn can be precisely dated in the law review literature between 1939 and 1949.[32] Whereas earlier writers and judges had invoked legislative purpose as important to statutory interpretation, this idea did not become central until 1939–40, after the modern regulatory state had been consolidated and right before the United States entered World War II.

The scholarship of the 1940s self-consciously viewed law as a purposive directive grounded in collective reason, not as official fiat. All branches of government "are directed toward facilitating and improving men's coexistence and regulating with fairness and equity the relations of their life in common," posited Lon Fuller.[33] Frankfurter similarly maintained: "Legislation has an aim; it seeks to obviate some mischief, to supply an inadequacy, to effect a change of policy, to formulate a plan of government."[34] Under such a purposive view of government, it made little sense to talk about the will or intention of the legislature.

Nor did scholars stress the primacy of the legislature; consistent with Radin, they saw purposive government acting through the cooperation of all three branches. For this generation a statute was a "ground design," an "instruction to administrators and courts to accomplish a definite result, usually securing the maintaining of recognized social, political, or economic values."[35] Thus, "[t]he 'law' of a statute is not complete when the legislative stamp has been put upon it; subsequent judicial decisions add meaning and effect to the statutory direction," argued Jones. "The interpretation of a statute with respect to wholly unforeseen issues requires the exercise of originative thinking on the part of those charged with its application to particular controversies, whether these be judges or administrative officers."[36]

This theory of government suggested to Jones and other scholars "the principle that in determining the effect of statutes in doubtful cases judges should decide in such a way as to advance the objectives which, in their judgment, the legislature sought to attain by the enactment of the legislation."[37] And these same scholars considered legislative history useful in figuring out statutory purpose. Indeed, "the purpose or policy embodied in a statute, is more often discoverable than is an understanding of legislators as to technical meaning or specific application" and creates the sort of "comprehensive and detailed . . . contextual setting" that protects against idiosyncratic interpretations by judges.[38]

Remarkably, at the same time that an academic consensus was forming against the plain meaning rule and in favor of interpreting statutes to fulfill their purposes as revealed by a comprehensive examination of the legislative history, the New Deal Court was writing that consensus into the United States Reports. The New Deal Court held in United States v. American Trucking Associations[39] that legislative history is always relevant to statutory interpretation, and that "even when the plain meaning did not produce absurd results but merely an unreasonable one 'plainly at variance with the policy of the legislation as a whole' this Court has followed that purpose, rather than the literal words." This is a far cry from either *Caminetti* or *Duplex*.

The Legal Process Era, 1950–1986: The Heyday of Legislative History's Policy Value

Scholars in the 1930s and 1940s developed a theory of legislative history as evidence of general intent. Their theory became the centerpiece for the teaching materials, "The Legal Process," developed by Henry Hart and Albert Sacks in the 1950s. But as the theory was applied in the courts and elaborated by Hart and Sacks, it became part of the larger battleground between conservative (e.g., Fuller and Frankfurter) and progressive (e.g., Radin and Douglas) visions of the legal process. The progressive vision was dominant in the 1960s but lost ground in the 1970s, and both strands of legal process came under fierce attack in the 1980s.

The Legal Process Synthesis and Its Fissures, 1950–1962

Although there appeared to be a consensus about the use of legislative history in the early 1940s, that consensus splintered after World War II, as illustrated by the debate in Schwegmann Brothers v. Calvert Distillers Corporation.[40] The Miller-Tydings Act of 1937[41] created an exception to antitrust liability for "contracts or agreements prescribing minimum prices for the resale" of certain commodities when under local law "contracts or agreements of that description are lawful as applied to intrastate transactions." A Louisiana statute permitted contracts to provide that the seller could control the resale price; the statute also had a nonsigner clause permitting the seller to control resale prices for buyers not parties to the contract. It was hard to fit the Louisiana nonsigner provision into the plain meaning of the Miller-Tydings Act,[42] but the debate within the Court focused on the statute's legislative history.

The opinion of the Court by Justice Douglas held that the apparent plain meaning of the statute was supported by its legislative history.[43] Justice Frankfurter dissented on the ground that a relevant committee report and statements by the bill's sponsor explicitly indicated that the bill applied to state fair trade laws having nonsigner provisions, as every state law (forty-two of them) did in 1937.[44] In short, Frankfurter invoked legislative history as evidence of specific legislative intent on the precise issue before the Court. Douglas responded that the purpose of the statute as revealed by its legislative history was to permit contractual freedom when permitted by state law—which would be inconsistent with allowing price-fixers to use state law to coerce nonsigners—and that Frankfurter's evidence of specific intent needed to be much clearer if it were to require the Court to sacrifice not only the apparent policy of the Miller-Tydings Act but also the long-standing policy of the Sherman Act.

Concurring Justice Robert Jackson agreed with the Court only because of the plain meaning of the statute.[45] He raised three significant points. First, he defended the plain meaning rule, a position rejected by seven Justices, who had reflexively turned to the legislative history. Second, Jackson argued that even when legislative history was consulted, the Court needed to consider the reliability and public availability of those sources; he suggested that the Court should not go beyond committee reports, which reflect sustained deliberation on an issue and are available to members of Congress. Third, Jackson feared that exploring the intricacies of legislative history would involve the Court in "political controversies" beyond its competence.

The foregoing helps describe the context in which Hart and Sacks were drafting their legal process materials in the 1950s. On the one hand, Hart and Sacks followed the scholarship of the late 1930s and the 1940s, using similar concepts and language as Frankfurter, Fuller, de Sloovère, and Jones in particular. Thus, Hart and Sacks posited that the role of agencies and courts is to implement statutes consistent with their purposes (see Chapter 5). "The internal legislative history of the measure . . . may be examined," they declared, but only "for the light it throws on *general purpose*. Evidence of specific intention with respect to particular application is competent only to the extent that the particular applications illuminate the general purpose and are consistent with other applications of it."[46]

Hart and Sacks showed greater caution about using legislative history than had other scholars of the 1940s. Their admonition that a statute should be interpreted to carry out its purpose was immediately qualified by the caveat "making sure, however, that it does not give the words . . . a meaning they will not bear."[47] Based on Hart's interpretation of the debate in *Schwegmann Brothers*, the legal process materials posed three requirements for using legislative history.[48] First, the material had to be *relevant:* only those "aspects of the internal legislative history which were officially before the legislature at the time of its enactment are part of its context." The second requirement was *competence:* relevant legislative history is also competent unless the legislative materials are inaccessible to persons subject to the statute. The third was *probative value:* "the internal legislative history of a statute should always be . . . used not as a separate and self-sufficient record of purpose and meaning but in the light of other relevant materials, and with the object only of resolving doubts emerging from the analysis of the problem as a whole." In short, Hart and Sacks excluded legislative history that was not part of the public process of reasoned elaboration within the legislature.

People speak of the legal process "consensus" in the 1950s, which is a misnomer. Legal process theory was a centrist theory, whose emphasis on contextualism, purpose, and process enabled it to reach out to two different strands of New Deal thought which had splintered in the 1950s. One strand, a remnant of the legal realists and left-wing New Dealers such as Jerome Frank, emphasized progressive dynamic policy. For them, legislative history was useful when viewed as evidence of general intent, permitting interpreters to update statutes and develop their policies progressively over time. Douglas's opinion in *Schwegmann Brothers* is an exemplar of this approach. Another strand, representing the opponents of the legal realists and the more conservative New Dealers such as Learned Hand, warned that a profligate use of legislative history would undermine rule of law values. These theorists viewed legislative history more cautiously because they still regarded it, at least sometimes, as evidence of specific intent, permitting interpreters to figure out exactly what the language of the statute was meant to cover. Jackson's opinion in *Schwegmann Brothers* illustrates how this strand of thought preserved a role for the plain meaning rule, while Frankfurter's opinion illustrates its ability to perpetuate imaginative reconstruction as a legitimate use of legislative history.

Although Douglas wrote the opinion for the Court in *Schwegmann Brothers*, a majority of the Court in that case (the Frankfurter group and the Jackson group) expressed a more conservative approach to legislative history. That balance generally characterized the Court in the 1950s, a period in which Frankfurter pulled the Court toward the political center in statutory interpretation cases.[49] The Court's practice roughly paralleled the academic compromises of the Hart and Sacks materials.

The Warren and Burger Courts, 1963–1986: Bursting with Legislative History

The Supreme Court's fairly cautious legal process approach to legislative history ended when Frankfurter left the Court in 1962, and the Court moved toward the approach Douglas had taken in *Schwegmann Brothers*.[50] Illustrative of this shift was Jones v. Alfred H. Mayer Co.[51] The Civil Rights Act of 1866 provides in part that "[a]ll citizens of the United States shall have the same right, in every State and Territory, as is enjoyed by white citizens thereof to inherit, purchase, lease, sell, hold, and convey real and personal property."[52] In an opinion by Justice Potter Stewart, the Court held that the statute creates a cause of action against private property owners who refuse to lease because of an applicant's race. Stewart briefly suggested that this is the plain meaning of the statute, which he supported with a detailed exploration of its century-old legislative history.[53]

Justice John Harlan's dissent relied on specific statements by the bill's sponsors that the statute would apply only to states having "black codes" placing disabilities on property ownership and transactions by former slaves, to which the Court responded that Congress in 1866 was generally concerned with private as well as public discrimination against African Americans. As evidence the Court relied on sponsor statements of the statute's broad purpose, the Schurz Report presented to Congress which described private violence against blacks, floor statements by both opponents and proponents of the bill, rejected proposals that would have limited the statute to invalidating state black codes, and even the president's veto message (the veto was overridden). Relying mainly on floor debate and sponsor statements, Harlan believed that Congress specifically intended to target only discriminatory state action.[54]

The debate between Stewart and Harlan in *Alfred H. Mayer* was representative of the Warren Court's progressive spin on process theory. During the 1960s the plain meaning rule became virtually a dead letter, as the Court was inevitably willing to look at relevant legislative history, even when the text was fairly clear.[55] The Court typically considered legislative history for its policy rather than its authority value. The Warren Court's interest was in the progressive evolution of legal policy, not in implementing the intentions of long-dead politicians. Consequently, the Justices seized on the law-as-purpose features of legal process thought to liberalize federal habeas corpus,[56] labor law,[57] antitrust statutes,[58] immigration law,[59] regulatory policy,[60] selective service requirements,[61] and civil rights statutes.[62] Like *Alfred H. Mayer* most of these opinions were strongly dynamic interpretations of the statutes they were construing (going against as well as beyond original legislative expectations), and like *Alfred H. Mayer* they often drew spirited dissents from Justices on the Court and from legal scholars.[63]

Reflecting a conservative shift in the nation's politics and in the Court's membership (when Rehnquist and Powell started voting),[64] the Court after 1972 moved back toward the conservative legal process approach of Frankfurter's dissent and Jackson's concurrence in *Schwegmann Brothers.* In a show of judicial restraint and strict construction, the Court under Chief Justice Warren Burger revived the plain meaning rule after a long slumber and turned to great masses of legislative history to recreate specific legislative intent.[65] The Burger Court would follow *both* Jackson *and* Frankfurter.

How the Burger Court could perform this conjuring trick is revealed in Tennessee Valley Authority [TVA] v. Hill.[66] Section 7 of the Endangered Species Act of 1973 required federal agencies to ensure that "action authorized, funded, or carried out by them do not jeopardize the continued existence of endangered species and threatened species or result in the destruction or modification of habitat of such species."[67] Soon after the act was passed, it was invoked by environmentalists to halt construction of an almost completed $107 million TVA dam that was threatening the habitat of the snail darter, a tiny and endangered fish. The Supreme Court affirmed that this harsh application of the statute was required by its plain language. "One would be hard pressed to find a statutory provision whose terms were any plainer that those in section 7 of the Endangered Species Act," wrote Burger, who applied the plain meaning rule because he felt it was required by the Constitution's separation of powers and by the principle of legislative supremacy in policy-making.[68]

Ironically, this leading plain meaning opinion lingered only briefly on the textual argument and instead lavished almost all of its analysis on an examination of the legislative history, which confirmed the statute's plain meaning.[69] This analysis was typical of the Burger Court. In almost all of its plain meaning cases, the Court checked the legislative history to be certain that its confidence in the clear text had not misread the legislature's intent. "The circumstances of the enactment of particular legislation may persuade a court that Congress did not intend words of common meaning to have their literal effect," the Court repeatedly said.[70] The Court sometimes admitted that it was displacing plain meaning with apparent legislative intent or purpose gleaned from legislative history.[71]

In short, the Burger Court's plain meaning rule was a very "soft" one, its particular rule of law ideology requiring that the legislative history be checked to make sure the Court was not reading its own values into statutory text. Like Frankfurter and Harlan, the Justices of the Burger Court sought evidence of specific intent when they searched legislative history but were just as interested in evidence of general intent when the former was not available. To discern intent, the Court was willing to look at almost anything.

Like prior Courts, the Burger Court considered committee reports to be the most "authoritative source for legislative intent,"[72] with statements by sponsors and floor managers being almost as authoritative,[73] since these were the best-informed and most publicized statements of the key players, and hence were most likely to reflect widely held legislative expectations. Less authoritative but also useful were rejected proposals, floor colloquy, and legislator statements in committee hearings.[74] These sources of legislative intent were accepted before the Court exploded with legislative history discourse. Other more unusual examples of legislative history were also emphasized, even in some plain meaning cases (such as *TVA v. Hill*).

Statements of Nonlegislator Drafters In reconstructing legislative intent, Burger's opinion in *TVA v. Hill* considered a wide array of hearing testimony, not only by members of Congress but also by an assistant secretary of the interior, the director of the Michigan Department of Natural Resources, and Defenders of Wildlife (a private group). Because much legislation is proposed or drafted by nonlegislators and adopted by Congress, what these nonlegislative drafters have to say about legislation is often of interest to the statutory interpreter. Hence, the Burger Court was willing to consider presidential transmission letters and veto messages[75] as well as statements by executive department drafters.[76] Also, the Court sometimes considered the views of private persons (especially law professors and groups that draft or lobby for legislation).[77] Nonlegislator statements were most useful to the Court as evidence that the statute embodied a certain political consensus or compromise whose details were worked out outside the formal legislative process.[78] Occasionally the Court would rely on such statements when other evidence of legislative intent or purpose was completely ambiguous.[79]

Legislative Silence The silence of legislators can be as significant as their utterances. In "Silver Blaze," Sherlock Holmes solved the case by making inferences from the fact that a dog did not bark. A dog's barking may be significant, suggesting that something (or a strange someone) has disturbed the household's status quo. A dog's failure to bark may thus be evidence that the status quo has not been disrupted. Following this logic, the Burger Court followed a principle of continuity: every time Congress enacts or amends a statute, it is acting against a background of legal rules and interpretations which Congress is presumed to know. When Congress wants to change one of these rules, it usually says something to suggest that intention in the statutory text or legislative history (that is, it barks). Often Congress talks about changing one of these rules but ultimately decides not to. More often still no one says anything, lending an equally strong inference that the preexisting rules are to be left in place: that is, the dog fails to bark in a situation where one would expect it to do so if there were a change in the status quo. Based on this analysis of silence in the legislative history, the Court opined that "[a] party contending that legislative action changed settled law has the burden of showing that the legislature intended such change."[80] The Burger Court was also sometimes willing to presume from Congress's silence over time that Congress "acquiesced" in judicial or agency interpretations of a statute (see the first section of Appendix 1) or from Congress's silence when reenacting or amending a statute that it wanted to carry over previous interpretations into the new statute (see the second section of Appendix 1).

Subsequent Legislative History   Most interesting was the Burger Court's willingness to consider "subsequent legislative history," the interpretation expressed by members of Congress after a statute has been enacted. Given the Court's focus on the original legislative intent or purpose and the possibility of manipulation, it sometimes said that "the views of a subsequent Congress form a hazardous basis for inferring the intent of an earlier one"[81] and refused to consider subsequent history probative, as in *TVA v. Hill*. Nonetheless, the Burger Court often considered subsequent legislative history when interpreting statutes.[82] The Court's stated reason was usually the dearth of other interpretive guides, but positive political theory suggests that the Court was also being attentive to current legislative signals in order to avoid overrides on issues about which Congress had intense preferences.[83]

The Burger Court's use of extrinsic sources was both open-ended and hierarchical. The Court preferred guidance from committee reports and sponsor statements but would consider almost anything else if those sources were unhelpful. Consider the graphic representation of the Court's hierarchy of extrinsic materials as shown in Figure 7.1 (page 222), a representation similar to the funnel of abstraction developed in Chapter 2.

Critiques of the Burger Court's Use of Legislative History, 1975–1986

The federal explosion in legislative history use paralleled a similar development at the state level. One commentator noted in 1981 that "[t]he trend in most [state] courts is toward a heavier reliance on recorded legislative history," a statement similar to Wald's description of Supreme Court practice two years later.[84] By 1980 most state systems were consulting extrinsic

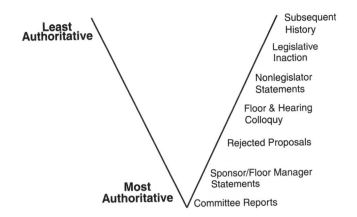

Figure 7.1   Hierarchy of legislative history sources, U.S. Supreme Court, circa 1982

materials, were following a soft plain meaning rule, and were willing to look at as many different sources as federal courts, even when those sources were not part of the public record or were unpublished.[85] Ironically, at the very time when both federal and state courts were bursting with legislative history, and commentators were proclaiming its triumph, it became controversial once again. Reliance on legislative materials to displace or even confirm statutory plain meaning was criticized from three different points of view in the late 1970s and early 1980s.

Reliability Criticisms   From a legal process perspective the main problem with the orgy of legislative history consumption was its reliability. Statements made during floor debates and committee hearings might not be reliable because they are often ill informed and tentative, are not widely known within the legislature or accessible to lawyers after the fact, do not necessarily represent the views of all legislators, and present opportunities for strategic behavior.[86] Though this criticism had been articulated in different forms by Radin, Hart and Sacks, and others, it gained new analytical bite as a result of legal interest in economic theories of politics.

Public choice theory (discussed in Chapters 1 and 5) questions the reliability of even the least controversial legislative history—committee reports and sponsor's statements—by suggesting that explanations in those sources may well be strategic rather than sincere expressions of the statute's meaning. *TVA v. Hill* relied on the House sponsor's statement that the bill would make the Air Force stop bombing whooping cranes in Texas and the Department of Agriculture protect grizzly bears in the West, notwithstanding heavy costs.

The Court assumed that this was a sincere statement by someone who represented a consensus on the issue and then inferred from it that Congress was intent on protecting endangered species whatever the costs. But because the sponsor may have a hidden agenda or may be acting pursuant to a secret logroll, the sponsor may not represent the consensus view. The sponsor of the Endangered Species Act may have uttered the broad species-protective language precisely because he realized he did not have the votes to put it in the statute itself. Or he may have been creating legislative history to pull in the votes of a few members who wanted to protect whooping cranes and grizzlies. Either of these explanations is as plausible as the Court's, but neither supports the Court's inference that Congress would have wanted to spend $100 million (costs already sunk in the Tellico Dam project) to save the snail darter.

Social choice theory provides another way of criticizing the reliability of legislative materials. Because several different choices are usually possible under majority voting, collective decision making often depends critically on who controls the agenda and how the person orders the choices (discussed in Chapter 1). It is very hard for a court to figure out how a legislature "would have decided" issues on which it never formally voted—for it depends on the order in which proposals are considered, which in turn depends on who controls the agenda. Hence, we have no way of knowing how Congress would have decided the snail darter issue in *TVA v. Hill*, notwithstanding a substantial amount of legislative history. The best one can say is that if the environmentalist-oriented House Merchant Marine and Fisheries Committee and the House sponsor of the Endangered Species Act had set the agenda on the issue, it is more likely that the snail darter would have been protected than if the budget-minded House or Senate Appropriations Committees had been setting the agenda. Indeed, at the behest of the Merchant Marine Committee, Congress in 1973 enacted the broadly phrased Endangered Species Act, while Congress later in the 1970s followed the Appropriations Committees to continue to fund the Tellico Dam, notwithstanding knowledge that its completion threatened the snail darter.[87]

The Historicist Critique A second source of doubt about the usefulness of legislative intent in the early 1980s was the law and interpretation movement. Even if collective intent or purpose were a coherent concept, no historically situated collective intent or purpose can be completely "reconstructed" by even the most "imaginative" jurist, for the latter's interpretation of the former's statements will inevitably be influenced by current context and other evolutive factors (recall Chapter 2). This concern is less applicable to cases such as *TVA v. Hill* and *Duplex*, where the Court was interpreting recently enacted statutes, than to cases such as *Alfred H. Mayer* or *Weber*, where the Court was interpreting older statutes.

Compare Jett v. Dallas Independent School District.[88] Norman Jett, a high school football coach, sued under the provision of the Civil Rights Act of 1866 which protects against racial discrimination in the making and enforcement of contracts,[89] alleging that the school's principal harassed him and ultimately discharged him because of race. A Dallas jury found racial harassment and awarded Jett damages against both the school district and the principal. The Supreme Court found that the statute does not hold municipal governments liable for the constitutional torts of their employees, even if *respondeat superior* precepts would normally impute liability to the employer. The plurality opinion examined the extensive legislative history of the 1866 act and found no evidence that the legislation's sponsors expected it to apply to municipalities. The plurality also relied on the subsequent enactment of the Civil Rights Act of 1871. Since the later Congress subjected municipalities to liability for a broad range of constitutional deprivations but did not "intend" to subject them to vicarious liability, the plurality reasoned that the earlier statute did not either.[90]

Problems of historicity exacerbate the reliability problems with the plurality's approach. The failure of the sponsors to talk about the statute's application to municipalities is consistent with several different inferences about what they thought. Either no one would have imagined that the bill would subject municipalities to vicarious liability (the plurality's inference), or everyone recognized that state and local governments were covered by the statute, and so the interlocutors didn't even bother to mention the issue (the dissent's inference). At least as likely is a historical reason not mentioned by either opinion: there were in 1866 serious questions about Congress's power to impose liability on municipalities for racial discrimination (questions that are no longer so serious), and so the sponsors kept the issue submerged.

The Formalist Critique   The legal process era saw a vast expansion in state regulation, often by dynamic agency and judicial interpreters operating under cover of supportive legislative history. A new generation of Reagan-era administrators, scholars, and judges[91] challenged the Burger Court's excessive reliance on legislative history. These critics expressed a nostalgia for the objectivity Holmes envisioned when he said, "We do not inquire what the legislature meant; we ask only what the statute means."[92]

Whereas Pound had urged imaginative reconstruction from legislative history as a way to *avoid* spurious interpretation, the new textualists of the 1980s believed that use of legislative history *invites* spurious interpretation.[93] By broadening the inquiry beyond the relatively concrete question of what the actual words of the statute mean, use of legislative history permits judges to justify a broader range of answers and makes it easier for them to read their own preferences into the statute. As Judge Harold Leventhal once said, citing legislative history is like "looking over a crowd and picking out your friends."[94] *TVA v. Hill,* for example, offered legislative history that provided companionship for virtually any view of the snail darter issue. The Court's opinion emphasized the House sponsor's view, while the dissenting opinion emphasized the views of the appropriations committees. Each side picked out its friends and ignored the rest of the crowd.

Jett offers a variation on this problem. The plurality and dissenting opinions picked out the same faces in the crowd but interrogated them differently. The plurality asked: What specific discussion of municipal liability can be found in the 1866 debates? None. Why, then, was municipal liability mentioned only in the 1871 debates and not in the 1866 debates? For historicist reasons I do not think the latter question is answerable, but it allowed the plurality to fall back on the assumption that Congress must have been unconcerned about municipal liability in 1866. The dissent asked different questions: What was the general purpose of the 1866 act? To root out and penalize racial discrimination in contracting. Would that general purpose be subserved by interpreting the statute to apply to municipalities? Yes. Which set of questions is truer to original legislative intent? The answer is unclear, even as it is likely that each set of questions is motivated by different judicial attitudes about the statute.

Spurious interpretation under the cover of legislative history is not just disingenuous but antidemocratic and unconstitutional, according to the new textualists.[95] Recalling Radin, they argue that such judicial lawmaking violates the separation of powers embodied in articles I–III of the Constitution, both by allowing courts to exercise legislative authority and by inviting Congress to control subsequent statutory applications through plants in the legislative history. Going beyond Radin, the new textualists object that use of legislative history amounts to an end run around the constitutionally mandated legislative process. By elevating language in a committee report to authoritative status, the Court allows lawmaking by legislative subgroups, in violation of the bicameralism and presentment requirements of article I, section 7.

The Post–Legal Process Era: The New Textualism and Legislative History's Normative Value

Although legal process approaches to extrinsic legislative materials—a soft plain meaning rule, use of legislative history as evidence of general as well as specific intent, and an expansive view of legislative context—have been subjected to the critiques I have developed, they retain considerable vitality. But since 1987 the center of discussion about extrinsic sources has been moving away from legal process's interest in purpose and toward a direct debate between a text-based formalism and a pragmatic functionalism.

The New Textualism within the Supreme Court

The formalist critique of legislative history has become the basis for a positive theory of extrinsic materials. Pioneered by Judge Frank Easterbrook, the new textualism has become prominent because an early adherent, Antonin Scalia, is now a Justice on the Supreme Court. During his tenure on the Court of Appeals for the District of Columbia Circuit, Scalia questioned the use of committee reports as evidence of legislative intent.[96] His main criticism was the legal process concern that such reports are not reliable.

Upon his elevation to the Supreme Court, Scalia's critique became more radical and more formalist.[97] For Scalia the constitutionally mandated role of the Court is only to interpret laws—the actual statutory language—rather than to reconstruct legislators' intentions. He draws this conclusion from article I, section 7 of the Constitution: the only legitimate statutory law is that which has been approved by both chambers of Congress and presented to the president. The only way we can know what the House, the Senate, and the president agreed to is by what the statutory language tells us. When the Court credits committee reports and floor statements, it is essentially equating the views of a legislative subgroup to the enactments of Congress, a move which was the basis for the Court's invalidation of legislative vetoes in INS v. Chadha. Legislative history is "a frail substitute for bicameral vote upon the text of a law and its presentment to the President. It is at best dangerous to assume that all the necessary participants in the law-enactment process are acting upon the same unexpressed assumptions."[98] By refusing to consult legislative history in all cases (except where the text suggests an absurd result), says Scalia, the Court can discourage legislative behavior that seeks to evade the constitutionally prescribed procedures of lawmaking. "I think we have an obligation to conduct our exegesis in a fashion which fosters the democratic process."[99]

Scalia is aware of the familiar precepts that words do not interpret themselves and that their meaning depends on context.[100] He probably would agree that a dictionary definition will not always answer the difficult interpretive questions, and would admit that context is necessary. Like the defenders of legislative history, therefore, Scalia admits "coherence" arguments, that is, arguments that an ambiguous term is rendered clear if one possible definition is more coherent with the surrounding legal terrain than other possible definitions. But, unlike defenders of legislative history, Scalia admits only arguments based on textual coherence (this meaning is consistent with other parts of the statute or other terms in similar statutes), and not those based on historical coherence (this meaning is consistent with the historical expectations of the authors of the statute). According to Scalia, the proper interpretation of a statute is that which is "(1) most in accord with context and ordinary usage, and thus most likely to have been understood by the *whole* Congress which voted on the words of the statute (not to mention the citizens subject to it), and (2) most compatible with the surrounding body of law into which the provision must be integrated—a compatibility which, by a benign fiction, we assume Congress always has in mind."[101]

The Supreme Court has not abandoned its practice of consulting extrinsic legislative materials even when there is a plain meaning,[102] but its practice after 1986 (when Scalia joined the Court) has reflected the influence of the new textualism. First, the Court has been somewhat more willing to find a statutory plain meaning and less willing to consult legislative history, either to confirm or rebut that plain meaning (see Figure 7.2). In short, the old soft plain meaning rule has become harder. One example is Pierce v. Underwood.[103] The Equal Access to Justice Act (EAJA) provided that a party prevailing against the United States should be awarded counsel fees, "unless the court finds that the position of the United States was substantially justified or that special circumstances make an award unjust."[104] The Court of Appeals had interpreted "substantially justified" to mean that the government's position "had a reasonable basis both in law and in fact." The prevailing party seeking counsel fees argued that the EAJA required a stronger position than simply a "reasonable" one, and relied on the House committee report accompanying the 1985 reenactment of the EAJA. The Supreme

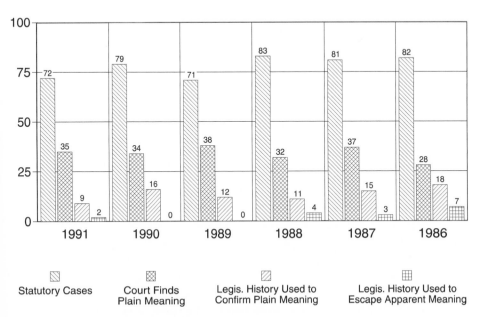

Figure 7.2 Supreme Court's legislative history practice, 1986–1991 terms

Court, in an opinion by Scalia, adopted the lower court's position, based on the plain meaning of "substantially justified." Scalia found the committee report unpersuasive in his interpretive inquiry, for essentially realist and practical reasons.[105] Because *Underwood* discussed the legislative history, it is a moderate version of the approach urged by the new textualism. More recent opinions have sometimes been more rigid, refusing even to discuss legislative history arguments, as the opinion for the Court did in *K Mart* (see Chapter 4).[106] And there is now strong resistance on the Court to "rewriting" statutes based on the legislative history.[107]

A second consequence of the new textualism for the Court's practice is the prominence of a "structural" view of what a statute's plain meaning is. "Statutory construction is a holistic endeavor. A provision that may seem ambiguous in isolation is often clarified by the reminder of the statutory scheme—because the same terminology is used elsewhere in a context that makes its meaning clear, or because only one of the permissible meanings produces a substantive effect that is compatible with the rest of the law."[108] For example, in finding a plain meaning, Scalia considers how the word or phrase is used elsewhere in the same statute, or how it is consistently used in other statutes. This was his approach in *Underwood*, which conceded that "substantially justified" could mean "justified in a high degree" (the view of the prevailing private party) *or* "justified in the main" (the government's view). Yet the opinion still found a statutory plain meaning by reference to the U.S. Code's use of "substantial" elsewhere.[109] It also relied on an analogy to the Federal Rules of Civil Procedure, which impose counsel fees for resisting discovery only when the loser's position is not "substantially justified." Scalia observed that no court had ever found this standard to require that the loser's position must be "justified to a high degree."

Scalia also considers how the possible meanings fit the statute as a whole.[110] Does one meaning render other provisions duplicative or superfluous? Is there a structure in the statute or a pattern of assumptions that supports one of the plausible meanings? Because statutes have become increasingly long and detailed in the last generation, this "whole statute" approach often generates interesting arguments. In Chan v. Korean Air Lines, Ltd.,[111] the issue was whether international air carriers lose their Warsaw Convention benefit of the limitation on damages for passenger injury or death if they fail to provide the passenger with the requisite notice of limitation on their ticket. Article 3(1) of the Convention requires the notice, and article 3(2) provides that if the carrier fails to deliver a ticket to the passenger, it cannot avail itself of the liability limits of the Convention. Although some courts had interpreted article 3(2) to include situations where the passenger received a ticket but without the requisite notice, Scalia's opinion for the Court found this view completely "implausible" on the grounds that it is inconsistent with the first sentence of article 3(2) and would produce absurd results if adopted.[112] He further reasoned that this conclusion is reinforced by comparing article 3(2) with other provisions of the Convention. Other sections provide parallel rules (including liability limitation and a notice requirement) for baggage checks and cargo waybills. The sections are identical in their requirements but not in their remedies. Section 1 (injury) provides no explicit remedy, yet sections 2 (baggage) and 3 (cargo) specifically waive liability limits for the airline's failure to include the notice requirements in the documents.[113] Having established the convention's plain meaning to his satisfaction, Scalia brusquely dismissed any effort to examine the legislative history.[114]

Scalia also relies on the interaction of different statutory schemes to determine statutory plain meaning. In *Jett*, for example, he refused to join the Court's legislative history discussion but concurred in its judgment on the ground that the 1866 act should follow the specific policy later adopted in the 1871 act because of the "principles of construction that the specific governs the general, and that, where text permits, statutes dealing with similar subjects should be interpreted harmoniously."[115] The eagerness of the new textualists to consider one statute's meaning in light of other statutes (a long-standing precept of statutory interpretation they have reinvigorated) has been especially influential on the Court.[116]

A third, but more subtle, consequence of the new textualism for the Court's practice has been an increased dependence on canons of statutory interpretation (discussed in greater detail in Chapter 9). Textual canons posit that Congress follows certain rules of grammar, language use, and punctuation when it writes statutes; the new textualists are keen on these rules, even where they are analytically questionable. For example, the canon "expressio unius est exclusio alterius" (the expression of one thing implies the exclusion of all others), which has long been the object of scorn by reflective academics and judges, has seen a revival. It was Scalia's key argument in *Chan:* because article 3(2) did not explicitly provide for negation of the liability limits for failure to provide proper notice, especially when other sections of the same convention did provide such an explicit remedy, Scalia inferred that the statute plainly meant to deny a remedy. *Chan* is no aberration, for *expressio unius* arguments have sprouted like mushrooms in the Rehnquist Court's statutory decisions.[117] So, too, have arguments based on other grammatical canons of construction, such as the punctuation canon, which presumes that the placement of every punctuation mark is significant.[118] In addition to reviving interest in textual canons, the new textualists have emphasized substantive canons of statutory construction; by deploying canons as clear statement rules rather than simple policy presumptions, the Court is able to eliminate reference to legislative history even when there is no statutory plain meaning (this theme is explored in Chapter 9).

Criticizing the New Textualism

Academia, an asylum for the contextually inclined, has not been receptive to the new textualism. Important criticisms have been that its rigid positivism is partisan, misunderstands the legislative process, and yields crazy results.[119] The criticism suggested in this book is that the new textualists' methodology is no more objective or constraining than other methodologies. Consider this criticism in light of Scalia's three main constitutional justifications for the new textualism.

The Bicameralism and Presentment Argument   According to Scalia, relying on committee reports and the like to determine a statute's meaning is tantamount to permitting lawmaking by congressional subgroups, which the Court found to be a violation of article I, section 7 in *Chadha*. Scalia reads too much into the bicameralism and presentment requirements, which support nothing more than the truism that legislative history does not have the same authority as statutory text. Itself quoting a Senate committee report, *Chadha* stated that bicameralism and presentment are only limitations on Congress's actions (the requirements are in article I), not the actions of branches of government regulated by articles II and III.[120] Bicameralism and presentment are formally and technically irrelevant as a limitation on the subsequent implementation and interpretation of legislation.

The purpose of the bicameralism requirement, as interpreted in *Chadha*, further undermines Scalia's position: "The division of Congress into two distinctive bodies assures that the legislative power would be exercised only after opportunity for full study and debate in separate settings."[121] The Constitution's contemplation of deliberative discussion in the legislature suggests an implicit tolerance for reviewing those deliberations on the part of those charged with interpreting and implementing the legislation. To the extent that committee reports and other legislative history shed light on the "study and debate" that Congress is supposed to engage in, the constitutional procedures of legislation would seem to support some consultation of legislative history.

Nothing in the Court's traditional practice is inconsistent with article I, section 7. If anything it is Scalia's theory that is inconsistent with the bicameralism and presentment requirements. Recall that his holistic textualism requires the Court to choose the interpretation "most compatible with the surrounding body of law into which the provision must be integrated—a compatibility which, by a benign fiction, we assume Congress always has in mind."[122] An assumption of this formulation is that, when Congress enacts statutes, it is omniscient about the law. Scalia therefore assumes that both chambers of Congress and the president are aware of judicial interpretations of provisions that a statute borrows or reenacts, of the canons of statutory construction (including grammar and punctuation rules) that might be applied to the statute, and of the surrounding legal terrain into which the statute must be integrated.[123]

Everyone knows that these assumptions have virtually no foundation in reality. Legal scholars, especially those who have actually been players in the legislative process, are scornful of them.[124] Judge Abner Mikva, a former member of the House of Representatives, says: "When I was in Congress, the only 'canons' we talked about were the ones the Pentagon bought that could not shoot straight."[125] Members of Congress and their staffs are not omniscient about legal rules, and the nature of the legislative process gives them incentives to focus on particular problems and not on future issues of interpretation. A member cutting deals in order to gain enough votes to secure enactment of her bill is relatively uninterested in how that bill will be "integrated" into the larger corpus of law, or in the wisdom of prior judicial interpretations of a provision she is borrowing. Often she has a positive incentive to suppress these facts, since they may raise problems with her bill which could defeat it.

Scalia knows this, for he calls his assumption "a benign fiction." Yet when he is discussing the Court's traditional use of legislative history, he is not so tolerant of fictive assumptions. "It is at best *dangerous* to assume that all the necessary participants in the law-enactment process are acting upon the same unexpressed assumptions,"[126] says Scalia, because that would be at odds with the policy of article I, section 7. How are the two fictions so radically different? The traditional approach assumes that members of Congress and the president have access to committee reports and rely on them as the best evidence of the purposes and at least some specific understandings embodied in the statute. Scalia assumes that members of Congress and the president *both* know the canons of construction, judicial interpretations of prior law, and the existing statutory terrain *and* draw the same conclusions from these sources about the probable meaning of the language they enact. Those are strong assumptions.

This analysis suggests a serious problem with Scalia's theory. In the name of bicameralism and presentment he applies a superrealist analysis of legislative history which enables him to question its legitimacy. But the same superrealism can be applied to his own assumptions. Dropping the sarcastic tone of his analytical scrutiny of legislative history, Scalia simply accepts the "benign fiction." Why accept one fiction and not the other? There may be good reason to prefer the fictions surrounding legislative history to those of the new textualism. At least legislative history is created within the legislative process and is subject to legislative reaction and correction.[127] Indeed, the Court often refuses to consider legislative history created under circumstances in which other legislators were not likely to have noticed or responded.[128] The canons of construction are, of course, created by judges over time and are much harder for legislators to negate.

The Separation of Powers Argument Scalia's main separation of powers argument is that consideration of legislative history creates greater opportunities for the exercise of judicial discretion, thereby enhancing the risk that the Court will exercise its own "WILL instead of JUDGMENT," effectively "substitut-[ing] [its own] pleasure to that of the legislative body."[129] Focusing on the text alone, in contrast, is a more concrete inquiry which better constrains the tendency of judges to substitute their will for that of Congress.

Even if one accepts Scalia's premise that separation of powers denies courts and agencies lawmaking functions (a premise refuted in Chapter 4), it is not clear that textualism advances his goal of more constrained judicial discretion. I find it mildly counterintuitive to posit (as Scalia seems to) that an approach asking a court to consider materials generated by the legislative process, in addition to statutory text (also generated by the legislative process), canons of construction (generated by the judicial process), and statutory precedents (also generated by the judicial process), leaves the court with *more* discretion than an approach that considers just the latter three sources. Scalia's approach requires choices among competing evidence just as much as the traditional approach, and potentially expands the judge's range of discretion by its revival of the canons of construction, which are notoriously numerous and manipulable. Indeed, it can be said that judicial use of the canons is like looking over a crowd and picking out your friends.

Consider Scalia's position in *Jett*. Section 1981 provides that "[a]ll persons within the jurisdiction of the United States shall have the same right in every State and Territory to make and enforce contracts . . . as is enjoyed by white citizens." The Supreme Court's interpretation of this svelte statutory scheme rested on an examination of the legislative history of the 1866 Civil Rights Act (of which section 1981 was a part) and of the 1871 act, which the Court held to have qualified the earlier statute to exclude municipal liability under a *respondeat superior* theory. Scalia refused to join any of this discussion and based his concurring opinion on two canons of construction: that the two statutes be construed harmoniously (the 1871 act has been construed to exclude vicarious liability for municipalities) and that the more specific statute (the 1871 act) govern the more general one.[130] His position in this case strikes me as arbitrary. Whereas Scalia invokes two widely used canons of construction, he neglects even to mention the canons that cut against his position. The canon that the earlier statute be interpreted in light of a later statute is inconsistent with the canon that repeals by implication are disfavored[131] and with the canon that a statute setting forth a general right presumably carries with it a remedy.[132] Apparently Scalia does not like these canons,[133] but his dislike for them reflects nothing more than his personal preferences. And his position is also at odds with a canon he does like: the actual text of the statute is controlling.

In endorsing the position that the 1871 act implicitly modified the 1866 act, Scalia makes no mention of the language of the 1871 act itself, which stipulates "[t]hat nothing herein contained shall be construed to supersede or repeal any former act or law except so far as the same may be repugnant thereto."[134] There is no repugnance in enforcing the 1866 act, while not enforcing the later act, against municipalities under vicarious liability, and so the text of the 1871 act has a plain meaning that Scalia ignores. Indeed, I do not understand how Scalia is faithful to the text of the 1866 act, which is as broadly written a statute as one will find and contains nothing in it that smacks of the policy line-drawing that Scalia endorses.

To be sure, in cases such as *Jett* the Court's use of legislative history is subject to quarrel because of selective use of evidence and questionable inferences drawn therefrom. But Scalia's claim is that textualism imposes more reliable constraints on judges. He fails to make his case, and performances such as his in *Jett* (and cases analyzed in Chapters 1 and 4) suggest that the new textualism is no more constraining than the traditional approach. In fact, so long as the new textualism relies heavily on the pliable canons of statutory construction, its methodology will often be more arbitrary and less constraining than that of the traditional approach (see Chapter 9).

The Democracy-Enhancing Argument   Scalia argues that statutory interpretation must be conducted "in a fashion which fosters the democratic process." That is, a method of statutory interpretation must be evaluated not just by its ability to constrain unelected judges but also by its ability to stimulate legislators to perform their functions better, as by drafting statutes more precisely. "What is of paramount importance is that Congress be able to legislate against a background of clear interpretive rules, so that it may know the effect of the language it adopts."[135] Hence, if Congress is aware that its statutes will be read with a strict literalism and with reference to well-established canons of statutory construction, it will be more diligent and precise in drafting them.

This is a nice economic argument (consider the ex ante affects of the rule you adopt), but the analysis in this book suggests doubts that an embrace of the new textualism would have much, if any, effect on the way Congress drafts statutes. Most of the Court's difficult statutory interpretation cases involve statutes whose ambiguity is either the result of a deliberate legislative choice to leave conflictual decisions to agencies or the courts *or* the result of social and/or legal developments not foreseeable by legislators. Clearer rules of interpretation would not eliminate such sources of ambiguity.

Furthermore, there is reason to doubt that the new textualism would provide Congress with a set of "clear interpretive rules." The new textualists are not only selective about which of the canons of construction they will use in any given case but are also inclined to tinker with some of the canons. As the canons change over time (it is inevitable that they will be dynamic), the background assumptions change. What, then, is the point of establishing clear background rules today when they are likely to be different tomorrow? This is one way to view *Jett*. When the 1866 Civil Rights Act was passed, the "clear interpretive rule" was that federal statutory rights usually carried with them a remedy.[136] When the Supreme Court interpreted the statute in 1989, the prevailing rule among the Justices was more restrictive.

The biggest problem I have with Scalia's new textualism is that it seems unfriendly to democratically achieved legislation and threatens to undo much of Congress's statutory work. Whatever the cogency of Scalia's indictment of legislative history, the fact remains that for most of this century the Court has told Congress, "We shall attend to committee reports, at least." That has encouraged Congress to develop conventions by which much of the elaboration of statutes—judicial decisions ratified or overruled, purposes to be fulfilled, specific issues thought to be resolved—has been put in committee reports rather than in the statutes themselves, where most of it would be cumbersome and out of place anyway. If the new textualism displaces the traditional approach entirely, it will undermine the expectations of decades of statutory drafting. This would not be a national calamity, but it seems insufficiently sensitive to the supremacy of Congress in making law.

Legislative History's Normative Value

Consider the use of legislative history, particularly *The Federalist*, in constitutional interpretation. The essays represent the views of three people, only two of whom were delegates to the Philadelphia convention; there is no way to tie the authors' views to the views of the framers. Nor are the authors necessarily representative of most ratifying delegates, even in New York (the intended audience). Nor can the views of Madison in his essays be confidently attributed to Hamilton or Jay; in fact, they cannot confidently be attributed to Madison himself, for the essays were after all propaganda documents. And they were written two hundred years ago, in defense of a constitution that was drafted by a convention that exceeded its powers authorized by Congress and that violated the Articles of Confederation in setting the terms of its own approval. In short, all the formalist, reliability, and historicist criticisms of statutory legislative history can be leveled at least as persuasively against *The Federalist*.[137]

Yet these essays are constantly cited and relied on in constitutional cases such as *Chadha*, and in the opinions of the new textualists.[138] Pragmatically I would advise lawyers to consult them because they are useful—and useful in some of the same ways that statutory legislative history often is. They have an authority value not because what the authors say is binding law (as the constitutional text is) but because the authors help us to understand the practical context of the constitutional text. The flexibility connoted by the "necessary and proper" clause and the sweeping power of the supremacy clause, the more limited power granted in the commander-in-chief clause, and the exacting requirements of the bicameralism and presentment clauses are all linguistic conventions associated with important terms of the Constitution's text, which *The Federalist* essays explicate and situate for the interpreter.[139] But the value of the essays is not just definitional, for they also suggest instances where the original participants expected to disrupt prior practice. The supremacy clause, for example, seems a rupture from the practice of the Articles of Confederation, and the essays of *The Federalist* reinforce that impression.

So, too, statutory legislative history is often useful in situating the statute's terminology within historical practice. If a statutory provision is a "term of art," with a specialized meaning that would not be apparent to a generalist, the legislative history may help avoid a disruption in social practice. In *Chan*, for example, the legislative history is relevant to test Scalia's proposition that defective notice in passenger injury cases has no legal consequences. Brennan's concurring opinion made out a persuasive case that the Warsaw Convention was not expected to unsettle traditional norms of waiver, and that the practice in this and other countries has been to penalize defective notice.[140] The legislative history is useful in *Duplex Printing* for the opposite reason, for it provides clues as to how much of a rupture in social practice—the labor injunction—Congress meant to create. The majority believed that the legislative signals were too weak to justify a departure from recent practice, and I believe that too is an admissible use of legislative history.

The essays of *The Federalist* are also cited for their policy value. The Constitution is a brief document, and this makes its structure and the policies of its various parts critically important to the interpreter. *The Federalist* often provides the interpreter with a theory of what function those provisions are supposed to be performing, and this purposive theory can be helpful, as it was to the Court in *Chadha*, which relied on the deliberative and faction-avoiding purposes of the bicameralism and presentment requirements. So, too, statutory legislative history often helps explain the reasons for enacting the statute, the structure of the statutory regime and why it was set up that way, and what at least some original legislators expected the statute to accomplish.

The main reason why all the Justices cite *The Federalist*, however, goes beyond its authority value or its policy value. The Justices cite the essays because of their normative value: they explicate theories of government that are unquestionably intelligent and far-sighted and that have proven robust over time. Chapter 2 of this book uses *The Federalist's* theory of lawmaking as the best way of explaining why statutory interpretation is dynamic, and Chapter 4 defends my interpretation of *The Federalist* against those who believe that the framers contemplated stagnant statutory interpretation. Though not penned by the likes of Madison and Hamilton, statutory legislative histories often explicate regulatory theories that are normatively robust. Note that the normative attractiveness of a statutory scheme often changes over time. The Endangered Species Act appeared more desirable in the abstract discussions of its 1973 enactment than it did in *TVA v. Hill*, when it meant flushing away a multimillion-dollar dam. Other statutes rest on a normative theory that grows in stature over time, as *The Federalist* has.

The Court's opinion in *Alfred H. Mayer* relied on legislative history to demonstrate that the policy of the Civil Rights Act of 1866 was to eradicate as completely as possible the continuing economic disabilities of African Americans; Harlan's dissent relied on legislative history to show that several of the key players expected the statute to apply only in states with formal legal barriers. Consider now the third opinion in the case, Douglas's concurring opinion, which critically interpreted the statute in light of the history of racism in America.[141] This opinion illustrates the normative value of legislative history.

Douglas joined the Court's analysis of the Senate and House materials, especially the Schurz Report on the private violence and discrimination against African Americans in the wake of the Civil War, but he supplemented that analysis with historical accounts of Reconstruction by African American historians William E. B. Du Bois and Frederick Douglass.[142] He also related these broader historical materials to subsequent developments. Although state-sanctioned racial discrimination was the object of most of the Court's attention in the modern era, Douglas argued that private discrimination, both antecedent to and nurtured by state discrimination, vigorously persists, "a spectacle of slavery unwilling to die."[143] Reflecting meticulous historical research and experience and written from the point of view of African Americans, the work of Du Bois and Douglass enabled the interpreter to trace a direct link between slavery in the past and current discriminatory attitudes. Specifically, these sources suggest that slavery was both a legal and a cultural institution resting equally on racial subordination and stereotypes about Africans, that the legal end of slavery did not end the entrenched cultural attitudes and soon enough gave way to the legal establishment of Jim Crow, and that the legal end of Jim Crow similarly failed to erase racist attitudes. This historical evidence is central to the Court's holding that private discrimination in housing is a badge of slavery which Congress can penalize pursuant to its powers under the Thirteenth Amendment.

A normativist approach recognizes that the historical evidence is filtered through the interpreter's point of view, which is both situated and critical. It is situated insofar as it reflects the interpreter's own horizon of assumptions and ideology. It is critical insofar as the interpreter privileges some of the historical evidence and subjects other evidence to doubt, if not disbelief. Harlan's dissent argued that interpreting the 1866 act to prohibit discrimination in private property transfers would be at odds with "the individualistic ethic of [that] time, which emphasized personal freedom and embodied a distaste for governmental interference," as well as with the customs of both North and South, which permitted private discrimination against African Americans as a matter of course.[144] This is a perceptive point, and one that undermines the Court's conclusion that interpreters in 1866 would have applied the statute to private transactions. But Douglas responded that the "customs" detailed by Harlan are themselves subject to critique, and "have no place in the jurisprudence of a nation striving to rejoin the human race."[145] His stance was explicitly normativist: the original purpose of the statute is one that looks even better today than it did in 1866, and should be interpreted even more broadly than its framers contemplated.

Douglas's normativist stance in *Alfred H. Mayer* is an attractive one, but recall that Justice Brewer in *Holy Trinity Church* took an equally normativist stance, which seems less defensible to modern sensibilities. The lesson he drew from the statute's legislative history was that limits on immigration should be applied liberally to "laborers" and the like, but not to "brain toilers"; the class and educational bias evident in this preference is questionable. Yet more strikingly, Brewer urged at the end of his opinion that it would be anomalous for our laws to exclude a man of the cloth, given our constitutional, legal, and cultural heritage as a "Christian nation."[146] This value is even more controversial. Doesn't the normativist approach invite such questionable second-guessing of prior legislative judgments?

Perhaps, but it is clear (from this book, I hope) that value judgments inevitably influence the way one reads the text and legislative history of a statute, as it did in *Jett*, for example. Like Douglas, the four dissenting Justices (Brennan, Marshall, Blackmun, and Stevens) consistently advocated a multiplicity of judicial remedies for civil rights violations, based on their substantive view that antidiscrimination laws are privileged and important in our legal system. Unlike Douglas, the four plurality Justices (Rehnquist, White, O'Connor, and Kennedy) have shown reluctance to expand antidiscrimination remedies beyond the ambit clearly defined by Congress. It is not surprising that the eight Justices read the same historical evidence and came up with such different stories about what the 1866 act means. All were acting in good faith as amateur historians. But the evidence each selected, the questions he or she asked of it, and the significance accorded it were decisively influenced by the different preconceptions held by each Justice.

The value of the normativist approach is that it would require statutory interpreters to articulate their presumptions more openly, to set out their substantive theory (based on legislative history and subsequent developments) so that it can be criticized, and to respond to criticisms on the merits. Generally, the more satisfactory Supreme Court opinions using legislative history are those that self-consciously place the history of the statute in the context of a larger historical and normative narrative.[147] I consider these opinions more satisfactory than other opinions (including other opinions in the same cases) not necessarily because I agree with their conclusions or normative frameworks, but because the opinions are candid about the values they are applying, use historical materials to highlight rather than submerge the policy tensions involved in cases, and are genuinely practical as well as informative about how the original legislative materials are related to subsequent developments (sometimes the answer is, refreshingly, not much).

The debate over the new textualism which raged in the 1980s should be ended with a concession that the new textualists were right to focus attention on the meaning of statutory language in the context of the whole statute, related or similar statutes, and the U.S. Code generally, but were wrong to dismiss legislative discussions as irrelevant. A pragmatic statutory interpreter is very much interested in the expectations of those who worked on the statute, the reasons why they made certain linguistic and structural choices, and their underlying normative presuppositions. A critical interpreter is also interested in how well those expectations, reasons, and presuppositions have met the test of time.

8 · Vertical versus Horizontal Coherence

Traditional liberal theory emphasizes vertical coherence in statutory interpretation. That is, the interpreter demonstrates that her interpretation is coherent with authoritative sources situated in the past: the original intent of the enacting legislature, previous administrative or judicial precedents interpreting the statute, and traditional or customary norms. This demonstration is important to liberal theory, and especially to the formalism popular at the end of the nineteenth century, for which the legitimacy of law rests on consent, either express (original text and intent) or implied (acceptance over time). Liberal theory also valorizes vertical coherence in order to ensure predictability and stability in the law.

The legal realists debunked arguments based on vertical coherence, arguing descriptively that there is no determinate "past" to which judges could link their current interpretations (vertical sources being manipulable) and then arguing prescriptively that law ought to be present-oriented rather than archaeological. Thus, the realists suggested that statutory interpretation depends more on horizontal coherence, or "consistency with the rest of the law" today.[1] The statutory interpreter demonstrates that her interpretation is coherent with authorities or norms located in the present: the statute's contemporary purposes, other statutes now in effect and their statutory policies, and current values. Because the realists considered law's legitimacy to be grounded in present policy needs, they were willing to throw over historical practice. They recognized the functional importance of private reliance interests predicated on law's stability, but believed that the public interest justifies overriding such private interests.

Although the realist critique revealed the importance of horizontal coherence for the legitimacy of law, its cynicism was not welcome within the mainstream legal academy or judiciary. Centrist, or legal process, scholars sought ways to reconcile the formal legitimacy and rule of law values subserved by vertical coherence with the functional legitimacy and efficiency values subserved by horizontal coherence. The key to the legal process reconciliation was a concept of *public reliance:* that is, the realists were right that the public interest could override private reliance on traditional rules, but the public interest itself may involve a reliance on those rules by state institutions. During the legal process era this idea accommodated realist policy thinking, but without requiring great shifts in public law.

Doctrinal debates about stare decisis for statutory precedents, the status of long-standing agency interpretations, and the retroactivity of new statutes were carried on within the legal process philosophy during the era of the Warren and Burger Courts, with public reliance serving as a conservatice process justification for preserving a status quo bias. Subsequently the debates moved away from the legal process synthesis. The Rehnquist Court is abandoning public reliance arguments but is replacing them with a curious blend of liberal rhetoric and realist judicial activism. This chapter develops the Court's doctrinal debates by analyzing Patterson v. McLean Credit Union.[2]

Brenda Patterson, a woman of color, sued her employer for harassing and firing her. She testified that her supervisor repeatedly impugned the competence of African Americans, humiliated her in public meetings, and passed over her for training and promotion opportunities because of her race. Patterson brought suit under section 1981 of Title 42, which assures everyone "the same right . . . to make and enforce contracts . . . as is enjoyed by white citizens."[3] The trial court held that her evidence did not make out a claim under section 1981, and Patterson appealed. An additional issue in *Patterson*, raised by the Supreme Court *sua sponte*, was whether it should overrule Runyon v. McCrary,[4] which had interpreted section 1981 to prohibit private as well as public discrimination in contractual relations. The Court declined to overrule *Runyon* but denied Patterson relief, holding that section 1981 does not cover racial discrimination during the operation of employment contracts. Congress overrode the Court's interpretation in 1991, and the courts were flooded with lawsuits raising the question whether the 1991 statute applied to pre-1991 discrimination.

Patterson reveals a Court with a skeptical attitude toward precedent even while it pays lip service to stare decisis, unwilling to bootstrap prior interpretations into settled law because of legislative inaction, and disinclined to apply statutes retroactively. This is a curious stance, combining confusion (the first point), superrealism (the second), and superliberalism (the third). My normative argument in this chapter is both pragmatic and critical. As a matter of pragmatism, I agree with the Court's willingness to rethink precedents and to consider legislative inaction arguments more reflectively, though its distaste for retroactive legislation is unpragmatic. As a matter of critical theory, I argue that the Court's peculiar doctrinal stance is related to an ideology of racial justice that is not openly disclosed and that is normatively unattractive.

Interpreting Legislative Inaction

Traditional liberal theories of statutory interpretation gave considerable meaning to Congress's silence. When Congress enacted a statute, it was presumed to be consistent with the common law, the canons of construction, and any long-standing interpretation of a similar statute or phrase.[5] Even while recognizing the legislature's prerogative to change legal rights and duties, liberal theory presumed continuity with previously established rights and duties. The liberal vision sought to protect vested private contract and property rights against abrupt shifts in legal rules. In contrast, the legal realists were eager for statutory policy to override the common law. Hence, they were less willing to presume that congressional silence left in place either the common law or judicial interpretations resistant to statutory policies that went beyond the common law. Legal realism was more interested in the ability of law to contribute to current policy goals and was tolerant of strong shifts in legal rules.

Legal process theory has been ambivalent about the meaning of legislative silence or inaction. Legal process Justices on the post–New Deal Court found legislative inaction a useful screening device for deciding which prior interpretations to privilege, namely, those for which there was some evidence (in legislative deliberations) of public reliance as well as the traditional private reliance. Legal process academics have been more skeptical of legislative inaction arguments, a skepticism that is supported by positive political theory. In this section of the chapter I propose a pragmatic reconciliation of the judicial practice and the academic skepticism, based on the idea that Congress has a duty to respond to building block interpretations if it disagrees with their policy. Yet the Court majority in *Patterson* unpragmatically refused to consider legislative inaction arguments, which I provisionally interpret as a signal that the Court is willing to take a more critical stance toward political practice.

The Legislative Inaction Doctrines

In the legal process era the Supreme Court developed three legislative inaction doctrines as a way of inferring public reliance: (1) the acquiescence rule that if Congress does not overturn a judicial or administrative interpretation it acquiesces in it; (2) the reenactment rule that a reenactment of a statute incorporates any settled interpretation of the statute by courts or agencies; and (3) the rejected proposal rule that proposals rejected by Congress are an indication that the statute cannot be interpreted to follow the rejected proposal. Consistent with legal process the Court has followed these doctrines only when it is satisfied that legislative inaction signals current congressional satisfaction with historic interpretations. All three of these doctrines seem at first glance to reinforce the *Runyon* interpretation of section 1981.

The Acquiescence Rule "The long time failure of Congress to alter the Act after it had been judicially construed . . . is persuasive of legislative recognition that the judicial construction is the correct one," Justice Harlan Fiske Stone wrote for the Court in Apex Hosiery Company v. Leader.[6] The *Apex Hosiery* principle is a distinctly legal process idea, protecting law's vertical coherence and private reliance interests, but for reasons of horizontal coherence and ongoing public reliance. During the legal process era this doctrine has often been cited as justification for the Court's refusal to reconsider its own precedents.

For example, in Federal Baseball Club v. National League[7] the Court held that baseball in the 1920s was not subject to the Sherman Act because its "exhibitions" were "purely state affairs" and not directly involved in interstate commerce, as required by the act. After the 1920s, of course, baseball grew into a highly popular interstate business. Yet the Court in Toolson v. New York Yankees[8] refused to overrule *Federal Baseball*, in part because "Congress has had the ruling under consideration but has not seen fit to bring such business under these laws." In the 1950s and 1960s, after *Toolson*, baseball added lucrative television contracts to its other interstate interests. This made *Federal Baseball* an increasingly anomalous opinion—especially after the Court applied the Sherman Act to other professional sports.[9] The Court in Flood v. Kuhn[10] again reconsidered *Federal Baseball* and again refused to overrule it, relying on both long-standing private reliance interests and the "positive inaction" of Congress.[11]

Congressional acquiescence has also been invoked to bootstrap settled lower court statutory interpretations into statutes, based on Congress's failure to override them after they had been brought to its attention. Additionally, the Court often finds that congressional failure to disapprove of executive department or agency regulations, while not dispositive, implies that the regulations accurately reflect congressional intent. The first section of Appendix 1 to this book collects the leading Supreme Court cases following the acquiescence rule since 1961. It also reports the equally numerous Supreme Court cases that refuse to follow the acquiescence rule.[12] The Court's justifications when not applying the rule have been consistent with the legal process philosophy: first, Congress was not aware of the judicial or administrative interpretation, or there was no sufficiently consistent line of interpretation that Congress could reasonably be charged with knowing; second, Congress has acted "as though" the interpretation were not the settled one; and third, the interpretation was so clearly erroneous that Congress could not be deemed to have ratified it.[13]

Three concurring Justices (the Brennan Justices) in *Patterson* invoked the acquiescence rule as a basis for reaffirming *Runyon*.[14] In 1968 the Supreme Court held in Jones v. Alfred H. Mayer Co.[15] that the section 1982 prohibition of discrimination in the sale or rental of property applies to private as well as public conduct. Since section 1982 is, like section 1981, apparently codified from section 1 of the 1866 Civil Rights Act, lower courts after 1968 interpreted section 1981 to apply to discrimination in private contract matters.[16] Congress was aware of this stream of lower court decisions, for when it was considering amendments to Title VII of the Civil Rights Act in 1971–72, it considered and rejected proposals to make Title VII the exclusive remedy for employment discrimination. The Supreme Court held that section 1981 applies to private contracts in three decisions between 1972 and 1976.[17] Soon after the Court's decision in *Runyon*, Congress enacted the Civil Rights Attorney's Fees Awards Act of 1976,[18] which assumed the correctness of *Runyon*'s interpretation and sought to encourage lawsuits pursuant to sections 1981 and 1982 by providing counsel fees to prevailing parties. Since 1976 the Supreme Court has repeatedly held or assumed that sections 1981 and 1982 apply to private discrimination.[19] Congress has done nothing to alter or overturn that interpretation, even though it has overturned other Supreme Court interpretations of civil rights statutes. This chronology seems to make *Patterson* much like *Apex Hosiery* and *Flood* and unlike the exceptions.

The Reenactment Rule   In many of the acquiescence cases, including *Apex Hosiery*, the Court has emphasized that legislative inaction was particularly meaningful because Congress had focused on the statute and amended it. Even though the amendments did not add to or detract from the prior interpretation at issue, Congress's failure to respond to that interpretation when it was considering the precise statute "is itself evidence that Congress affirmatively intended to preserve [the interpretation]."[20] This form of the acquiescence argument is closely related to the reenactment rule, in which "Congress is presumed to be aware of an administrative or judicial interpretation of a statute and to adopt that interpretation when it reenacts a statute without change."[21] The second section of Appendix 1 lists the leading Supreme Court cases since 1961 applying the reenactment rule.

Although the reenactment rule seems more procedurally attractive than the acquiescence rule (the congressional ratification occurs in connection with statutory enactment), it, too, is rather cautiously invoked by the Court. The Court usually cites evidence that Congress actually was or must have been aware of the previous interpretation when it reenacted the provision in question. An illustrative case is United States v. Board of Commissioners of Sheffield, Alabama.[22] Section 5 of the Voting Rights Act of 1965 provides for Department of Justice preclearance of specific electoral changes for "a State or political subdivision" covered by section 4 of the act. In *Sheffield* the Court held that municipalities within covered states are subject to preclearance review. The Court's main argument was that the attorney general, who is charged with enforcing the statute, had long interpreted preclearance to apply to municipalities and school districts and that Congress had reenacted the act in 1970 and 1975 without changing section 5 to overrule that interpretation. "When a Congress that re-enacts a statute voices its approval of an administrative or other interpretation thereof, Congress is treated as having adopted that interpretation, and the Court is bound thereby." The Court recognized the argument, made in a dissenting opinion, that unexplained inaction of Congress has little significance, but responded that Congress was specifically and repeatedly made aware of the attorney general's interpretation and apparently approved of it.[23]

Like the acquiescence rule, the reenactment rule is not always followed (see the cases in Appendix 1), and the three justifications for avoiding the acquiescence rule are also used to avoid the reenactment rule. The leading case is Girouard v. United States,[24] which held that the Nationality Act of 1940 did not require a noncitizen to take an oath to bear arms for this country in order to obtain citizenship. A dissenting opinion by Chief Justice Stone, the author of *Apex Hosiery*, relied on prior Supreme Court interpretations of the statutory oath requirement. Although Stone had not joined the earlier precedents, he felt bound by them, since Congress had adopted them by reenacting the provision without change in 1940. The Court rejected the reenactment argument. More persuasive for the Court than Congress's inaction in 1940 was Congress's action in 1942, when it specifically amended the act to permit noncombatants to become citizens.[25] *Girouard* represents the attenuated power of the reenactment rule when Congress has acted "as though" the prior interpretation were not settled law. Also, like the acquiescence rule, the reenactment rule is inapplicable to interpretations that Congress would not reasonably have known about or that are patently wrong.[26]

Under these reenactment cases the 1976 Fees Act lends some support to the acquiescence argument in *Patterson*, as the Brennan Justices argued. The statute provides counsel fees for prevailing plaintiffs in cases brought under sections 1981, 1982, and 1983 of Title 42. The Senate report suggested that the main reason sections 1981 and 1982 were included was to ensure that plaintiffs pursuing lawsuits against private discrimination (lawsuits that were not allowed before *Alfred H. Mayer*) would have similar counsel fee incentives as plaintiffs suing under Titles VII and VIII of the modern civil rights laws. The House report and floor statements by the House manager of the bill expressed congressional understanding and approval of the Supreme Court's interpretation of section 1981.[27]

The Rejected Proposal Rule   The Court sometimes fortifies its argument that legislative inaction has ratified the existing interpretation by pointing to the rejection of the opposite interpretation by either the enacting Congress or a subsequent one. For example, the "positive inaction" on which *Flood* relied was in part Congress's consideration of dozens of proposed bills seeking to overrule *Federal Baseball* and its refusal to enact any of them. The rejected proposal rule is not limited to these cases, however, and has evolved into an independent doctrine. "Few principles of statutory construction are more compelling than the proposition that Congress does not intend *sub silentio* to enact statutory language that it has earlier discarded in favor of other language."[28] The third section of Appendix 1 collects the leading rejected proposal cases since 1961.

In Sinclair Refining Company v. Atkinson,[29] for example, the Court held that in a lawsuit brought under section 301 of the Labor Management Relations Act of 1947 "for violation of contracts between an employer and a labor organization"[30] an employer could not obtain an injunction against a strike. The Court's main reason for not following the statute's apparent plain meaning was that such an injunction would be contrary to the Norris–La Guardia Act's general prohibition of federal injunctions in labor disputes (recall the denouement of Chapter 3). The Court also relied on a rejected proposal argument. The conference committee for the 1947 act rejected a provision in the House bill that would have made the Norris–La Guardia Act inapplicable to suits to enforce section 301 duties. "When the repeal of a highly significant law is urged upon [Congress] and that repeal is rejected after careful consideration and discussion, the normal expectation is that courts will be faithful to their trust and abide by that decision."[31]

Sinclair illustrates the Court's willingness to find significance in a conference committee's rejection of a specific provision. The Court may also infer meaning from the rejection of a specific proposal or interpretation by one chamber of Congress, or even by congressional committees.[32] In most of the cases where the Court has refused to draw significance from a rejected proposal, it has stressed that the proposal differed from the interpretive issue then under consideration, and hence Congress was not faced with a clear referendum on that issue.[33]

One of the leading rejected proposal cases is *Runyon*, and the Brennan Justices in *Patterson* relied on the rejected proposal doctrine. Proposals to render section 1981 inapplicable to private employment discrimination were rejected by Congress when it amended Title VII in the Equal Employment Opportunity Act of 1972.[34] During Senate deliberation on the bill, referring explicitly to the Civil Rights Act of 1966, Senator Roman Hruska introduced an amendment to make Title VII and the Equal Pay Act the exclusive remedies for employment discrimination.[35] The floor manager for the bill opposed the Hruska amendment, emphasizing the importance of section 1981 as an "alternative means to redress individual grievances" needed to supplement Title VII. The Senate twice rejected the Hruska amendment, the first time on a tie vote.[36] The House bill, however, included a provision making Title VII the exclusive remedy for employment discrimination complaints. But in conference committee the House receded from its position, and the final version of the statute had no exclusive remedy provision.[37] The defeat of the Hruska amendment and the conference committee's rejection of the House proposal (both proposing that section 1981 be inapplicable to private employment discrimination) "strongly militates against a judgment that Congress intended a result that it expressly declined to enact."[38]

Legal Process Debate over Legislative Inaction Cases

As formulated by the post-1938 Court, the legislative inaction rules mediate the tension between horizontal and vertical coherence by privileging prior statutory interpretations, but only when there is some evidence that they reflect current legislative intent. As to the latter point, the cases rely on a metaphor that goes something like this: Wadlington tells Krattenmaker, "Go fetch me some soup meat." Krattenmaker fetches beef and presents it to Wadlington with the query, "Isn't this the kind of meat you intended?" Wadlington says nothing. Under the acquiescence rule we can infer that it is more likely than not that Wadlington did mean beef. Suppose Wadlington issues the same directive every week for a year, Krattenmaker brings beef every time, and Wadlington keeps issuing the same directive. Under the reenactment rule we can infer that it is more likely than not that Wadlington did mean beef. Finally, suppose Wadlington's spouse suggests, "Dearest, why don't you have Krattenmaker fetch us some chicken instead of soup meat?" And yet Wadlington immediately turns to Krattenmaker and asks only for "soup meat." Under the rejected proposal rule we can infer that it is more likely than not that Wadlington meant beef. If one combines these three scenarios (as Brennan did in *Patterson*), the inference as to what Wadlington meant is powerful. She meant beef.

Notwithstanding this analogy, legal process academics have, at least since the early 1950s, been more skeptical of legislative inaction arguments than the legal process Court has been.[39] The argument is that Congress is materially different from Wadlington. To begin with, unlike Wadlington, Congress is a discontinuous decision maker. Wadlington is the same person, albeit older, year after year. Congress turns over every two years, and the only intent that is constitutionally authoritative is the intent of the Congress that actually enacts the legislation. Also unlike Wadlington, Congress is a collective decision maker. Whereas Wadlington may sometimes be "of two minds," Congress is always of two minds (the House and the Senate), and each of them contains many different minds, in good years. This makes it difficult to figure out what the intent of Congress is when it fails to do something. These are the arguments that the *Patterson* majority suggested when it declined to find that Congress had effectively "ratified" *Runyon*.[40]

The Hart and Sacks legal process materials, for example, questioned whether acquiescence and most rejected proposals are "competent" evidence of statutory meaning. Because article I, section 7 of the Constitution requires both bicameral approval and presentment to the president before a bill becomes a law, the failure of a later Congress to do anything has no formal bearing on what the original Congress enacted. If concurrent resolutions, passed by both Houses of Congress but not presented to the president, are not formally entitled to authoritative weight in statutory interpretation, how can congressional inaction be any more significant?[41]

Thus, Hart and Sacks, like *Patterson*, would question the competence of Congress's failure to override *Runyon* and even its rejection of specific proposals in 1971–72 at least as evidence of Congress's intent in 1866. The only competent argument would be the one based on the Fees Act, a new statute subject to interpretation. Although the reenactment cases are not subject to the formal competency objection, the Fees Act is not quite a reenactment of section 1981, although its inclusion of section 1981 was premised on the assumption that the section provided a remedy for private employment discrimination.[42] In short, Congress apparently was relying on *Runyon*'s interpretation of section 1981 when it adopted the Fees Act, and Congress's public reliance is entitled to consideration under the legal process philosophy.

Even if subsequent legislative inaction is held to be competent evidence of legislative intent, Hart and Sacks raised problems of relevance for such materials.[43] What does the inaction establish? There are as many reasons for Congress not to act as there are members of Congress—ranging from complete disinterest to indecision, higher priority for other measures, dislike of one feature of the bill, or approval of existing law.[44] Modern scholarship on the limited legislative agenda, the ease with which measures can be derailed by determined or well-placed factions, and the ways in which congressional leadership can stack the results of majority votes through procedural manipulations only reinforces Hart and Sacks's skepticism (recall Chapter 1).

Consider the relevance of the Hruska amendment's defeat. The amendment did not single out section 1981, nor did it posit that section 1981 should be reinterpreted to apply only to public discrimination. Hruska offered the amendment because then-current law permitted a "multiplicity of actions to be instituted against a respondent before a number of separate and distinct forums for the same alleged offense."[45] Although section 1981 was one of the "multiplicity of actions" that concerned Hruska, neither he nor his amendment expressed an opinion as to the ambit of section 1981. The Senate bill expanded Title VII to cover discrimination by state and local governments against their employees, and so section 1981 was a relevant statute however it was interpreted. Because the Hruska amendment did not present itself as a referendum on the correctness of *Runyon*-type interpretations of the 1866 act, its defeat was not inevitably a ratification of that interpretation.

But even if it had been such a referendum on section 1981's applicability, its relevance can still be questioned. While *Runyon* correctly stated that "Senator Hruska's proposed amendment was rejected," it did not mention that the amendment failed on a tie vote—thirty-three senators voted for it and thirty-three against.[46] Indeed, there were actually thirty-four senators on the floor in favor of the amendment, which means that a majority of those senators present supported it. But the thirty-fourth senator announced that he was a "live pair" for an absent senator.[47] It is unusual for a senator to agree to be a live pair when the outcome is affected, so probably some deal had been worked out by the Senate Democratic leadership to save the bill from the Hruska amendment. In any event, since at least half the voting senators agreed with the amendment, *Runyon*'s attempt to use it to prove legislative intent is questionable.

Like the Senate Labor and Public Welfare Committee, the House Education and Labor Committee had reported a bill that preserved existing remedies and refused to make Title VII the exclusive remedy for employment discrimination.[48] As I have noted, its bill was defeated on the floor by a substitute that contained (inter alia) an exclusivity provision. In the conference committee the House receded from its version, and the Senate nonexclusivity position prevailed. Though not mentioned in *Runyon*, Brennan's concurring opinion in *Patterson* invoked this outcome as evidence of congressional ratification.

But the public record contains no explanation of the conference's decision to choose the Senate position; any explanation would probably have been woefully general (such as a preference for a range of remedies for employment discrimination); and there is a likely procedural explanation for why the

Senate position prevailed, one that goes to the composition of the conference committee. The custom is to appoint as conferees members of the relevant committee in each chamber. Hence, the conference committee for the 1972 act consisted of the members of the House Education and Labor Committee, a majority of whom had opposed the exclusivity provision in committee and on the House floor, plus members of the Senate Labor and Public Welfare Committee, an overwhelming majority of whom had voted against the Hruska amendment.[49] Given this composition, the conference committee was unlikely to choose the Erlenborn-Hruska position. But should a proposal deleted by an unrepresentative collection of conferees be binding on the whole Congress?

Although these competence and relevance arguments may seem decisive in support of the majority's approach in *Patterson*, Brennan's position can also be articulated in legal process terms. The inaction of an actor—whether it be Wadlington or Congress—may have legal significance, not because it is evidence of actual intent but because it is evidence of an intent presumed by law. For example, criminal liability in Anglo-American law does not attach simply because an actor fails to save a dying person (even if the actor's intention is malicious)—unless there is a statutory or common law duty for the actor to do something. In Anglo-American contract law silence usually does not constitute acceptance of an offer (even if so intended), unless the parties' relationship has created a duty to respond negatively if the offeree wants to decline.[50] The best public law example is the president's use of the veto power. If the president does not veto a bill passed by Congress within ten days, the inaction is deemed an approval of the bill, which becomes law whatever the president's actual intent or the reason for the failure to act.

Thus, the legislative inaction cases, which usually speak in terms of *presumed* rather than *actual* intent anyway,[51] can be read as creating a duty for Congress to respond to judicial and agency interpretations of statutes when it disagrees. If Congress does not fulfill this duty, the Court is free to presume that the interpretations were correct, a presumption that can be rebutted by showing that Congress was not aware of the interpretation, or that Congress did send some signals of disapproval, or that the interpretations were incorrect and are now mischievous. The policy basis for such a legal process presumption is continuity in the law, especially when the continuity creates reliance interests that would be disturbed by a new interpretation.[52] Hence, the strongest case for application of the presumption is for a "building block" interpretation, namely, an agency or judicial interpretation (1) which is authoritative and settled, setting a firm, decisive direction for the statute's development; (2) on which persons subject to the statute have relied in structuring their conduct; and (3) on which public decision makers have relied in developing further legal rules. Conversely, the presumption of correctness does not inhere in a judicial, executive, or agency interpretation that is not authoritative and has not been the basis for private and public reliance. Such interpretations may in fact be correct, but they are entitled to no presumption.

Brennan's approach in *Patterson* is supported by a presumed intent approach, since *Runyon* was a building block interpretation. First, its interpretation was treated as authoritative by the Supreme Court and by lower courts applying section 1981. Second, there may have been some private reliance on *Runyon*. Brenda Patterson, for example, asserted that she waived her Title VII claims because she did not go through its procedural labyrinth, thinking that she could bring the same claims under section 1981.[53] Third, there was substantial public reliance on *Runyon*, for example, the Fees Act. More generally, Congress relied on *Runyon*esque multiplicity of remedies as a weapon in its increasing commitment to enforcement of antidiscrimination laws. Indeed, 66 senators and 118 members of the House filed a brief in *Patterson* asserting their continuing support for and reliance on the *Runyon* interpretation. The brief made it clear that many legislators considered overruling *Runyon* not only an error but an interference in Congress's agenda, and there was a similar consensus among the states.[54] Because *Runyon* was a building block interpretation, it was entitled to the presumption of correctness Brennan gave it under presumed intent theory.

Positive Political Critique of the Legislative Inaction Rules

Given the obvious legal process reasoning behind Brennan's concurring opinion, it is curious that the Court in *Patterson* brusquely dismissed the legislative inaction arguments in the opinion's only footnote. My hypothesis is that the Court was inspired by a third difference between Congress and my hypothetical Wadlington, a difference underappreciated in traditional legal process theory: what Wadlington wants has few if any third-party effects, while conclusions about congressional preferences have far-reaching third-party effects. A final way to criticize the legislative inaction rules is to view them as part of the structure of political decision making—and to consider how they might contribute to dysfunctions in the evolution of legal rules.

One dysfunction is that the interests of the "haves" (business, unions, the state) tend to be developed at the expense of the "have nots" (consumers, single-parent families, people with low incomes).[55] This occurs because "have" groups work the system—the legislature, agencies, and courts—more effectively to chip away at rules that hurt their interests and to advance rules that help them. Their instruments are lobbying, political action committees, and coordinated repeat-play litigation strategies. The legislative inaction rules can be a way for "have" groups to multiply their advantages. Thus, when "have" groups lose in judicial or agency forums, they often have a fighting chance to override their losses in the legislature. When they win, however, it is unlikely that Congress will override, for the legislature is loath to act decisively when interest group opposition is intense. Yet under traditional doctrine the Court might bootstrap this failure to act into a legislative ratification.

The history of baseball's exemption from the antitrust laws illustrates this phenomenon. Baseball may simply have been lucky to have had its antitrust status first litigated in the 1920s *(Federal Baseball)*, when its activities were localized and the Supreme Court took a restrictive view of the federal government's power under the commerce clause. Baseball's increasing interstate activities coincided with the New Deal Court's expansive interpretation of the commerce clause, yet baseball was able to keep its antitrust exemption through two Supreme Court reexaminations, even as other professional sports were found nonexempt. Both *Toolson* and *Flood* relied on congressional failure to override *Federal Baseball*, but the political process was stacked against an override. Baseball owners as a group were few in number, homogeneous, and wealthy, the classic ingredients for interest group power.[56] That alone would have been enough to block most override efforts. Moreover, serious efforts to override were not even attempted because there was no politically salient group demanding them.[57]

Thus between 1957 and 1965 the intense legislative interest was only in expanding baseball's exemption to other sports, since the owners were the best-organized players in the legislative ballgame. To consider this an example of "positive inaction" decisive in reaffirming the antitrust exemption, as *Flood* did, only reinforces a dysfunction in Congress. For this reason I propose that the presumption of correctness for a building block interpretation apply only when interests hurt by the interpretation have had meaningful access to the legislative process. This critique leaves the presumption in place for *Patterson*, since the employer groups harmed by *Runyon* had plenty of access. Hence, we still do not know why the *Patterson* majority was so dismissive of legislative inaction arguments.

Positive political theory suggests another line of critique that may justify the Court's action. An additional dysfunction in the legislative process— amply illustrated by the failed override efforts in 1971–72—is inertia: it is much easier to block congressional action than it is to obtain such action. From a liberal perspective legislative inertia can be useful insofar as it prevents the federal government from expanding state regulation until there is a strong political consensus in favor of such action. But the legislative inaction rules turn the impact of legislative inertia on its head: Congress's failure to act means not only that agencies and courts can greatly expand on regulatory directives without being overridden, but also that the failure to override itself becomes a barrier to subsequent deregulation.

Accordingly, *Patterson* became the occasion for the Court to deemphasize the legislative inaction rules as dysfunctional. As many as six of the nine Justices thought *Alfred H. Mayer* (interpreting section 1982) wrongly decided,[58] a Warren Court exhumation of Reconstruction-era statutes to provide more generous remedies than Congress was willing to do in the 1960s. Because the Democratic leadership and the gatekeeping committees in Congress were sympathetic to *Alfred H. Mayer,* it was never overridden. *Runyon* then used this inertia as a basis not only for preserving *Alfred H. Mayer* as a precedent but also for expanding its interpretation to section 1981, an arguably distinguishable provision. *Runyon* was a schools case, *Patterson* an employment case. To expand a decision that a majority of the Court thought wrong (and some thought a scandal) yet again, based on legislative inaction, must have been repugnant to as many as five Justices of the Court.

Overruling Statutory Precedents

Under traditional liberal theory the role of courts is to declare the law, not to change it. The doctrine of stare decisis requires that a court treat prior decisions as presumptively correct. Nineteenth-century liberal theory held that private law precedents, involving "vested rights" of contract or property, should almost never be overruled, although the Court had greater discretion to rethink constitutional precedents.[59] The same virtually absolute stare decisis applied to decisions interpreting at least some statutes: "After a statute has been settled by judicial construction, the construction becomes, so far as contract rights acquired under it are concerned, as much a part of the statute as the text itself, and a change of decision is to all intents and purposes the same in its effect on contracts as an amendment of the law by means of a legislative enactment,"[60] and hence unavailable under liberal premises.

The legal realists argued that judges are not constrained by precedent and that stare decisis should be more of a functional rule of thumb than a formal, iron-fisted command. A court is not, and should not be, "inexorably bound by its own precedents, but, in the interest of uniformity of treatment to litigants, and of stability and certainty in the law . . . will follow the rule of law which it has established in earlier cases unless clearly convinced that the rule was originally erroneous or is no longer sound because of changed conditions and that more good than harm would come by departing from precedent."[61] Realist Justice William O. Douglas urged that the Supreme Court should feel free to overrule statutory as well as constitutional precedents.[62]

The realists' willingness to reexamine precedents freely made the mainstream legal community nervous.[63] In response to that nervousness, legal process judges of the 1930s and 1940s suggested functional reasons for something like the old liberal position. Justice Louis Brandeis maintained that "in most matters it is more important that the applicable rule of law be settled than that it be settled right," and argued for strict stare decisis, except in constitutional cases, "where correction through legislative action is practically impossible."[64] In the 1940s Justices Stone and Frankfurter picked up on Brandeis's suggestion that the Court's statutory decisions are entitled to extra stare decisis deference because Congress is more institutionally competent than the Court to make policy corrections.[65] Also important was Edward Levi's argument that public as well as private decision makers rely on statutory precedents, which set a direction for the statute that ought not be unraveled unless it was unconstitutional. As he put it, a heightened adherence to stare decisis "marks an essential difference between statutory interpretation on the one hand and [common] law and constitutional interpretation on the other."[66]

Since the 1940s the Supreme Court has routinely cited the Brandeis-Levi rationale as the basis for what I call its super-strong presumption of correctness for statutory precedents.[67] The rule and its rationale, or even just the slogan that erroneous statutory precedents can be corrected by the legislature, have also been accepted by most legal process scholars and state courts.[68] Not surprisingly, *Patterson* invoked this reason as a justification for reaffirming *Runyon*.[69]

Other legal process scholars have been sharply critical of the super-strong presumption, however.[70] In this part of the chapter I explicate several process-based escape hatches from the super-strong presumption that the Court itself has created and argue that they reflect both an unease with the strict rule and the difficulty of applying it. I then develop an evolutive theory for overruling statutory precedents which I proposed in 1988 and which was apparently accepted in *Patterson*. I conclude with a critical analysis of *Patterson*'s use of stare decisis, arguing that the Court only gave lip service to the principle and was willing to throw it over for normative reasons.

Escape Hatches from the Super-Strong Presumption

There are two striking points about the super-strong presumption of correctness for statutory precedents: how often the Court invokes it like settled doctrine (as in *Patterson*), and how often the Court treats it like boilerplate, to be recited and then ignored (also as in *Patterson*, as we shall see). Appendix 2 lists decisions from the 1961 through 1991 terms in which the Court overruled (explicitly or implicitly) statutory precedents or important statements in such precedents. There are more than ninety such overrulings. This might be surprising in light of the Court's repeated endorsement of the Brandeis-Levi position, and one might conclude that the super-strong presumption is just a charade. That would be premature without an effort to reconcile the Court's frequent departures from strict stare decisis with the Brandeis-Levi rationale.

The Court's practice suggests a reconciliation: The Court might reconsider its earlier statutory interpretations provided (1) they are not legitimately binding precedents for the issue under consideration; (2) the statutory scheme represents a delegation of common law responsibilities to the Court; or (3) the interpretations have been undercut by subsequent statutory developments. It seems to me, however, that the escape hatches are just as malleable as the super-strong presumption. For example, two of the three escape hatches were applicable in *Patterson*, yet the Court failed to mention them.

The Procedural Exception   Justice Frankfurter accepted traditional stare decisis concerns (continuity in the law, protection of reliance interests) but believed a statutory precedent that did not reflect a complete and deliberative consideration of the issue by the Court was not entitled to strong stare decisis. Thus, for Frankfurter, "the relevant demands of stare decisis do not preclude considering for the first time thoroughly and in the light of the best available evidence of congressional purpose, a statutory interpretation which started as an unexamined assumption on the basis of inapplicable citations and has the claim of a dogma solely through reiteration."[71] This "proceduralist exception" posits that what the Court is overruling is not a rationally deliberated precedent, and hence not a "true" precedent under the legal process philosophy.

Frankfurter's proceduralist exception is the most widely invoked explanation used by the Court when it has overruled statutory precedents. There are three types of overrulings, all of which demonstrate the exception's elasticity. First, the Court often disapproves of "dicta," statements in statutory decisions which are not necessary to the decision of the case and/or not thoroughly briefed, and hence not entitled to full precedential effect. The third section of Appendix 2 lists several dozen cases in which the Court has disapproved of what I consider significant dicta in prior opinions. This finding is potentially troubling. Statements in Supreme Court opinions that the Court later characterizes as dicta are often treated as authoritative by lower courts, private parties, and Congress itself. By characterizing earlier statements as dicta, the Court seems at times too willing to shift directions.[72] This tendency is at odds with the Brandeis-Levi rationale for the super-strong presumption, or even with the rationale for ordinary stare decisis.

A second variation of the proceduralist exception permits the Court to overrule one statutory precedent that is inconsistent with others.[73] Like the exception for dicta, the exception for inconsistent precedents is plausible but manipulable (what constitutes "inconsistency"?). Also, once one realizes that the Court's interpretations of a statute often run in several different directions, this exception suggests the difficulty of realizing the goals of the super-strong presumption against overruling statutory precedents.

A third variation posits that statutory precedents may be overruled when "new" legislative history has been uncovered which undermines a rule created by old precedents.[74] This is the most questionable version of the proceduralist exception because the whole point of the Brandeis-Levi rule is to head off constant reappraisal of the historical evidence and to send a clear signal to Congress; a plain error exception, which this resembles, is not admissible in their theory. It is not surprising that this exception has been subject to quarrel.[75]

Frankfurter's proceduralist exception has been a very popular justification for overruling statutory precedents. Interestingly, it was arguably applicable in *Patterson*, which applied section 1981 to private employers. *Runyon*, the statutory precedent the Court called into question, applied section 1981 to private schools. The Court could have limited *Runyon* to nonemployment settings, based on a Frankfurteresque argument that *Runyon* and subsequent cases applying *Runyon* in employment settings did not address whether the Civil Rights Act of 1866 applies to private conduct for which the Civil Rights Act of 1964 provides a similar but more limited private right of action.

The Exception for Common Law Statutes   Frankfurter also argued that statutes having constitutional dimensions (such as section 1981) may be more freely reinterpreted than ordinary statutes.[76] The rationale is that statutes intimately tied to constitutional developments ought to be reinterpreted as constitutional law evolves. Since the Court follows a more relaxed stare decisis role in constitutional cases, it should take similar liberties in reinterpreting those related statutes, consistent with the Brandeis-Levi rationale for heightened stare decisis in statutory cases. This exception explains several of the Court's overrulings,[77] and it has spawned a related exception.

Justice John Paul Stevens has argued that the super-strong presumption should be relaxed for statutes (such as the Sherman Act and section 1983) phrased in "sweeping, general terms, expecting the federal courts to interpret them by developing legal rules on a case-by-case basis in the common law tradition."[78] Insofar as Congress expects the Court to develop statutory rules in a common law fashion, Stevens suggests Congress should expect the Court to rescind those rules much as it would overrule common law precedents. Just as administrative agencies which are delegated lawmaking responsibilities to fill statutory gaps are routinely allowed to change their interpretations of the statute, courts which are implicitly left with the responsibility for filling in the details of common law statutes should be given leeway to experiment.

About half the cases in which the Court has explicitly overruled statutory precedents are decisions interpreting common law statutes. But this exception has not been applied consistently. For example, it did not impel the Court to relax the super-strong presumption in *Flood*, which involved the quintessential common law statute (the Sherman Act), and which could also have justified more lenient stare decisis because the error of *Federal Baseball* rested in its outdated understanding of Congress's constitutional powers under the commerce clause.[79] Similarly, *Patterson* might also have invoked Stevens's exception for common law statutes, since the Reconstruction statutes (sections 1981, 1982, 1983, and 1985) are broadly phrased ones which the Court has developed in common law fashion, often in tandem with constitutional developments.

The Reliance Exception   The Supreme Court in Patsy v. Board of Regents[80] applied a balancing test to determine whether the super-strong presumption against overruling statutory precedents should be relaxed. Justice Thurgood Marshall's opinion considered whether the precedent represented a departure from prior decisions, whether the legislative history of the statute undermined the precedent, whether private parties had reasonably relied on the precedent, and whether subsequent statutory developments had built on or detracted from the principle(s) indicated by the precedent. Marshall incorporated features of Frankfurter's proceduralist exception but explicitly added inquiries into private and public reliance.

Marshall's exception for cases where there has been no public reliance on the precedent is consonant with the Brandeis-Levi rationale for the superstrong presumption, and with the legal process philosophy generally. Where Congress itself has relied on a precedent when it legislates, the precedent may be entitled to a super-strong presumption of correctness. Contrariwise, if Congress has clearly not relied on the precedent, it is entitled only to normal stare decisis protection. The exception also helps explain many of the cases that are not satisfactorily explained by the proceduralist exception and the exception for common law statutes.

For example, Marshall's exception provides the best argument for strong stare decisis in *Flood* (from which Marshall himself dissented). After *Toolson*, the Subcommittee on Study of Monopoly of the House Judiciary Committee held immediate hearings on the main alleged anticompetitive practice (the reserve clause) and urged no action to modify *Toolson*, on the grounds that "the overwhelming preponderance of the evidence established baseball's need for some sort of reserve clause."[81] And, as I noted earlier, legislative interest focused on expanding to other sports the antitrust immunity reaffirmed in *Toolson*, not on taking away baseball's immunity. In addition to baseball's private reliance on its antitrust exemption, it could be said that there was strong public reliance as well: congressional expectations were not disturbed when *Flood* refused to overrule *Toolson*. Much the same could be said of *Patterson*'s reaffirmation of *Runyon*, and the Court noted that there had been no intervening developments in law that would undermine presumptive reliance on *Runyon*.

An Evolutive Approach to Statutory Stare Decisis

Since the early 1960s the Court has sent mixed signals as to when it will relax the super-strong presumption of correctness. Its almost capricious treatment of stare decisis is open to question. The legal process tradition would counsel abandoning the Rube Goldberg contraption the Court has constructed—the super-strong presumption and then all the escape hatches to ameliorate the harsh rule—and would urge that the Court adopt for statutory precedents the evolutive approach it has long followed for reconsidering common law precedents.[82]

The Supreme Court treats its common law precedents as presumptively valid but will overrule them if they no longer fit into the evolving legal terrain and are producing anomalous policy results. In Moragne v. States Marine Lines, Inc.,[83] the Court overruled a hundred-year-old precedent denying wrongful death recovery under admiralty law, on the ground that the precedent rested on outdated legal assumptions and was obsolescent public policy in light of overwhelming acceptance of the wrongful death cause of action at the state and federal level. Justice John Harlan's opinion reasoned that the stare decisis concerns of excessive litigation, reliance, and respect for the judiciary are outweighed when the new rule is significantly more consistent with the "primary rules of behavior" which social mores and public policy have fostered over time. "If the new remedial doctrine serves simply to reenforce and make effectual less-understood primary obligations, the net result of innovation may be to strengthen rather than to disturb the general sense of security."[84] The Court found no clear congressional reliance on the outdated precedent.

Moragne and other common law decisions[85] suggest an evolutive approach to overruling precedents. Each decision of the Court is presumed to be correct and to stimulate private and public reliance. This gives rise to the stare decisis presumption against reconsidering precedents, which can be rebutted by a showing that the precedent was incorrectly decided and has not generated reliance interests. These two showings required to rebut the presumption are typically interconnected in this way: each decision rests on a complex array of assumptions about society and public policy. If those assumptions are shown to be wrong over time, reliance interests will usually be harder to uncover, since public lawmakers find it an unpersuasive policy paradigm, and private citizens are less likely to count on the precedent to make their plans. Hence, if society evolves "away" from the precedent, it is vulnerable to being overruled—unless it had become a cornerstone of legislative or judicial policy before its obsolescence became clear. In that event more powerful arguments are required to overrule the precedent.

Although this approach is mainly characteristic of the Supreme Court's treatment of common law precedents, several of the Court's statutory decisions have overruled Supreme Court interpretations of federal statutes for similar reasons.[86] An excellent example of such an approach is Justice Brennan's opinion in Boys Markets, Inc., v. Retail Clerks Union, Local 770.[87] The Norris–La Guardia Act of 1932 forbids federal courts from issuing injunctions in labor relations controversies (recall Chapter 3). The Supreme Court in *Sinclair* held that the act bars injunctive relief against a strike called in violation of a no-strike clause in the collective bargaining agreement and in the face of employer requests for arbitration pursuant to the agreement's arbitration clause. *Boys Markets* overruled *Sinclair,* notwithstanding the superstrong presumption and the Court's recognition that Congress had been urged to reevaluate the Court's decisions in this precise area. What was critical for the Court was that "in light of developments subsequent to *Sinclair,*" it had become clear that the precedent "frustrate[d] realization of an important goal of our national labor policy."[88]

When *Sinclair* was decided in 1962, a new but important development in national labor policy was the encouragement of peaceful resolution of labor disputes through private arbitration. In the "Steelworkers Trilogy"[89] the Court applied section 301 of the Taft-Hartley Act to authorize federal courts to enforce arbitration clauses of collective bargaining agreements. In the same year the Court decided *Sinclair,* it decided in Charles Dowd Box Co. v. Courtney[90] that state courts could enforce collective bargaining agreements and enjoin strikes in violation of no-strike clauses. There was some tension between the policy of the Norris–La Guardia Act as interpreted in *Sinclair* and the policy of the Taft-Hartley Act as interpreted in the Steelworkers Trilogy and *Charles Dowd.*

The tension demanded some resolution when the Supreme Court in 1968 held that state court lawsuits to enforce no-strike clauses could be removed to federal court.[91] This threatened to negate *Charles Dowd* because a union resisting a state court lawsuit to enforce a no-strike clause had only to seek removal to federal court, where *Sinclair* precluded such an injunction. This new development transformed *Sinclair*'s progressive obsolescence into an intolerable policy dilemma, which the Court resolved by overruling *Sinclair.* The Court chose to overrule *Sinclair* rather than *Charles Dowd* because it recognized an overall shift in national policy away from protection of the nascent labor movement (Norris–La Guardia) toward the encouragement of collective bargaining and peaceful resolution of industrial disputes (the Steelworkers Trilogy).

Under the evolutive approach suggested by legal process theory and the Court's common law decisions, the Court would overrule a statutory precedent only when the reasoning underlying the precedent has been discredited over time, when the precedent's consequences undermine current statutory policies and legislative purposes, and when practical experience suggests that the statutory goals are better met by a new rule that does not unduly negate public as well as private reliance interests in the old rule. Such an evolutive approach is a better way to protect the vertical coherence values embodied in stare decisis without unduly sacrificing the values of horizontal coherence. Indeed, the exceptions to the super-strong presumption suggest the logic of this approach. Thus, if a precedent can be overruled because the Court did not carefully consider all the arguments and evidence, why shouldn't a precedent be overruled when the assumptions of a careful consideration have been undone over time? If the exception for subsequent legislative developments may justify overruling a statutory precedent, why shouldn't subsequent social and policy developments also justify such overruling if they expose the precedent as a wrong turn in the judiciary's development of a statutory scheme? If precedents interpreting broadly drafted statutes can be overruled just as if they were common law precedents, why can't precedents filling any statutory gaps and ambiguities be treated similarly?

It was for reasons of horizontal as well as vertical coherence that the Court in *Patterson* declined to overrule *Runyon*. The Court found *Runyon* "entirely consistent with our society's deep commitment to the eradication of discrimination based upon a person's race or the color of his or her skin." This is good. The Court then said that "considerations of stare decisis have added force in statutory cases because Congress may alter what we have done by amending the statute."[92] This is bad. There is no reason to treat statutory precedents differently from common law precedents, since both can be and frequently are overridden by Congress. For example, *Moragne* applied normal stare decisis to a common law admiralty precedent, even though Congress had addressed wrongful death questions in the Death on the High Seas Act. Indeed, *Moragne* ruled that Congress's statutory action supported its result because it reflected the widespread acceptance of wrongful death recovery among modern policy-makers! Though the Court will hesitate to overrule its common law decisions if Congress has actually relied on them to pass or amend statutes,[93] it does not do so simply because Congress has legislated in the area and might choose to overrule the common law itself.[94] Note, too, that Congress has the authority to override most Supreme Court constitutional precedents,[95] yet the Court has not inferred heightened stare decisis for them. In short, *Patterson*'s statement is pointless, and the Court should abandon this long-standing rhetoric.

Antiaccommodationist Approaches to Stare Decisis and Legislative Inaction

Patterson's evolutive approach to stare decisis in statutory cases is connected to its refusal to credit legislative inaction arguments. On the one hand, both moves suggest that the Court is willing to jettison its own or other authoritative interpretations when they are not coherent with current policy. On the other hand, the two moves seem discordant under the pragmatic criteria developed in this book. A pragmatic approach to overruling statutory precedents, which the evolutive approach is, ought to be interested in the views of subsequent Congresses (see Part I). *Patterson* seemed both interested and uninterested in current legislative preferences—interested in *Runyon*'s favorable reception within the political system when the Court reaffirmed the precedent but uninterested in actual legislative deliberations about *Runyon* when the Court dismissed the legislative inaction arguments. The latter seems unpragmatic.

So is the former, when one examines *Patterson*'s actual fidelity to statutory text and precedent. *Patterson* specifically held that the alleged racial harassment, denial of promotion, and eventual discharge because of her race did not violate Brenda Patterson's right "to make and enforce contracts" with her employer under section 1981. The Court's rationale was that protecting Patterson's right to "make" a contract "extends only to the formation of a contract, but not to problems that may arise later from the conditions of continuing employment," and that protecting her right to "enforce" her contract prohibits only "discrimination that infects the legal process in ways that prevent one from enforcing contract rights."[96] The Court cited no precedent or any other authority (not even the usual dictionary) for this analysis.

Ordinary usage of the words *make* and *enforce* does not compel such a narrow reading. To say that Brenda Patterson has the "same right . . . to make . . . contracts . . . as is enjoyed by white citizens" implies a right to "make" the same kind of "contracts" that "white citizens" can make—namely, contracts with nondiscriminatory terms. The Court admitted that an employer who offered Patterson a contract that said, "We'll employ you, but we'll subject you to racial harassment on the job," has violated section 1981. Yet the Brennan Justices were claiming that McLean offered her such a contract, with the offensive term concealed. Why should her case be treated differently simply because the discriminatory term was concealed?[97] And to say that Brenda Patterson has the "same right . . . to enforce . . . contracts . . . as is enjoyed by white citizens" explicitly protects her right to "give effect to" (the dictionary definition of *enforce*) a nondiscriminatory contract. At the very least, employees should have a claim for discriminatory conduct amounting to a breach of contract.[98] For these reasons Patterson's reading of the statute is more faithful to its plain meaning than is the Court's. Indeed, her reading is the meaning that Senator Hruska ascribed to section 1981 when he objected to the fact that "a black female employee [claiming] a denial of either a promotion or pay raise . . . because of her color" could bypass Title VII by filing a complaint "under the provisions of the Civil Rights Act of 1866."[99] Hruska was describing Brenda Patterson.

More important, the Court's stingy interpretation of section 1981 was inconsistent with the Court's precedents. *Patterson* overruled *Runyon* in part. In *Runyon* the Court held that section 1981 prohibits private schools from discriminating against African Americans in their admissions. By implication *Runyon* interpreted section 1981 to prevent a school from admitting black children and then harassing them or expelling them because of their race.[100] It is ineluctable from the Court's result and reasoning that race-based harassment during the contract period would be a violation of the children's or parents' ability to "make and enforce" contracts. Indeed, *Runyon* relied on Johnson v. Railway Express Agency, Inc.,[101] to support its holding that section 1981 applies to private contracting. *Johnson* had applied section 1981 to a private employer's alleged racial discrimination with respect to seniority rules and day-to-day job assignments. Although the issue in *Johnson* was a statute of limitations question, the Court stated that section 1981 covered employment discrimination during the employment relationship. *Johnson*'s dictum was the basis for a holding to that effect in McDonald v. Santa Fe Trail Transporation Co.[102] *Patterson* therefore implicitly overruled *Runyon* in part, revoked dicta in *Johnson*, and overruled *McDonald* altogether.[103] Notwithstanding *Patterson*'s invocation of heightened stare decisis for statutory precedents, its holding left few of the precedents intact.

The most important thing about *Patterson*, and its most striking departure from the Court's post–New Deal practice, was how out of touch it was with the nation's political culture, which immediately recognized the decision as a renunciation of *Runyon*. During the Warren and Burger Courts the legislative inaction doctrines and heightened stare decisis for statutory precedents were pragmatic mechanisms by which the Supreme Court reconciled vertical and horizontal coherence in statutory cases, and did so in a way that facilitated the smooth evolution of the nation's public culture.[104]

The Court has traditionally been concerned not to overrule a precedent that enjoys current political support. The super-strong presumption represents the Court's (accurate) judgment that the safest policy is usually to leave the precedent alone. If Congress has not yet acted, there is a rebuttable presumption that it is not dissatisfied with the status quo and that an overruling might needlessly upset a policy equilibrium. The various legislative inaction doctrines (applicable to agency and lower court interpretations as well) then become occasions for the Court to inquire into the specific political history of the issue, if any. Evidence of public reliance on the challenged interpretation—like congressional rejection of proposals to override the interpretation (such as the fate of bills to override *Toolson*, the Hruska amendment) or legislation reenacting the statutory provision without change or legislation assuming the vitality of the challenged interpretation (such as the Fees Act of 1976)—is proof of current legislative equilibria and therefore relevant.

This was the point of Brennan's concurring opinion in *Patterson*. Whether or not it was correct in 1976, *Runyon's* interpretation of section 1981 was firmly accepted by the political culture. And what was accepted was not just the narrow holding of *Runyon* but its willingness to expand the remedies available to African Americans subject to continuing racial discrimination in contract-based relationships. This point was somehow lost on Justice Anthony Kennedy, concededly a newcomer to Washington when he wrote *Patterson*. But the political reaction to his decision was immediate and furious. Bills to override *Patterson* and other recent Supreme Court civil rights cases were developed during the summer and autumn of 1989, legislation denouncing as well as overriding the various cases was introduced in the House and Senate in February 1990, and in April 1990 the Bush administration went on record opposing most of the overrides but endorsing the override of *Patterson*. The 1990 bill was successfully vetoed, but a similar bill was passed the next year as the Civil Rights Act of 1991.[105] Section 101 of the act amended section 1981 to override *Patterson's* holding that section 1981 does not cover equal enjoyment of ongoing contractual benefits. The unexpected narrowing of section 1981 by *Patterson* and the curative override by Congress raise a final set of issues involving the legal process's mediation of the claims of vertical and horizontal coherence.

Prospective Judicial Decisions and Retroactive Statutes

Traditional liberal theory was hostile to retroactive lawmaking because it threatened to undermine private reliance on the previously existing law. Hence, liberals emphasized that statutes must have prospective effect lest they undermine private property and contract relationships. Indeed, retroactive legislation was potentially unconstitutional as an invasion of private vested rights.[106] Following Blackstone, traditional liberal theory assumed that judicial decisions were retroactive because they were mere declarations of law. But liberals realized that judicial decisions could shift legal terrain as radically as statutes, and some argued that such judicial decisions overruling earlier understandings should, like statutes, be given only prospective effect.[107]

The legal realists argued that prospective lawmaking was often justified by private reliance on the prior state of the law, but they argued in favor of retro-activity of either legislation or judicial decisions when private reliance was "unjustifiable" or when justifiable private reliance was outweighed by considerations of convenience, utility, or justice. Thus, the realists believed that judges often made new law, that this fact should be celebrated, and that prospective overruling of prior decisions was a useful device for ameliorating some of the drawbacks of shifts in judicial lawmaking. Similarly, they argued that statutes frequently reflected existing practice and, in any event, often required retroactivity to be effective. In short, courts should approach retroactivity questions functionally, and the public interest should presumptively be preferred to contrary private interests.[108]

Legal process theory, like realist theory, was open to both prospective over-ruling and retroactive statutes but urged a balance between public need and private reliance which emphasized the latter, ostensibly because of constitutional concerns.[109] For legal process the retroactivity of a new rule should turn, first, on whether retroactivity is necessary or useful in subserving the statutory purpose; second, on whether that public usefulness outweighs private reliance interests; and third, on whether retroactivity would be consistent with the institution's role. Solicitous of private expectations, legal process urged that statutes should "presumptively" apply only prospectively, and that decisions resulting in changes in people's "primary" substantive obligations should also normally be prospective, with changes in "remedial" rights easier to make retroactively.

The final part of the chapter relates this history of retroactivity theories to debates within the current Court as they concern *Patterson* and its statutory override. My thesis builds on legal process themes but spins those themes in light of economic and critical theory: choices between prospectivity and retroactivity often depend on a substantive evaluation of the policy being adopted. If the decision maker is proceeding experimentally and seeks to change social practice, the policy should be, and usually is, prospective. If the decision maker is merely adjusting legal rules to conform with social practice, the policy should be, and usually is, retroactive. Accordingly, the Court's decision in *Patterson* should have been prospective, since it unhinged social practice, whereas Congress's override should have been retroactive, since it was a curative statute.

Patterson foreclosed the first suggestion. In 1994 the Court rejected the second suggestion and held that the override applied prospectively, notwith-standing a good textual case for statutory retroactivity. The reasons why the Court is cool to statutory retroactivity relate to the Court's current doctrinal posture—a strong mixture of liberal and legal process positions. I interpret these positions as a substantive response by a Court skeptical of civil rights policy during the preceding generation. The Court's skepticism is normative, and it has implemented this normative vision through an activitist approach to statutory interpretation.

Prospective Judicial Decisions

Both state and federal courts have sometimes applied new judge-made rules prospectively, for essentially legal process reasons. The Supreme Court in Chevron Oil Co. v. Huson[110] held that a decision overruling prior precedents could apply prospectively if the overruling creates a new and unanticipated rule and the retroactive application of the rule would undermine statutory policy and produce hardship or inequitable results. *Chevron Oil* is a classic legal process statement. Although the Court during the legal process era sometimes emphasized the importance of private reliance interests, it most often stressed public reliance when it announced its new rules (especially new constitutional rules) prospectively. For example, in deciding whether to give new rules of criminal procedure prospective effect, the Court considered "the extent of the reliance by law enforcement authorities on the old standards" and "the effect on the administration of justice of a retroactive application of the new standards."[111]

In Northern Pipeline Construction Co. v. Marathon Pipe Line Co.[112] the Court carried the idea of prospective decision making one step further. It invalidated a portion of the Bankruptcy Act of 1978 which conferred on bankruptcy judges article III powers without providing them with article III protections of life tenure and nondiminishable salaries. Applying *Chevron Oil*, the Court declined to apply its decision retroactively, for such application of its relatively novel rule not only would have been unfair to litigants whose cases had already been or were being adjudicated, but would have unraveled the entire network for adjudicating bankruptcy disputes established by Congress. In addition to denying retroactive application of its holding, the Court also stayed its effect for several months so that Congress could adopt a new mechanism in an orderly fashion.[113] Pioneered at the state level, this idea of "prospective-prospective" overruling has a legal process appeal, since it protects public as well as private reliance interests and also fosters a dialogue between the Court and the legislature on issues of public importance.[114]

Patterson should have considered making its judgment prospective-prospective for pragmatic reasons. *Patterson* set forth a new rule for applying section 1981 to employment discrimination cases. Although the Court did not purport to overrule *Runyon*, it did overrule the implication that the courts of appeals had drawn from *Runyon*,[115] and it did overrule an understanding of the statute that the Supreme Court had adopted as dictum (*Johnson*) and holding (*McDonald*). Brenda Patterson herself had reasonably relied on this consensus to forgo her Title VII claims and concentrate only on her section 1981 claim. As in criminal procedure cases, the main reason for prospective application would have been the public reliance of Congress and the states (explained in detail by the amicus briefs filed for each). *Patterson* was a rupture in the law and should have applied only prospectively. Indeed, like *Marathon Oil*, the Court's decision should have been prospective-prospective, giving Congress an opportunity to override the Court's decision (which was virtually inevitable) before the decision's new and unexpected rule took effect.

Yet the Court's new interpretation in *Patterson* did not apply prospectively. Indeed, my suggestion would have been inconceivable to Justice Kennedy, for reasons that go well beyond any disagreement he might have with me concerning the novelty of the rule and its consistency with precedent. I develop two reasons here, and a third at the end of the chapter. First, although state courts have applied their overrulings of common law and statutory precedents prospectively, the United States Supreme Court rarely has. The Court has said that "decisions construing federal statutes might be denied full retroactive effect, as for instance where the Court overrules its own construction of a statute," but it has done that only in "rare cases."[116] The best-known case suggests how infrequently that occurs. In James v. United States[117] the Court overruled a tax precedent holding that embezzled funds do not constitute taxable income, but further held that the new rule could not fairly be applied to the tax defendant before the Court, who could not be charged with knowledge of the Court's new rule.

Justice Hugo Black's separate opinion in *James* argued that a purely prospective overruling was in conflict with heightened stare decisis for statutory precedents. As both liberal and legal process scholars had argued, Black maintained that prospective overruling made it too easy for the Court to rethink statutory precedents, a job better left to Congress under the Brandeis-Levi rationale for the super-strong presumption.[118] To the extent that the Court continues to treat constitutional and statutory precedents differently, it might confine prospective overrulings to the constitutional sphere. But this reasoning is not persuasive in *Patterson*, where the Court actually treated statutory precedents as if they were just as revisable as constitutional precedents.

Moreover, the Court has shown some nervousness about applying its constitutional precedents prospectively. In *James*, and in the criminal procedure cases of the 1960s, Justice Harlan argued that selective prospectivity (in which the case before the Court receives the benefit of the new rule but other pending cases do not) is in tension with the Court's article III obligations to adjudicate specific cases by declaring rather than making up the law and to ensure equal treatment of all similarly situated litigants.[119] The Supreme Court in the 1980s adopted Harlan's approach and his reasoning for criminal procedure cases on direct appeal, essentially ending the Court's long experimentation in that arena.[120] In Jim Beam Distilling Co. v. Georgia[121] a majority indicated that the Court would not follow selective prospectivity in civil constitutional cases either, effectively rejecting the *Chevron Oil* framework.

Three Justices would have abolished prospectivity of judicial decisions altogether as a violation of a court's duty to act "as if" it were doing nothing but declaring the law.[122]

This last-mentioned position, ascendant on the Rehnquist Court, may explain why the Court in *Patterson* would not have considered announcing its rule prospectively. But, as I have already shown, it requires a great suspension of disbelief to think that a statutory interpretation—such as *Patterson*—that is contrary to the statute's plain meaning, to several of the Court's precedents (including one that the same Court reaffirmed), and to the practice understood by the lower courts, Congress, the states, lawyers, and employers is either "declaring" the law or behaving "as if" it were declaring the law. The Court's performance in this and other cases lends no support to the legal process argument that prospective judicial decisions encourage judicial activism. I view *Patterson*'s retroactivity in normative terms: it signals the intensity of the Court's preferences as to civil rights policy in this country and reveals the Court's determination to set a new balance.

Retroactive Statutes

Patterson revolutionized section 1981 and, because it applied retroactively, affected hundreds of pending cases. For these reasons legislative override bills in both 1990 and 1991 were retroactive in their repeal of the new *Patterson* rule. Republican efforts to delete the retroactivity provisions were repeatedly defeated.[123] But the 1990 bill was successfully vetoed (the Senate override vote was 66–34), and one stated reason for President Bush's veto was the retroactivity provisions.[124] Although the 1991 bill, which was explicitly retroactive as to most issues, enjoyed majority support in both houses of Congress, it did not enjoy the two-thirds majority support required to override a presidential veto. This stimulated an intense round of bargaining among the sponsors, the administration, and a cluster of moderate Republican senators who held the balance of power because their support could ensure a veto override.

The final version of the bill, essentially hammered out in the Senate during the last ten days of October 1991, reflected compromises among the relevant bargaining groups. The bill dropped its original retroactivity provisions but did not add the nonretroactivity provisions desired by the Republicans. Neither was the final bill entirely silent on the issue, for it retained three "effective date" provisions: section 402(a), which provides as a general rule that "[e]xcept as otherwise specifically provided, this Act and the amendments made by this Act shall take effect upon enactment"; section 109(c), which provides that the extraterritoriality section "shall not apply with respect to conduct occurring before the date of the enactment of this Act"; and section 402(b), which provides that "nothing in this Act shall apply to any disparate impact case for which a complaint was filed before March 1, 1975, and for which an initial decision was rendered after October 30, 1983." The last provision was added at the insistence of the senators from Alaska to make sure that Wards Cove Packing Company (the winner in one of the overridden cases) would be protected against application of the new statute.[125]

Once the final bill was agreed to, the *Congressional Record* filled up with statements by the various players as to retroactivity. The statements suggest that almost all of the Democratic senators and almost none of the Republicans (including those who supported the bill) believed that it would apply retroactively; that the administration did not; and that more than one third (the number required to sustain a veto) of the Senate believed that the bill did not apply retroactively.[126] Everyone realized that the matter would be resolved in the courts, and dozens of judicial opinions addressed the issue within months of the statute's enactment. The Supreme Court held the *Patterson* override prospective in Rivers v. Roadway Express, Inc.[127]

Before *Rivers*, the *Patterson* override was the most litigated retroactivity issue, and the cases foundered on an ambivalence in the post-1950s legal process approach to statutory retroactivity. Although Congress has considerable authority to legislate retroactively in civil matters, the Court's opinions on the issue sweep both broadly and inconsistently. In Bowen v. Georgetown University Hospital[128] the Court held that the Department of Health and Human Services was not authorized by statute to issue a Medicare cost-reimbursement rule that applied retroactively. Although the Court's result is defensible as an interpretation of Congress's expectations in the authorizing statute, Kennedy's opinion created a clear statement rule: "Retroactivity is not favored in the law . . . [C]ongressional enactments and administrative rules will not be construed to have retroactive effect unless their language requires this result."[129] Contrast Bradley v. School Board of the City of Richmond,[130] where the Court retroactively applied an attorney's fees statute to a pending lawsuit. As it would later do (to the opposite effect) in *Bowen*, the Court eschewed narrow reasoning for the broad statement that "a court is to apply the law in effect at the time it renders its decision, unless doing so would result in manifest injustice or there is a statutory direction or legislative history to the contrary."[131]

The contrast between *Bowen* and *Bradley* reflects the ambivalence of the legal process tradition on the issue of statutory retroactivity: legal process scholars and judges, especially in the 1950s, recognized the quasi-constitutional presumption of retroactivity in general but also believed, especially in the 1960s and 1970s, that there are many classes of cases in which statutory retroactivity is justified. In Kaiser Aluminum and Chemical Corporation v. Bonjorno[132] the Supreme Court noted this tension between *Bowen* and *Bradley* but found it unnecessary to resolve the tension, though Scalia's concurring opinion gingerly protested that *Bowen's* clear statement rule best reflects Anglo-American (as well as ancient Roman) traditions and that the *Bradley* line of cases should be overruled.

How one sets the presumption in the *Patterson* override cases determined whether one found the 1991 act retroactive. For example, if you were to ask me whether the text of the 1991 act seems to apply retroactively to prior conduct, my naive reading of the text would suggest that it does. Section 402(a), the effective date provision for all the statutory provisions unless otherwise provided, is suggestive in its insistence that the statute take effect upon enactment. More important, sections 109(c) and 402(b) (described earlier) create specific nonretroactivity rules that would have been unnecessary if section 402(a) itself provided for general nonretroactivity. Stated another way, if I interpreted section 402(a) to render the act generally inapplicable to prior conduct, I would render sections 109(c) and 402(b) superfluous, violating what Scalia has described as "the cardinal rule of statutory interpretation that no provision should be construed to be entirely redundant."[133] Consequently, I should have thought the 1991 act generally retroactive under a plain meaning approach. The Supreme Court in *Rivers* found the act prospective, because this textual argument was insufficient to rebut the *Bowen* presumption.

One legal process answer to the retroactivity riddle would be to distinguish statutes altering rules of "primary" behavior (presumptively nonretroactive, with *Bowen* applicable) from statutes altering remedies (presumptively retroactive, with *Bradley* applicable).[134] But it is not clear where the *Patterson* override falls in this typology. On the one hand, section 101 expands section 1981's duty of nondiscrimination to include conduct during the contract period, which seems to affect primary behavior. On the other hand, in most employment cases (before the new remedies provisions in Title VII cases become applicable) section 1981 merely penalizes conduct already made illegal by Title VII, and in those cases section 101 simply expands the remedies (compensatory and punitive damages) available to a victim of racial discrimination in the workplace. But adding the damages relief of section 1981 to the back pay and injunctive relief of Title VII is in economic terms additional regulation of primary behavior.[135] This sort of analysis can be applied to a whole range of changes in this law. Because of the substantive relationship between rules of behavior and penalties for noncompliance, I do not consider the distinction between primary behavior and new remedy an analytically helpful one.

More helpful are decisions and commentaries positing that "curative" or "restoration" legislation should be applied retroactively.[136] Thus, where a statute simply codifies a congressional purpose long in place which Congress believed the Supreme Court had misinterpreted, it should presumptively be applied retroactively. Prospective interpretation of such statutes is unpragmatic, as it would undermine both vertical and horizontal coherence in law. It undermines vertical coherence by creating a legal whipsaw, in which one interpretation would govern for a number of years, to be displaced for a few years by an aberrant Supreme Court interpretation, itself displaced by a congressional override. If the congressional override "restores" the legal rule on which private and public decision makers have relied, and which the Supreme Court has upset, vertical coherence strongly supports retroactive application—as does horizontal coherence, of course. Because the 1991 act is not retroactive, the federal court system will long be clogged with two tracks of cases, one applying *Patterson* to pre-act conduct and cases pending in 1991, and another applying the 1991 act to post-act conduct. It will take years for the first track to clear out, and before it does there will surely be transitional difficulties to iron out, such as at what point some discriminatory conduct is pre-act and some is post-act.

Pragmatism would apply the *Patterson* override (as well as some other override) provisions of the 1991 act retroactively for a broader reason.[137] In the modern administrative state, with its ubiquitous regulation, the traditional presumption against retroactive legislation *(Bowen)* is not normatively supportable. Historically it rests on a common law conception of vested property and contract rights which did not survive the New Deal. Since then it has rested on a realist or process conception of private and public reliance on prior law, which is no longer a robust justification. It has long been recognized that reliance interests can be overborne when justice or social utility requires retroactive rule making. It is increasingly recognized that reliance interests themselves are contingent. Expectations cannot be considered a legally cognizable reliance interest unless they are "reasonable," but is it reasonable to act as though government rules will not change? A realistic view of the modern state would support the *Bradley* formulation: a statute or administrative rule can be retroactive, but not if it results in "manifest injustice" by unsettling social practice without a sufficient policy justification.

The reasonableness of expectations depends ultimately on an interplay between social and legal practice under a pragmatic philosophy. During my lifetime legal practice has progressively discouraged exclusionary employment policies and practices, especially those that directly or even indirectly prevent African Americans from getting jobs and promotions. I think that social practice has substantially assimilated the prohibitions against intentional discriminations on the basis of race and has been increasingly alert to policies having a discriminatory racial impact. The sort of openly harassing racial discrimination which Brenda Patterson complained of has long been unlawful in our society, has since *Alfred H. Mayer* been subject to multiple remedies, and is worth deterring under any of the conventionally respectable theories of racial justice and employment economics. The only legitimate objection is one of social cost: Does the extra amount of deterrence created by the additional remedy for black employees outweigh the administrative and other direct employer costs, as well as any intangible workplace costs? On that issue Congress has said that the costs are worth it—as an explicit matter since 1991 and implicitly ever since 1971, when the Senate defeated the Hruska amendment which described Brenda Patterson as its target.

Coherence and Ideology

An irony underlies the retroactivity litigation. The battle in the courts is over the presumption to be applied to the rules changed by the 1991 act, yet the choice of presumptions is driven by larger value choices and connections. I think section 101 of the 1991 act should have been applied retroactively for reasons that are related to my view that *Patterson* should have considered the legislative inaction arguments, should not have overruled *Johnson* and *McDonald* or retreated from *Runyon*, and should itself have been applied only prospectively. The Justices on the Court who felt differently about all these other issues also felt differently about the retroactivity issue.

That *Patterson*'s majority consisted of a bunch of conservatives raises an institutional irony. The archetype of respectable conservative judging has long been the pragmatic qualities associated with Justices Harlan and Powell—jurists who were deferential to Congress and genuinely interested in the deliberations of the legislative process, respectful of precedent and modest or tentative in their frequent reservations, legally innovative in increments and only after confirmation from a variety of different sources.[138] These legal process conservatives sought a practical balance between vertical and horizontal coherence. Doctrinally, Harlan and Powell gave due weight to legislative inaction, followed precedent even when they disagreed with it, overruled precedent only when the evidence suggested that it was inconsistent with social or legal practice, were willing albeit reluctant to announce some new judicial rulings prospectively, and followed an ad hoc approach to applying statutes retroactively. Their opposite on both the Warren and Burger Courts was Justice Brennan, a Houdini who never encountered a vertical coherence argument he couldn't escape. For thirty years Brennan and his allies gave short shrift to legislative inaction arguments, agitated to overrule or recharacterize precedents they disliked, embraced prospective overrulings, and were more than willing to apply reform legislation retroactively.

Ironically, the conservative *Patterson* Justices little resembled Harlan or Powell in that case—for they were dismissive of legislative inaction arguments as beneath their attention, recharacterized and overruled precedents with bland obliviousness, rigidly avoided prospectivity in their overrulings under the false cover that they were behaving "as if" they do not make new law, and would usually vote to deny corrective statutes retroactive effect. Also ironically, Brennan and Marshall in the late 1980s discovered the value of vertical coherence and took doctrinal positions more characteristic of Harlan and Powell (and quite contrary to their traditional ones), particularly in their new-found devotion to legislative inaction arguments and stare decisis.

The Rehnquist Court has been a rupture in the doctrinal history of statutory interpretation. Not only do conservatives usually win the cases, but they are recasting the doctrinal terms of the balance between vertical and horizontal coherence in neo-Blackstonian terms: judicial decisions will be retroactive, statutes will be prospective, and courts will be most solicitous of private reliance interests and less mindful of public reliance, unless captured in formally enacted statutes. The leading rupturer is Scalia, a conservative and an intellectual well schooled in the legal process (he took the course at Harvard, as did Justices Kennedy, Souter, Ginsburg, and Breyer), who is seeking to recast the horizontal-vertical coherence balance in ways that capitalize on the formalist features of process thought while rejecting or subordinating the realist influence.

For Scalia, horizontal coherence in law is critically important because law should be an internally coherent system of rights and duties, but the only admissible evidence of it is statutory and constitutional text. Hence, the judge's job is to make the best sense she can of this hard objective stuff, and she is barred from introducing soft stuff (context) both because it is not law and (relatedly) because soft stuff tends to be a reflection of what she would like the law to be rather than what the law actually is. Although traditional legal process tends to find open texture in every statute, Scalia rarely does. But he does admit the existence of open-textured statutes (such as the Sherman Act), and then he is interested in arguments from vertical coherence—precedent, history, tradition. Unlike realist theory, which tends to be more interested in yesterday's committee hearing than in nineteenth-century Supreme Court decisions, Scalia insists on a deep verticality; the mists of the Middle Ages may be more relevant to him than Warren Court decisions, and greatly more relevant than the unenacted current political consensus in Congress. But this deep verticality can be disrupted at any time by new political ruptures, so long as they are embodied in clearly written statutes.

In the 1980s and 1990s Scalia's distinctive combination of formalism, traditionalism, and rupture has riled legal academics of virtually all stripes. Yet his robust theorizing has had a constituency within the Court, even though he is not popular or even well understood by his colleagues. Why do they follow his lead, then? My hypothesis is that his approach to coherence issues offers a way for the Rehnquist Court to establish itself as a rule of law Court competent to deal with a better-defined judicial agenda, in contrast to the activist

Warren and Burger Courts. The legal community showed renewed interest in the rule of law and constrained judicial decision making in the 1980s, partly because many of the activist experiments of the Warren and Burger Courts have not turned out well and partly because liberals feared the consequences of an activist Reagan-Bush Court. As Mark Tushnet has suggested in an unpublished paper, the Court's composition makes it particularly responsive to rule of law talk. Populated now with lawyers whose previous reputation was largely regional or statewide, the current Court has neither the self-confidence nor the perceived intellectual stature to feel comfortable making policy decisions. Contrast conservative but assertive Justices Frankfurter, Harlan, and Powell, whose prominence may have given them some freedom to contextualize.

How should rule of law values be implemented? The experience of the Burger Court was not encouraging. Its moderates and conservatives were often seduced by Brennan's horizontal coherence arguments, while the staunchest rule of law advocate, Rehnquist, emphasized vertical coherence arguments (statutory precedents and legislative history) that had about them an air of mustiness and irrelevance. Scalia's strategy of text-based coherence is arguably a more determinate, harder-hitting way of enforcing rule of law values, and also an approach that does not make rule of law seem musty. Scalia's new formalism is an attractive approach for a rule of law Court, namely, one that is concerned about striking a balance between horizontal and vertical coherence, but without giving the impression that it is creating rather than finding the law.

Patterson and the Rehnquist Court's other civil rights decisions after 1989 provide a context for evaluating the new formalist approach to the balance between vertical and horizontal coherence (an inquiry I continue in Chapter 9). The civil rights decisions suggest that the new formalism is on the whole deregulatory, requiring clear statutory statements to justify regulation of employer policies that affect minorities. At the same time the Court was reading section 1981 narrowly in *Patterson*, it was also creating other procedural and substantive barriers to Title VII lawsuits.[139] In the two terms that followed, the Court handed down several more decisions reading Title VII narrowly in light of common law canons.[140] The pro-defendant bias in the Rehnquist Court's cases may be the result of the Court's methodology—its stingy textualism, its interest in traditions rooted in our nation's normatively ambiguous past, and its reluctance to credit public reliance arguments. But the results are not supported by its methodology. Recall my earlier discussion of the textual argument in *Patterson*. Kennedy's opinion amounts to virtually no positive argument for his interpretation, and the "plain meaning" of section 1981— as Brenda Patterson read it, as Senator Hruska read it in 1971, as the House and Senate committees read it in 1972, as the Supreme Court read it in *Johnson* and *McDonald*, as all the courts of appeals read it in light of those decisions and of *Runyon*, as Stevens read it in *Patterson* (and as Harlan and Powell would have read it), as I read it in light of the dictionaries and ordinary usage—is different from the interpretation reached by the Court majority. Although *Patterson* is an unusually weak application of textualist analysis, other anti-plaintiff decisions are similarly vulnerable to textualist counterarguments.[141]

In this light the Rehnquist Court's approach to vertical and horizontal coherence takes on a different, more substantive and more strategic, meaning. The Court's civil rights decisions from 1989 to 1991 do not represent its adherence to plain meaning. Instead, they represent its preference that civil rights statutes not "intrude" into employer decision making, and its strategic decision to create a "counter-rupture" in civil rights policy, correcting for its pro-minorities evolution during the Warren and Burger Courts, and basically daring Congress to resolve the divisive issues in an authoritative way.

The New Deal Court's rethinking of doctrines of vertical and horizontal coherence to privilege arguments based on public reliance was a political move, adapting doctrine to the modern administrative state. The Warren and (early) Burger Courts gave less emphasis to reliance arguments and were more willing to reconsider both agency and judicial precedents; that, too, was politically situated, as the Court updated statutory law to reflect progressive values. The Rehnquist Court's rethinking of the vertical and horizontal coherence doctrines arose in a third political setting: divided government in which progressives controlled Congress and conservatives controlled the Court and the presidency. And the Rehnquist Court between 1987 and 1993 behaved just as strategically as prior Courts in setting the balance between vertical and horizontal coherence.

In civil rights cases such as *Patterson* the Court between 1989 and 1993 could move civil rights policy strongly in a conservative direction so long as it was prepared to ignore Burger and Warren Court precedents and congressional signals in support of such precedents. Even though its decisions amounted to dramatic shifts in the law, the Court insisted that they be retroactive, but that any override be prospective unless there was a clear statement to the contrary. During divided government this doctrinal reconfiguration made congressional override of the Court's decisions triply difficult: an override must not only surmount interest group opposition and procedural hurdles in Congress, but must also have the supermajorities needed to override a presidential veto, and must last of all be able to muster the same supermajorities for an unambiguous retroactivity provision.

Once such strongly divided government ends (as it did in 1993), the possibility of another shift arises. The Rehnquist Court's approach to coherence issues will likely be modified. That it must now be associated with transparently anti–civil rights decisions, judicial activism, and conflictual overrides by Congress ought to undermine its appeal for one or two of the conservative

Justices, as well as for newly appointed Justices. To the extent that the Court seeks mooring in the pragmatics of the legal process tradition, I urge a common law approach to precedent (rather than the old super-strong presumption of correctness), a presumption of correctness for building block interpretations of federal statutes, and a more flexible treatment of the retroactivity issues raised by new statutes and judicial interpretations of them. To the extent that the Court is open to further rethinking, I urge it to develop substantive economic and critical analyses of civil rights and other policy concerns handled by the modern administrative state—and to be guided by those insights rather than by abstract procedural doctrines.

9 ▪ Canons of Statutory Construction as Interpretive Regimes

Anglo-American treatises on statutory interpretation from the nineteenth century to the present have relied heavily on the "canons of statutory construction," a homely collection of rules, principles, and presumptions.[1] The canons have served as a collective security blanket for lawyers and judges because they combine predictability and legitimacy in statutory interpretation: by applying the relevant canon(s), the lawyer can figure out what the legislature intended a statute to mean, which in turn is a sure prediction of how a judge will interpret it. The legal realists were skeptical that the canons render statutory interpretation a mechanical and determinate enterprise or meaningfully constrain judicial discretion. They viewed the canons as window dressing for decisions reached on other grounds. Karl Llewellyn's classic attack argued that "there are two opposing canons on almost every point" of statutory interpretation; he then proved his thesis by compiling a list showing every canon to have a counter-canon.[2]

Legal process thinkers agreed with Llewellyn that the canons do not mechanically determine interpretations reached by judges, but they believed that the canons had some value as rules of thumb, pointing to possible meanings that statutory language might have in context.[3] Although academic debate over the canons all but disappeared in the 1960s and 1970s, they came back in style during the 1980s, with law professors applying various legal process and post–legal process analyses to them[4] and the Supreme Court featuring them prominently in its opinions. The Rehnquist Court's vigorous use of the canons provides an excellent field on which the various academic theories can play. In this chapter I evaluate the Court's application of the canons by drawing on three theories of the 1980s: economics and public choice, republicanism, and postmodernism. Each section of the chapter explores what lessons, if any, each of these theories might have for understanding the value of the canons, but several general themes pervade the discussion.

275

First, the canons should no longer be treated as an undifferentiated lump, as Llewellyn considered them. They are readily segregable into three separate clusters: precepts of grammar, syntax, and logical inference (the textual canons); rules of deference to the interpretations others have placed on the statutory language (the extrinsic source canons); and policy rules and presumptions (the substantive canons). The substantive canons, in turn, can be further broken down into three categories based on the formal source of their policies, namely, the Constitution, statutes, and the common law. Different canons should be justified—or criticized—in different ways.

Second, understanding its use of the canons is essential to understanding the multiplex agenda of the Rehnquist Court. The Court's most defensible mission is to develop a transparent description of the "interpretive regime" (John Ferejohn's term) against which it interprets statutes. By developing such a thick description of its interpretive practice, the Court could provide Congress with more certain guidelines as to how it should expect to see its statutes interpreted. In addition, the Court is trying, especially in the extrinsic source canons and the constitutionally based substantive canons, to make the rules more democracy-enhancing. Finally, the evolution of the substantive canons is an expression of the Court's constitutional values, a way for the Court to conduct an illuminating discourse with the legislature about our nation's public values, but without seriously obstructing or intruding into the political system. The Court's expression of democratic and constitutional values is, in turn, an important component of the interpretive regime the Court is laying out for Congress.

Third, the Supreme Court's recent experimentation with the canons is a troubled one. The first two stated goals for the Court's interpretive regime, transparency and democracy enhancement, are only partially achievable through any set of canons, and it is unclear whether the Rehnquist Court has made genuine progress in this area. The third goal, expression of constitutional values, has been achieved, but is subject to criticism insofar as the underlying ideology of the Rehnquist Court rests on a controversial view of jurisprudence, politics, and civil rights. Some of the values fundamental to the Rehnquist Court's interpretive regime may not prove to be robust over time.

An Economic Theory of the Canons

The canons of statutory construction can be defended under simple economic theory. Drafting complete statutes that cover all contingencies is impracticable because of staff limitations and the inability of legislators to achieve consensus on all issues. This creates the possibility of numerous statutory ambiguities that might generate high costs.[5] Thus, courts have created "off-the-rack" gap-filling rules that are accessible ex ante to the drafters. These rules can reveal to the legislature the interpretive regime—the rules, presumptions, and practices—that a court will apply to the legislative product. Knowing the interpretive regime within which statutes will be developed over time, the players in the legislative bargaining process are able to predict what effects that different statutory language will have. This permits them to leave much unsaid in the statute itself, which in turn makes it possible to enact more statutes, and at a cheaper overall cost.

The efficiency of the canons under the foregoing theory does not depend on the Court's choosing the "best" canons for each proposition, as earlier economic thinkers have argued.[6] Instead, economic theory would suggest that the canons be treated as conventions, similar to driving a car on the right-hand side of the road. It is not so important to choose the best convention as it is to choose one convention and stick to it. As an agent of the legislature, the Court does its job best when it comes up with a transparent interpretive regime—a coherent and clear set of textual and substantive canons—for that allows legislators to coordinate their bargaining activities and predict the application of their statutes most easily.

This sort of analysis reflects the philosophy of at least some Justices of the Rehnquist Court. The Court has been codifying and clarifying a comprehensive set of grammar, deference, and substantive canons for the benefit of congressional drafters. "What is of paramount importance is that Congress be able to legislate against a background of clear interpretive rules, so that it may know the effect of the language it adopts."[7] Appendix 3 to this book collects and organizes the canons that have been recognized and applied by the Rehnquist Court through its 1992 term.

This economic theory suggests a possible justification for some of the Court's most widely criticized opinions, such as EEOC v. Arabian American Oil Company *(Aramco).*[8] In that case the Court interpreted Title VII of the Civil Rights Act of 1964 to be inapplicable to American employees working overseas for American companies—even though Title VII is broadly written, with specific reference to extraterritorial commerce and no indication that it was meant to apply only to domestic employment,[9] and even though ordinary choice of law analysis in such a case would suggest application of U.S. statutory law.[10] Yet Chief Justice William Rehnquist's opinion rejected these arguments not because he could demonstrate that they were wrong, but because they were not clear enough to rebut the canon presuming against extraterritorial application of United States statutes which he derived from the Court's prior opinion in Foley Brothers, Inc., v. Filardo.[11] The canon could of course be rebutted by a clear statement in the statutory text, but the text sent mixed signals in that regard. For example, Title VII as enacted in 1964 evidenced concern for the sovereignty of domestic "States" but not foreign states and failed to provide a mechanism for overseas enforcement. The grammar canon "expressio unius est exclusio alterius" (the expression of one thing suggests exclusion of others) then supported the inference that Congress had not focused on extraterritoriality in this statute, as it clearly had in others.[12]

Both canons invoked in *Aramco* are controversial. The extraterritoriality canon is in tension with the current internationalization of commerce,[13] and *expressio unius* is not considered a reliable maxim of logic or word usage.[14] They may not be the best canons, but economic theory might support the point of *Aramco:* because these two canons are the traditional ones, the Court should follow them faithfully so that Congress gets the point and its drafters can bargain around the canons. Or does it? For economic theory to justify a decision such as *Aramco* three conditions must be met: (1) Congress is institutionally capable of knowing and working from an interpretive regime that the Court is institutionally capable of devising and transmitting in coherent form; (2) the application of the interpretive regime, or the canons if you will, in concrete situations must be transparent to Congress; and (3) conditions 1 and 2 must be met for the enacting Congress as well as the current Congress— that is, the interpretive regime and its application should not change in unpredictable ways. On the whole I believe only the first condition can be satisfied, and even it offers difficulties; the second condition can rarely be satisfied; and *Aramco* and many other canons dramatically flunk the third condition.

Problems of Institutional Capability

The problem of institutional capability would appear to be easily answered. Once Congress becomes aware of the Court's easy-to-figure-out canons (hint: read Appendix 3), it can easily adjust its drafting process to take account of them. This is most apparent for the textual canons. To the extent that the Court can clearly signal to Congress the rules of grammar and syntax it will follow, such as *expressio unius*, statutory drafters ought to be able to adapt their drafting practice to conform to those rules. Indeed, the Court might consider adopting a standard style book as its presumptive reference point for rules of grammar, syntax, punctuation, and the like. The Rehnquist Court's main extrinsic source canon, that it will defer to agency decisions unless they are inconsistent with the plain meaning of a statutory text, also sends a plain message to Congress: expect agencies to be limited by your clear statutory directives (with clarity being defined in part through the textual canons); otherwise they will be free to make reasonable policy choices.

This is the theory. If state experience is any guide, the reality is more complicated. Even when the state judiciary has systematically developed grammar canons, state legislative drafters do not necessarily follow them, either because they remain uninformed about them or because the time pressures involved in putting together statutory deals and last-minute compromises mean that the rule book gets thrown out the window.[15] The first reason strikes me as superable at both the state and federal levels, whose staffs ought to be able to develop standard drafting handbooks or manuals that incorporate the canonical precepts.[16] The second reason poses a greater, more structural difficulty.[17]

The problem of institutional capability is more intractable for the substantive canons, but the opening pitch is the same: if the courts establish clearly defined baselines, legislative drafters ought to be able to anticipate their effect and to draft statutes accordingly. Although the reality of legislative drafting apparently does not live up to this theory, state legislatures have responded with statutory codifications of the canons and with drafting "checklists" of important issues and how the courts are likely to resolve them absent a clear statement on the part of the legislature. Similar proposals have been floated at the federal level in response to the Rehnquist Court's increased use of clear statement rules.[18] This is a useful idea, since the Court has set forth interpretive baselines on several dozen issues that recur across different kinds of statutes—such as preemption of state law, effect on immunities from suit, severability, availability of jury trials, the existence of a private right of action and remedies, standing to sue, and retroactivity. Armed with a drafting checklist and Appendix 3, federal legislative drafters ought to be able to predict how the Court would interpret various statutory approaches to the issue, including no statutory provision at all. Once the deal becomes clear, the drafters can simply plug in statutory boilerplate.

There is a further difficulty, however. Unlike the textual canons, which are on the whole neutral as to their allocational effects, the substantive canons do have such effects. The Court's choice of canons systematically affects the allocation of power, rights, and property in our society. The canon against extraterritorial application of United States law systematically advantages transnational companies, for example. Because the default rule is that there is no extraterritorial application, the burden of inertia is on those who want the statute to apply extraterritorially. In a legislative bargaining game every extra provision costs something, as it may trigger opposing votes and/or lobbying. The Civil Rights Act of 1964 was a particularly hard statute to get through Congress, with a two-thirds vote required in the Senate to overcome the southern filibuster (see Chapter 1). The last thing the bill's sponsors needed was opposition from business. So even if the extraterritoriality issue had been raised, a rational strategy might have been to duck the issue in order to forestall further controversy.

This problem of allocative effects is not fatal to an economic theory of the canons, for it does not deny that statutory drafters can work around any particular canon.[19] But it does suggest that the substantive canons the Court follows have allocational consequences that require normative justification.

The justification would be either that the canon reflects the probable assumption of the median legislator or that the canon is otherwise normatively attractive. I agree with Gary Born and Jonathan Turley that neither case can be made for the canon against extraterritorial application.[20] While the canon may well have reflected median legislative assumptions in 1949, when *Foley Brothers* was decided, it is much harder to make that case for 1964 or 1990, by which time transnational business operations had become an important part of most regulatory puzzles. Nor is the canon itself efficient unless it can be shown that domestic regulatory schemes cannot effectively be applied to nondomestic conduct, whether for administrative or other reasons. I doubt this showing could be made for the application of *American* law to *American* employees working overseas for *American* companies (the precise issue in *Aramco*).

Problems of Consistency

The theory of interpretive regimes cannot be completely successful unless the concrete application as well as the abstract content of the interpretive regime is transparent to Congress when it drafts statutes. This was the problem raised by Llewellyn's demonstration that for every canon there is a counter-canon. To illustrate, the plaintiff in *Aramco* relied on the canon that the Court should defer to the agency interpretation of the statute it is charged with enforcing, for the Equal Employment Opportunity Commission (EEOC) had interpreted Title VII to have extraterritorial effect.[21] But the canon of deference to agency interpretations is subject to several counter-canons, one of which was invoked by the Court: this deference rule is not applicable when the agency's interpretation has changed over time (the EEOC interpretation was promulgated in the 1980s) and does not represent an interpretation contemporaneous with the statute's early history.[22]

Llewellyn's chart of canon/counter-canon canvassed only textual canons (such as *expressio unius*) and extrinsic source canons (such as deference to agency interpretations) and tended to neglect the substantive ones. For instance, the presumption against extraterritoriality was notably absent from his chart, even though *Foley Brothers* was decided a year before the publication of Llewellyn's article. The substantive canons seem no more determinate, however. The main reason is that a variety of canons will typically be applicable to any given statutory issue, and they will often cut in different directions.[23] Not only does the Court have a choice as to which of two canons to emphasize (Llewellyn's point), but several and maybe even dozens of canons may be potentially applicable, and the Court's discretion extends not just to

which canons it will choose to emphasize but also to how much it will emphasize each canon, what relative weight each will have, and how the canons
will interact.

Thus in *Aramco* the Court's case consisted of (1) its invocation of one substantive canon and its interpretation of that canon to require a statutory clear
statement to rebut; (2) its invocation of textual canons to find the statutory
text insufficiently clear to overcome the substantive canon; and (3) its refusal
to credit the agency deference canon. Not only does every step of the Court's
canonical case rest on discretionary choices, but Congress in either 1964 or
1991 would probably have been surprised by the *Aramco* interpretation of
Title VII even if its drafters had been aware of the *Foley Brothers* presumption
(an awareness for which there is no evidence and little likelihood).

To begin with, a reasonable congressional observer in 1964 would have
thought that the *Foley Brothers* presumption was not good law *or* that the presumption would not apply to an American plaintiff suing an American defendant *or* that the broad jurisdictional grant, tying the jurisdictional term "employer" to foreign as well as interstate "commerce," would have been
sufficient to rebut any such presumption. In 1952, shortly after *Foley Brothers,*
the Court interpreted the Lanham Act to apply extraterritorially because of
its broad jurisdictional grant, which applied to "all commerce which may lawfully be regulated by Congress."[24] The Court did not mention the *Foley Brothers* presumption. By the 1960s it was clear from lower court opinions that
the antitrust and securities laws had extraterritorial effect, notwithstanding
similarly vague jurisdictional provisions.[25]

In 1953 and 1959 the Supreme Court declined to apply the Jones Act to
extraterritorial seaman's injury cases, but only because ordinary choice of law
principles suggested that non-American seamen injured on non-American
vessels should not have recourse to American law. Neither decision mentioned the *Foley Brothers* presumption, and the Court in 1970 applied the
Jones Act to an American seaman injured on a foreign vessel outside
the United States.[26] Relying on the *Foley Brothers* presumption, however, the
Court declined to apply the National Labor Relations Act to non-American
vessels employing non-American workers, and lower courts have applied the
presumption in Railway Labor Act cases even when the plaintiffs are American workers and the defendants American companies.[27]

In the judgment of the leading commentators, the Supreme Court's choice
of law jurisprudence in 1964 had all but abandoned the *Foley Brothers* presumption in favor of a balancing-of-contacts approach (the modern approach
to choice of law). The reasonable congressional observer in 1964 would likely
have assumed that United States civil rights statutes would at least apply to
extraterritorial discrimination by American companies against American employees. Indeed, it appears that the drafters of the statute had operated under

this assumption. Section 702 provided that Title VII "shall not apply to an employer with respect to the employment of aliens outside any State."[28] This "alien exemption" provision would have been unnecessary if Title VII had no extraterritorial effect because Title VII would not have applied to an employer "outside any State," whether "with respect to the employment" of aliens or "with respect to the employment" of Americans. The textual canons direct that the Court must, whenever possible, give effect to every statutory provision and must avoid statutory interpretations that render a provision superfluous,[29] as the Court's opinion did to section 702.[30] The provision's legislative history confirmed that Congress thought Title VII had extraterritorial effect and that Congress added the alien exemption "to remove conflicts of law which might otherwise exist between the United States and a foreign nation in the employment of aliens outside the United States by an American enterprise."[31] Indeed, Assistant Attorney General Antonin Scalia told Congress in 1975 that the alien exemption provision "implied that [Title VII] is applicable to the employment of United States citizens by covered employers anywhere in the world."[32] As a Justice, Scalia voted the other way in *Aramco*.

The Court overcame this canonical case for extraterritoriality by three maneuvers: trumping, recharacterizing, and ignoring. Thus, the Court trumped the canon of deference to agencies with the counter-canon of nondeference to a fluid agency interpretation. The Court's starting point, therefore, became *Foley Brothers*, which shifted the burden of persuasion onto the plaintiff to demonstrate that the statute has extraterritorial reach. The plaintiff presented such evidence (as noted earlier), but the Court was unpersuaded because the statute's text was insufficiently clear. Curiously, *Foley Brothers* itself created only a "presumption" against extraterritoriality, which the Court considered along with implications from the statutory text, the statute's legislative history, administrative interpretations, and statutory goals and purpose. *Aramco* transformed the *Foley Brothers* presumption into a "clear statement rule," which can be overcome only by a clear statement on the face of the statute.[33] Once the Court had created its new rule, it could more readily dismiss Title VII's general jurisdictional language, broad purpose, and occasional extraterritorial language as insufficiently focused to amount to a clear statement. Indeed, the *Aramco* rule is a "super-strong" clear statement rule as applied because it also rejected the structural argument based on the alien exemption provision, even though similar arguments have been successful in meeting other clear statement rules.[34]

There may be a justification for the Court's recharacterization of the extraterritorial effect canon. Telling Congress what the canons are is unhelpful unless the Court also gives Congress some idea of how the Court will apply them. That, in turn, would require the Court to develop a systematic set of harmonization rules to tell Congress how it will apply the canons when they cut in different directions. *Aramco* provides one harmonization principle: the rule against extraterritorial application trumps most other canons and can be overcome only by very explicit statutory language.

Nonetheless, the Court's current efforts to create *Aramco*-type harmonization rules may not provide Congress with a workable interpretive regime because Congress cannot rely on the abstract interpretive regime to figure out how the Court will apply the statute to specific cases. Most of the canons are highly context-dependent, and much of the context they depend on is unknowable to Congress when it enacts the statute. This unknowable future context includes the facts of the specific case, the administrative development of the statutory scheme and the credibility of the agency in the Court's eyes, and statutes later enacted by Congress.[35] Another part of that context is the Court's own development of the statutory scheme, and indeed the Court's attitude toward the statute. The Rehnquist Court does not have the same friendly attitude toward Title VII that the Burger Court usually did, and that grudging attitude cannot help but affect the way in which the Court applies the canons (which ones it emphasizes, which ones it ignores).

Finally, it is hard to escape the impression that *Aramco* is an expression of the Rehnquist Court's substantive preferences. But if that is true, the *Aramco* rule may have a limited life span. The decision itself was overridden by Congress less than a year after it was handed down,[36] and a different collection of Justices might well rethink its super-strong clear statement rule, particularly given the weak case for it on the merits and its inconsistency with the Court's approach in other cases of extraterritorial application. This particular harmonization rule, and others, may not be a sure guide for the future. If that is so, the canons become less useful as an interpretive regime on which Congress can rely.

From Presumptions to Clear Statement Rules: The Bait-and-Switch Game

Aramco suggests that the substantive canons, like the textual and extrinsic source ones, are plastic. Not only can they be invoked or ignored at will, but their weight in the overall balance can fluctuate over time. *Aramco* helps us see how this can work in a formal sense. Most substantive canons have traditionally been expressed as "presumptions" that can be rebutted by persuasive arguments drawn from the statutory text, legislative history, statutory purpose, or other sources. *Foley Brothers*' presumption against extraterritoriality is an example. Some canons, especially those grounded in constitutional concerns (such as the rule of lenity), have traditionally been expressed as clear statement rules, whose policy presumption can be rebutted only by clear statements on the face of the statute itself.[37] I think Title VII had such a clear statement, but *Aramco* required an unusually clear statement targeted at the issue. This is yet a third, and newer, type of canon, a super-strong clear statement rule.

In articulating an interpretive regime, it is rational for the Court to indicate clear statement and super-strong clear statement rules so that Congress may know not only what canons the Court will apply but also some of the harmonization and weighting rules. The problem is that Congress may be skeptical that such new clear statement rules will last any longer than the presumptions they replaced. This will undermine any advantage to be obtained from clarifying the canons, for Congress may be chary of trusting the Court to be consistent over time, much as the dupe burned in a game of bait and switch may be chary of playing again.

Consider the Court's decision in Dellmuth v. Muth.[38] The Court held that the Education of the Handicapped Act of 1975 (EHA) did not permit damage suits against the states, even though the EHA included a provision for judicial review of state decisions and was explained on the floor of the Senate as providing for lawsuits against the states.[39] The ground for the Court's decision was a new super-strong clear statement rule the Court had created in 1985. In Atascadero State Hospital v. Scanlon[40] the Court had held that federal statutes would be interpreted to abrogate state Eleventh Amendment immunity from suit only if the legislative intention to abrogate immunity were "unmistakably clear in the language of the statute." Based on the *Atascadero* rule, *Dellmuth* brushed aside arguments that its holding cut the heart out of the EHA, which requires state and local governments to provide fair educational opportunities to children with disabilities.

Dellmuth reveals how Congress can be frustrated by shifting interpretive regimes. Under the Supreme Court's prevailing Eleventh Amendment precedent in 1975,[41] when Congress enacted the EHA, the jurisdictional language covering actions against the states, plus the specific legislative history, were arguably enough to rebut what was then a "presumption" against congressional abrogation of the states' Eleventh Amendment immunity; such evidence was perhaps also enough to satisfy a traditional clear statement rule.[42] This was in fact the belief of the main Senate sponsor of the EHA. In 1985 the Court changed its approach, adopting the *Atascadero* rule and frustrating legislative expectations.

Responding to *Atascadero*, Congress in 1986 legislated that "[a] State shall not be immune under the Eleventh Amendment ... from suit in Federal Court" for a violation of statutes protecting people with disabilities, including the EHA.[43] Congress complained that its intent in the Rehabilitation Act had been thwarted by *Atascadero* and overrode that decision in a way that Congress expected would head off state immunity claims under other statutes protecting people with disabilities. Yet in *Dellmuth* the Court not only held that the 1975 EHA failed to abrogate state immunity but cited as evidence the

1986 statute, which contained the requisite clear statement but did not apply to the case in question.[44] Congress overrode *Dellmuth* a year later.[45] It is striking, and normatively troubling to a pragmatic philosophy of interpretation, that it took Congress three statutes to accomplish what it probably thought it had done in 1975.

Decisions such as *Dellmuth* and *Aramco* (in the latter case it took Congress just two statutes to accomplish what it probably thought it had done in 1964) send two different signals to Congress, one that the Court is creating not just clear canons but also clearer harmonization rules, and an opposite signal that the rules can be changed at the Court's whim. The second signal defeats the purpose of the first. This particular inconsistency could be rectified by the Court's announcing its new "clear interpretive rules" prospectively when they represent a break with past practice. This suggestion is related to my argument in Chapter 8 that the Court's refusal to announce statutory interpretation prospectively is unwarranted.

Republican and Quasi-Constitutional Theories of the Canons

Aramco and *Dellmuth* are not aberrations. The Supreme Court in the 1980s created a number of new constitutionally based canons that may trump apparent legislative expectations and hence are hard to justify under the economic theory I have articulated. Among the clear statement rules created or applied more aggressively in the 1980s were a super-strong rule against congressional derogation of presidential foreign affairs powers,[46] a strong rule deferring to agency interpretations,[47] a strong rule against congressional invasion of core executive powers,[48] a strong rule against congressional abrogation of the judiciary's inherent powers,[49] a super-strong rule against federal waiver of sovereign immunity,[50] a super-strong rule against congressional abrogation of the states' Eleventh Amendment immunity,[51] a strong rule against imposing conditions on state administration of federally assisted programs,[52] a strong rule against federal preemption of regulations traditionally left to the states,[53] a super-strong rule against federal regulation of core state functions,[54] a presumption against the applicability of federal statutes to state and local political processes,[55] a super-strong rule against federal habeas relief and in favor of established state procedures for adjudicating constitutional claims of convicted criminals,[56] a presumption that federal statutes touching on intergovernmental tax immunities hew to the constitutional lines established by Supreme Court precedent,[57] and a strong rule that federal statutory schemes are enforceable in state as well as federal court.[58]

The proliferation of these strong-arm canons, together with the vigorous use of the more traditional substantive canons (such as the rule of lenity), suggests that the Rehnquist Court is an activist Court in statutory cases. But this Court surely does not see itself as activist or, alternatively, thinks that whatever activism it has engaged in is justifiable. In the latter claim the Court may find support in neo-republican constitutional theory.

Neo-republican theory posits that constitutional law ought to promote both lawful government and self-government by an active citizenry.[59] Republicanism has equal relevance to issues of statutory interpretation, and the substantive canons may be understood through the prism of republican theory.[60] At least some of the Justices, particularly O'Connor and Scalia, view the constitutionally based canons as democracy-enhancing. In this section of the chapter I make out a case for three different republican goals which at least some of the substantive canons might serve: (1) focusing congressional attention onto underenforced constitutional norms, (2) encouraging policy-making by officials who are most accountable to the people, and (3) ameliorating systemic dysfunctions in the legislative process. On the whole I am skeptical that republican theory is a complete explanation for the Court's canonical activism.

The Canons as a Means for Implementing Underenforced Constitutional Norms

The Rehnquist Court's development of constitutionally based clear statement rules is a self-conscious effort to provide a subconstitutional way to enforce "underenforced" constitutional norms. Judicial review in a democracy is exceptional, and should be deployed by unelected judges only when there is a clear inconsistency between a statute or regulation and the Constitution. For this reason at least some constitutional values will remain "underenforced" by the Court.[61]

While a Court that seeks to avoid constitutional activism will be reluctant to invalidate federal statutes in close cases, it might seek other ways to protect constitutional norms. One way is through canons of statutory construction. A traditional example is the rule that ambiguous statutes should be interpreted to avoid constitutional difficulties (discussed in Chapters 5 and 6). The rule makes it harder for Congress to enact constitutionally questionable statutes and forces legislators to reflect and deliberate before plunging into constitutionally sensitive issues. Protecting underenforced constitutional norms through such clear statement rules is normatively attractive under republican theory (and under the critical pragmatism that I follow). It is not seriously undemocratic, since Congress can override the norm through a statutory clear statement. Additionally, such rules still provide significant protection for constitutional norms because they raise the costs of statutory provisions invading such norms. Ultimately, such rules may even be democracy-enhancing by focusing the political process on the values enshrined in the Constitution.

This theory is the best account of why the Rehnquist Court has created so many aggressive clear statement rules, but it is not a complete account. One difficulty is that the Court's overall practice is not perfectly consistent with the theory of underenforced constitutional norms. The leading theorists emphasize that constitutional provisions protecting individual liberties (free speech, equal protection) are underenforced,[62] but the Rehnquist Court is more reluctant to protect individual rights through clear statement rules than the Burger and Warren Courts were. Recall Rust v. Sullivan (discussed in Chapter 5), in which the Court upheld the Department of Health and Human Services (HHS) gag rule against medical counseling for women considering abortions. Because the agency's gag rule was not clearly authorized by the original statutory delegation and because it raised First Amendment as well as right to privacy issues, *Rust* presented an excellent opportunity for the Court to insist that Congress, rather than HHS, make the constitutional choice. Yet only O'Connor took this approach to the statute, and the Court deferred to the agency's interpretation, in striking contrast to its refusal to defer to the agency in *Aramco*, which presented no constitutional difficulty. *Rust* is not atypical of the Rehnquist Court, which has been reluctant to protect First Amendment, due process, and equal protection values through restrictive statutory interpretations, although it has been willing to enforce federalism and separation of powers norms in this way.[63]

A possible response to this difficulty is that structural constitutional norms are *more* underenforced than individual rights norms and hence require greater protection through clear statement rules. The nondelegation doctrine and federalism are almost never enforced through constitutional invalidation of federal statutes, and separation of powers limits are rarely enforced.[64] Though the equal protection clause and the First Amendment may be *under*enforced, they might have more bite than the virtually *un*enforced structural protections. Ergo, the Court should enforce the former through direct judicial review (constitutional law) and the latter through clear statement rules (quasi-constitutional law).

This appealing response becomes problematic if we take seriously the stated reasons why structural constitutional norms are *un*enforced. In Garcia v. San Antonio Metropolitan Transit Authority[65] the Court announced that limits on national power based on federalism are unenforceable against Congress because the Court has been unable to develop "principled constitutional limitations" from the Tenth Amendment and the commerce clause and because "the principal means chosen by the Framers to ensure the role of the

States in the federal system lies in the structure of the Federal Government itself." I shall focus on these federalism norms, but note that similar reasons underlie the Court's failure to enforce the nondelegation doctrine and separation of powers.[66]

These reasons for the nonenforcement of federalism norms through *constitutional* interpretation are equally valid arguments for the nonenforcement of federalism norms through *statutory* interpretation. Thus, if the Court refuses to enforce federalism through constitutional interpretation because it has found that the structure of the federal government sufficiently protects state and local interests, it is hard to see why the Court would feel required to enforce federalism through super-strong clear statement rules—unless the Court has second thoughts about how well protected state and local governments are at the federal level. Indeed, when *Garcia* was decided in 1985, four dissenting Justices were skeptical that the structure of the federal government provided much protection to state and local governments. Their views were rejected by the Court, and evidence since 1985 has done nothing to rehabilitate them. For example, Congress promptly overrode *Garcia*, at the behest of state and local governments, and recent studies indicate that state interests are exceedingly well represented in the national legislative process.[67]

Moreover, if the Court fails to enforce structural constitutional norms through judicial review because the Constitution provides little guidance as to their content in specific cases, how does the Court expect to come up with clear statement rules that are any more principled? Consider the Court's decision in Gregory v. Ashcroft,[68] which interpreted the Age Discrimination in Employment Act of 1967 (ADEA) to be inapplicable to state requirements that judges retire by age seventy. The Court could have reached this result by ordinary textual analysis, as Philip Frickey has argued.[69] Instead, the Court created a super-strong clear statement rule: "[I]nasmuch as this Court in *Garcia* has left primarily to the political process the protection of the States against intrusive exercises of Congress' Commerce Clause powers, we must be absolutely certain that Congress intended such an exercise."[70] The Court held in *Gregory* that Congress must speak super-clearly when it regulates the states directly.

But *Gregory* threatens to return the Supreme Court to the inquiry it found intractable in *Garcia*—of defining whether the subjects of regulation are "indisputably attributes of state sovereignty," whether state compliance with federal regulation "directly impairs" the state's ability "to structure integral operations in areas of traditional governmental functions," and whether the federal interest in regulation outweighs the state interest in autonomy.[71] *Gregory* itself provides little guidance on when to apply its new super-strong clear statement rule, referring at one time or another to "areas traditionally regulated by the States," state decisions of "the most fundamental sort for a sovereign entity," "authority that lies at 'the heart of representative government,'" and intrusion on "state governmental functions."[72] This would seem to run the gamut from everything within the traditional police power, to state operation of all its governmental processes, to state methods of selecting high officials.

Still, there might be clear cases. For example, one would expect *Gregory* to immunize state processes of selecting judges from all but crystal-clear federal regulation, yes? One would be wrong. The same day the Court decided *Gregory*, it decided Chisom v. Roemer.[73] *Chisom* held that section 2 of the Voting Rights Act,[74] which prohibits state electoral processes that result in the dilution of the voting strength of a racial minority, applies to the election of state judges. Justice Stevens's majority opinion approached the interpretive question quite conventionally, relying heavily on the legislative history and purpose of the statute. The majority never considered whether any super-strong clear statement rule about federal regulation applied. Indeed, it did not even cite *Gregory*.

O'Connor, the author of *Gregory*, silently joined the Court's opinion in *Chisom*. I believe that her votes can be explained by her opinion in *Rust* and her willingness to adopt narrowing interpretations that avoid constitutional difficulties. The ADEA was enacted under Congress's general commerce clause power, and any intrusion into state operations under that power is constitutionally more suspect (for O'Connor) than Congress's race-protective intrusion into state voting practices, which is specifically authorized by the Fifteenth Amendment. This explanation suggests some coherence in O'Connor's position but does not explain the Rehnquist Court's overall approach, for a majority of the Court seems reluctant to apply the rule to avoid constitutional difficulties in individual rights cases.

Constitutionally Based Deference and Substantive Canons as Democracy-Enhancing

Republican theory suggests a justification for the Rehnquist Court's activism through canons that protect structural rather than rights-oriented constitutional values. The best way to ensure individual rights is through ensuring democratic process in our polity. The best way to ensure democratic process is through protecting the Constitution's structures, as the framers anticipated. Given the virtual nonenforcement of such structures through direct judicial review, enforcement through clear statement rules becomes imperative. As Justice Scalia has put it, "I think we have an obligation to conduct our exegesis in a fashion which fosters th[e] democratic process."[75] Most of the Rehnquist Court's deference and substantive canons can be rationalized as fostering democracy. But the rationalizations do not rest on a sophisticated theory of democracy and, partly for that reason, may not be robust in practice.

Deference to Agency Interpretations   The rule of deferring to agency interpretations may be justified by a theory of comparative accountability. In Chevron U.S.A., Inc., v. Natural Resources Defense Council (discussed in Chapter 5), the Court held that it should defer to agency interpretations because unelected judges with life tenure are less democratically accountable than unelected agency heads, who are accountable to the democratically elected president. This justification for deference is incoherent, for theoretical as well as practical reasons. As a matter of comparative accountability the Court should mainly be deferring to Congress, whose members are elected by and accountable directly to the people. The Court's bow to this obvious point indicates that it will override the agency interpretation when it runs counter to the "plain meaning" of the statutory text. But the Court's purported plain meaning exception to deference only exacerbates its incoherent approach.

To begin with, what is or is not a plain meaning is to a large extent constructed, not found, by the Court. Recall *Aramco.* In that case the EEOC's interpretation (that Title VII applies to U.S. citizens employed by U.S. companies abroad) was consistent with the broadly written jurisdictional provisions of the statute. Yet the Court refused to defer to the EEOC, based on a plain meaning the Court created: the *Court's* clear statement rule was treated as the *statute's* plain meaning, unless it is rebutted by what *Congress* has written. That is a strange approach indeed to plain meaning, made even stranger by the Court's refusal to credit the alien exemption provision as a clear statement. The Court could have played this same game in *Rust* (do not defer to the HHS interpretation of a generally phrased statute when it would run afoul of the clear statement rule to avoid constitutional difficulties), but it chose not to.

The incoherence of *Rust* and *Aramco* as exercises in democratic theory is more striking when one considers the underinclusiveness of the plain meaning exception. *Chevron* establishes the case for deference to agency interpretations by contrasting current judicial preferences (not democratic) with current agency preferences (more democratic). This contrast is undermined by contrasting, instead, current agency preferences (more democratic) with past or current legislative preferences (most democratic). It is probable that Congress in 1964, and certain that Congress in 1991, preferred the position taken by the *Aramco* dissent to that taken by the majority. Hence, even if the EEOC had interpreted Title VII not to apply extraterritorially, the democracy-enhancing interpretation would have been one that deferred to Congress rather than to the agency.

Rust is a more difficult case, since it is unclear to me what Congress's preferences were when it enacted the enabling statute in 1970 (see Chapter 5). But it is clear that Congress in 1991 disagreed with the HHS gag rule. Hence, the main contrast in *Rust* is between current agency preferences and current congressional preferences. I fail to see how it is democracy-enhancing for the Court to defer to agency preferences when they are apparently inconsistent with legislative ones, as was the case in both *Rust* and *Aramco.*

Rule against Congressional Derogation from Executive and Judicial Powers Our polity is a democracy in which lawmaking powers have been deliberately fragmented so that ambition might counter ambition. Thus, the framers did not contemplate that what Congress desired as public policy would immediately become so. Instead, the Constitution makes congressionally chosen policy dependent on implementation by separate branches. This process yields less partial policy because Congress knows that biased policy can be turned against its allies, and it yields less radical shifts in policy because its message is filtered through officials not controlled by Congress.[76]

To preserve the vigor of the national government's separation of powers, the Court has created clear statement rules against congressional derogation of executive and judicial power. Thus, the Court presumes against congressional preclusion of judicial review, and against congressional invasion of the "inherent powers" of the judiciary.[77] Also, the Court presumes against congressional invasion of the president's executive powers and against congressional interference with the president's exercise of executive authority, especially in the foreign affairs arena.[78]

The goal of these canons is to preserve the integrity of the independent branches and an overall balance in the national government, lest one branch dominate the others. But as applied by the Court, these canons threaten to create new imbalances by aggrandizing executive and (to a lesser extent) judicial power at the expense of congressional power. For example, in Japan Whaling Association v. American Cetacean Society,[79] the Court held that the Department of Commerce had not violated the Packwood and Pelly amendments when it failed to certify Japan's allegedly excessive whaling practices to an international remedial body as an apparent violation of international agreements. Yet the Pelly Amendment on its face directed the department to certify if "nationals of a foreign country, directly or indirectly, are conducting fishing operations in a manner or under circumstances which diminish the effectiveness of an international fishery program."[80] The Court concluded that it was not clear that Japan's practices, which regularly exceeded the international limits, "diminish[ed] the effectiveness" of those limits within the meaning of the amendment.[81] The executive branch therefore enjoyed considerable discretion as to when it was required by statute to certify violations. This holding is a strained reading of the statutory text and contrary to the Pelly Amendment's legislative history.[82] *Japan Whaling* can be read to create a super-strong clear statement rule, either against congressional interference in the president's foreign affairs authority or in favor of deferring to agency interpretations in the foreign affairs arena. Either way, the Court's rule marginalizes Congress's role in foreign affairs, a marginalization contrary to the text of the Constitution and the expectations of its framers.[83]

I argued in Chapter 5 that, especially during periods of divided government, presidential preferences threaten to eclipse congressional preferences if the Court seriously applies the rule of deference to agency interpretations. To the extent that the Court also presumes against implementing congressional preferences in areas such as foreign affairs, the Court is compounding the difficulty. Neither *Chevron* nor *Japan Whaling* is democracy-enhancing because both undervalue congressional preferences, which are supposed to be most responsive to the people. In addition, the rules reflected in those decisions undermine the balance among the branches contemplated by the framers.

Canons Protecting Federalism Values   The Rehnquist Court's most appealing democracy-enhancing rules are the federalism canons. O'Connor's opinion in *Gregory* is the leading statement of the democratic values the Court hopes to engender:

> This federalist structure of joint sovereigns preserves to the people numerous advantages. It assures a decentralized government that will be more sensitive to the diverse needs of a heterogeneous society; it increases opportunity for citizen involvement in democratic processes; it allows for more innovation and experimentation in government; and it makes government more responsive by putting the States in competition for a mobile citizenry . . .
>
> Perhaps the principal benefit of the federalist system is a check on abuses of government power . . . Just as the separation and independence of the coordinate Branches of the Federal Government serves to prevent the accumulation of excessive power in any one Branch, a healthy balance of power between the States and the Federal Government will reduce the risk of tyranny and abuse from either front.[84]

This vision of federalism is an attractive one. It sounds a warning that the national government should not be able to cripple state and local governments by shifting costs onto those units. But this vision of federalism may not justify the Court's recent binge of federalism-based clear statement rules.

Chisom reminds us that the decentralization values of federalism must be balanced against the centralization values of the supremacy clause, which ought to be especially weighty when national legislation seeks to protect individual rights against state infringement. However much our polity might value federalism, it is a value we are prepared to sacrifice for some overriding national policies. The dissenting opinion in Coleman v. Thompson[85] argued that federalism "has no inherent normative value" beyond its practical value in "secur[ing] to citizens the liberties that derive from the diffusion of sovereign power" and in "realizing the concepts of decency and fairness which are among the fundamental principles of liberty and justice lying at the base of all our civil and political institutions." If federalism ultimately subserves the preservation of individual liberties, there seems scant reason not to sacrifice state sovereignty interests to individual rights in the name of, and not against, the norm of federalism.

Federalism can mean that individual liberties are doubly protected—through both local regulation and national superregulation. This is a reading of federalism the Court itself provided in *Tafflin v. Levitt*,[86] which created a clear statement rule, based on the supremacy clause, that federal statutory schemes must be presumptively enforceable in state as well as federal courts. Under this "dialectical federalism" the redundancy of state and federal courts serves a mutual checking function, with ambition countering ambition among judges in their protection of constitutional rights. Yet this vision of federalism does not yield much support for the Court's willingness to protect state entities from federal lawsuits seeking to enforce national rights, as in *Dellmuth*. This vision seems inconsistent, too, with decisions such as *Coleman*, which create barriers to federal habeas relief for constitutional errors in state criminal proceedings.[87]

There is a further difficulty with the Court's focusing on decentralization as a democracy-enhancing norm. Most grass-roots democracy occurs below the level of state government, and many national rules and statutes foster grass-roots democracy at the expense of the statocracy. Unless the Court retreats from *Gregory*'s functionalism and reverts to a pre–New Deal formalism, it must justify federalism-based canons on a case-by-case basis. Is national regulation unduly burdensome on the states, or does it instead encourage sub-state communities? For example, the EHA, the statute at issue in *Dellmuth*, can be viewed as democracy-enhancing because it empowered local communities of parents who have children with disabilities vis-à-vis the state. By refusing to permit lawsuits against the states, which Congress had legislated not once but twice, *Dellmuth* elevated a formalist federalism over the justifications articulated in *Gregory*.

The complexity of *Gregory*'s decentralization rationale is more clearly illustrated in the many canons involving state regulation of Native American territory. The Burger Court generally (but unevenly) followed traditional canons presuming against state regulation of tribal territory.[88] This stance can be justified not only by reference to the quasi-sovereign nature of tribal territory but also by the value of encouraging local Native American self-government—precisely the same value extolled in *Gregory*. Yet the Rehnquist Court has shown signs of trumping the traditional Indian law canons with its federalism-based canons. For example, in Cotton Petroleum Corp. v. New Mexico[89] the Court upheld application of a state severance tax on a non-Indian company under contract with a tribe to extract oil and gas in Indian country, even though the practical incidence of the tax fell largely on the tribe, and even though there was no congressional authorization of the sort the Burger Court had required for allowing states to impose tax burdens on Native American tribes. By presuming that states have concurrent jurisdiction over tribal territory,[90] *Cotton Petroleum* effectively trumped traditional canons preserving tribal autonomy with a new presumption derived from *Gregory*, even though the effect was greater centralization and a weakening of tribal self-government.

Substantive Canons to Ameliorate Dysfunctions in American Democracy

Republican theory would also support interpretive presumptions which correct for dysfunctions in the political process.[91] The Burger Court generally interpreted ambiguous statutes in ways that protected the interests of groups that had been subordinated in the political process, including African Americans, women, Native Americans, noncitizens, and nonmarital children. That such "discrete and insular minorities" were also entitled to heightened constitutional protection suggests a connection between these "*Carolene* canons" and the rule to avoid constitutional difficulties.[92]

The *Carolene* canons provide a republican theory for reconciling *Chisom*, a generous reading of the Voting Rights Act to cover state judicial elections, with *Gregory*, a stingy reading of the ADEA to exempt judges. Because the Court does not consider the elderly a constitutionally protected group, and because the elderly people who are judges are a politically powerful group, the Court was willing to sacrifice their interests to those of federalism and state regulation of local judicial systems. *Chisom*, by contrast, involved fundamental (voting) rights of the paradigm *Carolene* group, African Americans. That the Voting Rights Act was implementing the Fifteenth Amendment, a specific authorization for Congress to protect African American voting rights, made *Chisom* an especially attractive case for expansive rather than narrow interpretation.

Chisom is consistent with a proposition advanced in Chapter 5, that statutory interpretation may be representation-reinforcing, and that the Court may develop canons that correct for dysfunctions in the legislative and regulatory process. Thus, the Court ought to consider voices suppressed in the political process, and this suggests a meta-canon: decide close cases against politically salient interests and in favor of interests that have been subordinated in the political process. Congress can, of course, override the Court's decision, and indeed is more likely to do so if the loser is politically powerful.

This is fine under most versions of republican theory, if new perspectives are introduced into the political process.

This meta-rule provides interesting normative support for some of the Rehnquist Court's canonical jurisprudence. For the best example, it provides justification for the rule of lenity, that ambiguities in criminal statutes be construed against the government and in favor of the accused. Although the Rehnquist Court has cut back on procedural protections for accused as well as convicted criminals, the rule of lenity has flourished.[93] Representation reinforcement supports this development, since criminal defendants are poorly represented in the political process, while state and federal prosecutors (the losers in rule of lenity cases) are unusually well represented.[94] Representation-reinforcing concerns, however, do not perfectly well explain the Court's rule of lenity jurisprudence, for the big winners in these cases tend to be defendants with relatively more political clout. Consider the decisions in which the rule of lenity has protected state and local officials from federal prosecution.[95]

In McNally v. United States[96] the Court held that the federal mail fraud statute did not reach a scheme under which a state official and powerful persons in the state's dominant political party conspired to assign state insurance business to certain agencies that were required to kick back part of the insurance premiums. No monetary loss to the state was shown, and the federal prosecutor's theory of the case was that the conspirators had defrauded the state's citizenry of their intangible right to honest government. Even though the mail fraud statute reached "any scheme or artifice to defraud,"[97] and even though applying it to these facts would have been consistent with the background to the statute and the interpretations of it in the lower courts, Justice Byron White's majority opinion concluded that the statute protected only against fraud involving money or property rights. White relied on a strong version of the rule of lenity under which the harsher of two readings of a criminal statute should be chosen "only when Congress has spoken in clear and definite language."[98] He bolstered the application of the rule by noting that its use avoided involving the federal government in setting standards of disclosure and good government for local and state officials (implicating federalism values), and he seemed dubious that federal criminal law should be interpreted to reach acts of state officials and their associates which are not clearly in violation of the state's own laws. Stevens, in dissent, complained that the Court was using the rule of lenity to come to the aid of "the most sophisticated practitioners of the art of government," who must have known that their acts would be deemed unlawful based on precedents in the lower federal courts.[99]

Representation-reinforcement concerns cut several ways in *McNally.* On the one hand, the Department of Justice has the best legislative override record in recent history, and it is not politically unfair to place the burden on it to procure statutory language more specifically targeting intangible harms in the federal antifraud statutes. Indeed, the department did just that. Within a year Congress overrode *McNally* with more specific statutory language.[100] On the other hand, a broad interpretation of federal anticorruption laws may be representation-reinforcing by enabling federal prosecutors to break up patterns of political corruption which the local process is less likely to attack vigorously. It may also be true that local political moguls have relatively more clout, even on the national level, than run-of-the-mill criminal defendants, who tend to be poor and politically underrepresented.

Ironically, representation-reinforcing concerns may have contributed to the Court's decisions cutting back on civil rights statutes. In Wards Cove Packing Company v. Atonio,[101] for example, the Court reinterpreted Title VII to require that plaintiffs in disparate impact cases carry the burden of proving that racial imbalances are the result of specific discriminatory practices. At least some of the Justices probably saw the result as protecting a marginalized political group: blue-collar white men. This is how I have come to this conclusion: the main legal argument made in *Wards Cove* was that a lenient burden of proof for plaintiffs in disparate impact cases would put pressure on employers to adopt racial "quotas," which would be in tension with Title VII's provision that it not "require" racial preferences.[102] Invoking public choice arguments, some of the majority Justices had earlier criticized employment preferences on the ground that they penalized blue-collar white males.[103] The implication of this view is that, in the 1980s, blue-collar white men (a diffuse group) had less political clout than racial minorities (a group whose concentrated numbers contributed to greater political organization). According to this line of argument, a Court concerned with protecting the politically marginalized ought not to encourage racial workplace preferences.

Dellmuth and *Aramco* might be similarly explained as a judicial belief that many "discrete and insular minorities" (including people with disabilities as well as racial and ethnic minorities) not only have political clout these days but have more political clout than ordinary citizens.[104] That *Wards Cove, Aramco*, and *Dellmuth* were all promptly overridden by Congress does suggest that racial minorities and people with disabilities have more political clout than they did a generation ago. Nonetheless, it is not representation-reinforcing to protect powerful groups whose interests are well represented in the political process—such as state governments (the winners in *Dellmuth*) and transnational corporations (the winners in *Aramco*). The fierce battle to override *Wards Cove* is evidence that the winners in that case—companies with bad numbers and white male blue-collar workers—have plenty of political clout. These were, after all, the groups that had won five of the previous six presidential elections.

Thus, although some Justices may have a tendency to view their votes as representation-reinforcing in civil rights cases, they have a parochial under-standing of the "representation" they are "reinforcing." Conversely, in other lines of cases, where the representation-reinforcing strategy is clearer, the Rehnquist Court has created clear statement rules systematically advantaging politically powerful "have" groups at the expense of marginalized or ill-organized "have nots." For example, the Court has created new procedural presumptions barring recourse to habeas corpus remedies, even though state governments and law enforcement officials have much more clout in Con-gress than criminal defendants and their surrogates, the criminal defense bar and civil libertarians. The Court has also created a clear statement rule that federal jurisdiction cannot be invoked to enforce important national policies when there is a private agreement to arbitrate, even though the arbitration term is one of "adhesion" between a consumer and a corporation.[105] The Court has created a super-strong clear statement rule against federal waivers of the United States' sovereign immunity,[106] even though the diffuse citizenry suing the government is politically inchoate and the federal bureaucracy itself has the best override record in history.

A Postmodern Theory: The Canons as Expressions of the Court's Ideology

Llewellyn's argument that the canons are malleable is not the end of analysis, for malleable clay can be molded into coherent shapes. Although the canons do not constrain the Court or enable Congress to predict what the Court will do in particular cases, they may be connected in an important way with the results the Court reaches in statutory cases. Postmodern theory would draw from Llewellyn's game with the canons a critique of the cause-and-effect as-sumptions associated with traditional liberal theories of the canons—because there is this canon, then the decision maker reaches the following result. Such a critique does not prevent us from thinking about the canons in a noncausal way, or from thinking about an interpretive regime as something more than a grab bag of rules and presumptions. An interpretive regime is a means by which the Court expresses its underlying ideology in statutory interpretation cases. That ideology, in turn, should be understood not as a fixed set of politi-cal prejudices driving the Court's results, but instead as a web of beliefs about the world, the law, and the role of the Court—a web whose pattern has changed as new strands have been interwoven with older ones.

Because the Court is a collection of mysterious people, a thorough under-standing is beyond the scope of this chapter. Instead I focus on the Court's civil rights decisions, and suggest that the ideology that is part of the interpre-tive regime in those cases is not as simple as either the Court or its critics have maintained. The exercise that follows is an effort to make sense of the

Court's apparently arbitrary use of the canons by incorporating a story of the Court's evolving frame of vision in civil rights cases. I also seek to understand the Court's frame critically.

Conservative Process Statism

The Rehnquist Court's substantive canons help locate the Court in American jurisprudential history. The Rehnquist Court is not nostalgic for an era of libertarianism but is instead strongly statist. The starting point for analysis is no longer private interaction but public regulation, whether through common law rules, legislated statutes, or agency rule making. This is a legacy of the New Deal and the legal process school. The Court's statist pre-understandings are revealed in its tolerance of most state and federal regulatory schemes. The Court tends to strike them down or construe them narrowly mostly when regulations burden other governmental units (as in *Atascadero* and *Gregory*), and less often when they burden the citizenry or corporations (contrast *Rust*).[107]

If the Rehnquist Court is statist, what explains its reluctance in *Aramco* and *Wards Cove* (to choose two of several examples) to construe civil rights statutes broadly? My response to this complication consumes the remainder of this chapter. I begin by observing that the Rehnquist Court's statism is a legal process statism,[108] one in which private institutions are the first-order decision makers and in which the legitimacy of state decision making depends on the institutional competence of the decision maker and the regularity of the process. Legal process considers the legislature the institution most legitimate as well as most competent to make major policy decisions which have significant consequences for the allocation of rights, power, and/or wealth in our society (see Chapter 5). The role of courts is not to make policy choices but to see that the appropriate institutions are making those choices and are following the prescribed procedures for doing so. A "conservative" reading of the legal process philosophy emphasizes the presumptive desirability of the status quo, which includes both existing private power arrangements and pervasive state power. The presumptive desirability of the status quo means that any major policy shift must be made by the institution most competent to do it, following the prescribed procedures and after due deliberation.[109]

The meta-rule indicated by a conservative version of the legal process philosophy is that shifts in national policy should be made by the political process and not by the courts. One corollary to this meta-rule is that the political process must accomplish such shifts openly, deliberatively, and within the assigned competence of each institution. Two further corollaries, related to the first, are that the only institution competent to make important shifts in national policy is Congress and that Congress can do this only by enacting a new statute along the lines required by article I, section 7 of the Constitution. This meta-rule and its corollaries begin to make sense out of *Wards Cove*, in which the Rehnquist Court cut back on a policy innovation (disparate impacts on minorities can violate Title VII) accomplished by the EEOC and the Burger Court (see Chapter 1 for this story), as well as *Aramco*, in which the Court cut back on a policy innovation the EEOC was trying to make to extend Title VII overseas.

A more progressive understanding of the legal process philosophy suggests a counterargument: *Wards Cove* and *Aramco* are decisions inconsistent with the broad antidiscrimination purpose of Title VII, and the EEOC was acting both legitimately and competently when it adapted the statute to new circumstances in ways that subserve the statutory purpose. Emphasis on statutory purpose has a long legal process lineage (see Chapters 5 and 7) and was the Burger Court's prevailing approach to Title VII. It is not the Rehnquist Court's approach, which is skeptical of shifts in policy led by the Court, or even by agencies, unless justified by a specific legitimating "authority," such as statutory text, precedent, or tradition. This is where the canons come back into play. Consider one final decision.

The issue in Martin v. Wilks[110] was whether white firefighters could challenge employment decisions taken by Birmingham, Alabama, pursuant to a consent decree between the city and a class of black plaintiffs claiming to have been denied opportunities in violation of Title VII. Even though the plaintiffs were not parties to the original consent decree, Title VII's purpose of improving employment opportunities for African Americans (see Chapter 1) would arguably have been served by cutting off collateral challenges to consent decrees. But Rehnquist's opinion for the Court did not even mention statutory purpose and, instead, grounded the inquiry in the long-standing "principle of general application in Anglo-American jurisprudence that one is not bound by a judgment *in personam* in a litigation in which he is not designated as a party or to which he has not been made a party by service of process."[111] Finding that neither Title VII nor the Federal Rules of Civil Procedure contained language that satisfies this clear statement rule, the Court held that third parties can challenge Title VII consent decrees. In dicta the Court indicated that a "special remedial scheme . . . expressly foreclosing successive litigation by nonlitigants" would be given effect "if the scheme is otherwise consistent with due process."[112] The Court might have been suggesting that its interpretation of Title VII and the Federal Rules had the further advantage of avoiding difficult constitutional questions.

Wilks illustrates both the Rehnquist Court's conservative, tradition-based process approach to statutory issues and some of the problems with such an approach. The main objection posed by this book is that the Rehnquist Court's sources of authority—statutory text and tradition—are no "harder" or determinate than statutory purpose and are no better at screening out value judgments by judges. Although there is a tradition in United States law preventing people from being bound by judgments to which they were not parties, there is also a tradition in equitable relief cases of framing broad decrees which are binding on people not parties to the decrees. For example, school desegregation consent decrees regularly affect the rights of schoolchildren and parents whether or not they were parties in the lawsuit, as well as of future schoolchildren who could not have been parties to the original lawsuit. Partly for this reason, the large majority of federal circuit courts throughout the 1980s had refused to allow collateral challenges to Title VII consent decrees.[113]

A further problem is that the Court's approach discourages the sort of practical reasoning that can be a most productive way to analyze statutes (see Chapters 2 and 6). By overturning a decade's worth of lower court practice and prior understandings of the statute's purpose and operation, the Court created a rupture which both surprised and inflamed the political culture. Congress was quite surprised by *Wilks*, thoroughly disapproved of the decision, and angrily overrode it in 1991.[114] Of course, Congress's action was the institutionally legitimate way to make the policy change, and in this respect *Wilks*'s rupture was itself defensible under a conservative legal process philosophy. But was the cost (in unsettled consent decrees, years of expensive litigation, racial anger and distrust) worth this benefit? And what is the value of formal congressional action that merely restores the prior practice that the Court disrupted?

Scarcity and American Public Law

In the 1950s and 1960s, when the legal process philosophy was on the rise in law schools and the courts, the nation's potential and its resources seemed virtually limitless. The Warren Court and the early Burger Court seized on a liberal version of the legal process philosophy to stimulate public law litigation through bright-line constitutional lawmaking and aggressive procedural innovations to revive both old and new civil rights statutes through dynamic interpretation, and to open up statutory schemes to greater public participation by rethinking administrative law. This was exciting but expensive legal stuff. It crashed against the shoals of diminished expectations in the 1970s. After a generation of economic and legal binging (1945–1973), America rediscovered scarcity after bankrupting itself on a costly war and encountering a series of oil price shocks. Even a wealthy country cannot do all that it would like; the impact of that lesson becomes more profound once the country fears it may not be so wealthy in the future.

The rediscovery of scarcity by our political and economic culture has coincided with an increased emphasis on scarcity in our legal culture. In academic law this has been most apparent in the law and economics movement, which starts with the fact of scarce resources and asks how we can structure rules and procedures to maximize the happiness we can achieve through enjoyment of these scarce resources.[115] Doctrinally, concerns about scarcity have fueled a new generation of canons of statutory construction, a development that started in the Burger Court and accelerated in the Rehnquist Court.

Public law litigation, for example, becomes more problematic if one considers the state an institution with limited resources which might be drained away by the attorneys' fees, compliance costs, and agenda changes introduced by public law litigation. Whereas the cost-unconscious Warren Court encouraged public law litigation, the cost-conscious Burger Court was concerned that public law litigation threatened to overwhelm the state's ability to function efficiently. The Court expressed that concern by creating more restrictive standing and justiciability rules,[116] and by creating or clarifying substantive canons of statutory construction, including a presumption against implied causes of action from federal statutes,[117] a rule that federal jurisdiction be narrowly construed,[118] a presumption against federal common law in an area occupied by statute,[119] a presumption against federal abrogation of traditional official and state immunities from lawsuit,[120] and a rule against imposing federal conditions on state administration of federally funded programs.[121] The Rehnquist Court is even more acutely concerned with the costs of public law litigation and has applied most of these canons more strongly than the Burger Court did.[122]

Concern about scarcity also helps explain the decline of purpose-based process arguments in public law. Interpreting statutes to carry out their purposes becomes either question-begging or circular once one thinks about purpose in economic terms. Purpose-based interpretation may be question-begging because there is no purpose that is pursued at any cost. The economics-inspired analysis is that, given Congress's purpose and the trade-offs it was willing to make, which interpretation best fits the statutory balance? Thus, it is not fair to say that *Aramco* or *Wards Cove* or *Wilks* is wrong on the ground that any of these decisions thwarts Title VII's purpose to improve employment opportunities for blacks, when Congress was not willing to pursue that purpose at any price. Title VII is filled with procedural as well as substantive compromises detracting from that purpose (see Chapter 1). It is not clear how much Congress would have been willing to compromise the statutory purpose for overseas employment (*Aramco*) or for disparate impact lawsuits (*Wards Cove*) or for subsequent challenges to consent decrees (*Wilks*), since none of these topics was the focus of congressional negotiations in 1964. From a perspective of scarcity, interpreting a statute broadly to carry out its purpose poses the danger of overenforcement of the statutory mandate. The danger of overenforcement carries with it systemwide costs that undermine overall social utility.

The Rehnquist Court's attitude toward Title VII seems to have been specifically influenced by a scarcity-based concern that the statute has been overenforced. The early Burger Court tended to see Title VII not only as a statute enacted in the public interest, and hence to be construed liberally, but as something of a constitutional "moment" (to borrow Bruce Ackerman's term), and hence to be applied sweepingly. Even the Burger Court came to interpret Title VII more stingily by the early 1980s. Law and economics scholars tend to be even stingier, some arguing that Title VII is unnecessary because the market can resolve the most severe problems of discrimination; is extremely costly because of the many transaction costs it introduced, especially for small businesses; and is at bottom inefficient.[123]

For conservative legal process reasons the Rehnquist Court is not willing to question the legitimacy or desirability of Title VII in the way that some economists do. Scarcity concerns suggest a different economic theory of the canons of construction from the one developed at the beginning of this chapter. Canons such as the rule against extraterritoriality are not themselves efficient, but they can be applied in an efficiency-enhancing way. If the underlying statute (Title VII) is inefficient, then applying a narrowing canon is efficient because it limits the damage done by the rent-seeking. Hence, *Aramco*. By contrast, if the underlying statute is efficient, as the Sherman Act and the securities laws appear to be, application of the rule against extraterritoriality would be inefficient. Thus, lower courts have not applied the *Aramco* canon to those laws. In short, a theory of the canons (economic or otherwise) may be linked to theories of the different statutory schemes to which the canons are being applied. The Rehnquist Court's skepticism about Title VII as it was created in the 1970s fuels its willingness to cut back on the statute after 1989. My philosophy of critical pragmatism considers these to be appropriate questions. The Rehnquist Court's rupture in civil rights law is defensible if it can be justified by a robust critical appraisal of law's practice.

The question then becomes: Is the Court's substantive theory justified? Here, I am skeptical. Discrimination remains pervasive, is not corrected by the market, and creates three different kinds of inefficiencies that can be regulated by strong antidiscrimination laws (*Griggs* rather than *Wards Cove*).[124] First, employers still make decisions based on imperfect information, namely, stereotypes that undervalue the labor of minorities and women, or rely on information (such as prior work history) that reflects previous undervaluing of that labor. Disparate impact discrimination rules can ameliorate these informational problems by pressing employers toward experience with more diverse work forces. Second, structural barriers such as seniority systems and last-hired, first-fired practices still impede much minority entry into or advancement within the work force. By questioning customary practices which unnecessarily exclude people, disparate impact requirements may contribute to a more open employment system. Third, inefficiencies are introduced by status competition, in which groups vie for relative status rather than pure wealth increases. By working against status competition, antidiscrimination laws can channel competition into more productive uses.[125]

The normative case against the Title VII of the 1970s (disparate impact rules) is at this point underwhelming. If that is so, *Aramco* is a bad decision. *Wards Cove* is a bad decision. And so is *Wilks*. Even under a conservative legal process mindset and an understandable worry about efficient uses of scarce resources, the Rehnquist Court's "reneging on history" of civil rights enforcement may have been unjustified. Indeed, *Wilks* was an odd interpretation for a Court concerned with scarcity because the decision reopened hundreds of Title VII consent decrees for further adjudication. That in turn unsettled reliance interests of employers who have restructured their work force in compliance with the decrees and threatened to generate significant transaction costs with little payoff (few decrees rewritten). What inspired the Supreme Court in that case?

Civil Rights as Allocational Politics

Part I of this book suggested that *Weber* reflects a certain ideology of race relations in America. Likewise, *Wilks* reflects an ideology of race relations, albeit a competing one. Recall that Rehnquist wrote *Wilks* but dissented in *Weber*. Ironically, both ideologies arose from suppressed and unanticipated problems in the 1964 act's vision of discrimination (see Chapter 1). The civil rights bill's supporters sold it as a measure that mandated "color-blindness," elementary fairness. Such a mandate would affect only what Middle America could consider "the other"—Ku Klux Klan–style bigots. This consensus-oriented campaign suppressed points of view within civil rights activist communities which favored overhauling standard employer and union practices that created structural barriers to black workers, paying reparations to African Americans, and establishing proportional representation in the workplace and elite institutions. Such proposals were silenced because they would have been alarming to participants (such as unions, midwestern Republicans, churches) in the supercoalition supporting the bill.

Once the civil rights bill became law, the suppressed points of view came to the surface. Critics argued that "discrimination" was a more complicated concept than cross-burning bigotry. Discrimination could occur when well-meaning companies screened applicants through culturally biased tests or requirements of prior union membership. Also, if racism were deeply embedded in American social and economic structures, it would take more than color-blindness to unpack the deep historical effects. These critics believed that the antidiscrimination norm carried with it an implicit assurance of "group rights" to be free of historical as well as current discrimination. Group rights, in turn, suggested the desirability of proportional representation as a measure of progress. Within the Johnson and Nixon EEOC, a federal court system peopled with moderate Republicans and liberal Democrats, and the liberal gatekeeping congressional committees, the antidiscrimination concept gravitated away from the process vision of color-blindness to a pluralistic vision of proportional representation. During the 1970s the EEOC, the Supreme Court, and Congress worked together toward a proportional representation ideology, encoded in Title VII through the *Griggs* and *Weber* decisions making disparate impact a form of discrimination and allowing voluntary affirmative action.

Yet just as elite culture was coming to accept this ideology, it ran out of intellectual steam. Rehnquist's attack on "quotas" in his *Weber* dissent had a respectable audience in 1979 and was supported by more sophisticated arguments in the 1980s, when Scalia emerged as the Court's most eloquent critic of affirmative action. Whereas Rehnquist's brief against preferences was mainly a musty appeal to the original intent of the 1964 Congress, Scalia refined and updated the brief in 1987: by allowing employers to adopt racial preferences, *Weber* transformed Title VII from a public interest statute to a statute merely reallocating rights from one group to another. And the group that was paying the price for structural discrimination was made up not of those who had benefited from it (racist employees, unions, and businesses) but of "innocent" blue-collar white males—the new politically marginal minority for whom the Court should have sympathy.[126]

Scalia's charge is that elites in the 1970s transformed the antidiscrimination principle into allocational politics, in which benefits (job opportunities) are distributed from blue-collar white men to racial minorities and women and that this (re)distribution is normatively questionable. His charges resonate with academic theories that were becoming prominent in the 1970s, including public choice theory,[127] which suggests that even public-regarding government programs tend to become captured by client groups and turned into distributional rent-seeking programs; the new ethnicity in sociology,[128] which suggests a changing role for ethnicity (and race) from that of group identity to more instrumentalist goals; and theories of justice that emphasize individual liberty and personal responsibility.

Scalia's charges also resonate with the perceived experience of middle-class

America. People resent being passed over for jobs and promotions (especially in a slow economy), and they keenly resent it when they lose out to someone they consider socially subordinate. People are aware that there is a "civil rights lobby," and the Bork hearings not only publicized the political power of that lobby but also suggested that its lobbyists are willing to engage in the hyperbole characteristic of traditional rent-seeking groups.

Scalia's framework, that the EEOC and the Burger Court had cooperated in transforming a good, neutral statute with universal appeal into an unbalanced rent-seeking statute with partisan appeal, did not persuade five Justices to overrule *Weber* in 1987. A similar framework did prevail two years later, however, when the Court decided *Wards Cove* (in an opinion by White, who dissented in *Johnson*) and *Wilks* (in an opinion by Rehnquist, the third dissenter in *Johnson*).[129] Both decisions relied on canons of construction, and both can be criticized along Llewellyn lines for choosing one canon over other possible ones. In both cases what was driving the Court's choice of canons was a meta-canon against interpreting statutes to distribute rents to interest groups (a canon defended from a progressive point of view in Chapter 5). And that meta-canon's guidance, in turn, was informed by the understanding that liberals have changed Title VII into an allocational statute, which the Court considered both shortsighted and illegitimate.

Although Congress overrode these two decisions in 1991, it did so without a thoughtful response to the Scalia framework to justify the Court's giving the override legislation broad effect. One challenge for academics is to evaluate the Scalia ideology.[130] For example, the phenomenon of unconscious racism suggests that patterns of discrimination are culturally embedded and can be counteracted only by lived narratives of African Americans who achieve success in all aspects of the workplace. What Scalia considers allocational politics can equally be seen as a politics of presence, in which hiring and promotional preferences are justified to ensure that African Americans have an opportunity to create new workplace narratives that can undermine unconscious racism. Scalia's framework may also slight the positive value of diversity in the workplace, a value that has been widely recognized by employers. A particular value of workplace diversity is that it might help reduce general social instability. Perceived racial injustice has consequences in our society. Consider the Los Angeles riots in 1992. For traditional conservative pluralist reasons, our polity has a strong incentive to bring racial minorities "into the system," with the same sort of perceived opportunities that other groups have. A society divided along predictable racial lines invites mutual ignorance and loathing and squanders opportunities for productive cooperation.

Recall from the introduction the story of Hadrian's pardon of his would-be assassin. Following an early form of the rule of lenity, Hadrian refused to interpret the law "with savage rigor." Ever the pragmatist, Hadrian did so not out of compassion for the assassin but for the glory of Rome:

> All nations who have perished up to this time have done so for lack of generosity: Sparta would have survived longer had she given her Helots some interest in that survival . . . I wished to postpone as long as posible, and to avoid, if it can be done, the moment when the barbarians from without and the slaves within will fall upon a world which they have been forced to respect from afar, or to serve from below, but the profits of which are not for them. I was determined that even the most wretched, from the slaves who clean the city sewers to the famished barbarians who hover along the frontiers, should have an interest in seeing Rome endure.[131]

Like the Rehnquist Court in *Aramco* and *Wilks*, the Emperor Hadrian constructed his own interpretive regime pragmatically and critically. History evaluates his regime favorably. The Rehnquist Court awaits history's verdict.

Appendixes

Notes

Index

Appendix 1

The Primary Legislative Inaction Precedents, 1962–1992

This appendix collects the leading Supreme Court cases decided between the 1961 and 1991 terms of the Court in which the Court considered arguments based on the "inaction" of Congress.

Acquiescence Cases

Finding Acquiescence

Ankenbrandt v. Richards, 112 S. Ct. 2206, 2212–13 (1992) (Supreme Court interpretation)

Monessen Southwestern Railway v. Morgan, 486 U.S. 330, 336–339 (1988) (consensus of lower court decisions)

United States v. Johnson, 481 U.S. 681, 686 and n.6 (1987) (Supreme Court interpretation)

Johnson v. Transportation Agency, Santa Clara County, 480 U.S. 616, 629–630 n.7 (1987) (Supreme Court interpretation)

School Board of Nassau County, Florida, v. Arline, 480 U.S. 273, 279 (1987) (executive department interpretation)

United States v. Riverside Bayview Homes, Inc., 474 U.S. 121, 137 (1985) (executive department interpretation)

SEC v. Jerry T. O'Brien, Inc., 467 U.S. 735, 745–747 (1984) (agency interpretation)

Bob Jones University v. United States, 461 U.S. 574, 599–602 (1983) (executive department interpretation)

Herman & MacLean v. Huddleston, 459 U.S. 375, 384–386 (1983) (consensus of lower court decisions)

North Haven Board of Education v. Bell, 456 U.S. 512, 535 (1982) (agency interpretation)

Merrill Lynch, Pierce, Fenner & Smith, Inc., v. Curran, 456 U.S. 353, 381–382 (1982) (consensus of lower court decisions)

Haig v. Agee, 453 U.S. 280, 300–301 (1981) (executive department interpretation)

Dames & Moore v. Regan, 453 U.S. 654, 678–682 (1981) (presidential interpretation and practice)

United States v. Rutherford, 442 U.S. 544, 554 and n.10 (1979) (agency interpretation)

Cannon v. University of Chicago, 441 U.S. 677, 703 (1979) (consensus of lower court decisions)

Blue Chip Stamps v. Manor Drug Stores, 421 U.S. 723, 732–733 (1974) (agency interpretation and lower court decisions)

NLRB v. Bell Aerospace Co., 416 U.S. 267, 287–288 (1974) (agency interpretation)

Flood v. Kuhn, 407 U.S. 258, 280–285 (1972) (Supreme Court interpretation)

Red Lion Broadcasting Co. v. FCC, 395 U.S. 367, 381–382 (1969) (agency interpretation)

Blau v. Lehman, 368 U.S. 403, 412–413 (1962) (consensus of lower court decisions)

Zemel v. Rusk, 381 U.S. 1, 11–12 (1965) (executive department interpretation)

Sperry v. Florida, 373 U.S. 379, 388–395 (1963) (executive department interpretation)

Monroe v. Pape, 365 U.S. 167, 186–187 (1961) (Supreme Court interpretation)

No Acquiescence

Commissioner v. Fink, 483 U.S. 89, 101–106 (1987) (Stevens, J., dissenting from Court's failure to follow consensus of lower court decisions)

McNally v. United States, 483 U.S. 350, 376–377 (1987) (Stevens, J., dissenting from Court's failure to follow consensus of lower court decisions)

Shearson/American Express, Inc., v. McMahon, 482 U.S. 220, 234–238 (1987) (Supreme Court interpretation)

Aaron v. SEC, 446 U.S. 680, 693–694 and n.11 (1980) (executive department interpretation and consensus in lower court decisions)

Morton v. Ruiz, 415 U.S. 199, 212–230 (1974) (executive department interpretation)

Toussie v. United States, 397 U.S. 112, 120 (1970) (agency interpretation and consensus of lower court decisions)

Zuber v. Allen, 396 U.S. 168, 185–193 (1969) (executive department interpretation)

James v. United States, 366 U.S. 213, 220–221 (1961) (plurality opinion) (Supreme Court interpretation)

Reenactment Cases
Finding Ratification

Ankenbrandt v. Richards, 112 S. Ct. 2206, 2213 (1992) (Supreme Court interpretation)

Davis v. United States, 495 U.S. 472, 483 (1990) (executive department interpretation and lower court decisions)

Pierce v. Underwood, 487 U.S. 552, 566–568 (1988) (consensus of lower court decisions)

Midlantic National Bank v. New Jersey Department of Environmental Protection, 474 U.S. 494, 501 (1986) (consensus of lower court decisions)

FDIC v. Philadelphia Gear Corp., 476 U.S. 428, 437 (1986) (agency interpretation)

Lindahl v. Office of Personnel Management, 470 U.S. 768, 782–785 and n.15 (1985) (consensus of lower court decisions)

Herman & MacLean v. Huddleston, 459 U.S. 375, 384–386 (1983) (consensus of lower court decisions)

Merrill Lynch, Pierce, Fenner & Smith, Inc., v. Curran, 456 U.S. 353, 381–382 (1982) (consensus of lower court decisions)

Haig v. Agee, 453 U.S. 280, 300–301 (1981) (executive department interpretation)

Owen Equipment & Erection Co. v. Kroger, 437 U.S. 365, 373–374 and n.16 (1978) (Suprme Court interpretation)

United States v. Board of Commissioners, County of Sheffield, Alabama, 435 U.S. 110, 133–134 (1978) (executive department interpretation)

Lorillard v. Pons, 434 U.S. 575, 580 (1978) (dictum, but leading statement of reenactment rule)

Federal Energy Administration v. Algonquin SNG, Inc., 426 U.S. 548, 567–571 (1976) (agency interpretation)

Albemarle Paper Co. v. Moody, 422 U.S. 405, 414 n.8 (1975) (executive department interpretation)

Chemehuevi Tribe of Indians v. FPC, 420 U.S. 395, 410 (1975) (agency interpretation)

NLRB v. Bell Aerospace Co., 416 U.S. 267, 275 (1974) (agency interpretation)

Deepsouth Packing Co. v. Laitram Corp., 406 U.S. 518, 530 and n.10 (1972) (consensus of lower court interpretations)

Snyder v. Harris, 394 U.S. 332, 339 (1969) (Supreme Court interpretation)

Zemel v. Rusk, 381 U.S. 1, 11–12 (1965) (executive department interpretation)

Finding No Ratification

Demarest v. Manspeaker, 498 U.S. 184, 190 (1991) (executive department interpretation)

Lukhard v. Reed, 481 U.S. 368, 379 (1987) (plurality opinion) (agency interpretation)

Heckler v. Day, 467 U.S. 104, 125–128 (1984) (Marshall, J., dissenting from Court's refusal to find ratification of consensus in lower court decisions)

Dickman v. Commissioner, 465 U.S. 330, 346–348 (1984) (Powell, J., dissenting from Court's refusal to find ratification of consensus in lower court decisions)

Mohasco Corp. v. Silver, 447 U.S. 807, 829–832 (1980) (Blackmun, J., dissenting from Court's refusal to find ratification of consensus in lower court decisions)

Aaron v. SEC, 446 U.S. 680, 694 n.11 (1980) (agency interpretation and lower court decisions)

SEC v. Sloan, 436 U.S. 103, 119–120 (1978) (agency interpretation)

International Brotherhood of Teamsters v. United States, 431 U.S. 324, 391–393 and n.24 (1977) (Marshall, J., dissenting from Court's refusal to find ratification of consensus in lower court decisions)

Leary v. United States, 395 U.S. 6, 24–25 (1969) (executive department interpretation)

Commissioner v. Stidger, 386 U.S. 287, 292–295 (1967) (executive department interpretation) (tax code)

James v. United States, 366 U.S. 213, 220–221 (1961) (plurality opinion) (Supreme Court interpretation)

Rejected Proposal Cases

Finding Significance

Landers v. National Railroad Passengers Corp., 485 U.S. 652, 656 and n.3 (1988) (committee rejection)

Thompson v. Thompson, 484 U.S. 174, 183–185 (1988) (floor rejection in one chamber)

INS v. Cardoza-Fonseca, 480 U.S. 421, 442–443 (1987) (conference committee rejection)

United States v. Riverside Bayview Homes, Inc., 474 U.S. 121, 137 (1985) (bicameral and chamber rejection)

Heckler v. Day, 467 U.S. 104, 111–115 (1984) (committee rejection)

Bob Jones University v. United States, 461 U.S. 574, 601–602 (1983) (committee rejection)

Pacific Gas & Electric Co. v. State Energy Resources Conservation & Development Commission, 461 U.S. 190, 219–220 (1983) (conference committee rejection)

Illinois v. Abbott & Associates, Inc., 460 U.S. 557, 568–570 (1983) (conference committee rejection)

North Haven Board of Education v. Bell, 456 U.S. 512, 531–535 (1982) (floor rejection in one chamber)

Santa Clara Pueblo v. Martinez, 436 U.S. 49, 67–69 (1978) (committee rejection)

Runyon v. McCrary, 427 U.S. 160, 174 n.11 (1976) (floor rejection in one chamber)

Train v. Colorado Public Interest Research Group, Inc., 426 U.S. 1, 17–22 (1976) (floor rejection in one chamber)

Blue Chip Stamps v. Manor Drug Stores, 421 U.S. 723, 732–733 (1975) (committee rejection)

Gulf Oil Corp. v. Copp Paving Co., 419 U.S. 186, 199–200 (1974) (conference committee rejection)

National Railroad Passenger Corp. v. National Association of Railroad Passengers, 414 U.S. 453, 459–461 (1974) (committee rejection)

Flood v. Kuhn, 407 U.S. 258, 280–283 (1972) (failure of bicameral agreement and committee rejection)

S & E Contractors, Inc., v. United States, 406 U.S. 1, 11–12 (1972) (conference committee rejection)

Rodrigue v. Aetna Casualty & Surety Co., 395 U.S. 352, 358–359 (1969) (floor rejection in one chamber)

Fribourg Navigation Co. v. Commissioner, 383 U.S. 272, 283–286 (1966) (committee rejection)

FPC v. Union Electric Co., 381 U.S. 90, 108 and n.28 (1965) (floor rejection in one chamber)

Van Dusen v. Barrack, 376 U.S. 612, 635–637 (1964) (floor rejection in one chamber)

United States v. Muniz, 374 U.S. 150, 155–156 (1963) (committee rejection)

Blau v. Lehman, 368 U.S. 403, 411–412 (1962) (committee rejection)

Finding No Significance

Taylor v. United States, 495 U.S. 575, 589–590 (1990) (conference committee deletion)

California v. American Stores Co., 495 U.S. 271, 287–293 (1990) (committee rejection)

Communications Workers of America v. Beck, 487 U.S. 735, 757–758 (1988) (conference committee rejection)

Boyle v. United Technologies Corp., 487 U.S. 500, 515 and n.1. (1988) (Brennan, J., dissenting from Court's failure to credit committee rejection)

Agency Holding Corp. v. Malley-Duff & Associates, Inc., 483 U.S. 143, 154–155 (1987) (floor rejection in one chamber)

Firefighters Local 1784 v. Stotts, 467 U.S. 561, 619–620 (1984) (Blackmun, J., dissenting from Court's failure to credit floor rejection in one chamber)

Nachman Corp. v. Pension Benefit Guaranty Corp., 446 U.S. 359, 392–393 (1980) (Stewart, J., dissenting from Court's failure to credit conference committee rejection)

NLRB v. Catholic Bishop of Chicago, 440 U.S. 490, 512–516 (1979) (Brennan, J., dissenting from Court's failure to credit conference committee rejection and floor rejection in one chamber)

Monell v. Department of Social Services, 436 U.S. 658, 664–695 (1978) (floor rejection in one chamber, plus conference committee rejection)

Federal Energy Administration v. Algonquin SNG, Inc., 426 U.S. 548, 568–570 (1976) (conference committee rejection)

Connell Construction Co. v. Plumbers & Steamfitters Local 100, 421 U.S. 616, 652–655 (1975) (Stewart, J., dissenting from Court's failure to credit floor rejection in one chamber)

United States v. Enmons, 410 U.S. 396, 414–417 (1973) (Douglas, J., dissenting from Court's failure to credit floor rejection in one chamber)

Trbovich v. United Mineworkers, 404 U.S. 528, 532–535 (1972) (committee rejection)

Boys Markets, Inc., v. Retail Clerks Union, Local 770, 398 U.S. 235, 261 (1970) (White, J., dissenting from Court's failure to credit conference committee rejection)

Red Lion Broadcasting Co. v. FCC, 395 U.S. 367, 381 and n.11 (1969) (committee rejection)

United States v. Southwestern Cable Co., 392 U.S. 157, 169–171 (1968) (committee rejection)

NLRB v. C & C Plywood Corp., 385 U.S. 421, 426–429 (1967) (floor rejection in one chamber)

United States v. Philadelphia National Bank, 374 U.S. 321, 379–381 (1963) (Harlan, J., dissenting from Court's failure to credit committee rejection)

United States v. Wise, 370 U.S. 405, 411 (1962) (committee rejection)

James v. United States, 366 U.S. 213, 220–221 (1961) (plurality opinion) (floor rejection in one chamber)

Appendix 2

Supreme Court Decisions Overruling Statutory Precedents, 1962–1992

This appendix collects Supreme Court decisions overruling the Court's statutory precedents from the 1961 to 1991 terms of the Court. The appendix divides the cases into explicit overrulings, where the Court's opinion says it is overruling a precedent at least in part; implicit overrulings, where the Court does not announce the overruling, but it appears that at least one precedent has been effectively overruled at least in part; and renunciation of important dicta in statutory precedents.

Supreme Court Decisions Explicitly Overruling Statutory Precedents

Keeney v. Tamayo-Reeves, 112 S. Ct. 1715, 1717–19 (1992), overruling Townsend v. Sain, 372 U.S. 293 (1963)

Coleman v. Thompson, 111 S. Ct. 2546, 2563–65 (1991), overruling Fay v. Noia, 372 U.S. 391 (1963)

Exxon Corp. v. Central Gulf Lines, Inc., 500 U.S. 603 (1991), overruling Minturn v. Maynard, 17 How. 477 (1855)

Carden v. Arkoma Associates, 494 U.S. 185, 189–190 (1990), overruling Puerto Rico v. Russell & Co., 288 U.S. 476 (1933)

Rodriguez de Quijas v. Shearson/American Express, Inc., 490 U.S. 477 (1989), overruling Wilko v. Swan, 346 U.S. 427, 438 (1953)

Gulfstream Aerospace Corp. v. Mayacamas, 485 U.S. 271 (1988), overruling Ettelson v. Metropolitan Life Insurance Co., 317 U.S. 188 (1942), and Enelow v. New York Life Insurance Co., 293 U.S. 379 (1935)

Welch v. State Department of Highways & Public Transporation, 483 U.S. 468, 476–477 (1987), overruling in part Parden v. Terminal Railway, 377 U.S. 184 (1964)

316

Puerto Rico v. Branstad, 483 U.S. 219, 230 (1987), overruling Kentucky v. Dennison, 65 U.S. (24 How.) 66, 107 (1861)

Brown v. Hotel Employees International Union, Local 54, 468 U.S. 491, 504–505, 509–510 (1984), overruling Hill v. Florida ex rel. Watson, 325 U.S. 538, 541 (1945)

Copperweld Corp. v. Independence Tube Corp., 467 U.S. 752, 777 (1984), overruling Kiefer-Stewart Co. v. Joseph E. Seagram & Sons, Inc., 340 U.S. 211, 215 (1951), et alia

United States v. One Assortment of 89 Firearms, 465 U.S. 354, 361 (1984), overruling Coffey v. United States, 116 U.S. 436, 442–445 (1896)

Guardians Association v. Civil Service Commission, 463 U.S. 582, 611 (plurality opinion of Powell, J.), 612–613 (O'Connor, J.), 640–641 (Stevens, J.) (1983), overruling Lau v. Nichols, 414 U.S. 563, 568 (1974)

Trammel v. United States, 445 U.S. 40, 50–51 (1980), overruling Hawkins v. United States, 358 U.S. 74 (1958)

Monell v. Department of Social Services, 436 U.S. 658, 663 (1978), overruling Monroe v. Pape, 365 U.S. 167, 187 (1961)

Continental T.V., Inc., v. GTE Sylvania, Inc., 433 U.S. 36, 58 (1977), overruling United States v. Arnold, Schwinn & Co., 388 U.S. 365, 375 (1967)

Califano v. Sanders, 430 U.S. 99, 105–107 (1977), overruling in part Citizens to Preserve Overton Park, Inc., v. Volpe, 401 U.S. 402, 410 (1971)

Lodge 76, International Association of Machinists v. Wisconsin Employment Relations Commission, 427 U.S. 132, 154 (1976), overruling UAW Local 232 v. Wisconsin Employment Relations Commission, 336 U.S. 245, 265 (1949)

Braden v. 30th Judicial Circuit Court of Kentucky, 410 U.S. 484, 499–500 (1973), overruling Ahrens v. Clark, 335 U.S. 188, 193 (1948)

Andrews v. Louisville & Nashville Railroad, 406 U.S. 320, 326 (1972), overruling Moore v. Illinois Central Railroad, 312 U.S. 630, 633 (1941)

Griffin v. Breckenridge, 403 U.S. 88, 92–96, 101–102 (1971), overruling Collins v. Hardyman, 341 U.S. 651, 652 (1951)

Blonder-Tongue Laboratories, Inc., v. University of Illinois Foundation, 402 U.S. 313, 350 (1971), overruling Triplett v. Lowell, 297 U.S. 638, 642 (1936)

Boys Markets, Inc., v. Retail Clerks Union, Local 770, 398 U.S. 235, 238, 249–250, 254–255 (1970), overruling Sinclair Refining Co. v. Atkinson, 370 U.S. 195, 203 (1965)

Lear, Inc., v. Adkins, 395 U.S. 653, 671 (1969), overruling Automatic Radio Manufacturing Co. v. Hazeltine Research, Inc., 339 U.S. 827, 836 (1950)

Lee v. Florida, 392 U.S. 378, 385–386 (1968), overruling Schwartz v. Texas, 344 U.S. 199 (1952)

Peyton v. Rowe, 391 U.S. 54, 67 (1968), overruling McNally v. Hill, 293 U.S. 131, 138–139 (1934)

Carafas v. LaVallee, 391 U.S. 234, 240 (1968), overruling Parker v. Ellis, 362 U.S. 574, 576 (1960) (per curiam)

Brenner v. Manson, 383 U.S. 519, 526–527 (1966), overruling Postum Cereal Co. v. California Fig Nut Co., 272 U.S. 693 (1927)

Swift & Co. v. Wickham, 382 U.S. 111, 124 (1965), overruling Kesler v. Department of Public Safety, 369 U.S. 153, 157 (1962)

Harris v. United States, 382 U.S. 162, 167 (1965), overruling Brown v. United States, 359 U.S. 41, 51–52 (1959)

Fay v. Noia, 372 U.S. 391, 435–436 (1963), overruling Barr v. Burford, 339 U.S. 200, 208 (1950)

Local 438, Construction & General Laborers' Union v. Curry, 371 U.S. 542, 552 (1963), overruling Montgomery Building Trades Council v. Ledbetter Erection Co., 344 U.S. 178, 181 (1952)

Smith v. Evening News Association, 371 U.S. 195, 199 (1962), overruling Association of Westinghouse Salaried Employees v. Westinghouse Corp., 348 U.S. 437, 459 (1955)

James v. United States, 366 U.S. 213, 222 (1961), overruling Commissioner v. Wilcox, 327 U.S. 404, 409 (1946)

Supreme Court Decisions Implicitly Overruling Statutory Precedents

City of Burlington v. Dague, 112 S. Ct. 2638, 2642–43 (1992); see id. at 2645–46 and n.4 (Brennan, J., dissenting), implicitly overruling Pennsylvania v. Delaware Valley Citizens' Council for Clean Air, 483 U.S. 711 (1987)

McCleskey v. Zant, 499 U.S. 467 (1991); see id. at 506–511 (Marshall, J., dissenting), implicitly overruling Sanders v. United States, 373 U.S. 1 (1963)

Patterson v. McLean Credit Union, 491 U.S. 164 (1989), implicitly overruling McDonald v. Santa Fe Trail Transporation Co., 427 U.S. 273 (1976)

Wards Cove Packing Co. v. Atonio, 490 U.S. 642 (1989), implicitly overruling in part Griggs v. Duke Power Co., 401 U.S. 424 (1971)

United States v. Lane, 474 U.S. 438, 444–446 (1986), implicitly overruling McElroy v. United States, 164 U.S. 76, 81 (1896)

American Bank & Trust Co. v. Dallas County, 463 U.S. 855, 858, 862 (1983); see id. at 873–879 (Rehnquist, J., dissenting), implicitly overruling Society for Savings v. Bowers, 349 U.S. 143, 148 (1955), et alia

American Society of Mechanical Engineers, Inc., v. Hydrolevel Corp., 456 U.S. 556 (1982); see id. at 581–582 and n.5 (Powell, J., dissenting), implicitly overruling Coronado Coal Co. v. UMW, 268 U.S. 295, 304 (1925), et alium

Montana v. United States, 450 U.S. 544, 555–556 n. 5 (1981); see id. at 573–577 (Blackmun, J., dissenting), implicitly overruling Choctaw Nation v. Oklahoma, 397 U.S. 620, 634–635 (1970)

Wilson v. Omaha Indian Tribe, 442 U.S. 653 (1979); see id. at 680–681 (Blackmun, J., concurring), implicitly overruling United States v. Perryman, 100 U.S. 235, 236 (1880)

Parklane Hosiery Co. v. Shore, 439 U.S. 322, 326–328 and n.6 (1979), implicitly overruling Buckeye Powder Co. v. E. I. DuPont de Nemours Powder Co., 248 U.S. 55, 63 (1918), et alia

California v. United States, 438 U.S. 645, 670–675 (1978); see id. at 690–695 (White, J., dissenting), implicitly overruling Arizona v. California, 373 U.S. 546, 586–587 (1963), et alia

Stone v. Powell, 428 U.S. 465 (1976); see id. at 518–519 and n.14 (Brennan, J., dissenting), implicitly overruling Lefkowitz v. Newsome, 420 U.S. 283, 291–292 and nn.8–9 (1975), et alia

Barrett v. United States, 423 U.S. 212, 221–222 (1976); see id. at 229–231 (Stewart, J., dissenting), implicitly overruling Tot v. United States, 319 U.S. 463, 466 (1943)

Twentieth Century Music Corp. v. Aiken, 422 U.S. 151, 160–161 (1975); see id. at 166–167 (Blackmun, J., concurring in the result), 168–170 (Burger, C.J., dissenting), implicitly overruling Buck v. Jewell-LaSalle Realty Co., 283 U.S. 191 (1931)

Hamling v. United States, 418 U.S. 87 (1974); see id. at 142 (Brennan, J., dissenting), implicitly overruling Manual Enterprises, Inc., v. Day, 370 U.S. 478, 488 (1962)

Hagans v. Lavine, 415 U.S. 528, 543–545 (1974), implicitly overruling Brotherhood of Locomotive Engineers v. Chicago, R. I. & P. Railroad, 382 U.S. 423, 428 (1966), et alium

United States v. Chicago, Burlington & Quincy Railroad, 412 U.S. 401, 411–413 (1973); see id. at 417 (Douglas, J., dissenting), implicitly overruling Brown Shoe Co. v. Commissioner, 339 U.S. 583 (1950)

Hawaii v. Standard Oil Co., 405 U.S. 251 (1972); see id. at 268–270 (Douglas, J., dissenting); id. at 271–273 (Brennan, J., dissenting), implicitly overruling Georgia v. Pennsylvania Railroad, 324 U.S. 439, 447, 451 (1945)

Amalgamated Association of Street Electrical Railway & Motor Coach Employees v. Lockridge, 403 U.S. 274, 293–297 (1971); see id. at 302–303 (Douglas, J., dissenting), implicitly overruling International Association of Machinists v. Gonzalez, 356 U.S. 617, 621 (1958)

Jones v. Alfred H. Mayer Co., 392 U.S. 409, 419, 420 n.25 (1968); see id. at 451–452 and n.8 (Harlan, J., dissenting), implicitly overruling Corrigan v. Buckley, 271 U.S. 323, 331 (1926)

United States v. Arnold, Schwinn & Co., 388 U.S. 365, 379 (1967); see id. at 388–389 (Stewart, J., concurring in part and dissenting in part), implicitly overruling White Motor Co. v. United States, 372 U.S. 253, 263 (1963)

Sansone v. United States, 380 U.S. 343, 348–349 (1965), implicitly overruling Achilli v. United States, 353 U.S. 373, 379 (1957)

Simpson v. Union Oil Co., 377 U.S. 13, 22–24 (1964); see id. at 26–27 and n.1 (Stewart, J., dissenting), implicitly overruling United States v. General Electric Co., 272 U.S. 476, 488 (1926)

Aro Manufacturing Co. v. Convertible Top Replacement Co., 377 U.S. 476, 479–481 and n.1 (1964); see id. at 517–522 (Black, J., dissenting), implicitly overruling Aro Manufacturing Co. v. Convertible Top Replacement Co., 365 U.S. 336, 345 (1961)

Calbeck v. Travelers Insurance Co., 370 U.S. 114 (1962); see id. at 136–138 (Stewart, J., dissenting), implicitly overruling Hahn v. Ross Island Sand & Gravel Co., 358 U.S. 272 (1959) (per curiam)

Coppedge v. United States, 369 U.S. 438 (1962); see id. at 459 (Clark, J., dissenting), implicitly overruling Farley v. United States, 354 U.S. 521, 523 1957)

Supreme Court Decisions Disapproving Significant Reasoning in Statutory Precedents

Barker v. Kansas, 112 S. Ct. 1623–25 (1992), disapproving "dicta" in United States v. Tyler, 105 U.S. 244, 245 (1882), et alium

McCleskey v. Zant, 499 U.S. 467, 495 (1991), disapproving "some of the language" in Price v. Johnston, 334 U.S. 266 (1948)

Pennsylvania Department of Public Welfare v. Davenport, 495 U.S. 552, 561–562 (1990), refusing to follow "dictum" in Kelly v. Robinson, 479 U.S. 36 (1986)

Office of Personnel Management v. Richmond, 496 U.S. 414, 421 (1990), disapproving "dicta" in Montana v. Kennedy, 366 U.S. 308, 314–315 (1961), et alium

Crawford Fitting Co. v. J. T. Gibbons, Inc., 482 U.S. 437, 442–443 (1987), disapproving "classic *obiter*" in Farmer v. Arabian American Oil Co., 379 U.S. 227, 235 (1964)

NLRB v. International Brotherhood of Electrical Workers, Local 340, 481 U.S. 573, 591 and n.15 (1987), disapproving "dictum" in ABC v. Writers Guild, 437 U.S. 411, 436 (1978)

North Carolina Department of Transportation v. Crest Street Community Council, Inc., 479 U.S. 6, 13–14 (1986), disapproving "dicta" in New York Gaslight Club, Inc., v. Carey, 447 U.S. 54, 65–66 and n.6 (1980)

Southern Motor Carriers Rate Conference, Inc., v. United States, 471 U.S. 48, 57 n.21 (1985), disapproving "questionable dictum" in Cantor v. Detroit Edison Co., 428 U.S. 579, 597–98 (1976)

Local 82, Furniture and Piano Moving Drivers v. Crowley, 467 U.S. 526, 549–550 and n.22 (1984), disapproving statements in Trbovich v. United Mine Workers, 404 U.S. 528, 531 (1972), et alium

South Carolina v. Regan, 465 U.S. 367, 377 n.14 (1984), narrowing Bob Jones University v. Simon, 416 U.S. 725, 732 n.6 (1974)

Bowen v. United States Postal Service, 459 U.S. 212, 228–230 (1983), narrowing International Brotherhood of Electrical Workers v. Foust, 442 U.S. 42, 50 n.13 (1979), et alium

Zipes v. TWA, Inc., 455 U.S. 385, 392–393 n.6 (1982), disapproving dicta in International Union of Electrical Workers Local 790 v. Robbins & Myers, Inc., 429 U.S. 229, 240 (1976), et alia

NLRB v. Hendricks County Rural Electrical Membership Corp., 454 U.S. 170, 186–188 (1981), disapproving "dictum" in NLRB v. Bell Aerospace Co., 416 U.S. 267, 284 n.12 (1974)

McDaniel v. Sanchez, 452 U.S. 130, 141 and n.19 (1981), disapproving "dictum" in East Carroll Parish School Board v. Marshall, 424 U.S. 636, 638–639 n.6 (1976) (per curiam)

Rosewell v. LaSalle National Bank, 450 U.S. 503, 525 (1981), disapproving statements in Confederated Moe v. Salish & Kootenai Tribes, 425 U.S. 463, 470 (1976), et alia

Reiter v. Sonotone Corp., 442 U.S. 330, 341–342 (1979), disapproving dicta in Hawaii v. Standard Oil Co., 405 U.S. 251, 264 (1972)

Sears, Roebuck & Co. v. San Diego County District Council of Carpenters, 436 U.S. 180, 187–189 and n.13 (1978), declining to follow reasoning of San Diego Building Trades Council v. Garmon, 359 U.S. 236, 245 (1959)

City of Lafayette v. Louisiana Power & Light Co., 435 U.S. 389, 408–413 (1978) (plurality opinion), narrowing Parker v. Brown, 317 U.S. 341, 352 (1943)

Third National Bank v. Impac, Ltd., 432 U.S. 312, 319 n.9 (1977), disapproving "dictum" in Pacific National Bank v. Mixter, 124 U.S. 721, 727 (1888)

Stone v. Powell, 428 U.S. 465, 481–482 (1976), disapproving "dictum" in Kaufman v. United States 394 U.S. 217, 225–226 (1969)

Cantor v. Detroit Edison Co., 428 U.S. 579, 585–592, 600–603 (1976) (plurality opinion), narrowing Goldfarb v. Virginia State Bar, 421 U.S. 773, 790 (1975); Parker v. Brown, 317 U.S. 341, 350–51 (1943)

Runyon v. McCrary, 427 U.S. 160 (1976), disapproving dictum in The Civil Rights Cases, 109 U.S. 3, 16–17 (1883), et alia

United States v. United Continental Tuna Corp., 425 U.S. 164, 178 n.16 (1976), disapproving "dictum" in Amell v. United States, 384 U.S. 158, 164 (1966)

Barrett v. United States, 423 U.S. 212, 222–223 (1976), disapproving "dictum" in United States v. Bass, 404 U.S. 336, 342–343 (1971)

Warden, Lewisburg Penitentiary v. Marrero, 417 U.S. 653, 658–659 (1974), nullifying dictum in Bradley v. United States, 410 U.S. 605, 611 n.6 (1973,) et alium

Chicago & Northwestern Railway v. United Transportation Union, 402 U.S. 570, 577–578 (1971), disapproving "passing reference" in General Committee v. Missouri-Kansas-Texas Railroad, 320 U.S. 323, 334 (1943)

Younger v. Harris, 401 U.S. 37, 50–53 (1971), disapproving broad statements in Dombrowski v. Pfister, 380 U.S. 479, 486–487 (1965)

In re Permian Basin Area Rate Cases, 390 U.S. 747, 775 (1968), disapproving "imprecise" dictum in Bowles v. Willingham, 321 U.S. 503, 517 (1944)

United States v. Neifert-White Co., 390 U.S. 228, 231 and n.4 (1968), disapproving dictum in United States v. Cohn, 270 U.S. 339, 345–346 (1926)

United Mine Workers v. Gibbs, 383 U.S. 715, 722–725 (1966), rejecting reasoning of Hurn v. Oursler, 289 U.S. 238, 245–246 (1933)

Transportation-Communication Employees Union v. Union Pacific Railroad, 385 U.S. 157, 164 (1966), disapproving "dicta" in Whitehouse v. Illinois Central Railroad, 349 U.S. 366, 372–373 (1955)

Appendix 3
The Rehnquist Court's Canons of Statutory Construction

This appendix collects the canons of statutory construction that have been used or developed by the Rehnquist Court from the 1986 to the 1991 terms. The appendix divides the canons into three conventional categories: the textualist canons, which set forth conventions of syntax, linguistic inferences, and textual integrity; extrinsic source canons, which direct the interpreter to an authoritative source of meaning; and substantive policy canons, which embody public policies drawn from the Constitution, federal statutes, or the common law.

Textualist Canons

Plain meaning rule: follow the plain meaning of the statutory text,[1] except when text suggests an absurd result[2] or a scrivener's error.[3]

Linguistic Inferences

Expressio unius: expression of one thing suggests the exclusion of others.[4]

Noscitur a sociis: interpret a general term to be similar to more specific terms in a series.[5]

Ejusdem generis: interpret a general term to reflect the class of objects reflected in more specific terms accompanying it.[6]

Follow ordinary usage of terms unless Congress gives them a specified or technical meaning.[7]

Follow dictionary definitions of terms unless Congress has provided a specific definition.[8] Consider dictionaries of the era in which the statute was enacted.[9]

"May" is usually precatory, whereas "shall" is usually mandatory.[10]

Grammar and Syntax

Punctuation rule: Congress is presumed to follow accepted punctuation standards, so that placement of commas and other punctuation is assumed to be meaningful.[11]

Structural

Each statutory provision should be read by reference to the whole act.[12]

Avoid interpreting a provision in a way that would render other provisions of the act superfluous or unnecessary.[13]

Avoid interpreting a provision in a way that is inconsistent with the policy of another provision.[14]

Avoid interpreting a provision in a way that is inconsistent with a necessary assumption of another provision.[15]

Avoid interpreting a provision in a way that is inconsistent with the structure of the statute.[16]

Avoid broad readings of statutory provisions when Congress has specifically provided for the broader policy in more specific language elsewhere.[17]

Interpret the same or similar terms in a statute the same way.[18]

Specific provisions targeting a particular issue apply instead of provisions more generally covering the issue.[19]

Provisos and statutory exceptions should be read narrowly.[20]

Do not create exceptions in addition to those specified by Congress.[21]

Extrinsic Source Canons

Agency Interpretations

Rule of deference to agency interpretations unless contrary to plain meaning of statute or unreasonable.[22]

Presumption that an agency's interpretation of its own regulations is correct.[23]

Continuity in Law

Rule of continuity: assume that Congress does not create discontinuities in legal rights and obligations without some clear statement.[24]

Super-strong presumption of correctness for statutory precedents.[25]

Presumption that international agreements do not displace federal law.[26]

Borrowed statute rule: when Congress borrows a statute, it adopts by implication interpretations placed on that statute, absent express statement to the contrary.[27]

Reenactment rule: when Congress reenacts a statute, it incorporates settled interpretations of the reenacted statute.[28]

Acquiescence rule: follow unbroken line of lower court decisions interpreting statute.[29]

Extrinsic Legislative Sources

Interpret provision consistent with subsequent statutory amendments,[30] but do not consider subsequent legislative discussions.[31]

Consider legislative history when statute is ambiguous.[32]

Committee reports are authoritative legislative history[33] but cannot trump a textual plain meaning.[34]

The "dog didn't bark" canon: presumption that prior legal rule should be retained if no one in legislative deliberations even mentioned the rule or the question of changing it.[35]

Substantive Policy Canons

Constitution-Based Canons

Avoid interpretations that would render a statute unconstitutional.[36] This rule is inapplicable if the statute would survive constitutional attack, or if the statutory text is clear.[37]

Separation of Powers

Super-strong rule against congressional interference with the president's authority over foreign affairs and national security.[38]

Rule against congressional invasion of the president's core executive powers.[39]

Rule against review of the president's core executive actions for "abuse of discretion."[40]

Rule against congressional curtailment of the judiciary's "inherent powers"[41] or its "equity" powers.[42]

Rule against congressional expansion of article III injury to include intangible and procedural injuries.[43]

Presumption that Congress does not delegate authority without sufficient guidelines.[44]

Presumption against "implying" causes of action into federal statutes.

Presumption favoring severability of unconstitutional provisions.[45]

Federalism

Super-strong rule against federal invasion of "core state functions."[46]

Super-strong rule against federal abrogation of states' Eleventh Amendment immunity from lawsuits in federal courts.[47]

Rule against inferring enforceable conditions on federal grants to the states.[48]

Rule against congressional expansion of federal court jurisdiction that would siphon cases away from state courts.[49]

Rule against reading a federal statute to authorize states to engage in activities that would violate the dormant commerce clause.[50]

Rule favoring concurrent state and federal court jurisdiction over federal claims.[51]

Rule against federal preemption of traditional state functions.[52]

Presumption against federal preemption of state-assured family support obligations.[53]

Presumption against federal regulation of intergovernmental taxation by the states.[54]

Presumption against application of federal statutes to state and local political processes.[55]

Presumption that states can tax activities within their borders, including Indian tribal activities,[56] but also presumption that states cannot tax Indian lands.[57]

Presumption against congressional derogation from state's land claims based on its entry into the Union on an "equal footing" with all other states.[58]

Presumption against federal habeas review of state criminal convictions supported by independent state ground.[59]

Principle that federal equitable remedies must consider interests of state and local authorities.[60]

Presumption that Congress borrows state statutes of limitations for federal statutory schemes unless otherwise provided.[61]

Due Process

Rule of lenity: rule against applying punitive sanctions if there is ambiguity as to underlying criminal liability[62] or criminal penalty.[63]

Rule against interpreting statutes to be retroactive.[64]

Rule against interpreting statutes to deny a right to jury trial.[65]

Presumption in favor of judicial review,[66] especially for constitutional questions.[67]

Presumption against exhaustion of remedies requirement for lawsuit to enforce constitutional rights.[68]

Presumption that judgments will not be binding on persons not party to adjudications.[69]

Presumption against national service of process unless authorized by Congress.[70]

Presumption against foreclosure of private enforcement of important federal rights.[71]

Presumption that preponderance of the evidence standard applies in civil cases.[72]

Statute-Based Canons

Meta-Canons

In pari materia: similar statutes should be interpreted similarly.[73]

Presumption against repeals by implication.[74]

Purpose rule: interpret ambiguous statutes so as best to carry out their statutory purposes.[75]

Allow *de minimis* exceptions to statutory rules, so long as they do not undermine statutory policy.[76]

Presumption that federal private right of action (express or implied) carries with it all traditional remedies.[77]

Specific Statutory Schemes

Rule against state taxation of Indian tribes and reservation activities.[78]

Narrow interpretation of exemptions from federal taxation.[79]

Presumption against taxpayer claiming income tax deduction.[80]

Narrow interpretation of exemptions to Fair Labor Standards Act.[81]

Presumption that Bankruptcy Act of 1978 preserved prior bankruptcy doctrines.[82]

Federal court deference to arbitral awards, even where the Federal Arbitration Act is not by its terms applicable.[83]

Strong presumption in favor of enforcing labor arbitration agreements.[84]

Rule favoring arbitration of federal statutory claims.[85]

Strict construction of statutes authorizing appeals.[86]

Rule that Court of Claims is proper forum for Tucker Act claims against federal government.[87]

Presumption that statute creating agency and authorizing it to "sue and be sued" also creates federal subject matter jurisdiction for lawsuits by and against the agency.[88]

Construe ambiguities in deportation statutes in favor of aliens.[89]

Principle that veterans' benefits statutes be construed liberally for their beneficiaries (veterans).[90]

Presumption against application of Sherman Act to activities authorized by states.[91]

Principle that statutes should not be interpreted to create anticompetitive effects.[92]

Strong presumption that federal grand juries operate within legitimate spheres of their authority.[93]

Common Law-Based Canons

Presumption in favor of following common law usage where Congress has employed words or concepts with well-settled common law traditions.[94]

Super-strong rule against extraterritorial application of U.S. law.[95]

Super-strong rule against waivers of United States sovereign immunity.[96]

Super-strong rule against conveyance of U.S. public lands to private parties.[97]

Rule presuming against fee-shifting in federal courts, and narrow construction of fee-shifting statutes.[98]

Rule presuming that law takes effect on date of enactment.[99]

Presumption that public (government) interest not be prejudiced by negligence of federal officials.[100]

Presumption that federal agencies launched into commercial world with power to "sue and be sued" are not entitled to sovereign immunity.[101]

Presumption favoring enforcement of forum selection clauses.[102]

Presumption against criminal jurisdiction by an Indian tribe over a nonmember.[103]

Presumption that party cannot invoke federal jurisdiction until she has exhausted her remedies in Indian tribal courts.[104]

Presumption that federal judgment has preclusive effect in state administrative proceedings.[105]

Presumption importing common law immunities into federal civil rights statutes.[106]

Cases Cited

1. Estate of Cowart v. Nicklos Drilling Co., 112 S. Ct. 2589 (1992); United States v. Providence Journal Co., 485 U.S. 693 (1988) (compare Stevens dissent, invoking absurd result exception).

2. Holmes v. SIPC, 112 S. Ct. 1311 (1992).

3. United States v. Wilson, 112 S. Ct. 1351 (1992); Green v. Bock Laundry Machine Co., 490 U.S. 504 (1989).

4. EEOC v. Arabian American Oil Co., 499 U.S. 244 (1991); Jett v. Dallas Independent School District, 491 U.S. 701, 732 (1989); Chan v. Korean Air Lines, Ltd., 490 U.S. 122, 132–133 (1989). But see Burns v. United States, 111 S. Ct. 2182, 2186 (1991); Sullivan v. Hudson, 490 U.S. 877, 891 (1989).

5. Dole v. United Steelworkers, 494 U.S. 26, 36 (1990); Massachusetts v. Morash, 490 U.S. 107 (1989).

6. Hughey v. United States, 495 U.S. 411, 418–419 (1990).

7. Will v. Michigan Department of State Police, 491 U.S. 58, 64 (1989).

8. Pittston Coal Group v. Sebben, 488 U.S. 105, 113 (1988).

9. St. Francis College v. Al-Khazraji, 481 U.S. 604 (1987).

10. Mallard v. United States District Court for the Southern District of Iowa, 490 U.S. 296 (1989).

11. United States v. Ron Pair Enterprises, Inc., 489 U.S. 235, 241–242 (1989); San Francisco Arts & Athletics, Inc., v. United States Olympic Committee, 483 U.S. 522, 528–529 (1987).

12. Pavelic & Leflore v. Marvel Entertainment Group, 493 U.S. 120, 123–124 (1989); Massachusetts v. Morash, 490 U.S. 107 (1989).

13. Kungys v. United States, 485 U.S. 759, 778 (1988) (plurality opinion of Scalia, J.); South Carolina v. Catawba Indian Tribe, Inc., 476 U.S. 498, 510 n.22 (1986).

14. United Savings Association of Texas v. Timbers of Inwood Forest Associates, Ltd., 484 U.S. 365 (1988).

15. Gade v. National Solid Wastes Management Association, 112 S. Ct. 2374 (1992).

16. Eli Lilly & Co. v. Medtronic, Inc., 496 U.S. 661 (1990); Gwaltney of Smithfield, Ltd., v. Chesapeake Bay Foundation, Inc., 484 U.S. 49 (1987).

17. West Virginia University Hospitals, Inc., v. Casey, 499 U.S. 83 (1991).

18. Sullivan v. Stroop, 496 U.S. 478, 484 (1990); United Savings Association of Texas v. Timbers of Inwood Forest Associates, Ltd., 484 U.S. 365 (1988).

19. Green v. Bock Laundry Machine Co., 490 U.S. 504, 524–525 (1989); Crawford Fitting Co. v. J. T. Gibbons, Inc., 482 U.S. 437 (1987).

20. Commissioner v. Clark, 489 U.S. 726, 739 (1989).

21. United States v. Smith, 499 U.S. 160, 166–167 (1991).

22. Sullivan v. Everhart, 494 U.S. 83 (1990); NLRB v. Curtin Matheson Scientific, Inc., 494 U.S. 775 (1990); id. at 796 (Rehnquist, C.J., concurring); K Mart Corp. v. Cartier, Inc., 486 U.S. 281 (1988).

23. Mullins Coal Co. of Virginia v. Director, OWCP, 484 U.S. 135 (1987).

24. Green v. Bock Laundry, 490 U.S. 504, 521 (1989); Finley v. United States, 490 U.S. 545, 554 (1989).

25. California v. FERC, 495 U.S. 490 (1990); Maislin Industries, U.S., Inc., v. Primary Steel, Inc., 497 U.S. 116, 131–135 (1990).

26. Société Nationale Industrielle Aérospatiale v. United States District Court for the Southern District of Iowa, 482 U.S. 522, 539 (1987).

27. Molzof v. United States, 112 S. Ct. 711, 716 (1992); Metropolitan Life Insurance Co. v. Taylor, 481 U.S. 58 (1987).

28. Davis v. United States, 495 U.S. 472 (1990); Pierce v. Underwood, 487 U.S. 552 (1988).

29. Ankenbrandt v. Richards, 112 S. Ct. 2206 (1992); Monessen Southwestern Railway Co. v. Morgan, 486 U.S. 330, 337–339 (1988).

30. Bowen v. Yuckert, 482 U.S. 137, 149–151 (1987).

31. Sullivan v. Finkelstein, 496 U.S. 617 (1990); id. at 631–632 (Scalia, J., concurring in part).

32. Wisconsin Public Intervenor v. Mortier, 111 S. Ct. 2476, 2485 n.4 (1991).

33. Southwest Marine, Inc., v. Gizoni, 112 S. Ct. 486 (1991); Dewsnup v. Timm, 112 S. Ct. 773, 779 (1992).

34. Republic of Argentina v. Weltover, Inc., 112 S. Ct. 2160 (1992); American Hospital Association v. NLRB, 499 U.S. 606 (1991).

35. Chisom v. Roemer, 111 S. Ct. 2354, 2364 and n.23 (1991).

36. See Public Citizen v. United States Department of Justice, 491 U.S. 440 (1989); Edward J. DeBartolo Corp. v. Florida Gulf Coast Building and Construction Trades Council, 485 U.S. 568 (1988).

37. See Peretz v. United States, 111 S. Ct. 2661 (1991); Rust v. Sullivan, 111 S. Ct. 1759 (1991).

38. Department of Navy v. Egan, 484 U.S. 518 (1988); United States v. Johnson, 481 U.S. 681 (1987). See also United States v. Stanley, 483 U.S. 669 (1987) (LSD experiments by the military).

39. Morrison v. Olson, 487 U.S. 654, 682–683 (1988). See also Carlucci v. Doe, 488 U.S. 93, 99 (1988).

40. Franklin v. Massah, 112 S. Ct. 2767, 2775 (1992).

41. Chambers v. NASCO, Inc., 111 S. Ct. 2123 (1991).

42. California v. American Stores Co., 495 U.S. 271 (1990).

43. Lujan v. Defenders of Wildlife, 112 S. Ct. 2130 (1992); id. at 2146 (Kennedy, J., concurring in part and concurring in the judgment).

44. See Mistretta v. United States, 488 U.S. 361, 373 n.7 (1989).

45. Alaska Airlines, Inc., v. Brock, 480 U.S. 678 (1987).

46. See Gregory v. Ashcroft, 111 S. Ct. 2395 (1991).

47. Blatchford v. Native Village of Noatak, 111 S. Ct. 2578 (1991); Hoffman v. Connecticut Department of Income Maintenance, 492 U.S. 96 (1989); Dellmuth v. Muth, 491 U.S. 223 (1989); Pennsylvania v. Union Gas Co., 491 U.S. 1 (1989) (finding abrogation); see Atascadero State Hospital v. Scanlon, 473 U.S. 234 (1985) (leading case).

48. Suter v. Artist M., 112 S. Ct. 1360, 1366 (1992).

49. Finley v. United States, 490 U.S. 545, 552–553 (1989).

50. Wyoming v. Oklahoma, 112 S. Ct. 789, 802 (1992).

51. Tafflin v. Levitt, 493 U.S. 455 (1990); Yellow Freight System, Inc., v. Donnelly, 494 U.S. 820, 823–826 (1990).

52. Cipollone v. Liggett Group, Inc., 112 S. Ct. 2608 (1992); California v. ARC America Corp., 490 U.S. 93, 101 (1989).

53. Rose v. Rose, 481 U.S. 619, 636–637 (1987) (O'Connor, J., concurring in part and concurring in the judgment).

54. Davis v. Michigan Department of Treasury, 489 U.S. 803 (1989).

55. See City of Columbia v. Omni Outdoor Advertising, Inc., 499 U.S. 365 (1991) (Sherman Act); McCormick v. United States, 500 U.S. 257 (1991) (Hobbs Act); McNally v. United States, 483 U.S. 350 (1987) (mail fraud statute). But see Evans v. United States, 112 S. Ct. 1881 (1992) (Hobbs Act applied).

56. Cotton Petroleum Corp. v. New Mexico, 490 U.S. 163, 173 (1989).

57. County of Yakima v. Confederated Tribes and Bands of the Yakima Indians, 112 S. Ct. 683, 688, 693 (1992).

58. Utah Division of State Lands v. United States, 482 U.S. 193, 197–198 (1987).

59. Wright v. West, 112 S. Ct. 2482 (1992); Coleman v. Thompson, 111 S. Ct. 2546 (1991).

60. Spallone v. United States, 493 U.S. 265, 276 (1990).

61. Lampf, Pleva, Lipkind, Prupis & Petigrow v. Gilbertson, 111 S. Ct. 2773, 2778 (1991).

62. See Crandon v. United States, 494 U.S. 152, 158 (1990) (civil defendant but underlying liability criminal); United States v. Kozminski, 487 U.S. 931, 939 (1988).

63. United States v. R.L.C., 112 S. Ct. 1329 (1992). But see Chapman v. United States, 111 S. Ct. 1919 (1991) (rule of lenity not applicable when sentence is clearly stated).

64. Bowen v. Georgetown University Hospital, 488 U.S. 204 (1988). But see Kaiser Aluminum and Chemical Corp. v. Bonjorno, 494 U.S. 827 (1990) (conceding existence of separate line of decisions presuming some retroactivity).

65. Gomez v. United States, 490 U.S. 858, 864 (1989).

66. McNary v. Haitian Refugee Center, Inc., 498 U.S. 479 (1991).

67. Webster v. Doe, 486 U.S. 592 (1988).

68. McCarthy v. Madigan, 112 S. Ct. 1081 (1992).

69. Martin v. Wilks, 490 U.S. 755, 761–763 (1989).

70. Omni Capital International v. Rudolf Wolff & Co., 484 U.S. 97 (1987).

71. Wilder v. Virginia Hospital Association, 496 U.S. 498, 520–521 (1990) (very probably not a viable canon today).

72. Grogan v. Garner, 498 U.S. 279, 286 (1991).

73. Morales v. TWA, Inc., 112 S. Ct. 2031 (1992); TWA, Inc., v. Independent Federation of Flight Attendants, 489 U.S. 426 (1989); Communications Workers of America v. Beck, 487 U.S. 735 (1988); Wimberly v. Labor and Industrial Relations Commission of Missouri, 479 U.S. 511 (1987).

74. Pittsburgh & Lake Erie Railroad Co. v. RLEA, 491 U.S. 490, 510 (1989); Traynor v. Turnage, 485 U.S. 535 (1988); Atchison, Topeka & Santa Fe Railway Co. v. Buell, 480 U.S. 557, 564–567 (1987).

75. Reves v. Ernst & Young, 494 U.S. 56 (1990).

76. Wisconsin Department of Revenue v. William Wrigley, Jr., Co., 112 S. Ct. 2447, 2457–58 (1992).

77. Franklin v. Gwinnett County Public Schools, 112 S. Ct. 1028, 1033 (1992).

78. California v. Cabazon Band of Mission Indians, 480 U.S. 202 (1987) (may no longer be prevailing canon in Indian cases).

79. United States v. Burke, 112 S. Ct. 1866, 1877 (1992) (Souter, J., concurring in the judgment); United States v. Wells Fargo Bank, 485 U.S. 351 (1988).

80. Indopco, Inc., v. Commissioner, 112 S. Ct. 1039, 1043 (1992).

81. Citicorp Industrial Credit, Inc., v. Brock, 483 U.S. 27 (1987).

82. Dewsnup v. Timm, 112 S. Ct. 773, 779 (1992).

83. United Paperworkers v. Misco, Inc., 484 U.S. 29 (1988).

84. Groves v. Ring Screw Works, Ferndale Fastener Division, 498 U.S. 168, 175–176 (1990).

85. Gilmer v. Interstate/Johnson Lane Corp., 500 U.S. 20 (1991); Shearson/American Express, Inc., v. McMahon, 482 U.S. 220 (1987).

86. California Coastal Commission v. Granite Rock Co., 480 U.S. 572, 578–579 (1987).

87. Preseault v. ICC, 494 U.S. 1 (1990).

88. American National Red Cross v. S. G., 112 S. Ct. 2465 (1992).

89. INS v. Cardoza-Fonseca, 480 U.S. 421, 449 (1987) (perhaps questionable today). But see INS v. Elias-Zacarias, 112 S. Ct. 812 (1992).

90. King v. St. Vincent's Hospital, 112 S. Ct. 570 (1991).

91. City of Columbia v. Omni Outdoor Advertising, Inc., 499 U.S. 365 (1991).

92. Two Pesos, Inc., v. Taco Cabana, Inc., 112 S. Ct. 2753, 2761 (1992).

93. United States v. R. Enterprises, Inc., 498 U.S. 292, 299–301 (1991).

94. Nationwide Mutual Insurance Co. v. Darden, 112 S. Ct. 1344 (1992) (common law definition of employee); Kamen v. Kemper Financial Services, Inc., 500 U.S. 90 (1991) (state corporation law); Community for Creative Non-Violence v. Reid, 490 U.S. 730, 739 (1989) (common law of agency); Mississippi Band of Choctaw Indians v. Holyfield, 490 U.S. 30, 49 (1989) (domicile). But see Taylor v. United States, 495 U.S. 575 (1990) (not following common law meaning inconsistent with statutory purpose).

95. EEOC v. Arabian American Oil Co., 499 U.S. 244 (1991); Argentine Republic v. Amerada Hess Shipping Corp., 488 U.S. 428, 440–441 (1989).

96. United States v. Nordic Village, Inc., 112 S. Ct. 1011 (1992); United States Department of Energy v. Ohio, 112 S. Ct. 1627, 1633 (1992); Ardestani v. United States, 112 S. Ct. 515 (1991); United States v. Dalm, 494 U.S. 596, 608 (1990). But see Irwin v. Department of Veterans Affairs, 498 U.S. 89, 94–95 (1990) (once sovereign immunity is waived, equitable doctrines can be applied).

97. Utah Division of State Lands v. United States, 482 U.S. 193, 197–198 (1987).

98. West Virginia University Hospitals, Inc., v. Casey, 499 U.S. 83 (1991).

99. Gozlon-Peretz v. United States, 498 U.S. 395, 404 (1991).

100. United States v. Montalvo-Murillo, 495 U.S. 711 (1990).

101. Loeffler v. Frank, 486 U.S. 549, 554–555 (1988).

102. Carnival Cruise Lines, Inc., v. Shute, 499 U.S. 585 (1991); Stewart Organization, Inc., v. Ricoh Corp., 487 U.S. 22, 33 (1988) (Kennedy, J., concurring).

103. Duro v. Reina, 495 U.S. 676, 684–685 (1990).

104. Iowa Mutual Insurance Co. v. LaPlante, 480 U.S. 9 (1987).

105. Astoria Federal Savings and Loan Association v. Solimino, 111 S. Ct. 2166 (1991).

106. Burns v. Reed, 111 S. Ct. 1934 (1991); Spallone v. United States, 493 U.S. 265, 276 (1990); Forrester v. White, 484 U.S. 219 (1988).

Notes

Introduction

1. The annus mirabilis for this renaissance was 1982, for in that year were published J. Willard Hurst, *Dealing with Statutes* (1982); Guido Calabresi, *A Common Law for the Age of Statutes* (1982); Ronald Dworkin, "Law as Interpretation," 60 *Texas Law Review* 527 (1982); and Richard A. Posner, "Economics, Politics, and the Reading of Statutes and the Constitution," 49 *University of Chicago Law Review* 263 (1982).

2. Marguerite Yourcenar, *The Memoirs of Hadrian*, 113–114 (Grace Frick, trans., 1954).

3. About 50 percent of the decisions written by the United States Supreme Court each year involve statutory interpretation. Similar percentages have been reported for other common law systems. See D. C. Pearce, *Statutory Interpretation in Australia*, 1 (1981); A. A. Paterson and T. St. John N. Bates, *The Legal System of Scotland: Cases and Materials*, 286 (1986).

4. See Dred Scott v. Sandford, 60 U.S. (19 How.) 393 (1857) (opinion of Taney, C.J.) (African Americans are not "citizens" under the federal statute creating diversity jurisdiction); Swift v. Tyson, 41 U.S. (16 Pet.) 1 (1842) (Story, J.) (interpreting §34 of the Judiciary Act of 1789); Marbury v. Madison, 5 U.S. (1 Cranch) 137, 173 (1803) (Marshall, C.J.) (interpreting another provision of the Judiciary Act of 1789). See John Choon Yoo, "Marshall's Plan: The Early Supreme Court and Statutory Interpretation," 101 *Yale Law Journal* 1607 (1992) (student note).

5. For instance, the main protections for voting rights have come through the Department of Justice and Supreme Court interpretations of the Voting Rights Act of 1965, as amended, and not through the Court's constitutional jurisprudence. Compare Lassiter v. Northampton Election Board, 360 U.S. 45 (1959) (conservative interpretation of Fifteenth Amendment voting rights protections), with Allen v. State Board of Elections, 393 U.S. 544 (1969) (liberal interpretation of Voting Rights Act of 1965). Compare City of Mobile v. Bolden, 446 U.S. 55

(1980) (conservative interpretation of Fifteenth Amendment), with Thornburg v. Gingles, 478 U.S. 30 (1986) (interpretation of Voting Rights Act of 1982 to override *Bolden*).

6. Aristotle, *Rhetoric*, bk. 1, chap. 15 (W. Rhys Roberts, trans., rev. Oxford ed. 1984).

7. Aristotle, *The Nicomachean Ethics*, bk. 5, chap. 10 (W. D. Ross, trans., revised by J. O. Urmson, rev. Oxford ed. 1984).

8. Aristotle, *De Interpretatione* (J. L. Ackrill, trans., rev. Oxford ed. 1984).

9. See Alan Watson, ed., *The Digest of Justinian*, vol. 1, bk. 1 (1985).

10. See Geoffrey P. Miller, "Pragmatics and the Maxims of Interpretation," 1990 *Wisconsin Law Review* 1179, relying on Augustine, *On Christian Doctrine* (D. W. Robinson, ed., 1958) (early Christian hermeneutics); V. Sarathi, *The Interpretation of Statutes* (1981) (ancient Hindu law); A. Schreiber, *Jewish Law and Decision-Making: A Study through Time* (1979) (Jewish law).

11. Thomas Aquinas, *Summa Theologica*, quest. xcv; quest. xcvi, art. 4 (Anton C. Pegis, ed., 1948).

12. See Kurt Mueller-Vollmer, ed., *The Hermeneutics Reader: Texts of the German Tradition from the Enlightenment to the Present*, 3 (1988).

13. Reporter's Note to Eyston v. Studd, 2 Plowden 459, 465, 75 All E.R. 688, 695–696 (1574); for similar ideas, see Heydon's Case, 76 Eng. Rep. 637 (Exch. 1584); 1 William Blackstone, *Commentaries on the Laws of England*, 61 (1765).

14. Friedrich Daniel Ernst Schleiermacher, "Introduction," in *Compendium, 1819*, pars. 18–19 (James Duke and Jack Forstman, trans., 1977, from the Heinz Kimmerle ed.).

15. For the United States, see Chapter 7. For Germany, see Karl Larenz, *Methodenlehre der Rechtswissenschaft*, 301 ff. (1983). For France, see Michel Troper, Christophe Grzegorczyk, and Jean-Louis Gardiés, "Statutory Interpretation in France," in *Interpreting Statutes: A Comparative Study*, 171, 179–180, 185–186, 190 (D. Neil MacCormick and Robert S. Summers, eds., 1991).

16. François Gény, *Méthode d'interprétation et sources en droit privé positif* (1899).

17. Hans-Georg Gadamer, *Truth and Method*, xvi (Joel Weinsheimer and Donald G. Marshall, trans., 2d rev. English ed. 1989) (translators' preface).

18. William N. Eskridge, Jr., "Dynamic Statutory Interpretation," 135 *University of Pennsylvania Law Review* 1479 (1987), as well as William N. Eskridge, Jr., and Philip P. Frickey, *Legislation: Statutes and the Creation of Public Policy*, chap. 7 (1988).

19. See Richard A. Posner, *The Problems of Jurisprudence* (1990); T. Alexander Aleinikoff, "Updating Statutory Interpretation," 87 *Michigan Law Review*. 20 (1988); Daniel A. Farber, "Statutory Interpretation and Legislative Supremacy," 78 *Georgetown Law Journal* 281 (1989); John A. Ferejohn and Barry R. Weingast, "Limitation of Statutes: Strategic Statutory Interpretation," 80 *Georgetown Law Journal* 565 (1992); Philip P. Frickey, "Congressional Intent, Practical Reasoning, and the Dynamic Nature of Federal Indian Law," 78 *California Law Review* 1137

(1990); Bruce W. Frier, "Interpreting Codes," 89 *Michigan Law Review* 2201 (1991); Heidi M. Hurd, "Sovereignty in Silence," 99 *Yale Law Journal* 945 (1990); Alex M. Johnson and Ross Taylor, "Revolutionizing Judicial Interpretation of Charitable Trusts: Applying Relational Contracts and Dynamic Statutory Interpretation to Cy Pres and America's Cup Litigation," 74 *Iowa Law Review* 545 (1989); Donald C. Langevoort, "Statutory Obsolescence and the Judicial Process: The Revisionist Role of the Courts in Federal Banking Regulation," 85 *Michigan Law Review* 672 (1987); Francis J. Mootz III, "The Ontological Basis of Legal Hermeneutics: A Proposed Model of Inquiry Based on the Work of Gadamer, Habermas, and Ricoeur," 68 *Boston University Law Review* 523 (1988); William D. Popkin, "The Collaborative Model of Statutory Interpretation," 61 *Southern California Law Review* 541 (1988); Daniel B. Rodriguez, "Statutory Interpretation and Political Advantages," 12 *International Review of Law and Economics* 217 (1992); Edward L. Rubin, "Law and Legislation in the Administrative State," 89 *Columbia Law Review* 369 (1989); Peter C. Schank, "The Only Game in Town: An Introduction to Interpretive Theory, Statutory Construction, and Legislative Histories," 38 *Kansas Law Review* 815 (1990); Jeffrey W. Stempel, "The Rehnquist Court, Statutory Interpretation, and a Misleading Version of Democracy," 22 *University of Toledo Law Review* 583 (1991); Cass R. Sunstein, "Interpreting Statutes in the Regulatory State," 103 *Harvard Law Review* 405 (1989); Nicholas S. Zeppos, "Judicial Candor and Statutory Interpretation," 78 *Georgetown Law Journal* 353 (1989).

20. There is a rich literature in linguistics that is now being brought to bear on statutory issues. See Lawrence M. Solan, *The Language of Judges* (1993).

21. See Daniel A. Farber and Philip P. Frickey, *Law and Public Choice: A Critical Introduction* (1991); Herbert Hovenkamp, "Legislation, Well-Being, and Public Choice," 57 *University of Chicago Law Review* 63 (1990); Jerry Mashaw, "The Economics of Politics and the Understanding of Public Law," 65 *Chicago-Kent Law Review* 123 (1989); Edward L. Rubin, "Beyond Public Choice: Comprehensive Rationality in the Writing and Reading of Statutes," 66 *New York University Law Review* 1 (1991); Daniel N. Shaviro, "Beyond Public Choice and Public Interest: A Study of the Legislative Process as Illustrated by Tax Legislation in the 1980s," 139 *University of Pennsylvania Law Review* 1 (1990).

22. See "Symposium: Positive Political Theory and Public Law," 80 *Georgetown Law Journal* 457–807 (1992); Conference on "The Organization of Political Institutions," 6 *Journal of Law, Economics, and Organization*, special issue, 1–332 (1990).

1. The Insufficiency of Statutory Archaeology

This chapter draws from my article (coauthored with Philip P. Frickey) "Statutory Interpretation as Practical Reasoning," 42 *Stanford Law Review* 321 (1990), © 1990 by the Board of Trustees of the Leland Stanford Junior University; as well as from my article "Dynamic Statutory Interpretation," 135 *University of Pennsylvania Law Review* 1479 (1987).

1. 2A *Sutherland, Statutes and Statutory Construction*, §45.05 (Norman Singer, ed., 4th ed. 1984).

2. E.g., Commissioner v. Engle, 464 U.S. 206, 214 (1984).

3. Frank H. Easterbrook, "The Supreme Court, 1983 Term—Foreword: The Court and the Economic System," 98 *Harvard Law Review* 4, 60 (1984).

4. The earliest extended treatment is *A Discourse upon the Exposicion & Understandinge of Statutes With Sir Thomas Egerton's Additions*, a sixteenth-century manuscript edited and published in 1942 by Samuel E. Thorne. For early American expositions of an intentionalist approach, see, e.g., Theodore Sedgwick, *A Treatise on the Rules Which Govern the Interpretation and Application of Statutory and Constitutional Law*, 231 (1857); J. G. Sutherland, *Statutes and Statutory Construction*, 380 (1891); Roscoe Pound, "Spurious Interpretation," 7 *Columbia Law Review* 379, 381 (1907).

5. See Richard A. Posner, The *Federal Courts: Crisis and Reform*, 286–293 (1985); Martin H. Redish, *The Federal Courts in the Political Order: Judicial Jurisdiction and American Political Theory*, chap. 2 (1991); Daniel A. Farber, "Statutory Interpretation and Legislative Supremacy," 78 *Georgetown Law Journal* 281 (1989); Learned Hand, "How Far Is a Judge Free in Rendering a Decision?" in *The Spirit of Liberty: Papers and Addresses of Learned Hand*, 103, 105–110 (3d ed. 1960); Earl M. Maltz, "Statutory Interpretation and Legislative Power: The Case for a Modified Intentionalist Approach," 63 *Tulane Law Review* 1 (1988); Thomas W. Merrill, "The Common Law Powers of Federal Courts," 52 *University of Chicago Law Review* 1, 33–39 (1985); Daniel B. Rodriguez, "Statutory Interpretation and Political Advantage," 12 *International Review of Law and Economics* 217 (1992); Patricia M. Wald, "Some Observations on the Use of Legislative History in the 1981 Supreme Court Term," 68 *Iowa Law Review* 195 (1983).

6. 443 U.S. 193 (1979).

7. Codified at 42 U.S.C. §2000e-2(a)(1) (1976).

8. Compare *Weber*, 443 U.S. at 201–208 (Brennan's opinion for the Court), with id. at 219–220, 222, 226–255 (Rehnquist, J., dissenting). See also Hugh Davis Graham, *The Civil Rights Era: Origins and Development of National Policy, 1960–1972* (1990); Alfred W. Blumrosen, *Modern Law: The Law Transmission System and Equal Employment Opportunity*, chap. 16 (1993); Bernard Meltzer, "The *Weber* Case: The Judicial Abrogation of the Antidiscrimination Standard in Employment," 47 *University of Chicago Law Review* 423 (1980).

9. See Nicholas S. Zeppos, "The Use of Authority in Statutory Interpretation: An Empirical Analysis," 70 *Texas Law Review* 1073, 1099–1101 (1992). For some leading examples, see, e.g., Public Citizen v. United States Department of Justice, 491 U.S. 440 (1989) (Brennan, J.); United States v. Fausto, 484 U.S. 439, 443–448 (1988) (Scalia, J.); School Board of Nassau County v. Arline, 480 U.S. 273, 277–278 (1987) (Brennan, J.); Midlantic National Bank v. New Jersey Department of

Environmental Protection, 474 U.S. 494 (1986) (Powell, J.); NLRB v. Catholic Bishop of Chicago, 440 U.S. 490 (1976) (Burger, C.J.); Jones v. Alfred H. Mayer Co., 392 U.S. 409 (1968) (Stewart, J.); Schwegmann Brothers v. Calvert Distillers Corp., 341 U.S. 384 (1951) (Douglas, J.).

10. See generally Max Radin, "Statutory Interpretation," 43 *Harvard Law Review* 863, 870–871 (1930), discussed in Chapter 7.

11. House Report no. 914, 88th Cong., 1st sess., pt. 1, 69 (1963) (minority views), reprinted in 1964 *United States Code Congress and Administrative News*, 2431, 2438 (emphasis omitted).

12. 110 *Congressional Record* 2518 (1964) (Rep. Celler, D-N.Y., Judiciary Committee chair); id. at 2558 (Rep. Goodell, R-N.Y., supporter) (quotation in text).

13. *Weber*, 443 U.S. at 235–251 (Rehnquist, J., dissenting). The eleven saying the bill required quotas were all opponents of the bill (Senators Byrd, Ervin, Hill, Long, Robertson, Russell, Smathers, Sparkman, Stennis, Talmadge, Tower), while the eleven saying otherwise were supporters of the bill (Senators Allott, Carlson, Case, Clark, Humphrey, Keating, Kuchel, McGovern, Muskie, Saltonstall, Williams). Two opponents (Cotton and Curtis) engaged in a sarcastic colloquy on the quotas issue. None of this evidence has formal significance for vote-counting purposes of determining the actual intent of the Senate.

14. 42 U.S.C. §2000e-2(j) (1976) (emphasis added).

15. The most illuminating statements on the issue after §703(j) was added cut in different directions. Compare 110 *Congressional Record* 15,893 (1964) (Rep. MacGregor, R-Minn.) (Congress did not legislate on "preferential treatment or quotas in employment," issues better handled by state government and by private bargaining), with id. at 13,086 (colloquy of Sens. Curtis, R-Neb., and Cotton, R-N.H.) (the bill would "outlaw" employers "who provide jobs for a class of people who have perhaps not had sufficient opportunity for jobs").

16. 110 *Congressional Record* 6549 (1964) (Sen. Humphrey, D-Minn.), quoted in *Weber*, 443 U.S. at 238 (Rehnquist, J., dissenting).

17. 110 *Congressional Record* 7213 (1964) (interpretive memorandum on Title VII by Sens. Clark, D-Pa., and Case, R-N.J.), quoted in *Weber*, 443 U.S. at 239 (Rehnquist, J., dissenting).

18. Compare Kenneth A. Shepsle, *The Giant Jigsaw Puzzle: Democratic Committee Assignments in the Modern House* (1978) (committees dominated by "outliers" whose policy preferences are not representative of the chamber's), with Keith Krehbiel, *Information and Legislative Organization*, chap. 4 (1991) (outlier problem overstated). In 1963–64 it appears that the House and Senate Judiciary Committees in charge of civil rights legislation were preference outliers on civil rights issues, the House committee more liberal than its chamber, the Senate committee more conservative than its chamber. See Charles Whalen and Barbara Whalen, *The Longest Debate: A Legislative History of the 1964 Civil Rights Act*, 29–67 (1985).

19. See Krehbiel, *Information and Legislative Organization*, chap. 4; McNollgast,

"Legislative Intent: The Use of Positive Political Theory in Statutory Interpretation," 57 *Law and Contemporary Problems* 3 (Winter 1994); McNollgast, "Positive Canons: The Role of Legislative Bargains in Statutory Interpretation," 80 *Georgetown Law Journal* 705, 725–727 (1992).

20. See McNollgast, "Positive Canons"; McNollgast, "Legislative Intent."

21. *The Federalist Papers*, nos. 63 (Madison), 73 (Hamilton), 78 (Hamilton) (Clinton Rossiter, ed., 1961); INS v. Chadha, 462 U.S. 919, 950–951 (1983); see David F. Epstein, *The Political Theory of "The Federalist,"* 177–178 (1984).

22. *Weber,* 443 U.S. at 240 (Rehnquist, J., dissenting), quoting 110 *Congressional Record* 7213 (1964) (Clark-Case memorandum) (emphasis supplied by Rehnquist).

23. *Weber,* 443 U.S. at 241 (Rehnquist, J., dissenting).

24. Pound, "Spurious Interpretation," 381; see Posner, *Federal Courts,* 286–287; and discussion in Chapter 7.

25. See McNollgast, "Positive Canons."

26. See Hubert Horatio Humphrey, *Beyond Civil Rights: A New Day of Equality,* 85–86 (1968); Merle Miller, *Lyndon: An Oral Biography,* 370 (1980); Edward Schapsmeier amd Frederick Schapsmeier, *Dirksen of Illinois: Senatorial Statesman* (1985).

27. McCulloch had consistently put his neck on the line for civil rights bills and supported stronger bills than those acceptable to Dirksen. Mansfield, a liberal Democrat, was to the left on civil rights issues, as was the president. See Whalen and Whalen, *The Longest Debate.*

28. Humphrey persuaded Johnson that Dirksen had no choice but to support the bill and that the president should yield only token concessions to Dirksen. See Neil MacNeil, *Dirksen: Portrait of a Public Man,* 234–235 (1970); Whalen and Whalen, *The Longest Debate,* 171–172.

29. *Weber,* 443 U.S. at 209–216 (Blackmun, J., concurring).

30. This account is drawn from Graham, *The Civil Rights Era,* chaps. 9, 11, 12, 13, and 15; Herman Belz, *Equality Transformed: A Quarter-Century of Affirmative Action* (1991); Neal Devins, "The Civil Rights Hydra," 89 *Michigan Law Review* 1723 (1991) (reviewing Graham, *Civil Rights Era*). For an account of this transformation by a key player within the EEOC, see Alfred W. Blumrosen, *Black Employment and the Law* (1971).

31. 401 U.S. 424 (1971).

32. 30 Fed. Reg. 12,319 (1965), currently codified at 41 C.F.R. pt. 60:2 (1993).

33. *Weber,* 443 U.S. at 202, quoting United States v. Public Utilities Commission, 345 U.S. 295, 315 (1953).

34. Henry M. Hart, Jr., and Albert M. Sacks, "The Legal Process: Basic Problems in the Making and Application of Law," 166–167, 1148–79, 1200 (tentative ed. 1958) (forthcoming from Foundation Press, 1994, ed. William N. Eskridge, Jr., and Philip P. Frickey); see Lon L. Fuller, "The Case of the Speluncean Explorers," 62 *Harvard Law Review* 616, 620–626 (1949) (Foster, J.); Harry Willmer Jones, "Statutory Doubts and Legislative Intention," 40 *Columbia Law Review* 957

(1940); Max Radin, "A Short Way with Statutes," 56 *Harvard Law Review* 388 (1942). Chapter 7 discusses this development in greater detail.

35. Hart and Sacks, "The Legal Process," 1415.

36. See, e.g., Wilfred E. Binkley and Malcolm C. Moos, *A Grammar of American Politics* (1949); Earl Latham, *The Group Basis of Politics* (1952); David B. Truman, *The Governmental Process* (1952).

37. Richard A. Fenno, *Congressmen in Committees* (1973); see also John W. Kingdon, *Congressmen's Voting Decisions* (2d ed. 1981); Morris Fiorina, *Congress: Keystone of the Washington Establishment* (1977) (primary motive is reelection); David Mayhew, *Congress: The Electoral Connection* (1974) (similar to Fiorina).

38. See Fiorina, *Congress*; Michael Hayes, *Lobbyists and Legislators: A Theory of Political Markets* (1981); R. E. McCormick and Robert D. Tollison, *Politicans, Legislation, and the Economy* (1981). See generally Dennis C. Mueller, *Public Choice II* (1989).

39. Civil Rights Act of 1964, §703(h), codified at 42 U.S.C. §2000e-2(h) (1976).

40. Id. §702, codified at 42 U.S.C. §2000e-1 (1976).

41. Id. §701(b), codified at 42 U.S.C. §2000e(b) (1976).

42. Id. §703(e)(1), codified at 42 U.S.C. §2000e-2(e)(1) (1976).

43. Id. §706, codified at 42 U.S.C. §2000e-5 (1976).

44. Id. §703(j), codified at 42 U.S.C. §2000e-2(j) (1976).

45. *Weber*, 443 U.S. at 202–204.

46. 110 *Congressional Record* 14,510 (1964) (remarks of Sen. Dirksen), quoted in *Weber*, 443 U.S. at 254 (Rehnquist, J., dissenting).

47. For leading studies, see James Heckman and Brook Payner, "Determining the Impact of Federal Antidiscrimination Policy on the Status of Blacks: A Study of South Carolina," 79 *American Economic Review* 138 (1989); James P. Smith and Finis Welch, "Black Economic Progress after Myrdal," 27 *Journal of Economic Literature* 519 (1989). For further discussion, see Chapters 8 and 9.

48. See Robert Suggs, "Racial Discrimination in Business Transactions," 42 *Hastings Law Journal* 1257 (1991).

49. Richard A. Posner, "The Efficiency and Efficacy of Title VII," 136 *University of Pennsylvania Law Review* 513 (1987). But see John Donohue III, "Is Title VII Efficient?" 134 *University of Pennsylvania Law Review* 1411 (1985)

50. See T. Alexander Aleinikoff, "A Case of Race-Consciousness," 91 *Columbia Law Review* 1060, 1065–66 (1991); James P. Smith, "Affirmative Action and the Racial Wage Gap," 83 *American Economic Association Papers and Proceedings* 79 (1993).

51. Public Law no. 102–166, §105, 105 Stat. 1071, 1074–75 (1991), adding new §703(k), codified at 42 U.S.C. §2000e-2(k) (1992).

52. 480 U.S. 616 (1987).

53. See Whalen and Whalen, *The Longest Debate*, 115–117; Francis Vaas, "Title VII: Legislative History," 7 *Boston College Industrial and Commercial Law Review* 431, 441–442 (1966).

54. *Johnson*, 480 U.S. at 657 (Scalia, J., dissenting).

55. Leading cases along these lines include West Virginia University Hospitals, Inc., v. Casey, 499 U.S. 83 (1991) (Scalia, J.); Public Employees Retirement System of Ohio v. Betts, 492 U.S. 158 (1989) (Kennedy, J.); Board of Governors, Federal Reserve System v. Dimension Financial Corporation, 474 U.S. 361, 373 (1986) (Burger, C.J); United States v. Locke, 471 U.S. 84 (1985) (Marshall, J.); Consumer Product Safety Commission v. GTE Sylvania, Inc., 447 U.S. 102, 108 (1980) (Powell, J.); Tennessee Valley Authority v. Hill, 437 U.S. 153, 173–174 (1978) (Burger, C.J.); United Airlines, Inc., v. McMann, 434 U.S. 192, 199 (1977) (Burger, C.J.); Unexcelled Chemical Corp. v. United States, 345 U.S. 59 (1953) (Douglas, J.); United States v. Sullivan, 332 U.S. 689 (1948) (Black, J.); Packard Motor Car Co. v. NLRB, 330 U.S. 485 (1947) (Jackson, J.); Caminetti v. United States, 242 U.S. 470 (1917); United States v. Wiltberger, 18 U.S. (5 Wheat.) 76 (1820) (Marshall, C.J.).

56. 458 U.S. 564 (1982).

57. 46 U.S.C. §596 (repealed 1983).

58. Act of June 7, 1872, ch. 322, §35, 17 Stat. 269: "[E]very master or owner who neglects or refuses to make payment [of a seaman's earned wages within five days after a seaman's discharge] without sufficient cause shall pay to the seaman a sum not exceeding the amount of two days' pay for each of the days, not exceeding ten days, during which payment is delayed beyond [the five-day period]; and such sum shall be recoverable as wages in any claim made before the court."

59. Act of December 21, 1898, ch. 28, §4, 30 Stat. 756: "Every master or owner who refuses or neglects to make payment [of a seaman's earned wages within four days of the seaman's discharge] without sufficient cause shall pay to the seaman a sum equal to one day's pay for each and every day during which payment is delayed beyond the [four-day period], which sum shall be recoverable as wages in any claim made before the court." As the text indicates, the 1898 statute also changed the period of permissible delay (from five to four days) and made the penalty single rather than double wages. The latter change was reversed by the Act of March 4, 1915, ch. 153, §3, 38 Stat. 1164, which substituted "two days' pay" for "one day's pay."

60. *Griffin*, 458 U.S. at 588–589 and n.19 (Stevens, J., dissenting).

61. House Report no. 1657, 55th Cong., 2d sess. 2, 3 (1898).

62. See Public Law no. 98-89, 97 Stat. 566 (1983), now codified at 46 U.S.C. §10313(g) (1988). The House committee report suggested that "the literal language of the statute should control the disposition of the cases. There is no mandate in logic or in case law for reliance on legislative history to reach a result contrary to the plain meaning of the statute, particularly where that plain meaning is in no way unreasonable." House Report no. 338, 98th Cong., 1st sess. 120 (1983), reprinted in 1983 *United States Code Congressional and Administrative News* 932.

63. See Frank H. Easterbrook, "The Role of Original Intent in Statutory Construction," 11 *Harvard Journal of Law and Public Policy* 59 (1988); address by Antonin Scalia, "Speech on Use of Legislative History" (delivered at various law schools, 1985–86), both discussed at length in Chapter 7.

64. See my article "The New Textualism," 37 *University of California at Los Angeles Law Review* 621 (1990) (recent and stronger use of textualism since Scalia joined the Court); Richard Pildes, "Intent, Clear Statements, and the Common Law: Statutory Interpretation in the Supreme Court," 95 *Harvard Law Review* 892 (1982) (student note); Patricia M. Wald, "The Sizzling Sleeper: The Use of Legislative History in Construing Statutes in the 1988–89 Term of the United States Supreme Court," 39 *American University Law Review* 277 (1990); Nicholas S. Zeppos, "Scalia's Textualism: The 'New' New Legal Process," 12 *Cardozo Law Review* 1597 (1991).

65. See Kenneth A. Shepsle, "Congress Is a 'They,' Not an 'It': Legislative Intent as Oxymoron," 12 *International Review of Law and Economics* 239 (1992); see also Jerry Mashaw, "The Economics of Politics and the Understanding of Public Law," 65 *Chicago-Kent Law Review* 123 (1989).

66. See Kenneth Arrow, *Social Choice and Individual Values* (2d ed. 1963); Duncan Black, *The Theories of Committees and Elections* (1958). See generally Mueller, *Public Choice II*, 384–399.

67. The diehard supporters of the bill favored choice (2) over choice (3) or choice (1) because they wanted to gain jobs for African Americans. Diehard opponents preferred (1) to either (2) or (3) for the converse reason, and they preferred (2) to (3) on the ground that it would make the bill more vulnerable to their charge that it would create quotas. Moderates preferred choice (3) over choice (1) or (2) because it freed businesses from the broadest state intervention (the state would not force quotas on businesses, nor would it prevent them from adopting voluntary quotas); they preferred (1) over (2) because they feared government-imposed quotas more than they liked the flexibility of preferences at the discretion of employers.

68. Daniel A. Farber and Philip P. Frickey, *Law and Public Choice: A Critical Introduction*, 49–55 (1991); Kenneth A. Shepsle and Barry Weingast, "Structure-Induced Equilibrium and Legislative Choice," 37 *Public Choice* 503 (1981).

69. See Frank H. Easterbrook, "Ways of Criticizing the Court," 95 *Harvard Law Review* 802 (1982).

70. See Zeppos, "The Use of Authority in Statutory Interpretation," 1112–20. Examples beyond those discussed in this chapter are recounted in Eskridge and Frickey, "Statutory Interpretation as Practical Reasoning"; Donald Langevoort, "Statutory Obsolescence and the Judicial Process: The Revisionist Role of the Courts in Federal Banking Regulation," 85 *Michigan Law Review* 672 (1987); Nicholas S. Zeppos, "Judicial Candor and Statutory Interpretation," 78 *Georgetown Law Journal* 353 (1989).

71. *Weber,* 443 U.S. at 226 (Rehnquist, J., dissenting); *Johnson,* 480 U.S. at 670–671 (Scalia, J., dissenting) (same point); see also id. at 647–648 (O'Connor, J., concurring in the judgment).

72. See McDonald v. Santa Fe Trail Transportation Co., 427 U.S. 273 (1976).

73. See Thomas Sowell, *Civil Rights: Rhetoric or Reality?* (1984); W. Bradford Reynolds, "Individualism vs. Group Rights: The Legacy of *Brown,*" 93 *Yale Law Journal* 995 (1984).

74. See Patricia J. Williams, *The Alchemy of Race and Rights* (1991); Kimberlé Williams Crenshaw, "Race, Reform, and Retrenchment: Transformation and Legitimation in Antidiscrimination Law," 101 *Harvard Law Review* 1331 (1988).

75. See Randall Kennedy, "Persuasion and Distrust: A Comment on the Affirmative Action Debate," 99 *Harvard Law Review* 1327 (1986); Kathleen Sullivan, "Sins of Discrimination: Last Term's Affirmative Action Cases," 100 *Harvard Law Review* 78 (1986).

76. The material that follows is drawn from the Thurgood Marshall Papers, Library of Congress, Box 415, Folder 9 (Marshall's case file for *Johnson,* which includes a memorandum from Brennan, dated February 26, 1987).

77. *Johnson,* 480 U.S. at 657–677 (Scalia, J., dissenting).

78. Id. at 647–657 (O'Connor, J., concurring in the judgment).

79. Id. at 657 (White, J., dissenting).

80. Id. at 642–647 (Stevens, J., concurring).

81. The discussion that follows is drawn from Eskridge, "The New Textualism," 650–666, and is based on Scalia's opinions such as Finley v. United States, 490 U.S. 545, 556 (1989); Pierce v. Underwood, 487 U.S. 552 (1988); United Savings Association of Texas v. Timbers of Inwood Forest Associates, 484 U.S. 365, 371 (1988).

82. 490 U.S. 504, 528 (1989) (Scalia, J., concurring in the judgment); see also Chisom v. Roemer, 111 S. Ct. 2354, 2369 (1991) (Scalia, J., dissenting).

83. Codified at 42 U.S.C. §2000e-2(h) (1976).

84. Id. §2000e-2(e).

85. See Jett v. Dallas Independent School District, 491 U.S. 701, 738–739 (1989) (Scalia, J., concurring in part and concurring in the judgment) (narrowing interpretation of Civil Rights Act of 1866, based on canon that "the specific governs the general"); Chan v. Korean Air Lines, Ltd., 490 U.S. 122 (1989) (Scalia, J.) (narrowing interpretation of Warsaw Convention based on *expressio unius*).

86. *Johnson,* 480 U.S. at 676 (Scalia, J., dissenting).

87. Congress amended Title VII right after *Griggs.* No one in Congress said that *Griggs* was inconsistent with §703(j), either formally or practically, and the committee reports in both House and Senate described and praised *Griggs.* See House Report no. 238, 92d Cong., 1st sess., 21–22 (1971), reprinted in 1972 *United States Code Congressional and Administrative News,* 2137, 2156–57; Senate Report no. 415, 92d Cong., 1st sess., 14 (1971).

88. *Johnson*, 480 U.S. at 677 (Scalia, J., dissenting).

89. *Bock Laundry*, 490 U.S. at 524–527.

90. Id. at 527–530 (Scalia, J., concurring in the judgment).

91. Id. at 529.

92. Scalia mischaracterized the dissent's rewrite as changing "defendant" to "civil plaintiff, civil defendant, prosecutor and criminal defendant."

93. In full, Scalia's rewrite (with his addition emphasized) would read: "For the purpose of attacking the credibility of a witness, evidence that a witness has been convicted of a crime shall be admitted if elicited from the witness or established by public record during cross-examination but only if the crime (1) was punishable by death or imprisonment in excess of one year under the law under which the witness was convicted, and the court determines that the probative value of admitting this evidence outweighs its prejudicial value to the *criminal* defendant."

2. The Dynamics of Statutory Interpretation

This chapter is drawn from my articles "Gadamer/Statutory Interpretation," 90 *Columbia Law Review* 609 (1990), and "Statutory Interpretation as Practical Reasoning," 42 *Stanford Law Review* 321 (1990) (coauthored with Philip P. Frickey), © 1990 by the Board of Trustees of the Leland Stanford Junior University.

1. See, e.g., Benjamin N. Cardozo, *The Nature of the Judicial Process* (1921); John Chipman Gray, *The Nature and Sources of the Law* (2d ed. 1921); Charles P. Curtis, "A Better Theory of Interpretation," 3 *Vanderbilt Law Review* 407 (1950); Lon L. Fuller, "The Case of the Speluncean Explorers," 62 *Harvard Law Review* 616, 620–626 (1949) (opinion of Foster, J.).

2. See John Henry Merryman, *The Civil Law Tradition: An Introduction to the Legal Systems of Western Europe and Latin America*, 43–47 (2d ed. 1985); F. A. R. Bennion, *Statutory Interpretation* (1984) (United Kingdom); G. E. Devenish, *Interpretation of Statutes*, chaps. 1–2 (1992) (South Africa); 1 Henri DePage, *Traité élémentaire de droit civile belge* (1962) (Belgium); 1 H. Koziol and R. Welser, *Grundreiss des Gurgerlichen Rechts* (5th ed. 1979) (Germany); 1 J. J. Llambias, *Tratudo de derecho civil* (2d ed. 1964) (Argentina); Giovanni Tarello, *L'interpretazione della legge* (1980) (Italy); Michel van der Kerchove, ed., *Interprétation en droit, sous la direction de Michel van der Kerchove* (1978) (France); Jerzy Wróblewski, *Constitucion e teoria general de interpretation juridica* (1985) (Poland). See also D. Neil MacCormick and Robert S. Summers, eds., *Interpreting Statutes: A Comparative Study* (1991) (chapters on gap filling and evolutive interpretation in Argentina, Germany, Finland, France, Italy, Poland, Sweden, and the United Kingdom).

3. For the beyond/against distinction, see Daniel A. Farber, "Statutory Interpretation and the Principle of Legislative Supremacy," 78 *Georgetown Law Journal* 281 (1989).

4. Bennion, *Statutory Interpretation*, 356; see T. Alexander Aleinikoff, "Updating Statutory Interpretation," 87 *Michigan Law Review* 20 (1988) (similar nautical metaphor).

5. Aristotle, *The Nicomachean Ethics*, bk. 5, chap. 10 (W. D. Ross, trans., revised by J. O. Urmson, rev. Oxford ed. 1984).

6. See *Philosophical Writings of Peirce* (J. Bochler, ed., 1940); William James, *Pragmatism: A New Name for Some Old Ways of Thinking* (1907), analyzed and applied to legal reasoning in Michael Brint and William Weaver, eds., *Pragmatism in Law and Society* (1991) (esp. chaps. by Thomas Grey, Richard Posner, Margaret Radin, Richard Rorty, and David Hoy); Daniel A. Farber and Philip P. Frickey, "Practical Reason and the First Amendment," 34 *University of California at Los Angeles Law Review* 1615 (1987).

7. Arthur Phelps, "Factors Influencing Judges in Interpreting Statutes," 3 *Vanderbilt Law Review* 456, 469 (1950); see also Gray, *Sources of the Law*, 124–125, 172; Curtis, "A Better Theory of Interpretation," 415.

8. Aristotle, *Nicomachean Ethics*, bk. 6, chaps. 5–11 ("practical wisdom"); Ronald Beiner, *Political Judgment* 72–82 (1983).

9. House Conference Report no. 93-1597, 93d Cong., 2d sess., 9 (1974). For legislative debate, see 120 *Congressional Record* 2379 (1974) (House); id. at 3075–83 (Senate).

10. Immigration and Nationality Act of 1952, §212(a)(4), 66 Stat. 163, 182 (1952), codified at 8 U.S.C. §1182(a)(4), amended by act of October 3, 1965, Public Law no. 89-236, §15(b), 79 Stat. 911, 919 (1965), repealed by Immigration Act of 1990, Public Law no. 101-649, §601, 104 Stat. 4978, 5067 (1990).

11. Senate Report no. 1137, 82d Cong., 1st sess., 9 (1951); see Report of the Public Health Service on the Medical Aspects of H.R. 2379, attached to House Report no. 1365, 82d Cong., 2d sess., 47 (1952), reprinted in 1952 *United States Code Congressional and Administrative News*, 1653, 1701.

12. 302 F.2d 652, 657–658 (9th Cir. 1962), vacated and remanded on other grounds, 374 U.S. 449 (1963).

13. Act of October 3, 1965, Public Law no. 89-236, §15(b), 79 Stat. 911, 919 (new language emphasized).

14. Boutilier v. INS, 363 F. 2d 488, 490–492 (2d Cir. 1966) (describing medical affidavits), affirmed, 387 U.S. 118 (1967).

15. 387 U.S. 118 (1967).

16. American Psychiatric Association, *Diagnostic and Statistical Manual: Mental Disorders* 38–39 (1952) (characterizing homosexuality as a "sociopathic personality disturbance"); Edmund Bergler, *Homosexuality: Disease or Way of Life?* 28–29 (1956); Charles Socarides, *The Overt Homosexual* 6 (1968).

17. *Fleuti*, 302 F.2d at 658 and n.19 (citing medical experts discrediting "psychopathic personality" as a useful medical term); see Evelyn Hooker, "Male Homosexuality in the Rorschach," 22 *Journal of Projective Techniques* 33–54 (1958);

Evelyn Hooker, "The Adjustment of the Overt Male Homosexual," 21 *Journal of Projective Techniques* 18 (1957).

18. *Boutilier*, 363 F.2d at 497–498 (Moore, J., dissenting from the Second Circuit's decision), adopted in *Boutilier*, 387 U.S. at 125 (Brennan, J., dissenting from the Supreme Court's decision).

19. See Ronald Bayer, *Homosexuality and American Psychiatry: The Politics of Diagnosis*, 101–178 (1981).

20. The PHS relied on the 1974 and 1979 editions of the *Diagnostic and Statistical Manual: Mental Disorders* of the American Psychiatric Association, which stated that "homosexuality per se is one form of sexual behavior, and with other forms of sexual behavior which are not by themselves psychiatric disorders are not listed in this nomenclature." Memorandum from Julius B. Richmond, Assistant Secretary for Health and Surgeon General, to Dr. William Foege, Director, Centers for Disease Control, and Dr. George I. Lythcott, administrator, HSA (August 2, 1979), reprinted in 56 *Interpreter's Releases* 387 (1979). The memorandum also argued that the PHS could not in good faith continue to enforce the prior policy because "[t]he determination of homosexuality is not made through a medical diagnostic procedure."

21. See 8 U.S.C. §§1222, 1224 (1988) (repealed 1990).

22. Id. §1226(d) (if the PHS certifies that an immigrant "is afflicted with . . . any mental disease, defect, or disability" excludable under §212(a)(1)–(5), the INS decision to exclude "shall be based *solely* upon such certification"; emphasis added). Contrast id. §1225(a) ("inspection, other than the physical or mental examination," shall be done by INS).

23. Memorandum Opinion for the Acting Commissioner, INS (no. 79-85), 3 *Opinions of the Office of Legal Counsel* 457, 462 (1979).

24. See 62 *Interpreter's Releases* 166, 166–167 (1985).

25. 714 F.2d 1470 (9th Cir. 1983).

26. 716 F.2d 1439 (5th Cir. 1983), cert. denied, 467 U.S. 1219 (1984).

27. Immigration Act of 1990, Public law no. 101-649, §601, 104 Stat. 4978, 5067 (1990); see 135 *Congressional Record* S5040–42 (daily ed., May 9, 1989) (statement of Senator Simpson, R-Wyo., indicating that view of homosexuality as a "disease" was obsolete and old §212[a][4] was no longer acceptable policy).

28. Eskridge and Frickey, "Statutory Interpretation as Practical Reasoning," 353; see id. at 345–362.

29. Nicholas S. Zeppos, "The Use of Authority in Statutory Interpretation: An Empirical Analysis," 70 *Texas Law Review* 1073 (1992).

30. W. V. Quine and J. S. Ullian, *The Web of Belief* (1970); see Steven J. Burton, *An Introduction to Law and Legal Reasoning* 132–136 (1985).

31. Charles Sanders Peirce, *Collected Papers*, vol. 5, par. 264 (C. Hartshorne and P. Weiss, eds., 1960).

32. See Sanford Levinson and Steven Mailloux, eds., *Interpreting Law and Liter-

ature: A Hermeneutic Reader (1988); W. J. T. Mitchell, ed., *The Politics of Interpretation* (1983); "Interpretation Symposium," 58 *Southern California Law Review* 1 (1985); "Symposium: Law and Literature," 60 *Texas Law Review* 373 (1982); Francis J. Mootz III, "The Ontological Basis of Legal Hermeneutics: A Proposed Model of Inquiry Based on the Work of Gadamer, Habermas, and Ricoeur," 68 *Boston University Law Review* 523, 527–556 (1988); Dennis M. Patterson, "Wittgenstein and the Code: A Theory of Good Faith Performance and Enforcement under Article Nine," 137 *University of Pennsylvania Law Review* 335 (1988).

33. My discussion of hermeneutics is based mostly on Hans-Georg Gadamer, *Truth and Method* (Joel Weinsheimer and Donald Marshall, trans., 2d rev. English ed. 1989), analyzed in Georgia Warnke, *Gadamer: Hermeneutics, Tradition, and Reason* (1987). See also Diane Michelfelder and Robert R. Palmer, eds., *Dialogue and Deconstruction: The Gadamer-Derrida Encounter* (1989); Richard Bernstein, *Beyond Objectivism and Relativism: Science, Hermeneutics, and Praxis* (1983).

34. Horizon is context, "the range of vision that includes everything that can be seen from a particular vantage point," Gadamer, *Truth and Method*, 302, including "everything of which one is not immediately aware and of which one must in fact remain unaware if there is to be a focus of attention." Joel Weinsheimer, *Gadamer's Hermeneutics: A Reading of "Truth and Method"* 157 (1985).

35. See generally Miriam Allott, ed., *The Brontës: The Critical Heritage* (1974) (collection of nineteenth-century reviews of *Jane Eyre*).

36. See, e.g., Linda R. Hirshman, "Brontë, Bloom, and Bork: An Essay on the Moral Education of Judges," 137 *University of Pennsylvania Law Review* 177 (1988); Adrienne Rich, "Jane Eyre: The Temptations of a Motherless Woman," in *On Lies, Secrets, and Silence*, 89 (1979).

37. It is suggested by other passages as well. For example, the consumptive Helen dies while holding Jane in her arms like "a little child." As a matter of the novel's general themes, it is interesting to contrast the love Helen and Miss Temple bear for Jane with the love offered by St. John and Rochester later in the novel. The women offer love openly and generously; the men are not open (Rochester deceives Jane, and St. John deceives both himself and Jane) and seem more selfish in their dealings with Jane. They want her to play a role in their scenarios, whereas the women help Jane construct her own role.

38. See Anita L. Allen, "The Jurisprudence of *Jane Eyre*," 15 *Harvard Women's Law Journal* 173 (1992).

39. See Lillian Faderman, *Surpassing the Love of Men: Romantic Friendship and Love between Women from the Renaissance to the Present* (1981).

40. Gadamer, *Truth and Method*, 304.

41. Id. at 269.

42. Id. at 304.

43. Id. at 306.

44. Gadamer, *Truth and Method*, 517 (supplement 1 to the 2d ed., *Hermeneutics*

and Historicism [1965]). See also Richard A. Posner, *Law and Literature: A Relation Reargued* (1987).

45. See Hooker, "Male Homosexuality in the Rorschach" (psychiatrists could not distinguish the "homosexuals" from the "heterosexuals" by standard tests).

46. See Jonathan Katz, *Gay American History: Lesbians and Gay Men in the U.S.A.*, 197–316 (1976) (pt. 2, *Treatment, 1884–1974*).

47. See David Couzens Hoy, "Interpreting the Law: Hermeneutical and Post-structuralist Perspectives," 58 *Southern California Law Review* 135 (1985); Mootz, "Legal Hermeneutics"; Dennis M. Patterson, "Interpretation in Law—Toward a Reconstruction of the Current Debate," 29 *Villanova Law Review* 671 (1984); James Boyd White, "Law as Language: Reading Law and Reading Literature," 60 *Texas Law Review* 415 (1982).

48. Compare Boutilier v. INS, 363 F.2d 488 (2d Cir. 1966) (majority opinion by Kaufman, J.), affirmed, 387 U.S. 118 (1967), with id. at 496–498 (Moore, J., dissenting).

49. 363 F.2d at 497–498 (Moore, J., dissenting).

50. 363 F.2d at 496 n.15 (opinion of the court).

51. Senate Report no. 1137, 82d Cong., 2d sess., 9 (1952); see also House Report no. 1365, 82d Cong., 2d sess., 42–48 (1952), reprinted in 1952 *United States Code Congress and Administrative News*, 1653, 1701.

52. 1952 Senate Report, 9, quoted in *Boutilier*, 363 F.2d at 493.

53. Report of the Public Health Service on the Medical Aspects of H.R. 2379, appended to 1952 House Report, 48, reprinted in 1952 *United States Code Congress and Administrative News*, 1653, 1700 (emphasis added).

54. Gadamer, *Truth and Method*, 291; see David Couzens Hoy, *The Critical Circle: Literature, History, and Philosophical Hermeneutics* (1978); Warnke, *Gadamer*, 82–91.

55. Gadamer, *Truth and Method*, 329 (footnote omitted).

56. See E. D. Hirsch, "Meaning and Significance Reinterpreted," 11 *Critical Inquiry* 202, 216 (1984); Steven Knapp and Walter Benn Michaels, "Against Theory 2: Hermeneutics and Deconstruction," 14 *Critical Inquiry* 49 (1987).

57. Paul Ricoeur, "The Hermeneutical Function of Distanciation," in *Hermeneutics and the Human Sciences: Essays on Language, Action, and Interpretation*, 131–144 (John Thompson, ed. and trans., 1981).

58. See Hirsch, "Significance Reinterpreted," 218.

59. Warnke, *Gadamer*, 79; see Gadamer, *Truth and Method*, 276 (charge of subjectivity "is a distorting mirror" because the personal views of particular individuals are "only a flickering in the closed circuits of historical life").

60. Gadamer, *Truth and Method*, 329–330; see Stanley Fish, *Is There a Text in This Class?* (1980) (community of interpretation reflects constraints on interpreter).

61. See Gary Peller, "The Metaphysics of American Law," 73 *California Law Review* 1151 (1985).

62. See my review essay "A Social Constructionist Critique of Posner's *Sex and Reason:* Steps toward a Gaylegal Agenda," 102 *Yale Law Journal* 333 (1992); and see the medical sources in note 16.

63. See, e.g., Thomas Szasz, *The Manufacture of Madness* 170–174 (1970) (demonstrating that "psychiatric opinion about homosexuals is not a scientific proposition but a medical prejudice"); Judd Marmor, *Homosexual Behavior* (1980).

64. The original statute, act of June 27, 1872, chap. 322, §35, 17 Stat. 269, required a double wage penalty but only up to ten days' worth of double wages, and courts had discretion to award less than that (but not more). The act of December 21, 1898, chap. 28, §4, 30 Stat. 756, did three things: it changed the penalty from double wages to single wages (which Congress changed back to double wages in 1915); it eliminated the ten-day cap on the penalty period; and it eliminated reference to judicial discretion to shorten the penalty period. In *Griffin* the seaman obtained reemployment after about a month, but the Court held that the penalty period extended over several years, until judgment in the case. The 1898 Congress would have been astounded by such a result, given the very short penalty period contemplated in the 1872 act and the routine nature of the 1898 revision (no mention that this would result in a penalty period fifty or one hundred times the old ten-day cap), the controversial nature of punitive damages in law at the end of the nineteenth century, and the equities of the case, in which the seaman obtained reemployment within a month and the shipowner delayed payment because it contested the seaman's charge that the wages had been withheld "unlawfully."

65. See Charles Foster, "Rule 609(a) in the Civil Contest: A Recommendation for Reform," 57 *Fordham Law Review* 1 (1988).

66. Proposed new Rule 609(a)(1) was reported in the March 1, 1990, advance sheets for the *Supreme Court Reporter,* cxxvii. When Congress did not override the proposed rule within the statutory period, the Court reported that the new rule went into effect on December 1, 1990.

67. Apologies to Richard A. Posner, "Legal Reasoning from the Top Down and from the Bottom Up: The Question of Unenumerated Constitutional Rights," 59 *University of Chicago Law Review* 433 (1992), and Mari J. Matsuda, "Looking to the Bottom: Critical Legal Studies and Reparations," 22 *Harvard Civil Rights–Civil Liberties Law Review* 323 (1987).

68. See, e.g., Ronald Dworkin, *Law's Empire* (1986); Guido Calabresi, *A Common Law for the Age of Statutes* (1982).

69. Edward L. Rubin, "Law and Legislation in the Administrative State," 89 *Columbia Law Review* 369 (1989); Edward L. Rubin, "The Concept of Law and the New Public Law Scholarship," 89 *Michigan Law Review* 792 (1991); see Peter L. Strauss, "When the Judge Is Not the Primary Official with Responsibility to Read: Agency Interpretation and the Problem of Legislative History," 66 *Chicago-Kent Law Review* 321 (1990).

70. I have no direct evidence for this. In the late 1980s, when I was originally researching this topic, my associates and I spoke to several representatives of the

PHS, who admitted to some degree of embarrassment that the agency had ever cooperated in identifying and excluding bisexuals, gay men, and lesbians as afflicted with "psychopathic personality" or "sexual deviation." Although their level of embarrassment was surely less keen in the 1970s, they suggested that PHS doctors were unenthusiastic about the policy then as well, for similar professional and cultural reasons.

71. Michel Foucault, *Introduction*, vol. 1 of *History of Sexuality*, 94 (Robert Hurley, trans., 1978).

72. On the Stonewall riots and the ensuing politics of "coming out," see Martin Duberman, *Stonewall* (1993); John D'Emilio, *Sexual Politics, Sexual Communities: The Making of a Homosexual Minority in the United States, 1940–1970* (1983); Lillian Faderman, *Odd Girls and Twilight Lovers: A History of Lesbian Life in Twentieth-Century America* (1991). On Kameny's stunt, see Bayer, *Homosexuality and American Psychiatry*, 104–107. On the process by which the APA reversed its official stance toward homosexuality as an illness, see id. at 101–154.

73. This story is influenced by archival research set forth in Hugh Davis Graham, *The Civil Rights Era: Origins and Development of National Policy, 1960–1972* (1990), reviewed by Neal Devins, "The Civil Rights Hydra," 89 *Michigan Law Review* 1723 (1991).

74. See Civil Rights Act of 1964, §§703(a)(1), 706(g), 42 U.S.C. §§2000e-2(a)(1), -5(g) (1988); 110 *Congressional Record* 12,724 (1964) (statement of Senator Humphrey, D-Minn.).

75. See Civil Rights Act of 1964, §706(a)–(f), 42 U.S.C. §2000e-5(a)–(f) (1988); Graham, *The Civil Rights Era*, 146–149.

76. 2 *Public Papers: Lyndon B. Johnson, 1965*, 636 (1966) (June 1965 speech by President Johnson at Howard University).

77. See White House Conference on Equal Educational Opportunity (EEOC, 1965). Several key agency players published explications and defenses of this ideology. See EEOC Executive Director Herman Edelsberg, "Title VII of the Civil Rights Act: The First Year," 19 *New York University Conference on Labor* 289–295 (1967), and EEOC staff member Alfred W. Blumrosen, *Black Employment and the Law* (1971).

78. Memorandum from EEOC staff attorney Sonia Pressman to EEOC General Counsel Charles T. Duncan, May 31, 1966, quoted in Graham, *The Civil Rights Era*, 244–247.

79. EEOC Commissioner Samuel C. Jackson, "EEOC vs. Discrimination, Inc.," *Crisis* 16–17 (January 1968).

80. See, e.g., Quarles v. Phillip Morris, Inc., 279 F. Supp. 505 (E.D. Va. 1968).

81. 292 F. Supp. 243 (M.D.N.C. 1968), affirmed, 420 F.2d 1225 (4th Cir. 1970), reversed, 401 U.S. 424 (1971). The litigation is analyzed from the EEOC's point of view in Alfred W. Blumrosen, "Strangers in Paradise: *Griggs v. Duke Power Co.* and the Concept of Employment Discrimination," 71 *Michigan Law Review* 59 (1972).

82. *Griggs*, 420 F.2d at 1239–44 (Sobeloff, J., dissenting).

83. For support, see my articles "Reneging on History? Playing the Court/Congress/President Civil Rights Game," 79 *California Law Review* 613 (1991); "Overriding Supreme Court Statutory Interpretation Decisions," 101 *Yale Law Journal* 331, 391–397 (1991). For argument that a Court protecting original legislative expectations would attend to current legislative preferences, see John Ferejohn and Barry Weingast, "Limitation of Statutes: Strategic Statutory Interpretation," 80 *Georgetown Law Journal* 565 (1992).

84. See Brian A. Marks, "A Model of Judicial Influence on Congressional Policymaking: *Grove City College v. Bell*" (Ph.D. diss., Washington University, 1989), as well as John Ferejohn and Charles Shipan, "Congressional Influence on Bureaucracy," 6 *Journal of Law, Economics, and Organization* 1 (1990) (special issue); Ferejohn and Weingast, "Limitation of Statutes"; Pablo T. Spiller and Rafael Gely, "Congressional Control of Judicial Independence: The Determinants of U.S. Supreme Court Labor Decisions, 1949/1988" (July 1991).

85. The evidence for this proposition is the subsequent history of Fleuti v. Rosenberg, 302 F.2d 652 (9th Cir. 1962), where the appeals court ruled that the PHS could not enforce §212(a)(4) against gay men and lesbians without a clearer text. The PHS persuaded Congress to override *Fleuti* by amending §212(a)(4) to add "sexual orientation" to the list of medically excludable offenses. Act of October 3, 1965, Public Law no. 89-236, §15(b), 79 Stat. 911, 919 (1965).

86. See Jon Elster, *Sour Grapes* (1983); Amartya Sen, *Inequality Reexamined* (1992).

87. See Keith Krehbiel, *Information and Legislative Organization* (1991); Robert Katzmann, *Institutional Disability: The Saga of Transportation Policy for the Disabled* (1986); John W. Kingdon, *Agendas, Alternatives, and Public Policies* (1984); Arthur Maass, *Congress and the Common Good* (1980).

88. Positive political theory suggests that Congress would limit the agency's ability to shift policy immediately, through procedural as well as substantive provisions in the statute. See Matthew D. McCubbins, Roger G. Noll, and Barry R. Weingast, "Administrative Procedures as Instruments of Political Control," 3 *Journal of Law, Economics, and Organization* 243 (1987). Dirksen tried to do this with the EEOC by insisting on procedural rules limiting the EEOC's policymaking power.

89. Barbara Sinclair, "Agenda, Policy, and Alignment Change from Coolidge to Reagan," in Lawrence C. Dodd and Bruce I. Oppenheimer, eds., *Congress Reconsidered*, 291, 306–307 (3d ed. 1985).

90. See House Report no. 238, 92d Cong., 1st sess., 21–22 (1971), reprinted in 1972 *United States Code Congress and Administrative News*, 2137, 2156–57; Senate Report no. 415, 92d Cong., 1st sess., 14 (1971).

91. See Krehbiel, *Information and Legislative Organization*, 129 (Table 4.6) (House); Eskridge, "Overriding Statutory Decisions," 369 n.114 (Senate).

92. See Washington v. Davis, 426 U.S. 229 (1976) (disparate impact discrimination not actionable under equal protection clause); Personnel Administrator of Massachusetts v. Feeney, 442 U.S. 256 (1979) (applying *Davis* to constitutional gender discrimination cases). For the preference shift within the Court, see Jeffrey A. Segal and Albert D. Cover, "Ideological Values and the Votes of U.S. Supreme Court Justices," 83 *American Political Science Review* 557, 560 (1989) (Table 1).

93. Sinclair, "Alignment Change," 307 (big jump in civil liberties scores for House members, 1973–1976).

94. The Pregnancy Discrimination Act of 1978, Public Law no. 95-555, 92 Stat. 2076 (1978), overriding General Electric Co. v. Gilbert, 429 U.S. 125 (1976); see Eskridge, "Reneging on History," for analysis of this and other overrides of Burger Court decisions.

95. See Wygant v. Jackson Board of Education, 476 U.S. 267 (1986) (very stingy view of affirmative action under Fourteenth Amendment, by Powell, who joined the opinion in *Johnson,* and by O'Connor, who concurred in *Johnson's* judgment); Regents of the University of California v. Bakke, 438 U.S. 265 (1978) (balancing approach to affirmative action by Powell; Stewart, who joined *Weber,* voted against any affirmative action under Fourteenth Amendment, as did Stevens, who joined *Johnson* but did not vote in *Weber*).

96. This was implicit in *Weber's* refusal to credit the historical evidence marshaled by Justice Rehnquist. See *Weber,* 443 U.S. at 209–210 (Blackmun, J., concurring). It was explicit in *Johnson,* 480 U.S. at 629 n.7. Indeed, a proposal to override *Weber* in 1981 received the most slender support I have ever seen in formal congressional hearings. See *Affirmative Action and Equal Protection: Hearings before the Subcommittee on the Constitution of the Senate Committee on the Judiciary,* 97th Cong., 1st sess. (1981).

97. See Eskridge, "Overriding Statutory Decisions," 390 (thesis), 391–397 (evidence from interpretations of civil rights laws), 397–403 (evidence from Court's selective use of stare decisis and other doctrines).

98. This immediate shift was revealed in 1981 committee hearings which started out critical of the Burger Court's interpretation of §1983, see *Municipal Liability under 42 U.S.C. §1983: Hearings before the Subcommittee on the Constitution of the Senate Committee on the Judiciary,* 97th Cong., 1st sess., 1–2 (1981), but after reviewing the Court's decisions in 1981 concluded that the Court was responsive to conservative concerns. Id. at 380, 404–406, 444, 450–452, 458. Of the sixty-two civil rights decisions handed down by the Court in the 1980–1983 terms, 41 percent reached conservative results and 26 percent liberal results (the rest unclear). Contrast the thirty-seven civil rights decisions in the 1977–1979 terms (and decided by the same group of Justices), of which 33 percent reached conservative results and 47 percent liberal results (the rest unclear). Eskridge, "Overriding Statutory Decisions," 396 n.205.

99. 490 U.S. 642 (1989).

100. *Wards Cove* did not overrule *Griggs* explicitly and did not reject the disparate impact cause of action created by *Griggs*. Instead, *Wards Cove* redefined the plaintiff's burden of proof and the defendant's defenses in ways that made disparate impact cases much harder for plaintiffs to win.

101. President Bush vetoed the Civil Rights Act of 1990, whose primary goal was to override *Wards Cove*. His veto was sustained by the narrowest possible margin (sixty-six to thirty-four—one vote) in the Senate. See 136 *Congressional Record* S16,589 (daily ed., October 24, 1990).

102. Public Law no. 102-166, 105 Stat. 1071 (1991).

3. A Case Study

1. On this phenomenon generally, see Felix Frankfurter and Nathan Greene, *The Labor Injunction* (1930), as well as Daniel Robinson Ernst, "The Lawyers and the Labor Trust: A History of the American Anti-Boycott Association, 1902–1919" (Ph.D. diss., Princeton University, 1989); William E. Forbath, *Law and the Labor Movement* (1991); David Montgomery, *The Fall of the House of Labor: The Workplace, the State, and American Labor Activism, 1865–1925* (1987).

2. See Robert V. Bruce, *1877: Year of Violence* (1959); Gerald Gordon Eggert, *Railroad Labor Disputes: The Beginnings of Federal Strike Policy*, 24–53 (1967); Philip Foner, *The Great Labor Uprising of 1877* (1977); Karen Orren, *Belated Feudalism: Labor, the Law, and Liberal Development in the United States*, 164–171 (1991).

3. Bertholf v. O'Reilly, 74 N.Y. 509, 511 (1878); cases cited in note 5. For the views of two state judges, see Thomas M. Cooley, *A Treatise on the Constitutional Limitations Which Rest upon Legislative Power of the States of the American Union* (1868); David Josiah Brewer, "On the Individual and the State" (address June 16, 1883) (David Brewer Papers, Yale University, Document 3-126).

4. See Thomas M. Cooley, "Labor and Capital before the Law," 137 *North American Review* 506–508 (1884), and "Arbitration in Labor Disputes," 1 *Forum* 308 (1886).

5. State v. Donaldson, 32 N.J. 151 (1867) (conspiracy); Carew v. Rutherford, 106 Mass. 1 (1870) (civil damages); see Edwin E. Witte, "Early American Labor Cases," 43 *Yale Law Journal* 825, 829 (1935) (collecting other cases).

6. Thomas M. Cooley, "New Aspects of the Right to Trial by Jury," 11 *American Law Review* 705 (1877). See Clarence E. Bonnett, "The Origin of the Labor Injunction," 5 *Southern California Law Review* 105, 123 (1931).

7. See Eggert, *Railroad Labor Disputes*, 44–46; Walter Nelles, "A Strike and Its Legal Consequences—An Examination of the Receivership Precedent for the Labor Injunction," 40 *Yale Law Journal* 507 (1931). Drummund's order is reported in Secor v. Toledo, Peoria & Warsaw Rairoad, 21 Fed. Cas. 968 (C.C.N.D. Ill.

1877), and Gresham's order in King v. Ohio & Maine Railway, 14 Fed. Cas. 539 (C.C.D. Ind. 1877).

8. See [Pennsylvania Railroad President] Thomas Scott, "The Recent Strikes," 125 *North American Review* 351 (1877).

9. *Congressional Record*, 49th Cong., 1st sess., 4240, 4353, 4355–57 (1887), discussed in Eggert, *Railroad Labor Disputes*, 69–71.

10. See Donald L. McMurry, "The Legal Ancestry of the Pullman Strike Injunctions," 14 *Industrial and Labor Relations Review* 235, 239 (1961).

11. See Beers v. Wabash, St. Louis & Pacific Railway, 34 F. 244 (C.C.N.D. Ind. 1888), and Chicago, Burlington & Quincy Railway v. Burlington, C.R. & N. Railway, 34 F. 481 (S.D. Iowa 1888).

12. *Chicago, Burlington*, 34 F. at 481 (Judge Love); Toledo, Ann Arbor & New Mexico Railway v. Pennsylvania Co., 54 F. 730 (C.C.N.D. Ohio 1893) (Judge Taft).

13. Old Dominion Steam-Ship Co. v. McKenna, 30 F. 48, 50 (S.D.N.Y. 1887); see In re Higgins, 27 F. 443, 445 (C.C.N.D. Tex. 1886).

14. In re Doolittle, 23 F. 544, 547 (C.C.E.D. Mo. 1885); see also United States v. Kane, 23 F. 748 (C.C.D. Colo. 1885).

15. David Josiah Brewer, "The Liberty of Each Individual" (address July 4, 1893) (David Brewer Papers, Yale University, Document 3-133). Other Justices expressed similar libertarian fears. E.g., Henry Billings Brown, "The Twentieth Century" (1895 address at Yale University, where Brown and Brewer were classmates).

16. Cooley, "Labor and Capital," 508; see id. at 509.

17. Henry Billings Brown, "The Distribution of Property," in *Report of the Sixteenth Annual Meeting of the American Bar Association* 213, 237 (1893); accord, David Josiah Brewer, "The Nation's Safeguard," in *Proceedings of the New York State Bar Association* 37, 39 (Sixteenth Annual Meeting, January 17–18, 1893) (David Brewer Papers, Yale University, Document 3-132).

18. 21 *Congressional Record* 2456–2562, 2556–72 (1890).

19. See Hans Thorelli, *The Federal Antitrust Policy: Origination of an American Tradition*, 231–232 (1954); Charles Gregory, *Labor and the Law*, 206 (1946).

20. See House Select Committee, "Labor Troubles in the Anthracite Regions, 1887–8, Strikes and Lock-Outs in Pennsylvania," House Report no. 4147, 50th Cong., 2d sess., xxx (1889); Eggert, *Railroad Labor Disputes*, 98–103 (similar views held by Cooley when he headed ICC).

21. United States v. Patterson, 55 F. 605, 641 (C.C.D. Mass. 1893); Blindell v. Hagan, 54 F. 40 (C.C.E.D. La. 1893); letter from Richard S. Olney to D. S. Alexander, May 1, 1893, quoted in Gerald Gordon Eggert, "Richard Olney, Corporation Lawyer and Attorney General of the United States, 1893–1895," 386 (Ph.D. diss., University of Michigan, 1960).

22. See Arnold Paul, *Conservative Crisis and the Rule of Law: Attitudes of Bar and*

Bench, 1887–1895 (1960); Dianne Avery, "Images of Violence in Labor Jurisprudence: The Regulation of Picketing and Boycotts, 1894–1921," 37 *Buffalo Law Review* 1 (1988–89).

23. United States v. Workingmen's Amalgamated Council of New Orleans, 54 F. 994, 995 (C.C.E.D. La.), affirmed, 57 F. 85 (5th Cir. 1893).

24. Farmers' Loan & Trust Co. v. Northern Pacific Railroad Co., 60 F. 803, 809 (first quote), 821 (second quote) (E.D. Wis. 1894).

25. Arthur v. Oakes, 63 F. 310, 317–318 (7th Cir. 1894). Compare Plessy v. Ferguson, 163 U.S. 537, 552 (1896) (Harlan, J., dissenting).

26. Ames v. Union Pacific, 62 F. 7 (C.C.D. Neb. 1894).

27. The best contemporary account is United States Strike Commission, "Report on the Chicago Strike of June–July 1894," 53d Cong., 3d sess. (1895). See also Ray Ginger, *The Bending Cross: A Biography of Eugene Victor Debs* (1949); Almont Lindsey, *The Pullman Strike* (1939); Nicholas Salvatore, *Eugene V. Debs: Citizen and Socialist* (1982); Donald McMurry, "Labor Policies of the General Managers' Association of Chicago, 1886–1894," 13 *Journal of Economic History* 160 (1953).

28. See Thomas v. Cincinnati, Northern Ohio & Toledo Pacific Railway, 62 F. 803 (C.C.S.D. Ohio 1894) (Taft, J.); United States v. Elliott, 64 F. 27 (C.C.E.D. Mo. 1894) (Phillips, J.); In re Grand Jury, 62 F. 834 (S.D. Cal. 1894) (Ross, J.); United States v. Cassidy, 57 F. 698 (N.D. Cal. 1894) (Morrow, J.); United States v. Agler, 62 F. 824 (C.C.D. Ind. 1894) (Baker, J.).

29. Letter from William Howard Taft to Helen H. Taft (1894), quoted in Judith Icke Anderson, *William Howard Taft: An Intimate History*, 63 (1981).

30. Wire from Richard Olney to Edwin Walker, July 1, 1894, quoted in Eggert, "Richard Olney," 410. See also Gerald G. Eggert, *Richard Olney: Evolution of a Statesman* (1974).

31. Quoted in In re Debs, 158 U.S. 564, 570–571 (1895).

32. United States v. Debs, 64 F.724 (C.C.N.D. Ill. 1894), affirmed, 158 U.S. 564 (1895).

33. *Debs*, 158 U.S. at 582.

34. See United States v. Trans-Missouri Freight Association, 166 U.S. 290, 356 (1897) (White, J., dissenting); Loewe v. Lawlor, 208 U.S. 274 (1908).

35. Samuel Gompers, "Labor Organizations Must Not Be Outlawed—The Supreme Court's Decision in the Hatters' Case," 15 *American Federationist* 185–187 (March 1908). (Members of the Sherman Act Congress "again and again" assured labor that the statute would not apply to union actions.)

36. H. M. Gitelman, "Adolph Strasser and the Origins of Pure and Simple Unionism," 6 *Labor History* 71, 81 (1965); see Philip S. Foner, *History of the Labor Movement in the United States: From the Founding of the American Federation of Labor to the Emergence of American Imperialism*, 279–299, 345–368 (1955); Forbath, *Law and Labor Movement*; Herbert G. Gutman, "The Workers' Search for Power," in

The Gilded Age (H. W. Morgan rev. ed. 1970); Fred Greenbaum, "The Social Ideas of Samuel Gompers," 7 *Labor History* 35 (1966).

37. 156 U.S. 1 (1895).

38. 4 *American Federationist* 30 (1897) (Gompers editorial criticizing United States v. Trans-Missouri Freight, 166 U.S. 290 [1897], whose per se rule Gompers feared would extend to union activity).

39. 5 *American Federationist* 73, 75 (1898).

40. 28 *Congressional Record* 24, 54, 1001, 1072, 1163, 1214 (1896).

41. See 2 Arthur M. Schlesinger, Jr., and Fred L. Israel, eds., *History of American Presidential Elections, 1789–1968*, 1830 (1971) (reproducing Democrats' 1896 platform).

42. Pollock v. Farmer's Loan and Trust Co., 157 U.S. 429 (1895) (Court by 5–4 vote invaldiated federal income tax).

43. 2 Schlesinger and Israel, *Presidential Elections*, 1843 (Populist platform 1896, attacking "arbitrary judicial action," including "ruling by injunction"). The Populists had attacked the "Imperial Supreme Court" in the 1892 election as well. See James Weaver, *A Call to Action*, 133–135 (1892) (attack by the party's nominee).

44. Gilbert C. Fite, "Election of 1896," in 2 Schlesinger and Israel, *Presidential Elections*, 1787, 1823–24; Allan Westin, "The Supreme Court, the Populist Movement, and the Campaign of 1896," 15 *Journal of Politics* 3, 35–38 (1953). Conservative Democrats founded the National Democratic party, which endorsed the gold standard and free and independent courts: "We condemn all efforts to degrade that tribunal [the Court], or impair the confidence and respect with which it has been deservedly held." 2 Schlesinger and Israel, *Presidential Elections*, 1838.

45. Hopkins v. Oxley Stave Co., 83 F. 912, 931, 933, 936 (8th Cir. 1897) (Caldwell, J., dissenting). For other judicial critics, see also [North Carolina Supreme Court Justice] Walter Clark, "Constitutional Changes Which Are Foreshadowed," 30 *American Law Review* 702 (1896); Witte, "Early American Labor Cases," 835 and n.46.

46. Vegelahn v. Guntner, 167 Mass. 92, 106 (1896) (Holmes, J., dissenting); see also Plant v. Woods, 176 Mass. 492 (1900) (debate between court majority and Holmes, again in dissent). This idea had earlier been developed in Oliver Wendell Holmes, Jr., "Privilege, Malice, and Intent," 8 *Harvard Law Review* 1, 9 (1894).

47. See Mogul Steamship Co. v. McGregor Gow & Co., [1892] App. Cas. 25 (1891); Allen v. Flood, [1898] App. Cas. 1 (1897).

48. 170 N.Y. 315 (1902). Chief Judge Alton Parker's opinion held that "if the motive be to destroy another's business in order to secure business for yourself, the motive is good." Id. at 326. He then invoked Holmes for the idea that "free competition is worth more to society than it costs, and, that, on this ground the infliction of damages is privileged." Id. at 330. The concurring opinion by Judge John Gray more explicitly invoked Holmes's incidental effects concept. A dissenting opinion invoked economic libertarian concepts and *Debs*.

49. In addition to *NPA*, see also Jones v. Van Winkle Gin & Machine Works, 131 Ga. 336, 340 (1908); Karges Furniture Co. v. Amalgamated Woodworkers, 165 Ind. 421 (1905); Marx and Haas Jeans Clothing Co. v. Watson, 168 Mo. 133 (1902); Booth v. Burgess, 72 N.J. Eq. 181 (1906); Jersey City Printing Co. v. Cassidy, 63 N.J. Eq. 759 (1902); State v. Van Pelt, 136 N.C. 633, 649 (1904); Everett Waddey Co. v. Richmond Typographical Union No. 90, 105 Va. 188 (1906); Master Builders' Association v. Domascio, 16 Colo. App. 25 (1902); Mills v. United States Printing Co. of Ohio, 99 A.D. 605 (1904).

50. Samuel Gompers, "Conflicting Decisions on Labor's Rights," 8 *American Federationist* 80, 81 (1901).

51. 195 U.S. 194 (1904).

52. Id. at 203.

53. United States v. Addyston Pipe & Steel Co., 85 F. 271, 282–283 (6th Cir. 1898) (Taft, J.), affirmed, 175 U.S. 211 (1899) (Sherman Act does not prohibit activity whose competitive harm is "ancillary" to its main goal of profit and business); see William D. Guthrie, "Constitutionality of the Sherman Anti-Trust Act of 1890," 11 *Harvard Law Review* 80 (1897). In Northern Securities Co. v. United States, 193 U.S. 197 (1904), four dissenting Justices (including Holmes) signed on to a "rule of reason" interpretation of the Sherman Act similar to Taft's concept of ancillarity. Concurring Justice Brewer believed the Sherman Act carried with it a rule of reason but that the practice in *Northern Securities* was unreasonable. Id. at 361. The Court adopted the rule of reason approach to business combinations in United States v. American Tobacco Co., 221 U.S. 106, 177 (1911).

54. See Iron Molders' Union Local 125 of Milwaukee, Wisconsin, v. Allis-Chalmers Co., 166 F. 45, 51 (7th Cir. 1908); National Fireproofing Co. v. Mason Builders' Association, 169 F. 259, 265 (2d Cir. 1909); Shine v. Fox Brothers Manufacturing Co., 156 F. 357 (8th Cir. 1907).

55. See Homer Cummings and Carl McFarland, *Federal Justice: Chapters in the History of Justice and the Federal Executive,* 444–455 (1937).

56. Beck v. Railway Teamsters' Protective Union, 118 Mich. 497, 525 (1898); see Barr v. Essex Trades Council, 53 N.J. Eq. 101 (1894).

57. See Hopkins v. Oxley Stave Co., 83 F. 912 (8th Cir. 1897) (over dissent by Caldwell, J.); Casey v. Cincinnati Typographical Union No. 3, 45 F. 135, 144 (S.D. Ohio 1891).

58. The New York courts essentially adopted this approach. See Butterick Publishing Co. v. Typographical Union No. 6, 50 Misc. 1 (Sup. Ct. 1906) (discussing cases); Sinsheimer v. United Garment Workers of America, 28 N.Y.S. 321 (Sup. Ct. 1894).

59. E.g. Boutwell v. Marr, 71 Vt. 1, 8 (1899). See also Emack v. Kane, 34 F. 46 (C.C.N.D. Ill. 1888); Brown & Allen v. Jacobs' Pharmacy Co., 115 Ga. 429, 431 (1902); Doremus v. Hennessey, 176 Ill. 608, 614 (1898); Ertz v. Produce Exchange, 79 Minn. 140 (1900); Olive v. Van Patten, 25 S.W. 428 (Tex. Civ. App. 1894).

60. Quinn v. Leatham, [1901] App. Cas. 495, 514 (Lord Shand).

61. See Daniel R. Ernst, "The *Danbury Hatters'* Case," in *Labor Law in America: Historical and Critical Essays*, 180 (Christopher L. Tomlins and Andrew J. King, eds., 1992).

62. Loewe v. California State Federation of Labor, 139 F. 71 (C.C.N.D. Cal. 1905).

63. 208 U.S. 274 (1908).

64. It appears that Holmes was willing to defer to the Sherman Act's independent evolution on these issues. See letter from Oliver Wendell Holmes, Jr., to Professor E. R. Thayer, Jaunary 13, 1915 (Oliver Wendell Holmes, Jr., Papers, Harvard University).

65. *Loewe*, 208 U.S. at 297. Although the Court had applied the Sherman Act against a trade restraint in Northern Securities Co. v. United States, 193 U.S. 197 (1904), five Justices had indicated that the Sherman Act should be interpreted under a "rule of reason" that would allow pro-competitive activities even though they had an incidental restraint on commerce. See note 53.

66. 208 U.S. 161 (1908).

67. This was an action brought in local District of Columbia courts, essentially, by the National Association of Manufacturers (NAM) and the AABA to restrain an AFL boycott of the Buck's Stove & Range Company, whose president was also NAM's chief officer. 35 Wash. L. Rep. 797 (D.C. 1907). Justice Ashley Gould granted a preliminary injunction against Gompers in December 1907, and made it permanent in March 1908. The story of this lawsuit is told in Ernst, "American Anti-Boycott Association," 177–213. See also Barry F. Helfand, "Labor and the Courts: The Common-Law Doctrine of Criminal Conspiracy and Its Application in the Buck's Stove Case," 18 *Labor History* 94 (1977).

68. *Amendment of the Sherman Antitrust Law: Hearings before the Senate Committee on the Judiciary*, 60th Cong., 1st sess., 6 (1908); *Hearings on House Bill 19,745, An Act to Regulate Commerce, etc.: Hearings before the House Committee on the Judiciary*, 60th Cong., 1st sess., 64 (1908).

69. See *Hearings on House Bill 19,745*, 234. He also warned Congress that *Loewe* could be interpreted to outlaw industrywide collective bargaining, or even labor unions themselves. Id. at 49–51.

70. 2 Schlesinger and Israel, *Presidential Elections*, 2021 (Socialist platform 1908); see id. at 2112 (People's party platform 1908).

71. Id. at 2096–97 (Republican platform 1908).

72. William Howard Taft, "Labor and Capital," in *Present-Day Problems: A Collection of Addresses Delivered on Various Occasions*, 241, 272 (1908).

73. 2 Schlesinger and Israel, *Presidential Elections*, 2096–97 (Democrats' platform 1908, calling for "rigid impartiality" in labor dispute cases).

74. AFL v. Buck's Stove & Range Co., 33 App. D.C. 83 (1909); Gompers v. Buck's Stove & Range Co., 33 App. D.C. 516 (1909); see Ernst, "American Anti-Boycott Association," 186–193.

75. See Daniel McHargue, "President Taft's Apointments to the Supreme Court," 12 *Journal of Politics* 478 (1950).

76. 221 U.S. 418 (1911).

77. Id. at 437–439.

78. Gompers v. United States, 233 U.S. 604 (1914).

79. This story is told from Taft's point of view in Paolo E. Coletta, *The Presidency of William Howard Taft* (1973), and from Roosevelt's point of view in George Mowry, *The Era of Theodore Roosevelt: 1900–1912* (1958).

80. See William Jennings Bryan, "The Reason," in *William Jennings Bryan: Selections*, 113, 120–122 (Ray Ginger, ed., 1967); Theodore Roosevelt, "Charter of Democracy," *New York Times*, 5 (February 22, 1912). Most of the talk focused on state judges. See George Mowry, *The California Progressives*, 149 (1951) (California in 1911 passed a law for the recall of judges).

81. 202 F. 512 (N.D. W. Va. 1912), reversed, 214 F. 685 (4th Cir. 1914), reversed in part, 245 U.S. 229 (1917).

82. The party platforms are in 2 Schlesinger and Israel, *Presidential Elections*, 2179 (Republican), 2188 (Progressive), 2173 (Democratic), and 2199 (Socialist).

83. See, e.g., Meier v. Speer, 96 Ark. 618 (1910); Cohn and Roth Electric Co. v. Bricklayers, Masons & Plasterers Local No. 1, 92 Conn. 161 (1917); Saulsberry v. Coopers International Union, 147 Ky. 170 (1912); Roddy v. United Mine Workers of America, 41 Okla. 621 (1914). *NPA* was rejected in other states, most prominently Massachusetts. See Folsom v. Lewis, 208 Mass. 336, 338 (1911).

84. Kemp v. Division No. 241, Amalgamated Association of Street & Electric Railway Employees of America, 255 Ill. 213, 235 (1912) (Carter, J., concurring).

85. 221 N.Y. 342, 358–359 (1917), followed in Reardon v. Caton, 189 A.D. 501 (1919), but distinguished in Auburn Draying Co. v. Wardell, 227 N.Y. 1 (1919).

86. Especially in the Seventh Circuit, which had authorized draconian labor injunctions through the 1880s and 1890s. Roosevelt appointees adopted the *NPA* approach in Iron Molders' Union No. 125 of Milwaukee v. Allis-Chalmers Co., 166 F. 45 (7th Cir. 1908), and Wilson appointees expanded it to picketing in Tri-City Central Trades Council v. American Steel Foundries, 238 F. 728 (7th Cir. 1916), reversed in part, 257 U.S. 184 (1921).

87. Mitchell v. Hitchman Coal & Coke Co., 214 F. 685 (4th Cir. 1914), reversed in part, 245 U.S. 229 (1917).

88. Id. at 698–699 (first quote), 704 (second quote).

89. Gill Engraving Co. v. Doerr, 214 F. 111, 117 (S.D.N.Y. 1914).

90. 169 F. 259, 265 (2d Cir. 1909).

91. 214 F. 82 (2d Cir. 1914), affirmed, 244 U.S. 459 (1917).

92. On the history of the labor provisions of the Clayton Act, see generally Daniel R. Ernst, "The Labor Exemption, 1908–1914," 74 *Iowa Law Review* 1151 (1989); Alpheus Mason, "The Labor Clauses of the Clayton Act," 18 *American Political Science Review* 489 (1924). See also 2 Earl W. Kintner, *The Legislative History of the Federal Antitrust Laws and Related Statutes*, pt. 1, *The Antitrust Laws* (1978).

93. Arthur S. Link, *Woodrow Wilson and the Progressive Era, 1910–1917*, 20 (1954); Stanley I. Kutler, "Labor, the Clayton Act, and the Supreme Court," 3 *Labor History* 19, 23–28 (1962).

94. See Ernst, "Labor Exemption," 1163–65.

95. The Webb amendment was soon thereafter changed to substitute "any law of the United States" for "antitrust laws."

96. This was adopted from an amendment proposed by Senator Albert Cummins, described in Ernst, "Labor Exemption," 1171–72.

97. Ernst, "Labor Exemption," 1165–67, discussing William Howard Taft, "Recent Anti-Trust and Labor Injunction Legislation," 39 *American Bar Association Report* 370, 380 (1914), and George Wickersham, "Labor Legislation in the Clayton Act," 22 *American Federationist* 493 (1915).

98. Samuel Gompers, "The Charter of Industrial Freedom," 21 *American Federationist* 971, 971–972 (1914).

99. Ernst, "American Anti-Boycott Association," especially chap. 8 and the conclusion.

100. 244 U.S. 459 (1917).

101. Id. at 471. The drafting history of *Paine Lumber* is significant. See Oliver Wendell Holmes, Jr., Papers, Harvard University, Reel 70. Holmes originally wrote an opinion for the Court which avoided the Sherman Act issues and held that the plain meaning of Clayton Act §§6 and 20 "establishes a policy inconsistent with the granting of [an injunction] here." He reasoned also: "The only restraint of trade attempted was such restraint as follows from the members of labor unions refusing to work with non-union men or upon materials made by non-union men, for the sole purpose of strengthening the union. As was said by the defendants, that refusal is the principle upon which labor unions are based." Holmes did not obtain a Court majority for this draft opinion and recirculated it as a draft dissent. Finally he wrote for the Court, but on the Sherman Act ground, not the Clayton Act.

102. Hitchman Coal and Coke Co. v. Mitchell, 245 U.S. 229, 256–259 (1917) (relying on old authorities invoked in *Buck's Stove*); Barry Cushman, "Doctrinal Synergies and Liberal Dilemmas: The Case of the Yellow-Dog Contract," 1992 *Supreme Court Review* 235; Daniel R. Ernst, "The Yellow-Dog Contract and Liberal Reform, 1917–1932," 30 *Labor History* 251 (1989).

103. Coppage v. Kansas, 236 U.S. 1 (1915) (invalidating a state law prohibiting yellow dog contracts as a violation of liberty of contract).

104. Duplex Printing Press Co. v. Deering, 252 F. 722, 748 (2d Cir. 1918) (opinion of Hough, J.), reversed, 254 U.S. 433 (1921). Judge Hand concurred in the judgment (id. at 748), and Judge Henry Rogers dissented based on *Loewe*, *Paine Lumber*, and the common law cases (id. at 727–745).

105. 254 U.S. 433 (1921).

106. "I say again—and I speak for, I believe, practically every member of the Judiciary Committee—that if this section did legalize the secondary boycott there would not be a man to vote for it. It is not the purpose of the committee to

authorize it, and I do not think any person in this House wants to do it." Quoted in id. at 476–477 n.1.

107. E.g. Frankfurter and Greene, *The Labor Injunction,* 139–144 (legislative history of Clayton Act goes every which way).

108. See letter from Oliver Wendell Holmes, Jr., to Felix Frankfurter, January 30, 1921 (Oliver Wendell Holmes, Jr., Papers, Harvard University).

109. See Ernst, "Labor Exemption," 1167, 1169–72 and n.74.

110. 51 *Congressional Record* 9541 (1914). See generally id. at 9540–67, for the discussion of the Henry amendment. Just like the Webb amendment, which was subject to amendment to prohibit secondary boycotts, the Henry amendment was subject to amendment to provide more expansive protection for unions. The subsequent amendments were defeated because Henry, like Webb, interpreted his amendment to subsume the proposed replacements. See Joseph Kovner, "The Legislative History of Section 6 of the Clayton Act," 47 *Columbia Law Review* 749 (1947).

111. *Duplex,* 254 U.S. at 484, 486 (Brandeis, J., dissenting).

112. Id. at 469–471 (opinion of the Court).

113. See Taft, "Recent Labor Injunction Legislation." See also Truax v. Corrigan, 257 U.S. 312 (1921) (Taft, C.J., striking down state law abolishing injunctions in labor controversies).

114. 257 U.S. 184 (1921).

115. Id. at 209.

116. United Mine Workers v. Coronado Coal Co., 259 U.S. 344 (1922).

117. See Irving Bernstein, *The Lean Years: A History of the American Worker, 1920–1933* (1960); Forbath, *Law and Labor Movement,* 158–159 (over 2,100 anti-strike decrees in 1920s).

118. See Walter F. Murphy, "In His Own Image: Mr. Chief Justice Taft and Supreme Court Appointments," 1961 *Supreme Court Review* 159. See also Adkins v. Children's Hospital of the District of Columbia, 261 U.S. 525 (1923) ("Four Horsemen" joined by McKenna invalidated a state minimum wage law for women).

119. Coronado Coal Co. v. United Mine Workers of America, 268 U.S. 295 (1925).

120. See Frankfurter and Greene, *The Labor Injunction;* Robert H. Zieger, *Republicans and Labor, 1919–1929* (1969).

121. 274 U.S. 37 (1927), reversing, 9 F.2d 40 (7th Cir. 1925); see also United States v. Brims, 272 U.S. 549 (1926) (allowing antitrust action against a labor-management agreement).

122. *Bedford,* 274 U.S. at 48, arguing that since the strikes against users of Bedford stone were in several states, they disrupted interstate commerce.

123. Id. at 47.

124. Id. at 48–49; accord, id. at 55 (Sanford, J., concurring based on *Duplex);* id. at 55–56 (separate opinion of Stone, J.) (Court's result seems dubious in light of Sherman Act rule of reason and of Clayton Act policy, but bound by *Duplex).*

125. Id. at 63 (Brandeis, J., dissenting).

126. See "Injunctions in Labor Disputes," in 13 *Proceedings of the American Academy of Political Science*, 37–92 (1928); [former Senator] George Pepper, "Injunctions in Labor Disputes," in *Men and Issues*, 61–63 (1924).

127. *Limiting the Scope of Injunctions in Labor Disputes: Hearings before the Subcommittee of the Senate Committee on the Judiciary*, 70th Cong., 1st sess. (1928); *Hearings on the Shipstead Bill, S. 1482: Hearings before the Senate Committee on the Judiciary*, 70th Cong., 1st sess. (1928).

128. Frankfurter and Greene, *The Labor Injunction*, 207–228.

129. Labor unions and civil rights groups played key roles in defeating the nomination, the latter by publicizing the judge's decision in United Mine Workers of America v. Red Jacket Consolidated Coal and Coke Company, 18 F.2d 839 (4th Cir.), cert. denied, 275 U.S. 536 (1927), upholding a labor injunction against striking coal miners. See Peter Fish, "*Red Jacket* Revisited: The Case That Unraveled John J. Parker's Supreme Court Appointment," 5 *Law and History Review* 51 (1987).

130. Senate Report no. 163, 72d Cong., 1st sess., 8 (1931) (language quoted in text); House Report no. 669, 72d Cong., 1st sess., 7–8 (1931) (pointed criticism of Supreme Court decisions).

131. Act of March 23, 1932, §1, 47 Stat. 70 (1932), codified at 29 U.S.C. §101.

132. See Bernstein, *The Lean Years*, 414; Cummings and McFarland, *Federal Justice*, 460–461.

133. Justice Owen Roberts's "switch in time" upholding state minimum wage legislation, West Coast Hotel Co. v. Parrish, 300 U.S. 379 (1937), after President Franklin Roosevelt had proposed his Court-packing plan, was a signal that the Court majority was willing to override the libertarian wishes of the Four Horsemen and accommodate the New Deal. Justice Van Devanter retired later in 1937 and was replaced by New Deal Senator Hugo Black; Justice Sutherland left in 1938 and was replaced by New Deal Solicitor General Stanley Reed.

134. Lauf v. E. G. Shinner & Co., 303 U.S. 323 (1938).

135. 311 U.S. 91 (1940).

136. Thornhill v. Alabama, 310 U.S. 88 (1940); United States v. Hutcheson, 312 U.S. 219 (1941); Apex Hosiery v. Leader, 310 U.S. 469 (1940).

137. For the birth of this new regulatory regime, see Mark Barenberg, "The Political Economy of the Wagner Act: Power, Symbol, and Workplace Cooperation," 106 *Harvard Law Review* 1379 (1993).

138. William Howard Taft, *The Anti-Trust Act and the Supreme Court*, 47 (1914).

139. Id.

4. Liberal Theories

This chapter draws from my articles "Dynamic Statutory Interpretation," 135 *University of Pennsylvania Law Review* 1479 (1987), and "Spinning Legislative Supremacy," 78 *Georgetown Law Journal* 319 (1989), reprinted with the permission of the publisher, © 1989 The Georgetown Law Journal Association and Georgetown University.

1. See J. G. [Jabez Gridley] Sutherland, *Statutes and Statutory Construction* (1st ed. 1891 and subsequent editions); Roscoe Pound, "Spurious Interpretation," 7 *Columbia Law Review* 379 (1907); James M. Landis, "A Note on 'Statutory Interpretation,'" 43 *Harvard Law Review* 886 (1930); Frederick J. de Sloovère, "Preliminary Questions in Statutory Interpretation," 9 *New York University Law Review* 407 (1932); Learned Hand, "How Far Is a Judge Free in Rendering a Decision?," in *The Spirit of Liberty: Papers and Addresses of Learned Hand*, 103, 105–110 (3d ed. 1960); William M. Landes and Richard A. Posner, "The Independent Judiciary in an Interest-Group Perspective," 18 *Journal of Law and Economics* 875 (1975); Patricia M. Wald, "Some Observations on the Use of Legislative History in the 1981 Supreme Court Term," 68 *Iowa Law Review* 195 (1983); Earl M. Maltz, "Statutory Interpretation and Legislative Power: The Case for a Modified Intentionalist Approach," 63 *Tulane Law Review* 1 (1988); Frank H. Easterbrook, "The Role of Original Intent in Statutory Construction," 11 *Harvard Journal of Law and Public Policy* 59 (1988).

2. Thomas W. Merrill, "The Common Law Powers of Federal Courts," 52 *University of Chicago Law Review* 1, 19, 32–33 (1985); see also Martin H. Redish, *The Federal Courts in the Political Order: Judicial Jurisdiction and American Political Theory*, chap. 2 (1991) (reproducing and synthesizing Redish's prior work). Merrill and Redish also rely on the Rules Decision Act, 28 U.S.C. §1652, for their view that federal courts have no "lawmaking" powers. They represent the minority view in the academic debate on this issue, but I do not join the debate.

3. As well as its background history, see Gerhard Caspar, "An Essay in Separation of Powers: Some Early Versions and Practices," 30 *William and Mary Law Review* 211 (1989).

4. *Black's Law Dictionary*, 810–811 (5th ed. 1979); see 1 William Blackstone, *Commentaries on the Laws of England*, 63–70, 85–88, 91–92 (1765).

5. U.S. Const. art. I, §7, clauses 2–3 (requiring presentment of legislative bill to president before bill can become law).

6. Id. art. II, §2, clause 2, which explicitly gives the president, with the concurrence of the Senate, the power to make treaties, which are the "law of the Land" under the supremacy clause in article VI.

7. See, e.g., Dames & Moore v. Regan, 453 U.S. 654 (1981).

8. See, e.g., United States v. Maine, 475 U.S. 89 (1986) (interpreting the doctrine of "ancient title"); Illinois v. City of Milwaukee, 406 U.S. 91, 99–100, 104 (1972); Hinderlider v. La Plata River & Cherry Creek Ditch Co., 304 U.S. 92 (1938); Missouri v. Illinois, 200 U.S. 496 (1906).

9. For example, "Cases of admiralty and maritime Jurisdiction" had traditionally been governed by English judge-made law before American independence, and the common law of admiralty remains a lively area of law. See, e.g., American Export Lines Inc. v. Alvez, 446 U.S. 274, 275–276 (1980); Moragne v. States Ma-

rine Lines, Inc., 398 U.S. 375, 393–402 (1970). "Controversies to which the United States shall be a Party" might involve federal statutory law, but it is unlikely that the framers expected Congress to regulate all aspects of federal government affairs, such as government contracting, e.g., Clearfield Trust Co. v. United States, 318 U.S. 363, 367 (1943), or proprietary concerns, e.g., West Virginia v. United States, 479 U.S. 305 (1987). Even "Controversies . . . between Citizens of different States" were considered appropriate occasions for federal judicial lawmaking in the nineteenth century. See Swift v. Tyson, 41 U.S. (16 Pet.) 1, 18–19 (1842) (creating federal common law of commercial transactions in diversity suits), overruled, Erie Railroad v. Tompkins, 304 U.S. 64, 178–179 (1938). For an example of federal common law in diversity cases today, see Banco Nacional de Cuba v. Sabbatino, 376 U.S. 398, 424–425 (1964) (act of state doctrine).

10. *The Federalist*, no. 47, at 302–303 (James Madison) (Clinton Rossiter, ed., 1961), quoting and relying on Montesquieu, *The Spirit of the Laws*, bk. 11, chap. 6 (1765).

11. See *The Federalist*, no. 51 (James Madison).

12. *The Federalist*, no. 47, at 302 (James Madison).

13. See also *The Federalist*, no. 73 (Alexander Hamilton) (similar rationale supporting presidential veto); *The Federalist*, no. 78 (Alexander Hamilton) (similar rationale supporting judicial nullification or amelioration of "partial and unjust" statutes); see generally David F. Epstein, *The Political Theory of "The Federalist,"* 130–131 (1984).

14. The nondelegation doctrine theoretically limits Congress's ability to delegate without any policy guidance. See J. W. Hampton, Jr., & Co. v. United States, 276 U.S. 394 (1928) (Taft, C.J.). But even the most avid liberal adherents of the nondelegation doctrine believe it to be a minimal limitation on Congress's ability to delegate. See Mistretta v. United States, 488 U.S. 361, 415–416 (1989) (Scalia, J., dissenting from the Court's opinion but joining a unanimous Court in rejecting nondelegation challenge).

15. 275 F. 539 (2d Cir. 1921), reversed, 260 U.S. 689 (1923).

16. Act of June 17, 1930, §526, 46 Stat. 741, codified as amended at 19 U.S.C. §1526 (1988).

17. See T.D. 48537, 70 *Treasury Decisions* 336–337 (1936).

18. T.D. 53399, 88 *Treasury Decisions* 376, 384 (1953), currently codified at 19 C.F.R. §133.21(c)(1)–(2) (1993).

19. 790 F.2d 903 (D.C. Cir. 1986) (relying on the statutory text, background debates, and amendments to the bill in 1922, and the conference committee report), affirmed in part and reversed in part sub nom. K Mart Corp. v. Cartier, Inc., 486 U.S. 281 (1988).

20. 486 U.S. 281, 292–293 (1988) (opinion of Kennedy, J.); id. at 295, 297–312 (Brennan, J., concurring on this issue).

21. Osburn v. Bank of the United States, 22 U.S. (9 Wheat.) 738, 866 (1824). What Marshall meant by the "will of the Legislature" was probably *not* any sub-

jective intent of the enacting Congress (see John Choon Yoo, "Marshall's Plan: The Early Supreme Court and Statutory Interpretation," 101 *Yale Law Journal* 1607 [1992] [student note]), as is evident from Marshall's highly dynamic readings of statutes in decisions such as Marbury v. Madison, 5 U.S. (1 Cranch) 137 (1803) (Judiciary Act of 1789). For an example of Marshall's unconcern with the subjective expectations of the legislature when he was a private advocate, see Hooe v. Marquess, 4 Call (Virginia Reports, Annotated) 416, 419–421 (Virginia Court of Appeals, October 1798).

22. 1 Blackstone, *Commentaries*, 59–62, 91; see William S. Blatt, "The History of Statutory Interpretation: A Study in Form and Substance," 6 *Cardozo Law Review* 799, 802–805 (1985).

23. 1 Blackstone, *Commentaries*, 61; see id. at 87 (emphasizing Heydon's Case, 76 Eng. Rep. 637, 638 [Exch. 1584], which urges "construction as shall suppress the mischief and advance the remedy").

24. 1 Blackstone, *Commentaries*, 61.

25. Id. at 91; see College of Physician's (Dr. Bonham's) Case, 123 Eng. Rep. 928 (C.P. 1609), an authority well known to eighteenth-century American jurists. See Theodore F. T. Plucknett, "*Bonham's Case* and Judicial Review," 40 *Harvard Law Review* 30 (1926).

26. 3 Call (Virginia Reports, Annotated) 573 (Virginia Court of Appeals, December 1790).

27. Id. at 581.

28. *K Mart*, 486 U.S. at 299–309 (Brennan, J., concurring, joined on this issue by Marshall and Stevens, JJ.). Accord, Jamie S. Gorelick and Julia E. Guttman, "Parallel Importation after *K Mart v. Cartier* ('*COPIAT*')," 70 *Journal of Patent and Trademark Office Society* 696 (1988); Michael B. Weicher, "*K Mart Corp. v. Cartier, Inc.:* A Black Decision for the Grey Market," 38 *American University Law Review* 463, 469–471 (1989) (student note, surveying the academic literature). But see Vivitar Corp. v. United States, 761 F. 2d 1552, 1563 (Fed. Cir. 1985), cert. denied, 474 U.S. 1065 (1986) (legislative history sends no clear message).

29. *Bracken*, 4 Call (Virginia Reports, Annotated) at 580 (reporting Marshall's argument).

30. *The Federalist* no. 78, at 470 (Alexander Hamilton); see Epstein, *Political Theory of "The Federalist,"* 188–190 (Hamilton was suggesting that "courts may be lenient against the lawmakers' intention"; framers generally endorsed an equity-based approach to statutory interpretation).

31. *The Federalist*, no. 78, at 470 (Alexander Hamilton); see also *The Federalist*, no. 73 (Alexander Hamilton) (similar argument in favor of presidential veto).

32. *The Federalist*, no. 78, mostly deals with judicial review in enforcing the limitations on government imposed by the Constitution (id. at 466–470), and it is in that discussion that the language quoted in the text is found (id. at 469). Hamilton's subsequent discussion of statutory interpretation is brief (id. at 470), before he concludes generally (id. at 471–472).

33. Id. at 471 (the first constraint) and 465 (the second and third).

34. See *K Mart*, 486 U.S. at 295–296 (Brennan, J., concurring in part) (recounting COPIAT's extensive lobbying effort to override the common control exception in Congress).

35. The account that follows is developed in greater detail in Chapter 7 and in my article "The New Textualism," 37 *University of California at Los Angeles Law Review* 621 (1990).

36. Business Electronics Corp. v. Sharp Electronics Corp., 485 U.S. 717, 732 (1988) (Scalia, J.).

37. Green v. Bock Laundry Machine Co., 490 U.S. 504, 528 (1989) (Scalia, J., concurring in the judgment).

38. United States v. Fausto, 484 U.S. 439, 453 (1988) (Scalia, J.); see Jett v. Dallas Independent School District, 491 U.S. 701, 738–739 (1989) (Scalia, J., concurring in part and in the judgment).

39. *K Mart*, 486 U.S. at 292–293 (opinion of Kennedy, J., joined on this point only by White, J.).

40. This point was made by Scalia in a telling hypothetical (*K Mart*, 486 U.S. at 320), to which Kennedy lamely responded that the Customs Service can interpret the same statutory language ("merchandise of foreign manufacture") in different ways in the same set of regulations. See id. at 293 n.4; compare id. at 320 n.1 (Scalia, J., responding).

41. See *K Mart*, 486 U.S. at 300–307 (Brennan, J., concurring in part); T. Thomas Warlick IV, "Of Blue Light Specials and Gray-Market Goods: The Perpetuation of the Parallel Importation Controversy," 39 *Emory Law Journal* 347, 377–388 (1990) (student comment).

42. Antonin Scalia, "The Rule of Law as a Law of Rules," 56 *University of Chicago Law Review* 1775 (1989).

43. The Department of Justice in 1971 argued that the Tariff Act should be interpreted in light of antitrust policy and that such policy strongly supported the Service's proposed regulation codifying the common-control exception. See Memorandum from Walker B. Comegys, Acting Assistant Attorney General, Antitrust Division, to Myles J. Ambrose, Commissioner of Customs (April 19, 1971), reprinted in Joint Appendix, 68–74, *K Mart* (nos. 86–495 et al.). A more sophisticated and balanced analysis is Theodore H. Davis, Jr., "Applying Grecian Formula to International Trade: *K Mart Corp. v. Cartier, Inc.*, and the Legality of Gray Market Imports," 75 *Virginia Law Review* 1397, 1418–21 (1989) (student note).

44. See Daniel A. Farber, "Statutory Interpretation and Legislative Supremacy," 78 *Georgetown Law Journal* 281 (1989), as well as sources in note 1.

45. The subsequent discussion in text is derived from Aristotle's *Nicomachean Ethics*, discussed in this book's introduction. See also Ernest Bruncken, "Interpretation of the Written Law," 25 *Yale Law Journal* 129, 136 (1915); Marcus P. Knowlton, "Legislation and Judicial Decision," 11 *Yale Law Journal* 95, 100 (1901–2).

46. See Daniel A. Farber and Philip P. Frickey, *Law and Public Choice: A Critical Introduction*, 88–115 (1991); Gillian K. Hadfield, "Incomplete Contracts and Statutes," 12 *International Review of Law and Economics* 257 (1992); McNollgast, "Positive Canons: The Role of Legislative Bargains in Statutory Interpretation," 80 *Georgetown Law Journal* 705 (1992).

47. See Richard B. Stewart, "Regulation in a Liberal State: The Role of Non-Commodity Values," 92 *Yale Law Journal* 1537, 1551–53 (1983), as well as Eskridge, "Dynamic Statutory Interpretation," 1520–22.

48. See U.C.C. §2-208; *Restatement (Second) of Contracts*, §§222–223 (1981).

49. See U.C.C. §2-615 (excuse by failure of presupposed conditions); *Restatement (Second) of Contracts*, §261 (1981) (discharge by supervening impracticability); E. Allan Farnsworth, *Contracts*, 647, 677, 689 (1982); Robert A. Hillman, "Court Adjustment of Long-Term Contracts: An Analysis under Modern Contract Law," 1987 *Duke Law Journal* 1.

50. See U.C.C. §§1-203 (obligation of good faith), 2-302 (no enforcement of unconscionable terms); John P. Dawson, "Effects of Inflation on Private Contract: Germany, 1914–1924," 33 *Michigan Law Review* 171 (1934).

51. See Farnsworth, *Contracts*, 520–525.

52. Alex M. Johnson, Jr., and Ross D. Taylor, "Revolutionizing Judicial Interpretation of Charitable Trusts: Applying Relational Contracts and Dynamic Interpretation to Cy Pres and America's Cup Litigation," 74 *Iowa Law Review* 545, 579–586 (1989); Farber, "Legislative Supremacy," 309–314.

53. *Restatement (Second) of Trusts*, §381 (1959), analyzed in Johnson and Taylor, "Charitable Trusts," 565–566 (arguing that cy pres, which applies to a trust's substantive provisions, should be liberalized to be like deviation).

54. *K Mart*, 486 U.S. at 325 (Scalia, J., concurring in Court's holding as to authorized use exception) (emphasis added).

55. Frank H. Easterbrook, "The Supreme Court, 1983 Term—Foreword: The Court and the Economic System," 98 *Harvard Law Review* 4, 60 (1984). For other thoughtful works suggesting an honest agent metaphor (for judges anyway), see Richard A. Posner, *The Federal Courts: Crisis and Reform*, 286–293 (1985); Maltz, "Modified Intentionalist Approach."

56. Richard A. Posner, *The Problems of Jurisprudence*, 269–273 (1990). I posed a similar analogy between the statutory interpreter and a diplomat acting on orders from their national governments in Eskridge, "Dynamic Statutory Interpretation," 1554.

57. Posner, *Problems of Jurisprudence*, 270. Note the similarity to Aristotle's formulation in *The Nicomachean Ethics*.

58. See Ian R. Macneil, "The Many Futures of Contracts," 47 *Southern California Law Review* 691 (1974), as well as Ian R. Macneil, "Contracts: Adjustment of Long-Term Economic Relations under Classical, Neoclassical, and Relational Contract Law," 72 *Northwestern Law Review* 854 (1978).

59. Mark V. Tushnet, "Following the Rules Laid Down: A Critique of Interpretivism and Neutral Principles," 96 *Harvard Law Review* 781 (1983).

60. James Boyd White, *Justice as Translation: An Essay in Cultural and Legal Criticism*, 257–269 (1990); Paul Brest, "The Misconceived Quest for the Original Understanding," 60 *Boston University Law Review* 204 (1980).

61. See Bruncken, "Interpretation of the Written Law," 136.

62. Lawrence Lessig, "Fidelity in Translation," 71 *Texas Law Review* 1165 (1993); see id. at 1171–73 n.31 (earlier theories of law as translation).

63. Lessig, "Fidelity in Translation," 1182–92.

64. 19 C.F.R. §133.21(c) (1987) (withdrawn from the current regulations).

65. See *K Mart*, 486 U.S. at 293–294 (pt. II[C], the opinion of Kennedy, J., joined by Rehnquist, C.J., and Blackmun, O'Connor, and Scalia, JJ.); id. at 323–328 (opinion of Scalia, J., concurring on this issue and joined by Rehnquist, C.J., and Blackmun and O'Connor, JJ.). Compare id. at 312–317 (opinion of Brennan, J., dissenting on this issue and joined by White, Marshall, and Stevens, JJ.). The Brennan position originally commanded a majority of the Court on this issue, but Justice O'Connor switched her tentative vote because the agency position was "simply too far removed from the language and ordinary meaning of the statute." Memorandum from O'Connor to Brennan and Scalia, February 16, 1988, in Thurgood Marshall Papers, Library of Congress (Madison Building), Box 440, Folder 9.

66. First, goods made by a foreign-incorporated subsidiary (excepted under the common control regulation, which Kennedy upheld) are no less "merchandise of foreign manufacture" than are goods made by a foreign company authorized to make them abroad (excepted under the authorized-use regulation, which Kennedy invalidated). Second, there seems little reason to treat the two regulations differently; the U.S. trademark holder has functional control over the manufacture of its goods abroad in both cases, either by its control of the corporation or by the authorized use contract. Third, both situations are materially different from *Katzel*, the fraudulent bait-and-switch case that triggered enactment of the prohibition in the first place.

67. See Customs Commissioner Frank Dow to Senator Paul H. Douglas, March 23, 1951, reproduced in Joint Appendix, 52–53, *K Mart* (nos. 86–495 et al.).

68. *K Mart*, 486 U.S. at 325 (Scalia, J., concurring in part); see Frank H. Easterbrook, "Statutes' Domains," 50 *University of Chicago Law Review* 533 (1983).

69. *K Mart*, 486 U.S. at 325 (Scalia, J., concurring in part).

70. See generally David L. Shapiro, "Courts, Legislatures, and Paternalism," 74 *Virginia Law Review* 519 (1988), as well as H. L. A. Hart, *Law, Liberty, and Morality*, 30–34 (1963).

71. United States v. Rutherford, 442 U.S. 544, 554 n.10 (1979); see Chapter 8 for further elaboration, as well as Appendix 1 to this book for cases.

72. Compare *COPIAT*, 790 F.2d at 913–916 (Congress was never fully informed of Customs Service exceptions), with Brief for the Federal Petitioners, 36–43, *K Mart* (nos. 86–495 et al.) (congressional committees were informed of the exceptions and were friendly to them).

73. See Dow to Douglas, Joint Appendix, 52–54.

74. In connection with the Customs Procedure Reform and Simplification Act of 1978, Public Law no. 95-410, 92 Stat. 888, 903, the House report said that the act "has been consistently interpreted by the United States Customs Service for the past 20 years as excluding from protection foreign-produced merchandise bearing a genuine trademark created, owned, and administered by a citizen of the United States if the foreign producer has been authorized by the American trademark owners to produce and sell abroad goods bearing the recorded trademark." House Report no. 621, 95th Cong., 1st sess., 27 (1977). In connection with the Trademark Counterfeiting Act of 1984, Public Law no. 98-473, 98 Stat. 2178, the Senate report said that the new statute does not cover gray market goods: "The importation of such goods is legal under certain circumstances. For example, the Treasury Department has long interpreted [the Tariff Act] to permit the domestic importation of such goods when the foreign and domestic users of the trademark are affiliated through common ownership and control." Senate Report no. 526, 98th Cong., 2d sess., 3 (1984), reprinted in 1984 *United States Code Congress and Administrative News* 3627, 3629.

75. See John W. Kingdon, *Agendas, Alternatives, and Public Policies* (1984).

76. See *K Mart*, 486 U.S. at 325–328 (Scalia, J., concurring in part), citing United Drug Co. v. Theodore Rectanus Co., 248 U.S. 90, 100–101 (1918); Hanover Star Milling Co. v. Metcalf, 240 U.S. 403, 415 (1916). The analysis in text is drawn from Warlick, "Of Blue Light Specials and Gray Market Goods," 376 n.114, 406–409.

77. Compare *COPIAT*, 790 U.S. at 910–911 (legislative history suggesting purpose was to protect the American registrant's property rights in the trademark), with *K Mart*, 486 U.S. at 316–317 (Brennan, J., concurring in part) (other legislative history suggesting purpose was "America first" and protectionist). See also John A. Young, Jr., "The Gray Market Case: Trademark Rights v. Consumer Interests," 61 *Notre Dame Law Review* 838 (1986) (student note).

78. This parallels the dilemma faced by liberal theories of constitutional law. See Roberto M. Unger, *Knowledge and Politics* (1975); Mark V. Tushnet, "Darkness on the Edge of Town: The Contributions of John Hart Ely to Constitutional Theory," 89 *Yale Law Journal* 1037 (1980).

79. *K Mart*, 486 U.S. at 319–320 (Scalia, J., dissenting in part). See Lawrence M. Solan, "When Judges Use the Dictionary," 68 *American Speech* 50 (1993).

80. On the limited ability of judges to play these language games, see Lawrence M. Solan, *The Language of Judges* (1993); on Scalia's performance as a linguist, see id. at 113–117.

81. *K Mart*, 486 U.S. at 316 (Brennan, J., dissenting in part).

82. Id. at 324 (Scalia, J., concurring in part).

83. *Webster's New International Dictionary of the English Language*, 1736 (2d unabridged ed. 1961), defines "oven": "A chamber of brick or stonework used for baking, heating or drying; hence, any hot-air chamber used for such purposes; esp., a chamber in a stove used for baking or roasting, or a laboratory hot-air sterilizer." This dictionary definition could be used to justify several different regulatory choices.

84. *K Mart*, 486 U.S. at 324 n.2 (Scalia, J., concurring in part).

85. See *Weber*, 443 U.S. at 209–216 (Blackmun, J., concurring), drawing its argument from Judge John Minor Wisdom's dissenting opinion for the lower court. See 563 F.2d 216, 227 (5th Cir. 1977).

86. On "situation sense," see Karl N. Llewellyn, *The Common Law Tradition: Deciding Appeals*, 121–154 (1960).

87. See H. L. A. Hart, *The Concept of Law* (1961).

88. Earl M. Maltz, "Rhetoric and Reality in the Theory of Statutory Interpretation: Underenforcement, Overenforcement, and the Problem of Legislative Supremacy," 71 *Boston University Law Review* 767 (1991).

89. Id. at 788–789; Merrill, "The Common Law Powers of Federal Courts," 3–7.

90. For an example of this federalism-inspired precept as a basis for statutory interpretation, see Summit Health, Ltd. v. Pinhas, 111 S. Ct. 1842, 1849 (1991) (Scalia, J., dissenting).

91. Shapiro, "Courts, Legislatures, and Paternalism."

92. See Wesley Newcomb Hohfeld, "Some Fundamental Legal Conceptions as Applied in Judicial Reasoning," 23 *Yale Law Journal* 16 (1913).

93. David L. Shapiro, "Continuity and Change in Statutory Interpretation," 67 *New York University Law Review* 921, 942 (1992); see M. B. W. Sinclair, "Law and Language: The Role of Pragmatics in Statutory Interpretation," 46 *University of Pittsburgh Law Review* 373 (1985).

94. Shapiro, "Continuity and Change," 942; see John Paul Stevens, "The Shakespeare Canon of Statutory Interpretation," 140 *University of Pennsylvania Law Review* 1373 (1992).

95. *Griffin*, 458 U.S. at 588–589 (Stevens, J., dissenting).

96. A difficulty conceded in Shapiro, "Continuity and Change," 926 n.17.

97. Lon L. Fuller and William R. Perdue, Jr., "The Reliance Interest in Contract Damages," 46 *Yale Law Journal* 52 (1936).

98. Thomas W. Merrill, "Judicial Deference to Executive Precedent," 101 *Yale Law Journal* 969, 1007–12 (1992).

99. Thus, the agency establishes Rule A, the legislative committee holds hearings where it is informed of Rule A, and based on those hearings the committee proposes Rule {A + B}, which is enacted by Congress. Although Congress has not formally voted in favor of Rule A, the rule is a necessary part of a statute Congress has adopted, and under liberal premises this is a strong argument for

an implicit ratification of Rule A by Congress. See Franklin v. Gwinnett County Public Schools, 112 S. Ct. 1028, 1038–39 (1992) (Scalia, J., concurring in the judgment).

100. The agency establishes Rule C as an exception to its statute's broad reach; the legislative committee holds hearings to consider the breadth of the statute's reach, and the agency describes and defends its exception; and the committee proposes other exceptions (which Congress enacts) and accepts arguendo the legitimacy of Rule C.

101. See Brief Amicus Curiae of the American Free Trade Association, 3, *K Mart* (nos. 86–495 et al.) (trade association of independent American importers claiming that gray market accounted for up to $100 billion per year).

102. See Brief Amicus Curiae of the National Mass Retailing Institute, 3, *K Mart* (nos. 86–495 et al.) (association of 125 discount retailers with sales of $100 billion per year, some of which came from gray market goods); Amicus Curiae Brief of the National Association of Catalog Showroom Merchandisers, 1–2, id. (association of two thousand small discount retail stores with sales of $10 billion per year, much of which came from gray market goods).

103. Customs Procedural Reform and Simplification Act of 1978, Public Law no. 95-410, 92 Stat. 888 (1978), adding new 19 U.S.C. §1526(d).

104. House Report no. 621, 95th Cong., 1st sess., 27 (1977), quoted in note 74.

105. Senate Report no. 526, 98th Cong., 2d sess., 2 (1982), quoted in note 74.

5. Legal Process Theories

This chapter draws from my collaboration with Philip P. Frickey in the forthcoming publication of the Henry M. Hart, Jr., and Albert M. Sacks materials, "The Legal Process" (see note 3).

1. See, e.g., James Landis, "Statutes as the Sources of Law," in *Harvard Legal Essays*, 213 (1934); Harlan Fiske Stone, "The Common Law in the United States," 50 *Harvard Law Review* 4 (1936). See generally Neil Duxbury, "Finding Faith in Reason: The Process Tradition in American Jurisprudence," 15 *Cardozo Law Review* 601 (1993).

2. See Edward A. Purcell, Jr., *The Crisis of Democratic Theory: Scientific Naturalism and the Problem of Value* (1973).

3. Henry M. Hart., Jr., and Albert M. Sacks, "The Legal Process: Basic Problems in the Making and Application of Law" (tentative ed. 1958) (forthcoming from Foundation Press in 1994, ed. William N. Eskridge, Jr., and Philip P. Frickey); see also Lon L. Fuller, "Positivism and Fidelity to Law—A Reply to Professor [H. L. A.] Hart," 71 *Harvard Law Review* 630 (1958); Henry M. Hart, Jr., and Herbert Wechsler, *The Federal Courts and the Federal System* (1953).

4. Hart and Sacks, "The Legal Process," 2; see id. at 1.

5. Id. at 166; see Lon L. Fuller, "The Case of the Speluncean Explorers," 62 *Harvard Law Review* 616, 621 (1949).

6. Hart and Sacks, "The Legal Process," 3 (emphasis omitted).

7. Id. at 173, 183, 715–716.

8. Id. at 4–5 (principle of institutional settlement).

9. See Norman Dorsen, "In Memoriam: Albert M. Sacks," 105 *Harvard Law Review* 11 (1991); Robert Weisberg, "The Calabresian Judicial Artist: Statutes and the New Legal Process," 35 *Stanford Law Review* 213 (1983).

10. Hart and Sacks, "The Legal Process," 166–167; see id. at 1179–1200. For similar approaches to statutory interpretation by contemporaries and students of Hart and Sacks, see Alexander M. Bickel and Harry H. Wellington, "Legislative Purpose and the Judicial Process: The *Lincoln Mills* Case," 71 *Harvard Law Review* 1, 15–17 (1957); Felix Frankfurter, "Some Reflections on the Reading of Statutes," 47 *Columbia Law Review* 527 (1947); Fuller, "Speluncean Explorers," 623–626 (opinion of Foster, J.); Harry Willmer Jones, "Extrinsic Aids in the Federal Courts," 25 *Iowa Law Review* 737, 757 (1940).

11. Hart and Sacks, "The Legal Process," 1414–15.

12. Id. at 1157.

13. E.g., Lon L. Fuller, *The Law in Quest of Itself*, 9–10 (1940) (a statute is "a process of becoming"); Jones, "Extrinsic Aids," 761.

14. 197 Mass. 241 (1908), discussed in Hart and Sacks, "The Legal Process," 1214–15.

15. Hart and Sacks, "The Legal Process," 1215.

16. Although Hart and Sacks urged that the statute's words not be given a "meaning they will not bear" (id. at 1200, 1411), they eschewed any approach that sought a plain meaning divorced from statutory policy.

17. Id. at 1215; see Fuller, "Speluncean Explorers," 628–630 (opinion of Tatting, J.) and 634 (opinion of Keen, J.).

18. Hart and Sacks, "The Legal Process," 1215.

19. As are Hart and Sacks's analysis of the Female Jurors Cases, id. at 1203–14; Lon Fuller's analysis of the Vehicles in the Park Case, Fuller, "Positivism and Fidelity to Law"; see Steven L. Winter, "An Upside/Down View of the Countermajoritarian Difficulty," 69 *Texas Law Review* 1881 (1991); and the Brennan-Scalia debate over the Case of the Spewing Ovens, discussed in Chapter 4.

20. 461 U.S. 574 (1983).

21. After a preliminary injunction had been issued against the IRS's enforcement of its policy of giving tax exemptions to segregated schools (see Green v. Kennedy, 309 F. Supp. 1127 [D.D.C. 1970] [three-judge court]), the IRS on July 10, 1970, adopted a new policy of denying tax exempt status to such institutions.

22. Bob Jones is a fundamentalist college which before 1971 excluded African American students; between 1971 and 1975 it admitted married black students and unmarried blacks who had been staff members for four years or more; and after 1975 it admitted unmarried blacks, though not any African American who was a partner in an interracial marriage. See Philip B. Heymann and Lance M. Liebman, *The Social Responsibilities of Lawyers: Case Studies*, 139 (1988).

23. See Bruce E. Fein, Associate Deputy Attorney General, to Edward C. Schmults, Deputy Attorney General, December 7, 1981, reprinted in Heymann and Liebman, *The Social Responsibilities of Lawyers*, 156–158.

24. See House Ways and Means Committee, *Administration's Change in Federal Policy Regarding the Tax Status of Racially Discriminatory Private Schools*, 97th Cong., 2d sess. (1982); Heymann and Liebman, *The Social Responsibilities of Lawyers*, 141–152.

25. *Bob Jones*, 461 U.S. at 586; see id. at 593 n.20 (conceding that its interpretation is inconsistent with original intent); Mayer G. Freed and Daniel D. Polsby, "Race, Religion, and Public Policy: *Bob Jones University v. United States*," 1983 *Supreme Court Review* 1.

26. *Bob Jones*, 461 U.S. at 587–588, 591–592.

27. Id. at 592–596.

28. Walz v. Tax Commission, 397 U.S. 664, 689 (1970) (Brennan, J., concurring); see *Bob Jones*, 461 U.S. at 609–610 (Powell, J., concurring).

29. Hart and Sacks, "The Legal Process," 101.

30. Id. at 167; see id. at 1413, 1416.

31. Hart and Sacks observed that principles and policies form the basis for extending a rule or statute to a novel context (id. at 386–406); reformulating old rules or provisions (id. at 407–426); and replacing old rules or practices with new ones (id. at 565–589). Hart and Sacks's classic example is the Case of the Female Jurors, id. at 1203–15.

32. See, e.g., Guido Calabresi, *A Common Law for the Age of Statutes* (1982); T. Alexander Aleinikoff, "Updating Statutory Interpretation," 87 *Michigan Law Review* 20 (1988); Philip P. Frickey, "Congressional Intent, Practical Reasoning, and the Dynamic Nature of Federal Indian Law," 78 *California Law Review* 1137 (1990); Harold A. McDougall, "Social Movements, Law, and Implementation: A Clinical Dimension for the New Legal Process," 75 *Cornell Law Review* 83 (1989).

33. Ronald Dworkin, *Law's Empire* (1986); Dworkin, *A Matter of Principle*, pt. 1 (1985); Dworkin, *Taking Rights Seriously* (1977); see Vincent A. Wellman, "Dworkin and the Legal Process Tradition: The Legacy of Hart and Sacks," 29 *Arizona Law Review* 413 (1987).

34. Dworkin, *Law's Empire*, 176–184, 190–192.

35. Id. at 217; see id. at 225.

36. Id. at 348. Dworkin develops the metaphor of statutory interpretation as a "chain novel," in which a statute is the first chapter in the novel and subsequent authors, usually judges, are called upon to add new chapters. See id. at 228–275. These ideas are anticipated by Fuller, *Law in Quest*, 9–10.

37. Cooper v. Aaron, 358 U.S. 1, 19 (1958); see Norwood v. Harrison, 413 U.S. 455, 468–469 (1973) (same principle applies to nonpublic schools).

38. 468 U.S. 737 (1984).

39. After the IRS issued regulations in 1978–79 placing burdens on schools with a low percentage of African American students to "prove" their nondiscrimination, Congress attached the Ashbrook amendment to a 1980 appropriations

statute, effectively barring the IRS from implementing the regulations. Other "back door" restrictions followed. See *IRS Tax Exemptions and Segregated Private Schools: Hearings before the Subcommittee on Civil and Constitutional Rights of the House Committee on the Judiciary*, 97th Cong., 2d sess., 49–50 (1982).

40. See Milliken v. Bradley, 418 U.S. 717 (1974) (lower courts cannot require interdistrict busing to eliminate racial segregation); Pasadena Board of Education v. Spangler, 427 U.S. 424 (1976) (lower courts cannot adjust school boundary lines).

41. See Washington v. Davis, 426 U.S. 229 (1976), followed in Village of Arlington Heights v. Metropolitan Housing Development Corp., 429 U.S. 252 (1977) (state housing policies); McCleskey v. Kemp, 481 U.S. 279 (1987) (death penalty); Mobile v. Bolden, 446 U.S. 55 (1980) (voting rights).

42. See my article "Public Values in Statutory Interpretation," 137 *University of Pennsylvania Law Review* 1007 (1989); Cass R. Sunstein, "Interpreting Statutes in the Regulatory State," 103 *Harvard Law Review* 405 (1989), which was the basis for Sunstein, *After the Rights Revolution: Reconceiving the Regulatory State* (1990).

43. Owen M. Fiss, "The Supreme Court, 1978 Term—Foreword: The Forms of Justice," 93 *Harvard Law Review* 1, 9 (1979).

44. See Peter C. Schanck, "Understanding Postmodern Thought and Its Implications for Statutory Interpretation," 65 *Southern California Law Review* 2505, 2529–33 (1992) (also discussing deconstructions of the thirty-five-year-old requirement by my colleagues Gary Peller, Girardeau Spann, and Mark Tushnet).

45. See Eskridge, "Public Values," 1019–1161 (the first two points in text); William N. Eskridge, Jr., "Politics Without Romance: Implications of Public Choice Theory for Statutory Interpretation," 74 *Virginia Law Review* 275 (1988) (third point in text); Sunstein, "Regulatory State," 468–493, 506–508 (all three points in text).

46. See United States v. Wells Fargo Bank, 485 U.S. 351 (1988).

47. See Pilot Life Insurance Co. v. Dedeaux, 481 U.S. 41, 48–49 (1987); Wimberly v. Labor & Industrial Relations Commission, 479 U.S. 511 (1987).

48. Runyon v. McCrary, 427 U.S. 160 (1976). See also Civil Rights Restoration Act of 1988, Public Law no. 100-259, §8, 102 Stat. 28 (1988).

49. Green v. Connally, 330 F. Supp. 1150 (D.D.C. 1971), affirmed without opinion sub nomine Coit v. Green, 404 U.S. 997 (1971).

50. Karl N. Llewellyn, "Remarks on the Theory of Appellate Decision and the Rules or Canons about How Statutes Are to Be Construed," 3 *Vanderbilt Law Review* 395 (1950); Eben Moglen and Richard J. Pierce, Jr., "Sunstein's New Canons: Choosing the Fictions of Statutory Interpretation," 57 *University of Chicago Law Review* 1203 (1990).

51. Legal process scholars tend to grant the plain meaning rule less importance than traditional liberals do, since they emphasize the functional operation of the state. But the plain meaning rule does serve functional values associated with the rule of law, United States v. American Trucking Associations, 310 U.S. 534 (1940) (Stone, J., dissenting), and even Hart and Sacks urged against interpretations that

give the statutory words "a meaning they will not bear." See Hart and Sacks, "The Legal Process," 1200.

52. Alexander M. Bickel, *The Least Dangerous Branch: The Supreme Court at the Bar of Politics*, 16 (1962).

53. See, e.g., id. at 206; Harry H. Wellington, *Interpreting the Constitution: The Supreme Court and the Process of Adjudication*, 11 (1991); Abner J. Mikva, "How Well Does Congress Support and Defend the Constitution?" 61 *North Carolina Law Review* 587, 609 (1983); Note, "Congressional Reversal of Supreme Court Decisions: 1945–1957," 71 *Harvard Law Review* 1324, 1332–36 (1958).

54. See my article "Overriding Supreme Court Statutory Interpretation Decisions," 101 *Yale Law Journal* 331, 336–343 (1991); John Ferejohn and Charles Shipan, "Congressional Influence on Bureaucracy," 6 *Journal of Law, Economics, and Organization*, special issue, 1 (1990); Robert A. Katzmann, "Bridging the Statutory Gulf between Courts and Congress: A Challenge for Positive Political Theory," 80 *Georgetown Law Journal* 653 (1992); Michael E. Solimine and James L. Walker, "The Next Word: Congressional Response to Supreme Court Statutory Decisions," 65 *Temple Law Review* 425 (1992).

55. See Edward P. Schwartz, Pablo T. Spiller, and Santiago Urbiztondo, "A Positive Theory of Legislative Intent," 57 *Law and Contemporary Problems* 51 (Winter 1994), on which I comment in "Post-Enactment Legislative Signals," id. at 75.

56. The bookend hearings were *Equal Educational Opportunity: Hearings before the Senate Select Committee on Equal Educational Opportunity*, 91st Cong., 2d sess. (1970), and *Administration's Change in Policy Regarding the Tax Status of Racially Discriminatory Private Schools: Hearing before the House Committee on Ways and Means*, 97th Cong., 2d sess. (1982).

57. Public Law no. 94-568, 90 Stat. 2697 (1976), codified at 26 U.S.C. §501(i), enacted by Congress to override McGlotten v. Connally, 338 F. Supp. 448 (D.D.C. 1972) (three-judge court), which had interpreted §501 to permit segregated social clubs to enjoy tax exemptions.

58. The committee reports for new §501(i) specifically relied on *Green*, which had interpreted the code to prohibit tax exemptions to segregated schools. See Senate Report no. 94-1318, 94th Cong., 2d sess., 7–8 and n.5 (1976); House Report no. 94-1353, 94th Cong., 2d sess., 8 (1976), reprinted in 1976 *United States Code Congressional and Administrative News*, 6051.

59. See Eskridge, "Overriding Statutory Decisions," 348–353.

60. 472 U.S. 675 (1985).

61. 18 U.S.C. §1382 (1982).

62. *Albertini*, 472 U.S. at 697–699 (Stevens, J., dissenting); see id. at 683–684 (opinion for the Court).

63. United States v. United States Gypsum Co., 438 U.S. 422, 437 (1978), quoting Rewis v. United States, 401 U.S. 808, 812 (1971).

64. Of the 121 congressional overrides of Supreme Court statutory decisions

between 1967 and 1990, eighteen overrode interpretations of federal criminal statutes; fourteen of the eighteen overrode interpretations adverse to the position taken by the Justice Department (one was adverse to state prosecutors). See Eskridge, "Overriding Statutory Decisions," 362.

65. Calabresi, *Age of Statutes*, 96–97.

66. See "Affirmative Action: Substantial Majority of Americans Oppose Preferential Treatment for Women and Minorities," 224 *Gallup Report* 28–29 (1984) (Gallup polls in 1977, 1980, and 1984 yielded large majorities against preferences based on race).

67. See, e.g., Daniel Bell, *The End of Ideology: On the Exhaustion of Political Ideas in the Fifties* (1960); Robert A. Dahl, *Who Governs? Democracy and Power in an American City* (1961); Louis Hartz, *The Liberal Tradition in America: An Interpretation of American Political Thought since the Revolution* (1955).

68. 471 U.S. 84 (1985).

69. See Locke v. United States, 573 F. Supp. 472, 474 (D. Nev. 1983).

70. See *Locke*, 471 U.S. at 123 (Stevens, J., dissenting).

71. AMF, Inc., v. Jewett, 711 F.2d 1096, 1108, 1115 (1st Cir. 1983); see 24 C.F.R. §570.423(b) (1985); 31 C.F.R. §515.560(i) (1985); 40 C.F.R. §52.1174 (1985).

72. See William N. Eskridge, Jr., and Philip P. Frickey, *Legislation: Statutes and the Creation of Public Policy*, 634–635 (1988); T. Alexander Aleinikoff and Theodore M. Shaw, "The Costs of Incoherence: A Comment on Plain Meaning, *West Virginia University Hospitals, Inc., v. Casey*, and Due Process of Statutory Interpretation," 45 *Vanderbilt Law Review* 687, 701 n.61 (1992); Richard A. Posner, "Legal Formalism, Legal Realism, and the Interpretation of Statutes and the Constitution," 37 *Case Western Reserve Law Review* 179, 204–208 (1986–87). Peter Strauss suggests that the strange language seeks to accommodate bureaucrats, who might not want to work a full day on December 31, New Year's Eve. Perhaps; but I have found no evidence that this was the legislative purpose.

73. Examples include (1) the Electoral College for electing the president, with the House of Representatives, voting by state, as the fallback if no one receives a majority; (2) the Senate's blatant violation of the one-person, one-vote principle otherwise followed in our system; and (3) gerrymandering in the House. See "Symposium: Gerrymandering and the Courts," 33 *University of California at Los Angeles Law Review* 1 (1985).

74. Michael Parenti, *Democracy for the Few*, 49–55, 193–207 (1977); *How Democratic Is the Constitution?* (Robert A. Goldwin and William A. Schambra, eds., 1980).

75. *The Federalist*, no. 10, at 82 (James Madison) (Clinton Rossiter, ed., 1961); see also *The Federalist*, no. 62 (James Madison).

76. *The Federalist*, no. 78, at 470 (Alexander Hamilton).

77. Hanna F. Pitkin, *The Concept of Representation* (1967); see Bickel, *The Least Dangerous Branch*, 51; Michael Perry, *The Constitution, the Courts, and Human*

Rights: An Inquiry into the Legitimacy of Constitutional Policymaking by the Judiciary, 146–182 (1982).

78. United States v. Carolene Products Co., 304 U.S. 144, 152 n.4 (1938) (stricter scrutiny where "discrete and insular minorities" are penalized or where the statute restricts the political process); South Carolina State Highway Department v. Barnwell Brothers, Inc., 303 U.S. 177, 185 (1938) (stricter scrutiny of state laws that impose costs on out-of-staters unrepresented in the state political process); Minersville School District v. Gobitis, 310 U.S. 586, 603–607 (1940) (Stone, J., dissenting) (stricter scrutiny when political process picks on unpopular groups). See David M. Bixby, "The Roosevelt Court, Democratic Ideology, and Minority Rights: Another Look at *United States v. Classic,*" 90 *Yale Law Journal* 741 (1981).

79. John Hart Ely, *Democracy and Distrust: A Theory of Judicial Review* (1980); see Jesse H. Choper, *Judicial Review and the National Political Process: A Functional Reconsideration of the Role of the Supreme Court* (1980); Eugene V. Rostow, "The Democratic Character of Judicial Review," 66 *Harvard Law Review* 193, 202–203 (1952).

80. See James C. Buchanan and Gordon Tullock, *The Calculus of Consent: Logical Foundations of Constitutional Democracy,* 164–168 (1962) (game theory perspective); James Q. Wilson, *Political Organizations* (1973) (interest group perspective).

81. See Morris Fiorina, *Congress: Keystone of the Washington Establishment,* 40–49 (1977); Michael T. Hayes, *Lobbyists and Legislators: A Theory of Political Markets* (1981).

82. See John W. Kingdon, *Agendas, Alternatives, and Public Policies* (1984) (describing "garbage-can decisionmaking" in the legislative process, whereby Congress acts only when a problem smacks it in the face and there is a well-considered solution immediately available).

83. See Randall B. Ripley and Grace A. Franklin, *Congress, the Bureaucracy, and Public Policy,* 6–10, 13–28 (4th ed. 1987).

84. See Frank H. Easterbrook, "The Supreme Court, 1983 Term—Foreword: The Court and the Economic System," 98 *Harvard Law Review* 4 (1984); Eskridge, "Politics Without Romance," 295–301, 326–334; Jonathan Turley, "Transnational Discrimination and the Economics of Extraterritorial Regulation," 70 *Boston University Law Review* 339 (1990).

85. See William M. Baxter, "Separation of Powers, Prosecutorial Discretion, and the 'Common Law' Nature of Antitrust Law," 60 *Texas Law Review* 661 (1982) (antitrust); Karl N. Llewellyn, "Re: Possible Uniform Commercial Code," reprinted in William Twining, *Karl Llewellyn and the Realist Movement,* 524–529 (1973) (U.C.C.). For statements that the Court interprets general statutes in a common law way, see Business Electronics Corp. v. Sharp Electronics Corp., 485 U.S. 717 (1988) (Sherman Act); Bateman Eichler, Hill Richards, Inc., v. Berner, 472 U.S. 299 (1985) (Securities Act of 1934); Landreth Timber Co. v.

Landreth, 471 U.S. 681 (1985) (Securities Act of 1933); Alexander v. Choate, 469 U.S. 287 (1985) (Rehabilitation Act of 1973); Carey v. Piphus, 435 U.S. 247 (1978) (§1983).

86. See Jonathan A. Macey, "Promoting Public-Regarding Legislation through Statutory Interpretation: An Interest Group Model," 86 *Columbia Law Review* 223 (1986).

87. See Anthony Downs, *Inside Bureaucracy* (1967); William A. Niskanen, *Bureaucracy and Representative Government* (1971); George J. Stigler, "The Theory of Economic Regulation," 2 *Bell Journal of Economics and Management Science* 3 (1971); Sam Peltzman, "Toward a More General Theory of Regulation," 19 *Journal of Law and Economics* 211 (1976).

88. Mancur Olson, *The Logic of Collective Action: Public Goods and the Theory of Groups* (1965).

89. 467 U.S. 340 (1984).

90. Easterbrook, "The Court and the Economic System," 49–51; see Eskridge, "Politics Without Romance," 330–34, for an extended discussion of *Community Nutrition*.

91. Public choice theory provides an explanation for this paradox: discrete and insular minorities may in one period be persecuted for their distinctness, but that very distinctness, as well as the social stigma, stimulates political organization and often efficacy in the next period. See Bruce A. Ackerman, "Beyond *Carolene Products*," 98 *Harvard Law Review* 713 (1985).

92. Charles R. Lawrence III, "The Id, the Ego, and Equal Protection: Reckoning with Unconscious Racism," 39 *Stanford Law Review* 317 (1987).

93. Derrick A. Bell, Jr., "*Brown v. Board of Education* and the Interest-Convergence Dilemma," 93 *Harvard Law Review* 518 (1980).

94. See Gary Peller, "*Neutral Principles* in the 1950s," 21 *University of Michigan Journal of Law Reform* 561 (1988), as well as Mari J. Matsuda, "When the First Quail Calls: Multiple Consciousness as Jurisprudential Method," 11 *Women's Rights Law Reporter* 7 (1989); Catharine A. MacKinnon, "Reflections of Sex Equality under Law," 100 *Yale Law Journal* 1281 (1991); Martha Minow, "The Supreme Court, 1986 Term—Foreword: Justice Engendered," 101 *Harvard Law Review* 10 (1987); Gerald Torres, "Local Knowledge, Local Color: Critical Legal Studies and The Law of Race Relations," 25 *San Diego Law Review* 1043 (1988).

95. For a notable exception, see Richard D. Parker, "The Past of Constitutional Theory—And Its Future," 42 *Ohio State Law Journal* 223 (1981).

96. 467 U.S. 837 (1984).

97. *Pro:* Richard J. Pierce, Jr., "*Chevron* and Its Aftermath: Judicial Review of Agency Interpretations of Statutory Provisions," 41 *Vanderbilt Law Review* 301 (1988); Mark Seidenfeld, "A Civic Republican Justification for the Bureaucratic State," 105 *Harvard Law Review* 1511, 1543–50 (1992); Sidney A. Shapiro and

Robert L. Glicksman, "Congress, the Supreme Court, and the Quiet Revolution in Administrative Law," 1988 *Duke Law Journal* 819; Peter L. Strauss, "One Hundred Fifty Cases per Year: Some Implications of the Supreme Court's Limited Resources for Judicial Review of Agency Action," 87 *Columbia Law Review* 1093 (1987). *Con:* Stephen Breyer, "Judicial Review of Questions of Law and Policy," 38 *Administrative Law Review* 363 (1986); Cynthia R. Farina, "Statutory Interpretation and the Balance of Power in the Administrative State," 89 *Columbia Law Review* 452 (1989); Thomas W. Merrill, "Judicial Deference to Executive Precedent," 101 *Yale Law Journal* 969 (1992); Cass R. Sunstein, "Law and Administration after *Chevron,*" 90 *Columbia Law Review* 2071 (1990).

98. 42 U.S.C. §7502(b)(6) (1978).

99. See *Chevron,* 467 U.S. at 855–859.

100. Natural Resources Defense Council, Inc., v. Gorsuch, 685 F.2d 718 (D.C. Cir. 1982), following ASARCO, Inc., v. EPA, 578 F.2d 319 (D.C. Cir. 1978), and reversed in *Chevron.*

101. *Chevron,* 467 U.S. at 866.

102. Id. at 863–864; accord, e.g., NLRB v. Weingarten, Inc., 420 U.S. 251, 265–266 (1975). But see, e.g., Zenith Radio Corp. v. United States, 437 U.S. 443 (1978) (long-standing agency interpretation should receive greater deference).

103. Family Planning Services and Population Research Act of 1970, Public Law no. 91-572, 84 Stat. 1506 (1970).

104. According to the committee report for the act, the §1008 restriction was to ensure that Title X funds would "be used only to support preventive family planning services, population research, infertility services, and other related medical, informational, and educational activities." Conference Report no. 91-1667, 91st Cong., 2d sess. (1970), reprinted in 1970 *United States Code Congress and Administrative News* 5080, 5081–82.

105. 42 C.F.R. §59.8(a)(1)(1988) specified that henceforth a "Title X project may not provide counseling concerning the use of abortion as a method of family planning or provide referral for abortion as a method of family planning." See also id. §59.8(a)(2)–(3), (b)(5).

106. 111 S. Ct. 1759 (1991).

107. Id. at 1786–88 (Stevens, J., dissenting).

108. Id. at 1788–89 (O'Connor, J., dissenting).

109. Id. at 1778–86 (Blackmun, J., dissenting, joined on this issue by Marshall and Stevens, JJ.).

110. Farina, "Balance of Power in the Administrative State," 499–526.

111. The game explored in the text was suggested in my article coauthored with John Ferejohn "The Article I, Section 7 Game," 80 *Georgetown Law Journal* 523 (1992), and is revised here in response to criticisms from, e.g., Peter L. Strauss and Andrew R. Rutten, "The Game of Politics and Law: A Response to Eskridge and Ferejohn," 8 *Journal of Law, Economics, and Organization* 205 (1992). The game assumes that information is complete, in that the preferences of the

players, the structure of the game, and the rationality of the actors are all common knowledge. It also assumes that the players perfectly anticipate the future course of play, that no one is able to commit to future courses of action, and that all the actors in the model prefer that their decisions not be overturned.

112. See the concurring opinions by legal process Justices Felix Frankfurter and Robert Jackson in Youngstown Steel & Tube Co. v. Sawyer (Steel Seizure Case), 343 U.S. 579 (1952).

113. Congress passed a bill overriding the gag rule, "The Family Planning Amendments Act," S. 323, 102d Cong., 2d sess. (1992). President Bush vetoed it (138 *Congressional Record* S15,157 [daily ed. September 26, 1992]), and the House fell ten votes short of overriding the veto. Id. at H10,678 (daily ed. October 2, 1992) (override vote of 266–148).

114. See INS v. Chadha, 462 U.S. 919 (1983) (legislative veto violates art. I, §7).

115. Stevens seems right that Congress focused only on prohibiting Title X programs themselves from performing abortions and did not contemplate "gag rules" for doctors, but Rehnquist may be right that Congress would have assumed that Title X doctors would also not be encouraging abortions, which were illegal in most states when the statute was enacted (three years before Roe v. Wade).

116. For a more technical version of the following analysis, see William N. Eskridge, Jr., and John Ferejohn "Making the Deal Stick: Enforcing the Original Constitutional Structure of Lawmaking in the Modern Regulatory State," 8 *Journal of Law, Economics, and Organization* 165 (1992).

117. If the Court's preferences are anywhere between those of the two chambers ($H < \mathcal{J} < S$), one of the chambers will always object to any shift. If the Court's preferences are to the right of both chamber medians but not to the right of the veto median of the more pro-president chamber ($S < \mathcal{J} < s$), both chambers of Congress might want to override the Court's decision, but the president would veto the override, and one or both chambers would not be able to override the veto.

118. E.g., Rutten and Strauss, "The Game of Politics and Law."

119. In 1981 seven of the nine Justices were on record as supporting women's rights to abortion as expressed in Roe v. Wade, but five Justices also upheld Congress's authority to provide that federal funds not be used for abortions. See Harris v. McRae, 448 U.S. 297 (1980). Given the First Amendment implications, the Court in 1981 probably would not have upheld a gag rule such as that involved in *Rust*.

120. See Linda R. Cohen and Matthew L. Spitzer, "Solving the *Chevron* Puzzle," 57 *Law and Contemporary Problems* 65 (Spring 1994).

121. President Clinton's first flurry of policy-making actions included an executive override of the HHS gag rule. Memorandum on the Title X "Gag Rule" from William J. Clinton for the Secretary of Health and Human Services (January 22, 1993), reprinted in 139 *Congressional Record* H187 (daily ed., January 25, 1993).

122. Colin S. Diver, "Statutory Interpretation in the Administrative State," 133 *University of Pennsylvania Law Review* 549, 574–592 (1985); Jerry Mashaw, "Pro-Delegation: Why Administrators Should Make Political Decisions," 1 *Journal of Law, Economics, and Organization* 81 (1985).

123. Peter H. Schuck and E. Donald Elliott, "To the *Chevron* Station: An Empirical Study of Federal Administrative Law," 1990 *Duke Law Journal* 984, 1007–8.

124. George L. Priest, "The Common Law Process and the Selection of Efficient Rules," 6 *Journal of Legal Studies* 65 (1977); see John C. Goodman, "An Economic Theory of the Evolution of Common Law," 7 *Journal of Legal Studies* 393 (1978); Paul H. Rubin, "Why Is the Common Law Efficient?" 6 *Journal of Legal Studies* 51 (1977).

125. See Robert Cooter and Lewis Kornhauser, "Can Litigation Improve the Law without the Help of Judges?" 9 *Journal of Legal Studies* 139 (1980); William M. Landes and Richard A. Posner, "Adjudication as a Private Good," 8 *Journal of Legal Studies* 235 (1979).

126. See Gillian K. Hadfield, "Bias in the Evolution of Legal Rules," 80 *Georgetown Law Journal* 583, 594–596 (1992).

127. Paul H. Rubin, "Common Law and Statute Law," 11 *Journal of Legal Studies* 205 (1982); see Einer R. Elhauge, "Does Interest Group Theory Justify More Intrusive Judicial Review?" 101 *Yale Law Journal* 31 (1991); Mark Galanter, "Why the 'Haves' Come Out Ahead: Speculations on the Limits of Legal Change," 9 *Law and Society Review* 95 (1974); Georg V. Wangenheim, "The Evolution of Judge-Made Law," in *Papers on Economics and Evolution*, no. 9205 (European Study Group for Evolutionary Economics, 1993).

128. Richard A. Posner, *Economic Analysis of Law*, 21–22 (3d ed. 1986); see Robert Cooter, Lewis Kornhauser, and David Lane, "Liability Rules, Limited Information, and the Role of Precedent," 10 *Bell Journal of Economics* 366 (1979).

129. For samples, all without any empirical support, see Posner, *Economic Analysis of Law*, 505–507 (judges maximize their influence on policy); Robert D. Cooter, "The Objectives of Private and Public Judges," 41 *Public Choice* 107, 129 (1983) (judges maximize their prestige among litigants); Wangenheim, "The Evolution of Judge-Made Law" (German scholar asserts that judges seek good rules, high standing in legal community, promotion).

130. See Richard A. Posner, *Overcoming Law*, chap. 3 (forthcoming 1995).

131. See Richard B. Stewart, "The Reformation of American Administrative Law," 88 *Harvard Law Review* 1667, 1716 (1976).

132. 463 U.S. 29 (1983).

133. See Eugene V. Rostow, *The Sovereign Prerogative: The Supreme Court and the Quest for Law*, 24–39 (1962); Kent Greenawalt, "The Enduring Significance of Neutral Principles," 78 *Columbia Law Review* 982 (1982); and especially Herbert Wechsler, "Toward Neutral Principles of Constitutional Law," 73 *Harvard Law Review* 1 (1959), analyzed in Peller, "Neutral Principles in the 1950s"; Edward

L. Rubin, "On Beyond Truth: A Theory for Evaluating Legal Scholarship," 80 *California Law Review* 889, 917–918 (1992).

134. See William M. Landes and Richard A. Posner, "The Private Enforcement of Law," 4 *Journal of Legal Studies* 1 (1975).

135. See Gary Peller, "The Metaphysics of American Law," 73 *California Law Review* 1151 (1985).

136. See, e.g., Anthony Earl Cook, "Critical Race Law and Affirmative Action: The Legacy of Dr. Martin Luther King, Jr.," 8 *Harvard Blackletter Law Journal* 61 (1991); Kimberlé Williams Crenshaw, "Race, Reform, and Retrenchment: Transformation and Legitimation in Antidiscrimination Law," 101 *Harvard Law Review* 1331 (1988); Mari J. Matsuda, "Looking to the Bottom: Critical Legal Studies and Reparations," 22 *Harvard Civil Rights–Civil Liberties Law Review* 323 (1987); Patricia J. Williams, "*Metro Broadcasting, Inc., v. FCC:* Regrouping in Singular Times," 104 *Harvard Law Review* 525 (1990).

137. Thomas W. Merrill, "Judicial Deference to Executive Precedent," 101 *Yale Law Journal* 969 (1992), found that the Supreme Court before 1984 deferred to agencies in 75 percent of the surveyed cases, that the Court after 1984 usually did not cite *Chevron* or follow its framework in deciding whether to defer to agencies, and that when the Court did apply the *Chevron* framework, it deferred to agencies in only 59 percent of the cases, well below the pre-*Chevron* figure of 75 percent, and below the overall deference rate after 1984 of 70 percent. For different numerical calculations but a similar trend, see Cohen and Spitzer, "Solving the *Chevron* Puzzle." Cohen and Spitzer make the important point, neglected by Merrill, that the Court's failure to cite or follow *Chevron* in post-1984 cases tells us nothing about the *effect* of the decision on agencies, litigants, and lower courts. Their article is the critical first step in such an inquiry.

6. Normativist Theories

This chapter draws from my article, coauthored with Gary Peller, "The New Public Law Movement: Moderation as a Postmodern Cultural Form," 89 *Michigan Law Review* 707 (1991).

1. Joseph A. Schumpeter, *Capitalism, Socialism, and Democracy*, 242 (1961).

2. See Judith N. Shklar, "Political Theory and the Rule of Law," in *The Rule of Law: Ideal or Ideology?*, 1 (Allan C. Hutchinson and Patrick Monahan, eds., 1987), who contrasts a vision of the rule of law as fairness and justice (Aristotle) with one of the rule of law as checks against the exercise of state power (Montesquieu).

3. A term suggested to me by Alexander Aleinikoff and first used in my review "Metaprocedure," 98 *Yale Law Journal* 945 (1989).

4. See Henry M. Hart, Jr., and Albert M. Sacks, "The Legal Process: Basic Problems in the Making and Application of Law," 4 (tentative ed. 1958) (forthcoming from Foundation Press in 1994, ed. William N. Eskridge, Jr., and Philip

P. Frickey); Owen M. Fiss, "The Varieties of Positivism," 90 *Yale Law Journal* 1007 (1981).

5. See John Finnis, *Natural Law and Natural Rights* (1980); Philip Soper, *A Theory of Law* (1984); Lloyd L. Weinreb, *Natural Law and Justice* (1987); Heidi M. Hurd, "Relativist Jurisprudence: Skepticism Founded on Confusion," 61 *Southern California Law Review* 1418 (1988) (student note).

6. See, e.g., David A. J. Richards, *The Moral Criticism of Law*, 31–36 (1977).

7. For an excellent introduction to Fuller's thought, see Martin P. Golding, "Jurisprudence and Legal Philosophy in Twentieth-Century America: Major Themes and Developments," 36 *Journal of Legal Education* 441, 473–480 (1986). See also Robert S. Summers, *Lon L. Fuller* (1984); Kenneth I. Winston, ed., *The Principles of Social Order: The Selected Essays of Lon L. Fuller* (1981); Alfred S. Konefsky, Elizabeth B. Mensch, and John H. Schlegel, "In Memoriam: The Intellectual Legacy of Lon Fuller," 30 *Buffalo Law Review* 263 (1981).

8. Lon L. Fuller, *The Law in Quest of Itself*, 8–9 (1940).

9. Id. at 9–10. See also Lon L. Fuller, "American Legal Philosophy at Mid-Century," 6 *Journal of Legal Education* 457 (1954).

10. Compare Ronald Dworkin, *Law's Empire* 348 (1986) (law is like a "continuing story, and [one's] interpretation therefore changes as the story develops").

11. Fuller, *Law in Quest*, 111–112.

12. Lon L. Fuller, "Human Interaction and the Law," in Winston, *The Principles of Social Order*, 211–246.

13. 536 A.2d 1 (D.C. 1987) (en banc).

14. See Congregation for the Doctrine of the Faith, "The Pastoral Care of Homosexual Persons," 16 *Origins* 377 (1986) (letter to Catholic bishops urging them to exclude from pastoral programs organizations in which "homosexuals" participate "without clearly stating that homosexual activity is immoral"); Bruce Williams, "Homosexuality: The New Vatican Statement," 48 *Theological Studies* 270 (1987).

15. District of Columbia Code §1-2520(1); see id. §1-2501 (intent of Council).

16. *Gay Rights Coalition*, 536 A.2d at 5, 16–17, 21, 26–30 (opinion of Mack, J., delivering the judgment of the court); see id. at 39 (Pryor, C. J., concurring in the judgment and in most of Mack's opinion). Judge Newman concurred in the judgment; id. at 40 (Newman, J., concurring). Judges Ferren and Terry concurred in that part of the judgment requiring Georgetown to provide equal access and services and dissented its not requiring recognition; id. at 46 (Ferren, J., concurring in the result in part and dissenting in part); id. at 74 (Terry, J., concurring in part and dissenting in part). Judges Belson and Nebeker concurred in that part of the judgment not requiring recognition and dissented from its requiring equal access and services; id. at 62 (Belson, J., concurring in part and dissenting in part); id. at 75 (Nebeker, J., concurring in part and dissenting in part). Hence, although only three judges agreed with both parts of the judgment, there were five (of seven) votes for each part.

17. Id. at 21 (opinion of Mack, J.).

18. Id. at 30–37.

19. Id. at 49 (Ferren, J., joined by Terry, J., concurring in the result in part and dissenting in part).

20. *Gay Rights Coalition*, 536 A.2d at 63 (Belson, J., joined by Nebeker, J., concurring in part and dissenting in part); see id. at 72.

21. Id. at 73.

22. Id. at 75 (Nebeker, J., concurring in part and dissenting in part).

23. Id. at 76–78.

24. See Sissela Bok, *Lying: Moral Choice in Public and Private Life* (1978); David L. Shapiro, "In Defense of Judicial Candor," 100 *Harvard Law Review* 731 (1987). But see Nicholas S. Zeppos, "Judicial Candor and Statutory Interpretation," 78 *Georgetown Law Journal* 353 (1989).

25. See Lon L. Fuller, *The Morality of Law*, 33–38 (1964; rev. ed. 1969) (the "parable of King Rex"); also Lon L. Fuller, *Anatomy of the Law* (1968).

26. My discussion in this part draws primarily on Heidi M. Hurd, "Sovereignty in Silence," 99 *Yale Law Journal* 945 (1990), and "Challenging Authority," 100 *Yale Law Journal* 1611 (1991); Michael S. Moore, "A Natural Law Theory of Interpretation," 58 *Southern California Law Review* 277 (1985). See also Heidi M. Hurd, "Justifiably Punishing the Justified," 90 *Michigan Law Review* 2203 (1992).

27. Moore, "Natural Law Theory of Interpretation," 315–320.

28. Id. at 353–358, criticizing Keeler v. Superior Court, 2 Cal. 3d 619, 470 P.2d 617 (1970), for not considering evolving and improving modern insights about personhood when the court held that a person's attack on a woman such that her unborn child died in the womb is not statutory "murder" of the fetus.

29. Moore, "Natural Law Theory of Interpretation," 358.

30. Hurd, "Challenging Authority," responding to Joseph Raz, *The Authority of Law* (1979) and *The Morality of Freedom* (1986).

31. Hurd, "Challenging Authority," 1620.

32. Id. at 1667–77; Hurd, "Sovereignty in Silence," 995–997 (statutes are at best "signs" of optimal social arrangements; they cannot be "signals" because they do not meet the requirements of "communicative utterances").

33. Hurd, "Sovereignty in Silence," 1028 and n.177, citing Lon L. Fuller, "Positivism and Fidelity to Law—A Reply to Professor Hart," 71 *Harvard Law Review* 630 (1958), and Moore, "Natural Law Theory of Interpretation," 383–386.

34. The Law Center, where I teach, supported the students. The university administration was internally divided at various points of the lawsuit, perhaps no more so than after the Court of Appeals decision. My understanding is that the university's lawyers, several members of the board of directors, and many alumni wanted to continue to litigate through the U.S. Supreme Court but that university president Timothy Healy, much of the faculty, and several members of the board of overseers wanted to settle the case. After much debate the latter course prevailed.

35. *Gay Rights Coalition*, 536 A.2d at 11–12 (opinion of Mack, J); id. at 64, 67–68 n.9 (Belson, J., dissenting in part).

36. See id. at 69–72, relying on, e.g., United States v. Lee, 455 U.S. 252 (1982) (requiring compelling state interest to subject Amish to social security taxes at odds with their religious beliefs).

37. See Raz, *Morality of Freedom*, 47.

38. In 1988 Congress attempted to compel the District Council to amend the Human Rights Act to exempt religious institutions from the prohibition against discrimination on the basis of sexual preference by conditioning federal funding to the District on adoption of such an amendment. Public Law no. 100-462, 102 Stat. 2269 (1988). A federal appeals panel invalidated this under the First Amendment. Clarke v. United States, 886 F.2d 404 (D.C. Cir. 1989), vacated as moot, 915 F.2d 699 (D.C. Cir. 1990) (en banc). Congress then legislated the restriction by amending the D.C. Code directly. Public Law no. 101-168, §141, 103 Stat. 1267, 1284 (1989).

39. See Leslie Green, *The Authority of the State* (1988), and Joseph Raz, *Practical Reason and Norms* (1975). Hurd, "Challenging Authority," 1620–41, mounts an analytical attack on a technical version of this sort of argument.

40. Gary Peller, "*Neutral Principles* in the 1950s," 21 *University of Michigan Journal of Law Reform* 561 (1988).

41. The concept of dialogue is particularly important to feminist theories (see Martha Minow, "The Supreme Court, 1986 Term—Foreword: Justice Engendered," 101 *Harvard Law Review* 10 [1987]); hermeneutical theories (see Francis J. Mootz III, "The Ontological Basis of Legal Hermeneutics: A Proposed Model of Inquiry Based on the Work of Gadamer, Habermas, and Ricoeur," 68 *Boston University Law Review* 523 [1988]); republican theories (see Bruce A. Ackerman, *Reconstructing American Law* [1984]; Frank I. Michelman, "The Supreme Court, 1985 Term—Foreword: Traces of Self-Government," 100 *Harvard Law Review* 4 [1986]); and literary or theological theories (see Robert A. Burt, "Constitutional Law and the Teaching of the Parables," 93 *Yale Law Journal* 455 [1984]). See generally Mark V. Tushnet, "Anti-Formalism in Recent Constitutional Theory," 83 *Michigan Law Review* 1502 (1985).

42. See generally "Symposium: The Republican Civic Tradition," 97 *Yale Law Journal* 1493–1723 (1988); Michelman, "Traces of Self-Government"; Suzanna Sherry, "Civic Virtue and the Feminine Voice in Constitutional Adjudication," 72 *Virginia Law Review* 543 (1986).

43. Robert M. Cover, "The Supreme Court, 1982 Term—Foreword: *Nomos* and Narrative," 97 *Harvard Law Review* 4 (1983).

44. Id. at 12–13.

45. *Gay Rights Coalition*, 536 A.2d at 16 (opinion of Mack, J.), citing NLRB v. Catholic Bishop of Chicago, 440 U.S. 533 (1979) (the leading case for the canon, in which the Supreme Court refused to interpret federal labor law to regulate the employment conditions of lay teachers at parochial schools).

46. *Gay Rights Coalition*, 536 A.2d at 33–38 (opinion of Mack, J.); see Barry D.

Adam, *The Rise of a Gay and Lesbian Movement* (1987); Lillian Faderman, *Odd Girls and Twilight Lovers: A History of Lesbian Life in Twentieth-Century America* (1992); John D'Emilio, *Sexual Politics, Sexual Communities: The Making of a Homosexual Minority in the United States, 1940–1970* (1983). See also Steven Epstein, "Gay Politics, Gay Identity: The Limits of Social Constructionism," in *Forms of Desire: Sexual Orientation and the Social Constructionist Controversy*, 239 (Edward Stein, ed., 1990) (the gay, lesbian, and bisexual community shares most of the functional characteristics of the "new ethnicity").

47. *Gay Rights Coalition*, 536 A.2d at 36 (opinion of Mack, J.); see Commonwealth of Kentucky v. Wasson, 842 S.W.2d 487 (Ky. 1992); Janet Halley, "The Politics of the Closet: Towards Equal Protection for Gay, Lesbian, and Bisexual Identity," 36 *University of California at Los Angeles Law Review* 915 (1989).

48. See Frank I. Michelman, "Law's Republic," 97 *Yale Law Journal* 1493 (1988), arguing that state sodomy laws are invalid under modern republican theory.

49. Cover, "*Nomos* and Narrative," 40.

50. For an excellent essay drawing on comparative law to discuss conflicting and colliding norms, see Melvin A. Eisenberg, "Private Ordering through Negotiation: Dispute-Settlement and Rulemaking," 89 *Harvard Law Review* 637 (1976).

51. Michelman, "Traces of Self-Government," 21–24. See the discussion of Aristotle in the introduction and Chapter 2 of this book, as well as Richard A. Posner, *The Problems of Jurisprudence* (1990); Daniel A. Farber, "Legal Pragmatism and the Constitution," 72 *Minnesota Law Review* 1331 (1988); Dennis M. Patterson, "Interpretation in Law—Toward a Reconstruction of the Current Debate," 29 *Villanova Law Review* 671 (1984). See generally Michael Brint and William Weaver, eds., *Pragmatism in Law and Society* (1991).

52. Most useful for me have been Naomi R. Cahn, "The Case of the Speluncean Explorers: Contemporary Proceedings," 61 *George Washington Law Review* 1755 (1993); Cynthia R. Farina, "Conceiving Due Process," 3 *Yale Journal of Law and Feminism* 189 (1991); Margaret Jane Radin, "The Pragmatist and the Feminist," in Brint and Weaver, *Pragmatism in Law and Society*, 127; Judith Resnik, "On the Bias: Feminist Reconsiderations of the Aspirations for Our Judges," 61 *Southern California Law Review* 1877 (1988).

53. Cultural feminism is inspired by Carol Gilligan, *In a Different Voice: Psychological Theory and Women's Development* (1982), which contrasted an ethic of care (the voice of Amy in Gilligan's experiments) and an ethic of rights (the voice of Jake). See also Carol Gilligan et al., eds., *Making Connections: The Relational Worlds of Adolescent Girls at Emma Willard School* (1990). My application of cultural feminist insights to statutory interpretation draws from Cahn, "Speluncean Explorers"; Martha Minow and Elizabeth V. Spelman, "In Context," in Brint and Weaver, *Pragmatism in Law and Society*, 247; Radin, "The Pragmatist and the Feminist"; Sherry, "Civic Virtue and the Feminine Voice."

54. See *Gay Rights Coalition*, 536 A.2d at 67–70 (Belson, J., dissenting in part)

(repeated focus on Georgetown's "rights" and terribleness of "forced" subsidies or recognition); id. at 75 (Nebeker, J., dissenting in part) (similar).

55. Id. at 31 (opinion of Mack, J.); see id. at 30–39 (detailed analysis).

56. Id. at 41 (Newman, J., concurring) (first quotation); id. at 43 (second quotation), quoting Herbert Wechsler, "Toward Neutral Principles of Constitutional Law," 73 *Harvard Law Review* 1, 16 (1959).

57. Id. at 75–78 (Nebeker, J., dissenting in part) (explicitly objecting to "homosexual 'life-style'" and attaching pictures promoting a gay dance); id. at 72–73 (Belson, J., dissenting in part) (sexual orientation discrimination is more acceptable than other forms of discrimination).

58. Radin, "Pragmatist and Feminist," 1711. Feminism has recognized the ways in which homophobia is tied to patterns of gender oppression as well. See Suzanne Pharr, *Homophobia as a Weapon of Sexism* (1988); Ruthann Robson, *Lesbian (Out)Law: Surviving under the Rule of Law* (1992).

59. See Mari J. Matsuda, "Pragmatism Modified and the False Consciousness Problem," 63 *Southern California Law Review* (1990), and "When the First Quail Calls: Multiple Consciousness as Jurisprudential Method," 11 *Women's Rights Law Reporter* 7 (1989); Minow, "Justice Engendered"; Radin, "The Pragmatist and the Feminist."

60. Michelman, "Law's Republic," as well as Michelman, "Traces of Self-Government," 31–33.

61. Michelman, "Traces of Self-Government," 33 (emphasis added).

62. *Gay Rights Coalition*, 536 A.2d at 5–7, 8 (opinion of Mack, J.).

63. Id. at 10–11.

64. This and other sources quoted id. at 8.

65. *Undergraduate Bulletin*, 1, quoted id.

66. John Boswell, *Christianity, Social Tolerance, and Homosexuality: Gay People in Western Europe from the Beginning of the Christian Era to the Fourteenth Century* (1980), critically reviewed by Bruce Williams, "Homosexuality and Christianity: A Review Discussion," 46 *The Tomist* 609 (1982). See also Bernadotte J. Brooten, *The New Testament and Homosexuality: Contextual Background for Contemporary Debate* (1983); John McNeill, *The Church and the Homosexual* (1976); Denise Carmody and John Carmody, "Homosexuality and Roman Catholicism," in *Homosexuality and World Religions*, 135–138 (Arlene Swidler, ed., 1993); Lewis John Eron, "Homosexuality and Judaism," in Swidler, *Homosexuality and World Religions*, 103.

67. See my article "A History of Same-Sex Marriage," 79 *Virginia Law Review* 1419 (1993) (same-sex unions); John Boswell, "Homosexuality and the Religious Life: A Historical Approach," in *Homosexuality in the Priesthood and Religious Life*, 3, 11 (Jeannine Grammick, ed., 1989) (same-sex marriages).

68. See Richard A. Posner, *Sex and Reason*, 154–155 (1992).

69. *Gay Rights Coalition*, 536 A.2d at 49 (Ferren, J., dissenting in part).

70. The bases for the assertions in the text are my own experience within the gay, lesbian, and bisexual communities in Washington, D.C., during the 1980s;

my general reading about our history and from our literature; and my work with Bi-LAGA on an oral history of the *Gay Rights Coalition* lawsuit, which has included videotaped interviews with some of the plaintiffs.

71. Postmodernism challenges modernist claims about rationality, representation, and meta-narrative as ways to mediate between individuals and universals. Postmodernism is insistently skeptical that there can be successful mediation. See Pauline Marie Rosenau, *Post-Modernism and the Social Sciences: Insights, Inroads, and Intrusions* (1992). Implications of postmodernism for law are explored by Stanley Fish, *Doing What Comes Naturally: Change, Rhetoric, and the Practice of Theory in Literary and Legal Studies* (1989); Zillah R. Eisenstein, *The Female Body and the Law* (1988); Milton C. Regan, Jr., *Family Law and the Pursuit of Intimacy* (1993); Dennis M. Patterson, "Postmodernism/Feminism/Law," 77 *Cornell Law Review* 254 (1992); Gary Peller, "The Metaphysics of American Law," 73 *California Law Review* 1151 (1985); Peter C. Schanck, "Understanding Postmodern Thought and Its Implications for Statutory Interpretation," 65 *Southern California Law Review* 2505 (1992).

72. For applications of Derrida to legal interpretive issues, see J. M. Balkin, "Deconstructive Practice and Legal Theory," 96 *Yale Law Journal* 743 (1987); Clare Dalton, "An Essay in the Deconstruction of Contract Doctrine," 94 *Yale Law Journal* 997 (1985); Schanck, "Understanding Postmodern Thought," 2522–38; Girardeau A. Spann, "Deconstructing the Legislative Veto," 68 *Minnesota Law Review* 473 (1984); Mark V. Tushnet, "Critical Legal Studies and Constitutional Law: An Essay in Deconstruction," 36 *Stanford Law Review* 623 (1984).

73. See Antonin Scalia, "The Rule of Law as a Law of Rules," 56 *University of Chicago Law Review* 1175 (1989). The deconstruction in the text is inspired by my reading of Peller, "The Metaphysics of American Law."

74. Compare *Gay Rights Coalition*, 536 A.2d at 21–26 (opinion of Mack, J., finding required access and facilities constitutional but required endorsement unconstitutional), with id. at 52–62 (Ferren, J., dissenting in part, arguing that the free exercise clause permits required endorsement as well as required access and facilities), and with id. at 67–74 (Belson, J., dissenting in part, arguing that the free exercise clause disallows required access and facilities as well as required endorsement).

75. Compare id. at 27–29 (opinion of Mack, J., finding evidence in the record that Georgetown denied access to the gay and lesbian student groups in large part because of the sexual orientation of their members and that the university's "recognition" also included implied endorsement), with id. at 64–65 (Belson, J., dissenting in part, finding evidence in the record that Georgetown denied access only because of students' advocacy), and with id. at 74–75 (Terry, J., dissenting in part, finding no evidence in record that recognition meant endorsement).

76. Compare id. at 33–38 (opinion of Mack, J., finding compelling the District's purpose to end sexual orientation discrimination, based on her independent examination of the unjust treatment of gay men, lesbians, and bisexuals), with id. at

75 (Nebeker, J., dissenting in part, finding no state interest in protecting gay men and lesbians because the "homosexual 'life-style' is felonious").

77. Id. at 16–21 (opinion of Mack, J.).

78. See id. at 21–23 (synthesizing Supreme Court free speech as well as free exercise decisions).

79. Margaret Jane Radin, "Reconsidering the Rule of Law," 69 *Boston University Law Review* 781, 799–800 (1989). Other postmodern efforts at thinking about the rule of law include Geoffrey De Q. Walker, *The Rule of Law: Foundation of Constitutional Democracy* (1988); Fred Dallmayr, "Hermeneutics and the Rule of Law," 11 *Cardozo Law Review* 1449 (1990); William N. Eskridge, Jr., "Gadamer/Statutory Interpretation," 90 *Columbia Law Review* 609 (1990); David Couzens Hoy, "Interpreting the Law: Hermeneutical and Poststructuralist Perspectives," 58 *Southern California Law Review* 135 (1985); Francis J. Mootz III, "Is the Rule of Law Possible in a Postmodern World?" 68 *Washington Law Review* 249 (1993) (yes).

80. See Stanley Fish, *Is There a Text in This Class? The Authority of Interpretive Communities* (1980); Fish, *Doing What Comes Naturally.*

81. Fish, *Is There a Text in This Class?* 303–304.

82. See Roland Barthes, "The Death of the Author," in *Images, Music, Text* (Roland Barthes, ed., 1978); Michel Foucault, "What Is an Author?," in *The Foucault Reader,* 101–120 (Paul Rabinow, ed., 1984).

83. Modernist democratic theory can be deconstructed chiefly through challenging its claims of "representation." See Harry Redner, "Representation and the Crisis of Post-Modernism," 20 *PS: Political Science and Politics* 673 (1987).

84. See Michel Foucault, *Beyond Structuralism and Hermeneutics* (Hubert L. Dreyfuss and Paul Rabinow, eds., 1982); Edward Stein, ed., *Forms of Desire: Sexual Orientation and the Social Constructionist Controversy* (1981). For legal applications, see Jed Rubenfeld, "The Right of Privacy," 102 *Harvard Law Review* 737 (1989); Stephen J. Schnably, "Beyond *Griswold:* Foucauldian and Republican Approaches to Privacy," 23 *Connecticut Law Review* 861 (1991).

85. Michel Foucault, *Introduction,* vol. 1 of *History of Sexuality,* 94 (Robert Hurley, trans., 1978).

86. For details of this story, see my review essay "A Social Constructionist Critique of Posner's *Sex and Reason:* Steps toward a Gaylegal Agenda," 102 *Yale Law Journal* 333 (1992).

87. See Michel Foucault, "Afterward: The Subject and Power," in Dreyfuss and Rabinow, *Beyond Structuralism,* 208; Mary McIntosh, "The Homosexual Role," 16 *Social Problems* 182 (1968).

88. Charles R. Lawrence III, "The Id, the Ego, and Equal Protection: Reckoning with Unconscious Racism," 39 *Stanford Law Review* 317 (1987). See, e.g., Derrick A. Bell, Jr., *Race and Racism in American Law* (2d ed. 1980); Patricia J. Williams, *The Alchemy of Race and Rights* (1991); Anthony Earl Cook, "Beyond Critical Legal Studies: The Reconstructive Theology of Dr. Martin Luther King, Jr.," 103 *Harvard Law Review* 985 (1990).

89. Catharine A. MacKinnon, *Sexual Harassment of Working Women: A Case of Sex Discrimination* (1979). See, e.g., Drucilla Cornell, *Beyond Accommodation: Ethical Feminism, Deconstruction, and the Law* (1991); Mary Joe Frug, "A Postmodern Feminist Legal Manifesto (An Unfinished Draft)," 105 *Harvard Law Review* 1045 (1992); Joan Chalmers Williams, "Dissolving the Sameness/Difference Debate: A Post-Modern Path beyond Essentialism in Feminist and Critical Race Theory," 1991 *Duke Law Journal* 296.

90. See Lynn A. Baker, "'Just Do It': Pragmatism and Progressive Social Change," in Brint and Weaver, *Pragmatism in Law and Society*, 99; Schanck, "Understanding Postmodern Thought," 2569–70 (endorsing Fish as the most consistent postmodernist because he claims no theoretical payoff for postmodernism), 2589–95 (praising my work with Philip Frickey for its postmodern eclecticism and avoidance of strong normative agendas).

91. It is inspired in large part by William James, *Pragmatism* (Fredson Bowers, ed., 1975); Richard Rorty, *Contingency, Irony, and Solidarity* (1989); Cornel West, *The American Evasion of Philosophy: A Genealogy of Pragmatism* (1989). Among legal authors, critical pragmatism is related to themes developed in Jay Feinman, "Practical Legal Studies and Critical Legal Studies," 87 *Michigan Law Review* 724 (1988); Matsuda, "When the First Quail Calls"; Radin, "The Pragmatist and the Feminist"; Joseph William Singer, "Property and Coercion in Federal Indian Law: The Conflict between Critical and Complacent Pragmatism," 63 *Southern California Law Review* 1821 (1990).

92. See William N. Eskridge, Jr., and Philip P. Frickey, "Statutory Interpretation as Practical Reasoning," 42 *Stanford Law Review* 321, 339 n.69 (1990).

93. Marguerite Yourcenar, *Memoirs of Hadrian*, 113 (Grace Frick, trans., 1954) (imaginative reconstruction of Hadrian's philosophy of life, law, and love).

94. See Boutilier v. INS, 363 F.2d 488, 497–498 (2d Cir. 1966) (Moore, J., dissenting), affirmed, 387 U.S. 118 (1967).

95. Letter from Oliver Wendell Holmes, Jr., to Felix Frankfurter, January 30, 1921, in Holmes Papers, Harvard University. I am indebted to Daniel Robinson Ernst for bringing this letter to my attention.

96. See Johnson v. Transportation Agency, Santa Clara County, 480 U.S. 616, 642–647 (1987) (Stevens, J., concurring); id. at 647–657 (O'Connor, J., concurring in the judgment). As a pragmatist I harbor doubts about the result in that particular case, based on Marc Rosenblum, "Race-Conscious Employment Programs in the Post-Brennan Era: An End to Falsely Remedial Preferences?" 28 *Houston Law Review* 993 (1991).

97. Public Law no. 102-166, §107(a), 105 Stat. 1071, 1075 (1991) (adding new §703[m]); see also id. §105(a) (adding new §703[k] to define the burden of proof in disparate impact cases).

98. Compare Michael Stokes Paulsen, "Reverse Discrimination and Law School Faculty Hiring: The Undiscovered Opinion," 71 *Texas Law Review* 993, 1005–6 (1993) (new §703[m] overrules *Weber*), with Officers for Justice v. Civil Service Commission, 979 F.2d 721, 725 (9th Cir. 1992) (rejecting this argument).

99. 490 U.S. 228 (1989). On the intent to override only *Hopkins* and not *Weber,* see House Report no. 102-40, pt. 1, 102d Cong., 1st sess., 45–46 (1991) (Education and Labor Committee report); House Report no. 102-40, pt. 2, 102d Cong., 1st sess., 16–19 (1991) (Judiciary Committee report).

100. Civil Rights Act of 1991, §116, 105 Stat. at 1079; see House Report no. 102-40, pt. 2, 37 (referring to both *Weber* and *Johnson* as "the law" to be applied to affirmative action).

101. See Thomas Sowell, *Civil Rights: Rhetoric or Reality?* (1984); Walter E. Williams, *The State against Blacks* (1982).

102. See "Symposium: The Law and Economics of Racial Discrimination in Employment," 79 *Georgetown Law Journal* 1619–1782 (1991), especially David Strauss, "The Law and Economics of Racial Discrimination in Employment: The Case for Numerical Standards," id. at 1619; John I. Donohue III and James J. Heckman, "Re-Evaluating Federal Civil Rights Policy," id. at 1713.

7. Legislative History Values

This chapter draws from my articles "Legislative History Values," 66 *Chicago-Kent Law Review* 365 (1990), and "The New Textualism," originally published in 37 *University of California at Los Angeles Law Review* 621 (1990), © 1990, The Regents of the University of California. All rights reserved.

1. Patricia M. Wald, "Some Observations on the Use of Legislative History in the 1981 Supreme Court Term," 68 *Iowa Law Review* 195 (1983).

2. Richard Pildes, "Intent, Clear Statements, and the Common Law: Statutory Interpretation in the Supreme Court," 95 *Harvard Law Review* 892 (1982) (student note); see Jorge L. Carro and Andrew R. Brann, "Use of Legislative Histories by the United States Supreme Court: A Statistical Analysis," 9 *Journal of Legislation* 282, 291 (1982) (enormous increase in citation of legislative history 1973–74, then falling back slightly in the late 1970s).

3. Skeptical treatments of the new textualism include Stephen Breyer, "On the Uses of Legislative History in Interpreting Statutes," 65 *Southern California Law Review* 845 (1992); George A. Costello, "Average Voting Members and Other 'Benign Fictions': The Relative Reliability of Committee Reports, Floor Debates, and Other Sources of Legislative History," 1990 *Duke Law Journal* 39; Michael Livingston, "Congress, the Courts, and the Code: Legislative History and the Interpretation of Tax Statutes," 69 *Texas Law Review* 819 (1991); Abner J. Mikva, "A Reply to Judge Starr's Observations," 1987 *Duke Law Journal* 380; Stephen Ross, "Reaganist Realism Comes to Detroit," 1989 *University of Illinois Law Review* 399; Patricia M. Wald, "The Sizzling Sleeper: The Use of Legislative History in Construing Statutes in the 1988–89 Term of the United States Supreme Court," 39 *American University Law Review* 277 (1990); Nicholas S. Zeppos, "Justice Scalia's Textualism: The 'New' New Legal Process," 12 *Cardozo Law Review* 1597 (1991). Treatments generally sympathetic to the new textualism include

Frank H. Easterbrook, "The Role of Original Intent in Statutory Construction," 11 *Harvard Journal of Law and Public Policy* 59 (1988); Orrin Hatch, "Legislative History: Tool of Construction or Destruction," 11 *Harvard Journal of Law and Public Policy* 43 (1988); Jerry L. Mashaw, "Textualism, Constitutionalism, and the Interpretation of Federal Statutes," 32 *William and Mary Law Review* 827 (1991); Frederick Schauer, "Statutory Construction and the Coordinating Function of Plain Meaning," 1990 *Supreme Court Review* 231; W. David Slawson, "Legislative History and the Need to Bring Statutory Interpretation under the Rule of Law," 44 *Stanford Law Review* 383 (1992); Kenneth W. Starr, "Observations about the Use of Legislative History," 1987 *Duke Law Journal* 371.

4. Theodore Sedgwick, *A Treatise on the Rules Which Govern the Interpretation and Application of Statutory and Constitutional Law*, 247 (1857); see Fortunatus Dwarris, *A General Treatise on Statutes: Their Rules of Construction, and the Proper Boundaries of Legislation and of Judicial Interpretation*, 143–145 (1871); G. A. [Gustav Adolf] Endlich, *A Commentary on the Interpretation of Statutes* (1888). On the ambiguous status of legislative history in the United Kingdom, see Zenon Bankowski and D. Neil MacCormick, "Statutory Interpretation in the United Kingdom," in *Interpreting Statutes: A Comparative Study*, 359, 378–382 (D. Neil MacCormick and Robert S. Summers, eds., 1991). The House of Lords in 1992 announced that it would consult parliamentary debates under some circumstances. Pepper v. Hart, 3 W.L.R. 1032 (House of Lords 1992).

5. The Supreme Court occasionally referred to legislative materials as secondary evidence to figure out what the "plain meaning" of a statutory text might be; see Jennison v. Kirk, 98 U.S. 453, 459–460 (1879); Arthur v. Richards, 90 U.S. 246, 258 (1875); Dubuque & Pacific Railroad v. Litchfield, 64 U.S. 66, 87 (1860). I have, however, found no decision before 1892 in which the Court relied primarily on such materials or used them to support an interpretation contrary to the statute's apparent plain meaning. For stronger reliance on extrinsic materials by the Department of Justice, see "Interest on Demands against the United States," 3 *Opinions of the Attorney General*, 294 (1837).

6. J. G. [Jabez Gridley] Sutherland, *Statutes and Statutory Construction*, 309 (quotation in text), 380–384 (1st ed. 1891).

7. 143 U.S. 457 (1892).

8. Act of February 26, 1885, ch. 164, 23 Stat. 332.

9. Elsewhere, for example, the statute listed specific occupations excluded from the prohibition, and clergy were not mentioned. Id. §5 (excepting professional actors, artists, lecturers, and singers, among others).

10. *Holy Trinity Church*, 143 U.S. at 459 (first quotation in text), 464.

11. J. G. [Jabez Gridley] Sutherland, *Statutes and Statutory Construction*, 879 (quotation in text), 880–883 (John Lewis, ed., 2d ed. 1904). The treatise cited *Holy Trinity Church* repeatedly. Id. at 880 n.22 and 881 n.25 See also Henry Campbell Black, *Handbook on the Construction and Interpretation of the Laws*, 224 (1896) (similar acceptance of some extrinsic materials).

12. See United States v. Pfitsch, 256 U.S. 547, 550–551 (1921) (committee report, prior draft); United States v. St. Paul Minneapolis & Manitoba Railway, 247 U.S. 310 (1918) (changes considered by chamber); Lapina v. Williams, 232 U.S. 78, 88 (1914) (committee change and report); Omaha & Council Bluffs Railway v. ICC, 230 U.S. 324 (1913) (sponsor's explanation); Johnson v. Southern Pacific Railroad, 196 U.S. 1, 20 (1904) (floor debate); Binns v. United States, 194 U.S. 486, 495 (1904) (committee report); Chesapeake & Potomac Telephone Co. v. Manning, 186 U.S. 238, 245 (1902); Bate Refrigerating Co. v. Sulzberger, 157 U.S. 1, 42 (1895) (committee report, prior draft).

13. Harry Willmer Jones, "Extrinsic Aids in Interpreting Statutes in the Federal Courts," 25 *Iowa Law Review* 737, 737 (1940).

14. Compare Roscoe Pound, "Spurious Interpretation," 7 *Columbia Law Review* 379 (1907), with Roscoe Pound, "'Mechanical Jurisprudence,'" 8 *Columbia Law Review* 605 (1908). See also Ernest Bruncken, "Interpretation of the Written Law," 25 *Yale Law Journal* 129 (1915).

15. 254 U.S. 443 (1921).

16. The House floor manager opposed a proposed amendment that would have rewritten §20 to be inapplicable to secondary boycotts. He asserted that he and "practically every member of the Judiciary Committee" believed that §20 did not protect such boycotts. Id. at 476–477 n.1, quoting 51 *Congressional Record* 9658 (1914).

17. See *Duplex*, 254 U.S. at 486–487 (Brandeis, J., dissenting), relying on committee reports and hearings.

18. Oliver Wendell Holmes, Jr., "The Theory of Legal Interpretation," 12 *Harvard Law Review* 417, 419 (1899), reprinted in *Collected Legal Papers*, 207 (1920).

19. Max Radin, "Statutory Interpretation," 43 *Harvard Law Review* 863, 871 (1930).

20. Frederick J. de Sloovère, "Textual Interpretation of Statutes," 11 *New York University Law Quarterly* 538 (1934); see Frederick J. de Sloovère, *Cases on the Interpretation of Statutes* (1931) (especially Pound's introduction).

21. Boston Sand & Gravel Co. v. United States, 278 U.S. 41, 48 (1928).

22. Pound, "Spurious Interpretation," 381, following In re Clerkship of Circuit Court, 90 Fed. Cas. 248, 251 (C.C.S.D. Iowa 1898). See also Bruncken, "Interpretation of the Written Law," 135.

23. Learned Hand classics of imaginative reconstruction include Fishgold v. Sullivan Drydock & Repair Corp., 154 F.2d 785, 788–791 (2d Cir. 1946), affirmed, 328 U.S. 275 (1946); Lehigh Valley Coal Co. v. Yensavage, 218 F. 547, 553 (2d Cir. 1914). See generally Archibald Cox, "Judge Learned Hand and the Interpretation of Statutes," 60 *Harvard Law Review* 370 (1947).

24. 242 U.S. 470 (1917).

25. House Report no. 47, 61st Cong., 2d sess., 9–10 (1909), quoted in *Caminetti*, 242 U.S. at 498 (McKenna, J., dissenting).

26. Radin, "Statutory Interpretation," 870–871, anticipated in Marcus Knowlton, "Legislation and Judicial Decision," 11 *Yale Law Journal* 95 (1901). Recall similar points made in Chapter 1.

27. James M. Landis, "A Note on 'Statutory Interpretation,'" 43 *Harvard Law Review* 886, 888–889, 890 (quotation in text) (1930); see Jones, "Extrinsic Aids," 742.

28. SEC v. Collier, 76 F.2d 939, 941 (2d Cir. 1935) (L. Hand, J.). For clear explanations of the Court's practice, see Frederick J. de Sloovère, "Extrinsic Aids in the Interpretation of Statutes," 88 *University of Pennsylvania Law Review* 527 1940); Jones, "Extrinsic Aids," 748–749.

29. Benjamin N. Cardozo, *The Nature of the Judicial Process*, 166 (1921). Other realist works developed the same precept specifically in connection with statutory interpretation. See Morris Raphael Cohen, *Law and the Social Order: Essays in Legal Philosophy*, 131 (1933); Charles P. Curtis, *It's Your Law*, 65 (1954); Karl N. Llewellyn, *The Common Law Tradition: Deciding Appeals*, 382 (1960); Jerome Frank, "Words and Music: Some Remarks on Statutory Interpretation," 47 *Columbia Law Review* 1259, 1267–70 (1947). A leading prerealist statement of the idea that "courts put life into the dead words of the statute" is John Chipman Gray, *The Nature and Sources of the Law*, 124–125 (2d ed. 1921).

30. Knowlton, "Legislation and Judicial Decision," 100.

31. See Lon L. Fuller, *The Law in Quest of Itself*, 122–125 (1940). For the overall intellectual context, see Edward A. Purcell, Jr., *The Crisis of Democratic Theory: Scientific Naturalism and the Problem of Value* (1973).

32. The primary articles, in order of their publication, are Harry Willmer Jones, "The Plain Meaning Rule and Extrinsic Aids in the Interpretation of Federal Statutes," 25 *Washington University Law Quarterly* 2 (1939); de Sloovère, "Extrinsic Aids," 527; Henry M. Hart, Jr., "The Business of the Supreme Court at the October Terms, 1937 and 1938," 53 *Harvard Law Review* 579, 623 (1940); Harry Willmer Jones, "Statutory Doubts and Legislative Intention," 40 *Columbia Law Review* 957 (1940); Jones, "Extrinsic Aids"; Charles B. Nutting, "The Ambiguity of Unambiguous Statutes," 24 *Minnesota Law Review* 509 (1940), and "The Relevance of Legislative Intention Established by Extrinsic Evidence," 20 *Boston University Law Review* 601 (1940); Max Radin, "A Short Way with Statutes," 56 *Harvard Law Review* 388 (1942); Frank, "Words and Music"; Felix Frankfurter, "Some Reflections on the Reading of Statutes," 47 *Columbia Law Review* 527 (1947); Edward Levi, "An Introduction to Legal Reasoning," 15 *University of Chicago Law Review* 501 (1948); Lon L. Fuller, "The Case of the Speluncean Explorers," 62 *Harvard Law Review* 616 (1949); Frank E. Horack, Jr., "The Disintegration of Statutory Construction," 24 *Indiana Law Journal* 335 (1949). My assertion about the dramatic break in the literature is based in part on the great surge in articles with strikingly similar arguments in or around 1940 and in part on a comparison with earlier scholarship. Compare de Sloovère, "Extrinsic Aids," emphasizing legislative purpose, with the same author's earlier work emphasizing imagi-

native reconstruction, "Preliminary Questions in Statutory Interpretation," 9 *New York University Law Quarterly Review* 407 (1932), and "Textual Interpretation." A waystation article was "The Equity and Reason of a Statute," 21 *Cornell Law Quarterly* 591 (1936), which advocated the golden rule that statutes should be interpreted reasonably.

33. Fuller, "The Case of the Speluncean Explorers," 621 (opinion of Foster, J.).

34. Frankfurter, "Reflections on the Reading of Statutes," 538–539; see Radin, "A Short Way with Statutes," 398.

35. Radin, "A Short Way with Statutes," 407. The importance of institutional design was emphasized by Lon L. Fuller, *The Problems of Jurisprudence*, 693–743 (1949).

36. Jones, "Extrinsic Aids," 761; see Frank, "Words and Music," 1270 (legislature must delegate filling in statutory meaning to courts and agencies).

37. Jones, "Extrinsic Aids," 757; see Frankfurter, "Reflections on Reading Statutes," 538–539; Radin, "A Short Way with Statutes," 399.

38. Jones, "Extrinsic Aids," 761 (first quotation); de Sloovère, "Extrinsic Aids," 540 (second quotation); see Radin, "A Short Way with Statutes," 410–411.

39. 310 U.S. 534, 543 (1940).

40. 341 U.S. 384 (1951).

41. 50 Stat. 693, currently codified at 15 U.S.C. §1 (1988).

42. This is true for several reasons. First, the act exempts from antitrust prohibition only "contracts or agreements prescribing minimum prices for resale" sanctioned by local law; the state law's application to nonsigners, who are not parties to those precise contracts, seems beyond the Miller-Tydings authorization. Second, the proviso to the act says that local law cannot authorize contracts or agreements between retailers for horizontal price-fixing. The effect of the Lousiana statute would be to allow one vertical (distributor-retailer) contract to rope in all other retailers, producing the equivalent of the sort of horizontal price-fixing prohibited by the proviso. Third, a broad reading of the Miller-Tydings Act would swallow up not only its proviso but also the strong policy of the Sherman Act against horizontal price-fixing, long considered a per se violation. Statutory exceptions are presumed not to swallow up statutory rules.

43. *Schwegmann Brothers*, 341 U.S. at 390–395.

44. Id. at 398–401 (Frankfurter, J., dissenting).

45. Id. at 395–397 (Jackson, J., concurring); see Robert Jackson, "The Meaning of Statutes: What Congress Says or What the Court Says," 34 *American Bar Association Journal* 535 (1948).

46. Henry M. Hart, Jr., and Albert M. Sacks, "The Legal Process: Basic Problems in the Making and Application of Law," 1415–16 (tentative ed. 1958) (forthcoming from Foundation Press 1994, ed. William N. Eskridge, Jr., and Philip P. Frickey).

47. Id. at 1200.

48. Id. at 1284–86, a "tentative restatement" submitted by Hart for discussion

at the 1953 American Association of Law Schools' Legislation Round Table, "The Use of Legislative History in the Interpretation of Statutes: Where Are We Going? Where Should We Go?" See *Association of American Law Schools Proceedings*, 187–188 (1953), also reprinted in Frank C. Newman and Stanley S. Surrey, *Legislation: Cases and Materials*, 669–671 (1955).

49. See Bernard Schwartz, *Super Chief: Earl Warren and His Supreme Court—A Judicial Biography*, 214–215, 267–272 (1983).

50. See id. at 445–448 (shift in the Court's balance of power after 1962), 470–479 (immediate shift to left in statutory cases).

51. 392 U.S. 409 (1968).

52. 42 U.S.C. §1982 (1988).

53. *Alfred H. Mayer*, 392 U.S. at 420–422 (plain meaning), 427–436 (legislative history).

54. Compare id. at 426–437 (opinion of the Court) with id. at 454–476 (Harlan, J., dissenting).

55. See the cases cited in notes 56–62, as well as Leary v. United States, 395 U.S. 6 (1969) (Harlan, J.); Bank of Marin v. England, 385 U.S. 99 (1966) (Douglas, J., over excellent Harlan dissent); SEC v. New England Electric System, 384 U.S. 176 (1966) (Douglas, J., over excellent Harlan dissent); Waterman Steamship Corp. v. United States, 381 U.S. 252 (1965) (Goldberg, J.); Reed v. The Yaka, 373 U.S. 410 (1963) (Black, J.); FTC v. Sun Oil Co., 371 U.S. 505 (1963) (Goldberg, J.); Commissioner v. Bilder, 369 U.S. 499 (1962) (Harlan, J.); Coppedge v. United States, 369 U.S. 438 (1962) (Warren, C.J.).

56. Fay v. Noia, 372 U.S. 391 (1963) (Brennan, J., over excellent Harlan dissent); Townsend v. Sain, 372 U.S. 293 (1963) (Brennan, J.); Sanders v. United States, 373 U.S. 1 (1963).

57. See National Woodwork Manufacturers Association v. NLRB, 386 U.S. 612 (1967) (Brennan, J., over excellent Stewart dissent); NLRB v. Fruit & Vegetable Packers Local 760, 377 U.S. 58 (1964) (Brennan, J., over excellent Harlan dissent).

58. See FTC v. Fred Meyer, Inc., 390 U.S. 341 (1968) (Warren, C.J., over excellent Harlan dissent); United States v. Philadelphia National Bank, 374 U.S. 321 (1963) (Brennan, J., over excellent Harlan dissent); FTC v. Sun Oil Co., 371 U.S. 505 (1963) (Goldberg, J.); Brown Shoe Co. v. United States, 370 U.S. 294 (1962) (Warren, C.J.).

59. See INS v. Errico, 385 U.S. 214 (1966) (Warren, C.J.); Rosenberg v. Fleuti, 374 U.S. 449 (1963) (Goldberg, J.). But see Boutilier v. INS, 387 U.S. 118 (1967) (discussed in Chapter 2), one of the few cases in which the later Warren Court used legislative history to bend an ambiguous text in conservative directions.

60. See SEC v. New England Electric System, 384 U.S. 176 (1966) (Douglas, J., over excellent Harlan dissent); Sperry v. Florida, 373 U.S. 379 (1963) (Warren, C.J.); Arrow Transporation Co. v. Southern Railway Co., 372 U.S. 658 (1963) (Brennan, J.).

61. See United States v. Seeger, 380 U.S. 163 (1965) (Clark, J.).

62. See Griggs v. Duke Power Co., 401 U.S. 424 (1971); Allen v. State Board of Elections, 393 U.S. 544 (1969); United States v. Johnson, 390 U.S. 563 (1968) (Douglas, J.); United States v. Guest, 383 U.S. 745 and 774 (1966) (opinions of Clark, J., and Brennan, J.); Louisiana v. United States, 380 U.S. 145 (1965) (Warren C.J.).

63. For support of Harlan's reading of the Civil Rights Act of 1866, see Charles Fairman, *Reconstruction and Reunion, 1864–1888*, 1258 (1971); Gerhard Casper, "*Jones v. Mayer:* Clio, Bemused and Confused Muse," 1968 *Supreme Court Review* 89. More recent scholarship has been less supportive of Harlan. See Robert J. Kaczorowski, *The Politics of Judicial Interpretation: The Federal Courts, Department of Justice and Civil Rights, 1866–1876* (1985); Barry Sullivan, "Historical Reconstruction, Reconstruction History, and the Proper Scope of Section 1981," 98 *Yale Law Journal* 541, 546 n.36 (1989).

64. See Jeffrey A. Segal and Albert D. Cover, "Ideological Values and the Votes of U.S. Supreme Court Justices," 83 *American Political Science Review* 557 (1989).

65. See Carro and Brann, "Use of Legislative Histories," 285, 291 (Supreme Court legislative history averaged 360 citations per year for the period 1973–1979 but only 178 for 1966–1972).

66. 437 U.S. 153 (1978).

67. 16 U.S.C. §1536 (1976).

68. *Hill*, 437 U.S. at 173 (quotation in text), 194; see Paul N. Cox, "Ruminations on Statutory Interpretation in the Burger Court," 19 *Valparaiso University Law Review* 287 (1985); Charles F. Lettow, "Looking at Federal Administrative Law with a Constitutional Framework in Mind," 45 *Oklahoma Law Review* 5 (1992).

69. *Hill*, 437 U.S. at 174–193.

70. Watt v. Alaska, 451 U.S. 259, 166 (1981), quoted in FDIC v. Philadelphia Gear Corp., 476 U.S. 426, 432 (1986); see Consumer Product Safety Commission v. GTE Sylvania, Inc., 447 U.S. 102, 108 (1980), as well as United States v. James, 478 U.S. 597, 607 (1986); Board of Governors, Federal Reserve System v. Dimension Finance Corp., 474 U.S. 361, 368 (1986); Rubin v. United States, 449 U.S. 424, 430 (1981); United Airlines v. McMann, 434 U.S. 192 (1977).

71. See, e.g., Kelly v. Robinson, 479 U.S. 36 (1986); Offshore Logistics, Inc., v. Tallentire, 477 U.S. 207 (1986); Midlantic National Bank v. New Jersey Department of Environmental Protection, 474 U.S. 494 (1986); Bob Jones University v. United States, 461 U.S. 574 (1983); Dames & Moore v. Regan, 453 U.S. 654 (1981); United Steelworkers v. Weber, 443 U.S. 193 (1979); Simpson v. United States, 435 U.S. 6 (1978); United States v. Board of Commissioners of Sheffield, Alabama, 435 U.S. 110 (1978); Train v. Colorado Public Interest Research Group, 426 U.S. 1 (1976); Connell Construction Co. v. Plumbers & Steamfitters Local 100, 421 U.S. 616 (1975); Chemehuevi Tribe of Indians v. FPC, 420 U.S. 395 (1975).

72. Thornburg v. Gingles, 478 U.S. 30, 43–44 nn.7, 8 (1986); see Garcia v. United States, 469 U.S. 70, 76 (1984); Gulf Oil Corp. v. Copp Paving Co., 419 U.S. 186, 199–200 (1974); see Carro and Brann, "Use of Legislative Histories," 304 (over a forty-year-period more than 50 percent of the Court's legislative history citations were to committee reports).

73. See, e.g., North Haven Board of Education v. Bell, 456 U.S. 512, 526–527 (1982); Lewis v. United States, 445 U.S. 55, 63 (1980); International Brotherhood of Teamsters v. United States, 431 U.S. 324, 350–351 (1977); Piper v. Chris-Craft Industries, Inc., 430 U.S. 1, 26–27, 28–29, 31, 34 (1977); Huddleston v. United States, 415 U.S. 814, 828 (1974); Adickes v. S. H. Kress & Co., 398 U.S. 144, 164 (1970). Generally, clear committee report language was preferred over floor debate, even statements by sponsors. See Chandler v. Roudebush, 425 U.S. 840, 858 n.36 (1976); Zuber v. Allen, 396 U.S. 168, 186 (1969).

74. See, e.g., Amoco Products Co. v. Village of Gambell, 480 U.S. 531, 554 (1987) (refusing to rely on imprecise sponsor statement contradicted by statutory definitions and statements of other legislators); Clarke v. Securities Industrial Association, 479 U.S. 388, 407 (1987) (refusing to rely on sponsor statement uttered after statute was enacted but relying on colloquy during legislative consideration); BankAmerica Corp. v. United States, 462 U.S. 122 (1983) (relying on legislator statements during committee hearings); Trbovich v. United Mine Workers, 404 U.S. 528 (1972) (similar). Although statements of opponents are usually given no weight, the Burger Court would sometimes consider them. See, e.g., Sedima, S.P.R.L. v. Imrex Co., 473 U.S. 479, 498 (1985).

75. See, e.g., NLRB v. Local 103, International Association of Bridge, Structural & Ornamental Iron Workers, 434 U.S. 335, 347 n.9 (1978) (presidential transmittal letter); Connell Construction Co. v. Plumbers & Steamfitters Local 100, 421 U.S. 616, 629 n.8 (1975) (presidential message calling for legislation); McDonald v. Santa Fe Trail Transportation Co., 427 U.S. 273, 291 and n.26 (1976) (veto message).

76. See especially statements by Justice Department officials, e.g., United States v. Board of Commissioners of Sheffield, Alabama, 435 U.S. 110, 131–132 (1978); United States v. Feola, 420 U.S. 671, 679–684 (1975); Gaston County, North Carolina, v. United States, 395 U.S. 285, 289–290 (1969), but also statements by other executive department officials, e.g., Wright v. City of Roanoke Redevelopment and Housing Authority, 479 U.S. 418, 425 n.7 (1987) (HUD); BankAmerica Corp. v. United States, 462 U.S. 122, 134–135 (1983) (presidential adviser and drafter of legislation); United States v. Vogel Fertilizer Co., 455 U.S. 16, 31–32 (1982) (Treasury Department drafters); United States v. Sotelo, 436 U.S. 268, 276–277 and 287 (1978) (letter from Assistant Treasury Secretary Stanley Surrey); Piper v. Chris-Craft Industries, Inc., 430 U.S. 1, 27–28, 33–34 (1977) (SEC chair); Ernst & Ernst v. Hochfelder, 425 U.S. 185, 202–203 (1976) (refusing to consider views of legislative opponents of securities laws but giving extensive consideration to the views of the executive branch drafter, Tommy Corcoran).

77. For law professor drafters, see Piper v. Chris-Craft Industries, Inc., 430 U.S. 1, 29 (1977); United States v. Giordano, 416 U.S. 505, 517–519 (1974); Trbovich v. United Mine Workers, 404 U.S. 528, 535 (1972). For interest group drafters, see, e.g., Jefferson County Pharmaceutical Association v. Abbott Labs., 460 U.S. 150, 159–162 (1983); Dawson Chemical Co. v. Rohm & Haas Co., 448 U.S. 176 (1980); Group Life & Health Insurance Co. v. Royal Drug Co., 440 U.S. 205, 221–223 (1979).

78. See, e.g., Community for Creative Non-Violence v. Reid, 490 U.S. 730 (1989); Chicago & Northwestern Railway v. United Transp. Union, 402 U.S. 570, 576, 580 (1971); Nacirema Operating Co. v. Johnson, 396 U.S. 212, 217 and n.12 (1969).

79. See Kosak v. United States, 465 U.S. 848, 855–857 (1984), criticized in Alison Giles, "The Value of Nonlegislators' Contributions to Legislative History," 79 *Georgetown Law Journal* 359 (1990) (student note).

80. Green v. Bock Laundry Machine Co., 490 U.S. 504, 521 (1989); see Kelly v. Robinson, 479 U.S. 36, 51 n.13 (1986); John Paul Stevens, "The Shakespeare Canon of Statutory Construction," 140 *University of Pennsylvania Law Review* 1373, 1381–82 (1992).

81. United States v. Price, 361 U.S. 304, 313 (1960), quoted in cases such as Mackey v. Lanier Collections Agency & Service, Inc., 486 U.S. 825 (1988); Consumer Product Safety Commission v. GTE Sylvania, 447 U.S. 102, 118 (1980).

82. See, e.g., Bowen v. Yuckert, 482 U.S. 137, 148–152 (1987); School Board of Nassau County, Florida, v. Arline, 480 U.S. 273, 279 (1987); North Haven Board of Education v. Bell, 456 U.S. 512, 530–531 (1982); Andrus v. Shell Oil Co., 446 U.S. 657, 666 n.8 (1980); Seatrain Shipbuilding Corp. v. Shell Oil Co., 444 U.S. 572, 596 (1980); Cannon v. University of Chicago, 441 U.S. 677, 686 n.7 (1979); United States v. Board of Commissioners, Sheffield, Alabama, 435 U.S. 110 (1978); Red Lion Broadcasting Co. v. FCC, 395 U.S. 367, 380–381 (1969).

83. See Edward P. Schwartz, Pablo T. Spiller, and Santiago Urbiztondo, "A Positive Theory of Legislative Intent," 57 *Law and Contemporary Problems* 51 (Winter 1994), and my response, "Post-Enactment Legislative Signals," id. at 75.

84. Marc R. Perman, "Statutory Interpretation in California: Individual Testimony as an Extrinsic Aid," 15 *University of San Francisco Law Review* 241 (1981) (student comment).

85. See, e.g., Walter Kendall Hurst, "The Use of Extrinsic Aids in Determining Legislative Intent in California: The Need for Standardized Criteria," 12 *Pacific Law Journal* 189 (1980) (student comment); Donald E. O'Connor, "The Use of Connecticut Legislative History in Statutory Construction," 58 *Connecticut Bar Journal* 422 (1984); Robert M. Rhodes and Susan Seereiter, "The Search for Intent: Aids to Statutory Construction in Florida—An Update," 13 *Florida State University Law Review* 485 (1985); Laurel A. Wendt, "Researching Illinois Legislative Histories—A Practical Guide," 1982 *Southern Illinois University Law Journal*

601; William D. Popkin, "Statutory Interpretation in State Courts—A Study of Indiana Opinions," 24 *Indiana Law Review* 1155 (1991); Louise Stafford, "North Carolina Legislative History," 38 *North Carolina State Bar Quarterly* 22 (1991); Karen L. Uno and Mark Stapke, "Evaluating Oregon Legislative History: Tailoring an Approach to the Legislative Process," 61 *Oregon Law Review* 421 (1982) (student comment); William H. Nast, "The Use of Legislative History in Construing Pennsylvania Statutes," 4 *Pennsylvania Law Journal-Reporter* 18 (1981); Malinda Allison and James Hambleton, "Research in Texas Legislative History," 47 *Texas Bar Journal* 314 (1984); Arthur C. Wang, "Legislative History in Washington," 7 *University of Puget Sound Law Review* 571 (1984).

86. Reed Dickerson, *The Interpretation and Application of Statutes*, 155–158, 174–175 (1975); Abner J. Mikva, "Reading and Writing Statutes," 48 *University of Pittsburgh Law Review* 627 (1987). See also William S. Moorhead, "A Congressman Looks at the Planned Colloquy and Its Effect in the Interpretation of Statutes," 45 *American Bar Association Journal* 1314 (1959) (a classic objection to relying on floor debate).

87. The Appropriations Committees endorsed the TVA's position that the Endangered Species Act was inapplicable to the Tellico Dam, and Congress continued to fund the dam. See Brief for the Petitioner, 7–18, *Hill*, 437 U.S. 153 (no. 76-1701). The 1977 committee reports specifically disapproved of the lower court's decision to enjoin completion of the dam. Senate Report no. 301, 95th Cong., 1st sess., 98–99 (1977); House Report no. 379, 95th Cong., 1st sess., 104 (1977). Congress in 1977 appropriated $2 million for TVA to relocate endangered species threatened by the dam. Public Works for Water and Power Development and Energy Research Appropriation Act of 1978, Public Law no. 95-96, 91 Stat. 797, 808 (1977).

88. 491 U.S. 701 (1989).

89. 42 U.S.C. §1981 (1988).

90. *Jett*, 491 U.S. at 713–721 (history of the 1866 act), 722–731 (history of the 1871 act and its interpretation) (plurality opinion of O'Connor, J.).

91. The main critics were Judge Frank H. Easterbrook, e.g., In re Sinclair, 870 F.2d 1340 (7th Cir. 1989); Frank H. Easterbrook, "The Role of Original Intent in Statutory Interpretation," 11 *Harvard Journal of Law and Public Policy* 59 (1988), and "Legal Interpretation and the Power of the Judiciary," 7 *Harvard Journal of Law and Public Policy* 87 (1984), and Judge (now Justice) Antonin Scalia. See sources in notes 93 and 97. Other judicial critics included Judge (later Solicitor General) Kenneth W. Starr, e.g., American Mining Congress v. EPA, 824 F.2d 1177 (D.C. Cir. 1987); Kenneth W. Starr, "Observations about the Use of Legislative History," 1987 *Duke Law Journal* 371; Judge James Buckley, e.g., Overseas Education Association, Inc., v. Federal Labor Relations Authority, 876 F.2d 960, 974–975 (D.C. Cir. 1989) (Buckley, J., joined by Starr, J., concurring); IBEW, Local 474, v. NLRB, 814 F.2d 697, 715–717 (D.C. Cir. 1987) (Buckley, J., concurring); and Judge Alex Kozinski, e.g., Wallace v. Christensen, 802 F.2d 1539, 1559–

60 (9th Cir. 1986) (Kozinski, J., concurring in the judgment). See also United States Department of Justice, Office of Legal Policy (OLP), "Using and Misusing Legislative History: A Re-Evaluation of the Status of Legislative History in Statutory Interpretation" (1989).

92. Holmes, "Legal Interpretation," 419, quoted in *American Mining Congress*, 824 F.2d at 1190 n.19; Easterbrook, "Original Intent," 61; Starr, "Use of Legislative History," 378; Department of Justice, "Misusing Legislative History," 20. See also Chisom v. Roemer, 111 S. Ct. 2354, 2369 (1991) (Scalia, J., dissenting). Holmes himself relied on legislative history when he served on the Court. See note 21.

93. See Easterbrook, "Original Intent," 62–63; Antonin Scalia, "Speech on Use of Legislative History," delivered between fall 1985 and spring 1986 at various law schools (quoted and analyzed in Daniel A. Farber and Philip P. Frickey, "Legislative Intent and Public Choice," 74 *Virginia Law Review* 423 [1988]).

94. Quoted in Wald, "1981 Supreme Court Term," 214. For a different version, see Conroy v. Aniskoff, 113 S. Ct. 1562, 1567 (1993) (Scalia, J., concurring in the judgment).

95. Department of Justice, "Misusing Legislative History," 34; *Wallace*, 802 F.2d at 1560 (Kozinski, J., concurring in the judgment); Easterbrook, "Original Intent," 64–65.

96. Hirschey v. FERC, 777 F.2d. 1, 7–8 (D.C. Cir. 1985) (Scalia, J. concurring in the judgment); Scalia, "Speech on Use of Legislative History."

97. In addition to Scalia's separate opinions in *Bock Laundry* and *Johnson* (discussed in Chapter 1), in *K Mart* (discussed in Chapter 4), and in *Jett* (discussed in this chapter), see also Conroy v. Aniskoff, 113 S. Ct. 1562, 1567–72 (1993) (Scalia, J., concurring in the judgment); Wisconsin Public Intervenor v. Mortier, 111 S. Ct. 2476, 2487–90 (1991) (Scalia, J., concurring in the judgment); Chisom v. Roemer, 111 S. Ct. 2354, 2369 (1991) (Scalia, J., dissenting); West Virginia University Hospitals, Inc., v. Casey, 499 U.S. 83, 98–99 (1991) (Scalia, J.); Begier v. IRS, 496 U.S. 53, 67–71 (1990) (Scalia, J., concurring in the judgment); Blanchard v. Bergeron, 489 U.S. 87 (1989) (Scalia, J., concurring); United States v. Taylor, 487 U.S. 326, 344 (1988) (Scalia, J., concurring in part); Thompson v. Thompson, 484 U.S. 174, 188 (1988) (Scalia, J., concurring in the judgment); INS v. Cardoza-Fonseca, 480 U.S. 421 (1987) (Scalia, J., concurring in the judgment). See generally Eskridge, "The New Textualism"; Zeppos, "Justice Scalia's Textualism."

98. *Thompson*, 484 U.S. at 192 (Scalia, J., concurring in the judgment) (citing and relying on INS v. Chadha, 462 U.S. 919 [1983]); see *Chisom*, 111 S. Ct. at 2369 (Scalia, J., dissenting); *Cardoza-Fonseca*, 480 U.S. at 452–453 (Scalia, J., concurring in the judgment).

99. *Taylor*, 487 U.S. at 345 (Scalia, J., concurring in the judgment).

100. This is one line of criticism directed at Scalia's approach. See, e.g., Breyer, "Legislative History"; Wald, "The Sizzling Sleeper."

101. *Bock Laundry*, 490 U.S. at 507 (Scalia, J., concurring in the judgment)

(quoted at greater length in Chapter 1). See also Scalia, "Speech on Use of Legislative History," 9; *Chisom*, 111 S. Ct. at 2369 (Scalia, J., dissenting).

102. In *Mortier*, 111 S. Ct. at 2485 n.4, the other eight Justices reaffirmed the Court's traditional willingness to look at legislative history, in a clear rebuff to Scalia. Seven Justices repeated the rebuff in *Aniskoff*, 113 S. Ct. at 1566–67 n.12.

103. 487 U.S. 552 (1988).

104. 28 U.S.C. §2412(d)(1) (1982).

105. *Underwood*, 487 U.S. at 566–567 (1985 report cannot state intent of 1980 Congress, cannot overcome presumption of continuity in the statute's evolution, and cannot force on the Court an unadministerable test unsupported by statutory language).

106. See West Virginia University Hospitals, Inc., v. Casey, 499 U.S. 83 (1991) (Scalia, J.) (compare the legislative history invoked in the Stevens dissent); Public Employees Retirement System of Ohio v. Betts, 492 U.S. 158 (1989) (Kennedy, J.) (compare the legislative history invoked in the Marshall dissent); Hoffman v. Connecticut Department of Income Maintenance, 492 U.S. 96 (1989) (plurality opinion of White, J.) (compare the legislative history invoked in the Stevens dissent); Dellmuth v. Muth, 491 U.S. 223 (1989) (Kennedy, J.) (compare the legislative history invoked in the Brennan dissent); Chan v. Korean Airlines, Ltd., 490 U.S. 122, 134–135 (1988) (Scalia, J.) (compare the legislative history invoked in the Brennan concurrence); Pittston Coal Group v. Sebben, 488 U.S. 105 (1988) (Scalia, J.) (compare the legislative history invoked in the Stevens dissent).

107. See the sharp debate over the Court's rewriting in *Bock Laundry*, 490 U.S. at 527 (Scalia, J., concurring in the judgment), and Public Citizen v. United States Department of Justice, 491 U.S. 440 (1989) (Kennedy, J., concurring in the judgment). Also see Peretz v. United States, 111 S. Ct. 2661 (1991).

108. United Savings Association v. Timbers of Inwood Forest, 484 U.S. 365, 370 (1988) (Scalia, J.).

109. *Underwood*, 487 U.S. at 564–565.

110. United States v. Fausto, 484 U.S. 439, 449–451 (1988) (Scalia, J.). See Kenneth W. Starr, "Of Forests and Trees: Structuralism in the Interpretation of Statutes," 56 *George Washington Law Review* 703 (1988).

111. 490 U.S. 122 (1989).

112. Article 3(2)'s first sentence reads: "The absence, irregularity, or loss of the passenger ticket shall not affect the existence or validity of the contract of transportation, which shall none the less be subject to the rules of this convention." Scalia thought that this sentence clearly covers lack of notice on the ticket, as that is plainly an "irregularity." *Chan*, 490 U.S. at 127.

113. Warsaw Convention, art. 4(4) (if baggage check does not contain notice of liability limitation, carrier shall not avail itself of the Convention's liability limitations); id. art. 9 (similar rule for air waybill). The Warsaw Convention is reprinted in the note following 49 U.S.C. §1502 (1988).

114. *Chan*, 490 U.S. at 134–135. For a critique of Scalia's refusal to consider

negotiating materials in interpreting treaties, see Detlev F. Vagts, "Senate Materials and Treaty Interpretation: Some Research Hints for the Supreme Court," 83 *American Journal of International Law* 546 (1989).

115. *Jett*, 491 U.S. at 739 (Scalia, J., concurring in part and concurring in the judgment).

116. For the 1988 term alone, see United States v. Monsanto, 491 U.S. 600 (1989) (White, J.); Public Employees Retirement System of Ohio v. Betts, 492 U.S. 158 (1989) (Kennedy, J.); Patterson v. McLean Credit Union, 491 U.S. 164 (1989) (Kennedy, J.); Sullivan v. Hudson, 490 U.S. 877 (1989) (O'Connor, J.); Gomez v. United States, 490 U.S. 858 (1989) (Stevens, J.); Wards Cove Packing Co. v. Atonio, 490 U.S. 642 (1989) (White, J.); Asarco Inc. v. Kadish, 490 U.S. 605, 629–630 (1989) (Kennedy, J.); Mallard v. United States District Court, 490 U.S. 296, 305–306 (1989) (Brennan, J.); United States Department of Justice v. Reporters Committee for Freedom of the Press, 489 U.S. 749, 764–765 (1989) (Stevens, J.); TWA v. Independent Federation of Flight Attendants, 489 U.S. 426 (1989) (O'Connor, J.).

117. See e.g., *Jett*, 491 U.S. at 732 (plurality opinion of O'Connor, J.); Mississippi Band of Choctaw Indians v. Holyfield, 490 U.S. 30, 47 and n.22 (1989) (Brennan, J.); Coit Independence Joint Venture v. FSLIC, 489 U.S. 561 (1989) (O'Connor, J.); Karahalios v. National Federation of Federal Employees, Local 1263, 489 U.S. 527, 532 (1989) (White, J.); Pittston Coal Group v. Sebben, 488 U.S. 105, 115 (1989) (Scalia, J.); Mackey v. Lanier Collections Agency & Service, Inc., 486 U.S. 825, 836–837 (1988) (White, J.); Honig v. Doe, 484 U.S. 305 (1988) (Brennan, J.); Lukhard v. Reed, 481 U.S. 368 (1987) (plurality opinion of Scalia, J.).

118. See United States v. Ron Pair Enterprises, Inc., 489 U.S. 235, 241–242 (1989) (Blackmun, J.); San Francisco Arts & Athletics, Inc., v. United States Olympic Committee, 483 U.S. 522 (1987) (Powell, J.).

119. See, e.g., Daniel A. Farber and Philip P. Frickey, *Law and Public Choice: A Critical Introduction*, 95–102 (1991); Livingston, "Congress, the Courts, and the Code"; Mikva, "A Reply to Judge Starr's Observations"; Ross, "Reaganist Realism Comes to Detroit."

120. *Chadha*, 462 U.S. at 954, quoting Senate Report no. 1335, 54th Cong., 2d sess., 8 (1897). In footnote 16 *Chadha* addressed administrative "lawmaking" and observed that "[e]xecutive action under legislatively delegated authority that might resemble 'legislative' action in some respects is not subject to the approval of both Houses of Congress and the President for the reason that the Constitution," namely article II, which describes the president's powers, "does not so require. That kind of Executive action is always subject to check by the terms of the legislation that authorized it . . . A one-House veto is clearly legislative in both character and effect and is not so checked; the need for the check provided by Art. I, §§1, 7, is therefore clear." This same analysis could be applied to judicial interpretation of statutes.

121. *Chadha*, 462 U.S. at 951.

122. *Bock Laundry*, 490 U.S. at 527 (Scalia, J., concurring in the judgment). The complete quotation from which this is excerpted can be found in Chapter 1.

123. *Underwood*, 487 U.S. at 567 ("reenactment, of course, generally includes the settled judicial interpretation"); *Bock Laundry*, 490 U.S. at 527 (Scalia, J., concurring in the judgment) (canons and legal terrain).

124. The best source is Eric Lane, "Legislative Process and Its Judicial Renderings: A Study in Contrast," 48 *University of Pittsburgh Law Review* 639, 651, 656–657 (1987).

125. Mikva, "Reading and Writing Statutes," 629.

126. Thompson v. Thompson, 484 U.S. 174, 192 (1988) (Scalia, J., concurring in the judgment) (emphasis added).

127. That is, if a staff member or lobbyist "plants" something in a committee report or floor colloquy (see Blanchard v. Bergeron, 489 U.S. 87, 98–99 [1989] [Scalia, J., concurring in part and concurring in the judgment]), it is likely that staff for other members will notice the plant. If the members do not agree with it, there are ways for them to negate its force: by excising the plant from the committee report (if the member is on the committee) or by denouncing it on the floor. On legislative monitoring of committees and their chairs, see Keith Krehbiel, *Information and Legislative Organization* (1991); McNollgast, "Legislative Intent: The Use of Positive Political Theory in Statutory Interpretation," 80 *Georgetown Law Journal* 705 (1992).

128. See, e.g., Clarke v. Securities Industrial Association, 479 U.S. 388, 407 (1987); Board of Governors of the Federal Reserve System v. Dimension Financial Corp., 474 U.S. 361, 372 (1986); Costello, "Reliability of Sources of Legislative History," 43–59 (analyzing other cases).

129. *The Federalist*, no. 78, at 469 (Clinton Rossiter, ed., 1961) (Hamilton), quoted in *Public Citizen*, 491 U.S. at 471 (Kennedy, J., concurring in the judgment).

130. *Jett*, 491 U.S. at 738–739 (Scalia, J., concurring in the judgment).

131. Morton v. Mancari, 417 U.S. 535, 549–550 (1974) (leading case). For recent applications, see, e.g., Pittsburgh & Lake Erie Railroad v. RLEA, 491 U.S. 490 (1989); Traynor v. Turnage, 488 U.S. 535, 547–548 (1988).

132. See Marbury v. Madison, 1 Cranch 137, 162–163 (1803) (leading case); *Jett*, 491 U.S. at 742–743 and n.2 (Brennan, J., dissenting) (citing cases showing that this canon was the one that any reasonable legislator would have considered in 1866).

133. He clearly rejects the remedial canon because he believes Congress must explicitly provide for remedies, and his personal belief is one shared by a majority of the current Justices. I am not sure why Scalia does not mention the implied repeals canon, but there is a little evidence that he does not like this one either. Compare United States v. Fausto, 484 U.S. 439, 452–453 (1988) (Scalia, J.) (structure of statutory scheme trumps implied repeal canons), with id. at 461–462 and

n.9 (Stevens, J., dissenting) (Scalia is undermining legislative expectations because of his dislike of the implied repeals canon).

134. Civil Rights Act of 1871, §7, 17 Stat. 15.

135. Finley v. United States, 490 U.S. 545, 556 (1989) (Scalia, J.).

136. See Kendall v. United States, 12 Pet. 524, 624 (1838); Marbury v. Madison, 1 Cranch 137, 162–63 (1803); see also Texas & Pacific Railroad v. Rigsby, 241 U.S. 33, 39–40 (1916) (synthesis case).

137. Arthur Furtwangler, *The Authority of Publius: A Reading of the Federalist Papers* (1984).

138. See *Public Citizen*, 491 U.S. at 467–468, 471 (Kennedy, J., concurring in the judgment); Morrison v. Olson, 487 U.S. 654, 697–699 (1988) (Scalia, J., dissenting).

139. See *The Federalist*, nos. 33 (Hamilton), 44 (Madison), 69 (Hamilton), 73 (Hamilton).

140. *Chan*, 490 U.S. at 139–152 (Brennan, J., concurring in the judgment); see Breyer, "Use of Legislative History" (excellent examples of usefulness of legislative history in explaining specialized terms or usages).

141. *Alfred H. Mayer*, 392 U.S. at 444–449 (Douglas, J., concurring).

142. Id. at 444–447, quoting from William E. B. Du Bois, *Black Reconstruction in America* (1963), and Frederick Douglass, "The Color Line," *North American Review* (June 1881.)

143. *Alfred H. Mayer*, 392 U.S. at 445 (Douglas, J., concurring).

144. Id. at 473–474 (Harlan, J., dissenting).

145. Id. at 449 n.6 (Douglas, J., concurring).

146. *Holy Trinity Church*, 143 U.S. at 471.

147. See, e.g., Bob Jones University v. United States, 461 U.S. 574 (1983) (Powell, J., concurring); Smith v. Wade, 461 U.S. 30 (1983) (O'Connor, J., dissenting); United Steelworkers v. Weber, 443 U.S. 193 (1979) (Blackmun, J.); NLRB v. Catholic Bishop of Chicago, 440 U.S. 490 (1979) (Burger, C.J.); Leo Sheep Co. v. United States, 440 U.S. 668 (1979) (Rehnquist, J.); Morton v. Mancari, 417 U.S. 535 (1974) (Blackmun, J.); United States v. Wolf, 787 F.2d 1094 (7th Cir. 1986) (Posner, J.). For the record, I disagree with the ultimate positions taken by O'Connor in *Smith v. Wade* and Rehnquist in *Leo Sheep*, though I think both cases are close calls.

8. Vertical versus Horizontal Coherence

This chapter is drawn from my articles "Overruling Statutory Precedents," 76 *Georgetown Law Journal* 1361 (1988), reprinted with the permission of the publisher, © 1988 The Georgetown Law Journal Association and Georgetown University; and "Interpreting Legislative Inaction," 87 *Michigan Law Review* 67 (1988).

1. Charles P. Curtis, "A Better Theory of Legal Interpretation," 3 *Vanderbilt Law Review* 407, 423 (1950); see Benjamin N. Cardozo, *The Nature of the Judicial Process* (1921); Morris Raphael Cohen, *Law and the Social Order: Essays in Legal*

Philosophy (1933); Arthur W. Phelps, "Factors Influencing Judges in Interpreting Statutes," 3 *Vanderbilt Law Review* 456 (1950).

2. 491 U.S. 164 (1989).

3. 42 U.S.C. §1981 (1988).

4. 427 U.S. 160 (1976).

5. See, e.g., Hecht v. Malley, 265 U.S. 144, 153 (1924) (statute does not disturb settled judicial interpretations); United States v. Cerecedo Hermanos y Compañía, 209 U.S. 337, 339 (1908) (agency decisions).

6. 310 U.S. 469, 488 (1940).

7. 259 U.S. 200 (1922).

8. 346 U.S. 356, 357 (1953) (per curiam).

9. See Radovich v. National Football League, 352 U.S. 445 (1957); United States v. International Boxing Club of New York, 348 U.S. 236 (1955).

10. 407 U.S. 258 (1972).

11. See id. at 281–283.

12. The leading case is Helvering v. Hallock, 309 U.S. 106 (1940), decided the same year as *Apex Hosiery.*

13. The leading cases are Zuber v. Allen, 396 U.S. 168, 185 n.21, 192–194 (1969); Monell v. Department of Social Services of the City of New York, 436 U.S. 658, 696–699 (1978) (second reason); Aaron v. SEC, 446 U.S. 680 (1980) (third reason).

14. *Patterson*, 491 U.S. at 200–205 (Brennan, J., concurring in the judgment in part and dissenting in part). This part of Brennan's opinion was joined by Justices Marshall and Blackmun.

15. 392 U.S. 409 (1968), discussed in Chapter 7.

16. See Charles Abernathy, *Civil Rights: Cases and Materials,* 265–276 (1980).

17. Runyon v. McCrary, 427 U.S. 160, 168–175 (1976); Johnson v. Railway Express Agency, 421 U.S. 454, 459–460 (1975); Tillman v. Wheaton-Haven Recreation Association, 410 U.S. 431, 439–440 (1973).

18. Public Law no. 94-559, 90 Stat. 2641 (1976), codified at 42 U.S.C. §1988 (1988).

19. See, e.g., Saint Francis College v. Al-Khazraji, 481 U.S. 604 (1987); Shaare Tefila Congregation v. Cobb, 481 U.S. 615 (1987); McDonald v. Santa Fe Trail Transportation Co., 427 U.S. 273 (1976).

20. Merrill Lynch, Pierce, Fenner & Smith, Inc., v. Curran, 456 U.S. 353, 381–382 (1982); see CFTC v. Schor, 478 U.S. 833 (1986); Lindahl v. Office of Personnel Management, 470 U.S. 768, 782–783 and n.15 (1985); North Haven Board of Education v. Bell, 456 U.S. 512 (1982).

21. Lorillard v. Pons, 434 U.S. 575, 580 (1978) (dictum).

22. 435 U.S. 110 (1978).

23. See id. at 134 (quotation in text), 133–134 (House and Senate hearings heard testimony about the attorney general's policy, which was also reflected in committee reports).

24. 328 U.S. 61 (1946).

25. Compare id. at 73–76 (Stone, C.J., dissenting), with id. at 70 (opinion for the Court) ("affirmative action" by Congress in 1942 "negatives" inferences from reenactment rule).

26. See Leary v. United States, 395 U.S. 6, 24–25 (1969).

27. See Senate Report no. 1011, 94th Cong., 2d sess., 4 (1976), reprinted in 1976 *United States Code Congressional and Administrative News* 5908, 5911 (unfair that fees are authorized in "an employment discrimination suit under Title VII . . . but not in the same suit brought under 42 U.S.C. §1981, which protects similar rights"); House Report no. 94-1558, 94th Cong., 2d sess., 4 and n. 8 (1976) (citing with approval two cases holding §1981 applicable to private discrimination); 122 *Congressional Record* 35,122 (1976) (Rep. Drinan, the floor manager).

28. INS v. Cardoza-Fonseca, 480 U.S. 421 (1987), quoting Nachman Corp. v. Pension Benefit Guaranty Corp., 446 U.S. 359, 392–393 (1980) (Stewart, J., dissenting).

29. 370 U.S. 195 (1962).

30. 61 Stat. 156, codified at 29 U.S.C. §185(a) (1982).

31. *Sinclair,* 370 U.S. at 210.

32. The leading case for conference committee rejections is Gulf Oil Corp. v. Copp Paving Co., 419 U.S. 186, 200 (1974); for floor rejections, see North Haven Board of Education v. Bell, 456 U.S. 512, 531–535 (1982); and for committee rejections, see Blue Chip Stamps v. Manor Drug Stores, 421 U.S. 723, 732–733 (1975). Other examples of each are found in the third section of Appendix 1.

33. The leading case is NLRB v. Catholic Bishop of Chicago, 440 U.S. 490, 505–506 (1976); compare id. at 513–514 (Brennan, J., dissenting). See also cases cited in the third section of Appendix 1.

34. Public Law no. 92-261, 86 Stat. 103 (1972), codified as amended at 42 U.S.C. §§2000e-1 to -17 (1988).

35. 118 *Congressional Record* 3172–73 (1972) (Sen. Hruska).

36. Id. at 3371 (statement of Sen. Williams, D-N.J., floor manager), 3373 (Hruska amendment fails on tie vote), 3965 (Hruska amendment fails on reconsideration, 37–50).

37. See 117 *Congressional Record* 31,973 (1971) (under substitute offered by Representative John Erlenborn, "[t]here would no longer be recourse to the old 1866 civil rights act" in employment cases); id. at 32,111 (House passage of Erlenborn substitute, 200–195); House Conference Report no. 899, 92d Cong., 2d sess., 17 (1972) (House recedes from Erlenborn provision on exclusive remedy).

38. Gulf Oil Corp. v. Copp Paving Co., 419 U.S. 186, 200 (1974).

39. The leading critiques from a legal process perspective are Henry M. Hart, Jr., and Albert M. Sacks, "The Legal Process: Basic Problems in the Making and Application of Law," 1394–1401 (tentative ed. 1958) (forthcoming from Foundation Press 1994, ed. William N. Eskridge, Jr., and Philip P. Frickey) (criticizing *Toolson*); Reed Dickerson, *The Interpretation and Application of Statutes,* 181 (1975);

John Grabow, "Congressional Silence and the Search for Legislative Intent: A Venture into 'Speculative Unrealities,'" 64 *Boston University Law Review* 737 (1984); Lawrence Tribe, "Toward a Syntax of the Unsaid: Construing the Sounds of Congressional and Constitutional Silence," 57 *Indiana Law Journal* 515 (1982); Note, "Congressional Silence and the Supreme Court," 26 *Indiana Law Journal* 388 (1951). For friendlier fire, see Daniel A. Farber, "Statutory Interpretation, Legislative Inaction, and Civil Rights," 87 *Michigan Law Review* 2 (1988).

40. *Patterson*, 491 U.S. at 175 n.1.

41. Hart and Sacks, "The Legal Process," 1395, analyzing *Girouard* (subsequent acquiescence and rejected proposals are incompetent evidence of legislative intent); cf. id. at 1401 (reenactment is competent evidence of legislative intent). Also see Cleveland v. United States, 329 U.S. 14, 22 n.4 (1946) (Rutledge, J.); Grabow, "Congressional Silence," 748 (making the concurrent resolution point).

42. The main evidence for that is the legislative history; see note 27. There is also some textual evidence. If §1981 applied only to discriminatory laws, it would duplicate §1983, and there would be no need to include both.

43. Hart and Sacks, "The Legal Process," 1395–97 (acquiescence rule), 1404–5 (reenactment rule). See also Reed Dickerson, "Statutory Interpretation: Dipping into Legislative History," 11 *Hofstra Law Review* 1125, 1133 (1983).

44. Hart and Sacks, "The Legal Process," 1395–96.

45. See 118 *Congressional Record* 3173 (text of Hruska amendment), 3172 (quotation in text) (1972).

46. Compare *Runyon*, 427 U.S. at 174 n.1, with 118 *Congressional Record* 3373 (1972) (roll-call vote).

47. 118 *Congressional Record* 3372 (1972). A live pair is a senator who is present but declines to vote, pairing his vote with that of an absent senator.

48. House Report no. 238, 92d Cong., 1st sess., 18–19 (1971).

49. Of the twenty representatives named to the conference (118 *Congressional Record* 5187 [1972]), eleven (all but one of the Democrats) had voted against the Erlenborn substitute, which added the exclusivity provision (117 *Congressional Record* 32,111 [1971]). Of the twelve senators named to the conference (118 *Congressional Record* 5184 [1972]), ten voted against the Hruska amendment, one voted for, and one was absent (118 *Congressional Record* 3372–73 [1972]).

50. See *Restatement (Second) of Contracts* §69(1) (1979); Note, "The Language of Offer and Acceptance: Speech Acts and the Question of Intent," 74 *California Law Review* 189, 217–220 (1986).

51. See the leading cases, United States v. Rutherford, 442 U.S. 544, 554 n.10 (1979) (acquiescence); Lorillard v. Pons, 434 U.S. 575, 580 (1978) (reenactment); *Sinclair*, 370 U.S. at 210 (rejected proposal); *Apex Hosiery*, 310 U.S. at 489 (acquiescence); *Girouard*, 328 U.S. at 76 (Stone, C.J., dissenting).

52. On the values of continuity from a legal process perspective, see Moragne v. States Marine Lines, Inc., 398 U.S. 375 (1970) (relying on Hart and Sacks, "The Legal Process").

53. Petitioner's Brief, 8, *Patterson* (no. 87-107).

54. Brief of 66 Members of the United States Senate and 118 Members of the United States House of Representatives as Amici Curiae in Support of Petitioner, 20–28, *Patterson* (no. 87-107); Brief of New York, California, et alia as Amici Curiae in Support of Petitioner, 1–3, *Patterson* (no. 87-107) (brief filed by forty-seven states plus Puerto Rico, the District of Columbia, Guam, and the U.S. Virgin Islands).

55. See my article "Overriding Supreme Court Statutory Interpretation Decisions," 101 *Yale Law Journal* 331 (1991); Marc Galanter, "Why the 'Haves' Come Out Ahead: Speculations on the Limits of Legal Change," 9 *Law and Society Review* 95 (1974); Paul H. Rubin, "Common Law and Statute Law," 11 *Journal of Legal Studies* 205 (1982).

56. See Mancur Olson, *The Logic of Collective Action: Public Goods and the Theory of Groups* (1965).

57. We ticket buyers hurt by the exemption are unlikely to organize because we are ignorant of our injury, our individual stakes are very small, and there are so many of us (triggering the free rider problem in forming a powerful interest group). Even baseball players were for cultural reasons not politically organized until after 1966. When the players did get organized, they were able (after *Flood*) to end the reserve clause through arbitration—and keep the sport's antitrust exemption, which then benefited them as well as the owners.

58. See *Runyon*, 427 U.S. at 189 (Stevens, J., concurring); *Patterson*, 491 U.S. at 171–172 ("[s]ome Members of this Court believe that *Runyon* was decided incorrectly").

59. Smith v. Turner, 48 U.S. (7 How.) 283, 470 (1849) (Taney, C.J.); see The Propeller Genesee Chief, 53 U.S. (12 How.) 443, 487 (1851).

60. Douglass v. County of Pike, 101 U.S. 677, 687 (1879) (holding that state court reversals of Supreme Court interpretations of state law should be given only prospective effect). For later articulations of this theme, see Francis v. Southern Pacific Co., 333 U.S. 445, 450 (1948); Boys Markets, Inc., v. Retail Clerks Union, Local 770, 398 U.S. 235, 257–258 (1970) (Black, J., dissenting); Frank Horack, "Congressional Silence: A Tool of Judicial Supremacy," 25 *Texas Law Review* 247 (1947).

61. J. W. Moore and R. S. Oglebay, "The Supreme Court, Stare Decisis, and Law of the Case," 21 *Texas Law Review* 514, 539–540 (1943); see Cardozo, *The Nature of the Judicial Process*, 15.

62. William O. Douglas, "Stare Decisis," 49 *Columbia Law Review* 735 (1949); see Canada Packers, Ltd., v. Atchison, Topeka & Santa Fe Railroad, 385 U.S. 182, 186–187 (1966) (Douglas, J., dissenting).

63. See "The Status of the Rule of Judicial Precedent," 14 *University of Cincinnati Law Review* 203–355 (1940); Emmet H. Wilson, "Stare Decisis, Quo Vadis? The Orphaned Doctrine in the Supreme Court," 33 *Georgetown Law Journal* 251 (1945).

64. Burnet v. Coronado Oil & Gas Co., 285 U.S. 393, 405, 406–407 and n.2

(1932) (Brandeis, J., dissenting). See also Erie Railroad v. Tompkins, 304 U.S. 64, 77–78 (1938) (Brandeis willing to overrule statutory precedent [*Swift*] only because of constitutional problems).

65. See *Apex Hosiery* (written by Stone, joined by Frankfurter); *Girouard* (Stone dissenting, joined by Frankfurter); Helvering v. Hallock, 309 U.S. 106 (1940) (written by Frankfurter, joined by Stone).

66. See Edward Levi, "An Introduction to Legal Reasoning," 15 *University of Chicago Law Review* 501, 540 (1948).

67. For leading cases, see Square D Co. v. Niagara Frontier Tariff Bureau, 476 U.S. 409, 424 n.34 (1986) (quoting Levi); City of Oklahoma City v. Tuttle, 471 U.S. 808, 818 n.5 (1985) (citing Brandeis); Illinois Brick Co. v. Illinois, 431 U.S. 720, 736 (1977) (quoting Brandeis); Edelman v. Jordan, 415 U.S. 651, 671 n.14 (1974) (quoting Brandeis); *Flood*; Snyder v. Harris, 394 U.S. 332, 339–340 (1969); Monroe v. Pape, 365 U.S. 167, 220–221 (1961); *Toolson*, 346 U.S. at 356–357; United States v. South Buffalo Railway, 333 U.S. 771 (1948); Cleveland v. United States, 329 U.S. 14, 18 (1945) (plurality opinion).

68. For scholars, see, e.g., Frank C. Newman and Stanley S. Surrey, *Legislation: Cases and Materials*, 653 (1955); Robert Keeton, *Venturing to Do Justice*, 79–80 (1969); C. Paul Rogers III, "Judicial Reinterpretation of Statutes: The Example of Baseball and the Antitrust Laws," 14 *Houston Law Review* 611, 626 (1977). For state courts, see, e.g., Williams v. Ray, 246 S.E.2d 387 (Ga. App. 1978); Williams v. Crickman, 405 N.E.2d 799 (Ill. 1980); Libertowski v. Hojara, 228 N.E.2d 422 (Ind. 1967); Boston v. Mac-Gray Co., 359 N.E.2d 946 (Mass. 1977); Higby v. Mahoney, 396 N.E.2d 183 (N.Y. 1979); Fulton v. Lavallee, 265 A.2d 655 (R.I. 1970); Powers v. Powers, 123 S.E.2d 646 (S.C. 1962); McKesson & Robbins v. Government Employees Department Store, 365 S.W.2d 890 (Tenn. 1963); James v. Vernon Calhoun Packing Co., 498 S.W.2d 160 (Tex. 1973); Bischoff v. City of Appleton, 260 N.W.2d 773 (Wis. 1978).

69. 491 U.S. at 172–173.

70. Hart and Sacks, "The Legal Process," 1348–1407 (intense analysis of *Toolson* and *Girouard*). For more recent legal process critiques, see Dickerson, *The Interpretation and Application of Statutes*, 252–55; Frank H. Easterbrook, "Stability and Reliability in Judicial Decisions," 78 *Cornell Law Review* 422 (1988); Earl M. Maltz, "The Nature of Precedent," 66 *North Carolina Law Review* 367, 388–389 (1988).

71. Monroe v. Pape, 365 U.S. 167, 220–221 (1961) (Frankfurter, J., dissenting). See also Commissioner v. Church's Estate, 335 U.S. 632, 667 (1948) (Frankfurter, J., dissenting and articulating reasons for stare decisis).

72. Compare Cantor v. Detroit Edison Co., 428 U.S. 579 (1976) (narrowing precedent widely viewed as creating antitrust immunity for state-sanctioned regulatory programs), with Southern Motor Carriers Rate Conference, Inc., v. United States, 471 U.S. 48 (1985) (essentially overruling the reasoning in *Cantor* but admitting only to disapproval of "questionable dicta" in plurality opinion). See Eskridge, "Overruling Statutory Precedents," 1371–72.

73. See Guardians Association v. Civil Service Commission, 463 U.S. 582 (1983), where the nine Justices split three ways on the stare decisis issue, with four Justices seeking to overrule Lau v. Nichols, 414 U.S. 563 (1974), entirely in light of its inconsistency with Regents of University of California v. Bakke, 438 U.S. 265 (1978), with four Justices willing to overrule *Lau* in part, and only one Justice trying to reconcile the two precedents. See Eskridge, "Overruling Statutory Precedents," 1372–73.

74. See Monroe v. Pape, 365 U.S., 167 192 (1961) (Harlan, J., concurring); id. at 220, 224–246 (Frankfurter, J., dissenting).

75. Compare Monell v. Department of Social Services, 436 U.S. 658, 664–683 (1978) ("new" historical evidence as basis for overruling Monroe v. Pape), with id. at 720–722 (Rehnquist, J., dissenting) (the Court's "new" evidence was considered in *Monroe* and does not undermine the precedent).

76. *Monroe*, 365 U.S. at 222 (Frankfurter, J., dissenting).

77. See, e.g., *Guardians Association*, 463 U.S. at 611 (Powell, Burger, and Rehnquist), 612–613 (O'Connor), 640–641 (Stevens, Brennan, and Blackmun) (unlawful "discrimination" under Title VI); Wilson v. Omaha Indian Tribe, 442 U.S. 653, 680 (1979) (Blackmun, J., concurring) (Indian law); Stone v. Powell, 428 U.S. 465 (1976) (habeas statute); Hamling v. United States, 418 U.S. 87 (1974) (anti-pornography law); Braden v. 30th Judicial Circuit Court of Kentucky, 410 U.S. 484 (1973) (habeas statute); Griffin v. Breckenridge, 403 U.S. 88 (1971) (civil rights statute).

78. *Guardians Association*, 463 U.S. at 635, 641 n.12 (Stevens, J., dissenting).

79. For other cases where the super-strong presumption has protected precedents interpreting common law statutes, see, e.g., Square D Co. v. Niagara Frontier Tariff Bureau, 476 U.S. 409 (1986) (Stevens, J.) (Sherman Act); City of Oklahoma City v. Tuttle, 471 U.S. 808, 818 n.5 (1985) (§1983); Maine v. Thiboutot, 448 U.S. 1, 4–8 (1980) (§1983); Quern v. Jordan, 440 U.S. 332, 338–345 (1979) (§1983); Illinois Brick Co. v. Illinois, 431 U.S. 720, 729–748 (1977) (Sherman Act).

80. 457 U.S. 496, 501 and n.3 (1982), relying on Monell v. Department of Social Services, 436 U.S. 658, 695–701 (1978)

81. House Report no. 2002, 82d Cong., 2d sess., 229 (1952); see Philip L. Martin, "The Aftermath of *Flood v. Kuhn:* Professional Baseball's Exemption from Antitrust Regulation," 3 *Western State Univeristy Law Review* 262, 280 (1975).

82. See Parklane Hosiery Co. v. Shore, 439 U.S. 322 (1979) (collateral estoppel in federal question cases); United States v. Reliable Transfer Co., 421 U.S. 397 (1975) (admiralty); M/S Breman v. Zapata Off-Shore Co., 407 U.S. 1 (1972) (admiralty); Executive Jet Aviation, Inc., v. City of Cleveland, Ohio, 409 U.S. 249 (1972) (admiralty); Moragne v. States Marine Lines, 398 U.S. 375 (1970) (admiralty). See generally Guido Calabresi, *A Common Law for the Age of Statutes* (1982) (excellent explication of legal process philosophy of overruling).

83. 398 U.S. 375 (1970) (overruling The Harrisburg, 119 U.S. 199 (1886)).

84. Id. at 404 (quoting Hart and Sacks, "The Legal Process," 577).

85. Especially United States v. Reliable Transfer Co., 421 U.S. 397 (1975), overruling The Schooner Catharine v. Dickinson, 58 U.S. 170 (1854).

86. See Griffin v. Breckenridge, 403 U.S. 88, 95–96 (1971); Lear, Inc., v. Adkins, 395 U.S. 653 (1969); Carafas v. LaVallee, 391 U.S. 234, 237–240 (1968); Peyton v. Rowe, 391 U.S. 54, 60–67 (1968); Swift & Co. v. Wickham, 382 U.S. 111 (1965); Fay v. Noia, 372 U.S. 391, 435–438 (1963); Smith v. Evening News Association, 371 U.S. 195, 198–201 (1962); James v. United States, 366 U.S. 213, 217–222 (1961). See also Welsh v. United States, 398 U.S. 333, 344 (1970) (Harlan, J., concurring in the result); Zschernig v. Miller, 389 U.S. 429, 443 (1968) (Harlan, J., concurring in the result); Walker v. Southern Railway Co., 385 U.S. 196, 199 (1966) (Harlan, J., dissenting); Gillespie v. United States Steel Corp., 379 U.S. 148, 158–166 (1964) (Goldberg, J., dissenting in part); James v. United States, 366 U.S. 213, 241 (1961) (Harlan, J., concurring in part and dissenting in part).

87. 398 U.S. 235 (1970).

88. Id. at 240–241.

89. United Steelworkers v. American Manufacturing Co., 363 U.S. 564 (1960); United Steelworkers v. Warrior & Gulf Navigation Co., 363 U.S. 574 (1960); United Steelworkers v. Enterprise Wheel & Car Corp., 363 U.S. 593 (1960).

90. 368 U.S. 502 (1962).

91. Avco Corp. v. Aero Lodge no. 735, 390 U.S. 557 (1968).

92. *Patterson*, 491 U.S. at 174 (first quotation), 175 n.1 (second quotation); see id. at 172–173 (party seeking to overrule statutory precedent has a greater burden of persuasion).

93. See Edmonds v. Compagnie Générale Transatlantique, 443 U.S. 256 (1979).

94. Brandeis's dissent in *Burnet* (the standard citation for the argument that overruling statutory precedents should be left to the legislature) cited both common law and statutory overrulings as examples of cases where "correction might have been secured by legislation." 332 U.S. at 406 n.1. Yet in cases such as *Moragne* the Court follows ordinary stare decisis analysis.

95. Congress can usually override Supreme Court decisions that refuse to create or protect constitutional rights against the United States or the states that find state policies preempted by federal statute or violative of the dormant commerce clause, or that allocate jurisdiction among the states and Indian tribes. The only constitutional decisions by necessity beyond the possibility of legislative override are those creating constitutional rights against the United States.

96. *Patterson*, 491 U.S. at 176–178.

97. For the Court's admission, see id. at 177. Also, since she was an at-will employee, Patterson's contract was constantly in the process of being "made," again triggering the literal terms of §1981. See id. at 221 (Stevens, J., concurring in the judgment in part and dissenting in part).

98. Patterson did not allege this, but at conference on the case at least six Justices were willing to allow her to sue for racially harassing conduct amounting to breach of contract. See Memorandum from Justice Stevens to Justice Brennan, May 22, 1989, in Thurgood Marshall Papers, Library of Congress, Madison Building, Box 467, Folder 2. Brennan circulated an opinion for the Court to this effect in December 1988 but never obtained a majority, with Justices Byron White and Anthony Kennedy apparently switching their votes. See id., Folders 2–4.

99. 118 *Congressional Record* 3368–69 (1972).

100. See Fiedler v. Marumsco Christian School, 631 F.2d 1144 (4th Cir. 1980).

101. 421 U.S. 454 (1973).

102. 427 U.S. 273, 285–287 (1976) (holding that §1981 provides a cause of action for white employees alleging that their employer had fired them because they were white; relying on *Johnson*, 421 U.S. at 459–460).

103. *Patterson* also rewrote the rationale for Goodman v. Lukens Steel Co., 482 U.S. 656 (1987). Compare *Patterson*, 491 U.S. at 177, with id. at 221–222 (Stevens, J., dissenting).

104. See Eskridge, "Overriding Statutory Decisions," and "Reneging on History? The Court/Congress/President Civil Rights Game," 79 *California Law Review* 613 (1991).

105. Public Law no. 102-166, 105 Stat. 1071 (1991).

106. See Elmer E. Smead, "The Rule against Retroactive Legislation: A Basic Principle of Jurisprudence," 20 *Minnesota Law Review* 775 (1936). See also Bryant Smith, "Retroactive Laws and Vested Rights," 5 *Texas Law Review* 231 (1927) (part one) and 6 *Texas Law Review* 409 (1928) (part two).

107. See George F. Canfield, "Address at the Twenty-fourth Annual Meeting of the South Carolina Bar Association," *South Carolina Bar Association Reports* 17 (1917); Robert Hill Freeman, "The Protection Afforded against Retroactive Operation of an Overruling Decision," 18 *Columbia Law Review* 230 (1918); see also John Henry Wigmore, *Problems of the Law: Its Past, Present, and Future*, 79–82 (1920). Contra, Robert von Moschzisker, "Stare Decisis in Courts of Last Resort," 37 *Harvard Law Review* 409 (1924); Note, "The Effect of Overruled and Overruling Decisions on Intervening Transactions," 47 *Harvard Law Review* 1403 (1934).

108. See generally Cardozo, *The Nature of the Judicial Process*, 142–167. On retroactive lawmaking, see Robert L. Hale, "The Supreme Court and the Contract Clause" (parts 1–3), 57 *Harvard Law Review* 512, 621, 852 (1944); Ray H. Greenblatt, "Judicial Limitations on Retroactive Civil Legislation," 51 *Northwestern University Law Review* 540 (1956); Roger J. Traynor, "Unjustifiable Reliance," 42 *Minnesota Law Review* 11 (1957). On prospective overruling, see Benjamin N. Cardozo, "Address before New York State Bar Association," 55 *Report of the New York State Bar Association* 263, 294–296 (1932); Beryl Harold Levy, "Realist Jurisprudence and Prospective Overruling," 109 *University of Pennsylvania Law Review*

1 (1960); Roger J. Traynor, "Quo Vadis Prospective Overruling: A Question of Judicial Responsibility," 28 *Hastings Law Journal* 533 (1977).

109. See Hart and Sacks, "The Legal Process," 620–637 (warm endorsement of prospective overruling), 640–651 (guarded approach to retroactive statutes). See also Charles B. Hochman, "The Supreme Court and the Constitutionality of Retroactive Legislation," 73 *Harvard Law Review* 692 (1960); Note, "Prospective Overruling and Retroactive Application in the Federal Courts," 71 *Yale Law Journal* 907 (1962). For a legal process update, see Gregory J. DeMars, "Retrospectivity and Retroactivity of Civil Legislation Reconsidered," 10 *Ohio Northern University Law Review* 253 (1983).

110. 404 U.S. 97, 106–107 (1971), essentially overruled by Jim Beam Distilling Co. v. Georgia, 111 S. Ct. 2439 (1991).

111. Stovall v. Denno, 388 U.S. 293, 297 (1967), overruled in United States v. Johnson, 457 U.S. 537 (1982), and Griffith v. Kentucky, 479 U.S. 314 (1987). See also Miranda v. Arizona, 384 U.S. 436 (1966) (applying new constitutional rule only to the cases decided by the Court, and not to 129 cases pending before the Court).

112. 458 U.S. 50 (1982).

113. The Court stayed its judgment until October 2, 1982. When Congress had not acted by then, the Court stayed its judgment until December 14, 1982. *Marathon*, 459 U.S. 813 (1982). Although the Court did not extend the stay further, Congress did not act until June 1984.

114. See Calabresi, *A Common Law for the Age of Statutes* (detailed analysis of the various options in overruling prior precedents); Spanel v. Mounds View School District no. 621, 118 N.W.2d 795 (Minn. 1962) (leading state case, analyzed by Calabresi).

115. All the courts of appeals that considered the issue held or assumed that §1981 as interpreted in *Runyon* applied to racially discriminatory contract terminations. Anderson v. Group Hospitalization, Inc., 820 F.2d 465 (D.C. Cir. 1987); Fiedler v. Marumsco Christian School, 631 F.2d 1144, 1149–50 (4th Cir. 1980); Randle v. LaSalle Telecommunications, Inc., 876 F.2d 563 (7th Cir. 1989) (arguendo). Judge Posner described *Patterson*'s interpretation of §1981 as one that "could not reasonably have been anticipated" before 1989 and, indeed, as "peculiar and unexpected." McKnight v. General Motors Corp., 908 F.2d 104, 108 (7th Cir. 1990).

116. United States v. Estate of Donnelly, 397 U.S. 286, 295 (1970). See *Flood*, 407 U.S. at 293 and n.5 (Marshall, J., dissenting); Simpson v. Union Oil Co. of California, 377 U.S. 13, 25 (1964).

117. 366 U.S. 213 (1961). Two different majorities yielded each holding. Six Justices (Warren, Frankfurter, Clark, Harlan, Brennan, and Stewart) voted to overrule Commissioner v. Wilcox, 327 U.S. 404 (1946). Six Justices also voted to overturn James's criminal conviction for tax fraud—three (Warren, Brennan, and Stewart) because statutory "willfulness" could not be charged to James, and three

(Douglas, Black, and Whittaker) because they believed *Wilcox* should not have been overruled; two (Frankfurter and Harlan) voted to overturn the conviction but remand the case for a trial on the willfulness issue.

118. *James*, 366 U.S. at 224–232 (Black, J., concurring in part in the judgment and dissenting in part); see Note, "Prospective Overruling and Retroactive Application," 930–933.

119. See Mackey v. United States, 401 U.S. 667, 675 (1971) (Harlan, J., concurring in the judgments); Desist v. United States, 394 U.S. 244, 256 (1969) (Harlan, J., dissenting).

120. Griffith v. Kentucky, 479 U.S. 314 (1987); United States v. Johnson, 457 U.S. 537 (1982).

121. 111 S. Ct. 2439 (1991). There was no opinion for the Court, but five Justices followed the Harlan approach rather than *Chevron Oil*, which the dissenting Justices saw as the death knell of that opinion. See id. at 2442–48 (plurality opinion by Souter, J., joined by Stevens, J.); id. at 2449–50 (Blackmun, J., joined by Marshall and Scalia, JJ., concurring in the judgment). See also id. at 2451 (O'Connor, J., dissenting).

122. Id. at 2449–50 (Blackmun, J., joined by Marshall and Scalia, JJ., concurring in the judgment); id. at 2450–51 (Scalia, J., joined by Marshall and Blackmun, JJ., concurring in the judgment).

123. The House Judiciary Committee in 1990 defeated (on a tie vote) an amendment to delete these provisions. See Transcript of Committee Mark-Up, as well as House Report no. 101-644, pt. 2, 71 (1990). A similar amendment was withdrawn in the House Education and Labor Committee. See House Report no. 101-644, pt. 1, 90 (1990). A Republican substitute with explicitly nonretroactive statutory language was defeated on the House floor by a vote of 238–288. See 136 *Congressional Record* H6747 (daily ed. August 3, 1990). The House rejected a Republican substitute in 1991 with similarly explicit language against retroactivity. See 137 *Congressional Record* H3908 (daily ed. June 4, 1991).

124. See President's Message to the Senate Returning without Approval the Civil Rights Act of 1990, 26 *Weekly Compilation of Presidential Documents* 1632, 1634 (October 22, 1990).

125. Letter from Senator Murkowski (R-Alaska) to Colleagues, October 15, 1991, reprinted in 137 *Congressional Record* S15,954 (daily ed. November 5, 1991). The letter was inserted into the *Record* as part of the Senate's debate over reinserting §402(b), which had been inadvertently left out of the engrossed bill passed by the Senate.

126. 137 *Congressional Record* S15,485 (daily ed. October 30, 1991) (Sen. Danforth and six other moderate Republican co-sponsors indicated that the bill "shall not apply retroactively"). Cf. id. at S15,325 (daily ed. October 29, 1991) (Sen. Danforth urging courts to ignore insertions into the *Record* as unreliable cheap talk).

127. 114 S. Ct. 1510 (1994); see Landgraf v. USI Film Products, 114 S. Ct.

1483 (1994) (presumption against applying provisions of 1991 act retroactively); Fray v. The Omaha World Herald Co., 960 F.2d 1370 (8th Cir. 1992). Like *Fray*, most of the courts of appeals found no retroactivity. See Gersman v. Group Health Association, 975 F.2d 886 (D.C. Cir. 1992); Johnson v. Uncle Ben's, Inc., 965 F.2d 1363 (5th Cir. 1992); Vogel v. City of Cincinnati, 959 F.2d 594 (6th Cir. 1992); Luddington v. Indiana Bell Telephone Co., 966 F.2d 225 (7th Cir. 1992); Mozee v. American Commercial Marine Service Co., 963 F.2d 929 (7th Cir. 1992). The Ninth Circuit found the costs provision of §113(b) retroactive in Davis v. City and County of San Francisco, 976 F.2d 1536, 1549–56 (9th Cir. 1992).

128. 488 U.S. 204, 213–215 (1988).

129. Id. at 208; see William V. Luneberg, "Retroactivity and Administrative Rulemaking," 1991 *Duke Law Journal* 106.

130. 416 U.S. 696 (1974).

131. Id. at 711; see United States v. Schooner Peggy, 5 U.S. (1 Cranch) 103, 110 (1801); Thorpe v. Housing Authority of the City of Durham, 393 U.S. 268, 282 (1969).

132. 494 U.S. 827 (1990).

133. Kungys v. United States, 485 U.S. 759, 778 (1988) (plurality opinion of Scalia, J.); see Russello v. United States, 464 U.S. 16, 23 (1983); Colautti v. Franklin, 439 U.S. 379, 392 (1979). Employers maintained that §§ 109(c) and 402(b) would still serve a useful purpose as "insurance" provisions inserted because the *Bowen-Bradley* conflict in Supreme Court opinions rendered the general rule hard for Congress to determine.

134. Hart and Sacks, "The Legal Process"; Note, "Prospective Overruling and Retroactive Application," 948–950; see Henry Campbell Black, *Handbook on the Construction and Interpretation of the Laws*, 380, 385, 404–410 (2d ed. 1911). This idea was applied to the 1991 act in Johnson v. Uncle Ben's, Inc., 965 F.2d 1363, 1374 (5th Cir. 1992); Gersman v. Group Health Association, 975 F.2d 886, 898–899 (D.C. Cir. 1992) (Wald, J., dissenting).

135. In this way: Employer A will bear reputation costs in the labor market if it discriminates against employee B. By subjecting A to injunctive and back pay relief, Title VII makes it more expensive for A to discriminate, though many a rational A will continue to discriminate, perhaps incurring expenses to hide the discrimination. By subjecting A to compensatory and punitive damages in addition to back pay and other injunctive relief, the 1991 act makes it yet more expensive to discriminate, and more employers will change their primary behavior.

136. Compare Lussier v. Dugger, 904 F.2d 661 (11th Cir. 1990); Leake v. Long Island Jewish Medical Center, 869 F.2d 130 (2d Cir. 1989); Mrs. W. v. Tirozzi, 832 F.2d 748, 754–755 (2d Cir. 1987), with *Rivers*, 114 S. Ct. at 1518 (rejecting this argument). For commentary, see Lon L. Fuller, *The Morality of Law*, 53 (rev. ed. 1969); Julian N. Eule, "Temporal Limits on the Legislative Mandate: Entrenchment and Retroactivity," 1987 *American Bar Foundation Research Journal*

379, 447–448; Greenblatt, "Retroactive Civil Legislation," 556; Stephen A. Munzer, "A Theory of Retroactive Legislation," 61 *Texas Law Review* 425, 469–470 (1982).

137. The analysis in this paragraph is based on Louis Kaplow, "An Economic Analysis of Legal Transitions," 99 *Harvard Law Review* 509 (1986); Luneberg, "Retroactivity and Administrative Lawmaking"; and Munzer, "A Theory of Retroactive Legislation."

138. See Charles Fried, "The Conservatism of Justice Harlan," 36 *New York Law School Law Review* 33 (1991); Gerald Gunther, "In Search of Judicial Quality on a Changing Court: The Case of Justice Powell," 24 *Stanford Law Review* 1001 (1972).

139. The main decision is Wards Cove Packing Co. v. Atonio, 490 U.S. 642 (1989). See also Independent Federation of Flight Attendants v. Zipes, 491 U.S. 754 (1989); Lorance v. AT&T Technologies, 490 U.S. 900 (1989); Martin v. Wilks, 490 U.S. 755 (1989); Price Waterhouse v. Hopkins, 490 U.S. 228 (1989).

140. See EEOC v. Arabian American Oil Co., 499 U.S. 244 (1991); West Virginia University Hospitals, Inc., v. Casey, 499 U.S. 83 (1991). African Americans were on the losing end of many Court decisions beginning in 1991. The biggest loss for employers during this period was UAW v. Johnson Controls, Inc., 499 U.S. 187 (1991), in which the Court, with Scalia concurring in the judgment, enforced the plain meaning of the Pregnancy Discrimination Act of 1978 to protect women against employer policies that discriminate because of pregnancy.

141. For textualist critiques of Scalia's opinion in West Virginia University Hospitals, Inc., v. Casey, 499 U.S. 83 (1991), see Lawrence M. Solan, *The Language of Judges*, 113–117 (1993); T. Alexander Aleinikoff and Theodore Shaw, "The Costs of Incoherence: A Comment on Plain Meaning, *West Virginia University Hospitals, Inc., v. Casey*, and Due Process of Statutory Interpretation," 45 *Vanderbilt Law Review* 687 (1992).

9. Canons of Statutory Construction as Interpretive Regimes

This chapter draws from my coauthored articles "Quasi-Constitutional Law: Clear Statement Rules as Constitutional Lawmaking," 45 *Vanderbilt Law Review* 593 (1992) (with Philip P. Frickey), and "Politics, Interpretation, and Rule of Law," in *The Rule of Law*, 265 (Ian Shapiro, ed., 1994) (with John Ferejohn).

1. See, e.g., P. B. Maxwell, *Interpretation of Statutes* (1875, updated in thirteen subsequent editions); J. G. [Jabez Gridley] Sutherland, *Statutes and Statutory Construction* (1891, updated in subsequent editions).

2. Karl N. Llewellyn, "Remarks on the Theory of Appellate Decision and the Rules or Canons about How Statutes Are to Be Construed," 3 *Vanderbilt Law Review* 395, 401–406 (1950). See also Frank C. Newman and Stanley S. Surrey, *Legislation—Cases and Materials*, 654 (1955).

3. Henry M. Hart, Jr., and Albert M. Sacks, "The Legal Process: Basic Problems in the Making and Application of Law," 1221 (tentative ed. 1958) (forthcoming from Foundation Press 1994, ed. William N. Eskridge, Jr., and Phillip P. Frickey). See Reed Dickerson, *The Interpretation and Application of Statutes,* 228 (1975); J. Willard Hurst, *Dealing with Statutes,* 57–65 (1982); Samuel Mermin, *Law and the Legal System: An Introduction,* 264 (2d ed. 1984); Daniel A. Farber, "The Inevitability of Practical Reason: Statutes, Formalism, and the Rule of Law," 45 *Vanderbilt Law Review* 533 (1992); Quintin Johnstone, "An Evaluation of the Rules of Statutory Interpretation," 3 *Kansas Law Review* 1 (1954); Cass R. Sunstein, "Interpreting Statutes in the Regulatory State," 103 *Harvard Law Review* 407, 454–459 (1989).

4. See generally "Symposium: A Reevaluation of the Canons of Statutory Interpretation," 45 *Vanderbilt Law Review* 529–795 (1992).

5. The costs of statutory ambiguity include (1) difficulty of planning by affected persons and reliance costs; (2) legal costs of extra research and litigation; and (3) frustration of statutory purpose as the bad get away with violations and the good are chilled. See Gregory E. Maggs, "Reducing the Costs of Statutory Ambiguity," 29 *Harvard Journal of Legislation* 123 (1992).

6. See e.g., Richard A. Posner, "Statutory Interpretation—in the Classroom and in the Courtroom," 50 *University of Chicago Law Review* 800, 806–807 (1983).

7. Finley v. United States, 490 U.S. 545, 556 (1989) (Scalia, J.).

8. 499 U.S. 244 (1991).

9. The antidiscrimination rule of §703(a) of the act, 42 U.S.C. §2000e-2(a), applies to any "employer," defined in §701(b), id. §2000e(b), to be any "person engaged in an industry affecting commerce who has fifteen or more employees." Commerce is defined in §701(g), id. §2000e(g), to mean "trade, traffic, commerce, transportation, transmission, or communication among the several States; or *between a State and any place outside thereof*" (emphasis added).

10. See Gary B. Born, "A Reappraisal of the Extraterritorial Reach of U.S. Law," 24 *Law and Policy in International Business* 1 (1992); Larry Kramer, "Vestiges of Beale: Extraterritorial Application of American Law," 1991 *Supreme Court Review* 179.

11. 336 U.S. 281, 285 (1949), invoked in *Aramco,* 499 U.S. at 248.

12. *Aramco,* 499 U.S. at 251–256.

13. See Born, "Reappraisal of Extraterritorial Reach," 29–54.

14. See Richard A. Posner, *The Federal Courts: Crisis and Reform,* 282 (1985); Sunstein, "Interpreting Statutes in the Regulatory State," 455. But see Geoffrey P. Miller, "Pragmatics and the Maxims of Interpretation," 1990 *Wisconsin Law Review* 1179, for a defense of *expressio unius* as a maxim with a distinguished lineage.

15. Eric Lane, "Legislative Process and Its Judicial Renderings: A Study in Contrast," 48 *University of Pittsburgh Law Review* 639, 651 (1987); see Otto Hetzel, "Instilling Legislative Interpretation Skills in the Classroom and the Court-

room," 48 *University of Pittsburgh Law Review* 663, 682–683 (1987); Abner J. Mikva, "Reading and Writing Statutes," 48 *University of Pittsburgh Law Review* 627, 629 (1987).

16. For the superability of the first reason, see Janice M. Pueser, "Rules of Statutory Construction for Legislative Drafting," 7 Federal Rules Decisions 143 (1955). For an example of state drafting manuals, see State of Wisconsin, Legislative Reference Bureau, *Wisconsin Bill Drafting Manual, 1993–1994.*

17. See Stephen F. Ross, "Where Have You Gone, Karl Llewellyn? Should Congress Turn Its Lonely Eyes To You?" 45 *Vanderbilt Law Review* 561, 572–573 (1992).

18. On checklists generally, see Alfred R. Menard, "Legislative Bill Drafting," 26 *Rocky Mountain Law Review* 368 (1954). On federal proposals, see *Report of the Federal Courts Study Committee,* 91–92 (April 2, 1990); *Statutory Interpretation and the Uses of Legislative History: Hearing before the Subcommittee on Courts, Intellectual Property, and the Administration of Justice of the House Committee on the Judiciary,* 101st Cong., 2d sess. (1990).

19. Recall the Coase theorem, which states that setting legal baselines does not prevent efficient operation of the regulated community because those affected will bargain around any inefficient baselines to reach the efficient rule (assuming minimal transaction costs).

20. Born, "Reappraisal of Extraterritorial Reach," 59–79 (the territoriality presumption does not reflect private international law, statutory policy in this century, or the views of legislators); Jonathan Turley, "'When in Rome': Multinational Misconduct and the Presumption against Extraterritoriality," 84 *Northwestern University Law Review* 598 (1990); see Comment, "Title VII of the Civil Rights Act of 1964 and Multinational Enterprise," 73 *Georgetown Law Journal* 1465 (1985).

21. See *Aramco,* 499 U.S. at 256–257.

22. Id. at 257–258. There is some suggestion of another counter-canon in the majority's mention that the EEOC does not have formal rule-making power. But see id. at 259–260 (Scalia, J., concurring in part and concurring in the judgment) (denouncing this counter-canon).

23. See Eben Moglen and Richard J. Pierce, Jr., "Sunstein's New Canons: Choosing the Fictions of Statutory Interpretation," 57 *University of Chicago Law Review* 1203 (1990).

24. Steele v. Bulova Watch Co., 344 U.S. 280, 286 (1952), relying on the definition of "commerce" in 15 U.S.C. §1127. *Aramco* distinguished this case on the ground that its jurisdictional grant was broader than that in the Civil Rights Act, which the Court characterized as "boilerplate." 499 U.S. at 252. See also Vermilya-Brown Co. v. Connell, 335 U.S. 377 (1948) (applying the Fair Labor Standards Act extraterritorially, based on a statute that applied only to "any Territory or possession of the United States").

25. See Schoenbaum v. Firstbrook, 405 F.2d 200, reversed on other grounds, 405 F.2d 215 (2d Cir. 1968) (en banc) (securities laws); United States v. Aluminum Company of America, 148 F.2d 416 (2d Cir. 1945) (L. Hand, J.) (antitrust law), analyzed in Born, "Reappraisal of Extraterritorial Reach," 29–39, 45–48.

26. Hellenic Lines, Ltd., v. Rhoditis, 398 U.S. 306 (1970); Romero v. International Terminal Operating Co., 358 U.S. 354 (1959); Lauritzen v. Larsen, 345 U.S. 571 (1953).

27. The NLRA cases are McCulloch v. Sociedad Nacional de Martineros de Honduras, 372 U.S. 10, 13 (1963); Benz v. Compania Naviera Hidalgo, S.A., 353 U.S. 138, 146 (1957). The RLA cases are Air Line Stewards and Stewardesses Association, International, v. Trans World Airlines, Inc., 273 F.2d 69 (2d Cir. 1959), cert. denied, 362 U.S. 988 (1960); Air Line Stewards v. Northwest Airlines, Inc., 267 F.2d 170 (8th Cir.), cert. denied, 361 U.S. 901 (1959).

28. 42 U.S.C. §2000e-1 (1988).

29. Colautti v. Franklin, 439 U.S. 379, 392 (1979); see Kungys v. United States, 485 U.S. 759, 778 (1988) (plurality opinion of Scalia, J.); South Carolina v. Catawba Indian Tribe, Inc., 476 U.S. 498, 510 n.22 (1986); Mountain States Telephone and Telegraph Co. v. Pueblo of Santa Ana, 472 U.S. 237, 249–250 (1985).

30. In *Aramco* the Court responded that if it followed this argument to its logical conclusion, Title VII would apply to discrimination against American workers by foreign as well as American companies abroad. 499 U.S. at 255. Not necessarily, for federal courts in the antitrust and securities areas have developed a thorough set of principles to limit the extraterritorial application of statutes that do not set clear limits on their face. See note 25. Aramco argued that its interpretation did not render the alien exemption provision superfluous because it would still be necessary to prevent application of Title VII to aliens employed in lands controlled by the United States (such as possessions) but not within any "State." Brief for Respondents, 27, *Aramco* (nos. 89-1838 and 89-1845). But the *Foley Brothers* presumption against extraterritorial application applies to U.S. possessions just as it applies to foreign soil. *Foley Brothers*, 336 U.S. at 285.

31. House Report no. 570, 88th Cong., 1st sess., 4 (1963).

32. *Discriminatory Overseas Assignment Policies of Federal Agencies: Hearings before the Subcommittee on Government Information and Individual Rights of the Senate Committee on Government Operations*, 94th Cong., 1st sess., 88 (1975).

33. The Court performed this transformation by conflating the *Foley Brothers* presumption with the stronger rule against statutory interpretations that violate international law or treaties or otherwise implicate international comity and U.S. foreign relations. *Aramco*, 499 U.S. 248, 258, sharply criticized id. at 261–266 (Marshall, J., dissenting).

34. See Pennsylvania v. Union Gas Co., 491 U.S. 1, 8 (1989) (implication of statutory language deemed sufficient to meet clear statement requirement for congressional abrogation of state Eleventh Amendment immunity).

35. The analysis that best supports the result in *Aramco* is the Court's observation that Congress itself has drafted statutes clearly to apply overseas. *Aramco*, 499 U.S. at 258–259. The Court's list tellingly included the Age Discrimination in Employment Act (ADEA), which Congress amended in 1984 to extend to overseas American employees, precisely the rule urged on the Court by the plaintiff in *Aramco*. When Congress enacted the Civil Rights Act in 1964, of course, it could never have predicted this 1984 amendment to a statute it had not yet enacted; and when it amended the ADEA in 1984 (to override lower court decisions making the same interpretive error *Aramco* would later make) it probably did not realize that this action made it less likely the Court would recognize extraterritorial application of the 1964 act. See Turley, "When in Rome," 624–627.

36. The Civil Rights Act of 1991, Public Law no. 102-166, §109, 105 Stat. 1071, 1077 (1991).

37. See Astoria Federal Savings and Loan Association v. Solimino, 111 S. Ct. 2166, 2169–71 (1991); *Aramco*, 499 U.S. at 262–263 (Marshall, J., dissenting).

38. 491 U.S. 223 (1989).

39. 20 U.S.C. §1415(e)(2) (1988); 121 *Congressional Record* 37,415–16 (1975) (statement of Sen. Williams, D-N.J., Senate sponsor).

40. 473 U.S. 234, 242 (1985).

41. Employees of the Department of Public Health and Welfare v. Department of Public Health and Welfare, Missouri, 411 U.S. 279 (1973).

42. See Vicki C. Jackson, "One Hundred Years of Folly: The Eleventh Amendment and the 1988 Term," 64 *Southern California Law Review* 31, 82–87 (1990) (suggesting that *Dellmuth* required a clearer statement from Congress than even *Atascadero* had required).

43. 42 U.S.C. § 2000d-7(a)(1) (1988).

44. *Dellmuth*, 491 U.S. at 227–232.

45. Education of the Handicapped Act Amendments of 1990, Public Law no., 101–476, §103, 104 Stat. 1103, 1106 (1990).

46. Japan Whaling Association v. American Cetacean Society, 478 U.S. 221 (1986); Dames & Moore v. Regan, 453 U.S. 654 (1981).

47. K Mart Corp. v. Cartier, Inc., 486 U.S. 281 (1988); Chevron U.S.A., Inc., v. Natural Resources Defense Council, 467 U.S. 837 (1984).

48. Public Citizen v. United States Department of Justice, 491 U.S. 440 (1989); Morrison v. Olson, 487 U.S. 654, 682–683 (1988).

49. Chambers v. NASCO, Inc., 111 S. Ct. 2123 (1991).

50. United States v. Nordic Village, Inc., 112 S. Ct. 1011 (1992).

51. In addition to *Atascadero* and *Dellmuth*, see also Blatchford v. Native Village of Noatak, 111 S. Ct. 2578 (1991); Will v. Michigan Department of State Police, 491 U.S. 58 (1989); Jackson, "One Hundred Years of Folly."

52. Pennhurst State School and Hospital v. Halderman, 451 U.S. 1 (1981).

53. See Cipollone v. Liggett Group, Inc., 112 S. Ct. 3608 (1992).

54. Gregory v. Ashcroft, 111 S. Ct. 2395 (1991).

55. McCormick v. United States, 111 S. Ct. 1807 (1991); City of Columbia v. Omni Outdoor Advertising, Inc., 111 S. Ct. 1344 (1991); McNally v. United States, 483 U.S. 350 (1987).

56. Coleman v. Thompson, 111 S. Ct. 2546 (1991).

57. Davis v. Michigan Department of Treasury, 489 U.S. 803 (1989); Memphis Bank and Trust Co. v. Garner, 459 U.S. 392, 396–397 (1983).

58. Tafflin v. Levitt, 493 U.S. 455 (1990).

59. See Frank I. Michelman, "The Supreme Court, 1985 Term—Foreword: Traces of Self-Government," 100 *Harvard Law Review* 4 (1986); Frank I. Michelman, "Law's Republic," 97 *Yale Law Journal* 1493 (1988); Suzanna Sherry, "Civic Virtue and the Feminine Voice in Constitutional Adjudication," 72 *Virginia Law Review* 543 (1986).

60. This is the theme of my article "Public Values in Statutory Interpretation," 137 *University of Pennsylvania Law Review* 1007 (1989), as well as of Cass R. Sunstein, *After the Rights Revolution: Reconceiving the Regulatory State* (1990).

61. Lawrence Gene Sager, "Fair Measure: The Legal Status of Underenforced Constitutional Norms," 91 *Harvard Law Review* 1212 (1978); see Paul Brest, "The Conscientious Legislator's Guide to Constitutional Interpretation," 27 *Stanford Law Review* 585 (1975); Stephen F. Ross, "Legislative Enforcement of Equal Protection," 72 *Minnesota Law Review* 311 (1987); Nicholas S. Zeppos, "Scalia's Textualism: The 'New' New Legal Process," 12 *Cardozo Law Review* 1597 (1991).

62. See Brest, "The Conscientious Legislator's Guide"; Ross, "Legislative Enforcement of Equal Protection"; Sager, "Fair Measure."

63. See, e.g., Public Citizen v. United States Department of Justice, 490 U.S. 440 (1989). Compare Peretz v. United States, 111 S. Ct. 2661, 2666–67 (1991) (refusing to protect jury trial rights with canon to avoid constitutional difficulties). See Eskridge and Frickey, "Quasi-Constitutional Law," 611–629.

64. See Mistretta v. United States, 488 U.S. 361 (1989) (nondelegation, separation of powers); Morrison v. Olson, 487 U.S. 654 (1988) (separation of powers); Garcia v. San Antonio Metropolitan Transit Authority, 469 U.S. 528 (1985) (federalism); Heart of Atlanta Motel v. Katzenbach, 379 U.S. 241 (1964) (federalism).

65. 469 U.S. 528, 550 (1985). The Court may be in the process of retreat from *Garcia*. See New York v. United States, 112 S. Ct. 2408 (1992).

66. See Mistretta v. United States, 488 U.S. 361, 371–379 (1989) (nondelegation doctrine); Goldwater v. Carter, 444 U.S. 996 (1979) (opinion of Powell, J.) (separation of powers).

67. See my article, "Overriding Supreme Court Statutory Interpretation Decisions," 101 *Yale Law Journal* 331 (1991), as well as Carol F. Lee, "The Political Safeguards of Federalism? Congressional Responses to Supreme Court Decisions on State and Local Liability," 20 *Urban Lawyer* 301 (1988) (excellent case studies of state clout in Congress).

68. 111 S. Ct. 2395 (1991). My discussion of *Gregory* is drawn from my collabo-

ration with Philip Frickey. See Philip P. Frickey, "Lawnet: The Case of the Missing (Tenth) Amendment," 75 *Minnesota Law Review* 755 (1991).

69. Elected state judges would fall under the ADEA's exception for elected state officials, 29 U.S.C. §630(f) (1988), while appointed state judges could fall under the same subsection's exception for "appointee[s] on the policymaking level." Frickey, "Lawnet."

70. *Gregory*, 111 S. Ct. at 2403.

71. See *Garcia*, 469 U.S. at 537.

72. *Gregory*, 111 S. Ct. at 2400, 2402, 2406.

73. 111 S.Ct. 2354 (1991).

74. 42 U.S.C. §1973 (1988).

75. United States v. Taylor, 487 U.S. 326, 346 (Scalia, J., concurring in part).

76. See *The Federalist* (Clinton Rossiter, ed., 1961), nos. 51 (Madison) and 78 (Hamilton).

77. On the presumption of judicial review, see Webster v. Doe, 486 U.S. 592 (1988); Dunlop v. Bachowski, 421 U.S. 560 (1975); Abbott Laboratories v. Gardner, 387 U.S. 136, 140 (1967). On the presumption against abrogation of inherent powers, see Chambers v. NASCO, Inc., 111 S. Ct. 2123 (1991); Weinberger v. Romero-Barcelo, 456 U.S. 305, 319 (1982); Hecht Co. v. Bowles, 321 U.S. 321, 330 (1944).

78. See Morrison v. Olson, 487 U.S. 654, 682–683 (1988) (executive powers); Dames & Moore v. Regan, 453 U.S. 654 (1981) (foreign affairs); Haig v. Agee, 453 U.S. 280, 301 and n.50 (1981) (foreign affairs).

79. 478 U.S. 221 (1986).

80. 22 U.S.C. §1978(a)(1) (1988). The Packwood Amendment followed the same certification process but required that it be expedited and removed the president's discretion not to impose sanctions. 16 U.S.C. §1821(e)(2) (1988).

81. *Japan Whaling*, 478 U.S. at 232–233.

82. See id. at 247 (Marshall, J., dissenting).

83. See Harold H. Koh, *The National Security Constitution: Sharing Power after the Iran-Contra Affair* (1990).

84. *Gregory*, 111 S. Ct. at 2399–2400. See also New York v. United States, 112 S. Ct. 2408 (1992) (O'Connor, J.); Deborah Merritt, "The Guaranty Clause and State Autonomy: Federalism for a Third Century," 88 *Columbia Law Review* 1 (1988) (cited and relied on in *Gregory*).

85. 111 S. Ct. 2546, 2569–70 (1991) (Blackmun, J., dissenting) (objecting to the Court's cutting back further on habeas relief, based on "federalism").

86. 493 U.S. 455 (1990) (majority opinion and Scalia concurring opinion). See Robert M. Cover and T. Alexander Aleinikoff, "Dialectical Federalism: Habeas Corpus and the Court," 86 *Yale Law Journal* 1035 (1977); Barry Friedman, "A Different Dialogue: The Supreme Court, Congress, and Federal Jurisdiction," 85 *Northwestern University Law Review* 1 (1990); Judith Resnik, "Tiers," 57 *Southern California Law Review* 837 (1989).

87. See Cover and Aleinikoff, "Dialectical Federalism"; Barry Friedman, "Habeas and Hubris," 45 *Vanderbilt Law Review* 797 (1992).

88. See, e.g., California v. Cabazon Band of Mission Indians, 480 U.S. 202 (1987); New Mexico v. Mescalero Apache Tribe, 462 U.S. 324, 335 (1983); White Mountain Apache Tribe v. Bracker, 448 U.S. 136 (1980); Bryan v. Itasca County, 426 U.S. 373 (1976); McClanahan v. Arizona State Tax Commission, 411 U.S. 164 (1970). See Philip P. Frickey, "Congressional Intent, Practical Reasoning, and the Dynamic Nature of Federal Indian Law," 78 *California Law Review* 1137 (1990).

89. 490 U.S. 163 (1989).

90. Id. at 188–189, 192.

91. See Stephen Breyer, *Regulation and Its Reform* (1982); Richard B. Stewart, "The Reformation of American Administrative Law," 88 *Harvard Law Review* 1667 (1975); see also Sunstein, *After the Rights Revolution.*

92. Bruce A. Ackerman, "Beyond *Carolene Products*," 98 *Harvard Law Review* 713 (1985); Eskridge, "Public Values in Statutory Interpretation," 1032–34, 1047–48.

93. See, e.g., United States v. R.L.C., 112 S. Ct. 1329 (1992) (rule of lenity applied to sentencing); Crandon v. United States, 494 U.S. 152 (1990) (rule of lenity applied to protect civil defendant, where standard of conduct was borrowed from criminal statute); United States v. Kozminski, 487 U.S. 931 (1988) (rule of lenity applied to require scienter in statute prohibiting involuntary servitudes).

94. Thus, Congress often overrides rule of lenity cases and creates the clear statutory directive found lacking, though it rarely overrides criminal law decisions won by state or federal prosecutors. See Eskridge, "Overriding Statutory Decisions," 362.

95. See also Evans v. United States, 112 S. Ct. 1881 (1992); McCormick v. United States, 111 S. Ct. 1807 (1991).

96. 483 U.S. 350 (1987).

97. 18 U.S.C. §1341 (1988) then provided that "[w]hoever, having devised or intended to devise any scheme or artifice to defraud, or for obtaining money or property by means of false or fraudulent pretenses, representations, or purposes ... for the purpose of executing such scheme or artifice or attempting to do so, [uses the mails or caused them to be used]," was subject to criminal penalty.

98. *McNally*, 483 U.S. at 359–360.

99. See id. at 375 n.9 (Stevens, J., joined by O'Connor, J., dissenting).

100. Anti-Drug Abuse Act of 1988, Public Law no. 100-690, §7603(a), 102 Stat. 4181, 4508 (1988), adding 18 U.S.C. §1346.

101. 490 U.S. 642 (1989).

102. Id. at 652, citing 42 U.S.C. §2000e-2(j) (1988).

103. Johnson v. Transportation Agency, Santa Clara County, 480 U.S. 616, 675–677 (1987) (Scalia, J., joined by Rehnquist, C.J., dissenting). White (the au-

thor of *Wards Cove*) expressed sympathy with Scalia's arguments. Id. at 657 (White, J., dissenting separately).

104. Compare Ackerman, "Beyond *Carolene Products*," with Daniel A. Farber and Philip P. Frickey, "Is *Carolene Products* Dead? Reflections on Affirmative Action and the Dynamics of Civil Rights Legislation," 79 *California Law Review* 685 (1991).

105. See Gilmer v. Interstate/Johnson Lane Corp., 111 S. Ct. 1647 (1991) (age discrimination claim must be arbitrated); Rodriguez de Quijas v. Shearson/American Express, Inc., 490 U.S. 477 (1989) (securities law); Shearson/American Express, Inc., v. McMahon, 482 U.S. 220 (1987) (same).

106. United States v. Nordic Village, Inc., 112 S. Ct. 1011 (1992), a somewhat tougher version of earlier formulations, e.g., Library of Congress v. Shaw, 478 U.S. 310 (1986); United States v. James, 478 U.S. 597 (1986). The Court has similarly been stingy in construing the Federal Tort Claims Act, e.g., United States v. Johnson, 481 U.S. 681 (1987); Kosak v. United States, 465 U.S. 848 (1984).

107. See David L. Shapiro, "Mr. Justice Rehnquist: A Preliminary View," 90 *Harvard Law Review* 293 (1976) (Rehnquist himself favors state over federal interests, government over private interests, and corporate over individual interests).

108. Rehnquist was a law clerk and protégé of Justice Robert Jackson, a legal process hero on the bench. See William H. Rehnquist, "Robert H. Jackson: A Perspective Twenty-Five Years Later," 44 *Albany Law Review* 533 (1980). Stevens was a protégé of Edward Levi, another legal process pioneer, and the attorney general who allegedly pressed for Stevens's appointment. Five Justices (Scalia, Kennedy, Souter, Ginsburg, and Breyer) took the Hart and Sacks "Legal Process" course at Harvard.

109. See Alexander M. Bickel, *The Least Dangerous Branch* (1962); Lon L. Fuller, *The Morality of Law* (1964, rev. ed. 1969); Robert H. Bork, "Neutral Principles and Some First Amendment Problems," 47 *Indiana Law Journal* 1 (1971); Herbert Wechsler, "Toward Neutral Principles of Constitutional Law," 73 *Harvard Law Review* 1 (1959).

110. 490 U.S. 755 (1989).

111. Id. at 761, quoting Hansberry v. Lee, 311 U.S. 32, 40 (1940).

112. Id. at 762 n.2, citing NLRB v. Bildisco & Bildisco, 465 U.S. 513, 529–530 n. 10 (1984) (scheme of the Bankruptcy Act requires that the rights of unnotified interests be cut off at a certain time).

113. See *Wilks*, 490 U.S. at 762–763 and n.3 (seven circuits disallowing collateral attacks, two allowing them).

114. Public Law no. 102-166, §108, 105 Stat. 1071, 1076–77 (1991), adding a new §703(n) to Title VII, 42 U.S.C. §2000e-2(n).

115. See Guido Calabresi, *The Cost of Accidents* (1970); Richard A. Posner, *Economic Analysis of Law* (1st ed. 1973).

116. See Allen v. Wright, 468 U.S. 737 (1984); Simon v. Eastern Kentucky

Welfare Rights Organization. 426 U.S. 26 (1976); Warth v. Seldin, 422 U.S. 490 (1975); Abram Chayes, "The Supreme Court, 1981 Term—Foreword: Public Law Litigation and the Burger Court," 96 *Harvard Law Review* 4 (1982).

117. The Warren Court had liberally implied causes of action from federal statutes, e.g., J. I. Case Co. v. Borak, 377 U.S. 426 (1964), but the Burger Court retreated from a liberal approach, first with the four-factor test of Cort v. Ash, 422 U.S. 66 (1974), and then with a test essentially presuming against implied causes of action. See, e.g., Touche Ross & Co. v. Redington, 442 U.S. 560 (1979).

118. See Owen Equipment & Erection Co. v. Kroger, 437 U.S. 365 (1978); Zahn v. International Paper Co., 414 U.S. 291 (1973); Snyder v. Harris, 394 U.S. 332 (1969).

119. See, e.g., City of Milwaukee v. Illinois, 451 U.S. 304 (1981); Mobil Oil Corp. v. Higginbotham, 436 U.S. 618 (1978).

120. See Imbler v. Pachtman, 424 U.S. 409 (1976) (prosecutorial immunity); Employees of the Department of Public Health & Welfare v. Department of Public Health & Welfare, Missouri, 411 U.S. 279 (1973) (state Eleventh Amendment immunity).

121. Pennhurst State School & Hospital v. Halderman, 451 U.S. 1 (1981).

122. In addition to *Dellmuth*, see Lujan v. Defenders of Wildlife, 112 S. Ct. 2130 (1992) (clear statement rule against interpreting statutes to expand "injuries in fact" for standing purposes); Finley v. United States, 490 U.S. 545 (1989) (strong presumption against expanding federal jurisdiction); Thompson v. Thompson, 484 U.S. 174 (1988) (strong presumption against implying new causes of action from federal statutes). The Rehnquist Court has vacillated on some of these restrictions. See, e.g., Northeastern Florida Chapter of the Associated General Contractors of America v. City of Jacksonville, 113 S. Ct. 2297 (1993) (expansive notion of standing for contractors challenging ordinance setting aside contracts for racial minorities).

123. See Frank H. Easterbrook, "The Supreme Court, 1983 Term—Foreword: The Court and the Economic System," 98 *Harvard Law Review* 4, 55–56 (1984); Richard A. Posner, "The Efficiency and the Efficacy of Title VII," 136 *University of Pennsylvania Law Review* 513 (1987), responding to John Donohue III, "Is Title VII Efficient?" 134 *University of Pennsylvania Law Review* 1411 (1986). See also Richard A. Epstein, *Forbidden Grounds: The Case against Employment Discrimination Laws* (1992), arguing (inter alia) that there is an "efficient" level of workplace discrimination which Title VII impedes.

124. See John J. Donohue III and James Heckman, "Re-Evaluating Federal Civil Rights Policy," 79 *Georgetown Law Journal* 1713 (1991); James Heckman and Brook Payner, "Determining the Impact of Federal Antidiscrimination Policy on the Economic Status of Blacks: A Study of South Carolina," 79 *American Economic Review* 138 (1989); David Strauss, "The Law and Economics of Racial Discrimination in Employment: The Case for Numerical Standards," 79 *Georgetown Law Journal* 1619 (1991).

125. See Richard H. McAdams, "Relative Preferences," 102 *Yale Law Journal* 1 (1992). This third point does not seem to me as supportive of *Griggs* disparate impact rules, however.

126. Johnson v. Transporation Agency, Santa Clara County, 480 U.S. 616, 676–677 (1987) (Scalia, J., dissenting).

127. For the gloomy view of government suggested by public choice, see, e.g., Michael T. Hayes, *Lobbyists and Legislators* (1981); Mancur Olson, *The Rise and Decline of Nations: Economic Growth, Stagflation, and Social Rigidities* (1982).

128. See Nathan Glazer, Daniel P. Moynihan, and Corinne Saposs Schelling, eds., *Ethnicity: Theory and Experience* (1975), especially the editors' introduction and Daniel Bell's essay, "Ethnicity and Social Change."

129. Both decisions were decided by 5–4 votes. In the majority in both cases were the three *Johnson* dissenters, O'Connor (who concurred in the *Johnson* judgment, largely on the basis of stare decisis), and Kennedy (who replaced Powell, who provided the fifth vote for Brennan's opinion in *Johnson*). See also City of Richmond v. J. A. Croson Co., 488 U.S. 469 (1989) (O'Connor opinion striking down race-based set-asides and writing for the same five Justices who decided *Wards Cove* and *Wilks*). The four dissenters in *Wards Cove* and *Wilks* had (with Powell) formed Brennan's majority in *Johnson*.

130. A project well under way. See, e.g., Patricia J. Williams, *The Alchemy of Race and Rights* (1991) (especially the tale of the author's encounter with a bored Benetton sales clerk); Duncan Kennedy, "A Cultural Pluralist Case for Affirmative Action in Legal Academia," 1990 *Duke Law Journal* 705; Randall Kennedy, "Persuasion and Distrust: A Comment on the Affirmative Action Debate," 99 *Harvard Law Review* 1327 (1986).

131. Marguerite Yourcenar, *The Memoirs of Hadrian*, 114 (Grace Frick, trans., 1954).

Index

A. Bourjois & Co. v. Katzel, 114, 123, 131, 132–133
Absurd results, avoiding, 45–46, 134
Ackerman, Bruce A., 302
Acquiescence, congressional, 221, 242–244; Supreme Court cases finding acquiescence, 309–310, 324; Supreme Court cases not finding acquiescence, 310–311
Adair v. United States, 92
Affirmative action, 17, 29 and 341n, 35–41, 109, 203–204, 302–305; Scalia's ode to blue collar white males, 44. *See also* United Steelworkers v. Weber
Age Discrimination in Employment Act of 1967 (ADEA), 288–289, 422n
Agency lawmaking, 2, 51–55, 66–67, 69–74, 114–116, 161–173; comparative advantages over courts, 170 and 382n
Agenda control, legislative, 36–37
Agricultural Marketing Agreement Act of 1937, 159
Agriculture, Department of, 159, 222
Allen, Anita L., 59, 60
Allen v. Wright, 147, 172, 173
Altgeld, John Peter, 86
American Anti-Boycott Association (AABA), 91–92, 96–97
American Civil Liberties Union (ACLU), 154
American Federation of Labor (AFL), 87–89, 91–94, 103; "We Don't Patronize" list, 91
American Psychiatric Association (APA), 53, 72
American Steel Foundries v. Tri-City Central Trades Council, 100–101, 102, 104

Analogies to statutory interpretation, 120–121; chain novel, 374n; cy pres, 123, 129, 134; deviation, 123; long-term contracts, 122–123; relational agency, 123–129; retelling an anecdote, 176–177; three-legged chair, 200–201; translation, 128–130
Apex Hosiery Co. v. Leader, 242, 243
Archaeology, statutory, 13, 48. *See also* Originalist statutory interpretation
Aristotle, 3, 50, 200 and 387n, 367n, 368n
Armstrong amendment, 182 and 386n
Atascadero State Hospital v. Scanlon, 284, 298

Bait and switch, Congress fooled, 234, 283–285
Barking dogs and congressional silence, 220–221
Bedford Cut Stone Co. v. Journeymen Stone Cutters' Association of North America, 102–104
Bell, Derrick A., Jr., 160
Belson, James, 178, 186, 192, 195–196
Bennion, Francis, 49
Bicameralism and presentment, 17, 19–20, 34–35, 50, 117–120, 164–165, 226, 230–231, 235, 247; implications for agency deference, 164–170
Black, Hugo, 104 and 363n, 265
Blackmun, Harry, 24–25, 45–46, 164
Blackstone, Sir William, 116, 117, 262; neo-Blackstonian theory, 271
Block v. Community Nutrition Institute, 159, 172, 173

429